The Battle of the Crater

The Battle of the Crater

A Complete History

JOHN F. SCHMUTZ

McFarland & Company, Inc., Publishers
Jefferson, North Carolina, and London

LIBRARY OF CONGRESS CATALOGUING-IN-PUBLICATION DATA

Schmutz, John F., 1947–
The Battle of the Crater : a complete history /
John F. Schmutz.
p.   cm.
Includes bibliographical references and index.

ISBN 978-0-7864-3982-9
illustrated case binding: 50# alkaline paper ∞

1. Petersburg Crater, Battle of, Va., 1864.
I. Title.
E476.93.S35   2009
973.7'37 — dc22   2008048244

British Library cataloguing data are available

On the cover: *Mahone's Counterattack*, painting by Don Troiani
(www.historicalimagebank.com)

Manufactured in the United States of America

*McFarland & Company, Inc., Publishers
Box 611, Jefferson, North Carolina 28640
www.mcfarlandpub.com*

To my family

Contents

List of Maps

The loss in the disaster of Saturday last foots up about 3,500, of whom 450 men were killed and 2,000 wounded. It was the saddest affair I have ever witnessed in the war. Such an opportunity for carrying fortifications I have never seen and do not expect again to have.
— Lieutenant General Ulysses S. Grant to Major General Henry W. Halleck, August 1, 1864

Preface

A PHYSICALLY EXHAUSTED AND TOTALLY disheartened Lieutenant Colonel Henry Pleasants slumped on the parapets of the Union breastworks at Petersburg, Virginia, his hand blistered and sore from using the flat of his sword on the backs of recalcitrant Union soldiers hiding in the massive hole that was his creation in a futile effort to spur them forward to continue their assault on the Confederate works. As he reclined there, incapable of further movement, he witnessed the shattered remnants of four full divisions of the Army of the Potomac's Ninth Corps attempting to return to the Federal lines amid a murderous hurricane of lead and steel spewing forth from the Confederate line and from a horseshoe of artillery positions surrounding the Crater on three sides. How had events devolved to this sad state of affairs in what had been conceived as an ingenious plan to detonate a mine beneath the Confederate fort nearest the Union line in order to create a massive breach, thereby splitting that Confederate line and isolating a significant portion of the Army of Northern Virginia? The promise of this carefully devised plan was that the action would not only allow the Union to lift its siege on Petersburg, but would also result in the favorable resolution of that dreadful war, which had by then had entered its fourth year and had claimed 500,000 lives and countless wounded. By this time, the conflict was sorely testing the very foundations of the republic, with many Northerners questioning the merits of its further prosecution, regardless of the consequences to the Union.

Despite a total lack of support from the high command of the Army of the Potomac, and a number of active detractors, Pleasants had accomplished an engineering marvel in the construction of a tunnel over 510 feet in length without utilizing any visible ventilation system, the use of which would have alerted the enemy to the project thereby ensuring its demise. With very few exceptions, those Union officers with any engineering or mining experience had contended that a successful completion of the affair was an impossibility. Upon its completion, everything was in place for the assault subsequent to the mine's detonation on July 30, 1864, which was to result in a huge military victory and perhaps an end to the war. The majority of the Confederate forces had been drawn away from the Petersburg lines by a massive diversionary movement on Richmond. Fresh troops had been identified and trained to take the lead in assaulting the breach and rolling up any remaining Confederate opposition on both flanks of the breach. The Federals enjoyed overwhelming numerical superiority and had two more full corps to pour in on the flanks of the breach once the assault started, further to insure victory. Given these extremely favorable conditions, all elements seemed in place to assure a solid Union victory. Yet, as the afternoon shadows grew longer on the field of battle, Ambrose Burnside's corps was in shambles, with hundreds of dead, dying and wounded lying on the field out of reach of assistance by the Federals on the line. The magnitude of the defeat was decisive, almost too bitter to swallow, and thoroughly demoralizing. Lieutenant General Ulysses Grant, in command of all Federal forces, commented that this was "the saddest affair I have witnessed in this war." Instead of a decisive victory, the Union suffered a humiliating defeat and the bitter war waged on for almost nine more months, claiming perhaps another 100,000 lives with countless more wounded and maimed.

I was first attracted to this particular battle when my genealogical research disclosed that I had two direct ancestors in the battle, one with the 14th New York Heavy Artillery, which at the last minute, and without any preparation or forewarning, was chosen to lead the assault, with disastrous consequences. Of course, as a life-long Civil War aficionado, I had long been intrigued by the unusual circumstances surrounding this battle, and its consequences, despite the overwhelming odds in favor of the Federal forces. The Battle of the Crater is one of the lesser known and understood battles, but it is one of the most intriguing of the entire Civil War. It is set amongst the brutal and unendurable trench warfare at Petersburg, Virginia, which served as a remarkable foreshadowing of the situation faced by the adversaries in France fifty years later. The battle itself, and the machinations leading up to it, present a plot worthy of the most creative piece of fiction — so much so that one might find it incredible if it was not all proven fact. The plot has all the elements necessary for the weaving of a great novel — political correctness run amok, the commander of the critical lead element drunk and hiding in a bomb shelter as his troops pass into harm's way, a titanic clash of egos, as well as petty jealousy at the high command, and an unusually colorful cast of characters. Add to this mix the employment of some rather unique military tactics and movements, war atrocities, the destruction of the military career of one of the war's most famous generals, the further blundering of an officer considered the war's worst general, and then, at the end, throw in an intense Congressional investigation, and one has the makings of a remarkable novel, though perhaps one that strains credulity. However, these elements are all documented facts. The battle itself gained some recent notoriety with the release of the movie *Cold Mountain*, which opened with an eleven minute, spellbinding segment on the battle (which, interestingly, was not treated in the novel itself).

As I began writing this book, there were only two significant works dealing generally with the Battle of the Crater. The first, *The Battle of the Crater: "The Horrible Pit," June 25– August 6, 1864*, by Michael Cavanaugh and William Marvel, is part of the Virginia Civil War Battles and Leaders series. It is a remarkable but short study of this most intriguing battle, and one which I utilized to stay organized as I muddled through troop movements and time frames. Then, in 2002, John Cannan wrote *The Crater: Burnside's Assault on the Confederate Trenches, July 30, 1864*, another abbreviated work which was published in paperback format as part of the Battleground America Guides, and which contains additional reflections on the battle. While both of these works are scholarly endeavors, they are both quite brief in their presentation of the events leading up to the battle, and in the additional testimony of events by the participants themselves. Shortly after I completed my first draft of the manuscript, Jim Corrigan's *The 48th Pennsylvania in the Battle of the Crater: A Regiment of Coal Miners Who Tunneled Under the Enemy* was published. As the title suggests, this significant and worthy work focuses on a particular unit, and thus has a different vantage point from my more global treatment of the subject. The Cavanaugh/Marvel work consists of a mere 94 pages of text. The present work, at more than 400 pages, is considerably longer, with an expanded explanation of the relative positions of the two armies, based upon what had transpired in the two months leading up to the battle. The mood of the country at that time is carefully examined. Care is taken to discuss the brutality inflicted on the black troops, but also to put in perspective the atrocities committed by both sides, which has not been previously discussed in any detail elsewhere. Great care has been taken to bring in anecdotal material from the participants themselves, in order to give a first-hand perspective often missing from a discussion of the bare facts.

This book delves into the military and political background of the battle by tracing the rival armies through their bitter conflicts of the Overland Campaign, and it ends with the crossing of the James River and the onset of the siege of Petersburg. A hard look at the way the war was perceived by both sides after over three years of bloodletting is carefully laid out in order for the reader to appreciate the relative impact that the battle had on the body politic of both sides. Thus, while this work is lengthy for an analysis of a battle which lasted less than ten hours, there is a considerable investment of time in placing the battle in its proper perspective in history. No work to date has so treated this important, intriguing conflict, which has received far less than its due in serious academic analysis.

A great deal of assistance is required to complete a research project of this magnitude. I would like to acknowledge the great efforts extended on my behalf by many organizations and individuals, high among them being the staffs of the United States Army Military Institute at Carlisle Barracks, Pennsylvania, the Virginia Historical Society in Richmond, Virginia, the Peace Civil War Collection at Navarro College in Corsicana, Texas, the South Caroliniana Library of the University of South Carolina, and the Albert and Shirley Small Special Collections Library of the University of Virginia in Charlottesville. Also of great assistance were the able staffs of the McCain Library and Archives of the University of Southern Mississippi in Hattiesburg, the Center for American History of the University of Texas in Austin, and the Vermont Historical Society in Barre. Additionally, I could not have accomplished my objectives without the assistance of the great people at the Petersburg National Battlefield, the Museum of the Confederacy, the Special Collections Library at Duke University in Durham, North Carolina, and the Bentley Historical Library and Clements Library of the University of Michigan. A special thanks also goes to Ben Sewell of the Sons of Confederate Veterans, Ted Savas of Savas Publishing Company, Ron Lee for use of the Fannie Austin letters, Blake A. Magner for the use of his map of Confederate artillery positions, Amber Rhea and the trustees of the Westmoreland Club for permission to utilize John Adams Elder's painting *The Battle of the Crater*. Also, thanks to the folks at CJ & Friends LLC, who were excellent in transforming my maps into a publishable format.

Of course, my long effort would not have been possible at all without my long-suffering wife, Marie, whom I believe occasionally felt that the mounting stack of printed papers on my desk, if examined, would all read "All work and no play makes John a dull boy," to paraphrase Stephen King's demented author in *The Shining*.

CHAPTER 1

"If It Takes All Summer"

WITH THE ADVENT OF 1864, the American Civil War was entering its third year of bloody conflict with catastrophic losses on both sides. The two major armies in the east, the Army of the Potomac and the Army of Northern Virginia, had wintered on opposite sides of the Rapidan River in Virginia in a one hundred mile crescent stretching from Culpepper Court House to Alexandria. Despite considerable Union strides in the western theater, the Confederates still held firmly to most of the east, with the opposing armies standing in approximately the same position relative to each other as when the war began, "between the Federal and Confederate capitals." The hardened veterans on both sides knew that spring would bring another bloody year featuring the grim harvests of dead and wounded before any conclusion was reached. Men on both sides desperately hoped the conflict would end with the coming campaign and that they would somehow survive until then. Apart from its two incursions into the North, the Army of Northern Virginia had rather consistently gotten the better of the Army of the Potomac. Major General George Gordon Meade had proven to be a disappointment following Gettysburg, when he failed to close with and destroy Lee's weakened army. Thus, Lincoln had again begun to look elsewhere for a leader and finally settled on Ulysses S. Grant, the hero of Vicksburg and Forts Henry and Donelson. Grant was appointed general-in-chief of all Union armies, with the rank of lieutenant general, a position not utilized since the time of George Washington, and he assumed command of 553,000 men in nineteen diverse military departments. While civilian reaction in the North was well received, officers of the Army of the Potomac possessed strong reservations, as Grant was from the west, and he had not faced Bobby Lee. Grant's first order upon assuming command was to designate his headquarters in the field with the Army of the Potomac, thus indicating that the military focus would be in the east, with Lee's army as the primary objective.

As he assumed command, Grant enjoyed all the natural advantages, with twice the number of troops and an unlimited supply of available manpower; supplies for the troops, and munitions also appeared to be limitless. Lee, on the other hand, had no prospects for augmenting his depleted army. All able-bodied men seventeen to fifty years of age were already in service and were committed for the duration. He had difficulties feeding and supplying his depleted ranks. Given his numerical advantage, Grant's army could apply simultaneous pressure on numerous battlefields, thereby preventing Lee from being reinforced. Lee, however, had the advantage of geography and defending the interior lines. He also had the hearts and minds of the Army of Northern Virginia, whose soldiers were fierce in battle, entirely dedicated to the cause, and capable of working miracles for their beloved leader, as they had so often done in the past.

Grant instructed Meade that "Lee's Army will be your objective point. Wherever Lee goes, there will you go also." In the past, the main objective had always been the Confederate capital itself. Grant was dedicated to waging a war of attrition, which obviously weighed heavily in his favor. As a frontal assault along the Rapidan was injudicious, Grant had to discover a means to force Lee to open ground. He therefore devised a plan, or "grand design," involving three separate armies in the east working in concert. Major General Benjamin F. Butler's Army of the James would attack Richmond from the back door, moving 35,000 troops up the James River. Major General Franz Sigel, with 26,000 troops, was posted on the northern entrance to the Shenandoah Valley to prevent a movement down that corridor to threaten Washington. He was to move up the valley after meeting up with Brigadier General George Crook from west of the Allegany Mountains to strike Lee's flank while Meade engaged his front. Major General Ambrose E. Burnside's Ninth Corps of over 20,000 men was summoned from Tennessee with the capability either of reinforcing Butler or of joining the Army of the Potomac. Grant had a significant portion of the heavy artillery forces posted to defend the dozens of forts ringing Washington relieved of duty there to augment the Army of the Potomac. In the forts, soldiers had enjoyed a soft job with all the amenities. These pampered troops were used to posh conditions and had seen little or no action while manning the forts around Washington. The heavy artillery regiments often had headcounts of over 1,800 men, making them almost comically large when compared to the veteran regiments that had experienced almost three years of fighting. They were often referred to as "paper-collar" troops, and were the brunt of many jokes. As they encamped with the Army of the Potomac, many veteran soldiers laughed and asked what "division" it was as the "heavies" marched by them.

The average Southern soldier enjoyed a jaded view of the leadership of the Army of the Potomac's military commanders, having witnessed the failure of five prior to Meade. They expected little change with Grant. However, Lieutenant General James Longstreet, a longtime friend of Grant and a groomsman at his wedding, cautioned people not to underestimate the new Federal commander. "That man will fight us every day and every hour till the end of the war," he declared.[1]

As spring came to Virginia, it found Robert E. Lee aching to take the offensive again. However, his army was depleted in strength and was spread out over one hundred miles due to its inability to be supplied or to find adequate forage. He had, at most, 65,000 men organized into thirty-five under-strength infantry brigades and seven cavalry brigades, together with 224 cannon; he faced in his immediate front 116,000 men organized into 40 infantry brigades, seven cavalry brigades and 358 cannon. The ultimate strategist, Lee predicted multiple-pronged offensives against Richmond, but he was powerless to commence a preemptive offensive, due to the scarcity of supplies. By the spring of 1864, the South's fading hopes for independence lay in exploiting the perceived defect in the North's will to persevere by attempting to influence the presidential elections through further military setbacks. Northern resolve was, indeed, at low ebb. The hope was to effect a peace, as Clausewitz asserted, by pursuing "political goals by other means."

Lee decided to defend Richmond with freedom of movement rather than retiring behind a strong natural position like the North Anna River. He had good fortifications and could still move if the Rapidan line was lost. Grant was fine with this, and more than willing to wage a war of attrition on the Rapidan. However, he needed to maneuver Lee from behind his strong earthworks and into the open ground where Grant's own vastly superior numbers and artillery effectively could be brought to bear. There were two ways to maneuver around Lee's position on the Rapidan — upriver or downriver. By crossing upriver, Grant could shield Washington from any potential Confederate raids. However, he would then find Lee between Meade and Butler, and the Army of the Potomac would be dangerously dependent upon the Orange and Alexandria Railroad for supplies. Should he fail to seize the line below the Rapidan, the campaign would fail. Pivoting around Lee's downriver flank avoided these issues, although there was a serious problem with the terrain. Once across the Rapidan, the Federals would be immediately enmeshed in the Wilderness, a broad stretch of impenetrable thickets and dense second growth well known to the veterans of the Army of the Potomac. The previous year, almost to the day, Stonewall Jackson had routed the Army of the Potomac in the Wilderness at Chancellorsville, with a loss of 17,300 men.

Once out of the Wilderness, however, Grant knew the army would quickly encounter open country and he was confident he could get his army clear of the Wilderness before Lee could reach him. A third choice was to utilize McClellan's old route, traveling by water to the tip of the Virginia Peninsula and then marching between the James and the York rivers to Richmond. Grant chose the second option, primarily because it insured the optimum supply lines. Thus, he decided to go to his left where he could maintain the seacoast as a base for his supply lines as he maneuvered.

Tactical planning for the massive maneuver was entrusted to Major General Andrew A. Humphreys, Meade's chief of staff. Lee's set of options needed to be carefully considered, including ignoring Meade and making a dash toward Washington along the Orange and Alexandria Railroad or the Shenandoah Valley, or withdrawing behind another fortified line further south. Humphreys planned to slip the Army of the Potomac past Lee's right flank to bring him out of the Rapidan defenses and then scoop the Army of the Potomac below Mine Run to force the Confederates out of that line as well. "A well-executed move to the south, and then a turn to the west would flush Lee into the open country, thereby ensuring Grant of the fight he was seeking."[2]

The ultimate plan called for a crossing at Germanna Ford with the right wing of the army, the left wing pursuing a circuitous route through Ely's Ford and Chancellorsville to the Catharpin-Pawunkey corridor. The movement started on the evening of May 3; the troops were to be marched hard through the Wilderness and nearby Mine Run before sunset on the 4th. The objective was to get the army out of the thick woods in a timely fashion and thereby take Lee by surprise. Thus commenced Grant's Overland Campaign. The Army of the Potomac started with 127,471 men coupled with Burnside's 21,357, along with 825 ambulances and 609 ordnance wagons. The seventh "On to Richmond" campaign was thus commenced by the Army of the Potomac, the six others having failed miserably. As the massive Federal force started its movement, Lee could call upon 63,984 men.

Grant was so pleased with the initial performance that he predicted he could be in Richmond in four days if Lee "became a party to the agreement." However, Lee was not a willing participant. He decided to leave Longstreet in Gordonsville to preserve the link with Richmond as long as possible. He reluctantly decided not to contest the Federal river crossings due to the disparity in numbers, but rather to hit the Union flank as the Army of the Potomac negotiated the Wilderness where superiority of numbers and munitions counted less. Fortunately for Lee, given a late start, the Federal headquarters overruled Humphreys' ambitious schedule and instead stopped the troops in the Wilderness to allow the massive wagon train to catch up to the infantry. "Providence on this occasion seemed to restore the opportunity Lee failed to achieve through his own planning."[3]

As soon as Meade's movement was detected, Lee, anxious to attack the Army of the Potomac while it was entangled in the Wilderness, reacted accordingly. Longstreet was quickly ordered up, beginning a forty-two mile march to the front. The majority of the Army of the Potomac was then centered at the crossroads near the Wilderness Tavern where the Germanna Plank Road lead southeast across the Orange Turnpike. By 8:00 A.M. on May 5, the Federals were heavily engaged by the Confederate forces attempting to flank them. Lee realized the longer Grant could be delayed in the morass of the Wilderness, the more punishment he could inflict. Brigadier General John B. Gordon's brigade of Ewell's corps was able to overlap the Union right. The underbrush soon caught fire and many men who were wounded between the lines were killed. By May 6, Grant launched a brutal, smashing counterattack all along his lines. Major General Ambrose Powell "A.P." Hill was forced to pull back almost two miles to the west, almost as far as the Widow Tapp farm. Meanwhile, Longstreet's corps hurried to achieve the front, with Gregg's Texas Brigade leading the way. Gregg went in just as Lee was about to lead a countercharge, while the Confederates shouted, "Go back, General Lee, go back!," terrified for his safety. Longstreet's momentum quickly overlapped Major General Winfield S. Hancock's flank, forcing him to withdraw behind his lines on the Brock Road. Longstreet then maneuvered along an unfinished railroad bed to the right around Hancock's left flank south of the Plank Road. The resultant attack was successful, but as the Confederate forces closed on Brock Road, Longstreet was shot in the throat by his own men, an incident ironically similar to Stonewall Jackson's wounding almost exactly one year before. This caused the Southern momentum to ebb. Meanwhile, on the left front, Gordon had been advocating a flanking movement all day on the Federal right. He finally received approval to commence an attack at 5:30 P.M. However, darkness intervened before he could achieve total success, although his assault spread extreme panic among the Federal forces.

On May 7, after two days of heavy fighting, the Union casualties were 17,500 and Confederate losses amounted to 10,500. The Federals broke off contact. Lee had prevented Grant from breaking his lines; he had saved Richmond and forced Grant to abandon his campaign of direct attack from the north, all the while inflicting heavy losses on Grant's army. The kindest assessment to Grant would call the result a draw. He did achieve his objective in punishing Lee, who had difficulty recovering due to his supply issues and the lack of troop reinforcements. In the past, however, the Union commander routinely had sought the roads north after such a brutal encounter with Lee. However, Grant had promised Lincoln there would be "[n]o turning back" and spent the day of May 7 planning a march around Lee's right to seize the crossroads at Spotsylvania Court House. He had vowed to continue "until by mere attrition, if in no other way, there should be nothing left of him [Lee]."[4]

At 5:00 P.M. that same day, the Army of the Potomac was treated to a novel sight. A division of black troops under Brigadier General Edward Ferrero had "marched up and massed in a hollow nearby" to join Burnside's Ninth Corps, remembered Colonel Theodore Lyman of Meade's staff. The veteran soldiers were far from happy at this development. The white soldiers "were not disposed to let them [the blacks] pass without some 'chaffing,' to which the black men were quite equal," according to Lieutenant Freeman S. Bowley, a white officer of the 30th United States Colored Troops (USCT).[5] They were "the most talked-about troops in Virginia," comprised of freshly raised black regiments, primarily from occupied positions in the South. These troops were the first USCT units in the Army of the Potomac and had been held in reserve since joining. The blue-clad black soldiers would soon play a leading role in a fierce battle at Petersburg in late July.

Grant gave orders for a night march to Spotsylvania Court House at 6:30 A.M. At that same time, Lee predicted the movement. He also predicted that Grant was held in such high esteem that he would be able to draw without limit on massive resources in men and materials to keep his offensive moving, while the Confederates had already exhausted both.

Lee's objective was to keep the Southern forces between Grant and Richmond, checking Grant for several months, until some crisis in governmental affairs or further change in public opinion in the North would induce authorities in Washington to allow the South to go its own way rather than forcing its retention at so heavy a cost. For the next six weeks, Grant would repeatedly attempt to circumvent Lee's right flank and destroy it. Each time, Grant would find his adversary in possession of the coveted stronghold, resisting all efforts to dislodge him. Lee repeatedly read Grant's mind and developed his own plans accordingly. In a diagonal running from Germanna Ford all the way to Cold Harbor, a scant ten miles from Richmond, Grant repeatedly hit Lee's lines and was held and thrown back and subsequently moved further down the diagonal, with Lee racing on parallel lines to thwart him again.

President Lincoln had not heard from Grant since Grant had crossed the Rapidan on May 4. On May 7, the Washington newspapers finally reported "Grant Found." That night, the Marine Corps band played on the White House south lawn for the first time since 1861, and Lincoln appeared on the portico and led three cheers for General Grant and his command. At about that same time, Grant pulled out of line and proceeded to Spotsylvania amidst fields bearing the skulls and bones of the casualties from the prior year's fighting. Despite this grisly scene, the veterans of the Army of the Potomac commenced cheering once they realized their route was south rather than north, as had been the past routine. The outcome of the war could well have depended upon who arrived first to Spotsylvania Court House. If it was the Army of the Potomac, the Federals would stand between Lee and Richmond, forcing him to deploy against an entrenched Yankee line. However, Lee got there first with his I Corps, under Major General Richard H. Anderson,[6] achieving the high ground at Laurel Hill, one and one half miles from the crossroads, and was thus the victor of the fateful race.

By May 9, serious fighting had commenced at Spotsylvania. Lieutenant General Richard S. Ewell's II Corps' entrenchments ended in a U-shaped salient beyond the remainder of the Confederate lines. Dubbed the "Mule Shoe," it made an inviting target for the Federals. At 6:10 P.M. on May 10, the Union attacked the Confederate salient and quickly penetrated the angle and thus threatened to take the whole Confederate line from the rear. However, with no reinforcements, the Union was ultimately forced to withdraw. This limited success gave Grant an idea. Thus, on May 11, he wired Washington that "We have now ended the sixth day of very heavy fighting [and] the result up to this time is much in our favor. I intend to fight it out on this line if it takes all summer."[7] Grant finally decided to utilize the same tactic on a grander scale. Major General Winfield Scott Hancock's corps was to breach the salient at its weakest point, near its apex, supported by Burnside's and Brigadier General Horatio G. Wright's corps, with the whole army committed to achieving success.

On May 12, Hancock initiated his movement. Ewell had placed twenty-two guns in the apex of the Mule Shoe; due to inaccurate reports of a Federal flanking action, all were soon withdrawn. In a heavy downpour, the Federals hit the salient and threatened to cut Lee's army in two. The guns were hastily rushed back to the front, where twenty were captured. Lee, intent upon saving the day, attempted to lead the counttercharge. The timely arrival of reserves from Early's corps thwarted the advance and the Federals were driven back to the captured Confederate trenches. While unable to reclaim the former position, Lee was able to build a new works at the base of the Mule Shoe to straighten his line. To the west of the apex, Wright fought Ewell's troops in hand-to-hand combat, with some of the heaviest level of musketry of the war. Corpses were piled up several deep. Large trees were shattered and felled by small arms fire alone; the flags of both armies were often found in the same breastworks. Since that day, the area has been known as the Bloody Angle, and for good reason. That night Lee's men were able to withdraw to their new line at the base of the salient.

Even as Lee was struggling to save his embattled army that day, he received word that Major General Jeb Stuart had been killed at Yellow Tavern, news which affected him greatly. Following a quiet on the battlefield, while the surgeons on both sides preformed their gruesome work, Grant shifted to the left, causing Lee to divert his lines accordingly. On May 17, the roads finally were dry enough to break the stalemate. Grant ordered the troops to assail Lee's left on the 18th. However, Lee proved to be too strong at that point. On the 18th, a number of the newly arrived heavy artillery turned infantry units were indoctrinated in battle when Hancock attempted to break Ewell's new line. Again on the 19th, the "heavies" saw considerable action as Ewell attempted to find a weak spot on the Federal right but were repulsed. The battle of Spotsylvania Court House ended, with over 18,400 Union casualties as opposed to 10,000 Confederates. In the first two weeks of the campaign, Grant had lost over 36,000 men.

He then proceeded with a plan for a movement south on May 20, which he had sketched the previous night. Lee, however, was reluctant to react; but by 1:00 P.M. he ordered Ewell's corps to move south to Hanover Junction to protect the rail lines into Richmond. Ewell crossed the North Anna River at Chesterfield Bridge early on May 22. Major General John C. Breckinridge soon brought two brigades from the Shenandoah Valley after the Battle of New Market. Lee's lines were a mile and one half upstream to Ox Ford, where the south bank was higher than the north bank. No matter which route Grant chose, Lee was in a strong position to move against him. On the same day, Grant approached the North Anna in a wide front. The objective was to cross the river west of the Fredericksburg Railroad and then "to strike Lee wherever he could be found."[8] The scene was thus set for yet another bloody contest between the two armies striving for position as if they were pieces on a chess board.

While the Army of the Potomac was still slugging it out at Spotsylvania Court House, Grant received rather devastating news regarding the progress of his grand design on the other fronts. Benjamin Butler, a War Democrat with little military experience, but far too powerful to be removed due to his role in Lincoln's chances for reelection, had taken Bermuda Hundred and City Point, as planned, in early May. However, his attempts to move against Richmond from the south were halfhearted at best. He first moved against Petersburg, which was barely defended at the time as most of its defenders were called away to thwart an attack by Sheridan from the north. Butler then passed to the defensive on May 15, and Lieutenant General Pierre G.T. Beauregard went on the offensive from Drewrey's Bluff, driving Butler away from the James, while his forces around Petersburg were to cut off Butler's army from Bermuda Hundred. Due to a lack of numbers and failed coordination, the Confederates failed to cut Butler off, but they did force him back to Bermuda Hundred and bottled him up there on May 18. He had lost 4,160 men, including two general officers, in the Battle of Drewrey's Bluff. Grant declared when he received the bad news that Butler's army was so completely shut off from further operations directly against Richmond "as if it had been in a bottle strongly corked."[9]

Meanwhile, Franz Sigel's third element of the grand design proved no more successful than Butler in carrying out its assigned mission. Grant had Sigel assemble 8,000 infantry, 1,500 cavalry and three batteries of artillery under Major General Edward O.C. Ord, to advance on Covington, Virginia, destroy portions of the Virginia & Tennessee Railroad, and then proceed to Lynchburg and destroy the depot there. A second element of cavalry under Brigadier General George Crook would proceed from Charleston, West Virginia, against the same rail line at Dublin Station, hit important saltworks at Saltville and the lead mines at Wytheville, then turn northeast down the Shenandoah to Staunton. Sigel would move southward down the valley to meet up with Crook and Ord at Staunton, where the combined force would then hit Lynchburg. While Grant had little faith in Sigel achieving complete success, he felt the attacks would serve as a major distraction to the Rebels. He confided to Sherman: "In other words, if Sigel can't skin himself he can hold a leg while some one else skins,"[10] paraphrasing Lincoln.

Sigel's forces set out in late April. After destroying several railroad bridges and depots, Crook took it upon himself to return to West Virginia to draw supplies. He later defended his actions by claiming he had received dispatches indicating that Grant had been defeated and that Lee was threatening to cut him off. A cavalry force under Brigadier General W.W. Averill then bypassed Saltsville on May 8, deeming it too well guarded due to the presence of Brigadier General John Hunt Morgan, who was fresh from his breakout from the Ohio Penitentiary. Morgan hit him as he moved to Dublin, where Averill learned his superior had subsequently returned to West Virginia. He promptly decided to follow suit on May 15.

The Confederate Department of Southwestern Virginia had been commanded since March by General Breckinridge, a candidate for president of the Southern faction of the Democratic Party and runner up to Lincoln in the 1860 election. Breckinridge proceeded to Staunton, arriving on May 12, and then set off for New Market, some forty miles away. There, cavalry under Brigadier General John D. Imboden was skirmishing with the advance elements of Sigel's main body only some twelve miles away. The combined forces approached 5,000 men, which included augmentations of about 750 local militia and 247 members of the corps of cadets from the Virginia Military Institute, led by one of their professors. A desperate Breckinridge hoped to keep the fifteen to seventeen year old boys, "the seed corn of the Confederacy," out of the thickest of the fighting, but confessed that "should the occasion require it, he would use them very freely."[11]

New Market was important to Sigel; if he could take it he would gain control of the only road across Massanutten Mountain that paralleled his intended route, an action that would secure his left flank all the way up the Shenandoah to Staunton. Breckinridge studied the field at New Market and decided to go on the offensive with his smaller force. Brigadier General Gabriel Wharton's brigade, reinforced by the dismounted 23rd Virginia Cavalry, the 62nd Virginia Mounted Infantry and an independent company of Missouri cavalry, charged the main Federal lines, followed by the 26th Virginia Battalion under Brigadier General John Ecol, with the VMI cadets in reserve, and started up Manor's Hill with the rain falling hard. As the charge finally began to falter, Ecol's men became pinned by heavy fire. Breckinridge faced a critical situation. "Put the boys in," he commanded, "and may God forgive me for the order."[12] The cadets advanced to the crest of the hill, where they were hit by heavy fire. Temporarily faltering when their professor was cut down by an artillery shell, they continued to advance and took cover behind a fence on the north edge of the orchard and closed the gap between Wharton's brigade and Ecol's command. Sigel had ordered his main force to advance into the gap created between the two Rebel forces but found that the Confederates had closed it before his troops could achieve the gap. Then the Confederates advanced, with the agile cadets in the lead, and overran the Federal artillery position and turned the guns on the exposed elements of the Federal line. Sigel fell back across the North Fork of the Shenandoah River and retreated to Mount Jackson, having lost 831 men. Thus, on the same day Beauregard began plans to push Butler back to Bermuda Hundred, thereby ending any hope for an advance on Richmond from the south, Franz Sigel's element of Grant's grand design was eliminated. The wheat crop in Virginia's "bread basket" was saved; the Battle of New Market freed up a portion of Breckinridge's force to join Lee on May 17. Thus, two-thirds of Grant's grand design for the east was in shambles, leaving only one weapon still available to him — the Army of the Potomac.

Grant abandoned Spotsylvania as he had the Wilderness and stepped off to his left, again executing his "Jug-Headed" movement, as his men termed it, heading east and south. He detached Hancock's corps, hoping to lure Lee into attacking the isolated force and thereby becoming enmeshed in an open-ground battle without entrenchments and where Federal numerical superiority would prove the telling factor. Lee withdrew from the battlefield on May 20 and began a blocking position across the North Anna River near Hanover Junction. He moved parallel to Hancock on the interior line but without taking the bait, predicting to his staff that the armies would next meet along the North Anna River due to the topography of the countryside. On the 23rd, the Army of the Potomac approached the North Anna in a wide front. Major General Gouverneur K. Warren's Fifth Corps comprised the right side, with Wright close by him. Burnside's Ninth Corps was in the center and Hancock's corps, comprising the Federal left, was farthest east, traveling down the Telegraph Road. Their goal was to cross the river west of the Fredericksburg Railroad and then hit Lee "wherever he could be found." The common opinion of the Federals on May 23 was that Lee had retreated toward Richmond by then.

Later on the 23rd, Hancock attacked a smaller Confederate force on the north side of Chesterfield Bridge, quickly clearing it away and moving to the south side of the river. Meanwhile, Warren's corps was fighting for its life only five miles away near a ford at Jericho Mill. With his force divided on opposite sides of the river, Warren was extremely vulnerable. Once he finally got his whole force across, he was still isolated from the main Federal body. The Confederates reinforced and struck and shattered Warren's right, forcing a retreat to the river. Then Major General Charles Wainwright's Fifth Corps artillery was called into play and spewed canister into the attacking Rebels and the embattled corps rallied around the guns. Warren organized a countercharge and forced the Confederates back. The Battle of Jericho Mill was over. The Confederates withdrew during the night, leaving Grant to assume Lee had retreated from the North Anna front. Federals had reason to feel optimistic, given their success in achieving the south bank of the North Anna. Grant predicted in a telegraph to Stanton that "Hancock and Warren will reach the South Anna by nightfall." Plans were to combine the advance, with Hancock and Burnside moving south through Hanover Junction, and Warren and Wright crossing the South Anna west of Hanover Junction.

Lee was seriously ill and was forced to ride in a carriage rather than on his horse, Traveller. The Federals had by then crossed both upstream and downstream. Lee did not want to abandon the vital railroad center at Hanover Junction, thus ruling out a withdrawal across the South Anna. Consequently, he came up with yet another bold solution. The only point where the north bank of the North Anna was not higher than the south bank was at Ox Ford, where the Confederate batteries would definitely have a great advantage. His plan was to swing both of his flanks back from the river in an inverted V-shaped position similar to Spotsylvania. The right of the V was held by Anderson's and Ewell's corps; A.P. Hill made up the shorter, left leg. The apex was at the river and Anderson's left. In all, the formation was five miles in length and was strongly entrenched, superb for a defense but also for springing an offensive action. Lee could easily and quickly strip one leg of the formation to reinforce the other to defend an attack; moreover, it could be used to attack an isolated wing of the Federal army. It did not matter which wing, as either would have to cross the river twice in order to reinforce the other, and would thus be unlikely to arrive in time, as the Confederates had only to cross the four mile base of the V. Lee was setting a massive trap and was confident that Grant would march right into it.

Burnside's Ninth Corps in the center of the Federal front could not cross at Ox Ford, as it was vulnerable to Confederate artillery fire and sharpshooters on the high ground on the south bank at that point. However, Grant felt the evidence seemed to indicate the Southerners were retreating and he reported to Halleck to that effect. Lee's illness was worsening as he contemplated which Federal wing he would hit that day. None of his acting commanders were up to the task, which called for precision, boldness and military acumen. A.P. Hill was himself quite ill; Ewell was likewise physically exhausted and ill. Richard Anderson was new to command and was untested and uninspiring as a leader. Quick execution was the key, as once the Federals sensed the trap, it would be too late and they would merely entrench or fall back and search for a crossing downstream. Only Lee's illness could prevent the Rebels from obtaining a great victory by overwhelming Hancock's corps left wing on that fateful day at the North Anna.

Hancock had great difficulty in closing with Burnside on May 24, as he was met with stiff resistance. He soon learned that two Confederate corps, Anderson and Ewell's, were on his front and right. The trap was now right for springing, as Hancock was totally isolated from the rest of the army, with his back to the river and facing a superior force and with no hope of assistance nearby. If Lee had attacked at that moment, the heart and soul of the Army of the Potomac would have been in serious difficulty. However, Lee was still quite ill and had not taken any of his subordinates into his confidence. Only he could direct the assault, and he was bedridden and too sick to carry out the plan.

Brigadier General James H. Ledlie's brigade of the first division of Burnside's corps attacked the heavily fortified Confederate defenses at the apex near the river, where it encountered Mahone's men. Ledlie had been ordered not to move forward, but he was either ignorant of the corps' predicament or too drunk to care, having fortified himself with plenty of "Dutch courage." He was clearly intoxicated. The men charged into a lead storm in the midst of a rainstorm and the line was quickly shattered. "Every man became his own general," Captain John Anderson of the 57th Massachusetts later wrote.[13] These two men were to face each other two months later with even more deadly consequences. Hancock, meanwhile, probed and discovered the eastern edge of the inverted V, only 250 yards away. A fierce attack by the Rebels confirmed that he was exposed and in serious danger, but he was now cognizant of the trap and able to avoid disaster. However, by the twentieth day of constant conflict, from the Federal perspective the "showdown was no closer within their reach than at the outset. Dejection was taking its toll, along with the profitless wear and tear of the past three weeks."[14] For the third time in three weeks, Lee had foiled Grant, who had maneuvered offensively only to be stopped by Lee's masterful "grasp of terrain, tenacious fighting, and good luck."[15]

Having failed to spring the trap and deal the Army of the Potomac a devastating blow, Lee was now forced to wait for Grant to make the next move. Grant soon decided to move downriver and cross the Pamunkey River to avoid the natural obstacles on Lee's left flank. Hence, he decided on yet another swing to the east to preserve his supply lines, a move which he initiated on May 26. By then, Grant believed Lee was whipped, since he had failed to prosecute the springing of the obvious trap, and Grant so informed Washington. Lee himself received 10,000 reinforcements and Grant 40,000, roughly the number he had lost in the past three weeks. The next target was Cold Harbor, halfway between the Totopotomoy Creek and the Chickahominy rivers, where five roads converged, an area the battle hardened veterans of both sides knew well from two years before during the Seven Days campaign as the Gaines' Mill battlefield, Lee's first notable victory. Countless rusty canteens, moldy shreds of clothing and blankets, and cartridge boxes were strewn over the entire countryside. As Lee moved to block all the approaches to Richmond, he recalled a rise in the topography near the Chickahominy River called Turkey Hill. On June 2 he advanced Breckinridge's two brigades to his right flank, next to Hoke's division. Sensing Grant was withdrawing strength from his right, he followed those units up with Mahone's and Wilcox's Divisions of A.P. Hill's corps. At about 3:00 P.M., Breckinridge captured Turkey Hill on the north bank of the Chickahominy. From there, the Confederate artillery could dominate the river bottoms, thus securing Lee's right flank; his line was a full seven miles long and very heavily fortified.

Meanwhile, Grant tightened his own lines near Cold Harbor and was angered when a series of Rebel attacks were not countered by Meade's army. He saw the need to strike at Lee instead of moving south of the James without a fight, as the North was impatient at the apparent indefinite continuation of military operations. Thus the attractive option for Grant was to attack Lee's lines, however well fortified. The war by this time was costing over four million dollars per day. Breaking Lee's lines, according to Assistant Secretary of War Charles A. Dana, "meant his destruction and the collapse of the rebellion."

Grant decided to assault Lee where he stood. Meade reasoned that if Lee could strike as he had with his left, his right must have been weakened considerably. Thus, a thrust was planned for the next morning, June 3, against the Confederate right where the preliminary attack of the day before had put the Federals closest to Lee's lines. That night the battle hardened veterans of Grant's army were observed throughout the camp — men had "taken off their coats and seemed to be engaged in sewing up rents in them." On closer examination, it was discovered they were "calmly writing their names and home addresses on slips of paper and pinning them to the backs of their coats, so that their bodies might be recognized and their fate made known to their families at home."[16]

The Confederate engineers had perfected a means of laying out entrenchments with incredible accuracy. A complicated surveying process avoided any difficult-to-defend angles. By the night of June 2, they were successful "beyond their wildest imaginings; through a combination of chance and design, Lee's men had created the perfect killing ground."[17]

As a heavy rain ceased on the morning of June 3, and following an immense cannon barrage heard in Richmond some twelve miles away, more than 60,000 Federals comprising three blue-clad corps came on, striking for three points along the center and right center of the Rebel line, which had only half the number defending its whole than that which was assaulting half of it. They advanced under a murderous fire, and "were simply slaughtered," according to Captain Lemuel Abbot of the 10th Vermont. Grant lost over 7,000 men within one half hour, over half of those in the first eight minutes of the attack. The dead covered five acres of ground. Confederate Brigadier General Evander Law of Field's division gave the most poignant description of the result: "It was not war, it was murder."[18] One casualty found on the field later with a blood stained diary in his pocket had this gruesome final entry that typified the day's effects: "June 3. Cold Harbor. I was killed."[19] Grant later confessed to his staff: "I regret this assault more than any one I have ever ordered."[20]

The attack at Cold Harbor greatly increased the dissention among the officers of the army. Grant had suffered 59, 929 casualties in one month — a greater number than the total strength of the Army of Northern Virginia by then. The common soldiers questioned the skill of their leaders. Meade complained to his wife that he would bear the responsibility for the loss without having the ability to command his army. The Army of the Potomac was also about to lose its character, as thousands of three year enlistments were scheduled to expire in the next two months. Grant had an epiphany on June 5 and devised a new plan. He would move his army south of the James River. He had lost two men for Lee's one, and at Cold Harbor his losses were five to Lee's one. He had to take these statistics to heart. Preparations were made to move over 100,000 men on June 9 from close contact with the enemy to the south bank of the James. Disengaging a ten mile front and marching fifty miles across swampy, ravine-riddled ground and crossing a tidal river at a point where it was over one-half mile wide and ninety feet deep was no easy task. At the same time, Lee watched for signs of movement and withdrew Early's corps into a position behind Anderson's left as a ready reserve. Meanwhile, he sent Breckinridge back into the valley to counter Sigel's successor, Major General David Hunter, who had just marched into Lexington and burned down VMI and the homes of prominent Confederates. Lee reluctantly also sent Early's corps to reinforce Breckinridge, defeat Hunter and march north down the Shenandoah to threaten Washington. This would leave him without almost one-third of his infantry and two-thirds of his cavalry[21] at the very time he was starting his strategic defensive move to the James.[22]

At daybreak on June 13, Lee learned Grant's army had again slipped away in the night. Lee quickly crossed the Chickahominy and moved into the Charles City Road heading toward Frayser's Farm. Grant reached the James and began construction of a great pontoon bridge over 2,100 feet in length across the river. Lee anticipated that Petersburg would be Grant's new objective. Lee had indicated one week earlier to Jubal Early that if Grant got to the James, it would mean a siege, and then it would be only a matter of time before the end of the Confederacy. He moved below White Oak Swamp where he could block the eastern approaches to Richmond and be closer to Drewrey's Bluff for a crossing in case the blow was aimed at Beauregard in Petersburg. He agonized over recalling Early but in the end decided success in the valley would "relieve our difficulties that at present press heavily upon us." No matter when Grant moved, it would now come down to a siege, and as he had previously predicted, "The picture presented is one of ultimate starvation."[23] Southern hopes were now left to a battle of wills—North versus South. The coming months would prove critical for the South in convincing the North of its intractable determination for independence as the presidential election came more into focus.

CHAPTER 2

Enemy at the Gates

The stalemate at Cold Harbor was unendurable to Grant. His charge had been to break the fighting potential of the South, and he persisted in the belief that this feat could still be performed in one bold stroke rather than a slow, methodical process of grinding and strangling and eroding. From the campaign's inception, his objective had been to keep the Army of Northern Virginia so busy that Lee could never again seize the initiative, thus compelling Lee to fight the Confederate's battles at his own choosing rather than Lee's. Adhering to this plan was Grant's opportunity for a decisive victory, and it was imminently clear that no further offensive at or near Cold Harbor could produce such an effect. While Halleck was urging that the Army of the Potomac stay put and engage in a siege, Grant still adhered to the principles of a war of movement. This was how he had taken Vicksburg, and this was how he would finally beat Lee. He saw his opportunity to the south, across the James River in a peaceful, sleepy Virginia city named Petersburg lying some twenty-odd miles from Richmond on the southern bank of the Appomattox River, near where it flows into the James.[1]

Petersburg was a critical supply terminus for the Army of Northern Virginia. The Richmond vicinity did not produce enough forage to supply the army. Supplies thus had to come from two vital sources. One was the Shenandoah Valley, and those supplies moved over the Virginia Central Railroad and the James River Canal. Of even more significance, however, were those which arrived from the Deep South, primarily on railroads that ran through Petersburg. If Grant could seize that city, the Army of Northern Virginia and the government would be in difficult straits. If, at the same time, the Shenandoah could be plugged, Richmond would no longer be defensible. Lee's army was still Grant's main objective. He wanted to destroy it; for him to do so, he had to find a way to get Lee out of the trenches. By cutting off his supplies, he hoped to finally force Lee to move on his own terms. Thus, Petersburg became a key to forcing Lee out into the open, where Grant's numerical superiority would prove decisive in a fight to the finish. Therefore, the next objective for this 100,000 plus blue-clad army was Petersburg.

By the eve of the Civil War, Petersburg had become Virginia's second largest city after its capital, Richmond, with a population of 18,206, including 5,680 slaves and 3,164 free blacks, most of whom lived on Pocahontas Island in the Appomattox River. Of the white population, over 90 percent were native-born Virginians. For many years, Petersburg was one of the busiest ports in the United States, due largely to its location just below the falls of the Appomattox River, which enabled planters to transfer their goods to awaiting ships for passage to the James River and thence on through the Chesapeake Bay to the Atlantic Ocean. Nestled on the Appomattox's southern bank, Petersburg was only eight miles from City Point, where the Appomattox joins the James, and a mere 23 miles from Richmond.[2]

The city played a role in the American Revolution. Its militia, under Major General Frederick Wilhelm von Steuben, delayed the British a sufficient time for the Marquis de Lafayette to entrench on Richmond's heights, thus preventing the city from a second capture,[3] and ultimately enabling the Americans to shell the British in Petersburg from Archer's Hill.[4] It also played a significant role in the War of 1812. The Petersburg Volunteers, commanded by Captain Richard McRae, left the city on October 21, 1812, for the war in Ohio. There they achieved fame in the relentless defense of Fort Meigs on May 5, 1813, important because it marked the beginning of the end for the British in the Northwest Territories.[5] The Petersburg unit wore jaunty feathered hats with conspicuous rosettes, leading then President Madison, soon after their heroic deeds, to nickname their ancestral home the "Cockade City" in deference to this notable headgear.[6] Subsequently, the Cockade City sent two companies to the Mexican War. This contribution was in addition to the individual examples of the city's patriotism; Petersburg sent men such as Winfield Scott, overall commander of U.S. forces in in the Mexican War, a native of Dinwaddie County and former resident of Petersburg.

Five major railroads converged on Petersburg, leading to its strategic importance as a transportation hub vital to the continued war effort, and gave the city significance well beyond its size. Tracks radiated in all directions. The Richmond and Petersburg Railroad left the city and headed north to the capital city. The Petersburg and Weldon Railroad pointed south, providing unique access to the coastal regions of North Carolina and Georgia; the Norfolk and Petersburg Railroad passed east of the city before turning southeast and running through the scenic countryside west of the Blackwater River before entering areas then occupied by Union troops near Suffolk. The City Point Railroad emanated from that city at the junction of the James and Appomattox rivers, a total of eight miles from Petersburg, thereby providing Petersburg with access to a deepwater port. The Southside Railroad ran westerly and linked Petersburg with eastern Tennessee, and, through Burke's Station, with the Deep South via a junction with the Richmond and Danville Railroad.[7]

In addition to the railroads, at least nine significant wagon roads converged on the Cockade City. A number of these roads were constructed of logs laid laterally across the roadbed to form a hard surface and were aptly named "plank roads." Two of the most important of these arteries were the Jerusalem Plank Road, which connected the city with Jerusalem (Courtland), and the Boydton Plank Road, which led south through Dinwiddie Court House.[8] Petersburg was soon to become the object of the longest military campaign ever waged against a city in the United States. In terms of world history up to that point, it might be compared to Londonderry or Sevastopol, or even Troy itself.[9]

As the Civil War entered its third year, Petersburg had truly become the "last bulwark of the Confederacy."[10] The supply lines so vital to Richmond and the ongoing existence of the Confederate government all came through Petersburg, which was thus hailed as the "guardian of Richmond's lifeline." Without Petersburg, Richmond itself was doomed. All but one railroad still in Confederate control from the south and west passed through Petersburg by June of 1864 (that being the Richmond and Danville Railroad). By that time, Grant had succeeded in cutting off the two eastern tracks, being the eight mile track to City Point and the Norfolk line. The city's remaining three railroads still connected Petersburg to major supply sources in the lower South. The lines poured supplies, food and troops into the city and thence on to Richmond and all points beyond.[11] Thus, Petersburg was the vital lifeline for the capital, and the South could ill afford to lose it. Grant recognized this strategic importance and was intent on taking the city. Someone later remarked to Grant that the Petersburg siege brought to mind the "legendary Kilkenny cats, which fought until only their tails were left." Grant replied bluntly that the Federal "cat has the longer tail."[12] The importance of this city resulted in the siege of Petersburg, which was to last 292 days and cost over 70,000 lives (42,000 Union and 28,000 Confederate).

Prior to the siege, the city had already encountered the cost of war by the spring of 1862 when the Army of the Potomac reached the outskirts of Richmond during McClellan's Peninsular Campaign. In August of that year, a line of defenses was started by order of the Confederate Engineer Bureau under Captain Charles H. Dimmock, a Northerner by birth. The finished line thus earned the name the "Dimmock Line." When the work was completed, Dimmock had left ten miles of breastworks, fortifications and positions for 55 batteries beginning and ending on the Appomattox River, thus protecting all but the northern approaches to the city.[13]

Petersburg had not totally escaped Federal scrutiny before Grant's decision to invest the city was forced on him by his monumental failure at Cold Harbor. Its parks and warehouses had already served as hospitals for the multitudes of sick and wounded Rebel troops. Its industry had concentrated on munitions to further the war effort. Most of its able-bodied men were absent, fighting the Union invasion in diverse places. Again, in February 1864, the city was the target of a proposed seaborne campaign advanced by some of Grant's subordinates but rejected by the administration.

Then, on June 9, the city had to be stripped of virtually all its defenders, providing yet another threat with the makings of a disaster. Beauregard had accurately predicted the Federals' next step. Noting the arrival of a pontoon train on June 7, he wired Bragg:

> Should Grant have left Lee's front, he doubtless intends operations against Richmond along the James River, probably on south side. Petersburg being nearly defenseless would be captured before it could be re-enforced. Ransom's brigade and Hoke's division should then be returned at once.[14]

This prediction was actually not that original; the Richmond *Examiner* that same day opined of Grant's crossing of the James. On June 8, Beauregard reported heavily laden vessels and more pontoons along the James, which suggested supplies and transportation for Grant's coming. However, Bragg still refused to act on the request for the return of Hoke's and Ransom's divisions, referring the matter instead to Lee. General Wise had returned to Petersburg on June 1, with his brigade. The city was totally devoid of troops with the exception of Wise's men on the extreme left and Sturdivant's light artillery battery of four guns along with two battalions of town militia — in all, close to 1,000 men. All other troops had been sent across the James to aid Lee in his struggle with Grant. Wise was convinced the greatest threat came from City Point, so that most of his command was posted along the eastern Dimmock line to block routes from that direction. There was a gap of approximately one mile and a half to Redan 16, occupied by 30 home guard militia with four pieces of stationary artillery. One mile farther were lunettes 26, 27 and 28. For four miles to the right, there were no guns and no troops all the way to the Appomattox River.

Benjamin Butler concerned that with the arrival of the Army of the Potomac whatever success the Army of the James might thereafter enjoy would be totally eclipsed — dusted off his prior plan of June 2 for taking Petersburg. Brigadier General Edward W. Hincks would use a reserve brigade with troops from City Point and the river forts to distract the Confederates, while Brigadier General August V. Kautz's cavalry entered the city from the south. Once in the city, the plan called for burning the bridges over the Appomattox as well as all the city's public buildings. The infantry arrived at the city's eastern defenses at 7:00 A.M. on June 9 as planned. Colonel Joseph R. Hawley was on City Point Road and Hincks was on the Prince George Court House Road to Hawley's left. They had been briefed that they would encounter only infantry parapets over which a horse could jump. Instead, the Union commanders were confronted with parapets so imposing that none of them believed there was a chance of a successful assault if those fortifications were manned. Although the fortifications contained only the 46th Virginia, a company of the 23rd South Carolina, a battalion of reservists and a battalion of militia along its entire front, they still looked fully manned to the rather timid Federals. Thus, Gillmore waited to hear from Kautz while merely demonstrating halfheartedly in front of the works. Spear's brigade of Kautz's division did not arrive on the Jerusalem Plank Road fortifications until 11:30 A.M.[15]

Major General Benjamin Butler (Official Records).

At 9:00 A.M. on June 9, Petersburg heard a roar of cannon and musketry all along the lines, and the tolling of the city hall bell, a signal which summoned the city's old men and boys "to the defense of their homes." Word spread that a heavy force was advancing up the Jerusalem Plank Road and that a "few of the home guard are there to prevent their taking the town." The men stopped their business, grabbed their antique firearms and hurried over paths to rally with Major Fletcher H. Archer, commander of the militia camp (and a former commander of one of the city's companies in the Mexican War) about two miles along the Jerusalem Plank Road from the city limits.[16] The youngest was fourteen, and the oldest, William C. Banister, nearly deaf, was 61. Only the women, young children and those not able to take up arms were left in the city. The second class militia was directed to Rives Farm battery. At full strength, they would have numbered 170; however, only 125 showed up that day. The defenders included citizens from the hospitals and jails, aptly dubbed "patients and penitents." On Bragg's Hill, a band of black musicians under Philip Slaughter played "Dixie" and "The Girl I Left Behind" to boost the defenders' spirits and impress the enemy.[17]

The subsequent battle was over by early afternoon, with the Federals having been turned back. More than half of the 125 locals who made their stand near Battery 27 had been killed, wounded or captured, including William Banister. Anne Banister remembered her uncle pulling up with her father's body. He had been shot through the head: "That evening universal mourning was over the town, for the young and old were lying dead in many homes." Two days later there were funerals all day, with processions moving at intervals from different homes and churches. It was Butler himself who coined a phrase when he wrote that Petersburg was defended by "old men and boys, the grave and the cradle being robbed in about equal proportions." Wise, on June 12, 1864, in his Special Orders No. 11, proclaimed with Churchillian flourish:

Petersburg is to be and shall be defended on her outer walls, on her inner lines, at her corporation bounds, on every street, and around every temple of God and altar of man, in her every heart, until the blood of that heart is spilt. Roused by this spirit to this pitch of resolution, we will fight the enemy at every step, and Petersburg is safe.[18]

This minor engagement had momentous consequences for the overall Petersburg campaign, for it alerted Beauregard to the city's dire vulnerability, so that he continued pressing for reinforcements until Bragg finally, on June 11, released Gracie's brigade from the Department of Richmond. This allowed Beauregard to move the remainder of Wise's brigade to Petersburg from the Howlett Line, the fortifications opposite the Union at Bermuda Hundred. From then on, attacks would encounter much more than old men and boys, enough to slow any force down and allowing time for reinforcement.[19]

Once Grant set his sights on Petersburg, he immediately sent two of his staff officers, Lieutenant Colonels Horace Porter and Cyrus Comstock to reconnoiter south of the James and to coordinate the planned movement with Butler, as well as to inform Butler that Smith's Eighteenth Corps would soon be returned to him by transports up the James. The pair returned in the early hours of June 12, reporting that they had found a good site for the massive pontoon bridge across the James, just beyond Charles City Courthouse, about ten miles downriver from City Point. "Grant showed the only nervousness he ever manifested in my presence," recalled Porter. The two men could barely speak fast enough for Grant, who peppered them with questions. At the end of the meeting, Grant indicated he would commence the movement that night.[20]

By dawn on June 13, no Union troops were left at Cold Harbor. Rebel skirmishers crossing the strangely silent rifle pits found nothing but "empty trenches and the indescribable unseemly refuse left behind by a departing army."[21] As it appeared the Yankees were moving toward Richmond below White Oak Swamp, Lee pulled his army out of its trenches and moved south to protect the capital, occupying the ground from Glendale to Malvern Hill, scene of the intense fighting of 1862. But Lee was far from certain what his adversary had in mind. Prisoners taken in the exchange of June 13 indicated Grant was heading toward Harrison's Landing, which had been fortified by McClellan in 1862. Lee weighed Grant's options: he could pull back to McClellan's old fortifications and hold them with gunboats on the James, or he could cross the James "with a view of getting possession of Petersburg before we can reinforce it." By the afternoon of the 14th, he informed Richmond that Grant intended to cross the James River.[22]

The advance guard of the Union march reached the James in the late afternoon of June 13, passing a grand plantation once owned by President John Tyler. The James River here was a half mile wide and represented the first "pleasant-looking" body of water the troops had seen since the start of the campaign. Yankee warships were anchored in the river; as the navy men came ashore at Wilcox Landing, the army personnel gaped at the contrast of the clean, unfaded and unsullied, spotless uniforms with the ragged, dirty, unkempt condition of the combat-hardened soldiers arriving at the landing. Grant's men, after six weeks of continuous fighting and marching, were distrustful of "anyone not as grimy as themselves."[23] The engineers immediately began building an enormous bridge over the James. When completed, it would be 2,100 feet in length, from Wyanoke Neck to the base of Windmill Point and supported by 101 pontoon boats, which Brigadier General E. Porter Alexander dubbed the "greatest bridge of boats since the time of Xerxes."[24] In midstream, the bridge was additionally supported by anchored schooners above and below the span. By the next afternoon, the remaining three corps were there, and while the wharf was being repaired many men went swimming to wash off the grime of six weeks of fighting. Riverboats were utilized to transport the infantry across the river, as the bridge was used primarily for artillery and wagons. By the morning of the 15th, all of Hancock's infantry and four batteries of his artillery were across the river. By the morning of the 17th, substantially all of the Union army was south of the James. The success of the crossing amazed everyone from Grant on down. Charles Dana wired War Secretary Edwin Stanton on the 15th: "All goes on like a miracle."[25]

While the army's crossing commenced, Grant took a transport up the James to Bermuda Hundred on June 14 to have a personal discussion with Benjamin Butler concerning his plan for an attack on Petersburg utilizing Smith's Eighteenth Corps. Scheduled for the 15th, the plan was to repeat Butler's aborted attack of the 9th, but instead using Major General William F. "Baldy" Smith's Eighteenth Corps, who were familiar with the terrain in the area and at the time en route to Bermuda Hundred by steamers from White House Landing. Smith had been pleased to advance to Cold Harbor in support of the Army of the Potomac, reasoning that with considerably fewer troops, Butler was less likely to cause any serious harm to the war effort. Once there, however, Smith was even happier to be back, having suffered over 3,000 casualties in the battle; he had developed a contempt for Meade and his tactics of "butchering" so many men. He also found his reception in the clique-ridden Army of the Potomac lacking in warmth or sincerity. Smith believed in retrospect that he could have accomplished more had he remained with Butler in his futile attack on Petersburg.[26] Grant wanted Smith's corps to be reinforced by as many troops as Butler could spare, which he viewed as 6,000 men. He had already met with Smith and emphasized the importance of striking hard and fast. Grant had confidence in Smith, a fellow West Pointer, and felt that his military acumen along with the Union's considerably greater strength and knowledge of the defenses around Petersburg learned in the first attempt, would enable this assault to succeed where the other had failed. Additionally, if there was any considerable delay in the proposed reduction of the city, Hancock would arrive with his three divisions to add the weight of the hardest-hitting corps in the Army of the Potomac to the pressure Smith was already exerting. The other three corps, as they came up, could then be used as the situation dictated, most probably in a westward breakout from Bermuda Neck, in effect "uncorking" Butler's army, then turning against Drewrey's Bluff to prevent reinforcements from being sent south by Lee.[27]

At sunset on June 14, as soon as Smith had returned to Bermuda Hundred, he was ordered to proceed at 2:00 the next morning to attack Petersburg, as Butler explained that Grant "wanted Petersburg assaulted immediately." Smith's corps continued disembarking throughout the night at Broadway Landing, which was the southern terminus of a pontoon bridge from Point of Rocks on the Bermuda Hundred. Due to the severe mauling the corps had taken at Cold Harbor, there was considerable straggling en route back to Bermuda Hundred.[28]

Lee was presented with a difficult dilemma at the time. While the reports he was receiving all indicated what areas Grant had abandoned, they offered precious little real evidence on where he was actually going. While he believed Grant was planning to cross the James, Lee was still loathe to commit his army until the move was confirmed beyond the shadow of a doubt, for fear of being decoyed out of position, for his army was down to 30,000 men with Early's departure, and defense of the capital had to be his primary concern. His son, Major General W.H.F. "Rooney" Lee's two thinly spread cavalry brigades, all that was left after Fitzhugh Lee and Wade Hampton left to pursue Sheridan, probed unsuccessfully at the masses of Union troops coming down the Long Bridge Road toward Riddell's Shop. A.P. Hill's corps was posted in Rooney Lee's support, along the line of the Seven Days battle at Glendale, while Anderson's corps was off to the right, all the way to Malvern Hill, which the cavalry used as an observation post.[29]

By 4:00 A.M. on June 15, Hancock's infantry and four batteries of its artillery were successfully across the James at Windmill Point. Three ferryboats were added to the crossing to expedite its completion. However, the rations Hancock was told to await did not arrive. Finally, after repeated dispatches from Hancock, Meade authorized him to move immediately without the supplies. Hancock ordered the march to begin, but the couriers failed to deliver the orders. The Second Corps, consisting of 20,000 men, did not start its march until 10:30 A.M. on the 15th. Smith, too, had his problems getting started. When he learned of his new assignment, he attempted to redirect his transports closer to Point of Rocks, rather than to Bermuda Hundred. A number of the transports did not receive the word, however, with the result that his command was landing all along the Bermuda Hundred shoreline. In the confusion, with the transports disgorging their passengers at just about any point they chose, "It was impossible for any general to tell what troops he had or would have with him." Kautz, ordered to cross the Appomattox on Butler's pontoon bridge at 1:00 A.M. on the 15th and lead Smith's force, was also delayed. Thus, the advance from Broadway Landing did not begin until well after daylight.[30]

Beauregard was totally beside himself by this time. As Smith's corps approached the city, Petersburg was still defended by no more than 2,200 men, including Wise's Brigade.[31] From Battery 1 near the river to Butterworth's Bridge, an average of only one infantryman manned every four and one-half yards of the five-mile long fortifications from the lower Appomattox almost to the Jerusalem Plank Road. The seven and one-half miles of trenches south of the Appomattox required a minimum of 25,000 men to adequately defend them, in Beauregard's opinion. Between Wise's right and the upper Appomattox were over five miles of empty trenches; matters thus appeared extremely bleak for the beleaguered city. Beginning by 7:15 A.M. on June 14, Beauregard had wired Bragg from his headquarters south of Swift Creek that "[m]ovement of Grant's across Chickahominy and increase of Butler's force render my position here critical. With my present forces I cannot answer for consequences. Cannot my troops sent to General Lee be returned at once?" His request for a return of his troops from

Lee received no response. At 8:10 P.M., Beauregard bypassed the War Department and telegraphed Lee directly that "A deserter from the enemy reports that Butler has been reinforced by the Eighteenth and part of the Tenth Army Corps." This, too, elicited no response, so Beauregard dispatched his aides to Lee personally to explain the situation south of the James in detail.[32]

Lee, while stymied by a lack of knowledge of Grant's ultimate movement, fully appreciated the danger to Petersburg. At 12:10 A.M. on June 15, he wired Davis indicating his belief that Grant was moving south of the James and speculated that Grant might use Harrison's Landing as a base, an event which would prove too costly to attack him. However, he was still uncertain that more than one small part of the Union army was yet across the Chickahominy. He was equally unsure if Butler had been reinforced, and he was concerned that Petersburg was a target. Thus he indicated that he was moving Hoke's division to the vicinity of the Confederate bridge over the James River south of Richmond, in order to allow it to cross over and

Lieut. General Pierre G.T. Beauregard (USAMHI).

return to Beauregard if necessary.[33] "The rest of the army can follow should circumstances require it," he added.[34] However, Lee was still uncertain as to whether Grant intended a movement against the capital, in addition to a move on Petersburg. Wise still had a part of his force on the north side of the Appomattox, the remainder being in the lines facing the approaches from City Point. Beauregard finally indicated that he was moving Hoke's division from Bermuda Hundred to Petersburg, leaving only one brigade to watch the lines opposite the "bottled" Butler. At 11:45 A.M., Beauregard received word from Petersburg that the city was under heavy attack. In such circumstances, to hold the Bermuda Hundred lines and Petersburg, he believed, would be impossible. He exhorted Henry Wise to "Hold on at all hazards!" then gave Richmond a choice of saving Bermuda Hundred or Petersburg, but not both. At 1:00 P.M., he wired Lee that he would hold the Bermuda Hundred lines only "as long as practicable." Only three quarters of an hour later, he again warned Richmond that it must choose between the two areas to defend, indicating that "I fear my present force may prove unequal to hold both." Bragg made no reply at all, and while Wise's 2,200 men were outnumbered at least eight-to-one by the massing blue host in front of their trenches, "the Creole general fumed and fretted."[35]

As Smith prepared for the assault, the first of several serious "glitches" was encountered. Unaware an attack was in the works, the corps artillery chief had sent all the horses off for water. This meant there could be no support fire for the attackers until the teams could be returned to haul guns into position along the western fringe of the woods. In frustration, Smith postponed the attack until 7:00 P.M. While Smith fumed, word came that Hancock was on the way, but would not arrive until after dark. Smith considered another postponement in order to have a combined force of 40,000 men for the assault. However, the thought of Confederate reinforcements arriving in defense of the city, along with the fact that Hancock outranked him and would therefore eclipse his success, led Smith to move ahead. His revised order prescribed an attack to commence at 7:00 P.M. With the artillery up and firing, the Union lines moved forward. While the thinly manned Confederate lines put up a valiant fight, their mission proved to be impossible. The Union attackers swarmed over them, with Hincks' black troops advancing as fiercely as the rest. By 9:00 P.M. the line was in Union hands, with the Confederate defenders losing sixteen guns and several hundred prisoners. Brooks' division captured Batteries 5 and 6, along with four cannon and 200 prisoners. A total of seven of the redoubts fell in one hour, five of them, Batteries 7 through 11, to the left of the salient succumbing to the jubilant black troops. Hincks' troops had taken a total of twelve of the 16 captured guns and half of the prisoners. In what became a series of deplorable atrocities, the black troops of Hincks' command, perhaps enflamed by reports of atrocities at Fort Pillow and Poison Spring, bayoneted a number of the unarmed Confederate prisoners captured in their assault on the Dimmock Line, and finally had to be forcibly restrained by white troops of Smith's corps to protect the defenseless Rebel prisoners.[36]

Hincks was anxious to drive right into Petersburg, given the ease with which his men had shattered the eastern nose of the Rebel oval. He therefore requested two divisions to support him in this effort. Smith denied the request, more intent on concentrating on Lee, who by then reportedly had detached a sizeable portion of his army for a crossing of the James. Hincks felt there was a reasonable risk of an immediate counterattack by a superior Confederate force, and he thus believed they should brace for the shock of an attack and attempt to hold the captured works until Hancock's corps could arrive to even the odds. Smith sent Butler a wire, saying, "Unless I misapprehend the topography, I hold the key to Petersburg." Around 10:00 P.M., Hancock finally arrived with two divisions, both dusty and exhausted but still full of enthusiasm. In addition to the ration fiasco, his arrival was further delayed by inadequate maps that doubled the length of the route to Petersburg and faulty instructions that put Hancock's destination within territory held by the enemy. The Second Corps thus had a long day on the roads, often with considerable backtracking. Then at about 5:30 P.M., a message arrived from Grant ordering Hancock to hurry because Smith had carried the outer works of the Petersburg defenses and needed immediate assistance. Hancock had been informed by a courier from Smith at about 4:00 P.M. that if his corps could come up in the vicinity of the Norfolk & Petersburg Railroad, his attack would be successful. This was intended to be part of the assault that day on Petersburg. This was the first Hancock had heard that he was to be marching to take part in a fight that day. Had he known, he could have insured his arrival in time, bad maps notwithstanding. No one on Grant's staff had thought to tell Meade, however, who could scarcely be expected to pass along orders he himself had not received. Hancock had accelerated his approach once he was aware of the situation, but once there Smith only requested that he relieve Hincks' troops (as there was some considerable mistrust as to their fighting qualities and their treatment of prisoners), which was accomplished by 11:00 P.M.[37]

Beauregard's slim force remained alert and toiled hard throughout the night on a north-south ridge between the city and the works they had lost. The Dimmock Line north of the City Point Railroad was still in Confederate hands, and so Beauregard anchored his weak defense to the Appomattox River along those earthworks. About one half mile west of the lines, now in Federal possession, ran Harrison's Creek, which roughly paralleled the Dimmock Line. Beauregard's engineers, taking full advantage of the high ground along the creek's west bank, ran a new defensive line southward along this ridge to a point just north of the Baxter Road, where the original Dimmock positions remained in Rebel hands. He had opted to force the hand of the government and impose his will on Lee by presenting a fait accompli. At about 10:30 that night, Beauregard determined that he must make the difficult choice he had posed earlier to Bragg, and he decided to concentrate everything he had on the defense of Petersburg. Therefore, he issued orders to Major General Bushrod Johnson, commander of the Bermuda Hundred defenses, to abandon the Howlett Line and march south post haste. Only Gracie's brigade of 1,000 Alabamians remained there to hold the defenses until Lee's forces could occupy the trenches. Beauregard was relinquishing the vital communications corridor linking Richmond and Petersburg. Within forty-five minutes, Beauregard informed Lee as to what he had done, adding, "Cannot these lines be occupied by your troops?" To a great extent, Beauregard was remarkably fortunate at Smith's extreme caution earlier that day. As he later wrote, "Petersburg at that hour was clearly at the mercy of the Federal commander who had all but captured it, and only failed of final success because he could not realize the fact of the unparalleled disparity between the two contending forces." It was only through a combination of Smith's caution, heroic action by the small force of Rebel defenders, and sheer luck that Beauregard was able to "stave off defeat" on June 15.[38]

Once Lee was informed of Beauregard's act of stripping of the Howlett Line, he had no rational choice in order to save the capital but to send troops south of the James. A breakout by Butler west of Bermuda Hundred would give the Union control of the rail lines leading north from Petersburg, having the same effect as if the three lines to the south had been cut and thereby forcing the fall of Richmond for lack of food. Thus, Lee sent Pickett's division on in at 3:00 A.M. on June 16 and informed Anderson to follow promptly with one of his other two divisions, Field's, and to direct the action against Butler, who predictably would have overrun the Howlett Line by the time the Confederates could get there. After ordering A.P. Hill to continue shielding Richmond from a north-side attack by Meade, whose army, with one corps detached, was still twice the size of the Army of Northern Virginia, depleted by Early's departure, Lee moved from Riddell's Shop and shifted his headquarters to Chaffin's Bluff, where Anderson's corps could cross the pontoon bridge to recover the critical southside works Beauregard had abandoned.[39]

Lee had released Hoke's division during the night of the 14th, and by 11:30 A.M., it finally transferred south of the James and raced for the beleaguered Petersburg, arriving around 7:00 P.M. on June 15 in time to save the city, along with Johnson's division, which Beauregard had been forced to withdraw from the Bermuda Hundred.[40] Meade was also busy that night. Grant had advised him that Smith was heavily engaged and that the rest of the army needed to come into line as soon as possible; Burnside and his corps therefore crossed the James with orders to move up and take a position to Hancock's left. The Fifth Corps was to follow Burnside, with artillery and trains and cavalry to follow, and Wright's Sixth Corps was left to hold the north bank of the James until all the other corps were south of the river. Then it would cross the river, remove the bridge, and all of the Union forces then would be safely south of the James, with City Point as the supply depot.

When Lee reached Chaffin's Bluff around 9:30 A.M. on June 16 and crossed the James after Pickett's division and before Field, the din of battle informed him that Butler had overrun the scantly held Bermuda work, whose northern sector was six miles downstream, and that Beauregard was fighting a desperate battle to hold Petersburg, a dozen miles to the south. Kershaw's division was still in place at Malvern Hill, and A.P. Hill's men were at Riddell's Shop, as Lee was still not convinced that Grant was south of the James with his entire force. Anderson soon reported that Butler's uncorked troops had moved westward to Port Walthall Junction where they were engaged in tearing up tracks and entrenching to prevent Rebel reinforcements beyond that point by rail or turnpike. Lee indicated that they must be driven off, and by nightfall they had been driven back to the Howlett Line, which they held in reverse, firing west. Beauregard meanwhile continued his urgent pleas for assistance. Lee responded that he could not further strip the north bank of the James without clear evidence that more than one of Meade's corps had crossed. Beauregard responded that, while he was uncertain as to Grant's exact whereabouts, Hancock's and Smith's corps were both definitely in his front.[41]

What Lee did not know, because Beauregard was unaware of the fact, was that Burnside had also been in front of Petersburg since midmorning and that Warren was arriving at that time, bringing the total Union strength in front of the city to 75,000. Wilson's cavalry was also on the way, and Wright, representing the last of Grant's army, was then in the process of crossing the pontoon bridge. By this time, Beauregard's strength had increased to 14,000 with the arrival of Johnson from Bermuda Hundred and Ransom and Gracie from Richmond. However, his chances of working yet another miracle defense against the rapidly increasing opposition were diminishing by the hour. Beauregard had to be well pleased with the brilliant defense his meager forces put forth on the 15th. Wise and his 2,200 men had made a sufficient show of strength to make Smith blink before attacking the formidable-looking but lightly manned Dimmock Line fortifications. The delay allowed time for Hagood's South Carolinians of Hoke's division to arrive by rail and assist in the work on the secondary defenses to prevent further weakening of those defenses by filling in between the 59th Virginia and the rest of Wise's Brigade. Then the rest of Hoke's Division arrived around 2:00 P.M. and closed the breach between Redans 5 to 11 on Hagood's right. Wise's 2,200 men had prevented a force of 18,000 from breaking through to the city. His command had previously jokingly been referred to as the "Life Insurance Company," but that tag was no longer uttered after June 15.[42]

Smith's June 15 attack, while haphazard and not en masse, had still achieved great success. The powerful redoubts south of the City Point Railroad were taken and the Rebel defenses were rolled up as far south as the Jordan Point Road, with nearly three and a half miles of the city's eastern shield smashed in the two hours of fighting. Yet Smith was consumed with caution given the immensity of the Dimmock Line and his fear that Beauregard was continuously being reinforced.[43] He was also plagued by inadequate maps of the area and had little knowledge of the terrain. Finally, he professed that his newly acquired black soldiers could not be kept in order; his inspection of the captured works found the blacks camped, with weapons stacked and dinner fires blazing on the enemy's side of the earthworks. His displeasure at this situation was met with bewilderment by the black soldiers. Many other Eighteenth Corps soldiers were impatient to advance on Petersburg and finish things for good. George Ulmer, a Maine volunteer wrote that he "kicked and condemned every general there was in the army for the blunder I saw they were making. I only wished I could be the general commanding for one hour. But it was no use; I couldn't be."[44] Regardless of what his men may have thought, Smith was generally pleased with his performance that day, expressing in a dispatch to Butler that night that "I hold the key to Petersburg." Grant himself was quite pleased that night as well, opining that "I think it is pretty well, to get across a great river and come up here and attack Lee in the rear before he is ready for us."[45]

Smith spent the night of the 15th in a tent set well apart from any others and without anyone's knowledge. He later explained to one of Butler's aides, Lieutenant John Davenport, that he was very tired and "came ... [there] for the purpose of securing rest, and being where I would not be likely to be disturbed." The previous night, Davenport had delivered an angry message from Butler urging Smith to advance, as "Petersburg could be taken that night." Smith, however, told Davenport that "Hancock's arrival has left me the junior officer," implying Hancock was then in charge and had decided not to attack that night. Davenport immediately approached one of Hancock's staff officers, who assured him that Hancock had "waived his rank, [and] placed himself and his command at the service of Smith." Davenport rode back to Bermuda Hundred and duly reported this confusion directly to Butler, who then asked him to return with orders to attack Petersburg immediately.[46] Smith was by then nowhere to be found, however. Davenport had arrived back at Smith's camp around 2:00 A.M. on the 16th. His aides claimed to have no idea where he was; Davenport checked Hancock's headquarters, but no one there had seen Smith. Davenport, noticing the solitary tent apart from all others once the dawn finally broke, entered and found Smith, who had just risen. Davenport delivered Butler's order to attack at once, to which Smith replied that "he would look his position over and prepare to attack the enemy." Grant meanwhile ordered Meade to hurry Warren's corps to the Jerusalem Plank Road as soon as he received the wire, and to travel to Petersburg "to take command in person." About noon on the 16th, Meade met Grant returning from Petersburg. Grant told him that "Smith has taken a line of works there, stronger than anything we have seen this campaign. If it is a possible thing, I want an assault made at six o'clock this evening."[47]

Gibbon's and Birney's divisions of Hancock's corps sent out several reconnaissances in force at daybreak on the 16th. Gibbon's 3rd Brigade made little progress on the right; on the left, however, Egan's brigade of Birney's division captured Battery 12 after a hard defensive fight by Wise's brigade. This success temporarily opened a huge hole in the Rebel line, but Hancock failed to capitalize on the situation. Matt Ransom's brigade soon arrived after its all night march from Drewrey's Bluff and prevented any further Federal progress in the area. Johnson's division, minus Gracie's brigade, had by then crossed the Appomattox and headed for Beauregard's right, which extended beyond the Norfolk & Petersburg Railroad. Even with Ransom and Johnson in the works, manned entrenchments went only from the Appomattox to Redan 22, with Brigadier General Stephen Elliott's brigade in reserve. After that, there were five full miles of vacant line (half a mile east of the Jerusalem Plank Road westward to the Appomattox). Beauregard actually relished these high-risk situations and had coolly abandoned great portions of his line to concentrate his strength along the most likely avenues of approach. Beauregard again sought reinforcements from Lee, reporting that Union prisoners indicated Hancock had crossed the James two days previously. Lee wired back at 4:00 P.M. asking if Grant had been seen crossing the James. He was still uncertain of Grant's movements and still unaware that the Federals had already crossed the James and had three full corps assaulting Petersburg.[48] Even given the missed opportunity of the 15th, the Yankees might still have forced their way into Petersburg that morning. Barlow's division came up on Hancock's left after having initially lost its way to the front. By midmorning, the first of Burnside's troops were staggering into position on Barlow's left. They were so exhausted from the hard march, however, that they immediately went to sleep.[49] Hancock had delayed any follow up to the morning's successes. He was not the same aggressive warrior he had once been. The groin wound he had suffered at Gettysburg had never fully healed and continued to cause him severe pain. It recently had opened up, and it would soon cause him to temporarily relinquish command. The Overland Campaign had finished for Winfield Scott Hancock what a Rebel bullet at Gettysburg had begun, smothering the fires of ambition and reckless courage he had previously displayed. His corps had been savagely ground up in the heavy fighting of the previous forty days. When someone at Cold Harbor had asked him where the Second Corps was, he responded, "It lies buried between the Rapidan and the James." When Meade did come up, he advised him to avoid any further attacks until Burnside arrived.[50]

Once Meade assumed command on the 16th, and based upon Grant's request, he ordered the attack on the Rebel defenses to commence at 6:00 P.M. Two brigades of Smith's corps were placed in support of Hancock's right and two brigades of Burnside's Ninth Corps were placed in support of Hancock's left. Federal guns were in place in the captured works, and a "great thunder of gunfire rolled out as the artillerists began to hammer the new Rebel trenches, which lay on the far side of a shallow valley. The Rebels had made good use of their time and the new line of works was formidable. The sun was going down and the air was full of dust and smoke, and as Meade and his staff rode out to watch the fight there was a strange, coppery tinge in the atmosphere and on the landscape."[51] Hancock and Burnside sent their units forward while Smith demonstrated, and a bitter, somewhat inconclusive fight ensued. The overall engagement, though piecemeal, lasted over three hours. Birney's division finally succeeded in breaking into a part of the Rebel line and "effected a lodgement," at a cost of 2,000 casualties. More of the Dimmock Line south of that previously taken fell, along with Redans 4, 13 and 14 and their connecting lines, although the Union troops failed to break through Beauregard's Harrison Creek line.[52] Warren's Fifth Corps came up too late in the day to be a part of the fight. Charles Dana wired Stanton that night that "the town they cannot think of holding, for it lies directly under our guns."[53] However — despite their overwhelming numbers — conflicting orders, inadequate maps and unpleasant memories of Cold Harbor combined to keep the Federals from making any concerted assault on the severely weakened Dimmock Line. This, even though there were at least 90,000 Union troops in front of Petersburg facing not even 10,000 "exhausted, half-starved men, who had gone through two days of constant hard fighting and many sleepless nights in the trenches."

Beauregard did not have nearly the force adequately to man the entire Dimmock Line, and so he had massed his troops opposite the Federal concentration to the east of the city. The defenses were wide open to the south. The Jerusalem Plank Road went south from the city, and it and the country to its west held no Confederates at all except for a thin force of cavalry pickets. Beauregard was mindful of this dire situation and indicated that if Meade put so much as one corps on the Jerusalem Plank Road and had it march north, "I would have been compelled to evacuate Petersburg without much resistance." Warren's corps on Meade's extreme left might have been in a position to have made such a march, as it was fresh, having not been significantly engaged since Spotsylvania. Grant had ordered Meade to get Warren over to the Jerusalem Road as quickly as possible on June 16, for a surprise attack up this turnpike on the morning of the 17th. However, Warren found Confederate skirmishers in his front, and he became extremely concerned about pressing them too hard. Consequently, the country west of the Jerusalem Plank Road remained empty all day long.[54]

Meade had planned for Burnside's Ninth Corps, on Hancock's left, to launch a moonlight attack in the early morning hours of June 17. However, the plodding general let matters develop at their own pace, and it was thus near dawn before his assaulting columns were ready. Following a ravine leading deep into the Confederate position, Potter's men attacked at 3:00 A.M. on the 17th, taking four guns, five flags, 600 prisoners and 1,500 stands of arms. A mile of Beauregard's Harrison's Creek line now lay in Federal control.[55] The slashed timber in the ravine made it difficult for Ledlie's division to follow up on Potter's initial success, however. Potter had finally halted when he encountered the Rebels in a new line stretching from the Appomattox to Battery 3, and from there along the high ground west of Harrison's Creek to the Norfolk & Petersburg Railroad.[56]

One of Burnside's regiments which was key to the assault's initial success was the 48th Pennsylvania, commanded by then Lieutenant Colonel Henry Pleasants, soon to play a starring role in this drama. Pleasants considered the assault so dangerous that he supposedly gave his men the option of not participating, an option which went unexercised by everyone. Caps were removed from the rifles to avoid an unintentional discharge, which would have given their position away prematurely. This was analogous to the British attack on the Americans at Paoli during the Revolution, where the British were required to remove the flints from their muskets. After a successful charge up the hill into the works, Pleasants found that the total number of his prisoners exceeded that of his whole regiment. The 48th also recaptured the colors of the 7th New York Heavy Artillery, along with two Confederate flags and two cannons. Pleasants then ordered the 48th to take a redoubt which covered their current position, and this was also quickly accomplished, with the Confederate occupants rapidly fleeing toward Petersburg. The capture of these two forts later turned out to be the determining factor of the 48th Pennsylvania's greatest project, the Petersburg Mine.[57]

At 6:00 A.M., Hancock advised Meade that he could hardly ride or walk. His leadership on this critical day would be marked by "uncertainty, hesitancy, and lackluster inspiration." His corps, which was supporting Burnside's attacks, made little progress and suffered disproportionately large losses. By late morning, Warren's corps had moved into line on Burnside's left but held back from full coordination in support of Burnside's assaults. Meade did little to solidify Warren's assistance, and in the end his 20,000 men accomplished almost nothing that day. Burnside himself failed to alert his other two divisions as to Potter's advances and thus did not exploit the success.[58]

After daylight Burnside had Orlando Willcox prepare for another attack to the left of Potter's new line. Willcox spent so much time arranging his artillery support and questioning Burnside as to the exact point of attack that Major James St. Clair Morton, Burnside's engineer, had to walk out on the field with a compass and demonstrate to Brigadier General John F. Hartranft the direction he was supposed to take. Morton ultimately led the attacking column himself to insure it did not veer astray and was killed at its head.[59] Willcox's division attacked the new Rebel line at about 2:00 P.M. in front of Battery 14, a mile north of the redans on the extreme Confederate right. Barlow's division of Handcock's Second Corps supported Willcox on the right. But the assault failed when the Rebels enfiladed it with artillery from the redans near the Norfolk & Petersburg Railroad, together with an intense barrage of musketry from the front.

Near sunset, Ledlie's division assaulted the new line where Willcox's attempt had failed and was significantly mauled. Ledlie's division had suffered a number of casualties in the earlier attack. Colonel Elisha G. Marshall, commander of the second brigade was down, and only one brigade had a full colonel in command. While the division was able to take possession of the first line, the Confederates maintained a vigorous fire from their stronger works. Ledlie was clearly not functioning well that afternoon, with the common impression being that he was again drunk. This was later substantiated by a first division staff officer who complained about being left in virtual command of the division while Ledlie vanished from headquarters for several hours. He was finally found later that afternoon "in a stupor, safely out of harm's way," a prophetic prelude to his performance on July 30.[60]

Beauregard continued his brilliant defense of the city, making it still more difficult for the Federals to take. He had Colonel D.B. Harris, his chief engineer, lay out a new line on advantageous ground behind a ravine 500 to 1,000 yards in the rear of his position with a series of white stakes. This shorter line would stretch from the Dimmock Line at the Jerusalem Plank Road to the Appomattox River. Every available staff officer in Hoke's and Johnson's divisions were briefed so that each command could, at the appointed hour, easily retire to the new line "with order and precision and unperceived by the enemy." Bayonets, tin cans, knives, axes, split canteens, and anything else capable of moving earth were used to dig the new line that night. After midnight, Beauregard withdrew safely and silently from the Harrison's Creek line he had so stubbornly fought to keep and began entrenching in the newly laid out position considerably closer to the city near Taylor's Creek.[61]

Two divisions of Horatio Wright's Sixth Corps had arrived in front of Bermuda Hundred at 6:00 A.M. on the 17th pursuant to Grant's orders for them to hold the Confederate line of defenses which Butler had taken and thwart communications between Richmond and Petersburg. "It seems to me important that we should hold our advantage gained yesterday," Grant informed Butler at 9:15 A.M. Unbeknownst to Grant, Anderson's Confederates had already retaken the line except for a stronghold still in Union possession near the Clay house. Lee moved his headquarters from Drewry's Bluff to near the Clay house to oversee the reestablishment of the Rebel defenses. Grant directed Meade to return Baldy Smith's command to Bermuda Hundred as soon as possible to aid in blocking any movement south by Lee, while Butler rested the two exhausted divisions of Wright's corps sent to aid in resecuring the Howlett Line. Butler had asked Grant, "Shall we attack them in force?" Out in the field, Grant did not receive the message until 6:45 P.M., then promptly replied, "If possible the enemy should be driven back." At 5:30 P.M., while Wright's troops recuperated, Pickett's and Field's divisions came under fire from Federal pickets at Clay's farm. The Confederate troops reacted by storming the picket line despite having been instructed not to attack. Butler's subordinates did not have confidence in his tactical prowess, and when he finally ordered these commanders to retake the lost lines, Wright and Terry found Butler's orders for a counterattack to be impracticable. At 11:30 P.M., Butler wired Grant that "I am sorry to say nothing has been done, or even a vigorous attempt made." Pickett and Field, having retaken the Howlett Line from end to end, had effectively recorked Butler, and this time for good. There was now nothing to prevent Lee from strongly reinforcing Petersburg.[62]

Beauregard felt that with the assault of the 17th, given his scarcity of manpower, "the last hour of the Confederacy had arrived." He continued sending Lee urgent pleas for reinforcements, attempting to convince Lee that he was facing the whole of Grant's army with 11,000 men. At 9:00 A.M., Beauregard advised Lee that "nothing positive [was] yet known of Grant's movements." At 11:00 A.M., he advised that an unconfirmed report, and false, had the Fifth Corps on its way to the Shenandoah Valley. Lee responded to one of these telegrams at noon: "Until I can get more definite information on Grant's movements, I do not think it prudent to draw more troops to this side of the river." Lee, tired of working in a vacuum, at 3:30 P.M. ordered his son, Rooney, then at Malvern Hill to "push after the enemy, and endeavor to ascertain what has become of Grant's army." At 4:30, he telegraphed A.P. Hill at Riddell's Shop, indicating that Beauregard had reported that a large number of Grant's army had crossed the James above Fort Powhatan the day before: "If you have nothing contradictory of this, move to Chaffin's Bluff." Beauregard also relied on staff officers to personally plead his case with Lee. One of them, Major Giles B. Cooke, informed Lee that if he did not send troops immediately, only God Almighty could keep the enemy out of Petersburg. The deeply religious Lee replied, "I hope God Almighty will keep the enemy out of Petersburg."[63]

Finally, at 5:00 P.M., Beauregard sent Lee a telegram:

> Prisoners just taken represent themselves as belonging to Second, Ninth and Eighteenth corps. They state that Fifth and Sixth corps are behind coming on. Those from Second and Eighteenth came here yesterday, and arrived first. Other marched night and day from Gaine's Mill, and arrived yesterday evening. The Ninth crossed at Turkey Bend, where they have a pontoon-bridge. They say Grant commanded on the field yesterday. All are positive that they passed him on the road seven miles from here.

He followed up that message with one at 6:40 P.M. with a dire warning that "I shall hold as long as practicable, but, without reinforcements, I may have to evacuate the city shortly." Finally, after the Federal attacks of that night, and his movement to the new, shorter defenses, Beauregard telegraphed Lee at Drewrey's Bluff at 12:40 A.M. on the 18th: "I expect renewal of attack in morning. My troops are becoming much exhausted. Without immediate and strong reinforcements, results may be unfavorable. Prisoners report Grant on the field with his whole army." Lee responded that he was still not thoroughly convinced of Grant's movements, "but upon your representations will move at once to Petersburg." After five days, he finally had sufficient evidence that Meade's army was no longer in his front but totally in Beauregard's and he reacted accordingly.

Lee had already decided to dispatch Kershaw's division of Anderson's I Corps to Beauregard, based on his earlier reports. He then ordered Anderson's third division to proceed to Bermuda Neck, and for A.P. Hill to cross the James at Chaffin's Bluff and await instructions for a march in either direction on the Petersburg Turnpike, depending upon the situation they confronted at the time. He also communicated to Jubal Early at Lynchburg to move back to Petersburg without delay.[64] He later ordered Anderson to move on to Petersburg along with A.P. Hill, who was to leave one division north of the Appomattox in the unlikely event that Richmond was to come under attack. By 10:20 P.M., he finally received definitive word from Rooney Lee that "Grant's army is across the river," having crossed the James at Windmill Point. Therefore, by 3:30 A.M. on the 18 of June, Lee's whole remaining army, with the exception of one division left holding the Howlett Line against Butler, would be on the road to Petersburg within the hour.[65]

Kershaw reached Petersburg with about 5,000 men at 7:30 A.M. on the 18th to the cheers and waving flags of the residents of that city. Field's division of the I Corps arrived about two hours later. Both groups were immediately placed in the trenches to relieve Beauregard's exhausted troops. Some of Wise's men were withdrawn from the defenses, as for three days they "had practically nothing to eat, almost no water to drink, and no sleep at all except such little as we could snatch from the few short intervals of calm." Lee himself arrived at 11:30 and met with Beauregard, now relegated to second in command. Beauregard was most grateful, indicating that "My welcome to General Lee was most cordial. He was at last where I had, for the past three days, so anxiously hoped to see him — within the limits of Petersburg!"

The two went to Reservoir Hill to view the battlefront. Beauregard proposed that as soon as Hill's and Anderson's corps arrived, they should attack the Union flank, before it began to fortify. However, Lee rejected the proposal due to the fact that his troops were tired and needed to recuperate after the march, and as the defensive posture had been "so advantageous to him against Grant's offensive ... at Petersburg, he preferred continuing the same mode of warfare." Beauregard argued strongly that the Yankees were equally as tired and had yet to entrench. However, his "views did not prevail." A.P. Hill's corps arrived in the afternoon and was placed along the previously undefended Confederate right, south of town to the Weldon and Petersburg Railroad. Marching at the head of Hill's column when it entered the city was the 12th Virginia, including the Petersburg Rifles, almost all local boys who had enlisted back in April of 1861. The streets were almost blocked with reunions of families and soldiers, many of whom were hardly recognizable due to their war-weary appearance.[66]

By this time, Meade no longer believed Petersburg could be taken, but given Grant's orders he had no choice but to continue the effort. Thus, he persisted in carrying out his plan for an all out assault at 4 A.M. on the 18th. The Federals were in possession of a long ridge formed by the hills where the Hare and Shand houses were located and Beauregard's recently vacated line was on the opposite ridge. The troops went forward on schedule for once, under orders to take the Confederate works "at all costs," only to find them deserted and covered only by a scout force of pickets. This result proved to be as disruptive to the Yankees as if they had met stiff resistance. Hours were consumed in organizing a force to occupy the abandoned works to guard against a counterattack and regrouping to probe for the vanished enemy. It was midmorning, therefore, before the Rebels were discovered nearly a mile to the west. There the Federals found a new, shorter line, heavily entrenched with guns clustered thicker than before, and, while they were yet unaware, the line had been considerably reinforced. Due to the physical layout of the new line, the various Union attacking units had different distances to travel to close with their enemy. At around noon, an assault was finally begun. Spearheaded by Birney's division, who attacked with Gibbon's division, which had to cover only 300 yards from the Hare house, Gibbon's men attacked twice on the right of the Prince George Court House Road, but both attacks were quickly repulsed. Burnside's corps, on Birney's left, however, had to move nearly a mile before it encountered the enemy outposts in the Norfolk & Petersburg Railroad cut in a ravine. To the left of Burnside's position, Warren's corps had advanced farther yet, and the deep railroad cut and ravines, enfiladed from the north, drastically hindered his advance. Both Burnside and Warren found ample reasons to delay their attack given the intimidating terrain. The whole effort was ineffectual and cost a considerable number of casualties to the Second and Eighteenth corps. Union survivors also reported the distressing news that Beauregard had been joined by Lee.[67]

Following this botched attempt for a coordinated, unified assault by the Second, Ninth and Eighteenth corps simultaneously, an exceedingly frustrated Meade sent orders to each commander for an immediate assault with their total force. Finally, the how totally frustrated Meade wired the commanders that "I find it useless to appoint an hour to effect co-operation.... What additional orders to attack you require I cannot imagine.... Finding it impossible to effect co-operation by appointing an hour for attack, I have sent an order to each corps commander to attack at all hazards and without reference to each other." The attacks were finally made late in the afternoon. But by then it was too late, for Lee's veterans were now in the trenches and the eight-to-one odds against them had vanished forever. The new works were strong, and a fresh enemy was sighting their rifles along the parapets at the Union lines. It was Cold Harbor all over again, "with its cruel demonstration that trench lines properly manned could not be taken by storm." An attack now would result in nothing but devastating losses to the attackers.[68]

If the generals could not discern this, or chose to ignore it, the soldiers were well aware of the consequences. Birney massed his troops yet again at about 4:00 P.M. for a final assault. The principal column was formed in four lines, six veteran units in the first two, and two enormous heavy artillery regiments, the 1st Massachusetts and the 1st Maine, green but enthusiastic, in the last two. The lines were instructed to remain prone until the order was given to rise and charge. However, when the order came, the soldiers in the front ranks continued to remain prone, paying no attention to the shouts and exhortations of their sword-waving officers. The rear ranks of heavies had risen and were preparing to advance. "Lay down, you damn fools! You can't take them works!" the veterans bellowed over their shoulders. The 1st Massachusetts heavies accepted this gratuitous advice and proceeded to lie back down. The 1st Maine, however, valiantly remained on its feet, rushed forward through the rows of prone comrades, and advanced for the Rebel line. The Confederate works erupted into flame at their approach. The gun pits had been built low and the muzzles of the cannon protruded out of the embrasures a foot or two from the ground; when they were fired, their canister rounds came in just off the ground so that escape was next to impossible. "The whole slope was burned with fire," and none of the brave heavies made it to the Rebel line, and few of them made the return trip back to their lines. Of the 850 who advanced, 632 of the 1st Maine fell within ten minutes. "They were laid out in squads and companies," commented one astonished observer. A tearful Colonel Daniel Chaplin, commander of the unit, offered his sword to General Mott when he returned, indicating he had no further use for it. He then berated the veteran regiments in his brigade for not supporting his inexperienced heavies. "There are the men you have been making fun of," he chastised the old soldiers, "you did not dare follow them." At a casualty rate of 74 percent, this was the most severe loss suffered in a single engagement by any Union regiment in the entire war.[69]

Sporadic attacks continued throughout the afternoon. To Birney's right, Martindale's division advanced and captured some rifle pits but failed to assault the main Confederate line. On Birney's left, Potter's and Willcox's divisions of Burnside's corps drove the Rebels from the Norfolk & Petersburg Railroad cut. However, they were not able to reach within 100 yards of Kershaw's division. Farther to the left, Warren's men made it to within 20 feet of the works held by Field's division. By about 6:30 P.M., Meade knew the Army of Northern Virginia was confronting him in the trenches and nothing more would be accomplished by such assaults en masse. Orders then went out to entrench. At 9:45 P.M., Meade wired Grant a summary of the day's action, concluding that "It is a source of great regret that I am not able to report more success." Grant had maintained a curious, hands off attitude throughout the contest, "even as he watched his well-laid plan being frustrated by inept staff work and the bone-deep disconsolation of the troops—invoked no ifs and leveled no reproaches." He felt satisfied that all that could be done was done, and called a halt to rest the men "and use the spade for their protection until a new vein can be struck."[70]

Once Petersburg was heavily reinforced, the Army of the Potomac had simply exchanged one stalemate for another, twice the distance from Richmond and on the far side of a major river. In doing so, it had suffered 11,386 casualties just since crossing the James.[71] Since the start of the campaign on May 4, a period of only six weeks, Grant's total losses, including Butler's, totaled over 75,000 men, a number greater than Lee and Beauregard had in their combined armies at the start of the campaign. Of this total, 66,315 were from the five corps under Meade (including Smith's, which had been assigned to him). For this reason, among others, William Swinton, historian for the army, pronounced that at this juncture "the Army of the Potomac, shaken in its structure, its valor quenched in blood, and thousands of its ablest officers killed and wounded, was the Army of the Potomac no more."[72] By nightfall, A.P. Hill's corps extended the Confederate right south of town to the Weldon and Petersburg Railroad. With Hill and Anderson in place, "the spade took the place of the musket." To protect against the incessant mortar shelling the Federals were lobbing into the trenches, the Rebels constructed a labyrinth of deep, narrow trenches and mound-shaped "bomb-proofs" behind the front. Thus began the investment of Petersburg, because Grant now felt he could accomplish what was needed with less loss of life by flanking the enemy and cutting off its sources of supply by destroying the railroads running to and from the city. The length of time needed to accomplish this feat would be the length of the siege. However, the stalemate ultimately worked in Grant's favor. As Porter Alexander later explained:

> The position which he had now secured, & the character of the military operations he now contemplated, removed all risk of any serious future catastrophe, however bold we might be, or however desperately we might fight. We were sure to be soon worn out. It was now only a question of a few moves more or less.[73]

The defenses of Richmond now ran from White Oak Swamp east of the capital to south of the Jerusalem Plank Road, some 26 miles away. There were between 111,000 and 113,000 Union forces facing 50,000 Confederates. The fate of the capital and the Army of Northern Virginia itself would rest on the outcome of the drive against Petersburg. Grant's greatest achievement was that he had deprived Lee of the highly valued weapon of maneuver and had reduced him exclusively to the defensive. Given his inferior numbers and the government's policy of holding Richmond at all costs, there was little Lee could do but allow himself to be pinned down at Petersburg while Sherman sliced up the Confederacy elsewhere. Lee informed Davis that the enemy could do more injury in their current position than from any other point he had ever taken. Large attacks would not be necessary, but rather a series of "regular approaches." Clearly, the Confederacy was in for an extremely unpleasant time.[74]

CHAPTER 3

War in the Trenches

The Ninth Corps had turned in a valiant performance during the initial days of the fighting at Petersburg. Burnside's men had marched twenty-two very hot and dusty miles in fifteen hours, without a meal, in order to be in position for another attack on June 16. Its second division made a courageous predawn attack at the Shand House on a little more than an hour's sleep. Potter's division lost heavily that day, as did Ledlie's first division and Willcox's. However, unlike his fellow division commanders, Ledlie was either negligent or drunk, or, probably, both. By nightfall, his division had lost almost all that it had fought for that day. Burnside, with prompting from Ledlie's protective staff, attributed Ledlie's failure to the rather large complement of heavies in his division. Burnside had indicated that "[i]n the attack last night I couldn't find thirty of them."[1] While Ledlie's unit was placed in reserve on June 18, Burnside's other two divisions made a good stand, recovering the ground abandoned by the Confederates, until they encountered the new, heavily defended works on the far side of the Norfolk and Petersburg Railroad. Throughout the day, Meade attempted to achieve a coordinated assault. Finally, in frustration, he ordered each corps commander to undertake an assault without regard to the other corps—in essence, every general for himself. "It was an injudicious directive from a commander pushed to the edge of his patience, but Burnside's second and third divisions under Generals Potter and Willcox, respectively, dutifully braved devastating fire to cross an enfiladed cut in the bed of the Norfolk and Petersburg Railroad."[2] The Yankees "soon crouched behind the raw, steep slope of the antebellum engineering achievement." They then approached Taylor's Creek (also sometimes referred to as Poor's Creek), where the Confederates had reorganized their lines after abandoning the Dimmock Line. Willcox and Potter successfully crossed the creek and battled to within a hundred yards of the blazing Confederate fortifications. No other Union division came so near the new Confederate line as did Potter, "and nothing this side of hell could bring his men any closer." The fighting soon put an end to any further engagements that day. Meade subsequently issued a very complimentary order congratulating the Ninth Corps on its gallantry that day.[3]

When darkness fell that night, the Yankees began digging some works of their own. The Ninth Corps, which had advanced the farthest, was still "the one that did not feel itself a part of this army, the one that had something to prove about itself and its beloved commander."[4] In the four days of fighting, the Ninth Corps had suffered the most losses, with the sole exception of the Second Corps, which had eighty-three regiments to Burnside's thirty-nine. Five of its brigade commanders had been wounded, and only two of seven brigades still fought under the same men who had led them across the Rapidan. The corps engineer, Major James St. Clair Morton, had been killed on the 17th leading Colonel John Hartranft's brigade against the Confederate works. Indeed, it appeared as though the zenith of the Ninth Corps may have passed.[5]

In the early morning hours of June 19, General Potter surveyed the moist, red clay of "the freshly-banked trenches and noted just how close his lines were to the enemy's." This forward line was "the high-water mark for the IX Army Corps—the extreme limit of the advance, the place where tired men who had fired all their ammunition lay in the dark to build little breastworks out of earth scooped up with bayonets, tin plates, and bare hands."[6] A new Confederate redoubt was positioned less than one hundred yards from Burnside's main trench line. Burnside thus began planning a means to drive the Rebels from their most recent trenches west of Taylor's Creek "where he and Willcox had dug in during the night 'like badgers.'"[7] The Ninth Corps had entrenched in between Warren's Fifth Corps on its left, and the Second Corps, temporarily under the command of David Birney, on the right, with their advanced position on the western slope of the ravine west of Taylor's Creek. On the eastern side of the creek, the Norfolk and Petersburg Railroad ran through the deep ravine parallel to it, a little to the rear of the corps' forward lines. The corps' picket line was beyond Taylor's Creek, "which took its rise between the lines in front of Fort Rice," about a half mile to the left of Potter's division. Taylor's Creek ran in a northern and partially northwesterly direction, ultimately flowing into the Appomattox River. The high ground on either side of the valley was cleared and cultivated.[8] Above the railroad bed and to the right of Baxter Road stood the scorched chimneys of the Taylor House, the remnants of William Byrd Taylor's home that had been burned to the ground earlier in the war. Potter's men soon began constructing a fort at this location, a few hundred yards behind the front lines. It was subsequently named for the late Major Morton, who had been killed in the assault on the Confederate lines on June 17, and when completed was considered the strongest of the Federal forts at the Petersburg front.

In front of the former Taylor House, the Union lines pushed closer to the Rebel lines than at any other point, only one hundred plus yards from the Confederate lines. The Union breastworks here were on the crest of a ravine framed by the railroad cut and Taylor's Creek, and to an untrained eye, it presented the appearance of an irregular line of earth banks thrown up without any definite design as to where the line was going or what it was intended to protect.[9] Behind this the terrain consisted of low ground and woods, which afforded admirable opportunity for massing large bodies of troops. This advanced fort in the front line was called by the Union troops "the horseshoe." A strong line of rifle pits all along the edge of the dead space was fortified with elaborate loopholes and head logs to protect their sharpshooters; from it the sharpshooters maintained a close and accurate fire on all parts of the line near them. Lieutenant Colonel Henry Pleasants would soon identify this area as the beginning point of his magnificent excavation. Directly in front of this horseshoe, and opposite the Taylor House, upon a swell of ground rising some thirty-five to forty feet above Taylor's Creek, and 200 yards north of the Baxter Road, was a Confederate fort with a battery consisting of four pieces of artillery and several regiments of South Carolina infantry.

This fort formed a salient which pushed forward beyond the general trend of the Confederate line. This redan battery was thus in a commanding position, which became very active and very annoying to the Federal troops. The location of this redoubt was in many respects bad, as the salient was actually a reentrant salient, as opposed to a projecting one, reentering the general line of entrenchments. It, as well as the ground between it and Burnside's advanced line of entrenchments, was being exposed to a flanking fire on the right and left.[10]

The Federal line in front of Fort Morton (Library of Congress).

In its rear some several hundred yards back was a crest on a ridge of small hills where the Confederate infantry was entrenched and other artillery batteries were positioned. The fort, a "strong, bastioned work, became known as Elliott's Salient," for it was manned by Brigadier General Stephen Elliott's brigade, which included 300 men of the 18th and part of the 23rd South Carolina regiments who were actually located in and around the fort itself in the main works. This redoubt, or small earthen fort, was on an elevation in the Confederate position held by Ransom's brigade, at a point where the brigade had first taken its stand in the recent fighting.[11] This redoubt was also known to the Confederates as Battery No. 5, and eventually to the Union, as "the mined fort."[12] The overall position reminded one Union officer "of the ugly horns of a rhinoceros."

In the rear of the Salient was a small ravine, then gradually rising ground back to Cemetery Ridge, half a mile in the rear, which the Union hoped to crown with artillery should they gain the ridge through a breach in the Confederate lines. The right and left also contained ravines, with a small stream running through the one on the left, heading at a spring 200 yards above. On the left, the woods reached up to within seventy-five yards of the redoubt. About seventy-five feet to the rear was a wide ditch, with the bank thrown up on the side next to the fortifications. This ditch was to protect parties carrying ammunition and rations to the troops at the front. Between this irregular and ungraded embankment and the main line, the troops had constructed numerous caves where they slept at night. The embankment from the bottom of the ditch was about ten feet high and commanded the outer, or main, line. The space between the outside of the fortifications to the inner edge of the ditch was more than one hundred feet wide. By early July, a third line of entrenchments to the rear of Elliott's Salient was completed to the extent that it could be occupied by two full companies.[13] Some 800 yards to the rear of the Salient, the Jerusalem Plank Road was sunken about five feet below ordinary surface conditions, offering "a beautiful place for an ambuscade of artillery & infantry." In the immediate rear of the Salient, the ground dipped suddenly and broadened out into a meadow of some considerable size, making it a suitable site for massing large bodies of troops. The streets of Petersburg, the walls of Blandford Cemetery and the Jerusalem Plank Road made an almost perfect parallel to Taylor's Creek and the lines, beginning at zero distance at the Appomattox River, widening to more than 500 yards, and then just beyond Elliott's Salient, turning decidedly and crossing Taylor's Creek. The opposing lines on the western crest of Taylor's Creek ran southward, "rising and dipping as that crest rose and dipped because of some small side branches."[14]

The crest of Cemetery Hill, flowing with Confederate artillery, was not more than 800 yards distant from the advanced works of the Union, "and its gently sloping sides were welted with long rows of earthworks, pitted with redoubts and redans, and ridged with serried salients and curtains, and other skillful defences."[15] All ground between the Confederate lines and the Jerusalem Plank Road was exposed to their view and fire from their lines on the far side of Taylor's Creek. Thus, it was impossible to approach the Confederate lines from the rear except in two places. On the Confederate left was a ravine with a small stream where the Confederates constructed a regular trench that made a covered way. Some two-thirds of a mile to the right, a path was found wandering among some shallow hollows, which was also thoroughly covered from the enemy's observation.[16]

As soon as the momentum for further offensive operations waned, both sides quickly set about establishing improved entrenchments, fortifications and batteries, as well as backup positions, bomb-proofs and covered ways. Such activity, with a view toward making their respective positions impregnable, went forward throughout the rest of June and July. The Salient had a line of picket trenches in front connected with the lines by a zigzag trench or covered way. This picket line was quite close to the main line and only 113 yards from the enemy, across Taylor's Creek. About 150 to 200 yards to the rear of the battery at the Salient, the Confederates had "thrown up a work ... connecting with the main line on each side." This line was to play a critical role in the subsequent Union attack, and perhaps ultimately saved the day for the Confederate forces. It was known as a cavalier line, sometimes referred to as a "gorge line."[17]

Elliott's flank was one third of a mile long. Wise's brigade, then under the command of Colonel John T. Goode, was located on his right, occupying the eminence south of the Baxter Road about 200 yards from the Salient. Ransom's brigade occupied the front about 400 yards to the left of the Salient, running north and south along the western edge of woodland. Gracie's Alabama Brigade was positioned to the right of Wise's brigade, near where the Norfolk and Petersburg Railroad crossed the lines. Here a ravine passed through the breastworks, and a brook at the bottom had been dammed up, thus filling the ravine for a considerable distance and creating a pond. Between this pond and the railroad was a space of about 200 yards where the opposing sides' pickets were quite close together. Elliott's Salient was a high point in the line and there was a rapid dip toward Wise's position, and a gradual dip toward Ransom's on the other side. This dip toward Ransom was soon to take on great importance, for the majority of the impending battle would be from the Salient to the bottom of that dip. The dip favored the construction of a zigzag trench or covered way leading back from the

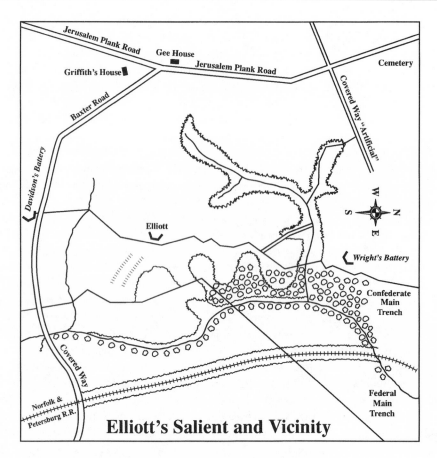

Elliott's Salient and Vicinity

front lines to the Jerusalem Plank Road (in fact, it passed under the road and on into the valley of Lieutenant Run). The little branch that caused the dip between Elliott's and Ransom's brigades came up from the lines and branched at the mouth of that covered way, "one branch turning south and making a depression, or swale, between the ... [Salient] and the Plank Road."[18]

As previously stated, Elliott's Salient was considered a reentrant salient, not a projecting one. At Wise's position, the entire Confederate line took a turn to the southwest, "which turn there, made an outward salient; but Wise and Ransom could look across Elliott's front at each other." The inward or reentrant curve there was slight, "but intentional—to enable the enfilade of Elliott's weak front." The lines had been meticulously laid out by Colonel Harris, the engineer-genius of Beauregard's command, and were approved by Lee as the best the terrain allowed.[19]

In the rear of the Salient was a ridge of small hills west of the Jerusalem Plank Road where "very active and annoying Confederate marksmen and several other Southern batteries were entrenched, trying to shoot anything wearing blue that moved. Everyone was constantly on the alert, and relaxation was virtually unknown in that part of the Federal forward lines."[20] In preparation for the defense of the Salient, a four gun battery was erected about 555 yards to the left, across the covered-way ravine and a little secondary hollow where it was entirely sheltered from enemy observation. It was occupied by Wright's battery of Coit's battalion, the same to which Pegram's battery in Elliott's Salient itself belonged. It was located on Beauregard's front, under instructions from General Gilmore, chief engineer, who took an active interest in all the operations around Petersburg.[21] In a depression on the Jerusalem Plank Road, 800 yards to the rear of the Salient, Brigadier General E. Porter Alexander had placed fourteen of Major John C. Haskell's guns. Another four were located out in front of the earthworks to sweep a sort of hollow out to the right. Out near the path, there were two more guns under Lieutenant John H. Chamberlayne to enfilade the Confederate trenches, in the event the enemy was to occupy them. Wright's guns to the left were in a position to flank and sweep the Salient and its approaches even better than Chamberlayne could do from the right.[22] Alexander then found an ideal site for a whole battery to give "the same sort of flanking fire which had been so effective at Cold Harbor — a random fire, which did not directly see the enemy (& consequently he could not reply to it) but every shot from which would come bouncing & skipping along, exactly parallel to the front of his brigades, killing bunches when they hit & demoralizing the troops by their very direction even when they went clear." This battery was placed at the end of the covered way where it could see little or nothing in front, as little knolls in front on each side of the winding creek cut off the direct view down the course of the stream, "but every shot fired over them would rake the dead space in front of Elliott's Salient." In order to prevent gunners from attempting to shoot at what they could see to their right flank and to confine the fire exclusively to raking the front of the Salient, where "the heart of the fight would be," Alexander ordered high and narrow embrasures to be built so the gunners could not see anywhere else. Another battery of four guns was placed in a smaller salient about 200 yards to the right of the Salient. The two left guns of the battery were "well traversed & their embrasures specially shaped to give a raking fire along the right flank of the Elliot [Salient] while the guns themselves should be protected from direct fire anywhere. At that close range their canister fire would be very effective."[23] There was also a mortar battery under Captain James N. Lamkin, consisting of four Coehorns on the Jerusalem Plank Road, and one Coehorn, and two twelve-pound mortars in the ravine 200 yards to the left and rear of the Salient, and two mortars to the left of Wright's battery. Additionally, there were three mortars on the right of Baxter Road under Lieutenant Jack Langhorne.[24]

Opposite Elliott's Salient, General Potter's second division of the Ninth Corps held the bulk of the line for the first few days of the Petersburg siege. (Interestingly, both Elliott and Potter had fathers who were Episcopal bishops.[25]) After the first few days, the disposition of the corps' line found the third division of General Willcox on the left, the second division under General Potter in the center, directly opposite the Salient, and General Ledlie's first division on the right of the corps. Potter's troops had borne the brunt of the campaigning thus far. Ledlie's troops consisted largely of greener troops who had not seen as much action. However, they had been on the front lines continuously and were quite skittish; the same situation existed with regard to Willcox's troops.

Brigadier General Henry J. Hunt, the army's chief of artillery, surveyed the Union lines on June 19 in order to initiate the armament emplacement for a long siege, which would take the next six weeks to fully accomplish. The following day, he sent for the heavy guns. A new siege train had been created, of even greater size and variety than its 1861–62 predecessor. The former siege train had come into being in late 1861, manned by the First Connecticut Heavy Artillery under Colonel Robert O. Tyler. In June of 1862, it massed the most mammoth display of ordnance in military history to that date to reduce Richmond to rubble as part of McClellan's Peninsula Campaign. The First Connecticut Heavy Artillery comprised the remnants of that siege train. Siege ordnance had been recognized as a vital ingredient to the 1864 campaign, and Hunt had devised a plan for an artillery train capable of being floated to the Richmond area by barges or 200 ton schooners. Hunt had suggested Colonel Henry L. Abbot to act as the new commander of the First Connecticut Heavy Artillery, now consisting of 1,700 men. Abbot was appointed and directed to prepare the siege train on April 20, 1864, and to report to General Hunt when the time was ripe to utilize the train. The train consisted of forty rifled siege guns (four and a half inch ordnance or 30 pound Parrots), ten, ten-inch mortars, thirty eight-inch mortars, twenty Coehorn mortars, and a reserve of six 100 pound Parrots. Each large cannon was accompanied by at least 1,000 rounds of ammunition, each large mortar by 600 rounds, and each Coehorn by 200 rounds. Abbot reported to Benjamin Butler on May 13, 1864, but by May 17 Butler was in flight back to Bermuda Hundred where Abbot was forced to spend the next month, "a siege artillerist nowhere near enough to his objective to lay effective siege." When Grant finally called for the siege train, it arrived on June 23, whereupon Abbot was ordered to report directly to Hunt, while storing all his ordnance at Broadway Landing. On June 27, much to Hunt's satisfaction, Grant placed him with authority over all siege operations south of the Appomattox, with the exception of Bermuda Hundred. This, in effect, took away the individual corps commanders' ability to control the artillery fire from the siege guns in their respective fronts. Lacking Meade's backing, Hunt did not exercise authority over the artillery still attached to the several corps, however.[26]

Hunt and Major James C. Duane, Meade's chief engineer, were ordered to make a lengthy reconnaissance of the Petersburg lines to determine if an offensive operation was feasible at any point along the Federal lines. On July 8, Hunt and Duane submitted a report that "a successful offensive might be conducted against the salient facing Burnside, but only if enough heavy cannon could be brought to bear on rebel flanking batteries north of the IX Corps' position and 'upon the salient and batteries in front of the Fifth and Eighteenth Corps.'"

Immediately following the report, Abbot sent up not only more cannon, but also ten more ten-inch mortars, in addition to six eight-inchers, all for use in the Fifth and Ninth corps sectors east and southeast of the city. Additional Coehorns were also sent up, "until virtually all Union-flanked reaches of the Confederate lines were susceptible to vertical fire."[27] All throughout July, the Union works were reinforced with even more 30 pounder Parrots, 4.5 inch rifles, heavy and light mortars and other instruments of death. Included in this array was the mammoth seacoast mortar, *Dictator*, a prized piece of Butler's ordnance cache at Bermuda Hundred, which was repositioned to the rear of Smith's corps on the extreme right flank. The weapon weighed 17,000 pounds and had a bore of thirteen inches. Mounted on a flatcar in between Petersburg and City Point on the Petersburg & City Point Railroad, with a charge of twenty pounds of powder, it could throw a 218 pound projectile over 3,600 yards (over two miles), providing "unholy terror" upon the subject of its fire once it went into action on July 9. The recoil produced by the gun's discharge sent it sliding back two feet across its platform and its car careening twelve feet down the track. "It made the ground quake," stated one infantryman posted near its position.[28]

Grant had seemingly given up on frontal assaults by June 19 and had become reconciled to settle in for a long siege. As both sides dug even deeper entrenchments and more infantry obstacles, the rolling farmland east and south of the city was soon churned into scenes resembling a moonscape. These tandem ramparts ran for twenty-six miles, crossed two major rivers, and traversed parts of four Virginia counties, from White Oak Swamp, east of Richmond, across Bermuda Hundred and south to the Jerusalem Plank Road below the city.[29] No campaign of the war quite equaled the siege of Petersburg, which was the object of the longest military action ever waged against an American city. More battles were fought and more lives lost there than in the defense of any better-known Southern cities such as Richmond, Vicksburg or Atlanta.[30] The two armies stood in their ever-increasing trenches, sniping at each other and writhing in the blistering sun in July temperatures that often topped 100 plus degrees.

The *Dictator.*

Soldiers in the trenches were constantly on the alert, especially around the Salient.[31] Anyone who exposed himself for an instant was the target for sharpshooters. An incident occurred when General Stevens, Lee's chief engineer, desired to take a close look at the enemy lines. He could not peer over the parapet, and it was dangerous even to look through a loophole. He thus cautiously held up a mirror at an angle so he could see the enemy's parapet down to his eye. Instantly, a bullet smashed through the glass in his hands, and a Union sharpshooter yelled out, "Set it up again, Johnny!"[32] Federal sharpshooters took a considerable toll even though the Confederate entrenchments were quite formidable and provided good protection. In most places they were seven feet high with a platform to step on while firing. A head above the ramparts would immediately draw fire from Yankees in the trees and trenches from some 200 to 600 yards away. O.T. Hanks of Company K of the 1st Texas found great sport in testing the Union sharpshooters' skills by hoisting his hat on a ramrod above the works and invariably he would have two quick holes in it where a bullet went through.[33] Corporal J.A. Watrous of the 36th Wisconsin of the Fifth Corps later related how the men on both sides had fun prompting the sharpshooters of the opposite side with caps propped on ramrods. One day in July the fourth division commander, Brigadier General Lysander Cutler, called "Old Pap Cutler" by the men, walked along the lines with his hands behind his back. The men in the trenches decided to have some fun and signaled for a "ramrod battle." Hats were quickly hoisted, bringing a hail of bullets over the general's head. He stood it for a couple of minutes and then went to the rear "at a much faster pace than he had displayed in coming up to the line, and his hands were not resting on his back either." The men "set up a shout and indulged in gyrations common to hilarity; he sighted the situation, looked daggers for an instant, and then joined in the laughter." One of his staff suggested that Cutler give an order prohibiting the ramrod exchanges, but Cutler said "No. Let the boys have all the fun they can get out of this serious business."[34]

In many places along the lines, the troops were not over 200 yards away, with advanced rifle pits only 100 yards apart. Trench life was terrible. In sunny weather, the reflected heat from the new red-clay embankments was intense and unrelieved by a breeze. In wet weather, one was always at least ankle deep in thick, clinging mud. Incessant shelling and picket firing made moving around extremely dangerous. The troops on both sides learned how to burrow like "conies" into the sides of the trenches with tin cups and bayonets to gain protection from the rain and the shells. One could look down a trench at a sultry mid-day or during a rain-fall and observe no one except a sentinel. At the sound of a drum, however, heads would pop out of the walls like prairie dogs. Sanitary conditions were so bad that the water supply from the nearby creek was almost immediately polluted, making drinkable water scarce. Trenches were often so narrow that two men could scarcely pass abreast; men were plagued by swarms of flies, lice, ticks and chiggers and the horrible stench of the latrines. There were traverses, narrow ditches, cross ditches, and mounds over officers' dens—a complete "system of bur-rowing, in imitation of rats and moles; literally living under ground; the impromptu bomb-proofs promiscuously thrown together, no ventilation and no light, damp and cold." Men were often careless about clothes and rations in the Union trenches. They would eat or throw away several days' rations without considering tomorrow, and would cast aside or give away clothes if warm, without thinking about cooler times to come.[35]

The trenches already ran south from the Appomattox River for five miles, following the highest terrain around Taylor's Creek. Each Union regiment would dig a broad trench, with a solid wall of logs facing the enemy, with dirt up banked beyond it. A number of yards in front of this would be a ditch, six feet deep by ten feet wide, with the excavated earth piled in front of the log wall until this embankment was from six to eight feet high and twelve feet thick. On top of the wall, sandbags or more logs would be placed, with slits or loopholes for troops to stick their muskets through. Just behind the wall would be a fire step — a low ledge of packed earth, fashioned so a man who stood on it could slide his musket through the loop-holes. At regular intervals, leading to the rear, would be covered ways, which were deep trenches zigzagged to take advantage of the lay of the ground, allowing troops to advance to their firing line without being exposed to the fierce enemy fire. In front of these trenches and earthworks, about fifty to one hundred yards nearer to the enemy, an abatis would be posi-tioned. To construct these formidable devices, the heavily wooded terrain was soon stripped of trees and the bushy tops pointed at the enemy. The butts of the trees were then embedded in shallow trenches to hold them in place, and the branches were sharpened and bound together so that it was next to impossible to proceed through the obstruction. In many areas, there were several rows of these entanglements, with narrow lanes cut at intervals to allow pickets to proceed to their stations. These abatis were supplemented by *chevaux-de-frise*, heavy logs laid end to end and bound together with chains, bristling with six-foot stakes sharp-ened to a point and projected in a manner so that a soldier attempting to negotiate over the obstruction would soon find himself entangled in the device.[36]

At periodic intervals, encompassing every hill was a fort, a square enclosure also of earth and logs with numerous openings for guns. The openings were constructed so that there was no place in front of the trenches that could not be reached by artillery fire. Farther back were pits like unroofed cellars where Coehorn mortars were mounted. In the forts and pits were bomb-proofs, which were square holes in the earth roofed with logs and dirt in which troops

Chevaux-de-frise before the Confederates' main works (Library of Congress).

could hide when the enemy shelled them. Their walls were constructed of logs heavily banked with earth and with a door or wide opening on the side away from the enemy. The roof was also made of heavy logs covered with several feet of earth.[37]

Lieutenant Robinson of the Ringgold Battery spoke of his experiences when his unit temporarily replaced Pegram's men in Elliott's Salient in July, recalling the incessant sharpshooting which continued through the night as well as the day: "[W]e had to sit down or kneel down all the time to keep from being shot. A hat on a stick shown above the breastworks was immediately perforated with bullet holes." He indicated that, while in the Salient, "officers were not allowed to go out at night. Our cooking was done at our horse camp in the rear.[38] The 'spat,' 'whiz,' 'zip' of hostile bullets would not even make ...[the soldier] quicken his pace. Mayhap he would take his short pipe out of his mouth and yell defiantly, 'Ah-h-Yank-yer-kain't shoot,' and go his way tempting fate, until a bullet struck him and he was dead, or maimed for life." It often seemed like men at times sought death or wounds as relief from "the torture of such intolerable life." It was enough to make most men reckless.[39] A Union soldier wrote that the "[m]ortar shells are constantly bursting over our heads. We eat our meals, and watch for them while swallowing our food, as cool as you please; sometimes it provokes a smile to think of the dire consequences that would happen to a dinner should a bomb descend upon it."[40]

Occasionally there would be a suspension of firing. Then, even ladies visited the Confederate trenches from Richmond. Pretty girls rode out on horseback and "dismounting, advanced boldly across the exposed ground, and stood for some time on our parapets watching the Union line." Union troops would then call out: "Hello, Johnnie! It's ladies' day, ain't it?" Often, the trenches would be lined with soldiers sunning themselves. They would talk to each other in familiar terms such as "Hello, Johnnie." "Sometimes our conversation was civil and kindly enough. Sometimes it was facetious. At others it was of the grossest and most unmentionable character." In this area, pickets of each army had made arrangements with each other, allowing common use of a stream between the lines. Corporal John L. Smith of Co. K, 118th Pennsylvania Infantry, wrote home on July 8 about his trading experiences with a Rebel, citing that "I had a very pleasant chat with him and found he was a mighty nice fellow." Smith told the Southerner that if he would come into the Union lines, "he could live like a white man then, but he respectively [*sic*] declined and said that he was a southern man and he would fight till the last, as he was sure that they would gain all their points."

The "rules" of this informal truce were faithfully observed. Those not abiding by them were dealt with by their own comrades. One day a recent Southern recruit was on line during a "truce" and, pursuant to the practice that had been drummed into him by his officers, he fired at the first Yankee he saw. The Federals jumped into their pits and prepared to retaliate in kind when the cry went up: "Don't shoot — you'll see how we fix him." Thereafter, the supposed foes "lounged on the grass, went for water, exchanged gossip, and kept a wary eye open for officers," while the "offending" Southerner was seen pacing back and forth along the firing line ignominiously shouldering a fence rail. Such truces would be terminated by someone calling from the rifle pits that orders had come in to reopen fire at a designated time, "sufficiently remote to allow everybody to seek cover."[41] These informal "truces" were exceptions to the rule elsewhere along the line. In most places, both sides continued to consistently "play for keeps," and it was negligent in the extreme to expose oneself for more than an instant.

Bombproof — Petersburg (Library of Congress).

When the lines at Petersburg were first manned by the Confederates, the thing most feared were the great mortar shells, which were particularly terrible at night. Their parabolas through the air were watched with great apprehension, "and their explosion seemed to threaten annihilation." However, as time went on these soon ceased to be of as great concern as the common minie ball. One could get out of the way of a mortar shell; the earth was so tunneled and pitted that the shells were more apt to fall in some depression where the fragments would be stopped and rendered harmless by the surrounding walls of dirt. Iron soon became scarce in the Confederate lines, and furloughs were granted for men who gathered certain quotas of shell fragments of certain limits for use in the foundries. Eager troops would often dangerously head for a shell even before it exploded. General Bushrod Johnson reported on July 19 that Gracie's brigade alone had collected 1,000 shells and solid shot on July 18, together with 350 to 400 pounds of lead. On July 22, Private Reamey, Company B, 34th Virginia of Wise's brigade, collected 1,567 minie balls, two shot and two shells. On the 23rd, Johnson's division reported collecting over 19,000 minie balls.[42]

The human cost of holding onto the opposing lines was tremendous; not a day went by without significant loss of life. This was particularly true for the opposing troops around Elliott's Salient, due largely to the proximity to each other and the fact that musketry and artillery fire was kept up continuously each day. The average loss of Potter's second division of the Ninth Corps alone was fourteen or fifteen men per day just from sniper fire and mortar fire. Divisional losses from sniper fire and mortar fire alone could easily run to 12 percent in one month. The corps reported losing an average of thirty to sixty men each day in this fashion.[43] On the other side of the trenches, the Confederate soldiers were not the only ones

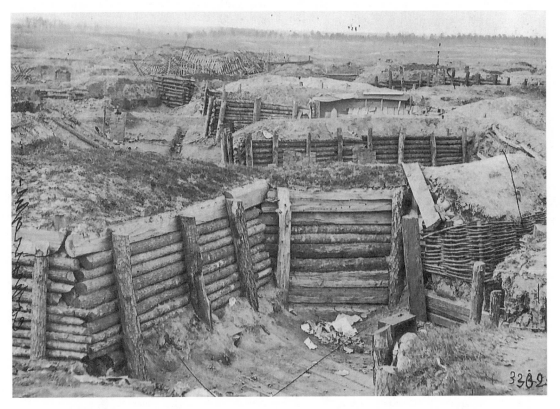

Confederate fortifications with chevaux-de-frise beyond (Library of Congress).

to suffer from the Union heavy artillery. Citizens were holding their breath for a rumored all-out assault to commence on the 4th of July, to match Grant's success at Vicksburg the year before. The rumor went on to indicate that, following a successful assault, the city would be put to the torch. "When July 4 had safely passed, life returned to what passed for normal under the siege."[44]

Both sides used various techniques to make their positions safer and to threaten the opposing force. Abatis were placed in front of the respective forward positions of each side to thwart attacks. Union troops began to approach Bushrod Johnson's rifle pits by means of sap rollers, which were large wicker cylinders ten feet long by seven or eight feet in diameter, made of straight hickory and oak poles, with hoop poles woven in like heavy wicker work and filled with poles big and small wedged in tight, which made the device virtually bulletproof. The sap rollers would be moved toward the Confederate lines with men hiding behind them in the process of digging a narrow trench toward the works. Close behind would be a string of more diggers to enlarge the trench. To combat the success of this endeavor, Confederate troops would run a "drift," or shallow mine, under them and blow the project up. Porter Alexander also sent to Richmond for hand grenades "of a pattern which Gen. Rains had recently devised." These devices were "thin, iron shells, about the size of a goose egg, filled with powder & with a sensitive paper percussion fuze in the front end, & a two foot strap, or strong cord, to the rear end." A man could swing one of these devices and hurl it over sixty yards. Alexander felt these would be ideal for use against sap rollers, although little record of their use is available.[45] Signal towers were also erected by the Union forces to study any evidence of a change in the Confederate lines. Whenever it "seemed to have any reference or relation to the defence of the salient, a great concentration, not only of siege & field artillery was prepared against it, but also a special one of heavy mortar fire."[46] Significant efforts were made to prevent any reinforcements, particularly from Elliott's Salient, by field, siege and mortar fire.[47]

As if these conditions were not next to unbearable in and of themselves, the weather became oppressively hot, often topping 100 degrees. No rain fell at Petersburg for forty-seven days—from the 3rd of June until the 19th of July. There was no surface water near the lines, as the springs, marshes, ponds and even streams went dry. An Alabama soldier wrote that the "heat was excessive, there was no protection from the rays of the sun...." Cordelia Handcock wrote to Joanna Dickeson, president of the Ladies Aid of Handcock's Bridge, New Jersey, that "[t]here were not surgeons near enough who were willing to stay in the sun and attend to the men and it was too awful to leave them uncared for."[48] A Union soldier wrote home that "I have not written home for a few days because it has been an impossibility; first, it has been too hot for mortal man to sit down with such an intention...."[49] Robert E. Lee worried about the effects of the hot, humid weather on the soldiers of his command digging "in the extreme heat," constantly to deepen and strengthen the trenches.[50] The light, sandy soil of the area was soon reduced to powder, and with a constant passing of mules, horses and wagons, huge clouds of dust arose which completely enveloped both armies. "At sunset this cloud would settle down and become so dense that one could not see objects twenty yards from him."[51] Cordelia Handcock wrote from City Point on July 1 that "the dust is shoe top deep, the sun just pours down, the smell is almost intolerable, and we have had no rain for nearly three weeks."[52] Abijah Marvin described the plight of the 21st Massachusetts:

> Exposed continually, day and night, they lay there in their trenches, not daring to lift their heads, so near were they to the enemy's sharpshooters. And all this during the scorching days of the last of June, and all of July, and the first part of August, when the trees were burnt, and the grass dead, and the heaven refused its rain, and the dust lay thick on all.[53]

Signal tower of the 14th New York Heavy Artillery (Library of Congress).

A New Yorker complained that the combination of 110 degree heat and four-inch deep dust "is killing more men than the Johnnies." Every day men toppled over with sunstroke and had to be carried to the rear. Soldiers took advantage of any creature comforts they could muster to make their plight more bearable. In a small grove of trees on the ridge in between Taylor's Creek and the railroad bed, to the right of Baxter Road, the men of the 45th Pennsylvania of Potter's division discovered a well-filled ice house near the picket line, but it was unfortunately in full sight of the enemy. In the bottom of this ice-well was a small quantity of ice, protected by straw. "Some of our fellows were killed by Rebel sharpshooters while trying to get ice for their lemonade, with maybe a 'stick' in it. All the same, the boys took chances and frequently brought chunks of ice into camp."[54]

Both armies were suffering greatly from over three years of continuous fighting with no end in sight. While the Army of Northern Virginia still remained high in spirit and devotion to the Cause, Lee was forced to work with stretched-out units which "bore little resemblance to the Army of Northern Virginia." Stonewall Jackson's old Second Corps, now under Jubal Early, was currently away, operating along the Potomac, desperately executing a diversionary threat on Washington. The remains of Longstreet's old First Corps were divided, with Anderson's control amounting to little more than administrative. Pickett's division, considered less than dependable by this time, occupied the Howlett Line taken in the June fighting against Butler. The divisions of Kershaw and Gregg were forced to alternate between holding the trenches at Petersburg and rushing to halt advances on Richmond.[55] Hoke's and Johnson's divisions of Beauregard's old command, together with batteries and brigades released from coastal garrisons, made up much of the trench defenses east of Petersburg, representing the first such trench warfare of this magnitude in world history. Lee's only intact corps was A.P. Hill's, currently dug in on the lengthening line southeast of Petersburg. "Hill's gaunt ragamuffins comprised the mobile force that was hurried at monotonous intervals to drive Federal infantry away from wrecking sections of the Weldon Railroad."[56] Hill was at his best when the greatest demand put upon him was to sustain the morale of his men, "while using every conceivable method of rotation to prevent their physical collapse." Yet, with his emotional nature, Little Powell was not the type with whom Lee could consult. Lee had to rely on this weakened remnant of his army to parry Grant's thrusts, at the same time maintaining a stable front.

Lee had little respect for Grant's generalship. In July, he wrote his eldest son, Brigadier General George Washington Custis Lee, then on President Davis' staff: "His [Grant's] talent and strategy consists in accumulating overwhelming numbers."[57] However, this strategy was working, in that Grant was wearing down the Army of Northern Virginia, now incapable of replenishing its dwindling numbers. Such a strategy would take a long time, far longer than "all summer," as Grant had proclaimed. However, unless the political situation could be drastically altered, Lee knew it was merely a matter of time. As he rode along the lines during that hot July, looking at the "toiling skeletons of men," observers found his expression careworn. On those rides, "there were more ghosts than soldiers 'present for duty' and, with more strangers than familiars among the officers, he must have sometimes seen the ghosts of 'the good and great Jackson' and the golden Stuart with laughter lightening his face."[58]

However, things were no brighter for the Army of the Potomac, which enjoyed a seemingly limitless supply of resources and an overwhelming, if not limitless, supply of soldiers. The army had truly changed forever after Cold Harbor; in fact, it was not the same. Replacements were conscripts and paid substitutes, who were "neither eager nor trained soldiers."[59] The provost general of the army, Brigadier General M.R. Patrick, wrote on July 18 that "[t]his army is nearly demoralized and the cavalry is no better than a band of robbers...." Meade later commented that the offensive spirit had been drained from the army, a belief which was substantiated by the willingness with which Federal infantrymen gave themselves up as prisoners. Between June 22 and August 24, eight thousand Federals surrendered.[60] The country itself was stuck in a morass. In the deeply gloomy months of July and August 1864, the barometric indicator of the economy, the price of gold, seemed to say that Lincoln and the Union government were failing. The significantly rising price of goods and services made life very difficult on citizens as well as on the soldiers.[61]

Some definitive action was necessary to break this stagnation and despair. For the South, it involved some measure which would cause the North, already teetering on the brink of despair, to lose heart completely, that is, a desertion of the Lincoln administration in the impending election. Such wishful thinking actually was quite close to being a reality. The situation required scoring a victory of sorts, which would cause a majority of the administration's remaining supporters to lose faith and cause a replacement of the administration in the fall elections with one prepared to sue for peace.

CHAPTER 4

The Earth Movers

After forty days of continuous fighting in the Overland Campaign, the two armies still found themselves facing each other from opposite breastworks outside Petersburg. The Ninth Corps, particularly the second division under Brigadier General Robert B. Potter, had advanced a short distance past the Norfolk and Petersburg Railroad bed and across Taylor's Creek. The Federal troops had established breastworks on the crest of a ravine, and, to the untrained eye, this line gave the appearance of an irregular array of earth banks thrown up without any definite design. In this ravine ran the tracks of the Norfolk & Petersburg Railroad, hidden from the Confederates' view by the outer Federal works. The most prominent forward earthwork was what came to be called "the horseshoe" by the men, built within one hundred yards of the Confederate lines near Elliott's Salient, directly opposite Fort Morton. This was the high-water mark for the Ninth Corps—the extreme limit of the advance of June 18, where tired men who had fired all their ammunition lay in the dark to build little breastworks with bayonets, tin plates and bare hands.

The Salient, on a swell of land thirty-five to forty feet above Taylor's Creek, was strengthened by the Confederates with a formidable redoubt holding a full battery and reinforced with smaller redoubts holding two guns each on the flanks.[1] The Confederate works had heavy guns capable of causing considerable damage to the Union fortifications and troops. Inside the Salient were 256 officers and men of the 18th and 22nd South Carolina regiments of Major General Bushrod Rust Johnson's division, together with two officers and twenty men of Captain Richard G. Pegram's Petersburg Battery.[2] Only 500 feet at most separated the two advanced lines of Fort Morton and Elliott's Salient, positioned one fourth of a mile east of the Jerusalem Plank Road, and one half mile southeast of Blanford Cemetery.

Due to the extremely close proximity of the opposing lines between the two forts, sniper fire was heavy and constant in this area. Potter's division was located in the ravine a little more than one hundred yards from Elliott's Salient, which itself was situated at an angle in the Rebel line of works, the closest at any part to the Union lines. Observers at the time felt the Union line had penetrated into the interior of the Confederates' lines in this area after the last battle and was thus occupying a tenuous position. The first unit assigned to the area, the 48th Pennsylvania Veteran Volunteer Infantry, of Potter's second division, was recruited largely from the coal mining area of Schuylkill County. During the fighting on the 18th of June, the 48th had pushed forward a little farther than the other units on either side of them. They had crossed the deep ravine formed by Taylor's Creek and struggled up the far slope to within 130 yards of the Confederate line. There, closer to the enemy than any other Federal unit, they dug in. Those daring to peer over their own parapets saw, on the crest of the rise, the redan containing Pegram's battery and the entrenchments stretching north and south, manned by South Carolina troops under Brigadier General Stephen Elliott, Jr., of Johnson's Division.[3]

The 48th Pennsylvania had been in the thick of the fight since the start of the war and fancied itself a crack unit. Pleasants and his men "were some very tough customers who had been in the war almost since the first shots of 1861."[4] After mustering in the fall of 1861, the unit served in coastal North Carolina under Ambrose Burnside, seeing significant action there. It took part in heavy engagements at Second Manassas, Antietam and Fredericksburg. In February 1863, the Ninth Corps was detached from the Army of the Potomac, and the 48th soon found itself in Lexington, Kentucky, where it was detailed for provost guard duty. In the fall of 1863, the unit moved with the Ninth Corps to Knoxville, Tennessee. Then, in the spring of 1864, the 48th went back to Pottsville, Pennsylvania, to recruit and "veteranize," in order to replace those lost as casualties as well as expired enlistments. The rejuvenated ranks soon rejoined the Ninth Corps at Annapolis in late March. The Pennsylvania minefields were full of strong young men of Copperhead sentiments. They demonstrated against the draft so violently that troops had to be sent from the front to keep order. The 48th, however, had no problem filling their ranks, quickly mustering over 400 men, many of whom knew how to dig mines. With its new recruits, the 48th crossed the Rapidan at Germanna Ford on May 5, 1864, with the rest of the Ninth Corps, on the extreme left of the first brigade of the second division. After participating in the battle of the Wilderness, the unit was soon heavily engaged at Spotsylvania Court House and by the end of that battle had lost 187 men just since the May 5 start of the current campaign. The unit took further significant losses at Cold Harbor; on June 17, it, along with the 36th Massachusetts of the first brigade, joined with a portion of the second brigade, and drove the Confederates back one half mile, while capturing four guns, fifteen hundred stands of arms and 600 prisoners, and recapturing the colors of the Seventh New York Heavy Artillery. The regiment took Battery No. 15, along with two sets of colors, two Napoleon cannon, and more prisoners than the number of men in the unit. After the Confederates withdrew to their new lines on June 18, a Union assault was attempted on the new lines, which resulted in the capture of the Norfolk and Petersburg Railroad, over which the men were then positioned.

The 48th Pennsylvania was at that time commanded by Lieutenant Colonel Henry Pleasants, who was born in the Argentine on February 16, 1833, the son of a Philadelphia businessman turned arms dealer (to the Spaniards operating out of Buenos Aires) who had married a Spanish woman. Pleasants lived in South America until he was thirteen, when his family sent him to Philadelphia for his education, in the care of his father's brother, Henry, a local physician. Henry and his wife, Emily, treated his young nephew as if he was one of their own; he was educated at Central High School in Philadelphia. He then took up a position with the Pennsylvania Railroad in the early 1850s as senior assistant engineer of the Pittsburgh & Connellsville Railroad, working on and accruing experience with the 4,200–foot Sand Patch Tunnel through the Alleghenies. There he first learned the principles of tunnel ventilation which would later serve him so well. He also became quite experienced in sinking deep shaft mines. Pleasants quit the railroad business to engage in anthracite coal mining, and thereafter made his home in Pottsville, Schuylkill County, devoting his attention to mining engineering with great success. There he met and soon married Sallie Bannon. When Sallie died at age thirty-one after contacting a sudden illness, Henry joined the army as a lieutenant in the 6th Pennsylvania Infantry, one of the early three month militia units, and subsequently joined the

48th as a captain when the 6th mustered out in July 1861. With the 48th, he participated in Burnside's North Carolina Expedition, Second Manassas and Antietam. Elevated to lieutenant colonel, he fought at Fredericksburg and then served in a detached capacity until the spring of 1864, when he rejoined the 48th for the Overland Campaign.[5]

At the time, Pleasants, although a relatively junior field officer, had inherited temporary command of the first brigade, due to the harsh attrition during the fighting in May and June. He then replaced Colonel Joshua K. Sigfried as commander of the 48th when Sigfried took command of a brigade in the new fourth division under Ferrero. Pleasants, while resting in a bombproof in the ravine one day, overheard one of his enlisted men of Company C discuss with his messmates the possibility that the fort in Elliott's Salient could be blown up by a mine. The man indicated that "[w]e could blow that damned fort out of existence if we could run a mine shaft under it with a mine."[6] As the thirty-one-year-old Pleasants passed along the trenches, "slim, dapper, dark and bearded," he kept thinking about what he had recently overheard regarding blowing up the Confederate fort in very close proximity to their front. To the right front of the 48th Pennsylvania's position was a deep ravine, or hollow, in which excavation work could be continually conducted without detection by the Rebels. Once the idea was conceived, Pleasants soon discussed the potential with Captain George Gowan of the 48th and Captain Frank Farquhar, chief engineer of the Eighteenth Corps, both men being his former townsmen and friends.

The outcome of that meeting was that all agreed the plan was feasible.[7] Their conclusion was that the "goddamned fort ... [was] the only thing between us and Petersburg, and ... [a viable plan could be fashioned to] blow it up." After exploring the ground that next morning of June 21, Pleasants then reviewed the possibility with General Potter and laid out the overall scheme before him, including tunneling up to the Confederate fort and blowing it up without loss of Union life. The Jerusalem Plank Road ran along a slight ridge roughly parallel to the line of works and only a few hundred yards behind Elliott's Salient. If this fort could be breached, a quick march would take the Federals to Cemetery Hill in Blanford where cannon could dominate the city of Petersburg. Potter was evidently favorably impressed, for he sent one of his staff officers, Captain Gilbert H. McKibben, to observe the situation firsthand with Pleasants. The next morning, these two men filed into the advanced trenches and proceeded as close to the Confederates as possible. McKibben pointed out the exact location of the nearest Rebel battery, an important point. As Pleasants jotted down a note, he heard a snap, and McKibben fell severely wounded in the face by a Rebel sharpshooter.[8] "All of Pleasants' subsequent triangulations had to be made under the same danger and subjected to the same chances." Back in his tent that day, Pleasants made a sketch of the terrain and relative positions of the opposing troops and forwarded it to Potter, who then sent a report to Burnside's chief of staff:

Lt. Col. Henry Pleasants (USAMHI).

Major Gen. John G. Parke,
Chief of Staff Ninth Army Corps

General: Lieutenant Colonel Henry Pleasants, of the Forty-Eighth Penna. Veteran Volunteers, commanding First Brigade, has called upon me to express his opinion of the feasibility of mining the enemy's works in my front. Colonel Pleasants was a mining engineer in charge of some of the principal works of Schuylkill County, Penna. He has in his command upwards of eighty-five enlisted men, and fourteen commissioned officers who are professional miners. The distance from inside our work, where the mine would have to be started, to inside of enemy's work, does not exceed one hundred yards. He is of the opinion that they could run a mine forward at the rate of twenty-five to fifty feet per day, including supports, ventilation, and so on. A few miners picks, which I am informed could be made by any blacksmith from the ordinary ones; a few handbarrows, easily constructed; one or two mathematical instruments, which would be supplied by the engineer department, and the ordinary entrenching tools, are all that are required. The men themselves have been talking about it, and are quite desirous, seemingly, of trying it. If you desire to see Col. Pleasants, I will ride over with him or send him up to you.

R.B. Potter, Brigadier-General[9]

At Burnside's request, Potter and Pleasants then reported to his headquarters on a sweltering June 24 evening to brief him on the plan. Burnside was in his tent with his coat off, his bald head glistening in the candlelight and a large cigar locked in the side of his mouth. Burnside listened intently while the plan was laid out, mopping beads of sweat off his forehead with a big silk bandana while they talked."[10] He immediately warmed up to the plan and told Pleasants to go ahead with his proposed work while he himself briefed General Meade on it. Pleasants therefore organized his miner-soldiers the next day and commenced the mining operation at noon on the 25th of June. Burnside formally notified Meade of Pleasants' initiative at 2:45 P.M. that same day. Meade, given his nature and general dislike for Burnside, took very little stock in the proposed project, however. His engineers reported "the new era in field works has so changed their character as in fact to render them almost as strong as permanent ones." Chief Engineer Major James C. Duane ridiculed the plan as a pipe dream. All concurred that a tunnel of that length was impossible and that the plan was "all clap-trap and nonsense."[11] Being the bureaucratic animal that he was, Meade never formally approved of the project, but he did not forbid the commencement of the work either. He was later to claim that the mine was started "without any reference to or any sanction obtained from the general headquarters of the Army of the Potomac." However, he did admit that "when the subject was brought to my knowledge [within twenty-four hours of commencement] I authorized the continuance of the operations, sanctioned them...." Thus, in Burnside's view, the work "was started and progressed with the full knowledge of General Meade."

Siege warfare required endless "dig-and fill routine," that is, an advance by regular approaches in military jargon, with the object to inch one's own lines forward far enough so that heavy guns could be mounted where they could destroy the enemy's works at short range. However, the trouble with this was that the conditions making siege warfare successful simply did not exist there. Petersburg was not surrounded at the time, and the Union did not have the necessary preponderance of force needed to succeed.[12]

George Meade was far from convinced of the probability of the success of such a bold plan, and he was reinforced by his West Point-trained professionals in the army's engineer corps, particularly Major Duane, who indicated that a tunnel of that length was totally impossible and that the plan was thus "all nonsense and an impossibility."[13] Mining an enemy's works was far from a novel idea; on the contrary, it was standard operating procedure once a besieging party had brought its own trenches up to within yards of its objective. However, no precedent existed for a tunnel of the length Pleasants was to undertake. The French had constructed a gallery of some 1,251 running meters, with some of it 50 feet underground, in the Crimea. More recently, the Union army had dug a number of mines at Vicksburg, but there the tunnels were started in approach trenches which had neared the Confederate works, and the plan had failed, at a cost of many Union lives. In any event, the Confederates were prepared and had previously constructed a second line.[14] Meade's advisors asserted that no army ever succeeded in carrying out a mining operation of this proposed length. "The army engineers were scornful. So long an underground passage had never been dug under such circumstances...." Thus, they would have none of it, dismissing the whole business as "visionary and impracticable."[15]

Meade had little faith in the project (especially as it originated with Burnside), "regarding it as an idle fancy of a disordered brain, the device of a crank," and his advisors did not conceal their derision of the plan.[16] He was so influenced by the army engineers' views "that he was grudgingly and coldly tolerant" to the idea. It was firmly believed by the corps' engineers that the miners would suffocate for lack of oxygen, or the mine would collapse somewhere along its extraordinary length in the process. Additionally, Meade's staff believed the Confederates were bound to discover the project before its completion and commence countermining to block the effort.[17] Meade also received a very lukewarm report from his chief artillerist on the prospect of a successful assault at the site of the proposed mine. It seemed that the problem was Rives' Salient, where the new Confederate works joined the old Dimmock Line near the Jerusalem Plank Road, flanking Elliott's Salient where the mine was being excavated. Given the configuration, any movement would be exposed to enfilading fire. Hunt and others on Meade's staff thus felt Rives' Salient would have to be reduced by regular approaches before any operation could be conducted from the tunnel, even if the same was successfully completed.[18]

Despite his lack of enthusiasm for the proposition, Meade had promptly briefed Grant, who was quite anxious to gain some momentum in the current stalemate any way he could. Meade was not confident there was any method to break through the Rebel lines, but told Grant that Burnside's men had commenced digging a mine "which General B. thinks when exploded will enable him by formidable assault to carry the line of works." Grant saw some credence in the plot and gave the go-ahead, over the reservations of Meade and his advisors. If nothing else, Grant reasoned, the project would bolster morale and "give them something to hang onto."[19] Pleasants was promised the full cooperation of the army's engineer corps and whatever materials and supplies he would require. Thus, with this tepid endorsement, due largely to the fact there was no other offensive option at present, Pleasants' miners began to take on importance.

Henry Pleasants began the project by having his company commanders assemble a roster of all the men in his command who were actually coal miners. Such miners were a strong and determined lot. They were generally inveterate tobacco chewers, "commonly seen with a greatly distended cheek, possessing a fine talent for spewing brownish streams." Pleasants organized shifts of several men each, with Sergeant Henry Reese as the mine boss. Reese was born in Wales in 1835 and had worked as a miner and bodyguard in the coal fields of Schuylkill County for a mine superintendent whose life had been threatened by the Molly Maguires. Known as "Snapper" to his friends and neighbors, Reese had seen some heavy fighting with the 48th. Though just shy of twenty-nine, with thick, red hair, his lungs were already full of coal dust that would ultimately claim him in his fifty-seventh year. Reese ate and slept at the site for the thirty-five days of its construction, personally supervising all the miners and keeping all interlopers out. Digging commenced at noon on Saturday, June 25, the diggers burrowing into the steep western slope of the railroad cut one hundred feet directly in the rear of the picket line of Potter's division, well hidden from the Confederate lookouts, with the miners initially using only their bayonets as picks.[20] The mouth was sufficiently below the Confederate line of sight that the men could come and go unmolested. The men worked in small shifts around the clock in three-hour intervals; each man would draw a dram of whiskey when his shift ended.[21] While the number of men employed was small at first, the numbers increased rapidly as the work progressed, until Pleasants was using his whole regiment in the enterprise. Pleasants and Potter initially expected to make forty feet of progress per day, although this estimate was soon reduced as the mine grew in length and the distance the men were required to stoop and carry out the excavated dirt increased considerably.[22]

To achieve speed and conserve timber, which was at a great premium in the area, the shaft was kept small. It was at most five feet tall and only four and a half feet wide at the bottom, while two and a half feet at the top, entering the slope roughly in the shape of a pyramid with its point cut off. It slanted upward toward the Salient in order to avoid drainage problems. As opposed to continuous supports along the whole length, the main support was the surrounding earth.[23] Day after day, the miners kept up their backbreaking work. One man dug, hunched over in the cramped gallery, while others carried away dirt, sand and gravel, which came out in a steady stream. Pleasants believed they could make forty to fifty feet per day in the soft Coastal Plain sediments. Fifty feet was achieved the first day and forty the next two days. But Pleasants had not calculated on the amount of dirt to be carried from the mine and the ultimate toll this would take on the men and their rate of progress. The further the stooping soldiers had to carry the debris, the less they could tunnel. Initially, the debris was loaded into sandbags for use along the parapets. Soon, however, there was a tremendous surplus of dirt, and another method of disposal had to be devised in order to avoid detection by the Confederate signal towers. The few remaining trees on top of the ridge offered the Confederates a clear view of the Union rear, and such a glimpse would reveal the fresh dirt and give the project away. Thus, the excavated material had to be carried far from the entrance of the mine to a location where other members of the 48th Pennsylvania cut bushes and trees from the rapidly deteriorating vegetation every day to hide the dirt before daylight.[24]

The miners continued to work in three-hour shifts. As work progressed, the length of the excavation grew, until the entire regiment was involved in the project. The regiment thus needed to be excused from picket duty, but they still remained targets for Rebel sharpshooters. Despite the intolerable conditions in the mine, the men of the 48th were used to such conditions, having sweated and strained through many long hours with considerably less headroom and under far worse breathing conditions back home in the Pennsylvania coalfields. The mine itself presented the men with suffocating closeness in the record-breaking heat wave. The only advantage to working in the tunnel was the miners' protection from the blaring sun and the record-breaking temperatures that July. An Ohio soldier recalled that the men "working in the mine had only shirts and drawers on, and some were minus shirt even. I used to watch them popping in and out of the hole like so many brown gophers."[25] Water in the tunnel made mud; as the men came out they were spotted and stained. Thus, it was quite easy to recognize a trooper of the 48th Pennsylvania by his muddy appearance. When the men would exit the tunnel after their three-hour shift, "the clay-caked crews would stumble like so many troglodytes into the raw daylight" and draw their allotment of whiskey. Many had their backbones shinned and were forced to take time off to recuperate. "Had they not been hardy miners, they would never have accomplished it," one contemporary observer noted.[26]

As work on the mine progressed, Pleasants found that the army was all too willing for

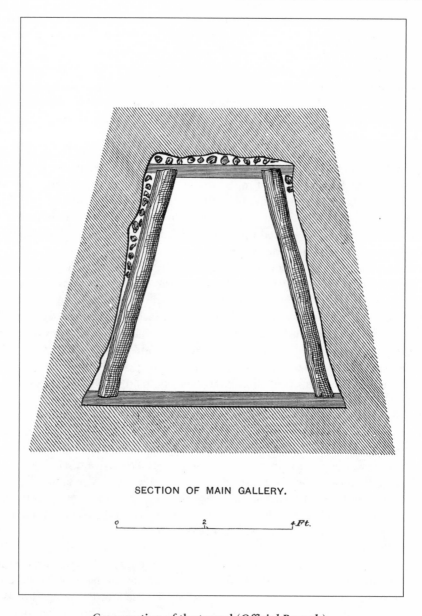

SECTION OF MAIN GALLERY.

Cross section of the tunnel (*Official Records*).

him to perform the job altogether, rather than assisting him in the process as had been proposed. Meade had reluctantly promised to send a company of engineers and other personnel, as well as to provide necessary materials and supplies. Pleasants later remembered that "Whenever I made application I could not get anything, although General Burnside was very favorable to it." Unfortunately, Burnside's word was not good for much with Meade or his staff. Major Duane, the staff officer most responsible for responding to Pleasants' requests, seemed to turn a deaf ear to any such reasonable pleas. Some years prior to this, Major Duane, then a captain, had written an extensive treatise titled *Manual for Engineer Troops—Practical Operations in Mining*. Under the "Tools of Mining Operations," he wrote (on page 208) concerning the "necessary" implements to a successful mining operation:

Pickaxe (common)	Miners wagon	Five foot rod	Needles, thread and
" (short handled)	Wheel barrow	Bellows (miner's)	scissors
Shovel (common)	Handsaw	Ventilating tube	Calico for hose
" (short handled)	Mallet	Flexible joints	Hatchet
Push-pick	Hammer (claw)	Iron candlestick	Tin funnel (for fitting
Rake	Rough plane (one	Lamp (miner's)	hose)
Canvas bucket	quarter inch)	Lantern	Rammers (short han-
Windlass and rope	Chisel	Oil can	dled)
Rope ladder	Gimlet	Measuring-tape	Helves (spare)
Wooden wedges and	Two foot rule	Compass	Sand bags[27]
pins	Plumb bob	Universal level	
" pickets	Boring rods		

Sadly and inexplicably, Pleasants' requests for even the most common and obviously necessary items such as wheelbarrows, picks, shovels, timber and sandbags went unanswered from headquarters of the Army of the Potomac. Thus, Pleasants was left to his own devices and without help, but still somehow he "continued his work with an unshakable perseverance."[28] When his request for wheelbarrows and sandbags went unanswered, he had the earth carried out in cracker boxes bound with iron hoops taken from old pork and beef barrels, with handles nailed on them and hickory poles nailed across the bottoms. When mining picks failed to arrive as requested, he had the common picks in the division straightened at the artillery batteries' blacksmith forge.[29]

Pleasants soon ran out of timber for shoring up the gallery of the mine, as the immediate area was quickly denuded of trees and no other building material was readily accessible. Again, his appeals to the army engineers went totally unanswered and he was soon forced to improvise. He sent a detail of his men down into the ravine behind the lines and tore down a railroad bridge over the Norfolk & Petersburg Railroad, using these timbers for as long as they lasted. Soon, reports of an abandoned sawmill approximately five miles to the rear provided a long-term solution to one of Pleasants' many problems. He obtained a pass from Burnside and sent two companies of his own regiment with wagons to operate the sawmill and return with lumber. Pleasants also requested a troop of cavalry to be assigned as guard, as the wagons would be exposed to reconnoitering parties of Confederate troopers. However, this request, as did all others, went totally ignored. By the time the mine was finally finished and ready for loading with gunpowder, insiders estimated that the work could have been accomplished in less one-third the time had any semblance of assistance been afforded to Pleasants and his men. "If ever a man labored under disadvantages, that man was Colonel Pleasants," Major William H. Powell of General Ledlie's staff later wrote of Pleasants' travails.[30]

When the tunnel had advanced 200 feet underground, Pleasants felt it was incumbent upon him to develop exact calculations to determine the exact location for positioning the powder magazine. Precision was required in any changes of direction and incline of the tunnel in order to avoid breaching the surface and thus being detected, or nearing the surface and thus precipitating a cave-in. Even more important, extreme care was required to avoid placing the powder magazine either in front or past the Salient. Such calculations had to be accurate to a fraction of an inch, which required the practice of triangulation, in surveying terms. The process, while a delicate bit of engineering, was at that time a routine process with the proper instrumentation. The instrument of precision at the time was known as a "theodolite,"[31] which was very routinely used on roads where grading was needed. The implement resembled a telescope mounted on a tripod with a plumb bob swinging underneath. By sighting through the instrument, calculations of the grade could be estimated. Taking additional readings at other points and coordinating these with a mathematical formula

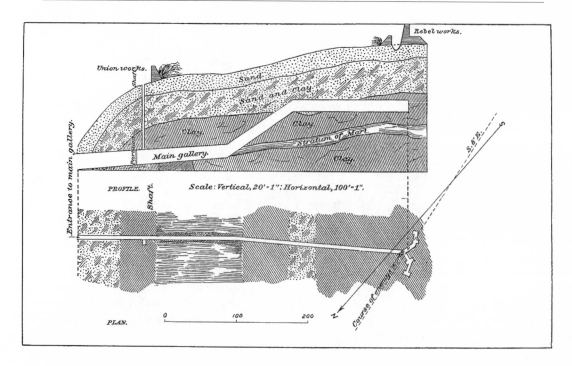

Cross section of the mine's main gallery (*Official Records*).

allowed a definite and accurate conclusion to be obtainable as the determining factor in the operation.

An infantry regiment would obviously not be equipped with a theodolite. However, as Pleasants knew, there was one at Meade's headquarters which was apparently not being used. Pleasants thus applied for temporary use of the instrument from the army's engineers, who were supposed to be assisting him in his efforts. Again, he heard no response to the inquiry and therefore advised Burnside of his plight. Burnside also made a request, but again to no avail, which came as no surprise to this patient individual. Burnside then solved the problem by telegraphing a friend in Washington who soon furnished Pleasants with an old-fashioned theodolite. Within a day or two, armed with the theodolite, Pleasants went about obtaining his needed measurements at the front lines. It was imperative that the measurements be made from the area where Captain McKibben had been severely wounded a short time before, as well as other equally dangerous points exposed to the relentless Rebel sharpshooters. To avoid detection of his purpose, Pleasants covered the instrument with a burlap bag, advanced to the front lines, set up the theodolite behind the parapet, and took his measurements while camouflaged with an additional piece of burlap topped by a clump of sod. He distracted the Rebel sharpshooters by having six of his men place their hats on ramrods and raise them above the parapets. While the Rebels methodically hit the hats, supposing they had dispatched unwary Federal soldiers, Pleasants was able to take the five necessary measurements while exposed to Confederate fire within 133 yards of the sharpshooters—sighting, calculating, triangulating, and rechecking until he was certain of the measurements. He then returned to his tent with the priceless notes and a "bullet pierced hat to show the accuracy of the enemy sharpshooters." [32]

One is left to question why the army's engineers would so completely ignore the repeated requests of a fellow officer assigned to carry out an offensive operation against the enemy, as well as how and why this undermining went on under Meade's nose. However, these staff officers, particularly Major Duane, had declared that the construction of a mine of the proposed length was an impossibility. As P. Regis de Trobiand, the French-born brigadier of Hancock's corps indicated:

> The chief engineers of the army and other authorities declared *ex cathedra* that the project was senseless and foolish; that a military mine as long as that had never been dug.... With *specialists*, the thing that has not been done cannot be done, and if you propose to them any innovation not found in their books, nine times out of ten they will tell you that it is impossible or absurd.[33]

Thus, the staff did not want any part of this enterprise that they had deemed to be absurd. Meade had little confidence in the mine's success, and undoubtedly felt reinforced by his staff's feelings, and they, reflecting his ambivalence, were unsupportive of the whole project from start to finish. As time progressed, they were concerned that Pleasants might, indeed, succeed, and therefore prove them wrong. Despite the total lack of cooperation, however, Pleasants proved himself "equal to every requirement without employing a person outside of his own regiment of four hundred men,"[34] according to a close observer, Captain John Anderson of the 57th Massachusetts.

In addition to this lack of confidence in the project, there was a significant lack of cordial harmony existing between Meade and Burnside. This friction was apparent from the very beginning of the campaign and became increasingly manifest by the time the mine project was undertaken. Burnside had been Meade's superior at Fredericksburg and was still his senior in rank, although he had willingly agreed to accept Meade's authority when his corps was folded into the Army of the Potomac. Fredericksburg still left a bitter taste with most officers and men of the army, and it remained Burnside's legacy. Meade by this time was also suffering the effects of being in Grant's shadow, where he felt, rightfully so, that he was deprived of credit for any success of the army while at the same time being the individual held responsible for all shortcomings, regardless of his ability to control or bring about the result. He was highly sensitive to perceived slights and firmly believed that he was not given due credit or the respect he so rightfully deserved. Meade was unjustifiably severe and sarcastic with Burnside, who was perceived as an "outsider" who had now been allowed to proceed with a project which Meade did not fully support. Friction such as this often has a marked influence on important military operations, which may have been the case here. It fosters a trickle-down effect, where any unfriendly or indifferent feelings of a commander towards one of his lieutenants is almost certain to manifest itself in some form and make its influence felt all down through the ranks until it reaches the private soldier, "who almost invariably shares the feelings of those nearest in touch with him."[35]

Meade's animosity spilled over to Major Duane, who spoke ill of Burnside at every chance provided him. Interestingly, Duane, while serving as George McClellan's chief engineer, had led Burnside to the wrong ford at Antietam Creek. The resulting incident was a contributing factor to the delay in the capture of the bridge over the creek that allowed time for Lee to receive much-needed reinforcements. Burnside consequently received much criticism for this development. Duane also had a role to play in Burnside's debacle at Fredericksburg. Despite the pleas of Handcock and others, Burnside postponed for days an attack on Lee's army while he awaited his pontoon bridges, which were inexplicably late in reaching the Army of the Potomac in December of 1862. One of Duane's last acts as McClellan's chief engineer was to order the return of the pontoon train from the upper Potomac to Washington. Rather than using telegraph or military messenger, he chose to transmit his order by regular mail, which added six additional days to the delivery time. The delay allowed Lee to strongly consolidate his forces around Fredericksburg, making his position impregnable. While Burnside had

The 48th Pennsylvania mining the Confederate works (*Harper's Weekly*).

never seen fit to criticize Duane, the disparaging tone the subordinate engineer always assumed with Burnside suggested severe defensiveness.[36]

Work on the mine initially progressed rapidly through the sand and soft clay of Din-widdie County soil, reaching 250 feet by July 2, when the miners encountered some extremely wet ground, described by some as quicksand, when the timbers gave way and the roof and floor of the shaft nearly met. The miners performed some rapid shoring with heavy posts, and from that point on they kept the supports closer together and planked the floor to achieve better weight distribution. Such shoring consisted of four parts: two props, one cap and one mud sill, notched into one another. Where the soil was very soft, the boards and planks were placed between the timbers and the top, bottom and sides so as to form a complete casing. As the gallery approached nearer the Rebel works, all timber was notched outside the mine and put in place without noise or jar of any kind. Almost immediately after the wet ground was encountered, another obstacle presented itself. The soil ceased to be of a sandy consistency and instead became marl, a putty-like consistency, making progress exceedingly slow. To extricate the shaft from this stratum of marl, Pleasants started an incline plane, raising the tunnel perpendicularly by thirteen and a half feet in one hundred feet of length, thus making it considerably higher than at the entrance. While slowing progress and adding to the travails of the miners, the marl had one beneficial impact; it provided a hobby and profit for some of the workers. The marl hardened to a rock-like substance with extended exposure to air and sunlight. When not on duty in the shaft, the men amused themselves making all types of artifacts such as pipes, crosses, figurines, and corps badges, sending them home as souvenirs.[37] Staff officer D.L. Way recalled how some men of the 48th Pennsylvania turned adversity to profit: "The sappers and miners around the entrance had brought the yellow clay out from under the Confederate fort, put the impression

MG George G. Meade (Library of Congress).

of the Ninth Corps badge on small pieces cut it out in shape of the badge (a shield) and dried it in the sun, selling them for 25 cents."[38] After traversing 100 feet of this marl stratum, the miners broke out into clay again, and the shaft was leveled off.

Perhaps the greatest of Pleasants' problems, and the conquest of which became his greatest engineering feat, was devising a mechanism to provide adequate ventilation to the miners working hundreds of feet into the hillside. The common belief was that a shaft of 400 plus feet would become too long to ventilate properly without vertical air shafts, and the miners would therefore suffocate for lack of clean air. Vertical air shafts were totally impractical, as they would give away the mine's location. Pleasants had explained his proposed solution to Major Duane in late June, but that officer still remained totally unimpressed and ridiculed the proposal. When another of Pleasants' requests for a miner's bellows went unanswered, he had his men sink a perpendicular shaft about two feet wide from one of the rifle pits twenty-two feet down into the tunnel at a point about one hundred feet into its length. The opening was carefully hidden in a clump of bushes. This air shaft opened directly into the tunnel wall. At the base of the shaft, or flue, attendants maintained a continuous fire in a grate. A small eight-inch square wooden duct which ran along a corner of the shaft was constructed from boards and was extended each day as the mine progressed. A partition of airtight burlap was hung across the shaft between the flue and the entrance to the mine. The fire caused the hot air to rise and increased its current, drawing the foul air up the chimney while simultaneously creating a draft and sucking fresh air from the outside into the void. The burlap partition prevented the escape of the good air and increased the effect of the ventilation system. To avoid detection due to smoke rising from the ground in this advanced position, Pleasants had a number of fires built and maintained on the surface in the area to avoid drawing special attention to the enterprise.[39]

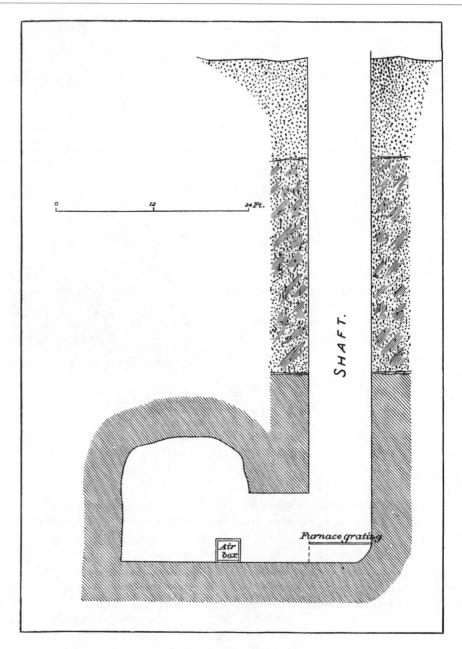

Ventilation shaft (*Official Records*).

While he and his men worked so feverishly on the mine, Pleasants was never certain if his efforts would ultimately be disapproved or the mine ever utilized for its intended purpose. On July 3, Grant inquired of Meade whether an assault on the Confederate works would be feasible on any part of the Union line. He desperately wanted to take the offensive again and to break out of the Bermuda Hundred bottleneck and invest Richmond from the south. Meade asked Burnside in writing if an assault on the enemy was "practicable and feasible at any part of the line held by this army." He specifically inquired as to the practicality of such an assault in Burnside's front by the Second and Sixth corps, in conjunction with the Ninth.

Burnside responded that same day, after obtaining the opinions of his division commanders and performing a personal reconnaissance of the Confederate lines. He indicated that the best option would be to await the completion of the mine, where there would be a "more even chance of success." If the assault had to be made immediately, he felt there was a "fair chance of success provided my corps can make the attack, and it is left to me to say when and how the other two corps shall come in to my support." The letter was carefully drafted and non-committal in many respects. Burnside asked that in the event he was responsible for an immediate assault that he be allowed to control the disposition of the supporting troops.[40] Meade shot back a response, indicating that he read Burnside's correspondence as being close to insubordination; he appeared indignant at the imagined presumption:

> The recent operations in your front, as you are aware, though sanctioned by me, did not originate in any orders from these headquarters. Should it, however, be determined to employ the army under my command in offensive operations on your front, I shall exercise the prerogative of my position to control and direct the same....

He went on to agree that the assault should be deferred until the mine was completed, "provided that it can be done within a reasonably short period — say a week." Interestingly enough, Pleasants was still hoping for the loan of a theodolite from Meade's staff even as Meade drafted his reply. Burnside instantly apologized for the unintended affront, explaining himself in such a humble manner that the gruff Meade thanked him for the apology and promised to do all in his power to promote "harmony and good feeling" among his corps commanders and himself.[41]

Pleasants and his men continued their backbreaking work around the clock. On July 6, Pleasants received a letter from Brigadier General John G. Barnard, the chief engineer of the U.S. Armies in the Field. Barnard posed a lengthy series of questions to Pleasants on the mining operation, "[i]n order to be enabled to have a clear judgment of the progress of the mining work in front of ... Burnside's rifle pits...." He requested detailed diagrams of the mine with dimensions and its position vis-à-vis the front lines. He also required information on the soil composition, the rate of progress, hours of operation, and number of men employed and when the mine would be completed. He wanted information on the charge, the means of tamping the mine, the method of firing, and the proposed timing of the explosion. Finally, he asked, "[What measures] are premeditated by the engineering department in accordance with the commanding General to secure the possession of the crater affected by the mine and to facilitate its defense?"[42] Considering his men had been "burrowing as if their lives depended on their efforts," for eight days by that time, Pleasants held his temper as a good and loyal officer and patiently responded to Barnard's questions as best he could on July 7. He indicated that the mine should reach the Confederate works in seven or eight days, and he described how the operation was progressing and the utilization of manpower. He indicated that answers to a number of the questions were still under consideration.[43]

Meanwhile, both Meade and Grant were seeking answers from their respective engineers and artillerists as to the potential for success of an assault on the Confederate works following the detonation of the mine in front of the Ninth Corps. Meade's staff still felt that Rives' Salient would need to be reduced by regular approaches before the explosion beneath Elliott's Salient would lead to a successful assault there. Henry Hunt, chief of artillery, presented his report to Meade on July 10, and siege operations against Rives' Salient were begun on July 11.[44]

Work continued in earnest, with virtually the entire 48th Pennsylvania employed in the task. Conditions continued to be insufferable in the intense heat and dust, coupled with the claustrophobic conditions in the tunnel. To distract the Confederates and prevent them from taking a prolonged look at what was going on in their front, the Ninth Corps kept up a constant fusillade of lead day and night. The Rebels, in turn, gave as well as they got; both sides remained on high alert, as casualties continued to mount. The Ninth Corps was losing over thirty men per day to sharpshooters. "You couldn't raise a hand over the breastworks without drawing the enemy's fire," reported Allen Albert of the 45th Pennsylvania Volunteers, of Potter's division.[45] Captain David Critchlaw, commander of Company C of the 100th Pennsylvania Veteran Volunteers, wrote to fellow member Corporal Frederick Pettit's parents on July 10, to tell them that "It becomes my painful duty to inform you that your noble son is no more. He was killed yesterday about seven o'clock P.M. ... sitting in his place reading at the time."[46]

Pettit had been wounded at Cold Harbor, and he had spent considerable time in the field hospital convalescing. He had just rejoined his unit the day before, and unfortunately was not yet accustomed to the rigors of trench warfare relative to one's personal safety. In addition to coping with the arduous work, punishing weather and the tensions of fierce trench warfare, the men of the 48th Pennsylvania were also worried about the folks back home. Jubal Early had moved up the Shenandoah and across the Potomac. The logical route to their apparent objective in Maryland and Pennsylvania was through Schuylkill County. Pleasants attempted to allay their fears with a "very friendly" speech which highlighted his appreciation for their hard work and sacrifice. Burnside visited the men on a number of occasions himself to bolster their spirits and check on their progress. On one occasion, he brought Senator Henry Sprague of Rhode Island and ex-governor David Tod. The general and his political friends were among the only celebrities "to brave the dank shaft, or even to sightsee at the maw, and they bantered with the miners, [jokingly] accusing them of laboring so hard just for a ration of whiskey." Apart from these few visits, few members of the Army of the Potomac ventured to view the progress or offer encouragement. It may well have been that many actually wished for the project to fail altogether.[47]

On July 17, one month after the last assault on the Confederates at the site, the main gallery was completed, being directly under the Confederate battery. The tunnel was exactly 510.8 feet in length and twenty feet below the enemy's breastworks. However, by then the Confederates had some knowledge of the mining operations, and Pleasants was ordered temporarily to halt operations and search for countermining efforts. Several Rebel deserters came into the Federal lines on the evening of July 16, including a miner who was detailed around the 12th or 13th to assist in countermining operations to discover the location of the Union mine. Pleasants made his personal investigation at midnight on the 17th — ordering all the men out of the tunnel — with just Captain William Winlack of Company C and one other man accompanying him. He crawled without lights to the head of the main shaft, where he remained flat on his face, ear to the ground, listening for countermining activity for thirty minutes. When a low whistle, the prearranged signal, was issued, the three then regrouped and Pleasants inquired if any countermining activity had been detected. Captain Winlack responded that apparently the Confederates "know no more of the tunnel being there than the inhabitants of Africa." Pleasants responded, "That's just what I believe." He then broke out in full voice, putting to flight all his notions cautioning extreme silence![48]

Following this brief hiatus, work commenced on July 18 on the lateral shafts at the tunnel's end underneath the redoubt. The right and left galleries were each nearly forty feet in length when completed. As had been the case with the prior shoring effort, timbers were cut and fitted together outside the mine, then dismantled, brought inside and reassembled in place, with almost no noise, under Henry Reese's close supervision. As the right gallery was being excavated, the men heard the sound of feet trampling overhead. Pleasants feared that the noise indicated the construction of a gun platform or a nearby countermine. As a countermine risked detection, and the recoil of a gun could collapse the tunnel, Pleasants curved the gallery around this disturbance and excavated a little beyond and in the rear of the works. This gallery was completed at 6:00 P.M. on July 23, being thirty-eight feet long. The left gallery, thirty-seven feet in length, was completed on Friday, July 22. The principal gallery of the mine thus ended in a transverse gallery seventy-five feet in length in the shape of the arc of a circle. In the walls of the latter, eight narrow passages were made facing each other, four on each side. *In toto*, Pleasants estimated that his men had excavated over 18,000 cubic feet of earth from the approximately 600 feet of tunnel. The mine that the army's experts had scoffed at as unworkable was fully completed on July 23 and ready for loading with powder. Pleasants stated that the mine could have been charged and exploded on that very date if so ordered.[49]

For the next four days, the men eased off on their efforts while awaiting further orders on loading the mine with powder. During this period, Pleasants had his miners timber and finish the eight magazines in the lateral galleries, four on each side. The ground was found to be quite damp in the magazine chambers; springs were discovered near the mine's head, which required men to drain and install sturdy framing to prevent cave-ins. Pleasants became extremely anxious awaiting the order to load the mine, fearing that the mine's walls might have been severely weakened by recent heavy rainfall. Both he and Burnside were also concerned that the mine might be discovered by the Confederates' countermining operation if it was not exploded soon. Burnside wrote Meade on July 26 indicating they might escape detection if the mine was used within the next two or three days. He cited the countermining efforts then known to be underway in the Confederate lines in order to emphasize the urgency of a detonation at the earliest possible occasion. Meade replied that the mine could be detonated if it was in danger of discovery, but such a premature detonation would not result in an assault. Meade then indicated that, if possible, the mine should be preserved for "use at some early future day when circumstances will admit of its being used in connection with other operations ... that you take no steps for exploding it as herein prescribed."[50] Burnside believed that the only thing which had saved the mine from detection up until then was that the Rebels believed the mining operations were farther to the southwest, nearer the Jerusalem Plank Road. Still, the powder was not forthcoming from headquarters, and no reason for the delay was forthcoming.

Finally, on July 27, Pleasants received permission to commence loading the powder. Burnside's proposal to Meade called for 1,200 to 1,400 pounds of powder allocated to each of the eight magazines, to be connected by a trough of powder instead of by a fuse. Pleasants had thus requested a total of 12,000 pounds of powder, as clearly shown on the invoice he presented. Somewhere in the process, however, Duane and others on Meade's staff had approved less without Pleasants' knowledge. The gunpowder arrived by mule train from Fort Monroe at Hampton Roads early on July 27. At this time, Pleasants learned that only 8,000 pounds of powder were delivered, rather than the 12,000 he had requested.[51] Pleasants had also requested 1,000 yards of safety fuse, only to find that Meade's headquarters had sent him common blasting fuse instead, which was cut into short lengths, requiring it to be spliced together down in the gallery. This substitution was not caused by unavailability — Henry Hunt's own inspector of artillery ordered the fuse directly from New York where it was manufactured.[52] Still, grossly inadequate material was delivered. The powder was delivered in twenty-five pound kegs. Corporal George Allen of the 4th Rhode Island was one of the men who were detailed to transport the explosives into the mine. He reported:

It was large, coarse blasting powder, and was placed in kegs of twenty-five pounds each. These kegs were then placed in bags and slung over our shoulders. We moved quickly over the space between the teams and traverse to avoid getting a bullet in one of these kegs of powder, as they were continuously flying all around us, and left the kegs at the mouth of the gallery. Here they were taken by the miners and carried into the magazine underneath the fort. In this manner four tons of powder were deposited in the large wooden tanks.[53]

The miners had built eight open-topped wooden boxes in the lateral gallery for magazines. The powder was carried into the mine and then poured into these eight wooden magazines approximately five feet high and six feet wide at the top. Once the powder was placed in the magazines, it was essential for the operation to be quickly concluded to avoid the charge from becoming damp.

Pleasants supervised the loading of the chambers, which took from 4:00 P.M. until 10:00 P.M. that day. It was by then very damp in the lateral galleries, so Pleasants placed wooden supports under the magazines and raised the trough for the powder, connecting each of the chambers several inches from the ground. Pleasants had specified safety fuse in lengths of 100 feet or more, rather than the common blasting fuse he received, which was not impervious to moisture. The inadequate quality fuse had arrived in short lengths, some less than ten feet. Pleasants erupted in rage when he discovered the "mistake," and dispatched two men to Meade's headquarters for the appropriate fuse. He later speculated that they had simply sent whatever was available from Fortress Monroe, where there would have been no need of such long lengths of fuse. Meanwhile, he had the available short lengths spliced together by practical miners accustomed to such tasks. He was soon thereafter informed that the safety fuse would not be obtainable in time for the planned detonation. Considering the number of splices in the fuse, Pleasants decided to lay three of them side by side on the floor of the main gallery, connected to the powder train in the laterals.

At 10:00 P.M., the miners went to work tamping the charge, avoiding any delays which would allow the charge to become damp. For twenty consecutive hours, 150 grimy, sweating miners hunched back and forth in the confined quarters stacking sandbags into the mouths of the magazines and at the deep end of the mine shaft itself. Pleasants was careful to have sandbags interspersed with long logs placed diagonally in such fashion that plenty of oxygen would reach the powder and thereby augment the force of the explosion. When finished, there was nearly 1,000 cubic feet of tamping to prevent the force of the blast from escaping down the tunnel. Thirty-four feet of main gallery was tamped, as well as ten feet of the entrance of each of the lateral galleries. The space between each magazine was left untamped. The only apertures were for the T-shaped trough of powder and the three knotted fuses. Tension mounted as the miners poured the loose powder into the wooden trough connecting the eight magazines. If, during the process, a lantern or candle lighting the chamber should be dropped, the premature detonation would ruin the mission, as well as obliterating all workers in the tunnel. Next, the powder-filled trough was connected to the three lengths of spliced fuse. Pleasants tied a fifty foot tail of additional fuses, strung them across the mine floor where it was still dry, and crawled out of the mine. At 6:00 P.M. on Thursday, July 28, an exhausted Henry Pleasants informed General Potter that the mine was, at last, ready to be exploded, and he suggested that it be done as soon as possible.[54] The stage was set for one of the greatest single dramas of the war.

While Pleasants and his men of the 48th Pennsylvania were hard at work on the mine, the Confederates were becoming more and more suspicious as to their activity. Brigadier General E. Porter Alexander, chief of artillery for the I Corps, was responsible for the artillery defenses at Petersburg, as well as all those from the Appomattox to the James, including those

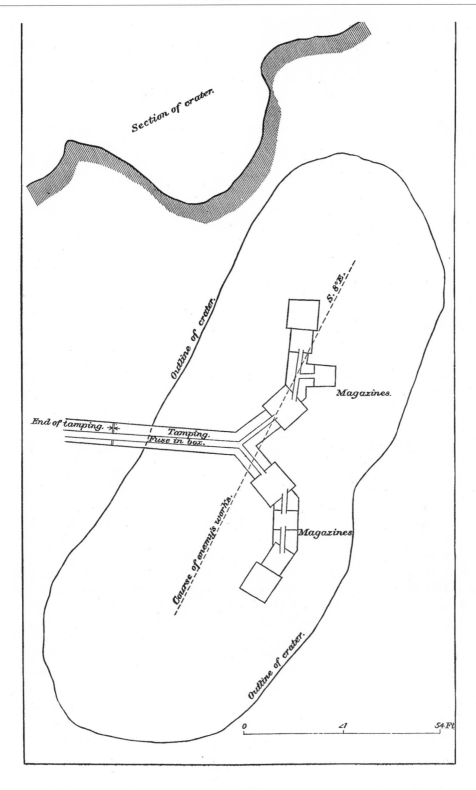

Sketch of magazines (*Official Records*).

batteries guarding the James at Drewrey's Bluff and Chaffin's Bluff. Alexander had experienced a varied and stellar military career thus far. The Georgia native graduated third in his class from West Point in 1857 and served under Albert Sidney Johnston in the Utah Expedition, where he became good friends with James Duane. He assisted Brigadier General Albert J. Myer in devising a system of communications over long distances, in so doing creating the U.S. Signal Corps. After resigning his commission when Georgia seceded from the Union, Jefferson Davis appointed him captain of the Confederate Signal Corps. At First Manassas, Alexander became the first to transmit a signal by the wig-wag method during the Civil War. After being assigned to Longstreet's First Corps, he observed the Battle of Gaines' Mill from an observation balloon while serving as chief of ordnance. He came to Robert E. Lee's attention with his masterful positioning of the artillery at Marye's Heights during the Battle of Fredericksburg, and commanded the 140 gun cannonade which signaled Picket's Charge at Gettysburg. He accompanied Longstreet to Tennessee in the fall of 1863, and after retuning to the Army of Northern Virginia for the 1864 spring offensive, he was promoted to brigadier general.

As Alexander scouted around Elliott's Salient on June 30, as was his practice every day, expecting to catch sight of a sap roller, he was surprised to find no evidence of fresh dirt in the front, despite ample time for such preparation on the Federals' part. As he loitered about and studied the Union lines from this advanced position for a long period of time, suddenly a light went off in his head. There was something exceedingly curious about this particular section of the line. Sharpshooter fire had diminished considerably all along the line by this time, except for a small area approximately one hundred yards on either side of Elliott's Salient. There, surprisingly, the fire had seemed to have increased. Alexander was therefore led to believe that the Federals planned to push forward from their position on this front in an assault. He felt that they would soon extend their trenches, and he anticipated that the movement would commence on June 30. In anticipation, he had countered by placing artillery covering the slopes in front of the Salient. Alexander was quite surprised, however, at the lack of fresh digging or apparent movement, despite the dramatically increased amount of small arms and mortar fire. He stayed there a long time studying the lines in all directions. Then he suddenly grasped the answer; his mind cried out: "They were coming, but it was not above ground or it would show. But they were coming underground. They were mining us!"[55]

Anxious to convey his deductions to his superiors, Alexander started back along the trenches to the path on the right of the Salient to where he had left his horse at the Raglan house. In his excited state, as he neared the path, he made a snap decision to cut across the ridge to the right in order to save time. While quite exposed to small arms fire, he reasoned that the sharpshooting had diminished considerably in that area. As he traversed the rising ground, he turned to catch a fleeting glimpse of the Union position. Then, from the rear of the lines, he heard a faint pop and soon the buzz of a bullet. The projectile hit the ground in front of him and ricocheted instantly into his shoulder. Alexander slowly walked down the hill to cover, attempting to convey the impression to his foes that he had not been hit. He returned to his camp, where the .58 caliber bullet, which had fortunately missed both bone and artery, was removed from the wound. Although he was granted a furlough to recuperate, Alexander still went first to Lee's headquarters before leaving for Richmond, in order to report his belief in the mining of Elliott's Salient. Lee was away at the time, so the report was given to his aide, Colonel Charles Venable. With Venable at the time was a correspondent of the London Times, Francis Lawley. Mr. Lawley was quite interested in Alexander's report, and he asked how far the enemy would have to tunnel to arrive beneath the fort thought to be

Men of the 48th Pennsylvania carrying powder into the mine (*Harper's Weekly*).

the target of the operation. Upon being informed that the distance would be over 500 feet, Lawley scoffed and indicated that the Union could not ventilate so long a gallery, that 400 feet was the maximum length for such a tunnel without external ventilation tubes, which had been proven during the siege of Lucknow, in India.[56] Alexander responded to Lawley that the Federal ranks contained many coal miners experienced in ventilating galleries in coal mines miles underground and that "they were up to devices to which 500 feet would be only child's play." Alexander later took note in his memoirs that the mine was suggested and constructed entirely by these miners and that their work had only commenced four days before he had predicted its existence.[57]

Lee and Beauregard both reacted to Alexander's report, in addition to the rumors and reports in Northern newspapers of such a mining operation, by ordering the army's engineers to commence countermining operations. By July 2, when Pleasants' men hit quicksand, the Confederates were already detailing men to train for countermining efforts.[58] Beauregard directed that countermines be sunk from all three salients on his front and that "gorge-lines" be constructed to which troops could retire in case of an explosion along the lines. Captain Hugh Douglas, a Virginia engineer, was ordered to Petersburg with his company of pontoniers, and by July 10 he had transformed the men into sappers, working on the three salients. Douglas, unlike his Union counterpart, did have the assistance of the army's chief quartermaster. However, that quartermaster did not have much equipment at his disposal, unlike *his* Union counterpart. Thus, similar to the plight of Pleasants' men, Douglas' had to carry dirt out of their mines in cracker boxes. There were insufficient men for the task on the Rebel side, and Douglas' examinations had to be made at point blank range. He, too, went to great lengths to conceal his excavated material, in order to catch the Yankees by surprise. His men, like those of Pleasants, also received whiskey rations to maintain their enthusiasm and vigor.[59]

All the countermines would commence behind the Rebel forward lines, where work would be undetected. There were a total of five mines at the front, two at Elliott's Salient on either side of the fort, and three at Colquitt's salient on the left of the Confederate line. When the proper distance to the front had been achieved, the tunnel was to turn right and left roughly parallel to the Confederate works, and then branch out "herring-bone fashion" or square, as the case might be. The ends of the shafts could be quickly charged with powder in case of the approach of the enemy under the surface. The main audits, or passageways, were generally cut four by six and framed up every four or five feet with four by four square timber frames, one-inch plank slipped in on top and often on the sides. Another plank on the floor served as a wheelbarrow runway. The debris taken from the shafts often differed among the various countermines, from soft sand to harder, sometimes "a very compact, pure clay of grayish brown color so tenacious that the picks had to be made with short blades, with widened chisel-like edges and short handles, and we had to chip the material out by inches."[60] This particular material was often called "pipe clay," as it was used to make pipes, and was similar to that encountered earlier by Pleasants' men. The Confederate mining squads normally consisted of a sergeant or corporal, and from four to six men, according to the nature of the material and the distance of the mine. According to M.W. Venable, Company H, 1st Regiment of Engineers, "[e]ach shift had to drive a panel, or cut off, of four or five feet, set up and line his timbers and make all secure for the next 'shift.'"[61]

The countermines were each sunk a few feet into the ground, similar to a well, from which galleries six feet in height and three feet wide were tunneled to the right and left, while others were started in the side of a ravine. Inside the gallery, Douglas would bore into the countermine's floor with a one-inch auger, seeking soft spots that would indicate the Union tunnel. Several of these shafts were excavated, including one on either side of Elliott's Salient.

The intention was to connect the shafts with a listening gallery "to run like a horseshoe around the front." Manpower was too limited for optimum effectiveness, however. Douglas did eventually receive a detail of 160 men from Henry Wise's Virginia brigade and Robert Ransom's North Carolinians on July 15. Soon thereafter, his complement was augmented by a hundred more men from Bushrod Johnson's division.[62] He was thus able to push his listening galleries nearly as far laterally as had Pleasants. The problem was, however, that Douglas did not dig deep enough, as his deepest tunnels were only ten feet deep and his auger would not have penetrated much beyond another five feet. As the closest the Union mine came to the surface was twenty feet, this resulted in negative readings from all of Douglas' efforts.[63]

By this time, the Union mine had ceased to be a complete secret to either side, as rumors proliferated through the ranks. The Union soldiers up and down the Federal line knew of the 48th Pennsylvania and "their mine." They even knew of the ventilation issue and its solution. It was an unfortunate fact that "secrets were practically impossible to keep in that army, and they made the rounds at dizzying speeds."[64] During July, it was common for Union pickets to taunt their Confederate counterparts with their intention to "send you to Heaven soon" or to threaten that they were "going to blow you up next week."[65] John Sergeant Wise, aide to his father, the former governor of Virginia and current Brigadier General Henry A. Wise, later pondered: "How soldiers get their information is one of the mysteries of the service, yet they are often in possession of more accurate knowledge than those high in authority."[66] A combination of Northern newspapers speculation, information from deserters and suspicions from vigilant observers such as Porter Alexander led most Confederate soldiers to believe that the Union was mining somewhere on their front. Colonel Charles Wainwright, chief of artillery in Major General Gouverneur K. Warren's Fifth Corps, wrote in his diary on July 21 that Rebel pickets were making good-natured inquiries as to "Burnside's mine."[67]

On July 16, three deserters from the 49th North Carolina jumped the Confederate picket lines and were quickly interrogated by Burnside's staff. One of the Tarheels had been working on a countermining operation. Thus, the Union had some sound notice that the Confederates knew their works were being undermined, although they obviously had not determined the location. The deserter's information also included evidence that countermining operations were underway.[68] The only consolation was that the Confederates appeared to believe that the mining was farther to the southwest, near the Jerusalem Plank Road. This knowledge ate at Pleasants, however. What little sleep he got was abbreviated by nightmares that the relentless countermining had struck his tunnel, thus obliterating a month's hard work and a priceless opportunity to strike a blow to end the war. It would take but one drive of a crowbar or a boring tool to undo the entire feverish labor of the past four weeks.[69]

As the month of July went into its last two weeks, and the mine had not been detected or detonated, doubts began to arise as to its existence. The Confederate experts began agreeing with their Union counterparts that a mine of that length was an impossible feat without visible ventilation. The rank and file Confederates thus began to treat the rumors as another camp rumor "and now and then they would call across and ask the Yankees when the big show was going to begin."[70] Rumors began to circulate that the talk of a mine was invented merely to scare the Rebels.[71] A joke in the Confederate lines had it that Grant had dug a tunnel under Petersburg and was running a train in it, and that smoke from that train could be seen rising through the cobblestones of Sycamore Street, a main thoroughfare in the city. "Greenhorns were assured they could hear a locomotive roaring in the tunnel if they listened carefully...."[72] With reservations as to the mine's existence abounding, many Rebel pickets began taunting their Ninth Corps counterparts between the lines, yelling and joking between shots with "When you'all Yankee nigger lovers again'ta blow us'ns up?" The Federal men would respond, "'Fore you know it, Johnny, you'll be chasin' after your rights with your tail between your legs, clean through Rebeldom!" The usual retort of the Rebels was then "Come on then, you damn Yanks!"[73]

The *Richmond Whig* on July 21, 1864, assured its readers that the soil was working against the Federal miners (the mine had actually been completed by then). Conversely, on July 28, the *Richmond Examiner* suggested it was time for Grant to spring some of his mines.[74] Whatever doubts the Rebel engineers and the press may have had, the privates knew where the works were being mined. Elliott's men educated the Confederate troops in the surrounding area as to its existence long before the explosion. Wise's and Elliott's men would lie down on the ground and listen for the work being carried on below ground, then return to tell about it.[75] The rumors led the men to devise their own novel ways to detect the mining operations. Behind the front lines, "pegs were driven deep in the ground. These pegs, when held in the teeth, were supposed to relay to the 'peg biter' the slightest vibration and enable the Confederates to locate the Yankee mining operation."[76]

The two South Carolina regiments posted in support of the four-gun battery did a large amount of the countermining. Captain George B. Lake of the 22nd South Carolina recalled that "[w]e sunk a shaft on each side of the four-gun battery [that of William J. Pegram], ten feet or more deep, and then extended the tunnel some distance to our front." Similarly, Samuel Catawba Lowry from Yorkville, South Carolina, a soldier of the 17th South Carolina, wrote his family from Elliott's Salient on July 20: "It is feared the enemy are tunneling under our lines, and as right in our front is the most favorable spot for such works, and as a battery is also here, we are preparing for such a device by digging a tunnel all along the whole face of the battery to meet theirs, if they have any."[77]

As the mining and countermining continued, a cat and mouse game ensued as the men strained their ears for the sound of the others' picks. Every fifteen minutes the workers were to stop digging and listen attentively. If they heard the sounds of picks, a charge could be detonated in the countermine to cave in the Union gallery. But as the days passed, the Confederates heard nothing. When the Confederate deserters were captured on July 16 and firm evidence of countermining was finally established, Pleasants ceased digging and listened for Confederate efforts. However, nothing was heard and work recommenced on the 18th. By July 21, the Rebel miners heard plainly underground "the sound of the picks and shovels of the Union sappers, but nowhere could the Confederates break into the enemy's gallery." Many thought they heard the "dull, faint sounds of digging and movement in the earth below them," encouraging more countermines.[78] But as the Confederate countermines were on a hill, the Union shaft was far below their efforts. The men of the 22nd South Carolina could hear the Union miners at work but could not find them. Captain George B. Lake of that regiment, aptly expressing the sentiment of the rank and file, observed that "[t]he idea of being blown into eternity without any warning was anything but pleasant."[79] At one point, the Confederates got within ten feet of the Union shaft, but they, of course, had no way of knowing this fact.

Many Confederate officers still insisted that the Union mine project could not be accomplished, and thus the support for countermining was considered somewhat halfhearted. When the sounds of picks and shovels ceased, the Confederates took this as an indication that the Yankees had given up. In point of fact, the reason was that the digging had been completed.[80] The countermining project was definitely not proceeding in a manner which would detect the Union mine unless it was left undetonated for a period of time. Some contemporary eyewitnesses such as Captain W. Gordon McCabe of Bushrod Johnson's division claimed the project was discontinued "owing to the lack of proper tools, the inexperience of the troops in such work, and the arduous nature of their service in the trenches."[81] Others supported this proposition that the countermining effort had ended prior to July 30. However, Porter Alexander strongly asserted that the project was still in process, though badly planned and slowly executed and not in a state of usefulness on that date.

Plans were still in place to connect the shafts on either side of the Salient with a listening gallery around the front. In fact, Alexander verified that when the Union mine was sprung on the 30, one shaft was immediately buried in debris. However, the other was far enough away that it was undamaged, and a number of Confederate sappers were indeed in the shaft at the time and were taken prisoner uninjured by the blast, later escaping in the confusion that fateful day.[82] Sergeant A.H. Smyth was actually in this countermine called by the Confederates "No. 2" supervising the digging at the time of the explosion, whereupon he related that he was "[s]tartled by the sound of a very heavy explosion and thrown from my feet by the shock, the ground or rather gallery heaved and waved as if from an earthquake. After recovering from our surprise I took the three men out who were at work in the mine...."[83]

In hindsight, Alexander believed that the countermining operation should have consisted of a single shaft sunk at the Salient angle and a listening gallery pushed forward until contact was established. A camonflet, or smothered mine, could then have been exploded, causing the enemy to abandon the project.[84] However, hindsight always makes for the right choice.

Loading powder into the magazines (*Harper's Weekly*).

While the countermining was underway, Beauregard ordered the construction of a gorge line, or retrenched cavalier, just behind Pegram's battery in the redoubt. The gorge line was a curved line of parapets in the rear of the Salient, connecting with the Confederate breast-works, so that if the Salient was blown up, dispossessed troops could occupy the gorge in the rear and resist an assault at the breach. Elliott had been ordered to man this gorge line in the event of an explosion and was in the process of carrying out that order when he fell wounded on the 30th. John Wise was surprised that the men and the guns in the Salient were not moved back to the gorge line prior to an explosion, to save them, as the artillery selection in front of the Salient indicated an assault there was anticipated and imminent.[85]

Colonel D.B. Harris, Beauregard's chief engineer, had responsibility for the gorge line, as well as the placement of a series of batteries covering the rear of the Salient. One of the most important decisions made in July was the erection of a four gun battery about 350 yards to the Salient's left, across the covered way ravine. This battery was located in a secondary hollow where it was totally sheltered from Union observation. It was occupied by Wright's battery of Coit's battalion, the same unit to which Pegram's battery belonged. From its loca-tion, the battery could flank and sweep the Salient and its approaches from the left, just as Lieutenant John Chamberlayne could from the right near the path. Thus, by this time, the Salient was a four-gun battery in a long trench line, with a picket trench in front, a zigzag trench on Ransom's side, a gorge trench in the rear and several countermines under the sur-face. In the rear, 600 or 700 yards away, was a horseshoe of artillery and mortars.[86] Thus, the Salient, while vulnerable due to its advanced location, was far from defenseless in the event of an attack, as Burnside's men were soon to discover.

CHAPTER 5

The Deep Bottom Diversion

Following the failed probe on the Weldon Railroad in late June, Grant was desperate for some type of offensive. On July 3 he asked his subordinates whether a successful assault could be made on their respective fronts. He desperately wanted to reclaim the initiative in Petersburg, and particularly to break out of the Bermuda Hundred bottleneck and to invest Richmond from the south, which had been his original plan. While others, including Warren, were quite pessimistic as to the success of such an assault, Burnside felt such an offensive could be successful in conjunction with the detonation of his mine. His specific response to the inquiry got him in considerable difficulty with George Meade, however. The staffs of both Grant and Meade had examined the sites of proposed attacks near Ware Bottom Church and Port Walthall on Bermuda Hundred, as well as Elliott's Salient. Their conclusion was that the chances of carrying the enemy's entrenchments were best at the mine site, although the existence of a second Rebel line made it "doubtful" whether such attempt would be "judicious." Meade, always the contrarian when it came to Burnside's opinions, disagreed. "He made it clear that he thought the odds favored failure in an assault at the site of the mine."[1] Meade was justifiably concerned that with the removal of Wright's Corps, which had been detailed to follow Early, the success of either a flank or frontal assault would have "the facility with which the enemy can interpose to check an onward movement." Lest Grant judge him to be without aggressive instincts altogether, however, Meade referenced Burnside's mining enterprise and the potential that a successful thrust might be made by undermining the Confederate entrenchments in combination with an offensive operation.

By the time the mine was near completion, Grant had become a "true believer" in the concept, although somewhat distracted by Jubal Early's threat to Washington. He decided he would take the offensive while that opportunity still presented itself, given his grave concern that any inertia would allow Lee to dispatch troops to reinforce Bragg in Georgia, particularly with Wright away stalking Early.[2] Grant felt there was an opportunity to take Petersburg with such an assault. To be successful, though, he had to convince Lee to shift as much of his army as possible north of the James River. There were miles of Confederate trenches in front of Richmond held only by a thin string of cavalry pickets. This was probably Lee's most sensitive spot, and a Union attack there was certain to pull Rebel strength into the area as fast as Lee could get there. So when Grant thought of ways to enhance Burnside's assault, his mind naturally turned to those nearly empty fortifications north of the James. However, he was also concerned with the failure of the divided Federal command in Washington to defeat

Early's threat to Washington. He thus decided that an assault would be made at Deep Bottom, about twelve miles to the northeast of Petersburg. The beauty of the operation was that it was a win-win proposition for the Union. If Lee failed to take the bait, the Union force could plunder Richmond and sever railroad connections with Lee at Petersburg. If, on the other hand, Lee reacted to the movement, the lines around Petersburg would be severely depleted, and consequently, the impact of the mine's detonation would be considerably enhanced.[3]

Ideally, Grant desired to make some assault in early July, but he decided to await the mine's completion in order to keep open as many of his options as possible.[4] His three-pronged plan in this regard was to (1) increase his ranks and stockpile the army for a long siege, (2) sever the railroads around Richmond, thereby starving the capital and its defenders, and, (3) deal directly with Lee by utilizing ingredients that Lee could not stop, that being constant pressure and the weight of numbers by striking one end of the defenses and then the other. To his significant advantage, Grant had the harbor at City Point and twenty-one miles of rail line from the docks at that harbor leading right up to the edge of his entrenchments. Federal strength was growing rapidly while that of the Confederates steadily declined, with absolutely no hope of replenishment. However, while Jubal Early had returned to the Shenandoah on July 16, Grant fully expected him to return to Petersburg, thereby allowing Lee to send troops to Georgia. Grant thus requested the return of the Sixth and Nineteenth corps from their Washington assignments. The Nineteenth was then en route to City Point from Louisiana where it had participated in the disastrous Red River campaign. Grant had previously ordered one of its divisions to Washington when Early threatened that city, along with two of Wright's divisions. The absence of these units had undermined Grant's plans for an earlier assault on the Petersburg lines on July 18 and 19. By July 23, Wright had returned to Washington after leaving Early at Strasburg, Virginia. This move convinced Grant that Wright's corps belonged back at Petersburg, for he believed Early would be returning to the city himself in order to allow Lee to detach men to Georgia for the defense of Atlanta. Thus, on July 24, he ordered Wright's corps back to Petersburg. He wished to explode the mine either as a diversion that would allow Sheridan to get cleanly off on a raid toward Richmond as far as Hicksford on the Weldon Railroad or as a means for another frontal assault against the Confederate lines at Petersburg to succeed.[5] Thus, as the mine neared completion, Grant felt the time was ripe to incorporate it into an important tactical operation.

Another reason for Grant's desire to initiate an offensive in the near future was his concern that Halleck might persuade Lincoln to lift the siege of Petersburg as a reaction to Early's threat. Consequently, he wanted to force Lee to recall Early or some of his troops, thus presenting yet another rationale for another Federal offensive operation. Grant's plate was clearly full of major issues impacting his military efforts. Early's offensive operations had also resulted in a controversy over who was to be placed in command of the Washington defenses. Grant wanted Major General William B. Franklin or another proven general in command. Edwin Stanton wanted Halleck, and Lincoln seemed to lean toward acquiescing to his secretary of war, thus casting his vote with the established politicos. While Grant desired for Franklin to head four consolidated military departments under one command, he indicated to the president that "[a]ll I ask is that one general officer, in whom I and yourself have confidence, should command the whole." He went on to suggest that if not General Franklin was not chosen, perhaps the four departments combined as a "military division" should be placed under General Meade, and General Hancock elevated to command of the Army of the Potomac. Brigadier General John A. Rawlins, Grant's chief of staff, delivered the request in person to Lincoln.[6] Stanton acquiesced to the proposed consolidation this time, but then he had Lincoln give Grant the last man Grant would want in charge—Halleck. That very day, July 27, Grant once again took to drink, ending a long state of abstinence. Rawlins, his aide and protector from the bottle, was away in Washington, which facilitated the fall off the wagon. Rawlins later wrote to his wife on July 28: "I find the General in my absence digressed from his true path." Grant was also suffering from more personal issues, which no doubt weakened his resolve. His close friend, Major General James B. McPherson, was killed on July 22 near Atlanta. Grant had planned for him to be Sherman's successor in the event the latter officer was disabled. Grant had "wet eyes" at the news, and his voice broke when he said, "The country has lost one of its best soldiers and I have lost my best friend."[7]

By July 25, Grant had fully formulated his plan for yet another Federal offensive designed to lift the siege on Petersburg which entailed a demonstration on the Peninsula by the Second Corps and two divisions of Sheridan's cavalry, plus Kautz's cavalry from the Army of the James. While Grant did not expect to invest Richmond, a strong attempt to do so would allow the cavalry to raid northward and wreak havoc with the Virginia Central Railroad between Charlottesville and Gordonsville, the only remaining link between Lee and Jubal Early's force west of Washington. Of course, if everything fell perfectly into place, Richmond was definitely a target of opportunity. Grant proclaimed, "It is barely possible, that by a bold move this expedition may surprise the little garrison of citizen soldiery now in Richmond and get in."[8] The secondary, but equally important and more realistic objective, was to divert troops from Petersburg, thus making the success of the mine's detonation much more likely. The distraction of the mine's explosion would at least allow Sheridan to get away on his raid on the railroads. This was the first of several operations which started by first threatening Richmond and subsequently threatening the Petersburg flank, later to become commonly known as "double-enders."[9]

On June 20, Benjamin Butler had established his bridgehead for future operations under Brigadier General Robert S. Foster, commander of the third division of the Tenth Corps on the north of the James on the west bank of Bailey's Creek, which flowed into the James at Deep Bottom. While it remained a threat to Lee's position, the Rebels did not have enough manpower to drive Foster out from his position. This minor success prompted Grant to order a second brigade up on July 23 to expand the occupation and suppress the harassing Confederate artillery fire. With the additional force, the Federals were quickly able to occupy the east bank of Bailey's Creek. A second pontoon bridge was constructed to link Jones' Neck to the Peninsula downstream from Bailey's Creek at Deep Bottom. The existence of such a bridgehead became a further threat to Lee's position, but he lacked sufficient forces to drive Foster back. Thus, on July 6, Lee sought assistance from General Ewell, then in command of the Department of Richmond, to push the Federals away; however, no sustained effort was undertaken in that regard. While unable to wrest the Federals from their positions, the Confederates were able to harass Federal shipping on the James with their artillery. The threat posed by this second force at Deep Bottom prompted Lee to dispatch Brigadier General Joseph Brevard Kershaw's division, joining Fulton's brigade of the Department of Richmond and Brigadier General James H. Lane's and Brigadier General Samuel McGowan's brigades of Wilcox's division under Brigadier General James Conner from the Petersburg lines back across the James, to move the Federals out. On July 25, Kershaw successfully drove the Union troops back from the east bank of the creek.[10]

Grant's plan called for Hancock's corps to be dispatched north of the James, accompanied by Sheridan and the cavalry. It would then cross the Appomattox below Petersburg, march north behind Butler's lines, and then cross the James by the new pontoon bridge at Deep Bottom, all without any attempt to conceal the movement from Lee. Lee would presumably be forced to move troops from Petersburg to meet this new threat on the Confederate capital. If they were very fortunate, the Federals might break through the lines in front of Richmond. If this did not succeed, it would be because Lee had severely weakened his front at Petersburg to meet this new threat, thus making the success of Burnside's assault all that much more likely.[11] At 4:00 P.M. on July 26, Hancock's corps commenced its march to Deep Bottom. Hancock had just returned to duty the prior week, still suffering from his Gettysburg wound. Thus, a force of 20,000 infantry and 5,000 cavalry was now headed north of the James to once again threaten the Confederate capital.

Hancock kept to roads well behind the Union lines in order to avoid the roving eyes of the Confederate signalmen. His troops all carried four days' ratios and 100 rounds of ammunition. To avoid detection en route, Hancock brought just a few engineer wagons carrying entrenching tools and twenty ambulances per division. Major Isaac Hamilton of the 110th Pennsylvania expressed the common belief that "desperate work lay before us."[12] Sheridan's force also started north, with Brigadier General Alfred T.A. Torbert commanding the first division and Brigadier General David McM. Gregg commanding the second division. The infantry began crossing the Appomattox on the pontoon bridge at Point of Rocks at about 9:30 P.M., followed by Sheridan's troopers crossing at Broadway Landing, the bridge being covered in hay to muffle the sound of movement. The march was, as General Barlow later remembered, a severe one, with "the roads in some places bad, and considerable falling out occurred."[13] The forces negotiated the difficult terrain of Jones' Neck—a peninsula formed by a loop of the James—in the dark of night, although Butler had eased the way to some extent by providing bonfires along the route to light the unfamiliar territory and had cavalry pickets interspersed along the route to serve as guides. Hancock had his infantry take the more difficult routes to give the cavalry a clearer passage.[14]

The head of Hancock's column reached the James at Jones' Neck at 2:30 A.M. on July 27, with Barlow's division in the lead. Butler had constructed and maintained two pontoon bridges to the north side of the James at Deep Bottom, with a portion of the Tenth Corps on that side under the cover of his gunboats and ironclads. One bridge was at the very tip of Jones' Neck; the second one was one mile downstream. General Foster's third brigade of the Tenth Corps curled around the end of both bridges, holding them for Hancock's arrival. For several days, Foster had been skirmishing along Bailey's Creek with Conner's brigade of Kershaw's division as well as Hardaway's and Cutshaw's battalions of artillery under the command of Lieutenant Colonel Thomas Carter of the II Corps, which remained behind when the rest of that unit went westward.[15] Grant's plan was for Hancock to cross at the upper bridge and then move due west to Chaffin's Bluff in order to cut off any Confederate movement to reinforce Richmond. Sheridan, in turn, was to lead his two cavalry divisions, in addition to Kautz's cavalry division from Butler's army over the lower bridge following an arc that would leave him north of Richmond, where he would therefore be in position to sever the Virginia Central Railroad.[16] However, when the Second Corps arrived, Foster reported that the Rebels were in force just beyond the upper bridge, and consequently, Hancock instead decided to cross at the lower bridge.[17]

This decision on Hancock's part presented rather significant issues, however, as the land between the far ends of the two bridges was traversed by Four Mile Creek, which made an excellent natural barrier for the Rebels. To reach Chaffin's Bluff from this approach, Hancock would be forced to swing around the Confederate left, thereby delaying Sheridan's cavalry from its appointed schedule and also effectively destroying the element of surprise. The topography of Deep Bottom negated the rapid movement essential to the Federal's chances of success.[18] The ground was low and quite marshy, bisected by several tributaries of Four Mile Creek to the west and Bailey's Creek to the east. Bailey's Creek was four miles long, running north and crossing Darbytown Road at Fussell's Mill, only twelve miles from Richmond. With the exception of three main roads leading to the northwest, it was very difficult for troops to move through the area. Hancock, for his march to Chaffin's Bluff, was to use the New Market Road, the closest of the three to the James. In the middle, above New Market Road was Darbytown Road. Then, five miles to the northeast was the Charles City Road, crossing through White Oak Swamp, which the cavalry would have to take in order to reach the railroads north of Richmond. The Long Bridge Road, which ran to the northeast, intersected all three of these routes. Hancock would have to hold the New Market Road in order to retain control of the central corridor, which was dominated by the Long Bridge Road.[19] By using the lower bridge, however, Hancock would more easily make contact with Sheridan's cavalry, operating to his right, and thus would afford the whole Federal force a better access to the three highways.

Therefore, Hancock immediately began crossing his corps on the lower bridge, which was also covered in hay to muffle the sounds of heavy movement on the wooden deck, thereby avoiding alerting the enemy. The bone-weary Federal troops fell out into an oak timberworks several hundred yards from the bridge, an area known as Curles Neck or Strawberry Plain, in hopes of obtaining a few hours' sleep prior to dawn. Foster's troops remained active during the move, both on the west side of Four Mile Creek and beyond Hancock's position, in an effort to maintain sufficient pressure on Kershaw so that he could not reinforce one wing of his then divided command with the other.[20] The Confederates were in the process of constructing an outer line of entrenchments on the west side of Bailey's Creek, as well as along New Market Heights. However, they lacked sufficient numbers adequately to maintain this front in addition to Petersburg and Bermuda Hundred, at the time having four or five brigades under Kershaw and a small cavalry force under Brigadier General Martin Gary west of Bailey's Creek, totaling approximately 4,700 men in addition to the two other brigades from Wilcox's division holding the lines at Chaffin's Bluff. With a strong assault, Hancock's 25,000 plus men should have found little difficulty in rolling up the Rebel lines covering the three main roads and thus allowing the cavalry to flow through to Hanover Junction on the object railroads.

The element of surprise was totally gone by this time, however. Lee had reacted swiftly to developments north of the James by sending Field's division of the I Corps, as well as Major General Henry Heth's division and part of Wilcox's from the III Corps to the scene, along with General Anderson, then commander of I Corps, designated by Lee to assume overall command of this hastily assembled force at 1:30 P.M. on the 27th. Along with the additional infantry units, Lee also dispatched the cavalry divisions of Major General Fitzhugh Lee as well as his son Major General W.H.F. "Rooney" Lee to support the infantry. He also requested that Richard Ewell send additional local defense troops down to Deep Bottom. Ewell gave this serious thought and actually called for an implementation of the request, but he was discouraged by Secretary of War Seddon, who felt the "derangement and confusion" of the government by taking all the clerks or starting a panic among the civilian population negated the military impact that the addition of these troops might contribute to the defense.[21] This significant movement north of the James left only Hoke's, Johnson's, Mahone's and part of Wilcox's divisions in the trenches at Petersburg, amounting to a force of under 18,000 men.[22] The image of the troops leaving the city was so significant that on July 29 the *Petersburg Express* reported that many in the city felt that the siege was over, although the newspaper itself disagreed with this position.[23]

At daybreak on July 27, Hancock, with Barlow's division in the lead, moved his force forward with a view of turning the left of the Confederate force holding the right bank of

Bailey's Creek, which ran at a right angle to the James and flowed into it at the northern end of Jones' Neck. It was immediately discovered, however, that Kershaw's division, together with some Confederate artillery, were behind the breastworks along New Market Road. Thus, the Federals knew that the element of surprise had most probably eluded them. The resulting fight was confused, and it was made even more so by the total absence of any clear definition of the relative authority between Anderson and Richard Ewell as commander of the Richmond defenses.[24] Hancock proceeded with Major General John Gibbon on the left, Brigadier General Gershom R. Mott's third division on the right, Brigadier General Francis C. Barlow in the center, and Sheridan's cavalry farther to the right of the infantry. The gunboats *Agawam* and *Mendote*, together with the Union artillery, opened up on the entrenchments while Hancock prepared for his assault. The gunboats proved particularly beneficial to the movement, hurling one hundred-pound shells at regular intervals from in between the two bridges at the Rebel forces. A soldier in Kershaw's division recalled years later that the "frying" noise the shells made as they traveled overhead, as well as their tremendous size, caused the Rebels to give them the name "camp kettles." He indicated that the shells traveled through their earthworks "like going through mole holes."[25]

Barlow's division led the advance, with a part of Brigadier General P. Regis De Trobriand's brigade of Mott's division acting as skirmishers, comprised of the 99th and 110th Pennsylvania, "to feel the woods bordering the New Market and Malvern Hill road," and the six companies of the 40th New York covering the flanks while maintaining contact with the James. Colonel Edwin Biles led his brigade of Foster's division in support, probing the wooded area in proximity of the junction of the New Market and Long Bridge roads. The objective was to link up with the remainder of Barlow's division on his left. Another skirmish line was thrown out from Gibbon's second division as it moved into the timber along the banks of Four Mile Run. De Trobriand's skirmishers became sharply engaged and were rapidly reinforced by the 73rd New York Volunteers. At the same time, the skirmish line of Brigadier General Nelson A. Miles' brigade of Barlow's division, consisting of the 183rd Pennsylvania, 28th Massachusetts and 26th Michigan Volunteers, engaged the enemy farther to the left, driving the Rebels back into their rifle pits along New Market and Malvern Hill roads. These regiments, led by Colonel John Lynch of the 183rd Pennsylvania, soon bested Brigadier General Benjamin G. Humphrey's Mississippi Brigade, which fell back, leaving Captain Archibald Graham's battery of the Rockbridge Artillery unsupported and out in the open. The Virginia artillerymen continued firing, totally oblivious of the fact they had been abandoned by their comrades. Eventually, sensing their extreme exposure, they, too, fell back, leaving behind their four undamaged U.S. twenty-pounder Parrotts together with their caissons, all of which had previously been captured at Winchester and Harpers Ferry. Graham begged for rifles for his men in order to rescue his battery. While he pleaded for assistance, however, artillerymen from the 10th Massachusetts hitched up the guns together with their caissons to their own teams and carried them away. Yet another Confederate battery opened on Mott's division on the left, but it was soon driven off by Mott's skirmish line, as well as Federal artillery fire, and retreated to the New Market and Long Bridge road. The fleeing Confederates fell into previously prepared breastworks on the west side of Bailey's Creek, a position offering great advantage for defense, and there the Union advance came to a halt.[26]

An advance in line of battle would find difficulty in crossing Bailey's Creek under fire; the situation was further compounded by the fact that the Confederate works were about 1,000 yards from the creek, with the ground in between quite open. The works appeared to General Hancock to be well-manned and supplemented with artillery. Following a careful examination, he decided the chances of a successful assault here were unlikely and opted on

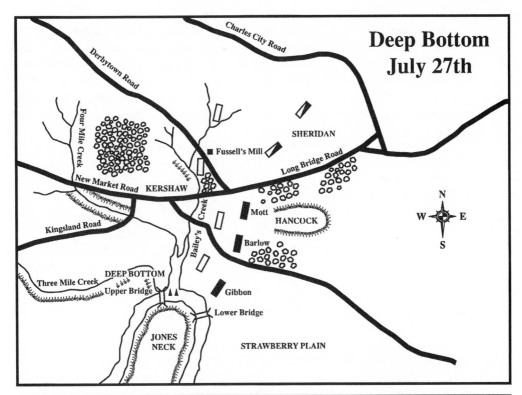

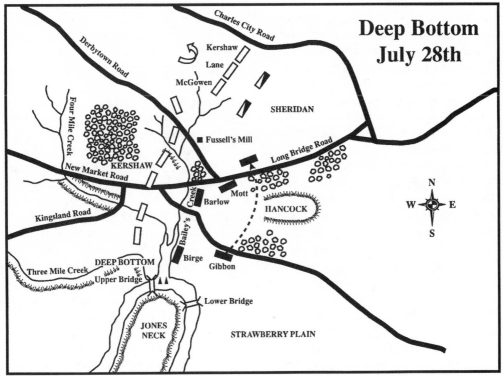

Deep Bottom Engagement

a maneuver to the right, with a view of turning the position. In the meantime, Sheridan's cavalry moved toward the extreme Federal right in the direction of Malvern Hill and to the front on the New Market and Long Bridge road, seizing the high ground along the Long Bridge and Darbytown road before the Rebels could recover. As Sheridan's column surged forward, the Union line stretched northward, which created a void on Barlow's left, soon filled by Gibbon's division. Gibbon's division then held the advance position on the New Market and Malvern Hill road, while Barlow's and Mott's divisions were pushed forward to the New Market and Long Bridge road, thereby connecting with the cavalry near the fork of the central road. The combined infantry and cavalry force continued up Long Bridge road, but it was unsuccessful in turning the Confederates' flank. Sheridan's troopers probed as far as Fussell's Mill, approximately four miles north of the James River, hoping to break through and gain the Confederate rear. However, the Confederates had refused their left there, so that Sheridan came up to a solid line of battle.

Brigadier General Martin W. Gary's assortment of cavalry from the Department of Richmond, including the Hampton Legion, the 7th South Carolina, the 24th Virginia and 25th Virginia Battalion Infantry enjoyed some success in driving the Union right back. Gary's force occupied the position given up by the left of Kershaw's line, about fifty yards from Tilghman's gate. He was soon ordered to withdraw to the Confederate's fortified line, having suffered significant losses, including six officers, one of whom, Lieutenant Hume of Texas, was from his own staff. At 3:30 pm, Grant arrived at the front, but he had difficulty locating Hancock. Consequently, he left a note after examining the Federal position, indicating that he did not feel much more could be accomplished that day. He requested that, if possible, the Confederate left should be doubled back toward Chaffin's Bluff in order to give the cavalry a good opportunity to complete its mission. Kershaw's division was still supported by the brigades from Wilcox's division, commanded by Brigadier General James Conner. In all, the force consisted of seven brigades in addition to a small force of cavalry. Given the Federal maneuver extending over a four mile front, the Rebel defenders were stretched thin. As night fell, both sides commenced digging in and making plans for renewing the fight the next morning.[27]

The Confederates began receiving reinforcements during the night; Heth's division arrived at Chaffin's Bluff at 8:30 P.M., along with Richard Anderson's corps. Hancock learned of this situation when Union signalmen reported twenty-nine rail cars loaded with men heading from Petersburg to Richmond. The Confederates had to move a much greater distance to reach the front, while Grants' forces could come and go by a more direct twelve mile route. This would soon prove to have an impact on the mine operation back in Petersburg. Brigadier General Henry W. Birge's brigade of the Tenth Corps, consisting of 2,500 men, reported to Hancock early on the 28th and relieved Gibbon's division from its advance position on the New Market and Malvern Hill road. This unit had been on its way from Louisiana to rejoin Emory's Nineteenth Corps in Washington until Grant intercepted it en route. Late on the 27th, Meade had passed along to Hancock a message from Grant. Grant realized that Sheridan could not continue toward Richmond in safety, as his force would be prevented from returning through Deep Bottom unless Hancock could drive the Rebels back to Chaffin's Bluff. This would require Sheridan to instead escape down the north side of the Chickahominy to Fort Monroe, and this would thus deprive Grant of that cavalry's services for several weeks. Therefore, Grant ordered Sheridan and Hancock to remain together for the time being and to attempt to force the Confederates back to Chaffin's Bluff or Richmond. However, Grant was emphatic that "I do not want Hancock to attack intrenched lines." While he still remained hopeful that Sheridan could later complete his raid, his immediate concern was for Hancock to keep the expanding Confederate presence occupied for a time, while Sheridan attempted to turn the Confederate flank.[28]

Both sides were thus stronger by the morning of July 28 and awaited movement by the other side. While fresh troops came up into the lines, McGowan's and Lane's brigades of Wilcox's division, joined by Kershaw's old brigade, under General Conner, moved to the extreme Confederate left, above Fussell's Mill, which at the time was held only by Gary's 600 cavalrymen, and assaulted Sheridan's right at 10:00 A.M. Kershaw's brigade was on the Confederate left, Lane's in the center and McGowan's on the right. As the column advanced about two hundred yards through the woods, it crossed the road and began to swing to the left. A gap opened in the line when Lane's men were momentarily bogged down by the marshy terrain, while McGowan's brigade emerged into an open cornfield and applied such a withering fire that the Union cavalry was quickly repelled. As the Confederates advanced over the ridge where Sheridan had fled, they suddenly came within short range of the Union's repeating carbines and were quickly stopped by the blazing fire enfilading McGowan's left flank. While the North Carolinians were temporarily able to drive the Union cavalry back, their success was short-lived.

Meanwhile, Gibbon's division was hurried up to the cavalry's support, but before it arrived, the Confederates had been disposed of by Brigadier General Alfred T.A. Tolbert's division, which made "a gallant advance of ... cavalry (dismounted), driving the enemy over a mile, capturing nearly 200 prisoners [mostly from Kershaw's division] and several colors."[29] The fight was thereafter most often referred to as the Battle of Darbytown. As a result, the two sides returned to the previous day's positions. Gibbon was ordered to hold the approaches to New Market and Long Bridge Road while Hancock had Sheridan reposition his men back in order to cover the New Market Road near Malvern Hill in an attempt to squeeze between the Union line and the lower pontoon bridge. Although a flurry of dispatches that the Confederates were massing for an attack were received, nothing further developed.[30]

Hancock had received numerous dispatches that the Confederates were massing for another assault to the east, in the direction of Malvern Hill, in order to get between them and the lower bridge. However, no further advances, other than some "crowding" of the cavalry skirmishers, occurred that day. In the afternoon, both Grant and Meade arrived on the front to confer with Hancock. By this time, Grant had lost all hope of pursuing the raid on the railroads. He did take great comfort in the fact that he had definitely achieved his alternate goal of drawing a sizable portion of Lee's army north of the James. Mott's division was ordered back to Petersburg that night to relieve the Eighteenth Corps, allowing Ord to shift south in accordance with the recently developed plan for the detonation of the mine. Mott departed the Peninsula at 8:00 P.M., recrossing the James on the lower pontoon bridge at Deep Bottom.[31] That same night, Rooney Lee's division of cavalry arrived at Deep Bottom — along with Lieutenant Colonel William T. Pogue's battalion, with Captain Nathan Penick's battery attached from its position north of the Appomattox — and reported to Lieutenant Colonel Thomas H. Carter. Throughout the 29th, Hancock demonstrated before the entrenched Confederates to keep up the illusion of a movement against Richmond.[32]

Hancock made a final, vigorous demonstration on the 29th in front of the Confederate lines. It included Foster's division, which cooperated with the 1st Maryland Cavalry and 24th Massachusetts regiments of the Second Corps near the Grover House. Foster placed four guns in position on the right of that house. The Confederates were driven from their main line of rifle pits, but it became impossible further to dislodge them with Foster's small force. After shelling the Rebel works for an hour, he withdrew to his original line. Grant then informed Washington that he was "yet in hopes of turning this diversion to account" by utilizing Pleasants' mine, and he thus ordered Hancock and Sheridan to return to Petersburg after dark on the 29th. The lightly regarded project of blowing up Elliott's Salient suddenly took on huge importance.[33] As Hancock's men were departing Deep Bottom, Major General Charles W. Field's division arrived at Fussell's Mill at sundown; Fitzhugh Lee's Division also crossed to the north side that evening. Hancock took a direct route back to Petersburg, while Sheridan's cavalry was ordered to move swiftly around the extreme left of the Rebels and threaten Petersburg from the southwest. Mott had already crossed the bridge near Point of Rocks on the 28th and relieved the Eighteenth Corps at dark on the 29th. Brigadier General John W. Turner's division of the Tenth Corps moved into the rifle pits, with its right resting on the Appomattox and the left connecting with the Ninth Corps. Also on the 29th, Grant directed Butler to order Ord to report to Meade for the attack on Petersburg, with the details to be left to Meade. Sheridan was to move his command to the left of Warren, while attempting to get around the Confederate's right flank. While Grant did not believe this effort would succeed, it would "detain a large force to prevent it." Ord had just recently been given command of the Eighteenth Corps after Baldy Smith's resignation on July 19. He brought the Eighteenth Corps over from the Bermuda Hundred to back up Burnside, including a division of the Tenth Corps, which marched up to join Ord behind the works of the Ninth Corps.[34] Ord put Mott's division in the entrenchments of the Eighteenth Corps and formed his troops to the rear of the Ninth Corps.

By 11:15 P.M. on the 29th, Hancock's total corps had crossed the James at Jones' Neck. It then marched all night to get into position at Petersburg so it could support the Eighteenth Corps. Sheridan's cavalry proceeded to Lee's Mill, a position on the extreme left of the Union. From this position, the horsemen could easily strike the Weldon Railroad when so ordered.[35] By daylight, the rear of Hancock's corps had passed Spring Hill. Its leading division, Gibbon's, moved into the rear of the Eighteenth Corps line, then held by Mott's division.[36]

Sheridan also withdrew from the James, with new orders to take a position on the left of the Union line well beyond Warren's Fifth Corps. Meanwhile, Birge, who was allowed to continue his original excursion, moved on to Washington. Foster, left with only 400 men at Deep Bottom, still was able to hold the bridges, while Butler's army was readily available at Bermuda Hundred. While Grant's diversion did not result in a demonstrable success as he had hoped, the Deep Bottom operation did serve a very useful purpose for both armies. While the Confederates were successful in preventing a raid on its railroad which they would have had difficulty opposing, at the same time, the movement compelled Lee to transfer a large portion of his troops north of the James. Grant therefore was able to feel free to unleash a direct attack on Petersburg using the mine as an offensive weapon. Five of Lee's eight Confederate divisions had been moved to Deep Bottom, where they were relatively helpless as events unfolded back at Petersburg on July 30.[37] As Hancock and Sheridan recrossed the James on July 29 and assumed their assigned positions for the mine explosion, they left the six Confederate divisions at Deep Bottom "with their thumbs to suck." Given Grant's strategy to denude Petersburg of a significant portion of the garrison, it would seem that the Federals could now count on a fairly easy victory.[38] Only three Confederate divisions remained in the Petersburg trenches on July 29 to oppose them, and by the early hours of July 30 these troops were confronted by three full Union corps crouched opposite them, awaiting the detonation of Burnside's solution to the stalemate.

CHAPTER 6

A Change of Plans

On July 3, as Pleasants' men feverishly continued their labors on the mine, Grant inquired of Meade whether a successful assault could be achieved against the Southern works. Meade reluctantly sought Burnside's opinion regarding the possibility of such a successful assault in his front, being closest to the enemy. The precise subject of the mine was not made a part of the inquiry by either commander. Apparently, both Meade and Grant were contemplating the potential for a frontal assault on the enemy's works without waiting for the benefit that a detonation of the mine would theoretically provide such an enterprise. Burnside responded that his sector of front was probably the optimum position to initiate such an endeavor, although he opined that it would be judicious to await the completion of the mine. However, his further opinion, that an assault on his front might still succeed without a detonation "if it could be supported in a specific way, and ... [he] could have the discretion of determining when the supporting columns should be put in,"[1] ended up setting off the prickly superior.

Burnside's last comment may have been the result of lessons learned from Antietam, where he was required to endure hours awaiting McClellan's supporting troops and ended up with a large share of the criticism for letting Lee off the ropes that day. However, given the already testy relationship the two shared as a consequence of Meade's sensitive ego, it was a response Burnside in retrospect might have couched in more diplomatic language. Meade immediately shot back, in words that Burnside later recalled to the Court of Inquiry, that "he [Meade] commanded this army and that he could not give to any one the authority to determine as to the time that his troops should be put in action; that he would be glad to receive from me at all times such suggestions as I might make, but that he himself would take the responsibility of re-enforcing any force that he should see fit to order in action, or words to that effect."[2]

Burnside instantly apologized for any unintended affront or disrespect, indicating humbly that he had no disposition to "claim the right to put other troops than my own in action." He went on to indicate that he had accorded other corps commanders the right to temporary command over portions of his troops, and he simply desired to "have accorded to me what I had accorded to them." Meade thanked him for his apology and pledged to do all in his power to promote harmony and good will among his corps commanders and himself and indicated that he hoped "all misapprehensions will be removed."[3] However, as Burnside's letter did not produce supporting evidence as to the basis for explanation, the suspicious Meade was probably left unsatisfied and convinced his subordinate had a "hankering for independence." The relationship between the two was, if anything, more fragile than ever after the apology. As historian William Marvel later wrote, "The good-hearted Burnside may have fallen for the rhetoric, but those who knew Meade best would have chuckled at the very thought."[4]

Ambrose Everett Burnside was born in a log cabin in Liberty, Indiana, in 1824 and was of Scottish descent. His great-grandfather was one of the outnumbered Scots who fought for Bonnie Prince Charlie and thereafter fled Scotland for the backwoods of South Carolina. Ambrose's father, Edghill, developed a strong distaste for slavery and moved the family to Indiana, where he taught school and later was elected as associate judge and then clerk of court. Ambrose, the fourth of nine children, was apprenticed to a tailor by the age of 15. In 1842, his father was serving in the state legislature and circulated a petition in that body, recommending his son for an appointment to West Point to Indiana's two senators. In March of 1843 the appointment materialized. A gregarious youth, Ambrose soon accumulated so many demerits that he was close to expulsion; he ranked 207 out of 211 cadets at the academy at the end of his first year. He did manage to graduate, in 1847, one year behind the class that contained such future generals as George McClellan, Winfield Scott Hancock, "Stonewall" Jackson, A.P. Hill, George Pickett and George Gordon, the famous "Class of 1846." Burnside was commissioned in the artillery and made his way to his unit, then fighting in Mexico. By the time he arrived, however, the war was all but over. With no fighting in Mexico City, he took up gambling and owed six months' pay by the time the war had officially ended. The following years were filled with garrison duty on various far-flung posts and included some Indian fighting.

After inventing a breech-loading carbine, which Burnside desired to market to the army through his company, the Bristol Rifle Works, he resigned his commission in 1852. Unfortunately, while the rifle received favorable reviews, Burnside's company was forced into bankruptcy. He thus sought employment from George McClellan, then vice president of the Illinois Central Railroad. With a rather lucrative position as cashier of the railroad's land department, Burnside eventually was able to repay all of his debts. He subsequently became treasurer of the railroad in 1860. Sensing war on the horizon, however, he set his business affairs in order and was soon offered command of the 1st Rhode Island regiment by Governor Sprague on April 15, 1861, and days later marched them into Washington. On May 2, 1861, the unit was mustered into Federal service for ninety days by Major Irwin McDowell, who soon thereafter assumed field command of all Federal forces. At First Manassas, Colonel Burnside commanded a brigade on the extreme right of Colonel David Hunter's division. Hunter was soon wounded, leaving Burnside in command of the division. Burnside performed admirably, although the battle ended in a Confederate rout, and he was quickly promoted to brigadier general. His next mission in March of 1862 was to organize an expedition against North Carolina, capturing Fort Macon and Roanoke Island and

MG Ambrose E. Burnside (Library of Congress).

thus becoming a sort of national hero in the process, given the paucity of Northern victories up to that point in the east. On July 27, 1862, President Lincoln offered Burnside command of the Army of the Potomac, which he declined, feeling unqualified for the role. Regardless, Lincoln did mark Burnside for greater things in the future. Burnside relinquished command of his North Carolina Department in July of that year and his former divisions were reorganized into the Ninth Corps, subsequently transferred to the Army of the Potomac. Following McClellan's defeat in the Seven Days Battle, John P. Pope was placed in charge of a new Army of Virginia carved out of McClellan's command. Soon thereafter the Union suffered a second defeat at Manassas. On September 5, 1862, Burnside was once again offered command of the Army of the Potomac, and again he refused the honor. This left only McClellan, who was again called upon to lead the army and ushered in a renewal of confidence by the rank and file.[5]

As Lee used his success at Second Manassas to invade the North, Burnside was dispatched to meet him with the First and Ninth corps. Following the discovery of Order No. 191, disclosing his movements and the splitting of his army into four parts, Lee entrenched at Antietam Creek, near Sharpsburg, Maryland, to await the impending Federal attack, with a large portion of his force still seventeen miles away at Harpers Ferry which it had just captured. Burnside was assigned the task of capturing Rohrbach Bridge, held by 350 soldiers of the 2nd and 20th Georgia under Colonel Henry L. Benning, and then moving against Lee's right. These Georgians were delaying the opportunity for McClellan to unleash his massed reserves in the center of the battlefield. The senior engineer on the general staff, one Captain James C. Duane, was ordered to position Burnside's divisions, but he soon left, thinly disguising his utter contempt for Burnside. Duane also failed to detect or pass along intelligence that the creek could be forded upstream and downstream. Adding to Burnside's frustration, the First Corps was detached and given to General Hooker. Burnside pouted over this decision, which made him somewhat sulky and hesitant when decisiveness was essential. Piecemeal attacks were made to cross Rohrbach Bridge but to no avail. Then at 1:00 P.M., one Union division crossed at a ford one mile downstream. The 51st New York, with Captain George Whitman and the 51st Pennsylvania, attacked across the bridge and finally established a bridgehead. Another critical delay then occurred when the lead division was forced to replenish its ammunition. At 3:00 P.M., Burnside finally got his whole line moving and he advanced. Then, at 4:00 P.M., just as it appeared he might cut off Lee's only means of retreat, A.P. Hill appeared from his forced march from Harpers Ferry and crashed into Burnside's troops. Burnside immediately sent to McClellan for support on his line of attack and McClellan replied that "I have no infantry." At the time Fitz John Porter was standing uncommitted nearby with two divisions. Burnside was ultimately driven back to Antietam Creek. Despite the role others played in the somewhat mismanaged assault, Burnside could be criticized for not having performed his own reconnaissance, for not advancing earlier in full force, and for continuing to act as a wing commander even after the First Corps was taken away from his command.[6]

Burnside was devastated by the severe damage his corps had suffered, in his eyes due to poor intelligence and lack of support at a critical juncture. Soon after the battle, Lincoln, displeased with McClellan in general and his failure to pursue Lee in particular, convinced an ever-reluctant Burnside to take command of the Army of the Potomac. McClellan had attempted to cast the blame for the failure to close with Lee on Burnside in his report on the battle, but Lincoln saw through the charges. In taking command, Burnside inherited many commanders whose primary loyalty was to McClellan and who resented the change and hoped he would fail, which would prove to be problematic to Burnside's ability to manage the army.

Lincoln's choice proved to be unfortunate. Although Burnside was honest, charismatic and industrious, "he lacked the intelligence and confidence to lead a great army. He was said to possess 'ten times as much *heart* as he has *head*,'" according to Fanny Seward, Secretary of State Seward's daughter and official hostess.[7] When McClellan offered Burnside his congratulations, Burnside retorted, "That, sir, is the last thing on which I wish to be congratulated." He later confessed to an officer-confidant that he was "not fit for so big a command, but he would do his best."

Under Burnside, the army was reorganized into three grand divisions under Franklin, Hooker and Sumner. Urged to be aggressive by Lincoln, Burnside's plan was to cross the Rappahannock at Fredericksburg in early December 1862 and attack the separate wings of Lee's army before it could consolidate in the vicinity. However, the pontoon train was late in arriving for the river crossing, allowing Lee to consolidate his forces on the opposite bank and fortify the heights behind the city. Burnside was not anxious to pursue a winter campaign, but he felt obligated to accede to Lincoln's strong desire for some rapid movement. His generals had implored him to cross with a portion of the army and attack before the Confederates consolidated, but Burnside was obstinately determined that the whole army mass together in front of Fredericksburg after crossing on the pontoon bridges. The bridges were finally positioned by December 13, and the army crossed the river and occupied Fredericksburg. Then, through poor communication and ineffective planning, attacks on Lee's more vulnerable left flank were not fully prosecuted, while the attacks concentrated on the highly fortified right at Marye's Heights, made nearly impregnable by a sunken road at its base bordered by a four foot high stone wall, could not succeed. Despite six grand, heartbreaking assaults against this position, the Confederate artillery and infantry fire was so severe nothing could be gained and no Union soldier came close to the stone wall. Men charged as if walking against a driving rain in a gale, with the rain being comprised of lead and iron. So many officers fell so quickly that the command of regiments sometimes passed to two or three men in a matter of minutes. After the last futile charge, Brigadier General William French rode through Fredericksburg with tears flowing down his cheeks, looking for his men and finally uttering, "My God, I am without a command." Federal losses amounted to almost 13,000 in the day's fighting. Many placed the figures even higher. Bodies littered the field between the stone wall and the city in rows as they had charged. John Hollensed of the 21st Mississippi talked to some Union prisoners who related that the men were totally demoralized following the devastating defeat and many asserted that "they never would cross the river no more to fight us in our present position; they call the battle field Burnsides Slaughter pen and they actually wrote on the head boards of their dead Burnsides Slaughter pen." The attack was "hopeless and useless, a waste of life, a horrible mistake that accomplished nothing, due primarily to Burnside's obstinacy."[8]

Burnside was soon thereafter replaced by Joseph Hooker and expressed a desire to retire, but Lincoln had other plans for him. He was transferred to the Department of the Ohio, headquartered in Cincinnati. In August 1863, he crossed the Cumberland Mountains and fought his way to and captured Knoxville, Tennessee. He repulsed an assault by Longstreet on November 1863, which facilitated the defeat of Braxton Bragg a short time thereafter. He then left the Tennessee and the Department of the Ohio in December and was sent east to recruit for the Ninth Corps. In April 1864, he resumed command of the Ninth Corps and chose Annapolis as the mobilization center for the burgeoning, newly organized corps. He met with Grant on March 11 and convinced him to release the rest of the corps from East Tennessee. Grant acceded, allowing Orlando Willcox to bring nearly 6,000 more men to Annapolis. With these new additions, the headcount of the corps reached nearly 20,000 men. Grant did not share his plans with Burnside but advised him to be ready to march by April 20 and to keep the news of the movement a secret. (Grant had by then decided to have Burnside alongside Meade and the Army of the Potomac for his Overland Campaign.)[9]

In early July, Meade believed that the mine was the best option at his disposal. Charles Dana had related this news in a July 5 dispatch to Edwin Stanton, indicating that all other options appeared fruitless to Meade. Soon thereafter, however, Meade reversed this thinking. He discounted the effectiveness of the mine operation, instead subscribing to a plan by Grant's chief engineer, General John G. Barnard, to attack a fortified position in front of Warren's line in conjunction with a mass bombardment of one hundred guns. Dana now reported that Meade felt the mine would prove of no value and that the salient angle on the Jerusalem Plank Road in Warren's front would prove to be the best point of attack. An ever cautious Meade did still remain of the opinion that a direct assault against Petersburg anywhere bore considerable risk. At this time, however, Grant returned again to his view of the mine as a strategic offensive maneuver and that Burnside's position offered the most likely position from which a successful attack could be launched. Two engineers assigned to investigate points at which to make an assault concluded that Burnside's front was definitely the best case.[10] Grant became convinced that the mine would be an integral feature in any offensive — either as a diversion or as part of a direct attack. He was also convinced that the army had to be ready to exploit a breakthrough, but if an attack were made and failed, the assaulting troops then had to be relieved as soon as possible to their respective entrenchments.

Meade remained unconvinced and discouraged any reliance on a detonation of the mine for an offensive operation. Based upon Major Duane's findings, the chances of a successful attack were minimal in conjunction with a detonation of the subject mine. Duane had opined that the Confederate works were in front of a crest between the fortifications and Petersburg. Thus, even if the Ninth Corps was successful in seizing the front line, heavy cannon fire from a secondary line of artillery on the crest near the cemetery at Blandford church, along with artillery fire from the left from Rebel forces facing Warren's Fifth Corps, would make this breakthrough untenable. Duane felt the issue could only be resolved if the lines were extended far enough to get around the enemy's southern flank. Meade had made a personal inspection of the front and wrote Grant that, while he did not find positive indications of such a secondary line 500 yards in the rear of the Rebel front line, he "became satisfied that a second line does exist on the crest of the ridge just in rear of the position of Burnside's mine." Meade believed they could "crown the crater, effect a lodgment and compel the evacuation of the enemy's present occupied line," but that the Confederate artillery fire from their redoubt on the Jerusalem Plank Road and their position at the Hare house would render this lodgment "untenable and compel our advance or withdrawal."[11] Meade thus advised against such an assault and asked that if an assault still needed to be made, that he be allowed to position sufficient artillery "to bear upon the lines not assaulted." He reluctantly indicated to Grant his belief that some offensive needed to be undertaken, however, and that the springing of Burnside's mine and an assault at that location would not "be hopeless." However, Meade concluded the chance of success was not "such as to make it expedient to attempt it."[12]

Based upon such a hollow endorsement, Grant was temporarily dissuaded from any reliance on Burnside's mine. That same day he remarked to Meade that "I am not willing to attempt a movement so hazardous as the one against entrenched lines against the judgment of yourself and your engineer officers, and arrived at after a more careful survey of the ground than I have given it."[13] However, Meade made yet another about face the next day, based upon an examination of the enemy lines from a signal station erected in a pine tree in front of Burnside's headquarters. This new intelligence yielded that, while the Confederates had detached batteries most likely in the rear of the front lines, there appeared to be no secondary, connected enemy line. Based upon this new analysis, Meade gave a favorable reevaluation to Grant on July 26. Grant thus decided to attempt his diversion. Meade, however, was still uncomfortable attacking without the Second Corps on hand to occupy the lines left vacant by the assaulting force; thus he felt that any assault should await the Second Corps' return following the diversion scheme.[14]

When it soon became apparent that the way to Richmond was well blocked, the troops were ordered back to Petersburg, and they recrossed the James on July 29 in accordance with Grant's previously agreed-upon commitment to Meade regarding the return the Second Corps if his ambitious plan could not be achieved. The diversion had worked exceedingly well in one respect, however, in that Lee had been forced to take the bait. Only three divisions of his army remained in the vicinity of Petersburg looking across the trenches at three full Federal corps! On July 28, Grant had dispatched Meade that unless progress was made toward Richmond that day, he could "withdraw Hancock, to be followed by Sheridan, make arrangements for assault as soon as it can be made."[15] He, too, was encouraged by the new intelligence on the lack of a secondary Confederate line, which increased the chances of an assault's success in connection with the springing of the mine. Thus, with the diversion stymied, Grant seized upon the mine's detonation as a means of keeping on the offensive and preventing Lee from releasing troops to Georgia. Meade would consequently have to "make use of the 'clap-trap' mine after all."[16]

Burnside had invited Brigadier General Edward Ferrero, commander of his fourth division, to recommend a plan of assault against Elliott's Salient around July 10, when the assault against Rives' Salient began, after having Ferrero reconnoiter the ground over which he would have to pass with his division. Ferrero presented Burnside with a plan calling for two brigades of the United States Colored Troops (USCT) of his fourth division to advance in parallel columns, with one regiment in each brigade to sweep down the Confederate trenches to the right and left of the crater formed by the detonation of the mine. The remainder of the division would then head for the crest behind the Salient occupied by the enemy at the Blandford Cemetery (sometimes referred to as Cemetery Hill).[17] Burnside subsequently approved the plan and adopted it as part of his requested recommendation to Meade, which he forwarded on July 26 through chief of staff Major General Humphreys. His recommendation was:

> [t]o explode the mine just before daylight in the morning or about 5 o'clock in the afternoon, mass the two brigades of the colored division in the rear of my line in column of divisions, double column closed en masse, the head of each brigade resting on the front line, and as soon as the explosion has taken place move them forward with instructions for the division to take half distance, and as soon as the leading regiments of the two brigades pass through the gap in the enemy's line, the leading regiment of the right brigade to come into line perpendicular to the enemy's line by the right companies, on the right into line wheel, the left companies on the right into line, and proceed at once down the line of the enemy's works as rapidly as possible, the leading regiment of the left brigade to execute the reverse movement to the left, moving up the enemy's line. The remainders of the two columns to move directly toward the crest in front as rapidly as possible, diverging in such a way as to enable them to deploy into columns of regiments, the right column making as nearly as may be for Cemetery Hill. These columns to be followed by the other divisions of this corps as they can be thrown in. This would involve the necessity of relieving these divisions by other troops before the movement, and of holding columns of other troops in readiness to take our place on the crest in case we gain it and sweep down. It would be advisable, in my opinion, if we succeed in gaining the crest, to throw the colored division right into the town.[18]

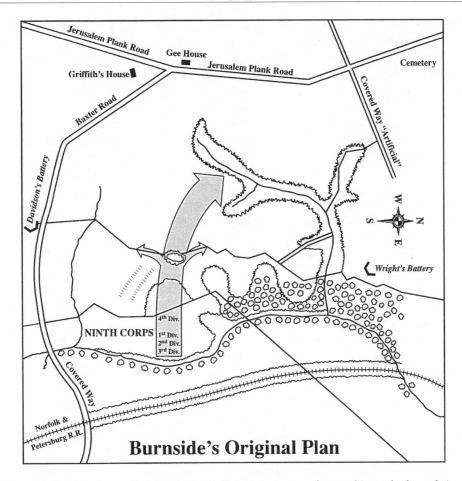

Burnside's Original Plan

Essentially, the plan called for the lead division to move forward into the breach immediately following the detonation of the mine, whereupon, reaching the vital point, they were to attack right and left, around the crater, to widen the breach made by the explosion. Those men would then lay down a sustained covering fire, flank and forward, for the other regiments in the division as well as the remaining divisions of the corps and the other corps, which would then push through to Cemetery Hill. This movement would eliminate the advantage the Confederates would otherwise enjoy in an attack on the concave salient, where Rebel troops on the right and left would be able to pour concentrated fire into the flanks of the attacking force, and ultimately to its rear. The subsequent divisions were then to continue on and spread out like a fan, smothering any opposition, and thereby providing the rapid advance of the last contingent consisting of all available forces to converge on Cemetery Hill. Such a coordinated movement would make Petersburg's capitulation inevitable and would, hopefully, precipitate the end of the war.

Burnside had already decided to initiate the assault with Ferrero's division consisting of U.S. Colored Troops in the lead. These troops had seen very little action up to that point, having served as guard for the Army of the Potomac's wagon trains from the Rapidan to the James, and were far fresher than any of Burnside's three other, white divisions.[19] Conversely, the white divisions of Burnside's corps were exhausted, decimated and thoroughly worn out and had "acquired the habit of sheltering themselves from the enemy's missiles." The black troops, on the other hand, had not been asked repeatedly to charge impossible fortifications as had the remainder of the corps. Burnside therefore believed that the black troops would be "least inclined to waver" under the exigencies of battle. The white troops, on the contrary, he felt, would advance so far and then seek a safe place for digging in.[20] As Henry G. Thomas, one of Ferrero's brigade commanders division put it, there are times when "the ardor, hopefulness, and enthusiasm of new troops not yet rendered doubtful by reverses or chilled by defeat, more than compensate in a dash, for training and experience."[21]

Burnside's plan as promulgated called for Ferrero's division to advance in a compact column of two brigades. Once in the breach, in order to protect the assaulting force's flanks, the lead regiment from the right brigade would "go right and sweep the enemy's lines in that direction, and the other was to go down the left and sweep the lines in that direction." He considered this essential due to the protruding nature of Elliott's Salient, which left the assaulting force enfiladed as it entered the breach. The remainder of those brigades and the rest of the division would then march forward in columns and carry the crest of Cemetery Hill, followed by the other three divisions in the corps, which would then charge directly for the summit of the hill. Then the Eighteenth Corps would advance into the city. If achieved, there would be no force between the Federal assaulting columns and the city. Once on the summit, the Confederates would be cut in two. The left, with its back to the Appomattox River, would be surrounded. The right could do nothing but make a prompt retreat. The tactical commands required to accomplish these maneuvers were necessarily complicated and the maneuvers themselves extremely confusing, especially when attempted in the heat of battle, even for troops well acquainted with the movements. Burnside therefore determined that the designated assaulting force, unaccustomed to operating under fire in any circumstances, should be allotted ample time to practice its footwork.

To obtain verification of his beliefs relative to which division was best suited to lead, Burnside asked his inspector general, Lieutenant Colonel Charles G. Loring, to inspect the lines and the divisions themselves with a view toward determining the most fit division to lead the attack. After completing his investigation, Loring's determination was that "the black division was the best prepared for this honor."[22] He officially informed Burnside that "the white troops of his corps were not in a fit condition to make the assault; that many of them had been for six weeks in close proximity to the enemy's lines, within one hundred and thirty yards; that all of them had been near the enemy's fire; and that when troops are exposed, as they were, day and night for six weeks to an incessant fire, it is impossible that they should have the same spirit as fresh troops."[23]

The commander of the designated fourth division, Edward Ferrero, was born in Grenada, Spain, in 1831 of Italian parents. Soon thereafter, the family moved to New York City, where Edward's father operated a successful dance instruction school, which was then among the most renowned in the country. Mr. Ferrero senior remained politically connected to Italy and often hosted such Italian luminaries as Garibaldi and Argenti, among others, in his home. Edward was raised on the dance floor and among high society of New York, and he developed into a dance master. Upon his parents' retirement, he carried on with the business, gaining fame as far as Europe and authoring books on dance, including a vastly popular work, *The Art of Dancing*, which remains in print today. In addition to his other accomplishments, he taught dancing at West Point.

Ferrero also had a military avocation, however, which was the complete antithesis of a dance instructor, and he advanced to lieutenant colonel in the New York militia. When war erupted, he raised the 51st New York Volunteers with his own funds and led this regiment in Burnside's North Carolina Expedition in 1861, and commanded the second brigade of the second division of the Ninth Corps at Second Manassas. As a brevet brigadier general, he led a brigade at Antietam, where he oversaw the taking of the Rohrbach Bridge (Burnside's Bridge), and also at the Union disaster at Fredericksburg. After a transfer to the western theater, he likewise commanded a brigade at Vicksburg. As the Senate had initially failed to confirm his promotion to brigadier, he served under Brigadier General Robert B. Potter in the division, who was his major in the 51st New York. After his reappointment to the rank and subsequent confirmation, he led a successful attack on the Confederates at Blue Springs, in eastern Tennessee. In a preview of events to come, as a division commander at Knoxville, he was accused by a subordinate of hiding himself in a bombproof during the entire battle. Burnside never ordered a court of inquiry, for reasons unknown, and soon relinquished command of the Department of the Ohio, effectively ending any possibility of an investigation. While Burnside did indicate that "the division of General Ferrero may justly feel proud of this great achievement" at Knoxville, he consciously did not commend Ferrero for his actions in the fighting.

BG Edward Ferrero (Library of Congress).

When Burnside and his Ninth Corps returned to the East in 1864 to serve under Grant, Ferrero received command of a new division consisting of black troops, many of whom were former slaves, recruited largely in Maryland and other parts of the North.[24] Burnside had ordered the fourth division to commence training in the rear areas of his front, where he met with Ferrero in early July regarding his recommendation. The officers of Ferrero's division expressed their confidence in the black soldiers to Burnside, and especially their ability to make the charge. Likewise, the black soldiers believed the officers "infallible." Unlike the remainder of Burnside's corps, they were relatively fresh and unscathed by previous battles. Their division consisted of only nine regiments, divided into two brigades. The first brigade was commanded by Colonel Joshua K. Sigfried from the 48th Pennsylvania, and was comprised of the 27th USCT under Lieutenant Colonel J. Wright, the 30th USCT, under Colonel Delevan Bates, the 39th USCT, under Colonel Ozora P. Stearns and the 43rd USCT, under Lieutenant Colonel H. Seymour Hall. The second brigade was commanded by Colonel Henry Goddard Thomas, and consisted of the 19th USCT under Lieutenant Colonel Joseph G. Perkins, the 23rd under Colonel Cleveland J. Campbell, the 28th USCT, a battalion of six companies, under Colonel Charles S. Russell, the 29th under Lieutenant Colonel John A. Bross, and the 31st USCT under Lieutenant Colonel W.E.W. Ross. At the time of the assault, the fourth division numbered 4,300 men, according to General Thomas, of which 2,000 belonged to Sigfried's brigade and 2,300 to Thomas's. The entire division began to be drilled with this special object in mind. Both officers and men, according to General Thomas, were eager to show their white comrades what the "colored division could do."[25]

At the inception of the war, the proportionately small number of blacks in the Federal army had been utilized largely as teamsters, cooks, laborers and servants. The idea of using them as soldiers was a radical departure from commonly accepted practice. However, as the war continued, the need for manpower increased geometrically, and as resistance to filling enlistment quotas and the draft increased, the concept of black fighting soldiers grew far less radical. By 1863, black regiments were making a good account of themselves in various theaters of the war, particularly in the west and along the Carolina coast. By the end of the war, over 180,000 blacks would have served in the Federal army in over 140 black regiments, the majority of them with a rifle. While the first black regiments were recruited primarily from free blacks in Louisiana and the Northeast, many of those recruited during and after 1863 were former slaves eager to derail their former masters and to ensure lasting freedom for their race. These black regiments were conspicuously absent from the Army of the Potomac until the spring of 1864, however. The Army's previous commanders had demonstrated very little enthusiasm for black soldiers.[26] Grant himself considered black soldiers fit for little more than digging ditches, and Meade's assessment was not much more advanced. In his drive to take Richmond, Grant had transferred some 20,000 plus soldiers from the southern and western armies to Virginia, many of them veterans of armed engagements of one sort or another, as opposed to relying on a greater involvement of black units.[27]

When the Ninth Corps was ordered east in 1864, Burnside received permission from Secretary of War Stanton to organize a new division consisting of the USCT. While the traditional Ninth Corps reorganized in Annapolis, Maryland, in preparation for the Overland Campaign, black regiments were then being recruited from various parts of the country, primarily from the ranks of former slaves. Maryland contributed the 19th, 30th and 39th USCT to the division. Ohio contributed the 27th USCT, and Pennsylvania the 43rd USCT. The 23rd USCT was organized in November 1863 at Camp Casey, Virginia, and the 28th USCT was from Indiana and had joined the corps only that July. Although the 31st was organized at Hart's Island, New York, it consisted of four companies from Connecticut. None of the units in the division had been in uniform prior to the previous Thanksgiving, and the majority only for a few months. The division first assembled as a whole at Annapolis in April, and it marched into Virginia as a new addition to the Ninth Corps. Soon thereafter, however, Grant commandeered the division for guarding the ammunition trains.[28] It was subsequently returned to Burnside only when the siege commenced at Petersburg, but it was then used largely for fatigue duties by the commanders of the other corps. Due to the fact that the unit was so new, it was significantly larger than other divisions in the Army of the Potomac, despite consisting of only nine regiments. While the division saw little fighting, its work was extremely difficult at Petersburg. It marched back and forth along the vast front, mainly digging trenches and fortifications and performing picket duties along the line.[29]

There was a prevalent feeling in the higher echelons of the army that black troops were best utilized as laborers and not as soldiers. While they had fought and died in large numbers at Fort Wagner and Fort Pillow, black soldiers were still shunned by the majority of Union officers. In fact, the best educated of Meade's staff officers regarded them merely as "hewers of wood and drawers of water," believing they could never withstand the rigors of combat.[30] Gouverneur Warren, who had recently worked Ferrero's men to the point of exhaustion building his fortifications, suggested they be converted permanently to engineer troops. While the Army of the Potomac's only black division continued to be completely untested in combat, however, the black regiments in the Army of the James' Eighteenth Corps had seen significant action thus far in the siege at Petersburg. Still, the attitude was pervasive among not only the generals but also the rank and file that the blacks were not up to the fight. Charles Henry Brewster wrote home on June 11, 1864:

You ask why they do not put the Negroes in the fights I imagine that they do not amount to any certain sum in a fight and in such tough battles as we have it will not do often times to put in troops which you cannot depend upon. ... though I have seen accounts of their fighting in the Northern papers I do not believe they have been in any fight at all.[31]

Similarly, Private Hermon Clark of the 117th New York wrote his father on June 23 describing the assault on the Dimmock Line on June 15: "I see the New York papers give the credit of the battle [on the] 15th to colored troops. Well, I think 2/3 the number of whites would have done the work."[32] Even Brigadier General Hincks of the Eighteenth Corps, whose black regiments of the Army of the James were baptized under fire on June 15, along with his superior, Major General William F. Smith, felt that the black regiments were far from being effective and desperately needed white officers lest the experiment prove a failure.[33]

Ambrose Burnside, by this time, however, was a true believer in the fighting ability and spirit of the black troops. He was also convinced that his three white divisions, all of which had been in daily contact with the enemy since early May, first in some of the fiercest assaults of the war and then in the arduous and deadly all-consuming trench warfare, were utterly exhausted. They were definitely in no condition, in his opinion, to lead an assault of this magnitude without sufficient rest. Additionally, given what these divisions had recently been through, he had good reason to doubt the experienced veteran's desire to execute such a frontal assault without seeking cover at the first opportunity. Added to all the above, these white divisions had been closest to the enemy in the trenches since mid–June and were fearful of even peering over the top of their entrenchments given the accuracy of the Rebel sharpshooters, who were then killing an average of thirty men a day in this enterprise. Thus, the men of these three divisions were considerably demoralized. Given these conditions, Burnside had good reason to seek Ferrero's counsel as to a plan, as well as to select his division to lead the assault. This tactical plan was subsequently given to the brigade commanders, Sigfried and Thomas, together with a rough outline map of the ground. The two brigade commanders were told to study the ground in order to supplement these maps with their own personal reconnaissance. This directive proved a very daunting task, given the expertise of the enemy's sharpshooters. Thomas was later to complete his mission by placing his own hat on a ramrod and lifting it over the ramparts, thus drawing fire. He would then proceed, "stepping quickly a few paces one side," take "a hasty observation," and repeat the process.[34] In this manner, Thomas and Sigfried ascertained what they needed to know of the ground to their front to execute the assault in an effective manner.

Burnside's plan called for the first brigade to execute "[r]ight companies, right into line wheel; left companies, on right into line, and go down the rebel works to the right," while the second brigade executed "[l]eft companies, left into line wheel, right companies, on left into line, and go down the rebel works to the left."[35] The plan called for the division to attack right and left to widen the breach already created by the mine's explosion. A portion of each brigade would split off to each side, wheel into line perpendicular to the main attack, and sweep the lateral trenches free of defenders. The Ninth Corps' other divisions would then follow into the breach, followed in turn by the other corps. While there was no written order from Burnside as to which brigade or regiment should take the lead, a verbal order was conveyed to Ferrero signifying that Sigfried's brigade should "take the lead" (it appears that this indicated that he was to initiate the assault to the right). Lieutenant Colonel H. Seymour Hall of the 43rd USCT reported he was ordered by Sigfried to have his regiment "[t]ake the lead of the brigade, for while I do not wish to disparage either of the other colonels or their regiments, I knew that I could rely on you in any emergency. You had full control of all your men, the discipline in your regiment was high up, your officers and men had implicit confidence in you as their colonel."[36] Hall was to take his position just before the mine was fired, in double column by division closed en masse, and to pass through the breach in the enemy works. He was then to take them in the flank and roll the enemy line up with the bayonet, by taking half distance, right companies right into line wheel, and left companies right into line.[37]

Brigadier General Ferrero, when informed that his division had been selected to lead the assault, initially expressed a strong objection. He indicated that his division had been previously utilized by the other corps commanders, especially General Warren, as laborers. Warren in particular had overworked them day and night to build improved fortifications and breastworks for their white troops. Ferrero implied that he would not have adequate time to train the men for such a complex assault if they were to continue thus as "slaves" for the other corps commanders. Burnside thereupon immediately called upon his assistant inspector general to file a report on this subject, essentially seeking a decision from headquarters as to whom Ferrero's division reported. Within a day, Ferrero's division was exempted from fatigue duty outside of the Ninth Corps.[38] This being finally settled, the fourth division then began to train in earnest for leading the assault. For almost three weeks before the assault, the troops drilled daily in accomplishing this mission.

Word of the plan trickled down to the troops of Ferrero's division. The white officers of the division were ecstatic that they were chosen to lead the assault. The black soldiers would often gather in the evenings; "the day's soldiering done, they liked to sit around the campfire and sing songs nobody ever heard before because they made them up, as they went along. They lifted their voices in music of a sweetness and sadness and depth that white men, listening, could not fathom." When these ex-slaves, who were now wearing blue uniforms, learned of their mission:

> [t]he news filled them too full for ordinary utterance. The joyous guffaw always breaking out about the camp-fire ceased. They formed circles in their company streets and were sitting on the ground intently and solemnly "studying." At last a heavy voice began to sing, "We-e looks li-ike me-en a-a marchin' on, we looks li-ike men-er-war." Over and over again he sang it, making slight changes. The rest watched him intently; no sign of approval or disapproval escaped their lips, or appeared on their faces. All at once, when his refrain had struck the right response in their hearts, his group took it up, and shortly half a thousand voices were upraised. It was a picturesque scene, these dark men, with their white eyes and teeth and full red lips crouching over a smoldering camp-fire, in dusky shadow, with only the feeble rays of the lanterns of the first sergeants and the lights of the candles dimly showing through the tents.... The sound was as weird as the scene, when all the voices struck the low "E" (last note but one), held it, and rose to "A" with a *portamento* as sonorous as it was clumsy.

The black soldiers were pleased at the prospect of the coming battle, and resolved to "demonstrate that Negroes would make good soldiers."[39] Colonel Pleasants felt that they were "brave, and almost primitively ruthless fighters; they stood up particularly well under the blazing heat of midsummer" and would follow their leaders into the jaws of death.[40]

> Every one of them understood that sooner or later he would have to pay the military debt he now owed for his liberty, and for that reason, in part, the blacks' original misgivings were suppressed, and their outlook on their role in the future battle gradually took on the enthusiasm of a religious crusade. They also felt strongly that a victory achieved by them would help dispel the deep prejudice held against their race by their white comrades in the Federal army.[41]

After all, they had a personal reason for wanting to perform well. "Only a few yesterdays ago they threw off their dreams every morning when the plantation bell rang; these mornings their dreams had form and substance, and the bugle blew Reveille to prove it; these were free men and the only U.S. Colored Troops in the Army of the Potomac. They gladly trained hard to be a worthy spearhead."[42] They looked forward "with determination and enthusiasm to winning a signal victory and to prove themselves worthy of the honor of being selected to lead the attack against the enemy."[43]

Each day that July, at least one black regiment was rotated to the rear to practice the drills and special movements required for the assault. They were drilled for two or three hours every day in such movements to familiarize them with the work to be done in leading the charge. The units would at the very least have to master a right or left wheel in double column, which was difficult enough for a veteran unit with considerable training under its belt. The "movements in which these troops were daily instructed were the very movements to be executed after the explosion of the mine.[44] The most critical maneuvers were required of the first brigade, and, therefore, Sigfried's men underwent special training not required of the second brigade. The first brigade drilled for nearly one month with these plans. Sigfried's men received training in sweeping right and left after the explosion, while Thomas' brigade drilled under more ordinary conditions, although some of the officers believed they might still lead the assault. The division practiced the maneuvers until they could execute them perfectly in the dark, with a view toward gaining and occupying Cemetery Hill, rehearsing day after day until they knew that "[t]hey were ready." They were "imbued with a tremendous spirit of enthusiasm over the great honor that had been conferred upon them, and each day they went through their secret rehearsals as if it were some tremendous religious ceremony, their black faces serious, almost reverent; and their burly non-commissioned officers relaying commands in low gruff voices that brought clocklike precision of response."[45]

Throughout the training, the enthusiastic troops of the fourth division went about their assignments cheerfully, with a view on the mission and their place in history. Until the assault on the crater, they continued to sing their special song every night, to the exclusion of all other songs. "After that defeat," General Thomas noted, "they sang it no more."[46]

On July 28, after Colonel Pleasants informed him that the mine had been completely charged, Burnside rode to Meade's headquarters to finalize preparations. Relations between the two men were still quite testy, despite Burnside's sincere attempts to humor Meade's fragile ego. Meade, with his low opinion of Burnside, and his ultrasensitive ego, continued to meddle in Burnside's plan any way he could. He changed the level of the powder charge Burnside had specified from 12,000 pounds to 8,000, after originally arguing against charging the mine at all. He remained cynical and skeptical, if not openly hostile. When Burnside arrived at his headquarters on the 28th, Meade dropped a final bombshell by indicating that he could not "approve of your placing the negro troops in the advance, as proposed in your project." When Burnside asked why, Meade responded that he did "not think they should be called upon to do as important work as that which you propose to do, certainly not called upon to lead."[47]

Burnside was utterly flabbergasted by this last minute refusal to allow the black division to make the assault at this late date. Meade also insisted that the assault column must immediately press on to the crest behind Elliott's Salient, instead of fanning out right and left as Burnside had specified, a move for which his troops had been training incessantly for nearly three weeks. Meade felt that the fourth division, all untested soldiers without battle experience, was not capable of leading the charge. He preferred more experienced troops and later explained that as the operation "was one requiring the best troops, I thought it impolitic to trust it [the black division]." Meade's feeling was that Ferrero's men were completely inexperienced and that the assault needed to be led by veteran troops. At this particular moment, his prejudice against the black troops certainly came out. Meade indicated that he had "yet to see African American troops do anything that would induce him to set aside his doubts regarding their ability to fight as well as white soldiers, which had been manifest in his making a point throughout the Overland Campaign of keeping Ferrero's division in the rear, guarding supply trains, and thus well away from the fighting."[48]

There were yet further considerations on Meade's mind for his refusal. Ferrero's division represented the only black division in the Army of the Potomac. Meade reasoned that, if things went badly, as they historically had a tendency to do, "it would then be said, and very properly, that we were shoving those people ahead to get killed because we did not care anything about them, but that could not be said if we put white troops in front."[49] This was indicative of the pervasive politics which affected command decisions by this time in the Army of the Potomac. The Joint Congressional Committee on the Conduct of the War, thoroughly dominated by Radical Republicans, had spent considerable time in the winter of 1863–1864 investigating Meade's conduct at Gettysburg, with some consideration to a recommendation to replace him. While this objective failed, it left an indelible impression on Meade. Thus, when faced with approving a plan prescribing black troops spearheading an attack for which he had no heart, he did not want to give the committee any ammunition suggesting that he was willing to sacrifice black troops in a questionable enterprise. He felt that the abolitionists would later accuse him of needlessly sacrificing black soldiers.

Burnside protested vehemently in favor of the plan to utilize his black division. He refused to retreat from this plan, as he felt the white troops were used up and too experienced not to take cover immediately once they were exposed to heavy fire. They had been under fire constantly since early May without any respite and had taken heavy casualties.[50] Burnside argued adamantly for the use of the fourth division, given the conditions of the remainder of the corps and the fact that Ferrero's men had been training daily for almost three weeks to make the complicated assault. Confronted with this powerful argument, Meade promised Burnside to lay the entire matter before Grant. He indicated that he was scheduled to meet with Grant at the lieutenant general's headquarters at City Point, about seven miles distant, at 1:00 P.M. that day, and would return later that evening. Thus, Burnside assumed that Meade would relay Grant's decision when he returned that very evening. When Meade arrived back that evening and Burnside did not hear anything, he assumed that his argument had prevailed, and that he retained the authority to commence his assault with the black division as planned.[51]

To the contrary, however, Meade had lobbied Grant that if the blacks headed the assault and it failed, this would give the impression that they were using these troops for "cannon fodder." Years later, Grant recalled Meade arguing that if the blacks were allowed to lead and the operation failed, it would be said that the command was unconcerned about them, which could not be argued if the white troops were utilized.[52] Meade had promised Burnside to present both sides of the debate to Grant, and the unfortunately trusting Burnside believed him. He did not insist, therefore, to present his case personally to Grant or to be present during the conversation. In his absence, "Meade's objectivity fell short of complete," however, and he gave Burnside's argument a very slight report. In fact, Meade never even revealed Burnside's plan to Grant, instead representing his own orders for the implementation of a plan as the original. Meade also could not resist adding political expediency to the equation when he feared that his arguments were not enough, "reminding Grant of the backlash which might follow any disaster that befell the black division."[53] Grant, forced to ponder the consequences of a failure of the tunneling operation and anticipated assault, reasoned that if it looked "as if black men had been deliberately chosen to die futilely, the fury of the abolitionists back home would descend on them."[54] He did not want the risk of giving any opposition on the issue to Lincoln, who was then beginning an extremely difficult campaign for a second term. "It must not appear that Lincoln the emancipator was careless with black lives."[55] Thus, the decision was ultimately made upon a widespread fear that black soldiers were an unproven quality and that should the assault result in a slaughter, the Union high command would be subject to charges of sacrificing black troops indiscriminately.[56]

Burnside heard nothing more from Meade on the 28th, although he was cognizant of the fact that his superior had returned from City Point that evening. By noon on the 29th, he thus began to relax. With the attack set for 3:30 the next morning, he "imagined that no further action was to be taken in the matter, and that ... [he] was to be allowed to place the Fourth Division in the advance."[57] Burnside began a meeting with Generals Willcox and Potter regarding their role in the upcoming assault.[58] He told them that he had "been very much worried and troubled the day before lest General Meade would overrule that part of my plan which contemplated the putting in of the colored troops, but that I hoped nothing further would be heard from it because ... the matter was to be referred to General Grant, and that inasmuch as I had not heard from General Meade I took it for granted that he had decided to allow the thing to remain as it was."[59] Burnside was so confident in his operation's success as planned that he had previously packed all his baggage for the journey into Petersburg.

Burnside was still in the process of explaining his concerns for the assault when he looked up as Meade appeared in his tent accompanied by Major General O.C. Ord, the new commander of the Eighteenth Corps, with their respective staffs. Meade informed Burnside that Grant had concurred with him and that the black division would not be allowed to lead the advance.[60] Burnside, visibly devastated, asked Meade if the decision could yet be changed. Meade replied, "No, general, it cannot; it is final, and you must put in your white troops." Meade also emphasized that there were to be no lateral movements in the assault to clear the enemy trenches, and that the troops must take Cemetery Hill at all costs, without reference to formation. Burnside indicated that this decision would necessarily call for changes to his plan, which Meade thereupon left him to resolve for himself. Burnside finally acknowledged the order, bowed his head, and replied, "Very well, General, I will carry out this plan to the best of my ability."[61] Meade and Ord thereafter departed with their staffs, leaving Burnside to "pick up the pieces." Many officers in the Ninth Corps felt that Meade and even Grant sometimes were somewhat ambivalent about Burnside's plans in general, seemingly determined to doubt the chances of success of any plan that did not originate with themselves. George Allen of the 4th Rhode Island later commented that he did not know if it emanated "from a feeling of jealousy on the part of Meade, or apathy and arrogance on the part of Grant."[62]

With fewer than fifteen hours left before the assault, Burnside was left without a contingency plan, which was totally inexcusable on Meade's part (and, arguably, on Burnside's). Other plans had to be substituted so late "that sufficient time could not be given to provide for their proper execution," commented Captain John Anderson of the 57th Massachusetts. Meade had ordered a replacement of the force which had been trained to make the initial assault only hours before the troops were scheduled to move toward their jump-off positions. Burnside had always excelled at making plans on paper, and the subject plan had been a good one. Conversely, though, he had never functioned well when forced to improvise, "and Meade's changes unraveled him completely."[63] Still, the assault was on and he had to designate a replacement division to lead the charge which would take place early the next morning.

After some preliminary discussions with Generals Willcox and Potter as to which division should take the advance, one of them indicated that Brigadier General Ledlie, current commander of the first division, should also be included in the conversation, and Ledlie was therefore summoned.[64] Ferrero's temporary replacement, already briefed on the division's role as lead division in the former plan, was no longer a part of the equation and thus remained absent. Seymour Hall indicated that Ferrero himself was in Washington on the 29th and did not learn of the change until shortly before the assault was to commence. The three commanders of the white divisions then commenced an analysis as to which division should take the lead. None displayed any apparent willingness to step forward. The four men wrangled over the issue for several hours, repeatedly returning to the conclusion that Ferrero's division was in the best position to lead the advance. Burnside was thus unfortunately left with three bad choices. Ledlie's first division was strong in numbers and comparatively well-rested, having joined the corps a little later, and since June 17 had been farther away from the sharpshooting near Elliott's Salient. They were, therefore, theoretically less jumpy and consequently had better morale. However, the division had a string of disappointing performances culminating in its role in the attack on June 17. A large portion of the division was made up of two heavy artillery regiments whose only function to date had been to guard large fortifications. There was a considerable element of German-speaking troops, which frequently was the source of serious communication difficulties. The division was also physically removed from the front and would thus require several hours to be placed into position. The second division, under Potter, had been the corps' most dependable, but it had been decimated in the fights in May and June and its survivors seemed shell-shocked. Potter, however, felt his division would nonetheless win the honor by default, but he apparently did not speak up in favor of this result.[65] Willcox's third division was in the best physical location to commence the assault, but it, too, was considered badly depleted and demoralized.[66]

The debate continued for hours with the same inescapable conclusion — the fourth division should lead the assault.[67] As it was by then three in the afternoon, with only twelve hours before the assaulting force had to be in position, Burnside grew extremely frustrated. With the same degree of frustration that had driven Meade to issue his attack-at-will orders of June 18, Burnside finally threw up his hands and indicated that he could not choose one unit over another. He thus indicated that "[i]t would be fair[est] to cast lots." He thereupon threw three scraps of paper into his hat and told the others to turn their faces away and draw. Willcox picked first, followed by Robert Potter. James Ledlie, the last to choose, however, "won" the honor by selecting the short straw by default.[68] Unfortunately, as Regis de Trobriand, the French-born brigadier general in Hancock's corps later pointed out, "The lot — which is of course blind, and sometimes is pleased to give us some severe lessons — fell upon the very division which, if it was not worse than the others, was certainly worse commanded."[69]

James Hewitt Ledlie was born in 1832 in Utica, New York, and graduated from the Scientific Department of Union College. He became a railroad engineer, working on the Erie Canal and later supervising the draining of marshlands for the Seneca River Improvement Company. At the outbreak of hostilities, he joined the 19th New York as a major and soon was promoted to colonel and its commander. At Fredericksburg, he commanded a brigade of New York troops. He subsequently served in several artillery units along the Carolina coast, being promoted to brigadier general of volunteers in December of 1862. Like Ferrero, however, the appointment expired without Senate confirmation the following spring. He was then reappointed and confirmed in that grade in October of 1863. He received a brigade command in the Ninth Corps at Spotsylvania Courthouse in May 1864, and in June was given command of the first division of the Ninth Corps. It appeared his political connections greatly assisted in his advancement, despite a relatively lackluster military career. His subordinates frequently complained of his drinking habits and poor performance on the battlefield. Ledlie's staff did a considerable job in protecting him, however. Burnside was apparently relatively unaware of his considerable shortcomings. Thomas L. Crittenden, the division's former commander, had previously informed Burnside that Ledlie was qualified to replace him. The Ninth Corps commander was well aware of Ledlie's aggressive, albeit unsuccessful charge on the fortified works at Ox Ford on May 26 in the North Anna campaign. He had even gone to bat for Ledlie in early June, writing Grant a laudatory letter regarding his subordinate's performance, when Ledlie's congressional confirmation was still in doubt.[70] With the advantage of hindsight, many subsequent critics observed that "[h]ow a man so incompetent came to command a division late in the war is the story of political influence and the frequent blindness of military bureaucracy." Ledlie was often away from his unit visiting with his neighbor, William H. Seward (secretary of the treasury), as well as George McClellan. Seward and Lincoln took a special interest in his situation and in the movement to make him a brigadier.[71]

But Ledlie was definitely not the person whom Burnside apparently thought that he was. As the Federals moved into Lee's trap at the North Anna, Ledlie's brigade made an unauthorized attack against the virtually impregnable entrenchments held by A.P. Hill. Ledlie's bellicosity that day was totally owed to what a Massachusetts soldier described as "artificial courage known throughout the Yankee army as 'Dutch courage.'" There Ledlie advanced without support and charged into the heavy storm of rain and lead. The Confederates had quickly mounted a counterattack and soon thereafter "[e]very man became his own general" in the predictable Federal retreat. Ledlie quickly lost control over events and let the men fall back toward Quarles Mill to rejoin the rest of the corps. Lieutenant Colonel Stephen Weld of the 56th Massachusetts, soon to be caught up in the impending assault, succinctly indicated that Ledlie "made a botch of it. Had too much booze on board, I think."[72] While Ledlie received some praise for his actions at North Anna, Charles Dana informed Stanton that Ledlie's brigade had lost so many men because it was attacking instead of being attacked. Nothing at all was accomplished by the assault, according to Captain John Anderson, then a lieutenant with the 57th Massachusetts.[73] Again on June 17, Ledlie's division was "severely roughed up while assaulting the Rebel lines, losing 841 men." While he was not on the field at the time, but instead in a bombproof and clearly drunk, he later seized a number of prisoners captured by one of his regiments, and claimed credit for the capture.[74]

Whatever possessed Burnside to overlook this very serious fault in the subordinate Ledlie, General Grant, who had previously been responsible for bringing Ledlie to the Ninth Corps, was well aware of these shortcomings. He knew that Ledlie was without question Burnside's worst division commander and should not be entrusted to carry out so critical a mission. In his memoirs, Grant wrote that "Ledlie besides being otherwise inefficient proved also to possess disqualifications less common among soldiers." This was a polite way of indicating that Ledlie was a coward. Grant was aware of the manner in which the first division had been chosen to lead the assault, but he did nothing to replace it or Ledlie, apparently due

BG James H. Ledlie (Library of Congress).

to the "demoralizing effect of all the previous meddling."[75] Thus were laid the seeds for one of the greatest disasters of the war. The change was made so late that there was not sufficient time to provide the white troops with any familiarization of the executions needed for success.[76] A large portion of the night before the assault was taken up revising the plan of attack and issuing new orders to the various troops which would take part in the grand assault in a matter of hours.

At some point, while Burnside was still meeting with his division commanders, Meade returned again to the Ninth Corps headquarters to meet with them to insure that they fully comprehended what was now expected of them. At this time, he discussed with them "the tactical maneuvers to be made between that crater and the crest; that the only thing to be done was to rush for the crest and take it immediately after the explosion had taken place, and that any attempt to take time to form their troops would result in a repulse."[77] He also indicated that the operation was "one purely of time; that if immediate advantage was not taken of the explosion of the mine, and the consequent confusion of the enemy, and the crest immediately gained, it would be impossible to remain there" and the troops should thus be withdrawn immediately to the protection of their trenches. He emphasized that there was absolutely no time for maneuver.

The substitution in the lead division also changed the choreography of the upcoming assault. Meade thus directed Burnside to forego the "fancy footwork" entailed in pairing off those two lead regiments that he had intended to use for clearing the Confederate trenches. Instead, the troops were all to simply rush for the cemetery's crest, "devil take the hindmost." To Meade, the lack of white troops trained in the flanking maneuvers prescribed in Burnside's plan was irrelevant, as he envisioned the taking of the crest at Cemetery Hill as the sole objective. Meade was so vehement in achieving this result that Burnside felt obligated to abandon the plan for sending one regiment from each of his brigades right and left in a sweep, instead making a plan to "accord with General Meade's views." This, too, would play a key role in the ensuing disaster. Meade later denied interfering "in any way" with Burnside's plans for tactical formations, indicating that while he disapproved of the use of colored troops in the lead, "no control was exercised over General Burnside in the tactical formation of his columns."[78] In light of the overall extent of his consistent interference, this statement appears totally incredulous.

After this discussion with Burnside and his commanders, Meade retired to his headquarters, where he met with General Grant at 4:00 P.M. Meade showed him his written order for the next day's assault, which had just been finalized. Grant read the order and expressed his satisfaction with it. The order read:

The following instructions are issued for the guidance of all concerned:

1. As soon as dark, Major-General Burnside, commanding Ninth Corps, will withdraw his two brigades under General White, occupying the intrenchments between the plank and Norfolk roads, and bring them to his front. Care will be taken not to interfere with the troops of the Eighteenth Corps moving into their position in the rear of the Ninth Corps. General Burnside will form his troops for assaulting the enemy's works at daylight of the 30th, prepare his parapets and abatis for work in opening passages for artillery, destroying the enemy's abatis, and the intrenching tools distributed for effecting lodgments, &c.

2. Major-General Warren, commanding Fifth Corps, will reduce the number of his troops holding the intrenchments of his front to the minimum, and concentrate all his available force on his right and hold them prepared to support the assault of Major-General Burnside. The preparations in respect to pioneers, intrenching tools, &c., enjoined upon the Ninth Corps, will also be made by the Fifth Corps.

3. As soon as it is dark Major Ord, commanding Eighteenth Corps, will relieve his troops in the trenches by General Mott's division of the Second Corps, and form his corps in rear of the Ninth Corps, and be prepared to support the assault of Major-General Burnside.

4. Every preparation will be made for moving forward the field artillery of each corps.

5. At dark Major-General Hancock, commanding the Second Corps, will move from Deep Bottom to the rear of the intrenchments now held by the Eighteenth Corps, resume the command of Mott's division and be prepared at daylight to follow up the assaulting and supporting column, or for such other operation as may be found necessary.

6. Major-General Sheridan, commanding Cavalry Corps, will proceed at dark from the vicinity of Deep Bottom to Lee's Mill, and at daylight will move with his whole corps, including Wilson's division, against the enemy's troops, defending Petersburg on their right, by the roads leading from the southward and westward.

7. Major Duane, acting chief engineer, will have the pontoon trains parked at convenient points in the rear, prepared to move. He will see that supplies of sand bags, gabions, fascines, &c., are in depot, near the lines, ready for use. He will detail engineer officers for each corps.

8. At 3:30 in the morning of the 30th Major-General Burnside will spring his mine, and his assaulting columns will immediately move rapidly upon the breach, seize the crest in rear, and effect a lodgment there. He will be followed by Major-General Ord, who will support him on the right, directing his movement to the crest indicated, and by Major-General Warren, who will support him on the left. Upon the explosion of the mine the artillery of all kinds in battery will open upon those points of the enemy's works whose fire covers the ground over which our columns must move, care being taken to avoid impeding the progress of our troops. Special instructions respecting the direction of the fire will be issued through the chief of artillery.

9. Corps commanders will report to the commanding general when their preparations are complete, and will advise him of every step in the progress of the operation and of everything important that occurs.

10. Promptitude, rapidity of execution and cordial cooperation are essential to success, and the commanding general is confident that this indication of his expectation will insure the hearty efforts of the commanders and troops.

11. Headquarters during the operation will be at the headquarters of the Ninth Corps.[79]

The order was signed by S. Williams, Assistant Adjutant-General, on Meade's behalf. Burnside was therefore to form his troops for the assault and prepare his parapets and abatis for the passage of the columns, and have pioneers so equipped to open passages for artillery, destroy all enemy abatis and distribute intrenching tools for the expected lodgments. Following the detonation of the mine, he was to move rapidly into the breach, "seize the crest in the rear, and effect a lodgment there." Ord would then follow in support on the right and Warren on the left. Thus Burnside, with close to 15,000 men, would rush into the opening made by the explosion and charge toward Cemetery Hill, 500 to 600 yards in the rear of Elliott's Salient. Ord would then follow with his corps of 10,000 men. Meade's plans were definitely simpler, easier to execute and less liable of complication with regard to the Ninth Corps' role in the operation. Burnside's plan, on the other hand, had depended on everything working in mechanical order "like the works of a clock."[80] However, the latter effort had much more thought and rehearsal behind it.

Burnside explained to his three division commanders what his revised plan entailed, having dispensed with the notion of sending troops perpendicularly down the right and left to clear the way, in accordance with Meade's views. His revised plan thus did not call for troops "to pass down to the right and left, but to make at once for the crest," which harbored the seeds for a disaster. His original plan had been to skirt the crater. Now, with Meade's change, the emphasis was instead all on capturing Cemetery Hill as the main objective. Ledlie's division was to lead and move forward to crown the crest behind Elliott's Salient near the Blandford Church, by then known to the men as Cemetery Hill. Then Willcox's division was to follow Ledlie around the abandoned Confederate works, bearing to the left flank of the first division's column, to make a lodgment to the left of Ledlie, along the Jerusalem Plank Road. Then Potter's division would move to the right of the first division as soon as his troops would not interfere with Willcox's men, to protect the left flank and establish a line to run from Cemetery Hill nearly at right angles with the enemy line. Ferrero would then move his fourth division immediately after Willcox until he reached the Union advance lines, when they were clear of the other three divisions, and then move forward over the same ground Ledlie had covered, passing through the Ninth Corps lines and if possible moving down to occupy the city of Petersburg itself.[81]

Aside from the lack of a sweep of the lead division's regiments right and left to clear the Confederate trenches, the plan remained rather close to Ferrero's original plan. The crucial difference, however, was that the lead assaulting force now would not have prepared in advance for the attack they were to carry out, nor would they be even adequately briefed as to their mission. Additionally, the lead element would not enjoy the "freshness and élan that Burnside considered essential to success."[82] With his verbal instructions completed, Burnside sent his commanders back to their respective headquarters to await further written orders. Given the depleted and demoralized state of the white troops, and Ledlie's poor performance in the Overland Campaign and the considerable rumors of drunkenness on duty, the new plan "had terribly little to recommend it."[83] Ledlie grumbled before he left that he was the unlikely victim of the lottery. Burnside in turn offered the services of his inspector general, Colonel William W. Loring, to go over the ground he desired Ledlie to take with him and his brigade commanders. Ledlie then left Burnside's headquarters sometime after 3:00 P.M., in what was later reported to be a very cheerful mood, to make his final arrangements.

Ledlie returned to his headquarters and summoned his two brigade commanders, Brigadier General William F. Bartlett and Colonel Elisha G. Marshall, the former commander of the 14th New York Heavy Artillery, and a number of staff officers to meet on the impending actions. They went up to the front near Fort Morton to observe the planned battlefield. Ledlie's assistant adjutant general, Captain Thomas W. Clark, commander of Company A, 29th Massachusetts, later recalled that Ledlie's plan was for Marshall's second brigade to be formed in column of battalion front. After the explosion, it was to move forward and occupy the Confederate works on the right of the crater, skirting its rim, without going into it. Marshall's brigade consisted of one worn-out battalion from Maryland, an incomplete New York regiment with a single day of combat, and the two huge but relatively untested heavy artillery regiments, considered less than anxious for undertaking this type of work. The first brigade was to follow with the same front and occupy the work on the left of the crater, likewise without going into it. With this lodgment in place, it was then to be secured and connected to the Federal line by the designated engineer regiment, the 35th Massachusetts. Ledlie indicated that the second division was then to extend this lodgment still more to the right, while the third division extended it to the left in the enemy's works by a frontal attack. Ferrero's division was then to pass through the crater and assault the crest at Cemetery Hill.

Marshall's distinct instructions to his brigade indicated "that the security of the lodgment was the primary duty of the First Division and the hill was a subordinate object."[84] Marshall was explicit that his brigade was to confine its attention to seizing and holding as great a length of the line on the right of the crater as possible, leaving the work beyond, i.e., seizing Cemetery Hill to the rear, to be done by other troops. The tactics of the first division, accustomed to line attacks as opposed to regimental column maneuvers, were not adapted to the formation designed for the black division, with its complicated tactical movements to the right and left after the works were seized. The ultimate effect of the maneuvers was to be about the same, however. Ledlie's instructions to his brigade commanders were in direct contradiction to those of Generals Meade and Burnside. Captain Thomas Clark confirmed that Ledlie had given positive orders that the first division should not go forward past the crater. Despite this inconsistency, "[n]evertheless, late in the evening of July 29, Bartlett and Marshall, in turn, gathered their respective commanders and explained the secret plan as revealed by James Ledlie." Following this meeting with the regimental commanders, they informed the other officers of the plan and told them to prepare the men to move at a moment's notice, but not to inform the men of the plan. However, the men knew almost as much as the officers knew, and sometimes more, "and the officers knew that they knew." They were also fully aware of Burnside's rift with Meade over the changes to his plan.[85]

It was after 9:00 that night when Burnside's written orders, which dealt with movements that were to commence almost immediately that night, were issued to his commanders. The orders read:

I. The mine will be exploded tomorrow morning at 3:30, by Colonel Pleasants.

II. General Ledlie will immediately upon the explosion of the mine move his division forward as directed by verbal orders this day, and if possible, crown the crest at the point known as Cemetery Hill, occupying, if possible, the cemetery.

III. General Wilcox will move his division forward as soon as possible after General Ledlie has passed through the first line of the enemy's works, bearing off to the left so as to effectually protect the left flank of General Ledlie' column, and make a lodgment, if possible, on the Jerusalem plank road to the left of General Ledlie's division.

IV. General Potter will move his division forward to the right of General Ledlie's division as soon as it is apparent that he will not interfere with the movement of General Will Cox's division, and will as near as possible protect the right flank of General Ledlie from any attack on that quarter and establish a line on the crest of a ravine which seems to run from the crest of Cemetery Hill nearly at right angles to the enemy's main line directly in our front.

V. General Ferrero will move his division immediately after General Wilcox's until he reaches our present advanced line, where he will remain until the ground in his front is entirely cleared by the other three divisions, when he will move forward over the same ground that General Ledlie moved over; will pass through our line and, if possible, move down and occupy the village to the right.

VI. The formations and movements of all these divisions, together with their places of rendezvous, will be as near as possible in accordance with the understanding during the personal interviews with the division commanders. The headquarters of the corps during the movement will be at the fourteen-gun battery in rear of the Taylor house. If further instructions are desired by division commanders they will please ask for them at once.[86]

Burnside later indicated there were details not entered in the order "in consequence of the verbal understanding which existed between [him] ... and ... [his] division commanders...." The repetition of the words "if possible" left a feeling to weaken the impact of the ultimate objective. Such orders in military parlance should normally be positive and never bear any "ifs." In retrospect, Burnside should probably have stated the obvious and ordered that division and brigade commanders should accompany their commands in person and that they would be held strictly responsible for the prompt and faithful execution of the order.[87]

Burnside ignored Meade's explicit orders as to the opening of his parapets and abatis for the attackers to pass through and made absolutely no such plans in his written orders. His rationale was that such preparations would alert the Rebels to the planned assault, and most of the obstructions had already been blown apart by the relentless rifle and mortar fire over the past six weeks, as a result of which the troops would have little difficulty passing through them. Thus the abatis remained extant. One other obstruction Burnside allowed to remain in place was a large, tall stand of pine, which obscured the view of the only Union battery that bore on the shallow depression south of Elliott's Salient. Henry Hunt, chief of artillery, reminded him about the copse on July 28, but Burnside feared that this (felling the trees), too, would alert the enemy of his plans "and the pines still stood as the sliver of waning moon rose July 29."[88] While fatigue details piled sandbags to form stairways in front of Ledlie's division, and parapets elsewhere were leveled somewhat, to a significant degree Burnside did not insist that his division commanders remove their defensive impediments. The engineers promised by Meade from headquarters never materialized, at least according to the Ninth Corps officers, and Burnside failed to order his own engineers to accompany the assault to assist with opening the enemy works. He did not even distribute entrenching tools for use on the bare hilltop that was the objective. He simply left such details to the division commanders after indicating the order in which they should make the assault.[89] All of these oversights added to the difficulties faced by the assaulting force the next morning and contributed to the impending disaster.

To add even further to the confusion, General Ferrero finally arrived back at Petersburg after 7:00 that night and immediately reassumed command of his division, which was already, by that time, on the move. He had relinquished command around July 22, when he received word that his appointment as a brigadier general had been revoked by Lincoln following the Senate's refusal to confirm him. Burnside was ordered to assign a "suitable" officer to replace him, and he appointed Brigadier General Julius White to that position. White had recently been assigned to the Ninth Corps after a stint as commander of a recruiting function in Springfield, Illinois. White was somewhat notorious for having surrendered Harpers Ferry to the Confederates in 1862. Now, at the most inappropriate time, Ferrero was back after finally having his appointment confirmed. Meade's headquarters approved Ferrero's reinstatement to command barely eight hours before the mine was to be exploded. At the time, he had not yet been briefed on the changes to Burnside's plan. In fact, the corps' brigade commanders were not informed until 11:00 P.M., and as the officers were asleep, many of then did not learn of the change until later still in the early morning hours. With Julius White thus out of a job, Burnside quickly appointed him as his acting chief of staff, in place of John G. Parke. Parke, who had proven indispensable to Burnside for the better part of two years, was quite ill with an attack of malaria and had been granted twenty days' leave on a surgeon's certificate of disability on July 4. White was soon to play a key role in the confusion in communication occurring in the next day's battle.[90] Thus, the scene was set for what was rapidly developing into a major fiasco on the part of the Union army.

CHAPTER 7

*The Men Are Ready —
Are the Generals?*

With the digging and planning accomplished, it was time to place the mechanics of the assault into motion, to be ready for the pivotal event — the springing of the mine at 3:30 the next morning. Ledlie's first division, having drawn the distinction of leading the assaulting force, was to be put in motion first. Orders were received by regimental and company commanders of the division late in the evening of the 29th to move at a moment's notice. The order came under the cover of secrecy and the officers were instructed to withhold the information from the enlisted men. Even the company grade officers were given no detailed plan of operations to protect the secrecy of the plan. John Anderson, then a lieutenant with the 57th Massachusetts Volunteers, recalled later that "[n]ever shall we forget that night of waiting."[1] Secrecy was an impossible objective, as the troops had received an inkling of it beforehand and the order to be ready revealed as much as the company officers knew at the time. Sometime after 10:00 P.M., the first division was relieved by the black troops of the Eighteenth Corps. They lined up, filled their cartridge and cap boxes with ammunition, topped off their canteens from the adjacent wells, and stuffed three days' worth of cooked rations into their haversacks.[2] The operation was underway!

As a measure to compensate for a dirth of good brigade commanders, Burnside had recently consolidated Ledlie's division of ten regiments into two large brigades. Consistent with his chronic poor judgment, Ledlie had decided to initiate the assault with his second brigade, led by Colonel Elisha Marshall, who had just recently recovered from serious wounds suffered at the head of an attacking column on June 17. Marshall's command consisted of one battered battalion from Maryland, an incomplete New York regiment with but a single day of combat experience, and two thoroughly demoralized regiments of heavy artillery. Even their comrades in the first division noticed the artillerymen's aversion to this sort of work. In an appraisal eerily similar to Burnside's private comment regarding the "heavies," made after the bungled assault on June 17, one regimental historian remarked simply that the men "had not enlisted for it." They were a rather dejected lot by this time. "Until a couple of hours before, these soldiers had expected Ferrero's black regiments to lead the charge: they themselves entertained only the vaguest notion of what was expected of them, and they had little confidence in James Ledlie," who had been in command of the division for only for six weeks.[3] For that matter, Ledlie had little confidence in himself. He had been working hard to have his resignation from the army accepted, perhaps to evade further combat, as well as the humiliation of seeing his commission expire unconfirmed by the Senate for a second time. On the eve of his last battle, he again "relied upon a heavy draught of artificial courage." "In a few hours this bilious brigadier would come to epitomize the weakness in Ambrose Burnside's laissez-faire style of management: a little meddling on Burnside's part would have been most welcome just now."[4]

Burnside's plan for the massing his corps for the attack on the Salient was for Potter's second division to mass to the right, or south, of the covered way on Ledlie's left, while Willcox's third division would form in the covered way itself and in the railroad cut to the right of Ledlie's division. Ferrero's fourth division was to remain in reserve to the rear of the covered way. Ord's Eighteenth Corps, together with Turner's division of the Tenth Corps, which had recently been attached for this operation, stood ready to support the assault on the right. General Ord had just taken command after Baldy Smith's dismissal earlier that month. On the left, Warren's Fifth Corps was poised on the front lines to take advantage of any success Burnside's men achieved in penetrating the Confederate defenses. Hancock's Second Corps were straggling back into position behind Ord's command after their arduous march back from their role in the aborted move on Richmond. Still farther to the rear, the army's engineers were preparing pontoons in the event the Confederates destroyed the bridges over the Appomattox in their anticipated retreat from Petersburg.

The men were required to leave the front lines under stealth, march to their rear, and then assemble for the movement back to the front opposite the doomed fort at the Salient. Major Charles Houghton of the 14th New York Heavy Artillery reflected that the rank and file knew that important work was immediately ahead for them:

> The men were cautioned to prevent the rattling of tin cups and bayonets, because we were so near the enemy that they would discover our movements. We marched with the stillness of death; not a word was said above a whisper. We knew, of course, that something very important was to be done and that we were to play a prominent part.[5]

The men of the first division marched to what was the widest covered way, which zigzagged to the extreme forward breastworks, which was then commonly referred to as Willcox's covered way. As Marshall's men began their journey back toward the front in the covered way to a ravine in front of Willcox's front line around midnight, Lieutenant William H. Powell described these passageways as "almost as puzzling to the uninitiated as the catacombs of Rome." Having been up all night, the men, as they moved forward, were now in a feverish state of expectancy.[6]

The designated jumping off point for the assault was considered by the division commanders to be inadequate for launching the attack due to its rather small area. When Burnside informed Potter and Willcox of the ground where they were to mass, Potter was immediately skeptical about the amount of space to the right of the covered way for his men to form upon emerging from their designated covered way. Burnside agreed with this assessment but indicated that they would unfortunately have to make do. The area where Ledlie's men were to form was only forty yards deep. They were ordered to be prone and to keep quiet as they emerged into the ravine.

The first brigade of the first division, under Brigadier General William Francis Bartlett, moved back from the front line around midnight[7] and was assembled outside the woods close to the base camp. After the troops had lain on the sandy ground for about one hour, at about 2:00 A.M. they were given instructions and moved out silently and cautiously in a southerly direction, careful to avoid making noise with tin cups, bayonets or canteens. They followed

Interior Confederate works — Petersburg (Library of Congress).

the same route as the second brigade along the rough and narrow army road cut through the piney woods, passing behind Taylor's scorched chimneys and Fort Morton. They were directed through Willcox's covered way to the ravine behind Potter's front lines at the Norfolk and Petersburg Railroad cut. The men were unfamiliar with this stretch of the Union trench work and were entirely disoriented in them.[8] In the 57th Massachusetts Volunteers of Bartlett's brigade, only ninety men remained to answer the call to duty in what had been a "splendid" regiment three months before. Captain Dresser, who had been temporarily acting as ordnance officer, asked to be relieved from this staff duty when he heard his regiment was going into action, even though Albert Prescott, who was his subordinate, had been promoted to major in his absence. This meant Dresser would be serving under one who, until recently, had been his junior in rank. However, such considerations mattered not to Dresser when his unit was entering into harm's way.

Marshall, upon arriving at the jumping off point, formed his brigade into columns of battalion front, with three lines of 400 men each. In the first line was the Provisional 2nd Pennsylvania Heavy Artillery, with Marshall himself in charge. The second line was comprised entirely of the 14th New York Heavy Artillery,[9] new to the Army of the Potomac and already badly beaten up in the campaign, particularly in the June 17 assault. The regiment was so large that it was split into two battalions for the fight, with Captain Lorenzo I. Jones commanding the first and Captain Charles H. Houghton in command of the second. Jones was considered an "officer of fiery zeal, but of no great experience at the time," and the same could also be said for Houghton. Marshall, therefore, placed his adjutant, Captain John Anderson, in charge of the second line of the attack. The third line consisted of the 3rd Maryland Battalion and the 179th New York, led by Lieutenant Colonel G.P. Robinson of the 3rd Maryland, an experienced and competent soldier.

As the second brigade formed in front of the Salient, the first brigade under Brigadier General Bartlett began to arrive out of the covered way. With his brigade consisting of almost all Massachusetts troops, Bartlett divided his organization into two wings. This brigade had recently been reorganized and now consisted of the 21st, 29th, 35th, 56th, 57th and 59th Massachusetts, as well as the 100th Pennsylvania, with the nickname of the "Roundheads." The latter, with 500 men, was the best regiment in the brigade, having just returned from a reenlistment furlough. Bartlett assigned the right wing of the brigade to Colonel J.P. Gould, consisting of the 29th, 57th and 59th Massachusetts, from left to right. The left wing, in turn, was assigned to Colonel Stephen Weld and consisted from left to right of the 100th Pennsylvania, the 56th Massachusetts, and the 21st Massachusetts. This second wing was placed temporarily in the first brigade's second battle rank until it cleared the trenches. Behind the second wing the 35th Massachusetts was assigned duty as the brigade pioneers to assist in clearing away the abatis and other impediments in front of the Confederate works.

The 21st Massachusetts was an old regiment, having fought with Burnside in the North Carolina campaigns, and had remained assigned to him thereafter. The 29th Massachusetts, with a current strength of 125 men, was the oldest of the three year regiments—perhaps the oldest in the country. It had first served six months in the Irish Brigade under McClellan and then had seen hard service at Vicksburg before heading east. The 56th and 57th Massachusetts each had between 200 and 300 men, while the 57th had 97 officers and men, including many new recruits. The 56th, 57th and 59th, comprised mainly of re-enlisted nine-month veterans, were raised in the early months of 1864 and had amassed a good record up to that time.

The 57th Massachusetts and the 29th Massachusetts deployed in regimental lines beside each other immediately to the rear of the 14th New York Heavy Artillery of the second brigade. They were to lead off the first brigade, with the 59th Massachusetts changing position just to the right rear of the 57th Massachusetts. The second brigade and the first line of the first brigade consisting of the 57th and 29th Massachusetts laid down in tight double ranks with their file closers on the flanks in the extremely tight area of formation, barely forty yards in depth, leaving only very narrow intervals between the lines. Given the extremely tight conditions of this formation area, the 21st, 56th, 59th Massachusetts and the 100th Pennsylvania were unfortunately forced to lie down still inside the covered way, packing themselves tightly against the walls, waiting in front of the Salient at the point of assembly. The exact order in which the regiments stood inside the covered way was uncertain.[10] There the men of the first division waited, tense and uneasy in the thick, dusty air:

> Their morale was at rock bottom, and they cursed their orders to lead the assault. All along, around every flickering campfire, the rumor had been that the 4th Division was to lead the charge, and the white soldiers felt it deeply that, once again, they were to be sacrificed for the blacks' emancipation while the Negro regiments would remain, once again, safely in the rear — or so the soldiers thought.

Added to this despair was the fact that the first division no longer had any confidence in their commander. He had thrown them to the wolves once too often, "and they knew intuitively that today would be no exception." Adding to the discomfort, the men of the first division were rightfully concerned that they were so close to the doomed fort that they might be atomized right along with the Confederate foes opposite them.[11]

General Potter had met with his brigade commanders and directed them as to where to mass their troops. The plan was for the entire division to mass between the railroad and the advance line of works on the right-hand side of the northernmost covered way, which he often referred to as "his" covered way in subsequent reports and testimony. The whole division was to have been formed "left in front to move forward by the flank, so that when ... [the] troops had passed the line of the enemy's intrenchments by fronting their front would be to the right," in order to enable it to cover the main assault on the right. The divisions of Ledlie and Willcox were to move out prior to this under Burnside's revised plan. Recognizing that this would hinder his division from moving forward for a long time, Potter ordered Brigadier General Simon G. Griffin to move down his covered way and put out a line of skirmishers to the right of the fort. In such a manner, Griffin would be in position to move in simultaneously on the right of Ledlie's assault, without the necessity of waiting for the other divisions to clear. These men were in place by 2:30 A.M. on the 30th. Potter did not, however, communicate this change in plans to Burnside. In addition to the question of whether there was enough room for the three divisions to mass in front of the Salient, Potter was likewise concerned about the topography to the west of his front. The troops would be forced to pass through a wooded ravine and swamp on their way to the Confederate works. These natural obstructions could cause considerable delay and result in disorganization of the ranks when passing through them. Thus, he believed that greater success could be achieved by attacking farther to the right, and he massed his troops in order to set up such a movement.

Colonel Zenus R. Bliss' first brigade was to be held in their trenches immediately in front of the mine and extending around to the railroad, and was to have been relieved by a division of Ord's corps under General Joseph Carr. This was the third division, consisting of seven regiments of colored troops. At about 2:45 A.M., General Carr himself came up and informed Potter that part of his division, its second brigade, had gotten lost. A portion of Carr's men, two small regiments under Colonel Samuel A. Duncan, subsequently relieved Bliss's line to the right at midnight, which formed with the second brigade in the front.[12] He cleared the trenches immediately in front of the Confederate fort, leaving a strong picket line there. Frederick E. Cushman of the 58th Massachusetts remembered being relieved by the colored troops at midnight, then moving cautiously to the breastworks in the woods through a long covered way which led from the trenches to the front: "There, the men turned in for the night, only to be awakened at 1 A.M. with orders to 'fall in' and move to the left and take position behind a covered way and wait for further orders."

Then, at 3:00 A.M., General Carr finally returned, indicating that he had found the rest of his command and that they would be up in a half hour to relieve the rest of Bliss's brigade. Potter told Carr that it was too late to make the change, given the scheduled time for springing the mine. He therefore indicated that he would charge forward from his present location instead of the designated locus, with the remaining portion of Bliss' brigade. The 7th Rhode Island of the division was designated to act as engineers, and was in the breastworks with their tools, ready to prepare the breastworks for the passage of field batteries in the event the initial assault was successful. [13]

General Potter was under orders not to engage at least two regiments into the action. One of these was the 36th Massachusetts Volunteers, which had not been relieved from duty in the front trenches; it remained on duty in that line between the railroad on the right and the ravine on the left. The other regiment which was excluded from participation in the coming assault was the 48th Pennsylvania, which was by this time utterly spent from its arduous task of digging the mine and preparing it, in large measure without any outside assistance. Rather, Potter assigned the unit as the provost guard for the division. Resting on the satisfaction of a job well done did not appeal to the 48th's energetic commander, however. Colonel Pleasants instead volunteered to serve on Potter's staff on the day of the assault, where he could be in the thick of things.[14]

Potter then established his headquarters at a clump of trees near the batteries on the right of his covered way.[15] Robert Brown Potter was born in 1829 and attended Union College in Schenectady, New York, and practiced law in New York City until the outbreak of the war. After initially enlisting as a private, he was commissioned a major in the 51st New York Infantry and was rapidly promoted to lieutenant colonel. He served under Burnside in North Carolina and then as colonel of the 51st New York at Antietam, where he subsequently got his troops across Burnside's Bridge after several failed attempts. He commanded a division during the siege at Vicksburg and, briefly, the entire Ninth Corps at Knoxville. When the Ninth Corps then returned east in the spring of 1864, Potter was given command of the second division.

Burnside's directive to Orlando Willcox, commander of the third division, was "to occupy his covered way and such positions of the railroad cut as was necessary," with room for Ledlie on his right. Pursuant to these orders, the division's sergeants moved quietly among the men of the third division, prodding them awake: "The men rolled to their feet, grumbling and growling. They had slept in the open under a fringe of trees, without tents or blankets, their arms and knapsacks at their sides. But the grass was soft, the night warm and still. The Third had slept in worse places."

The men of the Third Division were preparing for another epoch movement, desperately hoping for a means to shorten the war and its continuous bloodletting. They were tired of the war. The wind from the east brought the smell of the backwaters and salt marshes of the inlets of the James, a mere five miles distant. This was an alien smell to the midwesterners accustomed to the tanginess of the pine and tamaracks of the Michigan forests:

> As eyes became accustomed to the dark, they began to discern familiar outlines. Directly ahead, on slightly rising ground, stood the solid bulk of Fort Morton, one of the several strong points in the Federal lines composed of an intricate net of connecting trenches, rifle pits and bomb shelters. Beyond, but hidden by the gradual works—the first line, which at places almost touched the Confederate defenses.

The crest of a low hill, four hundred yards distant, was faintly visible. This prominent location was crowned by a cemetery where for many years before the war the people of Petersburg were buried. Now, it was the prime objective of the day's critical assault, in which the division was to play a prominent role.

From the rear the cooks came up, carrying huge kettles of steaming coffee. Here and there a man dug into his knapsack for a piece of hardtack. However, most of the troops had no interest in food. There were knots of nervousness in their stomachs. Some men pulled out their watches. It was by then 4:00 A.M. The day was July 30, 1864, and the division was about to embark on a gamble, which unfortunately was destined to end in "dismal failure and spread an ineradicable stain of Michigan blood on the red soil of Virginia."[16] Brigadier General John Hartranft formed his brigade in the rear and left of the first division in one or two regiment fronts (having put two small regiments together). Hartranft's brigade consisted of the 8th and 27th Michigan (with first and second companies of Michigan sharpshooters attached) under Captain Edward S. Leadbeater, the 109th New York under Captain Edwin Edwards, the 13th Ohio Dismounted Cavalry under Colonel Noah H. Hixon, the 51st Pennsylvania under Colonel William J. Bolton and the 37th and 38th Wisconsin (five companies) under Colonel Samuel Harriman and Lieutenant Colonel Colbert K. Pier, respectively. His instructions were that, after his force passed through the crater created by the explosion, he was to form to the left of the first division, protecting its left flank while they were advancing, and to form his own line of battle on its left.[17]

Colonel William Humphrey, commanding the second brigade of the third division, moved his troops into the covered way "leading by the right of Roemer's Battery to the front" before daylight on the 30th. The second brigade consisted of the 1st Michigan Sharpshooters under Captain Elmer C. Dicey and the 2nd Michigan under Captain John L. Young, along with the 24th New York Cavalry (Dismounted) under Lieutenant Colonel Walter C. Newberry, and the 46th New York under Captain Alphons Serviere. It also consisted of the 60th Ohio (9th and 10th companies of sharpshooters attached) under Major Martin Avery and the 50th Pennsylvania under Lieutenant Colonel Edward Overton, Jr. The 17th Michigan under Colonel Constant Luce acted as engineers for the division. Luce's orders were to wait in the covered way until Hartranft's brigade moved forward from the ground where they had formed and then move to this area and form his own brigade. His brigade was to then follow Hartranft's as closely as possible, and on passing through the Rebel lines, to take a position to Hartranft's right, "forming the connection between him and the left of the First Division." At 4:00 A.M. the troops left the

BG Robert B. Potter (Library of Congress).

bivouac area, minus knapsacks, and then halted in the covered way near Roemer's battery, there to await the springing of the mine and forward movement of the third division. The regimental commanders finally learned of the plan for springing the mine and their precise role at about 3:00 that morning.[18]

Orlando Bolivar Willcox was born in Detroit, Michigan, in 1823, and graduated from West Point in 1847. A veteran of the Mexican and Seminole wars, he later resigned his commission to practice law. With the advent of war, he reentered the army as Colonel of the 1st Michigan Infantry, which participated in the capture of Alexandria at the start of the conflict. While leading a brigade in Heintzelman's division at First Manassas, he was captured and held prisoner for over one year. Upon his release in August 1862, Willcox was commissioned a brigadier general of volunteers retroactive to the day of his capture. He was given command of the first division of Burnside's Ninth Corps, and led the division at Antietam, Fredericksburg and Knoxville, among other significant battles. From April to June 1863, he commanded the entire Ninth Corps. He moved east with the Ninth Corps in early 1864, and, as Burnside's most experienced commander, assumed command of the third division.[19] On the eve of this critical battle, after the plans were changed at the eleventh hour, Willcox definitely desired more than one night to prepare "for one of the most difficult feats to perform in the art of war," which had failed the year before at Vicksburg, in the Netherlands, in the Crimea, and in almost every siege where it was attempted. Normally, such desperate attempts were limited to gaining or destroying some important part of the enemy's works.[20] But Willcox was not to have the time or further input into the impending assault, other than to play his part, which was to place his men in harm's way for the sake of victory.

The fourth division began to pull out of line at nightfall, moving to the open ground near a belt of woods in front of Fort Morton. The 43rd USCT of Colonel Joshua K. Sigfried's first brigade led the advance to the left of the entrance to the covered way leading to the advanced line in front of the targeted Salient. As the white divisions continued to crowd into the ditches, and filled the covered ways leading forward, the fourth division massed on the open hillside below the ruins of the Taylor House, near the mouth of both covered ways. All around "could be heard the shuffling tread of the troops, but it was so dark that nothing could be seen." Lieutenant Freeman S. Bowley recalled halting in the massing area listening to the spent bullets droning overhead as the unit lay down and soon was asleep. Bowley's unit was on the front line entrenchments about half a mile from the railroad on the Ninth Corps' extreme left, which it connected with the Fifth Corps, and was one of the last regiments to be relieved by the white troops of the Eighteenth Corps. Sergeant Joseph H. Payne of the 27th USCT held a prayer service which was "short but not without good and lasting impressions being made upon the hearts and minds of many."[21]

At this point, the rank and file of the fourth division incredibly were still laboring under the impression that theirs was the honor of leading the assault in a few hours. They had continued their careful preparation and training up until they moved into position on the 29th. They were in good physical shape, with regiments at full strength and eager to prove themselves and their morale had never been higher. Only the day before, the 19th USCT had been drilled by Major Rockwood in forming double columns and charging, in preparation for their big day. Brigadier General Ferrero learned that his division was not to lead the charge — and, in fact, was to move in only after the three white divisions of the corps — only when he arrived at the jump area around Fort Morton after 7:00 P.M. and assumed command of the division again. In fact, the brigade commanders themselves learned of the change sometime after 11:00 P.M. on the 29th, when Colonel Thomas was "officially informed that the whole plan had been changed, and our division would not lead." He returned to the bivouac area "dejected and with an instinct of disaster for the morrow." He and his men were "keenly disappointed at losing an opportunity to prove themselves to the remainder of the Army of the Potomac. Nevertheless, they loyally took position behind Potter's Second Division in the darkness and waited for the new orders."

As most of the line officers and men were asleep when the brigade commanders came back to the bivouac area, they were not apprised of the change in plans until early the morning of the 30th as the battle was due to commence. Colonel H. Seymour Hall of the 43rd USCT in Sigfried's brigade indicated later that no "hint of change of plans had reached" him that night and he never heard of any change "till the morning of July 30," when Sigfried came to him in person with two or three of his staff officers and ordered Hall to "[b]e ready to advance when I order you formed, with muskets loaded, but not capped, bayonets fixed, and when the order is given, move your regiment by the flank, through the covered way over our outer works, directly to and through the breach made by the mine, form line beyond, and strike for the cemetery."[22] The men of the fourth division spent the night and early morning hours in the area adjacent to the Taylor House.

Upon learning of the change in plans, the men of the fourth were very disappointed and bitter, to say the least. Captain James Rickard of the 19th USCT related that "we had expected we were to lead the assault, and had been for several weeks drilling our men with this idea in view, particular attention being paid to charging." He related that "there was not an officer but would have staked everything that we would break through their lines and go to Cemetery Hill, as proposed." Rickard was confident that had "the plan been followed no doubt the war would have been ended on that day."[23]

Early the next morning, Lieutenant Fred A. Chapman of the 29th USCT recalled that everyone "felt the danger awaiting him, and there was unusual silence. All seemed occupied with their own thoughts." Colonel Thomas joined his staff for a soldier's breakfast of "Hardtack with a slice of raw, fat salt pork between — not a dainty meal, but solid provender to fight on," all of which was moistened with black coffee from their canteens. As a special treat, Thomas had a bottle of cucumber pickles which he shared with his staff. At daybreak, having formed by division in the timber in the rear of the covered way, the fourth division was to move in rear and left of the third division. Ferrero's new orders were to move forward immediately following Willcox's until he reached the advance line, and to remain there until the ground in his front was entirely cleared by the other divisions. At that point, he was to move forward over the same ground over which Ledlie had just moved, passing through the Federal line, and if possible, moving down to occupy the city to the right.[24]

Upon being relieved by Mott's division of the Second Corps, General Ord moved his three divisions of the Eighteenth Corps and Brigadier General John W. Turner's second division of the Tenth Corps south to support Burnside pursuant to Meade's orders. Ord's first and third divisions of the Eighteenth Corps were placed in the trenches of Burnside's front, relieving portions of his command to mass for the assault. Meade had indicated that Burnside could begin moving troops out of the trenches before Ord's men came up. This division had been relieved in the trenches on the 29th, issued rations and cartridges and told to be ready to march at a moment's notice. Between 8:00 and 9:00 P.M., it began to march along the rear lines toward the left. Soon after midnight, however, it halted behind the trenches near the railroad in an open wood, and the men were told to make themselves comfortable. With this invitation, the men lay down and were soon fast asleep. The second division, under Brigadier General Adelbert Ames, and Turner's division of the Tenth Corps were both placed in Burnside's rear as reserve supports and were instructed to await Burnside's orders as to where they were needed.

The Eighteenth was designated to support the Ninth when it had effected a lodgment on the crest of Cemetery Hill, whereupon Ord was to move his men up and support the other troops on the crest. Meade had met with Ord several times on the 28th and 29th, and had pointed out his position on the exact ground and furnished him all the intelligence available to the Army of the Potomac. Turner moved his division on the evening of the 29th to a point in front of the Ninth Corps where the covered way commenced. There he was to hold his division "in hand till ... [he] received further orders, which ... [he] might expect as soon as the mine was sprung and the assault made." His division was to follow the Ninth Corps, move off to the right and cover the movement on Cemetery Hill on its right flank. In the event the assault did not take Cemetery Hill, his division would "probably not be brought into the engagement." Turner carefully reviewed the route he was to take, especially through the woods, to arrive at the point where he was to mass his division. He had asked Burnside if any other troops were to pass over this same road during the night and was informed that Ledlie's first division would be the only troops on the road. Turner had a keen sense for the confusion encountered in moving troops in the dark and wanted no mistake which could impair his being in proper position at the time the attack was to be made. After nightfall he withdrew his troops from the trenches and moved them to a point just in the rear of where he was to mass them, where the road led into the woods. There he halted and waited for Ledlie's division to pass, which Burnside had assured him was the only other division to be on the road. He had been told to wait for Ledlie, and that once the first division had passed nothing would impair his taking up his position.

After waiting for a time, he dispatched a staff officer to Ledlie's headquarters to ascertain when the first division moved, as it was quite dark and thus difficult to distinguish troops, and even more so to identify their division. However, it was not until 2:00 A.M. when Ledlie's division commenced passing, leaving Turner with the thought that "it was pretty late for that division to pass to get into its position to move out at the time designated (at half past three) to make the assault, knowing the difficulties of the road." When Ledlie had passed, Turner immediately moved his division to the designated point, that being the commencement point of the covered way which led to the immediate front, through which all the troops had to pass. At daylight, Turner reported to Ord that his troops were in place in the woods, some 500 to 600 yards in the rear of where Potter's men were massed. Here they massed fifteen columns deep behind the Ninth Corps. There were now close to 50,000 Union troops ready and awaiting the springing of the mine as a signal to commence their grand assault.[25]

As the rest of Hancock's Second Corps began to arrive from north of the James, along with two divisions of Sheridan's cavalry, they were to position themselves in support of Mott's division on the right, which had just relieved the Eighteenth Corps in the trenches. Hancock was to be prepared to "follow up the assaulting and supporting columns, or for such other operations as may be found necessary." The two divisions arrived in time for the springing of the mine. All three of Sheridan's divisions were to make an assault on the Weldon Railroad from the southwest. However, Sheridan's two divisions from the Deep Bottom diversion could not cross the James until after the Second Corps, and consequently it was late in the day when they came up. General James Wilson, commanding Sheridan's third division, was ordered to be in readiness, and in view of the unavoidable delay of Sheridan's troops, orders were sent to Wilson not to await Sheridan's arrival but rather to push on himself to the Weldon Railroad on the western defenses, from the south and west roads. A minor attack was subsequently made at Lee's Mill, but none on the railroad itself. Most of Warren's Fifth Corps massed on Burnside's left, ready to exploit his success. Brigadier General Romeyn B. Ayres' second division was massed on the right of the Fifth Corps, on the left of the Ninth Corps in the railroad cut, in order to carry out Meade's order for concentrating the Fifth Corps on the right and holding them in preparation to support the assault. Ayres was directed by Warren to make his headquarters with the five gun battery in the corner of the woods in front of the Avery house. Warren's orders were to attack if he could "see a good chance to attack; ... [later, when asked,] he reported no chance to attack, and was asked what force he had available, he reported that he had no force available except [if] he moved Ayres...." By this time, he was instructed not to move him.[26]

This frenzied movement was not limited to the troops designated to take part in the assault. Fort Morton, as it came to be called, was 600 yards behind the front lines and afforded a panoramic view of the mined fort and the surrounding topography. It had been constructed by Potter's troops near the ruins of the Taylor house behind Taylor's Creek, and contained fourteen embrasures protecting fourteen Federal guns in place as of July 26. Burnside announced on the 29th that he was moving his headquarters there for the operation against the Confederate works. Meade then decided to shift his own headquarters from a protected point in the center of the army's rear lines on a knoll behind the Dunn house, near Harrison's Creek to Burnside's headquarters, on a knoll behind the Dunn house, near Harrison's Creek. Burnside's tent was still erect there. This positioned Meade three-quarters of a mile closer to the scene, though he was still a mile from the Salient. Unfortunately, the location was plagued with poor visibility, which disappointed his staff. Theodore Lyman, one of Meade's aides, commented that "you can see nothing from here." Meade's staff arrived at the location just after Burnside's departure, at almost the appointed time for the springing of the mine. To secure speedy communication of intelligence, Meade "took the precaution to have a telegraph run from ... [his] headquarters, in General Burnside's camp, to where General Burnside had established his headquarters for the day, in the 14-gun battery."[27] This last measure was to spell trouble for Burnside before the day was out.

Henry Hunt had spent two days in early July touring the front with Major Duane with a view towards supporting the breakthrough on Burnside's front following the detonation of the mine. Their finds were that a successful offensive could be conducted against the Salient, but only if enough heavy cannon could be focused on Confederate flanking batteries north of the Ninth Corps' position, as well as the salient and batteries in front of the Fifth and Eighteenth corps. Hunt had Colonel Henry L. Abbot of the First Connecticut Heavy Artillery, who was in charge of the siege train, bring up not only additional cannon, but also more 10-inch mortars and 8-inch guns, all for use in the Fifth and Ninth corps sectors.

Additional Coehorn mortars were also sent for, until virtually all of the Confederate line was susceptible to vertical fire. Soon thereafter, Abbot succeeded in lining the works with 30-pounder Parrotts, 4.5 inch rifles, more heavy and light mortars, and "various other instruments of death," in addition to the *Dictator* located behind the Eighteenth Corps lines. However, Hunt was unsuccessful in reining in the power of the individual corps commanders over their artillery units. In late June, Grant had instructed that Hunt would thereafter possess authority over all siege operations south of the Appomattox, which encompassed all forces around Petersburg except the corps at Bermuda Hundred under Butler. However, due to Meade's failure to support him, Hunt was unsuccessful in gaining full control over the artillery at the individual corps level. Recognizing that Grant generally deferred to Meade whenever possible, and particularly when it involved the Army of the Potomac, Hunt did not refer the controversy to the commanding general: "Thenceforward, he exercised control over only Abbot's siege batteries, not the artillery still attached to the several corps."[28]

By the eve of the assault, Hunt had worked wonders with the artillery support. There were some eighty-one siege guns and mortars, in addition to, in his estimation, over eighty field cannon trundled into position. "Armed and fully manned, each weapon, from the smallest Coehorn to the seventeen thousand-pound mortar on its flatcar, prepared to subject the enemy lines to the most concentrated barrage ever unleashed." Hunt's hands were all over the operation. As Theodore Lyman of Meade's staff later remarked, Hunt had "been everywhere and arranged his artillery like clockwork; each chief of piece knew his distances and his directions to an inch," all with the objective of silencing the Confederate artillery, especially those bearing on the ground in front of the mine.[29] Abbot's troops, including Companies A, B, C, D, F, G, I, and M of the First Connecticut Heavy Artillery and Companies C, H, and K of the 4th New York Artillery, consisted of eighty-one guns and mortars interspersed throughout the six mile line of entrenchments. Henry Matrau, a soldier of the 6th Wisconsin of the Second Corps, wrote home after rejoining the siege on the night of the 29th in the vicinity of the trenches occupied by the Eighteenth Corps:

> [t]o give you an idea of the noise we had, I will tell you the number of guns, & c, we had in the line of our brigade alone. There were 12 mortars, 24 pounders's, 12 brass 12 pound Napoleons guns, 6 iron, 10 pound rifled guns, and seven 32 pounder rifled siege guns in the rear of us that threw shells directly over our heads, beside big Cohorn iron mortars on each flank.[30]

Colonel Charles S. Wainwright, commanding the Fifth Corps Artillery Brigade, which included two batteries of the Sixth Corps, reported that he commanded fifty-two fieldpieces (twenty-four 12 pounders and twenty-eight rifled guns) and seventeen siege guns and mortars (six 4.5 inch siege guns and eleven Coehorns) in the action, not counting a further number held in reserve. Lieutenant Colonel J. Albert Monroe, commanding the Ninth Corps

Artillery, reported that he had thirty fieldpieces (twenty rifled guns and ten 12 pounders) as well as six Coehorns ready for action apart from Abbott's guns. Colonel Alexander Piper, chief of artillery, Eighteenth Corps, reported that his front included sixteen fieldpieces (six rifled guns and ten 12 pounders), and four 20-pound Parrotts in addition to Abbott's guns in the sector. Thus, in addition to Abbot's eighty-one siege guns and mortars, the individual corps engaged in the action appeared to have a total of ninety-eight field guns and an additional twenty-seven siege guns and heavy mortars ready for the assault. There was a total of over 200 guns trained on Elliott's Salient, the batteries defending the forts and the troops, and on the city of Petersburg itself.[31]

By sunup on "D-Day," Hunt had issued detailed instructions to all artillerymen in Burnside's front and on his flanks, listing targets in order of priority and suggesting the best methods of achieving maximum effect in laying down a supporting barrage for the Ninth Corps' assault. The fire was to be directed at the fort and works on each side of the Salient, as well as preventing reinforcements from coming up following the explosion. Many of the Fifth and Sixth corps' batteries were focused on the Confederate batteries along Jerusalem Plank Road or against those in the works near the fort. Grant had signal towers built overlooking the Rebel positions and at the proper time observers were to direct artillery to concentrate fire on every gun in the Confederate line which could be used for the defense of the Salient.[32]

The men on the opposite side of the trenches were spread dangerously thin as a result of Grant's Deep Bottom diversion toward Richmond. Lee had been forced to treat the movement as a wholesale attack on the capital, requiring the rapid deployment of troops to check the advance. This action left only three divisions remaining in the Petersburg trenches on July 29. Lee's men at Deep Bottom were unaware that Hancock and Sheridan had hastily withdrawn from their immediate front and were in the process of rejoining the Union lines at Petersburg. Only Hoke's and Johnson's divisions of Beauregard's Department of North Carolina and Southern Virginia, and Anderson's division of A.P. Hill's III Corps, currently commanded by Brigadier General William Mahone, a total of approximately 13,000 to 18,000 men (depending on whether all of Willcox's division had been sent away), were left in the trenches to face an advance which could encompass over 50,000 men. Hoke's division held from the Appomattox River to east of Blandford Cemetery. Bushrod Johnson's troops held from the right of Hoke's flank to where the Jerusalem Plank Road met the Confederate works southeast of Rives' Salient. Brigadier General Alfred H. Colquitt's brigade of Hoke's division, temporarily assigned to Johnson as of July 28, was in the line on the right of Henry Wise's Virginia Brigade, joining with the left of Anderson's Division under Mahone (for simplicity's sake, hereinafter referred to as "Mahone's division"), the right of the division being approximately one and one half miles from Elliott's Salient. One of Mahone's brigades was a full four miles to the right on the Weldon Railroad. Bushrod Johnson's division, in the center of the line, near the mined fort, had Ransom's North Carolina Brigade under Colonel Lee M. McAfee to the north, extending northward from the field in front of the Blandford Cemetery, followed by Stephen Elliott's South Carolina Brigade, then followed by Wise's Virginia Brigade under Colonel J. Thomas Goode, which began and extended southward to just where the line crossed the Jerusalem Plank Road.[33]

Elliott's front itself was one third of a mile long, with Wise's brigade on the right and Ransom's on the left. The distance to Wise was 200 yards and to Ransom, approximately 400 yards. There was a gradual dip toward Ransom's Brigade and a rather rapid dip toward Wise's unit. The regiments of Elliott's brigade were positioned in the trenches with the 26th South Carolina on the far left, followed by the 17th, 18th, 22nd South Carolina, with the 23rd South Carolina on the far right. The various companies in Elliott's regiments had been formed with interesting names, such as the Mounted Guards, the Catawba Light Infantry and Broad River Guards of the 18th South Carolina, the Indian Land Tigers, and Carolina Rifles of the 17th South Carolina. The fort containing Pegram's battery sat directly in between the 17th and 22nd South Carolina, with the 18th South Carolina, together with a portion of the 22nd positioned directly in and about it, and contained a total of 300 men on the night of July 29. The 22nd extended out some seventy yards beyond the right gun in the battery. Captain Richard Pegram had an additional thirty gunners in the fort, comprising a part of Major Coit's battalion.[34] Captain John Reed of the 8th Georgia, which had rotated out of the fort a few days before, later remembered that "[s]omehow I have always regretted that we missed that wild morning."[35] Samuel Catawba Lowry of Yorkville, South Carolina, a soldier with the 17th South Carolina, wrote his family on July 20 in the trenches that "[i]t is feared the enemy are tunneling under our lines, and as right in front is the most favorable spot for such works, and as a battery is also here, we are preparing for such a device by digging a tunnel all along the whole face of the battery to meet theirs, if they have any."[36]

Ransom's North Carolina Brigade was located on part of a "haphazard" line which ran north and south along the western edge of woodland, and the men, when in line, faced east toward the Union line. It consisted of the 24th, 25th, 34th, 49th, and 56th North Carolina regiments. The Tarheels had made their stand in June to the south where Elliott's Salient now stood. Wise's Virginia Brigade to the south of Elliott consisted of the 26th, 34th, 46th and 59th Virginia Infantry regiments. The 34th Virginia had taken some good-hearted ribbing from the veterans in the brigade for its lack of preparedness for the harsh warfare, which the other regiments in the brigade had long experienced. It used to be the 4th Virginia Heavy Artillery, and, like the transformed heavy artillery units in the Army of the Potomac, had previously enjoyed a less dangerous duty in the defensive works about Richmond.

Ransom and Wise's troops could fire obliquely at an enemy force attacking the Salient. Elliott's front had a line of picket trenches in front connected by covered ways, only 113 yards from the Union lines at their closest. A covered way ran back to the Jerusalem Plank Road (in fact, it passed under it and on to the valley of Lieutenant Run to the west). The dip on Ransom's side favored the construction of the trench, for the branch that caused the dip came up from the lines and branched at the mouth of the covered way, one branch turning south and making a depression, or swale, between the crest of the Salient and the Jerusalem Plank Road. Wise and Ransom could look across Elliott's front and observe each other's positions. The inward, or reentrant, curve was slight, but definitely intentional. The enfilade it provided for Elliott's weak front was a definite mastermind of Colonel Harris' engineering skills.[37]

When Beauregard learned of the Union mining operations, he had immediately ordered a trench dug just behind Pegram's battery, the trench commonly referred to as a gorge or cavalier line. Elliott was ordered to man the line in the event of an explosion in his lines. Reinforcements could be brought in through the covered way up to this line in a formation at least two brigade fronts wide, as Mahone later demonstrated. The cavalier line was approximately seventy-five feet in the rear of the supporting earthworks of the redan. It was a wide ditch with the bank thrown up on the side next to the fortifications, and was constructed to protect parties carrying ammunition and rations to the troops, to be manned as a fall back position in the event of an explosion. The embankment from the bottom of the ditch was about ten feet high and commanded the outer, or main, line. The space from the outside of the fortifications to the inner edge of the ditch was more than one hundred feet.

Captain Richard G. Pegram had placed four Napoleons belonging to the Virginia battery of Major James C. Coit's (Branch's) artillery battalion in the redoubt at the Salient.[38] Coit's overall command consisted of three batteries of four guns each, in addition to Pegram's: Bradford's Mississippi battery with four 20-pounder Parrotts, Wright's Halifax (Virginia) battery, consisting of four 12-pound Napoleons and Kelley's South Carolina battery, which was not present at the time. Bradford's battery was on the north side of the Appomattox opposite Federal Battery No. 1. The artillery was concentrated in order to defend the weak nature of the Salient. Batteries ran in a horseshoe curve from Wright's Battery on Ransom's line to the "Two-Gun" battery, as it came to be known on Wise's front, although on July 30 only one gun was operated. It was said at the time that "not a chicken could pass to the Plank." A total of fifty-two guns and mortars bore on the field that fateful day in July.[39]

Haskell's battalion, under the command of Major John C. Haskell, was positioned just west of the Jerusalem Plank Road, some 800 yards from the Salient. The unit was a part of the I Corps artillery temporarily under the command of Lieutenant Colonel Frank Huger in Porter Alexander's absence, following his wounding on June 30. Haskell had lost his right arm at Gaine's Mill in 1862 but none of his fighting spirit. Mahone considered him a brilliant soldier, "always hunting a place where he could strike a blow at our adversary." Haskell kept part of his command in the west side of a ravine which paralleled the Jerusalem Plank Road. In this area, the plank road was sunken to about five feet below the ordinary surface, which afforded very effective protection for the batteries, and a number of gun pits had been constructed in front of the road. The covered way in this area extended across the road and into the ravine, allowing for protection for the gun crews. The area was "a beautiful place for an ambuscade of artillery & infantry."

Alexander had previously positioned fourteen of Haskell's guns in this area. Another four were placed in the earthworks out in front to sweep a hollow out to the Confederate right. These placements included the battery of Captain Henry G. Flanner, which was comprised entirely of North Carolina artillerymen from Company F, 13th Battalion North Carolina, and that of Captain James N. Lamkin's Virginia Light Artillery (Co. B). This unit had been made into sharpshooters because they were unequipped with artillery. However, as soon as Alexander received twelve mortars on June 25, he began to train Lamkin's men in their use. They were soon firing at the huge Union forts arising all along the lines, as well as the strong rifle pits in front of Elliott's Salient. Haskell had received orders to keep two batteries harnessed, with the men sleeping by their guns, thereby allowing for a rapid deployment in the event of an assault.

The 13th Battalion Virginia Light Artillery, consisting of eight of these batteries with 12-pound Napoleons, was also a part of I Corps artillery, under the command of Major Wade Hampton Gibbs. Alexander had recently positioned two guns of Davidson's Virginia Battery out near a path (an extension of Baxter Road) which wound among some shallow hollows up to the front lines, hidden from Union observation some 373 yards to the right and south of the Salient. Lieutenant John H. Chamberlayne had taken temporary, "unofficial" command of Davidson's Virginia Battery on July 28 when the battery's commander, Captain George S. Davidson, was granted a furlough while he awaited his resignation to take effect; Chamberlayne, however, was ill and convalescing in a hospital on July 29. Lieutenant James Otey, next in line of command, had waived his right to promotion, and the other lieutenant, Thomas W. Powell, had failed the promotional examination. Major Gibb thus handpicked Chamberlayne for the position from outside the command. Alexander found what he conceived to be a beautiful place near the end of the path for a whole battery to give the same type of flanking fire which had proven so effective at Cold Harbor. Every shot over the small knolls masking their position would rake the dead space in front of Elliot's Salient. To prevent the gunners from attempting to rotate their guns to shoot at to the Union lines to their right, Alexander

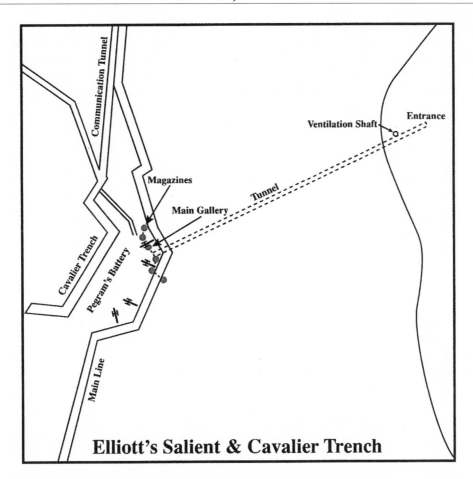

Elliott's Salient & Cavalier Trench

ordered that high and narrow embrasures be constructed for the guns to obscure the view to the right. This forced them to confine their fire exclusively to raking the front of the Salient "where the heart of the fight would be." Alexander had earlier instructed Captain Davidson that in case of an attack, he was to fire rapidly every round he had of shot, shell, shrapnel and canister right straight down the valley. Alexander later confided that "[i]t was near about the very prettiest artillery position I saw in the whole war."

Otey's Battery, considered one of the best in the Army of Northern Virginia, was positioned 473 yards to the south of the Salient and one hundred yards farther to the south from Davidson's Battery. Named for a former commander, Captain George Gaston Otey (wounded in the battle of Lewisburg, West Virginia, on May 23, 1862, and dead from those wounds by October 1862) it was currently commanded by Captain David Norvell Walker. The next two guns in a salient angle 573 yards on the right and south of the Salient, and 200 yards to the south of Davidson's Battery were part of the Ringgold Battery consisting of four 12-pound Napoleons. Interestingly, Lieutenant W.P. Robinson, a member of the Ringgold Battery commanded by Captain Crispin Dickerson, had just recently been sent to relieve Pegram's battery in the Salient. Rather than change out the guns, Dickenson decided to use Pegram's, as the enemy was too close and the guns were all 12-pounder Napoleons in any event. While Pegram's men went to the rear for a well-needed rest, Robinson and the men worked night and day to improve the breastworks, under constant sniping. The Ringgold Battery was then moved to the right of the Salient with their own four Napoleons. The guns were all loaded with a double shot of grape and canister and maintained a position aimed at Elliott's Salient. Together, these batteries completely enfiladed the Federal position, and when the Federals obtained temporary possession of the Crater on July 30, they decimated the attacking troops between the lines, and could also throw shells right on top of the troops in the Crater.[40]

Probably the most important work completed by the Confederates in July in preparation for the defense of the Salient was the erection of a four gun battery to its left and across the covered way ravine. It was in a secondary hollow where it was entirely sheltered from the enemy's observation. It was above the ravine and just to the rear of the main Confederate line behind Ransom's right. This position bore directly on the Salient at very close range, which was the reason for its construction. This battery was manned by the Halifax Artillery of Halifax County, under Captain Samuel T. Wright, a part of Branch's Battalion, commanded by Mayor James C. Coit, the same unit to which Pegram's Battery belonged. This artillery was part of Beauregard's Department of North Carolina and Southern Virginia, and was about one hundred yards behind McAfee's North Carolina Brigade and 555 yards to the northwest of the Salient. The location was positioned by General Gilmer, chief engineer, who took a close interest in all the Petersburg operations.[41]

Lieutenant Colonel William J. Pegram's Battalion (he was a cousin of Richard Pegram) was a part of the III Corps artillery under Colonel Rueben Lindsey Walker, consisting of two batteries of four Napoleons each: Captain Thomas Ellet's Company of Virginia Light Artillery, formerly Crenshaw's company, and the Letcher Artillery, Richmond, also known as Davidson's Company Va. Light Artillery, was commanded by Captain Thomas Alexander Brander. Both Brander and Ellet's units were brought up following the explosion at the Crater through the streets of Petersburg to Johnson's headquarters at 7:00 A.M. and ultimately positioned east of the plank road on Cemetery Hill. However, they were never brought into play in the engagement, although they received scattered shelling during the battle.[42]

The Army of Northern Virginia seldom used secondary lines for artillery defense except at Petersburg, because it rarely had sufficient troops to spare from the front line. Even the second line at Petersburg was built principally as a means of covered communications and was occupied by only a few guns in the rear of the most exposed points of the first line, designed to check the Union troops if they should penetrate the front lines. The Battle of the Crater was the only time when the Confederate lines ever had detached batteries in the rear of a point where the enemy succeeded in obtaining possession of the point. Porter Alexander later reflected that it was an excellent plan to place all the rifled guns in detached batteries in the rear of the exposed points where they could have excellent effect checking the enemy advance.[43]

As the Union prepared to unleash the assault after the springing of the mine, Burnside made several fateful decisions relative to obstacles, natural and otherwise, in his front. Meade's orders of July 29 had specified that Burnside would "prepare his parapets and abatis for the passage of the columns, and have the pioneers equipped for work in opening passages for artillery, destroying enemy's abatis & c., and the intrenching tools distributed for effecting lodgment, & c." Ultimately, a court of inquiry concluded that Burnside failed to obey this order, as well as not employing engineering officers to lead the assaulting columns or providing proper materials necessary for crowning the crest of Cemetery Hill. The extent to which failing to remove his own abatis hindered the operation is open to question; the fact that he did not obey the order is not. The other corps commanders involved in the assault carried out their orders to clear the abatis and parapets for the passage of troops in their front. Only Burnside decided to ignore this direct order from his superior.

Burnside later acknowledged that he clearly had been ordered to "level the breastworks and to remove the abatis before the explosion, so the troops could pass quickly to the front."[44] However, he firmly believed that this "[p]art of the order was necessarily inoperative, because of lack of time and the close proximity to the enemy, the latter of which rendered it impossible to remove the abatis from the front of our line without attracting, not only a heavy fire of the enemy, but also his attention to that point, and letting him know exactly what we were doing."[45] Robert Potter recalled that he had specific orders from Burnside "not to disturb anything immediately in the vicinity of the mine so as not to attract the attention of the enemy to that point." He had his pioneers ready for any orders to remove the obstructions. Instead, he was told to withdraw everything along that line for a space of 200 to 300 yards except a thin line of skirmishers and not to attract the enemy's attention.

Meade was highly critical of Burnside for his disregard of the orders to clear the abatis and make the parapets ready in preparation for the assault, contending that the Federal abatis and the high parapets were quite formidable and needed to be removed to insure the troops could move out rapidly from the front breastworks. Instead, when the time came for the assault, Meade contended there was only a small opening made by which 15,000 men were required to move out by the flank, whereas it should have been large enough to have allowed the whole corps to move out and to have obtained the crest in thirty minutes. While Meade conceded that removing the obstacles would have drawn the enemy's attention, "it was one of the risks which we had to run." Likewise, failing to level the parapets at various locations or constructing a method to rapidly *debouche* certainly caused some delay in the assault. Grant did not believe that removing the abatis would have caused a problem and could have been performed under the cover of darkness, which the Confederates would not have noticed. Gouverneur Warren, on the Federal left, concurred with this assessment, indicating that the obstructions had to be removed at any hazard, the enemy would not have benefited much from the knowledge that an attack was being prepared, and the whole process would have only taken a half hour.[46]

In addition to disregarding the order to clear the Federal abatis and raise the parapets prior to the assault, Burnside also failed to remove a large copse of trees in his front which obstructed the artillery's field of fire to the right. According to Henry Hunt, due to Burnside's stubbornness a "thick grove of trees had been allowed to remain in front of a crucial sector in the IX Corps' front, blocking the field of fire of a fourteen-gun siege battery" he had painstakingly erected. Burnside refused to send men to level the timber, despite Hunt's persistent entreaties, because he was concerned the Confederates, upon hearing the noise, would suspect something was amiss and it would thus alert them to the attack planned at the mine's explosion. The need to remove these trees was raised with Burnside on a number of occasions as being necessary for Hunt's men to "use the battery to advantage." On July 27, working parties were detailed to cut down the trees but they were driven off. Hunt telegraphed Burnside on the 28th, urging him to remove the trees. Captain Pratt of Abbot's command was so desirous of clearing the field of fire that he took out troops at night and cut some of them down; Lieutenant Colonel J. Albert Monroe of the First Rhode Island Artillery, and chief of artillery for the Ninth Corps, also went to Burnside and offered to muster a large party and take down the trees. However, Burnside was adamant that it not be done until after the explosion. This refusal did have considerable consequences, as the trees in question helped to mask Wright's battery, which enfiladed the Federal advance and inflicted a murderous fire, jeopardizing the overall success of the assault.[47]

Meade's orders were also specific regarding pioneers being ready and equipped for work in opening passages for artillery, and for destroying the enemy's abatis, and for entrenching tools to be distributed for effecting lodgments. Burnside failed to order his own engineers to accompany the assault and to assist with the opening of the Confederate works. In fact, he did not even distribute entrenching tools for use on the barren hilltop that was the ultimate objective. Some disputed whether Meade had the Army of the Potomac's engineers available to Burnside. Major Duane testified to the congressional hearing that Burnside took it upon himself to oversee the engineering operation of the Ninth Corps, and that the other corps had engineers assigned to them. In fact, Lieutenant W.H.H. Benyaurd of the U.S. Engineers testified that he was with Burnside on the 30th at Duane's request, but Burnside had not availed himself of any offered assistance from Benyaurd, including the construction of covered ways to the Crater or reducing the Confederate defenses or clearing the abatis. Benyaurd reported that he did not see any tools such as picks, shovels or axes assembled for the operation. Humphreys also reported that Burnside's pioneers were not effectively prepared for their work and no entrenching tools had been distributed.[48]

However, Robert Potter later testified at the court of inquiry that Burnside's verbal orders included that pioneers or the engineer regiment in each division be prepared with tools to prepare the breastworks for passage of field batteries in case the assault were successful. Potter indicated that his own pioneers were ready to carry out these orders. Clearly, Burnside had refused to have his own breastworks prepared for the coming assault and refused to level the copse of trees to insure adequate lines of fire for the artillery before the explosion. There was thus a delay of some undetermined duration while the obstructions were removed to allow the assault to commence and continue. The advancing troops did encounter difficulty in getting through the abatis in their front. General Ames of the Eighteenth Corps suggested that men with shovels go out and throw up rifle pits on the left of the Crater to protect the assaulting force once the battle began. He was told there were no tools available and when they were finally obtained, it was too late.[49]

Except for the usual artillery duels at sundown, the night of July 29 was relatively quiet. The sky was clear and a three-quarter waning moon was rising in the east over the forest which skirted the nearly open area between the opposing forces. All was in place for the impending assault following the springing of the mine. At the mouth of the covered way, Elisha Marshall's brigade, the forlorn hope, awaited the onslaught — two little, battered battalions of infantry and two huge, heavy artillery regiments. It was these "heavies" Burnside had cursed after the bungled assault on June 17, stating then that these heavies "had not enlisted for it." Minus their white cross belts and brass shoulder scales, these parade-field soldiers had been accustomed to service in the forts encircling Washington or on the Carolina coast, carrying out their service polishing the big coastal guns and sleeping in comfortable, wooden barracks. Now, huddled in the dense, heavy air of the Union defenses at Petersburg, almost suffocating in the hot, still air, with eyes stinging from fatigue and the ever-present dust, "these demoralized and disillusioned artillerymen were General Ledlie's choice to carry the Confederate works and Cemetery Hill." Grant had given them rifles and made them infantrymen, but, for many, their hearts were not in it, and they lacked the training necessary to emulate the veteran infantrymen of the old Army of the Potomac. Added to this unhealthy mix was the fact that the rank and file of the division had only contempt for its commander. His regimental commanders and even some of his staff felt him totally incompetent. Such assessments rarely failed to filter their way down to the average soldier, as was the case here.

Thus, standing in the hot, suffocating trenches after a night of shuffling and standing, then bunching up like stockyard cattle at the loading gate, the Ninth Corps were the only troops certain to partake of the morning's bloodbath. By now, veterans dreaded the open battle in a manner which would have undoubtedly been considered cowardly a year before. However, the veterans of a year before had not yet experienced the Wilderness, Spotsylvania, and, most notably, Cold Harbor. They were ready, if not totally willing, to do and die for the war to end. But they were certainly not looking forward to the experience, nor was their commander, James Ledlie. Described by Burnside as "cheerful" at the afternoon's council when informed that his division would lead the assault, those who saw him in the ensuing day would certainly use other adjectives to embody his character and demeanor.

CHAPTER 8

Inferno at Petersburg

As the men of the first division awaited the detonation of the mine and their impending appointment with destiny, many of them looked upon Colonel Pleasants, the mastermind of the mine concept and therefore the inspiration for the instant operation, as he personally manned the parapets awaiting the mine's explosion. Some viewed his nervous examination of his watch in the moonlight as the sign of a rash and irresponsible man who would stop at nothing to bring attention to himself. His gallantry, determination, steadfastness and independence were lost on many of those who were soon to be sacrificed in this latest testament to the high command's determination to win at all costs. The first division had been rather excited with the prospect of blowing up the Salient when it was to be another division which was to go in first. Now the tables were turned and none of the officers of the Army of the Potomac had any idea of the effect of the mine's detonation. Many felt that it was deeply unfair that, once again, they were to be sacrificed for the blacks' emancipation while the black regiments were to remain safely in the rear — or, at least, so they thought. Not surprisingly, "the boys were not eager to be in the position that they were currently occupying":

> Licking their dry lips and restlessly shifting the weight of their bodies around as they impatiently withstood the suspense, apprehension, and anticipation of what they sensed to be their certain death, the soldiers believed that Armageddon was at hand. The Irish cursed their luck on the one hand, and on the other fervently crossed themselves and said their Hail Marys and Our Fathers, as a hedge, while the Protestant comrades silently said their own prayers.[1]

They all nervously awaited the time for their fate to be carried out in the crowded, hot, suffocating area where they awaited the signal to commence their attack.

By the very early morning hours of July 30, the moon was down and it had become extremely dark, so much so that Henry Pleasants needed a candle to enter his mine. With him were Sergeant Reese and Lieutenant Jacob Douty, both of the 48th Pennsylvania. Pleasants took out a match from a tin container, dropped it and took another, struck it on the side of a wooden box and with a burst of acrid smoke, the line of glowing fire crept forward from the three, separate fuses into the pitch-black depths of the gallery. Pleasants said he would give it twenty minutes, as there was over ninety feet of fuse. "Half of that, Colonel, if the fuse is any good," replied Douty, prophetically, as it turned out. The time was 3:15 A.M. The men immediately ran out of the tunnel to await the impending explosion. At 3:20 A.M., Meade informed Burnside that, if it was still dark, revealing a certain ignorance of the detonating process, he could postpone firing the mine if he thought it proper. However, Burnside promptly replied to Meade that he intended to fire the mine at the time designated. It was by then too late to postpone the explosion, even if he had so desired.[2] The word had spread rapidly as Pleasants stood on the breastworks looking at his watch awaiting the explosion. A great ripple of excitement ran through the Union lines, but not enough to overcome the uneasiness of those who would soon be in harm's way:

> For days a rumor had been going around that Army of Potomac Headquarters considered the mine unsafe, had been reluctant to sanction it on grounds that the explosion might spread destruction through the Union lines, and had finally permitted the project to go only after a lot of harangue over something that nobody knew about — the amount of powder that could be used with responsible safety.

It was widely known that Pleasants' requisition of gunpowder had been significantly reduced. There was uneasiness on the part of the soldiers outside the division from those who mistook Pleasants' "boldness and courage for irresponsibility, and judged him out of hand as a brash young officer who would stop at nothing to get himself noticed in Washington." As the men anxiously waited in the trenches, they reflected on the latest gossip circulating among the ranks that the army's top brass thought the mine dangerous. "If something did go wrong, they reasoned, because they were so close to the site of the nearing explosion, they might be atomized right along with the Rebel fort." Just then, a jumpy soldier accidentally

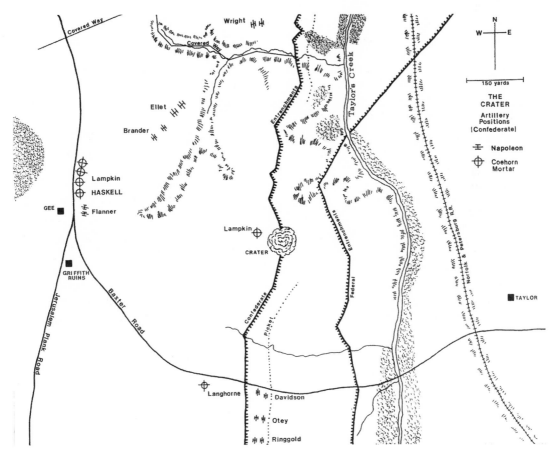

Confederate artillery placements (Blake A. Manger/ H.E. Howard, Inc.).

fired his rifle, sending shock waves through the impatient and edgy ranks. And so, while the fuse continued burning in the tunnel, there was apprehension in the outward wave of excitement shared by the troops. No one knew exactly what would soon take place; time seemed to stand still as the minutes ticked away. On the eastern horizon, the blackness of night was turning gray. Invisible objects were beginning to reveal a suspicion of shape. First Lieutenant William Baird of Company K, 23rd USCT reported that "it was so silent you could almost hear each man's heart beat."[3]

In the deadly silence at 3:30 A.M. "every eye was turned toward the doomed fort, but contrary to our expectations no explosion took place." The cause of this delay "was asked from one to another, no one, of course, being able to give any reason for this unaccountable delay." As the massed troops awaited their fate, no explosion occurred and the east was streaked with gray; "yet the tender beauty of the dim tranquility remained unvexed of any sound of war, save one might hear a low hum amid the darkling swarm as grew the wonder at delay."[4] Given the growing light, the massed troops were ordered to lie down on the ground as a precaution against being seen by the unsuspecting Rebels.[5] Pleasants anxiously watched as the minutes went slowly by without a sign of a successful outcome. He noted with dismay that it was quarter to four. Something was most definitely wrong! Could it be that the powder was too wet and the whole enterprise was doomed? Burnside would be laughed at and Pleasants himself would be totally disgraced. Such thoughts drove him nearly frantic. Pleasants became like a manic — and felt assured he knew the cause of the problem now, and that "those spliced fuses would defeat his great project!" Reese and Douty glanced at Pleasants nervously at the mouth of the mine. Burnside himself grew uneasy at Fort Morton as his watch swept toward 4:00 A.M., and he thus ordered Major James Van Buren of his staff to seek out Pleasants and ascertain the exact cause of the delay. Almost simultaneously, two staff officers from Meade's staff arrived at Fort Morton, seeking the same information. Burnside informed Meade's officers that he was then uncertain as to the problem, and sent yet another officer from his own staff to interview Pleasants.

At about 4:00 A.M., Pleasants rather anxiously started toward the tunnel, but Douty and Reese, already racing ahead of him, reached the entrance first and "volunteered to enter" in his stead. Captain Joseph H. Hoskings of Company F laid a hand on Pleasants and stated, "Stay here, Colonel. Two are enough. Three are too many." However, Pleasants still would not allow them to enter the tunnel until he was positive the fuse had failed. Finally, at about 4:15 A.M., he allowed Reese to crawl in with a lighted lantern. As he approached the adit, Reese indicated that "I'm going into the mine. If it don't blow up, give me time to reach the splice in the fuse and then come to me with fresh fuse and twine." Meanwhile, back at Burnside's headquarters, a dispatch arrived from Meade, who had as yet not heard back from his staff officers. He was extremely anxious to learn if there was going to be an explosion. At the time, Burnside had no idea of the nature of the problem and thus did not send an immediate response to the inquiry. Meade had added to his problems by being "unmindful of the dictum of Napoleon, that 'in assaults a general should always be with his troops,' and had fixed his headquarters full a mile away."[6]

Snapper Reese entered the dark tunnel and soon discovered where the fuse had stopped burning. He found a section of spliced fuse that had been wound too tightly so that the fire had failed to burn through the two spliced sections. As a result, "the fuze had died out about a hundred feet from the mouth of the main gallery. This was a thing that would not have occurred had ... [they] had material enough to have laid four or five fuzes; and ... would [not] have occurred had the fuze been continuous, or in but two or three pieces, instead of being, as it was, in so many pieces. It dried out at one of the points of contact, where two of the

Left: Lieut. Jacob Douty (Gould—*48th Pennsylvania*). *Above:* Sgt. Harry Reese (Gould—*48th Pennsylvania*).

pieces had been spliced together either by the failure to put in powder, or by the powder becoming damp."[7]

He could not relight the fuses without discarding the wads that had caused the problem. However, when he went into his pocket for his knife, he unfortunately found that he had neglected to bring it with him. Reese therefore went toward the mouth of the mine and asked for a knife, indicating that the problem was with the fuse and that he and Douty would fix it. Pleasants immediately declared that "I knew it" through his teeth. "That fuse! All that splicing! Hoskings [Captain Joseph H. Hoskings], sometimes I wonder why the hell ... ," he vented. Douty soon arrived next to Reese with an extra fuse and a knife and they cut away the charred portions of the fuse and made a fresh splice. They relit the fuse again and scrambled out of the tunnel to safety "as the blue flame hissed its way along its charted course toward the deadly black gunpowder kegs."[8]

While these two extremely brave men[9] were in the tunnel relighting the fuse, Pleasants received a message from General Burnside seeking to answer Meade's inquiry of him as to whether there was a problem with the mine. Grant himself had arrived at Meade's temporary headquarters at 4:00 A.M. and requested to know what was wrong with the mine: "General Meade shrugged his shoulders and said 'I don't know — guess the fuse has gone out.' Which was a true guess."[10] As Douty and Reese entered the abyss, Pleasants found the waiting almost unendurable, and as he stood beside Captain Hoskings, every step in the mining operation, "from inception to finish, flashed through his mind." Pleasants took a sheet of paper and scribbled a note to Burnside as to the situation and that the explosion should take place shortly. Meanwhile, at 4:35 A.M., Meade telegraphed Burnside that "if your mine has failed that you make an assault at once [without the detonation], opening your batteries." About this time, Douty and Reese came bursting out of the tunnel covered with mud, choked by fumes, and gasping for breath. Douty reported that "It's all right, Colonel, She's burning." Word quickly spread to the assembled troops to be ready to go. Cries of "On your toes, now!" and "Stand by to charge!" reverberated up and down the crowded lines. Pleasants informed Major James Van Buren at 4:33 A.M., in answer to Burnside's inquiry, that in "eleven minutes now the mine will explode." Looking at his watch, Pleasants indicated that "[i]t lacks a minute yet." Douty cried "Not a second ..." and the mine suddenly erupted at precisely 4:44 A.M.[11]

Pleasants had specifically utilized three separate lines of fuse, commonly referred to as blasting fuse. He had specifically requisitioned safety fuse but the Army had instead sent him common blasting fuse. From where the two lateral galleries joined there were two troughs with fuses in them running from one magazine to the other, half filled with fine powder. From a certain distance therefore there were just the three fuses, without any powder. The fuse as received had been cut into small sizes, which caused great consternation on Pleasants' part. There was little or no certainty about the ignition of powder using these fuses, unless they were spliced. So, quite unfortunately, Pleasants had to splice these small sections of fuse to make one fuse ninety feet long, which burned for about forty feet before it went out. Who was responsible for the failure to provide adequate and acceptable fuse? Burnside said he was told to requisition the fuse from the chief of artillery of the Army of the Potomac, and that he did so at the appropriate time. He informed Hunt of the exact number of feet and quality of fuse needed for the operation and that he "wanted enough to run three or four fuzes in to the charge." Meade later testified that he believed there had been enough material supplied for three fuses, but he was uncertain that had occurred. He did concede that ordinary prudence would have dictated three fuses would have been ignited, so as to secure three charges for the explosion of the mine, instead of one.[12] Meade claimed that the inadequacy of the fuse, such as it was, was no one's fault. Hunt later claimed that he furnished the requested fuses, and it was enough to make three or four lines. "But I understand that it was determined, instead of using this safety fuze, to use an inadequate pipe filled with powder."

Hunt never actually saw the fuse itself. He had ordered it from City Point on June 29, specifying safety fuse, and his order was handed over to an ordnance officer. The fuse was ultimately sent by Burnside's ordnance officer, Captain W.H. Harris.[13] By this time, it was too late to procure unspliced fuse due to the timing of putting powder into the mine. The fuse would have been sufficient had it not been cut. Pleasants prepared three fuses and laid them out as best he could to make certain that the enterprise would work. Unfortunately, considering the inherent defects in the furnished equipment, all three ultimately went out. Pleasants later testified at the congressional hearing that it was quite unusual to requisition fuse in that length.[14] While the blame may be distributed among several individuals, once again the army's failure adequately to supply the mining operation had manifested itself in growing difficulties for the success of the mission. One has to wonder to what extent Meade might have influenced the end result by his distain for the mining enterprise.

Meade was becoming frantic while reports of the mine's status were slowly on their way to him. He was eager to learn whether something had gone wrong, and when Grant joined him, he dispatched another officer to Burnside seeking answers to the delay in the explosion. Burnside informed this aide that he did not have any answers at the time but had sent ahead to find out what was wrong. Unfortunately, Meade apparently did not receive this particular reply. Thus, he nervously waited while dawn was about to announce its appearance without an attack. He was no doubt extremely annoyed that Burnside had not seen fit to keep him adequately informed, particularly since he was so predisposed to detect a slight on his subordinate's part. Finally, after much frustration, he had Chief of Staff Andrew Humphreys telegraph Burnside's headquarters asking, "Is there any difficulty in exploding the mine? It is three-quarters of an hour later than that fixed upon for exploding it." As previously mentioned, a somewhat addled Burnside chose not to respond; as he had no idea what the problem was at that time, he therefore perceived no necessity in responding to Meade with such an answer.

Having received no response to his inquiry, Meade very soon thereafter sent another terse message which evidenced his increasing frustration with Burnside and the situation. He addressed this one to "Operator at General Burnside's Field Headquarters," and having not heard from his subordinate, asked if Burnside was at his headquarters. Van Buren, then on his way with the information from Pleasants, had not yet arrived at Fort Morton. While Meade said that he would wait for word from Burnside before giving any orders for an assault, in his utter frustration he did not wait. At 4:35 A.M., the same time as his last telegraph was headed, he told Burnside to commence the assault at present if he could not light off the mine. Meade's orders to Burnside to make the assault at once and open his batteries were simultaneously sent to Generals Warren and Mott, for the Fifth Corps and fourth division of the Second Corps respectively to join in on the attack, and to open up with the artillery. Meade was at the time preparing an order for Ord, also giving him orders to attack. Such prospect undoubtedly was not well-received by Burnside, who was concerned as to his corps' ability to take the objective with the fort and its surrounding works yet undestroyed. "The idea of taking those same works intact bordered on preposterous," as Lee was to discover the next March in front of Fort Steadman. However, while Burnside may have been less responsive than Meade would have liked, he was paying attention to his orders; after receiving Meade's order to attack without the mine explosion, he prepared to launch the ordered attack. He resolved that the mine had failed, and sensing the urgency of acting very quickly, he was "on the eve of sending an order for the command to be ready to move forward. However, he delayed for enough time to ascertain the reason for the mine's lack of an explosion." Soon, Van Buren arrived and informed Burnside that the mine was scheduled to detonate at 4:45 A.M., which filled Burnside with hope and considerable relief.[15]

Due to the lengthy and frustrating delay in springing the mine, dawn was fast approaching, and the slight mist of night was very rapidly disappearing, so that the Federal troops massed in front of the Salient could actually see the enemy works and vice versa. The sun was about to rise above the horizon, and some of the garrison in the fort and along the Confederate works on either side could be seen moving about while their bugles began to sound reveille. The morning was cloudless and "a deep and ominous stillness reigned everywhere, yet within half a mile of the mined fort were not less than 45,000 men ready to spring forward in a moment's notice." At precisely 4:44 A.M., farmer William Griffith's war-torn farmland began to tremble as Henry Pleasants' deadly weapon finally came to life, producing what was "perhaps the greatest man-made explosion that had ever occurred" to that date.

Pleasants was standing on the parapet of the advanced Federal lines with some of his comrades "watching with intense solicitude the culmination of their five weeks' labors," while 15,000 Union infantry stood in hushed expectancy, poised to immediately leap over the breastworks and advance at the explosion, over ground where, for weeks, certain death had "awaited any man who trod it." Someone on the Federal line yelled, "There she goes!" As the ground began to tremble, Pleasants himself struggled to keep from falling. Then came "a dull grinding roar that grew in volume, swelled to a mighty crescendo, and finally broke away in waves of rolling thunder." Most observers described the initial reaction as resembling a rather severe earthquake.[16] Then:

[w]hile the earth rocks with a swaying motion like that which precedes the earthquake, a huge black mass suddenly shoots up two hundred feet into the air from the left of Elliott's salient. Seams of fire were glistening from its dark sides, flashes of light rise above it on the sky, and the whole mass of earth, broken timbers, military equipments, and human bodies hangs so like a huge monster over our heads.[17]

The ground for half a mile around shook as though moved by an earthquake. William H. Osborne of the 29th Massachusetts Volunteer Infantry of Ledlie's division observed that there was first:

> ... a deep, prolonged rumble, like the sound of a distant thunder, then the whole surface of the ground for many yards in the immediate vicinity of the galleries of the mine began suddenly to heave and swell like the troubled waters of the sea. The Confederate line, which up to this moment had been silent, was now thoroughly aroused; and their men lining the breastworks, were seen peering over the parapets, filled with wonder and alarm at the terrible sounds that were issuing from the earth....
> Large masses of earth, guns, caissons, tents, and human bodies filled the air. The first explosion was quickly followed by others of lesser magnitude, but it was all over in a few minutes.

An enthusiastic, if not articulate Lewis Crawford of Company M, 3rd Pennsylvania Heavy Artillery, part of Abbot's siege train, wrote his friend Samuel P. on August 16: "You aut to seen the jonys fly up in the are som went up in the are a bout twenty to thirty feet and som was bered fifty feet under ground I tell you that it was a big thing to see thay was a grate meny killed and wounded."[18]

Garland H. White, chaplain of the 28th USCT and a Methodist minister and former slave, felt that the phenomenon was as though "the hand of God intended a reversal of the laws of nature. This grand convulsion sent both soil and souls to inhabit the air for a while, and then return to be commingled forever with each other, as the word of God commands 'From dust thou art, and unto dust thou shalt return.'" Those near the spot said that "clods of earth weighing near a ton, and cannon, and human forms, and gun-carriages, and small arms, were all distinctly seen shooting upward in that fountain of horror, and fell again in shapeless and pulverized atoms." Brigadier General P. Regis De Trobriand, commander of the first brigade of the third division, Second Corps, described the shapeless mass as a "bed of lightning flashes" spreading into an immense mushroom whose stem seemed to be of fire and its head of smoke. Suddenly, everything appeared "to break up and fall back in a rain of earth mixed with rocks, with beams, timbers, and mangled human bodies, leaving floating in the air a cloud of white smoke which rose up to the heavens, and a cloud of gray dust which fell slowly towards the earth." This cloud floated to the north, "as if shrinking from the carnage and destruction it had created," tinged by the first faint rays of sunrise, which colored the cloud blood red.[19]

The Confederate soldiers of the 18th South Carolina and Pegram's battery slept in the doomed fort "as the fuse sparked and sputtered inch by inch towards the four tons of Gunpowder which were to rend with the violence of an earthquake the spot on which they were resting." Major James Coit, commander of Branch's battalion, had remained in Pegram's battery that night until midnight, after which he returned to his headquarters. All was quiet on the lines, and the men were in "remarkably good spirits, singing songs, &c., all unconscious of the fate that awaited them with the dawn." A sergeant in the 26th Virginia of Wise's Brigade had just stepped up on the breastworks when he heard "a tremendous dull report and at the same time felt the earth shake beneath me. I immediately looked down to our left & to my sorrow I saw an awful scene, which I never witnessed before."[20] Sergeant John W. Callahan of the 22nd South Carolina was buried in the explosion. His friend Daniel Boyd, a sergeant

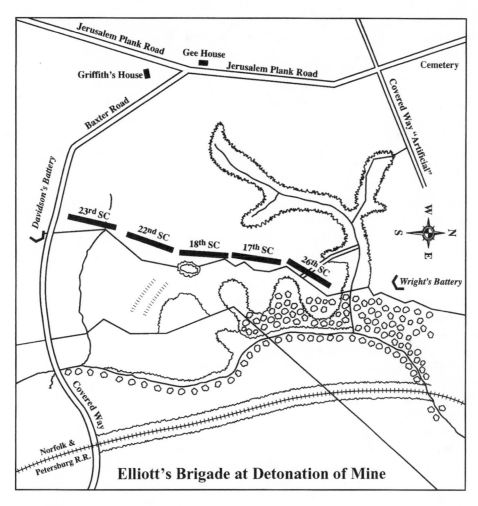

Elliott's Brigade at Detonation of Mine

in Joseph Kershaw's old brigade of the I Corps wrote: "J W Calahan Was Kild by the blowing up of our breast Works he was buried wit[h] the dirt. When they found him he was Standing Strait up the ditch."[21]

Two cannon, each weighing a ton, "went whirling over the parapet that had been, and dropped between the picket lines." William P. Hopkins of the 7th Rhode Island Volunteers later wrote that "Lairy Chandler, who was sleeping beneath one of them, was hurled so high and so far he fell within the Union lines. Another Johnny subsequently captured, said the first he knew he was blown up a right smart distance, and when he was coming down he met others going up, too." An Irishman in the South Carolina Brigade was completely stunned for a considerable time. When he recovered his senses, he found himself in a mixture of Federals and Confederates, without knowing exactly what had occurred. He nudged a comrade and asked, "I say, Byes! Have we tuk them or have they tuk us?"[22] One Confederate who was blown unharmed into the Federal rifle pits said that "he thought it was rather unceremonious to send a man kiting through the air in that shape before he had eaten his breakfast."[23]

The effects of the resultant explosion were devastating and horrific to behold. The force had "rent in twain Elliott's brigade." A crater 200 feet long, 70 feet wide and over 30 feet deep displaced Pegram's former battery, together with its former guns. The surface, instead of being smooth, was a mass of clods of earth of all shapes and sizes from small to the size of a house.

John A. Elder's famous oil painting accurately depicts one large clod on the crest, which remained a fixture for months thereafter. The 18th South Carolina and Pegram's battery were entirely destroyed, along with two-thirds (three companies) of the 23rd South Carolina and a part of the 17th South Carolina. Lieutenant A.B. Thrash's company of North Carolinians was on picket duty a couple of hundred yards north of the fort. Thrash was leaning on the breastworks when the explosion erupted. He could distinguish two objects climbing skyward in the faint light, one a carriage of the twelve-pounder Napoleons, and the other the body of a man. A member of a nearby artillery battalion recalled the wreckage descending, "hurtling downward with a roaring sound showers of stones, broken timbers, and blackened human limbs, ... the gloomy pall of darkening smoke flashing to an angry crimson as it floods away to meet the morning sun."

Some were unfortunately blown into the air with the debris and some were sleeping in bombproofs and were therefore buried with it, still alive. A few were later dug out and made prisoners. A few feet of Pegram's line and the gorge line in the rear were left intact, a space which "made a fine rallying point for troops and the Federal writers confound it with the crater proper." At least 300 yards of the Confederate lines were destroyed or seriously affected and left at the mercy of the Federals. Beyond that breach not a Confederate infantryman stood to dispute the passage of the Federals into the heart of Petersburg. "A prompt advance in force, a gallant dash, not into the crater, but around it and three hundred yards beyond it, would have crowned the great explosion with a victory worthy of its grandeur." Confederate troops on the line to the right and left of the huge abyss recoiled in terror and dismay. Their reaction was forgivable, "for so terrible was the explosion that even the assaulting column shrank back aghast and nearly ten minutes elapsed ere it could be reformed." From Blandford Church and its cemetery the Federals might have looked back on the Confederates within ten minutes, "stunned, paralyzed and separated; and, looking forward, they might have seen the coveted city undefended and at their mercy."[24]

Some 300 men of Elliott's brigade were unceremoniously rocketed into the sky, or buried in the bowels of the works where they slept, with a mere handful surviving. In all, 278 men were lost in the explosion itself. Company B of the 22nd South Carolina, positioned directly over the mine's gallery, had thirty-one of its thirty-four men killed by the blast. Captain George Lake and W.J. Lake, his lieutenant, both of Company B, were asleep when the mine went off and knew nothing of what had happened until Captain Lake was dug out and became fully conscious. He indicated that they "knew we were buried, discussed the probabilities of getting out, and thought they were very slim. His thigh was broken, and he was otherwise badly injured, but finally recovered. The brave fellows who took us out of the ground, working away while exposed to shot and shell, I think were members of a New York heavy artillery regiment [most likely the 14th New York Heavy Artillery]. The weight of the earth was too great for them to budge."

Captain Lake indicated that when he learned "that nearly all my men had been killed, and the remaining few, with myself, were prisoners, it was gloomy indeed." Wilson Moore of Company B, 22nd South Carolina had only recently been relieved from guard duty and was fast asleep in a ditch behind the main trench. As everyone else had stretched out lengthwise, he found just enough room to sleep sitting up. When tons of the yellow clay and sand suddenly buried the ditch, the others were helplessly buried alive. Moore, however, threw his hands over his head, and although the falling dirt and debris covered him completely, a comrade could still observe his hands wriggling on the surface, and he excavated Moore's face, though he was unable to extricate him at the time. The two Lakes and Private Moore were the only survivors of Company B. A very fortunate Corporal William Green of Company B,

22nd South Carolina, who was recuperating from wounds and thus absent from his unit on the 30th wrote his parents:

> My company was all Blowen up and all Buried under the dirt....
> They say they never herd Such praying on all thare Lives as the men dad under the ground. Ough it is two Sad a picture to write about But it is neverlefs a true one....
> Tell Mrs. Ellis I had just Stated to her in the Last Letter I wrote to you that Judge & James Duncan was well But now I have the Sad Entelligence to communicate to her that they are Boath Dead and Buried Beneath the ruins. Judge I think had joined the church and was a good Boy.

Lieutenant J.W. Pursley of the 18th South Carolina wrote home on August 1 that he had just lain down to get some sleep early that morning when the mine exploded to his right. At the first noise he thought a bomb had just hit his bomb-proof. This was quickly followed by a much larger concussion and "[j]ust as I lit in to the ditch there came another blast & God only knows how high it sent me. I spread out my wings to see if I could fly but the first thing I knowed I was lying on top of the works." Captain Floyd of that same doomed regiment was hurled to the ground so violently that he lost consciousness:

> When I came to myself again I saw masses of earth and pieces of large timbers lying all around me and I was covered up from head to foot with earth and debris. Tremendous firing and shouting was going on and the fierce, distant yells of contending men, intermingled with the groans of the wounded and dying, constituted a perfect pandemonium not inferior in intensity to "Dante's Seven Circled Hell."[25]

Private Tom Wilkins of the 11th Mississippi recalled that he and his friends were whispering to each other to keep from falling asleep, when all of a sudden the ground began to shake, accompanied by a deep rumble:

> Then a great upward bulge occurred on our line of trenches right where we had manned the line a short while ago. The huge, round column of earth now rose straight up like a picture of the Italia volcano, Vesuvius, I once saw in Papa's Matte-Brun's Geography book.

Wilkins recalled that as "human bodies looking like little rag dolls tossed end over end high in the seething air," his detail guard stood trembling in stunned silence. C.S. Cooper yelled, "It's an earthquake!" G.B. Triplett screamed, "It's a volcano!" "It's the end of the world and I ain't repented yet!" wailed Wilkins' cousin James Norwood. Wilkins "just stood there stunned." Lieutenant Robinson of the Ringgold battery indicated that he was asleep under one of the guns and his men were all around them, some asleep and others watching the Federals, given that the lines were so close at that point and there was no picket line. They slept in their clothes, ready, with the guns double-shotted with grape and canister to meet any enemy advance. The explosion caused the earth to heave and stagger. As he jumped up and looked down the line to the left he saw "my conception of a volcano. I saw what appeared to be arms and legs and cannon all going up in the air." One survivor of the blast was taken prisoner with his face much begrimed. A Federal soldier addressed him: "'Say, Johnny! Guess you got blown up!' 'Well,' replied Johnny with an oath, 'I should just say so; but somehow I got the start of the other fellows, for when I was coming down I met the regiment going up, and they all called me a blasted straggler!'"[26]

Colonel David G. Fleming of the 22nd South Carolina was in a bombproof near the epicenter of the blast. He was so completely buried that a diligent search was made for three days thereafter, and yet his body was never found. A soldier of the 36th Massachusetts regiment reported that the bodies of the Confederate garrison in the fort were strewn around and stripped of all clothing by the blast. He felt movement under him and soon uncovered a rebel soldier who soon rallied in the fresh air and was able to tell his plight and opinion on this novel form of "rapid transit." He indicated that he was "standing near one of the guns, with one foot on the hub of a wheel; all was quiet, and he was thinking of home, when the earth seemed to give way, a terrific noise, and he lost consciousness. How far skyward he went, he had no means of knowing. His escape from death was most remarkable."

A surgeon of the 18th South Carolina later recalled two men who had an experience worse even than the soldier just mentioned, yet obviously better than Colonel Fleming's. Lieutenant Willard Hill of Company E and Sergeant Greer of Company A, 18th South Carolina, were sleeping in a bombproof just to the left of the mine after being relieved from watch duty. They awoke to find that they had been completely buried alive under tons of rubble and dirt: "Their first impulse was a deep, indescribable despair — heart-sickening, heart-rending hopelessness, that left them almost powerless for a time." They had nothing with which to dig themselves out but a bayonet Greer had on his belt. While the battle raged overhead, Greer dug with that instrument, while Hall passed back the excavated dirt. Often hope would flood their hearts, only to give way to despair again. Finally, they moved a huge boulder and they could see light, which caused them to faint. They awoke to the clash of arms, but they could not extricate themselves. "At last the cry of victory rose high above everything else. They knew that someone was vanquished, and that somebody was victor; who, they knew not." When they were finally extricated with assistance and carried to the field hospital, the surgeon said they were "the most sadly changed men that I ever beheld." Hill, a young man, had not a single gray hair prior to the explosion, and now his head was almost "as white as snow."[27]

There were thirty artillerymen on duty in Pergam's battery that morning. Of these, twenty of the men and two officers were killed by the blast. Only the crew on the extreme right gun and one other man survived. Almost all of the 18th South Carolina on duty in the fort were annihilated. Lieutenant Smith Lipscomb of Company F was the only man in his company to escape death or capture. He dashed back to his own side up the works with a handful of survivors of his regiment and some of the 17th South Carolina, found a rifle and prepared to repel the impending Federal assault. One of counterminer Captain Douglas's sergeants, A.H. Smyth, was with the night's countermining detachment on the evening of July 29, along with eight men working in mine No. 2 to the front and side of the Salient. Smyth was suddenly startled by the "sound of a very heavy explosion and thrown from my feet by the shock, the ground or rather gallery heaved and waved as if from an earthquake." Upon recovering from the shock, he took three men who were actually in the countermine at the time, and upon reaching the surface found the works "utterly destroyed for a distance of 100 or 150 yards." The detail had to flee the destroyed portion of the line rapidly, as a squad of Union troops who had rushed through the gap was pursuing them. The other workers had fled while Smyth and his comrades were still underground.[28]

The scene of devastation was like nothing these battle-hardened veterans had ever witnessed. Charles W. Trueheart of the 8th Alabama observed giant clods of earth, timber fragments from the bomb-proofs, pieces of guns and small arms strewn amongst a sea of human arms and legs, all mangled and blackened:

> Sticking out of the ground here and there, are the bodies of the poor fellows, so suddenly launched into Eternity by the explosion. Some of the men were thrown to a distance of 75 yards. One of the cannons was thrown 35 yards from its place towards the enemy.

The explosion accomplished what was intended: it demolished a four gun battery and its garrison of troops and acted as a wedge, opening the way for the much awaited assault.[29]

Captain B. Lewis Beaty, commander of Company K, 26th South Carolina, recalled that for a short time after the explosion, great consternation prevailed among those close to the Crater. Some were awakened from sleep, while others, taken by surprise "were filled with consternation and demoralized at the terrible calamity and awful destruction caused by this, to them, new and powerful mode of warfare." Many of the stunned men came rushing back covered with earth and "wild with fright." Colonel Fitz William McMaster of the 17th South Carolina also observed this unfettered "consternation" among the Confederate soldiers: "Some scampered out of the lines; some, paralyzed with fear, vaguely scratched at the counter-scarp as if trying to escape. Smoke and dust filled the air." Tom Wilkins of the 11th Mississippi reported that "[t]he whole company was running around like a chicken with his head cut off." The Confederate troops occupying the lines to the right and left in the immediate vicinity of the mine had fled precipitately because of fright and fear of further explosions. Major Walter Newberry of the 24th New York Cavalry (Dismounted) noted that the destruction and the noise "were appalling and the Confederates for the time completely stunned into apathy and silence."[30]

Following the explosion, there was no infantry fire from the front for approximately half an hour, and none from the left for twenty minutes, and just a slow rate of fire from the right. At least 300 yards of the lines were destroyed or temporarily left to the mercy of the assaulting party: "Beyond that breach not a Confederate infantryman stood to dispute their passage into the heart of Petersburg." To the south of the Crater the lines were unmanned even as far as Wise's Brigade and so, too, to the north, at least 300 yards were deserted by the defenders. The way was completely open to the summit of the hill, "which was protected by no other line of works."[31]

At the instant the mine was sprung, the Federal artillery along the whole length of the line opened a terrific fire on the Confederate works, one of the largest single assemblies of artillery in the Civil War. "Along a six-mile line, the field batteries, plus the 4.5 inch guns, the 10-inch mortars, the 30-pounders and all other siege pieces, sent a huge converging fire at positions adjacent to the leveled salient."[32] The "sounds were perfectly deafening." Lieutenant Colonel William Stewart, who was sleeping with Mahone's Brigade at the Wilcox farm, observed that the Federal barrage appeared "as if every lanyard had been pulled by the same hand. The grey fog was floating over the fields, and darkness covered the face of the earth, but the first bright streak of dawn was gently lifting the curtain of night.

The fiery crests of the battlements shone out for miles to our left, and the nitrous vapors rose in huge billows from each line of battle, and sweeping together formed one vast range of gloom." The barrage was "one of the greatest single artillery barrages of the war. Plumes of white smoke, mixed with the red sandy soil of Virginia, floated in the sky, turning the rising sun blood-red."

An unknown Federal soldier who signed his letter home just "John A.M." said that "[a]s soon as it [the fort] was blown up all our artilery opened nearly two hundred[33] pieces it made a awful noice. I never heard more cannonading in my life the Rebs dident Reply very fast for they were scared of the Explosion."[34] Howard Aston, of Company F, 13th Ohio Volunteer Cavalry, noted that "our forts all along the line opened out, with every gun, apparently from the sound, and they were almost immediately answered by the Confederates. The solid shot and shell howled and shrieked over our heads, and balls could be seen ricocheting along the front line of works from an enfilade fire on our right front."[35]

Henry Matrau of the 6th Wisconsin wrote home that the explosion of the mine was the signal for the entire Federal artillery and mortar batteries to open, including thirty-one in back of his brigade alone throwing shells directly over the troops' heads: "The sudden transition from utter silence to fiercest clamor was terrible." The guns "belched out sheets of flame and milk-white smoke, while the shot and shell sped forward, screeching, howling, rumbling, like the rushing of a hundred railroad trains. The Federal lines were on fire from one end to the other: "Answering to the quake that shook every spire of Petersburg and was felt as far away as Richmond, came the roll and roar of Grant's artillery. A pall of smoke and dust covered, as with a kindly vent, the central horror, yet in each redan and each redoubt men staggered and shrunk back from the sudden and awful scene."[36]

Colonel McMaster indicated that he had "scarcely ever heard a more crushing roar of big guns. Very soon the little valley along which the entrenchment ran was covered by a heavy pall of black smoke which lay suspended but a short distance above the earth, which, with the thunderous roar of the artillery, made one of the most magnificent war pictures I have ever beheld." James H. Clark, of the 115th New York, had a good position with which to observe the bombardment. He remarked:

> What a fearful thunder, and what a terrible concentration of iron, lead and fire, and yet men live. See how it tears and sweeps and mows through human flesh and blood, dealing out death, destruction and slaughter with an unsparing hand. The awful, sickening sight gives us a sort of sadness; yet we know that unless we kill them, they will do their best to kill us, and destroy the beloved fabric of liberty.[37]

The batteries burst forth in one massive roar, and "there was nothing but the banging of the guns and the distant hum of the shells!" While some accounts indicate a delay before the Confederate artillery responded to this artillery attack, Sergeant C. Thomas Bowen wrote to his mother that both sides' artillery "opened fire in one simultaneous roar all along the line & the air was in a moment alive with rushing iron, shrieking & whistling around in all directions."[38] Colonel Charles Wainwright, chief of artillery for the Fifth Corps, observed that "[t]he roar was not greater if equal to that at Gettysburg, but there was more variety of notes in it."[39] The Union artillery believed that the enemy guns that might have borne upon the Ninth Corps attackers were silenced within ten minutes. In actuality, they were not yet prepared to respond.

Understandably, the massive explosion, together with the physical effects it had upon the Confederate line and followed immediately by the tremendous artillery barrage, produced unparalleled consternation, despair and disorganization in the Rebel troops. Unfortunately for the Union, these conditions were felt with almost the same degree on the attacking force. The Ninth Corps was almost as badly disconcerted as their Confederate counterparts. Lieutenant William Powell, an aide to General Ledlie, observed that it "appeared as if ... [the debris of the explosion] would descend immediately upon the troops waiting to make the charge." Many of the troops in the front lines of the second brigade of Ledlie's division broke, scattered to the rear, and became intermingled, thinking the debris was about to rain down on them.[40] Benjamin A. Spear of Company K of the 57th Massachusetts observed that "[i]t seemed for a moment or two as though Co. K would be covered with dirt, fragments of gun-carriages, timbers and distorted fragments of human beings." This was a reasonable fear, as a cannon and fragments of gun carriages were later found over one hundred feet inside Federal lines, so terrible was the force of the concussion, reported Private Warren Goss, a Massachusetts soldier. Union soldiers "ducked as bits of men and equipment rained among them."[41] Others were too stunned to move. The almost simultaneous impact of the Federal artillery barrage added to this sense of panic and despair. The barrage was deafening. Many men clapped their hands over their ears for protection from the din. Then the smoke began to clear and the effect was that the rising sun appeared blood-red through the orange haze.[42]

CHAPTER 9

The Attack Begins: The First Division Enters the Breach

The first division had been formed at midnight and was soon advanced through the covered ways and into position behind the Union breastworks before daybreak on the 30th. According to General Ledlie's later testimony at the court of inquiry, the first division was to lead the advance, pass over the enemy works, and charge Cemetery Hill some 400 yards to the right—which was approached via a slope comparatively free of obstacles—and occupy this objective. The 35th Massachusetts, as the engineer unit, was then to be set to work throwing up entrenchments at the site. This plan was, by his account, supposedly disseminated in detail to his subordinates. The first division's advance was to be immediately followed by the advance of Willcox's third division to the left of the works as soon as the first had cleared, to provide protection on the left flank. Potter's second division was to move simultaneously in the same fashion to the right.[1] By 3:30 A.M., Ledlie's division was in position, with Colonel Elisha G. Marshall's second brigade in front, followed by the first brigade commanded by Brigadier General William F. Bartlett.

Elisha Gaylord Marshall was born in Seneca Falls, New York, in 1829, and graduated from West Point in 1850. He was then assigned to frontier duty at various posts in the West. In 1858, he was detailed to accompany the Utah expedition, and then he held various positions in garrison duty in California and the New Mexico Territory, where he had his first skirmish with hostile Indians. Historical accounts portray him as a gruff, no-nonsense type of leader. He considered himself a fighting man and not a talker. Promoted to captain in May of 1861, after initially supervising recruitment in Rochester, New York, he received a commission as lieutenant colonel of the 13th Regiment New York Volunteers in April of 1862, which then became part of the Army of the Potomac. In this position, he led his regiment through some of the bloodiest fighting of the war, until he was seriously wounded at Fredericksburg, where he also earned a commission as brevet lieutenant colonel in the regular army. After some minor postings while recuperating from his wounds, Marshall accepted a commission as colonel of the 14th New York Heavy Artillery in January 1864, and thereafter commanded the brigade to which his regiment was attached at the Wilderness, and saw significant action in all the other battles of the Overland Campaign. He was wounded again at Petersburg in the Ninth Corps' June 17 attack, and spent a month convalescing at home on sick leave, returning just in time to participate in the assault on July 30.[2]

William Francis Bartlett, commander of the first brigade of the division, was born in Haverhill, Massachusetts, in 1840, and when the war broke out in 1861 was a member of the class of 1862 at Harvard College. On the day Fort Sumner fell, Bartlett enlisted as a private, and soon became a captain in the 20th Massachusetts. During the Peninsular Campaign, he was shot in the knee and lost a leg as a consequence. He was fitted with a cork leg with a spring which did not adapt well to scurrying around on midnight expeditions. While recuperating, he received his degree from Harvard and became colonel of the 49th Massachusetts in November of 1862. He took part in the siege and capture of Fort Hudson in July 1863, where he was wounded twice more, and he was thereafter compelled to enter his battles on horseback, making him a prime target for sharpshooters. In battle, Confederate officers repeatedly ordered their men not to fire on him due to the courage he displayed. In the spring of 1864, Bartlett organized the 57th Massachusetts, which he led into the Wilderness, sustaining yet another, fourth, wound. He was appointed a brigadier general of volunteers in June, and had just rejoined his brigade from sick leave one week before the assault on July 30.[3]

The second brigade had been formed in three lines, each with approximately 600 men, behind the breastworks of the advanced Union line, with the Pennsylvania Provisional Heavy Artillery (112th Pennsylvania) in front with Marshall in charge, the 14th New York Heavy Artillery under the command of Captain Jones comprising the second line, and the 3rd Maryland, a veteran unit, and the 179th New York, consisting of six companies under the command of Lieutenant Colonel Gilbert P. Robinson, comprising the third line. Marshall, however, detailed his adjutant general, Captain John Anderson to lead the second line, given Jones' relative inexperience.[4] The 3rd Maryland was the only genuine veteran unit in the brigade. The heavies were totally new to this type of warfare, having been trained to operate big guns inside fortified positions. The 179th New York was also quite new and untested. Thus, not only was the assault to be led by the corps' worst division commander, but also by a relatively inexperienced body of men. Historian George Agassiz once described this brigade as "good for nothing, over which Marshall, a severe, courageous man had been put, with inconceivable fatuity," having been selected by lot.

The first brigade was placed in the rear of the second, in columns formed of three lines of battle with the 57th Massachusetts and the 29th Massachusetts in the first line, and the 59th Massachusetts temporarily in the rear of the 57th, due to the crowded conditions in the staging area. The 57th Massachusetts, under Major Albert Prescott, was comprised of three-year veterans and had only 125 men left in the ranks (of which 91 participated in the engagement). The second line was still positioned in the covered way, there being no more room in the field. The 29th Massachusetts was led by Captain Willard D. Tripp, as its commanding officer, Lieutenant Colonel Joseph H. Barnes, had been acting as officer of the day in charge of the division pickets. The 21st Massachusetts was under the command of Captain William H. Clark, the 56th Mass-

Col. Elisha G. Marshall (Library of Congress).

achusetts under Colonel Stephen M. Weld, the 59th Massachusetts under Colonel Jacob Patrick Gould and the 100th Pennsylvania under Major Thomas Jefferson Hamilton. The 56th and the 59th Massachusetts were new units, consisting mainly of reenlisted nine months troops. The 100th Pennsylvania had 500 men present under arms. Colonel Gould from the 59th Massachusetts was in charge of the brigade's right wing, with the line consisting of the 29th, 57th, and 59th Massachusetts from left to right. Colonel Weld was in charge of the left wing, which consisted of the 21st Massachusetts on the right, then the 56th Massachusetts and the 100th Pennsylvania on the left. The 35th Massachusetts was in the rear acting as engineers. The "men and officers [were] in a feverish state of expectancy, the majority of them having been awake all night."

The location and condition of the Confederate fort was not pointed out to the men of the second brigade, who were not entirely familiar with this portion of the line, nor was any notice taken as to what would soon occur or what was expected of them. The men dozed and rested for a couple of hours before daylight, awaiting subsequent developments. Daylight slowly came, and still they

BG William F. Bartlett (National Archives).

"stood with every nerve strained prepared to move forward the instant an order should be given." By 4:00 A.M. the men were extremely edgy, having been on their feet for four hours, and still no explosion had occurred.[5] Suddenly, the earth trembled and a black pyramid rose into the air. When the explosion occurred at 4:44 A.M., it seemed so close to the advanced Federal lines that it appeared it would descend on the troops of the second brigade. This caused many of them to break and scatter to the rear. It seemed so close that the men in front would be crushed by the raining debris. Officers screamed orders and curses, desperately trying to untangle the confused mass and straighten the lines, "but it took several minutes before a semblance of order was restored." George L. Kilmer of the 14th New York Heavy Artillery later said that the explosion "was so startling that the first two lines of men broke, for it was believed to be an earthquake or a Confederate mine springing upon us. No one believed that a Confederate fort was so near."[6]

Due to the confusion that the explosion precipitated, the attacking forces, "instead of drawing inspiration from the sight of the breach they had effected, actually appeared to recoil from the havoc." While the front lines broke and fled in panic, the 14th New York Heavy Artillery, with the familiar presence of their commander, Colonel Marshall, to encourage them, remained comparatively steady, although there was still some confusion for a brief spell. Between five and ten minutes was thus consumed in reforming and reorganizing the front lines.[7] The men stood motionless and awestruck for a few minutes after the lines were reformed, overwhelmed at the sights and sounds in front of them. There was little time actually lost, as it took this long for the explosion's massive cloud of dust to begin settling, thus allowing for a troop movement to commence.[8]

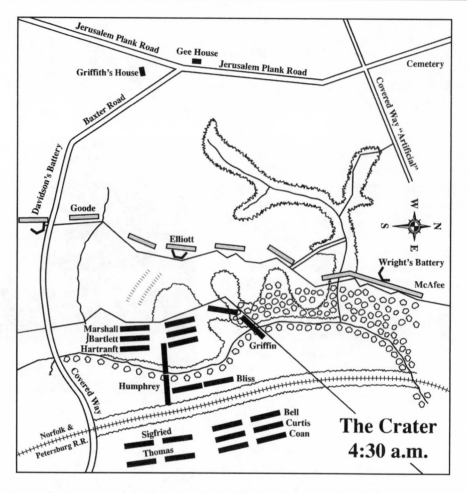

Many observers noted an "incomprehensible delay (usually described as at least twenty minutes)." Many others would argue the delay was of a significantly lesser duration. One Lieutenant Thompson in the front line was thrown into a mud hole by the shock of the explosion, and just as he emerged blinded and bespattered, a call rang out "Forward!" and the second brigade began its advance, accompanied by the sound of the massive Federal bombardment. They advanced "not with eagerness but with rushes & pauses of uncertainty." The division "had nothing in front of it. The Confederate troops occupying the lines to the right and the left in the immediate vicinity of the mine had fled precipitately through fright and fear of further explosions." The way was completely open all the way to the summit of Cemetery Hill.[9]

Immediately after seeing his men off, Ledlie retired to a bombproof approximately ten yards behind the front lines, which had once served as a regimental headquarters and was then serving as an aid station, where he was soon joined by General Ferrero, whose men were still lying flat in the covered way. Ledlie had found solace in this shelter that had been designated to be used as an operating room once the fighting commenced. Sick with fright, he talked Surgeon Hamilton E. Smith of the 27th Michigan Volunteers, in charge of the field surgeons of the third division, into giving him a bottle of medicinal rum under the pretext that he had been injured by a spent bullet, as well as having experienced a flair-up of malaria, causing him to be seriously ill. While the physician prepared field dressings, Ledlie, soon accompanied by General Ferrero, sat in a corner nursing his "medicine." He remained there

Eruption of the mine at Elliott's Salient and the initial assault on Cemetery Hill (*Harper's Weekly*).

for almost the whole battle, except for an occasional trip outside to ascertain the status of his men. At one point, he apparently inquired as to the whereabouts of General Bartlett with the intent of handing command over to him so that he could retire from the front altogether.[10]

Just before 5:00 A.M., Colonel Marshall gave the order for the second brigade to move out. He exclaimed, "Gentlemen, take command of your lines. 2nd Pennsylvania, rise up. Forward, March! By the right flank; march. Over the parapet and swing up your left!" The men, "uttering a mechanical cheer," slowly mounted the crest and passed "unmolested across the intervening space." In the lead, the 2nd Pennsylvania Provisional Heavy Artillery attempted to climb out of the Federal breastworks, but had considerable difficulty as the trenches were eight feet deep at this point and the men were loaded down with all their gear, too encumbered to readily negotiate the parapet. No one had thought of ladders. Thus, the men stood around dumbly until someone had the inspiration of sticking bayonets in the logs of the front wall while other men held the opposite ends at both knee and shoulder length, creating makeshift ladders. Sandbags were also arranged as steps while men who had scaled the wall assisted others up from the top. Still others stood on the backs and shoulders of their comrades to surmount the parapet. The less strong and agile had to be pulled up and boosted by the noncommissioned officers.

All this took time, and time was not a luxury the Army of the Potomac could afford if the assault were to succeed. This obstacle seriously broke the ranks of the second brigade and yet no time was subsequently taken to stop and re-form once out of the works. As about twenty men of Company B of the 14th New York Heavy Artillery joined their commander on the wall, he ordered them to align, but Colonel Marshall called out, "No time for that, Lieutenant. Go for the crest." Thus was the case for the whole brigade, with only handfuls of an entire regiment ready at the first jump.[11] The men, already deployed by the flank and forced to move forward in columns, dashed forward in ragged spurts, between the two lines, two and three at a time. To add to this confusion, the troops behind the 2nd Pennsylvania moved too fast, and had to check and halt, which caused them to become tangled up and intermingled, thereby causing yet further delay.[12] Colonel de Chanal, standing with Colonel Lyman of Meade's staff "was frantic over the loss of precious moments ... [negotiating obstacles which should have been readied in advance]. '*Mais, cette perte de temps!*' [But, what a waste of time!] he kept uttering."[13] Little by little, while the pall of dust and smoke settled even thicker around them, and confused officers shouted orders that were difficult to understand and sometimes impossible to obey, the bewildered troops of General Ledlie's task force managed to move out in a pattern very roughly approximating the paperwork plan.[14]

Immediately after negotiating the unprepared parapets of the Union advanced line, the men of the second brigade of the first division were then confronted with the obstructions between the lines. The lead elements of the second brigade found that the Federal sappers had removed only a small section of the heavy collection of abatis, chevaux-de-frise and the strong wire which held them together in front of the breastworks. Consequently, the brigade also had to deal with these obstacles, which further prevented them from adequately forming battle lines in front of the Crater. These obstacles were supposed to have been removed well in advance of the assault. By restricting the breach to a narrow passage through the Union abatis, the focus of the assault was constricted, causing considerable disorganization. In the process, all semblance of order that remained after negotiating the parapets was lost. Colonel Weld later related that his brigade had been told that the works would be fixed so the troops could advance in line and the abatis would have been removed and "everything would be made ready for an unobstructed advance, as far as our lines were concerned."[15] Yet another critical problem during this initial process was the narrowness of the covered ways themselves. Many participants later argued that they should have been made much wider, given the necessity of a rapid movement through the lines by an assaulting force of over 15,000 men. Nonetheless, "[h]alf-strangled by the acrid powder fumes, choking and coughing in the dense curtain of dust, the first wave of troops finally moved forward, slowly, blindly, hardly knowing which way to go."

There has been considerable debate over the role that the failure to remove the obstacles from the Federal lines, as well as those of the Confederates, played in the ultimate outcome of the battle. Burnside openly agreed that he did not remove his obstacles to the degree that Meade had ordered. However, he later contended that any delay caused by this failure was of five minutes duration or less.[16] Captain John Anderson of the 57th Massachusetts agreed the "abatis and other obstructions in front of our intrenchments were [partially] removed, allowing only a sufficient space for the passage of the charging column." In other accounts, the abatis and cheavaux-de-frise in front of the enemy's works were sufficiently covered by the debris from the explosion that they did not pose a significant issue for the impending assault. The degree of the problem caused by the failure adequately to remove Federal obstructions is open to debate. However, the individual in charge of clearing any such obstructions later did acknowledge a possible delay of at least five minutes in order to remove them. Given the premium placed upon the speed of execution of this assault, the loss of even five minutes could still have resulted in disastrous effects on the eventual success of the mission.[17]

With all semblance of organization lost negotiating the Federal breastworks and abatis, the advancing troops were unable to form battle lines. Instead, with bayonets fixed, rifles at right shoulder-shift position in order to avoid sticking the men to their front, the troops had to move out in column toward the destroyed fort, while gagging and coughing in the thick, acrid smoke and choking fumes and dust. With Meade's strict and explicit orders issued for the removal of nearly 200 yards of the defensive material totally ignored, "[n]ow a full frontal assault was reduced to men double-quicking in columns three and four abreast toward the objective. Nothing, it seemed, was going right for the attackers." The attack went forward by the flank, as opposed to going in solid column "as we expected they would do," according to then Lieutenant George M. Randall, acting as an aide to Ledlie that day. Fortunately, most of the Confederate chevaux-de-frise in front of the enemy works had been covered by the debris from the explosion.[18] However, the advance in some places was still held up for considerable time periods due to ground impediments, placed by the Rebels, which had not been removed by Federal pioneers ostensibly assigned for the task. Burnside had ignored Hunt's repeated advice that the troops be armed with axes to use in cutting their way out of the man-made obstructions, both Federal and Confederate.[19]

Thus, amid "[c]louds of dust and gunsmoke [that] still choked the air as the first Federal troops—Brigadier General [*sic*] Elisha Marshall's men, who made up the Second Brigade in Ledlie's division—lurched from their trenches and scrambled across the open ground toward the smoldering crater."[20]

> The next moment came the roar of a gun, and then another, till a hundred cannon along our line were playing upon the rebel batteries. The bugles rang out, the drums beat, and in dashed Ledlie's division, Marshall's brigade leading the advance.... The Fourteenth New York Heavy Artillery first entered the gap, followed by Marshall's second brigade, which men [rushed] pellmell into the smoking crater, from the bottom of which protruded half buried limbs and mangled bodies of men.[21]

The 14th New York Heavy Artillery had entered the campaign that spring with 1800 men, divided into three battalions led by five field grade officers and twelve captains. As the regiment advanced on the Crater that morning, it contained a little over 300 men, and with its commander in charge of leading the second brigade, it had no field officers present, the last major having been killed in the assault on June 17; moreover, only two of its twelve captains remained.[22]

At about 5:00 A.M., as soon as the second brigade had cleared the parapets, General Bartlett gave the order "First Brigade, forward!" and the first line, consisting of the 57th and 29th Massachusetts scrambled over the top in the same manner as the second brigade had accomplished the feat. The other regiments of the first brigade had a more bewildering time getting out. They had been crowded into the covered way in a rather careless fashion behind the leading units and now had to be sorted out first, then formed into regimental lines and finally moved forward to scale the trench wall. This drill cost the division another ten minutes. The space to get over the breastworks was not over ten feet wide where the sandbags had been piled up by the second brigade. This resulted in a charge by the flank, instead of line of battle, with not more than four men at a time, given the extremely tight space and none of the abatis removed. This, according to Colonel Stephen Weld, also delayed the advance of the first brigade considerably. It broke the regiments up, considerably scattering the troops and with little organization being brought to bear on the advance.[23] With Bartlett in the lead, the first brigade then quickly moved forward behind Marshall's brigade, about thirty degrees to the right. The men cheered loudly as Bartlett struggled to stay in the lead, battle flags streaming proudly. The men lost no time crossing the one hundred plus yards to the destroyed fort. The Confederate opposition was very light at this point, and the movement was virtually unopposed due to the scarcity of Confederate troops remaining directly in the front. What opposition there was could be seen running to the rear as the blue lines advanced. For several hundred yards to the right and left, the works were virtually deserted.[24]

As Marshall's men reached the outer fringes of the destroyed fort to the right of the Crater, they encountered still more trouble. The area had been densely obstructed by a broad barricade of felled trees and interlaced branches, creating "an almost impenetrable jungle."

Once the air cleared, it was apparent that, while the fort had been largely obliterated, much of the barricade remained. The blast had torn only a narrow corridor in the Rebel abatis and the troops had to thread their way cautiously to approach the destroyed fort. Colonel Robinson indicated that "[b]y keeping a strong right oblique we arrived at the crater formed by the mine, to the right of which the orders for the assault had directed us to form."[25] As the lead regiments approached the Crater, the makings for disaster arose. Instead of skirting the edge of the Crater, fanning out into and beyond the Confederate trenches before the Confederates could reorganize, the troops headed for the pit itself and halted. They arrived there in great disorder due to the manner in which the debouch took place. If the regiments had been in their places when they arrived, they could have been led and taken to the crest. However, they arrived scattered and disorganized, and it was impossible to get the regiments together, according to then Lieutenant Randall. Randall also indicated that it was the general impression among the troops that one good regiment in solid column could have gone forward without any difficulty, given the initial lack of opposition. Unfortunately, there was little genuine leadership exhibited, and the exact opposite occurred.[26]

Everything started to unravel as the second brigade came up the final yards of the slope in front of the Crater in unavoidable disorder after its charge. As the men reached the lip, most of the men just came to a complete halt. Instead of shaping their efforts toward their objective, the crest, the Federals broke their remaining ranks and began milling about, marveling at the size of the hole. A serious bottleneck developed, for the men could not be encouraged to move forward. Units began crowding up and piling in together and the officers were no longer urging them on. All were instead looking down in awe at the phenomenon that obviously blocked their progress. Major Powell later recalled the fantastic scene which greeted Ledlie's men that morning:

> [a]n enormous hole in the ground ... filled with dust, great blocks of clay, guns, broken carriages, projecting timbers, and men buried in various ways—some up to their necks, others to their waists, and some with only their feet and legs protruding from the earth. One of these near me was pulled out, and proved to be a second lieutenant of the battery which had been blown up. The fresh air revived him, and he was soon able to walk and talk. He was very grateful and said that he was asleep when the explosion took place, and only awoke to find himself wriggling up in the air; then a few seconds afterward he felt himself descending, and soon lost consciousness.
>
> The whole scene of the explosion struck every one dumb with astonishment as we arrived at the crest of the debris.

George L. Kilmer, Company I, 14th New York Heavy Artillery, noted that "in the pit, powder smoke issued from the crevices; guns were seen half buried; the heads and limbs of half-buried men wriggled in the loose earth." What little sense of purpose and organization the Federals had possessed as they straggled forward was now completely lost.[27] The second brigade could not move forward in line. Given the broken state they were in, every man crowding up to look into the hole, and being pressed by the first brigade in their immediate rear, it was equally impossible to move by the flank by any command around the Crater. Before the brigade commanders could assess the situation, the two brigades became inextricably mixed due to a morbid desire to look into the hole. Thus, Marshall yelled to the second brigade to move forward and the men did so, "jumping, sliding, and tumbling into the hole, over the debris of material, and dead and dying men, and huge blocks of solid clay."[28] As the first brigade pushed forward toward the Crater, the milling masses of the second brigade, "in the midst of the shock of the artillery, through the dense clouds of flying dust, and clambering violently pushed down into the yawning crater." The 14th New York Heavy

The Ninth Army Corps charging the Confederate works immediately after the explosion of the mine (*Harper's Weekly*).

Artillery was the first unit into that frightening abyss. Once inside the abyss, the men largely became sightseers, milling about and hunting for souvenirs. The scene of devastation, death and destruction paralyzed the Federals, mangled human bodies scattered all over. Instincts of humanity also got priority and further delay ensued while many of the unfortunate victims were unburied. During this time, there was still only scattered artillery fire on the assaulting force.

The 14th New York Heavy Artillery was then largely engaged in a rescue and mop-up operation regardless of what the senior officers may have desired of them at the moment. Bartlett's second brigade, "with the stupidity of sheep, followed their bellwethers into the crater itself, where huddled together, all semblance of organization vanished, and company, regimental and brigade commanders lost all power to reorganize, much less control, their respective troops." One enterprising noncommissioned officer began gathering up the dazed Confederates, getting them into a formation and sending them to the rear. An observer at the time noted that "he seemed to be 'drilling troops in squads.'"[29]

In addition to the awesome scenes of destruction, the Crater presented physical obstacles to the effective movement of troops through its ragged terrain. The sides of it were composed of jagged masses of hardened clay projecting from loose sand. The upper surface had been composed of sand, with a lower stratum of clay furnishing scarcely a foothold. Lieutenant Colonel Charles G. Loring, the Ninth Corps' assistant inspector general, who had followed the second brigade in its initial assault, indicated that:

It was an obstacle which it was perfectly impossible for any military organization to pass over intact, even if not exposed to fire. The nature of this ground itself was enough to cause confusion among men accustomed to seeking shelter from constant exposure to fighting for the last five or six weeks. The men, upon entering this abyss, became confused and it was impossible to get then out, a phenomenon which could have happened with the best of troops. The second brigade went blindly into the Crater and filled it and were almost immediately "utterly immovable and sullen!"[30]

A handful of officers yelled themselves hoarse trying to get the soldiers out of the hole and on with the attack. Loring related that "[t]he whole brigade was broken up in confusion, and had utterly lost its organization. The officers were endeavoring to reform their men, but it was an exceedingly difficult operation."[31] The objective, Cemetery Hill, was about twenty-five degrees to the northwest (right) of the Crater, and approximately 1300 yards distant. The opportunity to rush and capture it at that time was ripe, given that the explosion had confounded the Rebels in that sector of their line.[32]

Some of Bartlett's men had crossed the open space by the right flank and moved forward in support of the second brigade. They were forced momentarily to halt in front of the destroyed fort, as what was left of the fort was unable to contain more troops at the time. While this was occurring, the Federals began to suffer severe artillery and rifle fire from the flanks as the stunned Confederates recovered their senses and started to protect the breach in their lines. They were required to hold this position for about twenty minutes when they were finally ordered into the fort and to take up a position on the left. Bartlett may have misunderstood his orders, which were to advance to the left of the Crater and secure as much of the Confederate works as possible. But with Ledlie nowhere to be found, there was no one present to question a mistake, and thus the first brigade blindly followed the second brigade into the depths of the Crater. Bartlett came up at the lead of his brigade, hopping along cheerfully, aiding himself with a stout Malacca cane with an ivory cross handle.[33] The regiments then began to dig in, as the 57th Massachusetts' Company K, armed with Spencer repeating rifles, provided some cover by firing effectively into the Confederate artillery to their front. The primary mission, however, was not to occupy the Crater, but to press on to the crest and Cemetery Hill (or at least that is what the commanders back at Fort Morton believed it to be). But instead of passing over this chaotic scene, Bartlett's men piled into and among the stalled second brigade, thus becoming completely intertwined with it and defying any and all efforts to bring order to the chaos. All organization ceased to exist. Captain Stephen M. Weld of the 56th Massachusetts observed the scene as:

> ... a confused mob of men continually increasing by fresh arrivals. Of course, nothing could be seen from this crater of the situation of affairs around us. Any attempt to move forward from this crater was absolutely hopeless. The men could not be got forward. It was a perfect mob, as far as any company or regimental organization was concerned, and that necessarily from the way we went forward. And not from any fault of the officers or men. To ask men to go forward in such a condition was useless. Each one felt as if he were to encounter the whole Confederate force alone and unsupported. The moral backing of an organized body of men, which each would sustain his companions on either side, was wanting.[34]

Despite the reigning confusion and disorganization, a large portion of the maligned "heavies" made an excellent accounting of themselves in the initial moments in the Crater. They had gone in on the advance with a cheer that urged an observing Fifth Corps officer to exclaim that he heard it over two miles distant, over the tremendous roar of the Federal artillery barrage. As Marshall led a mixed band of men with the colors, at the command "Go ahead!" these men headed for a section of the exploded works which remained intact. Marshall ordered Major Charles Houghton, with his "battalion" of the 14th New York Heavy Artillery, to charge with what men he had on hand. There were still Confederates in this work and in the breastworks alongside of it. The men in the works either surrendered or fled, and the flag of the 14th New York Heavy Artillery was planted on the outer site of the demolished fort, being the first Union banner to be seen flying from the Crater.[35] The Confederates remaining in the vicinity, upon seeing the colors, commenced firing into the oncoming men. In the Crater, "[t]he Northerners were captivated by the destruction caused by the mine, and most of them continued in their role as tourists, ignoring their pleading officers.... One Southern boy was found, with both legs blown off, helplessly trying to crawl to safety, all the while leaving two wakes of blood behind him from his dragging stumps."

Others of the 14th New York began breaking into small rescue squads, digging out as many of the buried Confederates as possible. While these 14th New York heavies were so engaged, the 2nd Pennsylvania Provisional Heavy Artillery under Lieutenant Colonel Benjamin Griffin Barney moved around their Empire State counterparts and attempted to scale the steep, slippery slope of the Crater's far perimeter, which ran for 125 feet along the old Confederate works. This wall formed a formidable obstacle. Forged out of the Virginia clay by the blast, the wall made it almost impossible for the men to get their footing as they attempted to emerge from the Crater to continue on towards Cemetery Hill. They finally succeeded in scaling the high walls, passing the far western reaches of the pit, but they soon took a position behind the demolished fort, digging in just as Burnside had predicted.[36] In this process, the unit had the distinction of making the farthest advance of the first division toward Cemetery Hill.

By now, the Confederates had recovered from their initial shock and fear, and the disorganized mass of the first division saw all around them that the enemy was superior in number. Still, the men pushed on with Marshall's urging. Part of the 14th New York Heavy Artillery, diverging slightly to the left, upon reaching the far side of the Crater moving with other units stopped to excavate two dismounted guns from the left wing of the fort, which Major Houghton, Sergeant Wesley Stanley of Company D and two of his men struggled to place into position. Major Houghton detailed Stanley and the others to retrieve a magazine, and with his converted artillerymen got the two Napoleons operational and established a clear field of fire. He began firing on a Confederate battery which had only recently opened up on the Federals in the vicinity of the Crater.[37] Major Houghton later recalled that "We then hauled back the pieces of artillery to get a range over the top of works on a Confederate gun on our left that was throwing canister and grape into us. We loaded and fired and silenced the gun, and at our first fire forty-five prisoners came in, whom I sent to our lines."[38]

Another portion of Marshall's brigade clambered up the far side of the Crater wall and began to form for a further advance. Atop this wall thrown up by the blast, the men gazed on "a perfect honeycomb of bombproofs, trenches, covered ways, sleeping holes and little alleys running in every direction." Behind this vast honeycomb, "forming a rear wall to the area of devastation stood the newly built cavalier and retrenchment." It was thus "exceedingly difficult for troops to spread themselves either ... to the right or to the left." Marshall eventually got some of his available men into a rough semblance of a battle line with great difficulty and pushed forward into the trenches and covered ways.

Three distinct trenches, or covered ways, ran from the northwest side of the fort. The trench nearest to the Federal lines was actually a part of the Confederate main line of works. Another led to the rear at an angle of about twenty degrees, while a third, still more to the rear, was at an angle of about fifty degrees with the main line. As the 14th New York Heavy Artillery went over the western rim of the Crater, Lieutenant Green Smith, one of Marshall's aides, informed them that they were designated to occupy the center trench. This covered way, entered by the 14th New York "heavies," was a cul-de-sac about 300 to 400 feet long and ended in a heavy traverse. The regiment went to the end of the ditch, manned the traverse and commenced a fire on Confederate troops in a nearby flanking work.

Marshall himself had gone to the farthest trench with the 2nd Pennsylvania Provisional Heavy Artillery. Lieutenant Colonel Robinson's troops, the 3rd Maryland and the 179th New York, were directed into the nearest trench, which was actually a partial covered way running back 350 yards and dead-ending in a protective traverse. Robinson's men rushed into the trench as far as a right-angled earthwork and opened fire on the flanking Confederate soldiers who, after recovering their senses, were rapidly returning to the front lines to repel the Federal advance. The Marylanders were also armed with Spencer repeating rifles, and were able to force their way forward by leapfrogging from traverse to traverse and "demonstrated the advantage of an organized corps of sharpshooters." Soon, a second brigade officer yelled for the men to move again. They were by then totally intermingled with the first brigade, which had arrived at the Crater by this time. The men of the first brigade commenced climbing up the far side of the Crater. Private Josiah N. Jones of the 6th New Hampshire observed, "[t]here was now a crowded jumble of men in the crater and around it."

Once Bartlett's first brigade came in, the 29th, 56th and 57th Massachusetts were directed into the covered way occupied by Robinson's men, while the 21st Massachusetts and part of the 100th Pennsylvania went into the ditch where Marshall had led the 2nd Pennsylvania Provisional "heavies," while yet another portion of the 100th Pennsylvania remained to man the edge of the Crater on the Confederate side. The 57th Massachusetts soon followed the rush and occupied one hundred yards of the trench, capturing fifty Rebel prisoners in the process. Bartlett soon got some of the 59th and 29th Massachusetts into the trench with Robinson's men, but this did little more than add to the pandemonium, and they were finally pushed back into the Crater, which continued to fill up with the disorganized and disoriented men of the first division. Only the line now consisting of the 2nd Pennsylvania, the 21st Massachusetts and the 100th Pennsylvania had an open field of fire to their front. Robinson and his men moved on in the main line, charging around several traverses, with the sharpshooters in his command armed with Spencer repeaters. Robinson and Lieutenant Randall of the 4th U.S. Infantry led small squads in charges around the various traverses. Before he was finally halted, his men had gained over 350 yards of the covered way to the right of the Crater.[39]

Soon after the first brigade came in, Marshall felt that a further advance should be made, and he sent Lieutenant Green Smith to Ledlie for permission to carry works to the right. Unfortunately, Smith fainted from sunstroke before reaching Ledlie. From the 2nd Pennsylvania Provisional Heavy Artillery's position one could make out a covered way or sunken road leading from Cemetery Hill down to the destroyed fort, which was full of Rebel defenders. A very formidable enfilading fire could thus be brought to bear on the Federal troops, rendering an advance up the hill that much more dangerous. Thus, the elimination of this target was deemed "the first condition of further success, and Marshall and Bartlett ordered their brigades to be ready to attack this covered way obliquely." Robinson was to move out and forward, supported by the 56th, 57th and 29th Massachusetts, who were to form Robinson's second line by moving to the right, along the Confederate front line. The 2nd Pennsylvania Provisional, the 21st Massachusetts and the 100th Pennsylvania were to swing up their left and thereby align with Robinson, and the 14th New York Heavy Artillery was to file over the traverse at the end of the covered way and form the second line for this detachment. While these movements were taking place, the 35th Massachusetts was vigorously working to run a flying sap from a point to the right of the mine towards a point to the right of the Crater and was making considerable progress. However, this enterprise became untenable after the loss of Robinson's position and was totally abandoned shortly thereafter.

The various interdependent movements that were thus attempted in the early going resulted in heavy flank fire from a covered way leading from the crest as the first brigade became engaged. Colonel Stephen Weld of the 56th Massachusetts was aware of the need to move the men quickly out of the Crater to be an effective fighting force. He later recounted that:

> [a]s soon as possible I got my men out of the crater into the works on the right, and tried to re-form there. A second line or parapet, some feet higher than the enemy's front line, led from the crater obliquely to the rear. This would have given us a good line of defense had it not been taken in rear of the enemy's front line, which was occupied by them some 200 yards from the crater. The intervening space between this rear line and the front line was cut up in every way by bombproofs, traverses and pits. I pushed my regiment down to the right, and endeavored to clean out the pits still further. The fire was too hot to do much, and the ground too broken. The enemy by this time was using artillery, chiefly canister.

Thus Weld's position was far from improved even as his men got outside the Crater. He later remarked that the lack of leadership, with "each regiment fighting on its own account with the few men that could be gotten together," was a monumental problem for the mission's success, and ultimately for its survival. The 100th Pennsylvania also attempted to break out of the Crater, moving over the open space to the rear of the fort, only to ultimately fail for lack of support. Joseph Nelson, Company F, later professed:

> We were not supported as we were to be, and were obliged to fall back to the fort, and after being near enough to Petersburg to see into its streets, I mean part of the troops were, as part had to remain in the fort to defend it from the flanks, as the enemy still occupied the right and left of the blown fort, so we fell back to the fort and helped out many "Johnnies" who were still buried up to their knees, waists and armpits.

The color bearer of the 21st Massachusetts was killed and its commander, Captain William H. Clark, was mortally wounded. The two Pennsylvania units lost heavily and Robinson's command and the 14th New York "heavies" were also badly mauled by the flanking and rear fire. After ultimately being repulsed, Robinson and Randall made their way back to Colonel Marshall, who ordered his whole command to fall back and re-form. Thus, the division by and large forced to fall back into the Crater. Only a relatively few men in the advance got as far as the maze of works beyond the Crater, where they began exchanging fire with a handful of the enemy that had not fled. Unit leaders were for the most part ignored as they shouted and pointed swords at the hill, as no one of superior authority was at hand to save the situation. In the area where the 14th New York Heavy Artillery had retrieved the Rebel cannon, the second brigade broke out of the Crater, but it was quickly enfiladed by the fire from the traverses running toward their own lines which sheltered Confederates while they fired across the plateau and into the Crater.[40]

Wherever the first division attempted to advance out of the Crater, they were soon met by intense fire from the Confederate infantry, which had by then recovered its composure after the explosion and bombardment, as well as the Rebel artillery, which had found the range on the Federals in the Crater. Many were hit not only from the exposed flanks, but also from the rear, as the Confederates reoccupied the transverses and entrenchments to the right and left of the Crater. These men had recovered their equanimity and when the Union attempted to re-form on the Confederate side of the Crater, the Rebels had faced about and delivered a fire into the backs of the Federals.

Coming so unexpectedly, this caused the forming line to fall back into the Crater. Only 1600 feet beyond the pit was the Jerusalem Plank Road and one half mile along it was Cemetery Hill. But the men of the first division had unfortunately hesitated too long. Valuable time was lost in the disorganization which had accompanied the advance to and into the abyss, as well as the efforts required to deploy the men to counter the new threat from the now-recovered Confederate forces in the vicinity of the Crater. By this time, only thirty minutes had expired since the explosion; however, the momentum which Meade stressed as essential was now seemingly lost. Meade later testified before Congress that the charge he required was never made. The troops instead kept crowding into the Crater until it was filled up, and there they remained, while there would have been "nothing but marching ahead for the first half hour"[41] had they advanced on from the pit itself.

One could also easily speculate that had Burnside's original plan, calling for two regiments to sweep down inside the Confederate lines to the right and left of the Crater, not been rejected by Meade, the first division could well have re-formed its two brigades and still moved on to Cemetery Hill before the Rebels fully realized what was intended. However, the next-to-unchallenged reoccupation of the trenches to the right and left of the Crater by the Confederates prevented such an impromptu organized re-formation under the new plan of battle. Further, there being no division, corps or army commander present at the Crater to give the appropriate orders to other troops to clear the trenches. A formation under fire from the rear was something no troops could accomplish. Additionally, there was the issue of a failure of leadership from those in the Crater and a lackluster performance by many of the demoralized Union forces. Confederate artilleryman Colonel John Haskell, who soon managed to lay an extremely effective artillery fire on the men in the Crater and who was in quite close proximity to it early in the battle, observed that:

> Even after I got my guns in position, a couple of good companies, deployed as skirmishers, could have taken them with little trouble; the ground was rough and broken, for protection, and the distance not over three hundred yards, but they did not attempt it. Time after time, they did come part of the way, only to break as we threw a few shots into them, and the only cries we heard were appeals for quarter of a good many who saw the way shorter into our lines than back into theirs.[42]

By 5:30 A.M., the air began to clear of dust and one could see the Crater being rapidly clogged with the puzzled and idling men of the first division. They were not moving, even though the Confederate fire was still somewhat light and sporadic at that point. Neither men nor officers appreciated the urgency required of them at this early hour of the battle, and without a division commander being present on the scene, they remained almost static, despite the effort of the brigade commanders. A large part of the problem could be attributed to the men's long stay in the trenches in the worst part of the Federal line. They had been harassed day and night by the Rebels, and their physical condition had deteriorated from the terrific heat and the constant construction of the defenses under the intense gunfire, thus causing lethargy and tepidness, as Burnside had feared.

Yet the individual units and the men could not be blamed for this performance. They had little idea as to what their objective was or how to achieve it. They had performed adequately in all prior engagements, by and large, regardless of the inadequacies of their division commander. Captain John Anderson spoke for his unit, the 57th Massachusetts, regarding their inability to advance, citing that there were few left to go forward: "Call the roll over the unknown graves, call it from battlefield, hospital and prison pen, and the answer will tell how it went forward."

After falling back into the Crater, a partial line was formed by Bartlett and Marshall with some of the troops, "but owing to the precipitous walls the men could find no footing except by facing inwards, digging their heels into the earth, and throwing their backs against the side of the crater, or squatting in a half-sitting, half-standing posture, and some of the men were shot even then by the fire from the enemy in the traverses." A virtual "catch-22" existed, as Ledlie later testified that he could not advance his division, as the enemy were in the same trenches as his men, "starting from the point where the right of my division rested and extending thence to the left (our right)." He indicated that it was impossible for his line to dislodge the enemy; had he moved forward, the enemy, merely by filing to the right in the same trench, would have occupied his position and then poured deadly fire into his rear. Yet nothing else could be accomplished until the first division performed its part. Without it, all movements made to the right or left exposed the advancing ranks to attack. Josiah Jones of the 6th New Hampshire describes how the "...troops in the Crater were in a confused mass, and not only did not advance beyond, but, hindered every other force from attempting it." Confederate resistance was increasing rapidly and was thus able to thwart an advance in any direction. Men were returning to the trenches and the heavy guns and mortars were increasingly being brought to bear on the crowded Union troops in the Crater. The crest in front was now occupied by a strong force, while the batteries stationed there delivered a raking fire on the men in and around the Crater: "It was a veritable 'leaden rain and iron hail.'"

So crowded were the men in the Crater that only those in front could use their arms to advantage. Marshall and Bartlett tried in vain to get the troops back out of the abyss so some semblance of organization might be attempted, as all order had been lost by that time. Only fragmented groups were able to make disorganized movements outside the Crater, and only then to meet stiff resistance. Neither officers nor men knew what was really expected of them. Ledlie was not present and had not entrusted either of his brigade commanders with proper instructions. "The division was simply there, a mass of brave men without orders and without a head." It was wound like a machine, set in motion, launched through the breach and then left to run down without any hand to guide it. Bedlam reigned supreme in the bloody Crater! To add to this confusion, the details of Meade's revised plan had not been explained to the commanders. John Anderson recalled that "[e]very officer from colonel down to second lieutenant was giving orders of some kind, most of them being contradictory." At one time you would hear officers shout "halt and intrench," while others yelled "forward" and still others "give way to the right." By then, Bartlett's artificial leg had been crushed by a flying shard of boulder and he was lying on his back in the Crater as helpless as the buried Confederates around him. It was entirely useless to attempt to push this disorganized force against the enemy's lines and batteries. In this situation, it could be said that "[t]he greater the number the greater the disadvantage."[43]

One reason for the apparent lackluster effort to proceed to Cemetery Hill instead of securing and remaining in the Crater and its adjacent works was the exact nature of the instructions Ledlie had imparted to his subordinates the evening before the assault. Ledlie later emphatically testified that he had ordered his men not to halt in the environs of the Crater, but rather to push through to Cemetery Hill. However, many of those present when Ledlie met with his brigade commanders on the evening of the 29th clearly indicate that he gave positive orders *not* to go beyond the Crater after the assault. Marshall, Bartlett and a number of staff officers met just before dark on the 29th at Fort Morton, where the plan of the movement was discussed. Then Marshall and his adjutant general, along with one or two others, went to the front across from the Salient for personal reconnaissance. Marshall then met with his battalion commanders at 8:00 P.M. and then the brigade marched to the front at 11:00 P.M. Captain Thomas W. Clarke, an assistant adjutant general for one of Ledlie's brigades, recalled specifically that Ledlie gave orders *not* to go forward. Clarke recalled this in detail:

> The plan as given by General Ledlie to Bartlett and Marshall, and as given by Marshall to his battalion commanders, was to this effect, and it was on this plan that Marshall and Bartlett worked. The Second Brigade was to be formed in column of battalion front. [It made three

lines of about four hundred men each.] On the explosion of the mine it was to move forward and occupy the enemy's works on the right of the crater, skirting its edge, but not going into it. The First Brigade was to follow with about the same front and occupy the works on the left of the crater, but not going into it. When the lodgment had been made, it was to be secured and connected to our lines by our engineer regiment, 35th Massachusetts. The Second Division was then to extend this lodgment still more to the right, the Third Division was to extend it to the left in the enemy's works by a front attack, and the colored division was then to pass through the crater and assault the hill in the rear. Marshall's distinct instructions were that the security of the lodgment was the prime duty of the First Division and the hill was a subordinate object; and General Ledlie's instructions, as heard, conveyed no other meaning to me, or, as will appear later, to General Bartlett or Adjutant Warren [Bartlett's adjutant].

The drill and habits of the First Division, accustomed to line attacks and not to regimental column maneuvers, were not adapted to the plan of formation designed for the colored division, with its proposed tactical conversions to right and left after the works were reached, but the ultimate effect of the maneuvers was to be the same. The flanks were to be cleared before the attack on the hill. Marshall was explicit that his brigade was to confine its attention to seizing and holding as great a length of line on the right of the crater as possible, and that the work as great a length of line on the right of the crater as possible, and that the work beyond [Cemetery Hill], to the enemy's rear, was to be done by other troops. His phrase about it was this: "When we have secured the lodgment, Ferrero will take the negroes through the crater, which we shall have left clear for them, and see what they can do beyond it."[44]

Lieutenant Colonel Joseph H. Barnes, who succeeded to command of the first brigade following Bartlett's capture, supported this proposition that the first division was instructed *not* to advance beyond the Crater. He disputed the criticism that the first division halted in the Crater against orders. He indicated that it "was not a part of the plan of battle for that division to advance after reaching the crater. The orders issued to the division were distinctly not to *advance*." He further indicated that historians who cite the opposite did an injustice to the division in implying they failed to carry out orders. Rather, he indicated that "this division executed its orders to the letter, that it led the assault and occupied the crater, and is entitled not to censure but to praise." Barnes indicated little was said in the meeting with Bartlett regarding minor details. There was no misunderstanding that Ledlie's division was to capture the front line as their part of the battle:

> To expect them to immediately charge another line would have been unreasonable. It was fair to presume, and it was presumed, that the division which led the assault would be roughly handled by the enemy, and that if they succeeded in obeying their orders, and did secure and hold the front line, it would be done with considerable loss; that the division would not be in condition for further immediate aggressive action.

Regardless of the instructions given the brigade commanders, it is unlikely any regimental commanders ever "knew the objective point they were expected to make, or that even the regimental commanders were so informed. General Ledlie, the responsible head of the division, was inexcusably absent behind our breastworks; all was confusion in the fort."[45]

By 5:30 A.M., however, the initial efforts to expand the breach beyond the Crater had begun to meet with significant enemy resistance. Thus, Marshall called upon Powell to report back to Ledlie the status of the situation, since he was there on the scene and fully appreciated the situation. The enemy was far from idle at that point. It had bought up artillery from its left to bear on the Crater, and that position was currently being swept "with as heavy a fire of canister as was ever poured continuously upon a single objective point." While the Federal battery gave this battery particular attention, they could not silence it. Powell found Ledlie and part of his staff "ensconced in a protective angle of the works."[46] He explained Marshall's reasons for being unable to advance from the Crater and its adjoining works. Ledlie did not evidence much compassion or concern for his men; he ordered Powell to return to Marshall and Bartlett immediately and advance in obedience to General Burnside's orders. Powell returned and delivered the message.

With the incessant fire on the Crater, it was now, according to Major Powell, as totally impractical to re-form a brigade inside the pit as it would be "to marshall bees into line after upsetting the hive; and equally as impracticable to re-form outside of the crater under the severe fire in front and rear, as it would be to hold a dress parade in front of a charging enemy."[47] Here the second point of advantage was lost by the lack of a leader to change the program to meet the existing circumstances. Had a prompt attack been made to the right and left of the Crater as soon as possible when the lead brigade passed into it, thereby clearing out the enemy and diverting the fire of the Rebels, success would have been inevitable (particularly on the left, "as the small fort immediately in front of the Fifth Corps was almost, if not entirely, abandoned") for a time.

Powell was unaware as to whether or not Ledlie informed Burnside of the affairs as reported by him. By then, Burnside had heard again from Meade, who directed him that all of his troops "be pushed forward to the crest at once." Powell believed it likely that Ledlie did report, as not long after he himself returned to the Crater with Ledlie's orders, a brigade of the second division under Brigadier General Simon G. Griffin advanced its skirmishers and followed them immediately to the right of the Crater, significantly adding to the turmoil.[48]

CHAPTER 10

The Initial Response in Defense of the Breach

The Confederate forces recovered quickly from their consternation, shock and fear following the explosion, bombardment and oncoming assault. The remaining officers of Elliott's brigade, which lost 457 men dead and wounded in the explosion itself,[1] soon realized what had actually occurred and rose to the occasion. Considering their plight, the South Carolinians were remarkably cool and self-possessed, and much of the ultimate success of the Confederate defense can be attributed to them. Major James C. Coit, commanding Branch's battalion of artillery came upon the scene within ten minutes of the explosion and found Elliott's men "standing firm and undaunted, almost up to the very borders of the crater." Captain John Floyd, commanding Company I of the 18th South Carolina, as officer of the day had just arisen that morning when he was hurled to the ground so violently that he temporarily lost consciousness.

When he awoke, he saw masses of earth and pieces of large timbers lying around him and that the whole right of the regiment which rested on Pegram's battery had been totally blown apart. The air was so filled with smoke and dust that visibility was down to ten feet, but Floyd could tell that the Federals were upon them. He promptly ordered the men to commence firing over the breastworks. With assistance from Adjutant Clough L. Sims, Lieutenant John M. Anderson[2] and Sergeant T.W. Berry, Floyd gathered all the men who could be spared from the left of the regiment and occupied a line of works to the rear of the destroyed fort. Floyd, recounted that he, Sims and Berry were all bareheaded "and looked like ... [they] had just emerged from a clay hole." He observed that "[t]he dust and smoke were still dense, in fact we were groping in the dark." They soon came in contact with 200 Union troops who ordered them to surrender, and "in reply we gave them the contents of our rifles," according to Floyd. They returned the fire and once the Confederates' guns were empty, the opponents engaged in hand-to-hand combat. Soon a shell from one of the Confederate batteries fell among the contestants, hurling blue and gray right and left, killing and wounding a number of them.[3]

The Federals then dashed into the Crater itself where they could continue fighting with protection, while Floyd's men were totally exposed. Thus, Floyd ordered his survivors to fall back to the cavalier line one hundred feet to their rear and 150 feet from the main Confederate breastworks, which presented excellent cover: "The fire from the Crater was very severe

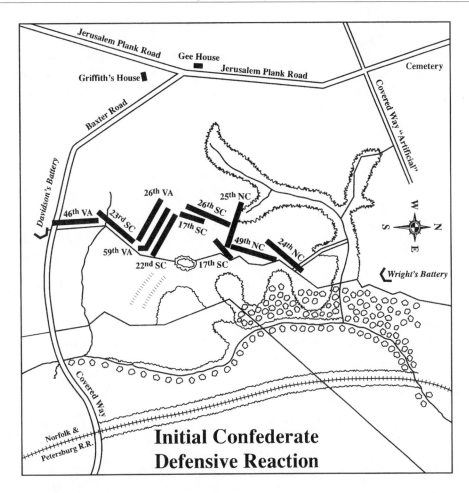

Initial Confederate Defensive Reaction

and we retired walking backwards, fighting as we fell back, the officers using their revolvers, while the men fought with their rifles." Half of his men, including Lieutenant Anderson, were killed before they could reach the trench, and Adjutant Sims was mortally wounded. Upon reaching the cavalier trench, this small remnant of the 18th South Carolina met the 17th South Carolina, which had spread into the connecting trenches and traverses to confront the oncoming Federal assault.[4] Colonel Fitz William McMaster, commander of the 17th South Carolina, later recalled receiving Ledlie's charge soon after the explosion. Inspired by the regiment's officers, he related that:

> Our men bounded on the banquette and commenced firing on the ranks of men who were rushing in without firing a gun. By this time some of the men of the gallant Eighteenth, who extricated themselves from the bank which covered them, came rushing down the trenches, and as many as could picked up guns and began firing. For a considerable time the firing was done entirely by the infantry.[5]

No more than fifteen minutes had passed before the Confederates recovered from the initial shock and were prepared to defend their positions against the onslaught. While Floyd's survivors reached the cavalier line, still other scattered remains of the 18th South Carolina reached the 26th South Carolina to their right. The brigade had been trained on what to do in the event of a breach, and Elliott's men not physically affected by the explosion maintained the ground with remarkable steadfastness. The 17th South Carolina had remained in their trenches to the left of the Salient and in the immediate proximity to it.[6] The dusty survivors of the 22nd South Carolina, under its sole surviving officer, Captain James N. Shedd, retreated to the left where the 23rd South Carolina was located, and together they threw up a barricade of sandbags across their main trench south of the breach, eighty-eight yards to the right of the Crater. Still other remnants of the 22nd found their way to the cavalier trench. General Elliott had issued orders for them to hold the position and "to fire only when the enemy showed themselves or attempted to cross the hill towards Petersburg." Several attempts were made by Union troops to cross the hill, but the fire from the ditch was so intense that they quickly returned to the Crater.

Elliott and two staff officers had been sleeping in a bombproof on the line in full uniform that night, ready at an instant, when the explosion occurred. Elliott's adjutant, A.L. Evans, went to place a guard at the covered way to prevent flight, while his aide rushed with orders to his subordinates. Elliott himself went to the breach, near the gorge line, where he was soon joined by Evans. The surviving men of Elliott's brigade bravely manned the works up to the border of the Crater over the roar of the Federal bombardment and a torrential hail of bullets. In so doing, they left no front for the entrance of Federals except such as had been made vacant by the explosion. Any further Federal advance was checked by Elliott's men and supporting artillery.[7] Major James C. Coit, commander of Branch's artillery battalion, to which Pegram's battery belonged, later reported that:

> [s]o stubbornly did Elliott's men contest every inch of ground, that the enemy failed to press them down the line from the direction of the crater, resorted to the expedient of rushing from the crater down the front of our works, and then by a flank movement mounting the works and jumping pell-mell upon Elliott's men in the trenches. ... In this manner did they gain the little ground they held of our lines to the left of the crater.[8]

Meanwhile, General Johnson reported that he had immediately contacted the brigades on both wings of the division, directing them to extend their intervals and to reinforce the wings of Elliott's Brigade in order to strengthen the force where the weight of the impending assault was to bear. He also dispatched staff officers to the divisions on either side for reinforcements. From Hoke's Division on his left, he received word that no assistance could be furnished, "as the line was already too weak." From the right, he heard that support would ultimately arrive in the form of two brigades from Mahone's division of the III Corps.[9]

Stephen Elliott, Jr., was born in Beaufort, South Carolina, in 1832, the son of Stephen Elliott, the first bishop of the Episcopal diocese of Georgia,[10] and the grandson of a distinguished naturalist. He attended Harvard College and graduated from South Carolina College in 1850. Elliott was a very successful sea cotton planter and state legislator on Parris and Davis islands in Port Royal Harbor who had devised a method to utilize the tides to gin cotton. When the war threatened his native state, although he was personally opposed to secession, he organized a light battery, the Beaufort Volunteer Artillery, and was present at the bombardment of Fort Sumner in April 1861. He was instrumental in the defense of Port Royal in late 1861, and following the Federal occupation of coastal South Carolina, Elliott was responsible for a number of successful raids on coastal towns as well as on Federal shipping. He was placed in charge of the garrison at Fort Sumner in September 1863, then "a crumbling morass of brick masonry into an impregnable earth work with masonry, the old walls as backing," and captured several ships that had been dispatched to capture his command.[11] With a total force of 300 men, he held the Federal army and navy at bay for over eight months, "which will, if justice be done, rank beyond any defense of a besieged position in history." He never gave up against overwhelming forces and the Federals finally abandoned their attacks.[12] In May of 1864, he was appointed colonel of Holcombe's Legion and was soon there-

A dead Confederate soldier in a trench in front of the main line (Library of Congress).

after placed in charge of Evans' Brigade when its temporary commander, Brigadier General William S. Walker, was wounded at Warebottom Church on May 20, 1864. Elliott was soon thereafter promoted to brigadier general.[13] When it became evident Evans could not resume command of the brigade, Elliott's appointment was considered permanent and the unit was officially changed to "Elliott's Brigade," which was then ordered to Petersburg on June 16, 1864.[14]

Meanwhile, Major John Haskell traveled down the covered way toward the Salient, finding the shattered brigade in various trenches in front of the Crater. Elliott at the time was re-forming his men and dispatching them as best he could to resist the Federal advance. Haskell pointed out the defenseless position of the guns on the Jerusalem Plank Road and asked for Elliott's assistance in the form of sharpshooters to harass those Federals who were making demonstrations toward his batteries. Elliott at once agreed that he would attempt to provide such protection with two regiments of the shattered remnants of his brigade, despite viewing a dozen or more stands of Federal colors in his front. However, he indicated that his men were very demoralized and that he doubted that he could do much to help for some time yet to come.[15]

As he stabilized the remnants of his shattered command, Elliott determined to deal with the exposed position of the artillery along the Jerusalem Plank Road, as Haskell had pointed out, as well as his troops' own exposure to a potential Federal flanking movement which might roll up his thin gray line. He thus determined to arrange a counterattack with the remnants of his brigade which were isolated north of the Crater. He therefore ordered Colonel Alexander D. Smith, commander of the 26th South Carolina, to move from its position on the left of the breach, and together with the 17th South Carolina to form a line on the brow of the hill and charge the enemy in the Crater with the object of retaking all of the occupied works. The commanders found it difficult to strip their trench line in order to get the men to go with Elliott to retake the gorge line, at least until some

BG Stephen Elliott (USAMHI).

reinforcements were obtained from Ransom's Brigade. However, Colonel Smith jumped up on the parapet and exhorted the men to charge.

Elliott and Smith, with the 26th and a small portion of the 17th South Carolina, marched up the line of breastworks under a very severe enfilading fire from the Federals to within fifty to seventy-five yards of the Crater. As the regiment then filed out of the entrenchments to the rear and into the open field, they came under full and complete exposure to the Federal guns in that portion of the Confederate lines which the Federals occupied, as well as those in lines still partially in Confederate possession, all of whom redoubled their deadly efforts until "it was a terrible hailstorm of death." So severe was the fire that Elliott did not wait for the 17th South Carolina, or even the rest of the 26th South Carolina, to arrive, but charged instead with but 200 men. Captain B. Lewis Beaty of Company K of the 26th indicated that the men were being killed so fast "that as soon as five of nine companies were formed we charged upon them. It was indeed a forlorn hope."[16]

The men were literally mowed down, at the cost of great numbers of officers and men. Colonel McMaster reported that "No troops could stand a moment exposed to such a fire, and such as did not fall were immediately withdrawn."[17] Major Coit, observing the actions from Wright's battery, felt it was a mistake for the 26th South Carolina to leave the line and reoccupy the open ground between the Crater and Elliott's headquarters. He later remarked that "It was an effort gallantly made to interpose and prevent the advance of the enemy in the direction of Cemetery Hill and the plank road."[18] Elliott was among one of the earliest to fall, within thirty yards of the Crater, and was carried from the field with a severe shoulder wound. The few remaining men pushed clear up to the edge of the Crater, and several who went in were quickly made prisoners by the Union troops there. Beaty's company was on the left of this line in the charge and struck a little to the left of the Crater where it joined the Confederate trenches. After the line was thoroughly repulsed, with terrible carnage, the men found themselves in the traverses very close to the Crater, between the works occupied by the enemy and the Confederate position. There, though there were but few Rebel troops left, Captain Beaty recalled that "[w]e held our position, loading and firing into the masses of the enemy in our immediate front by elevating our guns over our heads, as there was a constant stream of death-dealing missiles passing over our heads from front and rear of us, from friend and foe."[19]

Command of the brigade then devolved upon McMaster, who later related that as soon as Elliott was shot, "he was borne past me, and told me to take charge of the brigade. His aides reported to me immediately and rendered good service during the day." However, others nearby reported overhearing Elliott say to his subordinate, "Not a word from you.... If you had obeyed orders, this would have never happened." Elliott had indeed long shared a low opinion of McMaster. Earlier that month, Elliott had written his wife regarding McMaster: "[h]e is a hypocrite and I strongly, yea powerfully, suspect that his regard for his hide is paramount.... If you do not think much of a man in college the Chances are that you never will at any subsequent time.... Pshaw! I ought not to waste half a page on so poor a subject."[20]

This deep-seated, intolerant opinion went back in part to a court-martial of McMaster in April of 1863 on charges preferred by General Evans, former commander of the brigade. Evans believed that McMaster was the mastermind behind a movement whereby most of the brigade's officers petitioned the War Department for transfers to another command over issues relating to Evans' leadership following a battle at Kinston, North Carolina. When the court declined to take any action, an infuriated Evans published a general order explaining in detail his disagreement with the court's decision. This, in turn, enraged McMaster, who wrote a twenty-six page pamphlet entitled "Colonel McMaster's Rejoinder to Brig. Gen. Evans," and had the manuscript published and distributed. Evans thereupon challenged McMaster to a duel, which the latter declined to accept after considering the matter for a week, citing religious reasons. Despite the passage of time, there was still apparently a large amount of ill will remaining in the brigade over the incident.[21]

McMaster had organized the 17th South Carolina along with former South Carolina governor John Hugh Means, and was elected its major in November 1861, and soon elevated to lieutenant colonel. Colonel Means was mortally wounded at Second Manassas on August 30, 1862, and command of the 17th devolved upon McMaster, who was soon promoted to colonel. He was in command of the regiment through all the fighting thereafter and was considered a very capable commander.[22] Recognizing the "rashness and hopelessness of the efforts to dislodge such a large number of the enemy in our lines," upon assuming command of the brigade McMaster quickly countermanded Elliott's order. At that time, he could see over fourteen Federal regimental flags flying in his front. McMaster feared the Federals could rush down the hill and thereby get in the rear of the Confederate lines and thus push across the field and into the city itself. He therefore ordered Colonel Smith to take as much of his regiment as he could muster, along with three companies of the 17th South Carolina under Captain E.A. Crawford, and proceed immediately down the ditch to where General Elliott's headquarters were located, and then up the ravine one hundred yards to the east, extending somewhat parallel with and in the rear thereof, form in line, and resist every effort of the Federals to advance from behind the cavalier trench. He believed that the fate of Petersburg, as well as, perhaps, the entire Confederate line of defense, depended upon filling in this gap in the rear of the Crater and holding firmly onto this position. The men under Colonel Smith of the 26th South Carolina were ordered to lie down behind the cavalier trench and to rise up and fire only when necessary, "so as to prevent the enemy from rushing down the hill and getting in the rear of ... [the Confederate] lines." This order was promptly executed by the designated regimental commands. For the time being, these two hundred plus soldiers were the only infantry between the Federal assault around the Crater and the city of Petersburg itself. It was this sparse gray line that met and repulsed the 2nd Pennsylvania Provisional Heavy Artillery's assault west of the Crater. Meanwhile, the remainder of the 17th and 18th South Carolina was spread out along the line of the main breastworks until they struck Ransom's brigade on the left, giving them more operating room to use their rifles. At various places, barricades were thrown across the trench. Thus began a long struggle to keep the Federals from coming in, both down the trench way as well as by jumping the breastworks.[23]

McMaster then sent a courier to General Johnson for reinforcements and dispatched a soldier of Company I to the right of the Crater to inform the Brigade's troops there that Elliot had been shot and that he himself was in command, to report their condition as soon as possible, and to resist as best they could until the reinforcements arrived which General Johnson promised were coming. Many of the Federals jumped over the back part of the Crater and thus got into the rear ditch, which communicated with the trench leading into Pegram's salient, thereby pressing McMaster's position from his right flank. Nearly all of his right two companies were killed, wounded or captured in the successive, hand-to-hand fights with the advancing Federals. Some of these men had been so close to the explosion they were still covered with earth, and yet they resisted violently. One, a Private R.S. Hoke, refused to surrender "to a damned Yankee," and was instantly knocked down by four Federals with the butt of his own musket and bayoneted. At one point, McMaster himself was left alone between the enemy and his command. He soon became anxious about Smith and his men in the ravine to the west and rear of the Crater, so he "took to a sink, from which position I made a reconnaissance of the ravine. On my return up the little ditch to the main trench, I observed the trench for twenty yards free of men. As soon as I got back to my men, we made a new barricade."[24] The cavalier line formed a diamond-shaped fortification, which connected the main breastworks in the Salient.

After Colonel Smith reached the ravine where he was ordered by McMaster to position the 26th South Carolina and portions of the 17th and had established their position, he personally went north to where Ransom's North

Col. Fitz William McMaster (courtesy Amber Rhea — Family Photograph).

Carolina Brigade was located and came in contact with the 25th North Carolina. He requested Major William Simmons Grady, in command of the regiment, to assist him in defending the area west of the Crater. Grady replied that, without orders from his superiors, he dared not leave his own position. Soon thereafter, however, Colonel Lee M. McAfee, then commanding Ransom's brigade, acquiesced, and the regiment, consisting of about 250 men, was by the right flank formed, facing just to the rear of the Crater, next to and left of the 26th South Carolina, and ordered to lie down, where they remained for several hours fending off a number of Federal advances. McAfee also aided in the effort to repel the Union assault by forwarding regiments down the line to bolster the South Carolinians on their right flank.[25]

After the three companies of the 17th South Carolina joined the 26th in the ravine, the 24th North Carolina under Colonel William John Clarke and 49th North Carolina under Lieutenant Colonel Fleming, both of Ransom's brigade, closed in on the remainder of the 17th North Carolina at the point where the 25th North Carolina had vacated its position in the trenches and repulsed a number of Federal charges from these new positions. The 35th North Carolina under Colonel James Theodore Johnson and 56th North Carolina under Captain Lawson Harrill fought from their established positions in the trenches north of the breach. Soon the Federals threw out a force to the rear of the Confederate works, and attempted to charge to the Rebel left along their breastworks in both front and rear. The assault was successfully met and repulsed by the Confederates in front, while the 26th South Carolina was equally successful in the rear. The 25th North Carolina now fronted to the south, while the rest of Ransom's brigade fronted to the east, its left extended nearly to the rear of the right of the 49th North Carolina, forming a right angle, which was nearer the Crater than any other part of the brigade. The 49th North Carolina had "moved rapidly along the works, which made a bend just above the ravine in front of Capt. Wright's battery and soon came in full view of the crater over on the other hill," recounted Private W.A. Day of that regiment.

As the 49th North Carolina came to the aid of their Palmetto State comrades, it was then light enough to see some distance, and they could see their fellow soldiers openly running to the rear, while the Yankees charged up to the Crater. The 49th filed right along the covered way, and its men were able to see at least twelve United States standards flying in the Crater. Commanded by Lieutenant Colonel John A. Fleming, who had taken command when McAfee took over command of the brigade, the 49th filed to the right in line and then halted with half the regiment in the cavalier line and the other half at an angle in the main works on the left, with the colors at the apex of the unit's position. With the two brigades thus effectively joined, they met and "repulsed the terrible onslaught of the enemy." Several assaults were made. If the Federals moved south or southwest, they met Elliott's men. If they moved north or northwest, Ransom's Tarheels were there to repel such attempts. If they advanced directly toward Petersburg, they were on top of the ridge and under the deadly crossfire from both lines. By 6:45 A.M., the Union troops first commenced breaking to the rear singly and in squads. This brought them in range of cross fire from the Confederates still occupying the old lines, and as many were cut down attempting such a retreat as reached their own lines.[26]

Meanwhile, the 23rd South Carolina under Captain E.R. White and a number of the 22nd under Captain James N. Shedd, also aided by the 26th Virginia and portions of 46th Virginia of Wise's Brigade under the command of Colonel J. Thomas Goode, bravely defended the trenches to the right of the breach. Elliott's men had successfully placed a barricade in the trenches on the side of a hill and positioned themselves behind it and in the *boyaux* which ran to the rear. There they maintained their position within thirty yards of the Crater for well over five hours. During this time, the Federal troops were unable to move them at all to the right, although they made several assaults in addition to attempting several moves to the rear of the works so as to move on the flank and rear of the regiments. Goode additionally ordered the 59th Virginia under Captain Henry Wood to form in the covered way running perpendicular to the rear of the main work, "with orders to cut down any of the enemy attempting to form in the rear of the crater...." When the Federals attempted to form with the intent to charge to the right, this regiment — along with the 26th Virginia under Captain Napoleon Street, combined with the 23rd South Carolina and in coordination with the two guns near Baxter and Jerusalem Plank Road — opened a fire that drove them precipitously back into the Crater. Five times that morning the Federal troops attempted this charge and each time they were driven back at great loss.[27]

From the explosion at 4:44 A.M. until 10:00 A.M., there were no reinforcements and absolutely no force to hold the enemy into the Crater but these few South Carolina troops, together with the North Carolina and Virginia troops on the flanks — Ransom's on the left and Wise's on the right, plus several batteries of artillery. These few hundred scattered troops were all that lay between the Army of the Potomac and the streets of Petersburg all that time. The hand to hand fighting was fierce; Federal officers continuously exhorted their men to leave the Crater, where they were so tightly packed, and move according to the plan, but whenever they tried, the 26th and 17th South Carolina regiments rose up from the depression or ravine where they lay and poured fire so rapidly that, along with the artillery, the Federals would break and rush back to the cover of the Crater and nearby breastworks. In the rear of Pegram's destroyed battery was a breastwork which was not completely destroyed by the blast. Here, in the open field, the Federals would attempt to form their lines of battle, each attempt foiled by the men of the 26th and 17th South Carolina. As Captain Beaty of the 26th South Carolina later pointed out, the rest of Elliott's Brigade:

> ...aided by Ransom's on the left and Wise's on the right, hemmed them in to within about 100 yards on each side of the Crater, while our cannon and mortar hurled and rained shot, shell and canister upon this seething mass of humanity. Their commanding officers continuing to rush their men into the Crater, with the intention to form and charge to the right and left and double up our line, hold as far as captured, and then with the balance of the 65,000 men massed for the occasion, push on through, take and hold Cemetery Hill, break up our line of defense, and capture the city. For four hours, from about 5 A.M. until 9 o'clock, we fought them foot by foot, from the line of our breastworks and the ravine in rear of the Crater, succeeding in confining them to and adjoining the breach in our line made by the springing of the mine.

To Elliott's Brigade belonged the glory of the Battle of the Crater, at least according to Captain William H. Edwards of the 17th South Carolina. If Elliott's brigade had been driven from its position early in the attack, the integrity of the battle line would have been gone and the weight of Grant's army would have made the whole line untenable. To Edwards, "[n]o command during the Confederate war or any other war of modern times ever opposed successfully greater odds or fought with more distinguished gallantry than did Elliott's Brigade at the Battle of the Crater."[28]

This small band of infantrymen was not without assistance from their brothers in arms, however. A small portion of the Confederate artillery at Petersburg played a major role in fending off the Union assault, especially in the critical early hours. Immediately after the mine explosion, Major Coit, commander of Branch's Battalion, which included the ill-fated Pegram's Petersburg Battery, as well as the Halifax battery under Captain Samuel T. Wright,[29] immediately went to the site of Pegram's battery to see if any of the guns were unharmed. There he was met by the few men of the battery who had survived the explosion, and he witnessed the devastation of what had until moments before been one of his batteries. The enemy was already pouring over the Confederate works and into the crater left by the explosion. Despite the tremendous Federal artillery barrage and the oncoming assault, he found Elliott's men bravely manning the works up to the border of the Crater, "leaving no front for the entrance of the enemy except such as had been made vacant by the up-heaval of the earth." He also encountered Captain Richard G. Pegram, who had only recently, to his great fortune, been relieved in the battery along with First Lieutenant Melvin A. Martin by Lieutenants William B. Hamlin and Christopher S. Chandler. Pegram had retired to his headquarters near Mr. William Cameron's house at the head of Adams Street. Upon being awakened by the explosion, he also went toward his battery. There he encountered Major Coit, who ordered him to return to his headquarters and to ascertain how many of his men may have escaped and the extent of the loss, as well as to prepare a third battery not then placed in the trenches, in readiness to move as soon as ordered.[30] Pegram later placed his losses by the mine explosion at seventeen men and two officers killed, as well as three men captured.[31]

Coit then made his way 300 yards down the lines to the left to Wright's Battery, consisting of four guns, which was a few yards in the rear of the main line where it bore directly upon Elliott's Salient at close range, having been constructed to defend that front of the works. The battery was located atop a knoll to the left and near the ravine, or covered way, to Ransom's right. It was at a higher elevation than the Salient and was completely masked by trees. Given the gradual ascent from the ravine to the Crater, Wright's guns could sweep the front of the Confederate works over the heads of the Rebel defenders in the line occupied by Elliott's Brigade. Coit arrived at this battery within twenty to twenty-five minutes of the explosion. From this vantage point, Coit had a great view of the fighting to his right, where there was a relatively clear field of fire and the artillerymen could safely wreak carnage on the advancing Federals. Coit ordered the battery to open up with shrapnel and canister, sweeping the ground in front of Elliott's line and salient: "At this time, the enemy were still pressing their columns from their lines over the intervening space to the crater. This fire, together with the musketry from Elliott's brigade and other troops along the line within reach, soon checked the advance of the enemy from their own lines." By this time, the Crater had completely filled and thousands were crowded over its interior rim and stood in the rear totally disorganized in one dense mass. "Wright's fire was rapid, incessant, and accurate," according to Sergeant Joseph Gould of the 48th Massachusetts of Potter's division, "causing great loss." While the Federals made a vain attempt to locate it with mortar shells, which tore up the ground all around it, they could never silence it.[32]

Having checked the Federals' advance from their lines, Wright's guns were then turned directly on the Crater and the mass of humanity accumulating in its rear. Wright's battery completely swept the ground between the Federal lines and the Crater, the Crater itself and the ground to the right, firing over the heads of Ransom's men formed in the covered way along the ravine. "The fire from this battery was unremitting from the time it opened until the close of the engagement by the surrender of the crater, having thrown during the time from five to six hundred shell and canister." Major Coit, feeling the safety of the Confederate position depended "upon our success in preventing the formation of the enemy, ... watched their movements closely, and redoubled the fire when ... [he] saw any indication of formation or attempt to advance in the direction of the plank road." The work of Wright's battery was superior in the manner it was served, and the rapidity and consistency of its fire astonished the Federals that day.[33]

Major Wade Hampton Gibbs commanded the 13th Battalion Virginia Light Artillery in the I Corps of the Army of Northern Virginia. Gibbs was a twenty-seven year old South Carolinian and a West Point graduate from the class of 1860. He fired one of the first shots at

Fort Sumter, making his wartime experience one of the longest of any Southern officer. He was married to a sister of General Porter Alexander and was highly respected as an accomplished artilleryman.[34] The 13th Battalion was comprised of Company A, Otey's battery, under the command of Captain David Norvell Walker, with four 12-pound Napoleons; Company B, Ringgold's Battery, under Captain Crispin Dickerson, with four 12 pound Napoleons; and Company C, Davidson's Battery, then under the temporary command of Lieutenant James C. Otey, with two 12 pound Napoleons. Additionally, the Battalion contained a battery of mortars manned by men from the Otey and Ringgold Batteries under the command of Lieutenant Jonathan B. "Jack" Langhorne. Lieutenant John Hampden "Ham" Chamberlayne was about to formally take over command of Davidson's Battery, with its four Napoleons[35] and one hundred men, after Captain George S. Davidson went on leave pending his resignation becoming effective. He later wrote his mother that the unit was in a "loose, disorganized state."

Chamberlayne, a Richmond teacher and lawyer, had extensive wartime experience, and had been recommended for the position by A.P. Hill, Colonel Reuben Lindsey Walker, commanding the III Corps Artillery, and Major Gibbs. He had previously served with Purcell's and Crenshaw's batteries in the III Corps, and as adjutant for Colonel Walker. Otey had recently waived his right to promotion to the position, and the only other internal candidate, Second Lieutenant Thomas W. Powell, had failed the promotional examination. Chamberlayne himself was on sick leave in a field hospital on July 30, and Lieutenant James C. Otey was temporarily in command of its two 12-pound Napoleons, located just south of Baxter Road, 373 yards from the Crater, looking down a shallow ravine. This particular battery was on a knoll on the front line and thus quite prominent, with their only protection being their own parapets and traverses. Only the left gun was properly positioned to "throw canister-shot into the enemy's left flank, and [together] with Wright's battery to sweep the ground in front of the breach with a destructive cross-fire." Following the explosion, and after discharging a few rounds, Otey and his men unfortunately "acted as cowards and left their guns…" in the face of the intense Federal artillery barrage.[36] Soon thereafter, Major Gibbs moved to the gun along with some of Alexander's staff, including Captains Steven Winthrop and Joseph Cheves Haskell (brother of Major Haskell), Private L.T. Covington of Pegram's destroyed battery, and Lieutenant Edward Norvell from the Otey Battery. Soon Lieutenant Colonel Frank Huger, commanding the I Corps artillery in Alexander's absence, arrived and assisted in operating the gun. Later, Chamberlayne himself also came "spurring hard from the hospital…," against doctor's wishes, and in his own words, "so handled these abandoned guns that from that day the battery bore his name, and he wore another bar upon his collar."[37]

The gun was "now firing fast and with the deadliest precision," and the Federals could not put it out of commission, even though their shells were crashing all around it. After firing about forty rounds, Gibbs was severely wounded in the arm, and the gun was thereafter commanded by Colonel Huger. Upon learning of Gibbs' wounding (perhaps from Chamberlayne), and of the need for more experienced artillerymen to man the gun, Colonel J. Thomas Goode, commanding Wise's brigade, dispatched Captain Samuel D. Preston with his Company C of the 34th Virginia Regiment to take charge of Davidson's guns and relieve Huger, Winthrop and Haskell. Under his command, the gun then mowed down the advancing Federals with great slaughter until Preston was wounded.[38] Meanwhile, Goode had caused the 59th Virginia to form in the ditch running perpendicular to the rear of the main works, in front and slightly east of Davidson's Battery.

The Federals attempted five times to form in the rear of the breach and had planted four sets of colors on the line, but the 59th and 26th Virginia, along with the 22nd and 23rd South

Carolina, opened up a severe fire and drove them perpendicularly back into the Crater.[39] When Preston was wounded, command devolved upon Adjutant Edward "Ned" Bagby, aid-de-camp to Colonel Goode, whom Goode had just ordered to the aid of the battery upon learning of Preston's injury. Bagby, whose father was a veteran of the War of 1812 and whose great-grandfather was a settler at Jamestown in 1628, had volunteered for the King and Queen Artillery Company, and served without absence in the 34th Virginia until July 30, 1864. Enlisting as a private, he was subsequently detailed as an aide-de-camp for Henry A. Wise, the commander of the brigade.[40] Bagby was supervising the operating gun as ordered when a Federal shell exploded nearby and a fragment took off a portion of his head, killing him almost instantly.[41] Goode then dispatched Captain Alexander Fleet Bagby, Ned's cousin, along with his Company K, 34th Virginia, who then continued to man the gun with murderous fire on the Federals until the end of the fight.[42] Captain David N. Walker, from the Otey Battery, who took command of the battalion when Gibbs was wounded, wrote that the battery, together with Wright's, "were sweeping the open field like a tornado." Walker wrote that the field soon "looked like an inclined plane of dead men," despite the losses suffered by the battery itself.[43]

Lt. John H. Chamberlayne (*Ham Chamberlayne—Virginian*).

The Otey Battery was under the command of Captain Walker, with four 12-pound Napoleons located 473 yards from the Crater. Occupying a position on the Confederate main line on the right of Baxter Road, it was admirably adapted to throw canister into the Federal left flank and was commonly considered one of the best artillery units in the army. The Ringgold Battery under Captain Crispin Dickenson was located 573 yards to the south of the Crater and was equipped with four 12-pound Napoleons; it completely enfiladed the enemy.[44] The battery was divided into two sections, with two guns under the command of Captain Dickenson and the other two under First Lieutenant W.P. Robinson. Given the manner in which the guns had been positioned by General Alexander, only the two in Robinson's section were able to fire on the Federals in and around the Crater.[45] The men had slept in their clothes, with their guns double-shotted with grape and canister to meet the enemy in an emergency.

Upon the explosion, Lieutenant W.P. Robinson jumped up and looked down the line to the left and "saw my conception of a volcano." He could see the Federals charging the Crater, and he immediately opened with the two guns in his section with spherical case shells. Being 573 yards from the target was "just the right distance for using shells with the greatest effect, and ... [they] got the range at once." The Federal artillery soon opened on the two guns with murderous fire, but the brave Confederate artillerymen kept firing, throwing shell into the Crater and surrounding areas swarming with Union troops. Robinson saw mortar shells "as large as nail kegs" raining down on their position. Sergeant Kerr of the battery later stated that his gun kept on firing until it ran out of shells, whereupon they began using "log chains." Robinson's section was guarded by the Richmond Blues of Wise's Brigade, located directly behind their four guns, which made Robinson feel safe and even to wish for the Federals to attack them. General Wise once referred to this 75 years old unit (Company A, 46th Virginia

Infantry) as "the damnest hardest set of men to manage he ever had anything to do with, but they were perfect devils in a fight.[46]

A detachment of three Coehorn mortars from the "Mortar Train" under the command of Lieutenant Langhorne were manned by men from the Otey and Ringgold batteries. The unit was located behind the Otey Battery near the south side of Baxter Road and behind a bombproof, approximately one hundred yards from the main Confederate line and some 400 yards from the Crater. When Langhorne was ordered by Major Gibbs to return to his own unit, supervision of the battery passed to Sergeant A. Whit Smith of Otey's Battery.[47]

Major Haskell's Battalion had only Flanner's Battery, Company F, 13 Battalion North Carolina Artillery, and Captain James Nelson Lamkin's Company, Virginia Light Artillery (Co. B), also known as Captain Woodville Latham's Company, present and ready for action at Petersburg on July 30. Porter Alexander had assigned Lamkin's battery sixteen mortars, as his fieldpieces had not left South Carolina where his unit had been on detached service until rejoining the Army of Northern Virginia just before the Battle of the Wilderness. His unit was considered to be the first in the Southern army to be furnished with these small mortars. According to Bushrod Johnson's subsequent report, Lamkin's ordnance consisted of four Coehorns on the Jerusalem Plank Road, one Coehorn and two 12-pounder mortars in a ravine 200 yards to the left and in the rear of the Crater, and two mortars to the left of Wright's battery.[48] Behind the Salient, the Jerusalem Plank Road was sunken about five feet below the surrounding surface, offering a "beautiful place for an ambuscade of artillery & infantry." Alexander placed fourteen of Haskell's guns here and four in an earthwork out in front to sweep a sort of hollow out to the right. Alexander had approved the placement before he went on sick leave after being wounded, and he had ordered that Haskell not dig in or throw up breastworks in order to avoid the enemy detecting their location. Flanner's battery was posted on the Plank Road near the Gee house, forming a second line — but one which had no infantry support. He had a total of six 12-pound Napoleons at this location.[49]

Major John C. Haskell (Wise — *The Long Arm of Lee*).

Haskell had been aroused from sleep by the explosion, which he said was followed by others in rapid succession. He ran from his tent and gave orders to his orderly for the bugler to sound the alarm. The whole sky was lighted by the massive explosion, and from nearly a mile away one could see the fearful sight of men being blown into the air. Haskell rushed up the hill with two light batteries which were standing ready and took position on the Jerusalem Plank Road, occupying the half-completed gun pits. There he placed some guns in a shallow sink in the road, which made pretty effective protection. The Federals did not discover Haskell's guns in the sunken portion of the plank road until they opened up on the assaulting force outside the Crater. Once they opened up, the Federal artillery, thinking them to be fresh batteries brought up for that purpose, concentrated on them with devastating fire, and Haskell was required to pull back all but Flanner's six guns which were positioned in the sunken road. He asked for volunteers to man these and to his delight "every gun detachment volunteered to remain." Flanner's men opened with double canister on the troops attempting to move out of the Crater toward the Jerusalem Plank Road and Cemetery Hill. Despite being an inviting target for over one hundred Federal guns trained on their position, the "brave North Carolinians stood to their guns and repulsed every advance made by the enemy, holding them in check alone, and without infantry support…" for several hours. During this time, the battery was firing not less than fifty shells per minute at the advancing Federal troops.[50]

After seeing to his guns, Haskell had gone forward to seek out Elliott for infantry support for his exposed battery, as he believed that "a couple of good companies, deployed as skirmishers, could have taken them with little trouble; the ground was rough and broken, for protection, and the distance not over three hundred yards…." Haskell desperately wanted sharpshooters to keep the advancing enemy demonstrations down. Meanwhile, Captain Lamkin's battery of mortars on the plank road opened on the enemy and did great work demoralizing and damaging the Federal advance at a close distance, dropping shell after shell into the enemy and taking the fight out of them. Finally, Langhorne's 10-inch mortars from the Baxter Road behind Otey's battery and 8-inch mortars from behind Wright's Battery also joined in the dreadful chorus. One of Langhorne's men stated that they used almost a wagonload of shells in the process. Finally, Confederate batteries from across the Appomattox on the Federal right from Bradford's Battery consisting of four 20-pounder Parrots kept up a constant reply to the Federal cannonade, hitting the Federal line as far as the Hare house, and were thus able to prevent their total concentration opposite the Crater.[51]

General Johnson later memorialized in his report on the battle that the assaulting Union forces directed at the Crater consisted of the Ninth Corps and ultimately portions of two other corps. This large force was held in check "by little more than three regiments of Elliott's, two regiments of Ransom's, and two regiments of Wise's brigades, with the efficient aid of artillery, especially of Wright's battery and the our mortars, under Captain Lamkin, on the Jerusalem plank road" for over five hours! Their Herculean efforts and the effect were similar to those later described by Winston Churchill some seventy-five years later: "Never in the field of human conflict was so much owed by so many to so few."[52] This small band poured such a heavy fire on the Federals attempting to emerge from the Crater and adjoining works that the Federals were forced to seek protection in the Crater.

The combined fire made Bartlett's and Marshall's repeated attempts to reorganize their men into a fighting force and thus to move out of the Crater and its environs next to impossible. All attempts to revive the first division were thwarted by the hail of bullets and the blasts of grape and canister which tore its ranks to shreds and sent them flying for protection. Elliott's men and Wright's guns mowed the Union troops down like wheat in the harvest. Thus the first division of Burnside's corps was stalled by a combination of the resultant disorganization and the surprisingly effective defensive show of the Confederates at the breach. Of course, Burnside had many more men at his disposal, ready to enter the fray, and Meade had other corps which could play an effective role. Thus, while stalled, the offensive was far from played out by 6:30 A.M.

CHAPTER 11

"Push Forward to the Crest at Once"

As Ledlie's division slowly surged forward, Robert Potter's second division prepared to advance almost simultaneously. Pursuant to the revised plan, the corps had been formed in the shape of a triangle or wedge, with Ledlie's division at the point. It was now to push directly for Cemetery Hill. Potter's second division was to form on Ledlie's right, completing the line down to the base of the triangle or right side of the wedge to protect Ledlie's right flank and wipe out the exposed lines in the ravine running on that side of the Salient. Willcox's third division was to do the same on the left and attempt to seize the Confederate line on the plank road. Under the plan of attack, Potter's division was intended to be the third one to advance, awaiting the forward movement of Willcox's division before he advanced through the same small breach in the lines. Believing that this would result in too long a wait before his division could move forward, Potter, at a meeting around midnight of the 29th, "took the liberty of altering the programme a little," and instructed Brigadier General Simon Griffin to deploy a line of skirmishers to the right of where he was expected to make his attack and "if they found the enemy were stunned by the explosion, not to wait for the advance of the other troops ... [but] to push ahead immediately with his brigade and make a lodgment to the right, and establish a line on the crest of the ravine running nearly at right angles to the enemy's line."

Potter impressed upon Griffin "the importance of time, for the success of this movement depended mainly upon it being a surprise." If the assault seemed to be a success and Ledlie moved forward, Griffin was to advance from that position on the right. Thus, Griffin's orders were to move to the right of the mine and to make his attack there *on his own account*, emphasizing "that it was important to press forward as quickly as possible before the enemy recovered." Potter, however, did not see fit to advise Burnside of this alteration in the overall plan.[1] Griffin later related that "[t]he ground where they were was broken up with covered ways and numerous rifle-pits of the rebels. We had just driven the rebels out, and my troops occupied their places; therefore in that position, disconnected, as many of them were, it was difficult and almost impossible to form them to make a direct charge."[2]

Immediately following the explosion, Potter was concerned that his men were not advancing as he had ordered. Colonel Pleasants, whose regiment had been exempted from participating in the assault, given their tireless efforts in the mining operation, had volunteered to serve on Potter's staff for the assault. He had thus gone forward to ascertain the difficulties, and observed the awful carnage caused by the detonation of his mine. For many years thereafter, he would remember the sight of a Rebel without legs trying to crawl away and a dismembered arm still clutching a musket whose rope still entwined the man's fingers. Once oriented to the surroundings, he quickly noted that Ledlie's first division was completely disorganized. Pleasants drew his saber and commenced hitting the wallowing troops of the first division with the flat of the blade to spur them forward. He grabbed a lieutenant by the arm, ordering him to "Get your men together! Move out! On the Double!" Continuing to shout, and "striking out with saber and fists like a wild man," Pleasants' efforts were to no avail, as Ledlie's men soon were tumbling into the Crater and milling about, reacting as men do to a natural disaster.[3] They had "apparently ... forgotten that this situation was deliberately created to abet a campaign in which they were engaged. It was monstrous and it was useless."

Pleasants climbed out of the pit and reported back to Potter that the whole division was hopelessly mired in the Crater, without a division commander to lead them. Potter indicated to Pleasants that he was ready to move out but had orders to await Willcox's advance, and that the third division was slowly coming through the covered way and thus there would not be enough room for his men to get through. Willcox's troops were squeezing through these narrow ditches and just beginning to emerge two and three at a time near the front of the slope. Potter reiterated to Pleasants that he was to move forward in this improvised position but unfortunately he had orders to await Willcox. He then indicated that "I'll take a chance on something else," and substituted common sense for absurdity. Thus, he decided to abandon the covered way, where troops were required to go through like cattle through a chute, and bypass the bottleneck and instead advance across open ground in order to move forward. He thus implemented his alternative plan.[4]

Given the change in plans ultimately implemented by Potter, his first wing, the second brigade, under General Simon G. Griffin, was fortunately ready to move out soon after Ledlie's men advanced. (Potter later put the time when his men moved out at not more than eight to ten minutes after the explosion, or very soon after Ledlie's advance.)[5] The 9th New Hampshire under Captain Andrew J. Hough was in the first line of the division, having been on the brigade's skirmish line that morning, immediately in front of the Salient, when the division massed for the assault. The 9th had been reduced to no more than 200 men by the fighting of the last two months, with not one field grade officer left and only one other captain. Sergeant George L. Wakefield indicated that he was the sergeant of the guard on skirmish duty on the night of the 29th, as no relief came, and so his unit pushed forward from there.

Sergeant Franklin C. Burnham of the unit recalled that the brigade had massed that morning in a ravine just behind the first line of rifle pits. Following this advanced regiment in line was the relatively new yet battle-tempered 31st Maine, with Captain James Dean commanding, and the battle-weary 2nd Maryland under Lieutenant Colonel Henry Howard, Jr. This lead wing of Griffin's attacking force was led by Colonel Daniel White of the 31st Maine. White's instructions were to attack to the right of the Crater, thereby protecting Ledlie's right flank. The 32nd Maine, reduced to only 150 men under Colonel Mark F. Wentworth, the 17th Vermont under Major William B. Reynolds, the 6th New Hampshire under Captain Robert L. Ela and the 11th New Hampshire under Captain Arthur C. Locke, were all together right behind the lead element and prepared to march when called upon. At 5:00 A.M., Captain Hough cried "Forward!" and the 9th New Hampshire sprang to its feet and started forward over its own entrenchments. Corporal Newell Dutton later recalled that "[t]he first object that met my eyes as I jumped over our fortifications was a rebel, stretched out at full length, having been blown a hundred and fifty yards." Simultaneously, Colonel Wentworth commanding the 32nd Maine shouted "Forward!" and "with a fierce yell which could be but faintly heard owing to the deafening thunder of artillery, with all possible haste ... [they] rushed for Cemetery Hill. Yelling and shouting [they] rushed on by the entrance of the tunnel and over the earth-works at the point where ... [Lieutenant Chase had] joined ... [his] company on ... [his] arrival eight days previous."[6]

Simon Goodell Griffin, born in 1824 in Nelson, New Hampshire, had two grandfathers who fought in the Revolution. With no formal education, Griffin was still able to become a lawyer through hard work and intensive study. He enlisted as a private in the Goodman Rifles in Concord at the inception of the war and was soon elected a captain and took part in First Manassas with the 2nd New Hampshire. In late 1861, he was promoted to lieutenant colonel, and soon to colonel and commander of the 6th New Hampshire. He led the 6th through many significant battles, and brought off the colors himself from the field in the Union's defeat at Second Manassas. In late 1863, he was assigned to the Ninth Corps and was placed in command of the first brigade, second division, at Vicksburg. Upon coming east in 1864 with the Ninth Corps, Griffin was assigned to command of the second brigade of the division. He brought his brigade to Hancock's aid at a critical junction of the fight at Spotsylvania, enabling Hancock to hold his position, and was therefore promoted to brigadier general of volunteers for his gallantry. On June 17, 1864, his charge at Petersburg, together with Colonel John I. Curtin's first brigade of the division, created a breach in the Confederate works for one mile in length; many guns, prisoners and colors were captured. Griffin was a gallant leader, who had two horses killed, and another five wounded under him, and who, according to Henry C. Houston of Company C, 32nd Maine, "from first to last, whenever his men were ordered to go under fire ... went with them. Yet he never received a wound, and was never absent from his command on account of illness."[7]

Regardless of the imposing parapets and obstructions in their path, Griffin's men lined up in columns of regiments as they prepared to advance. The second brigade quickly stepped away on a line obliquely to the right. There was no time for regimental battle formations, however, given the considerable obstructions left on the field. Rather, the brigade ran single file through the narrow openings and rushed ahead in rather disorganized clusters. By the time the third division had funneled through the narrow covered way, both divisions would thus be ready to press forward around the Crater in support of the first, saving valuable time. The brigade immediately rushed for the right, with its pioneers organized from the brigade clearing the way. As they went forward, Griffin's men were almost suffocated by the immense clouds of smoke and dust. Their advance was further slowed by Burnside's lack of attempt to remove the abatis and chevaux-de-fries in front of the Rebel works. Lieutenant Chase reported that, almost immediately after they left their own breastworks, when they had scarcely charged over twenty-five yards, a murderous fire opened on their right flank, and then soon thereafter "another volley similar to the fight was poured into ... [their] left. The effect of this volley was horrible, men appeared to be falling in every direction and the shrieks and groans of the wounded were heartrending."[8]

The situation seemed like it was rapidly beginning to turn against the Union. The volleys were coming from the ravine approximately 400 yards to the left, directed mainly at the remnants of the first division, which had begun to organize itself and was slowly starting to skirt the rim of the Crater. The Confederates, having largely recovered from the effects of the explosion, were pouring fire into the blue-clad ranks as Elliott's shattered brigade rallied into a ravine to the Crater's rear. The Federals dropped in their tracks, and when a concealed battery opened up and dropped shells directly in their midst, the survivors of the disorganized first division broke and scrambled for the nearest cover, back over the rim of the Crater. The situation was rapidly deteriorating from bad to worse. Griffin's men made slow progress in their oblique advance, as the terrain was difficult and the slope steep, even though the men were fairly well shielded from the fire for the time being. As they marched forward, Sergeant

John Hilling of the 32nd Maine wrote, on August 1, 1864 that "[o]ur batteries and those of the enemy were now in full play, and with rifle firing the din was deafening. Shot and shell flew thick and fast. It was truly terrific. Two or three forts were firing on us, while our forts were firing on them and the town of Petersburg, part of which was set on fire." After briefly having his men lie down as ordered, Colonel Wentworth of the 32nd Maine shouted "Quick to the fort for your lives, boys!" The men sprang again to their feet, and they were very quickly hit by the murderous hail of lead.[9]

BG Simon G. Griffin (USAMHI).

Although Potter issued clearer instructions on where to focus his assault on the Confederate line than Ledlie's regimental commanders received, the dense smoke and dust, coupled with the spirited defense from Elliott's shattered brigade, caused Colonel White's advance began to veer south, or left, toward the Crater. There they became enmeshed with some of the scattered regiments of Bartlett's first brigade led by Weld, which was then struggling to move out of the Crater and into the rifle pits to the north of the Crater and adding considerably to the confusion that Griffin's lead elements were already experiencing. Coming upon the smoldering, gaping hole, Griffin's brigade overlapped it on the left, and thus two or three of its regiments, or at least certain portions of them, poured into the already crowded Crater. At least two of these regiments claimed to have been the first into the Crater, a claim that was certainly disputed by the 14th New York Heavy Artillery and other units of Ledlie's division. The two commands quickly became thoroughly confused and unmanageable.

To that point, Sergeant Burnham of the 9th New Hampshire, in his diary, later wrote that "We immediately advanced, leaped on works, and charged the fort. I am confident that the colors of our regiment were the first inside of it." Burnham, upon entering the pit, accepted the surrender of one man who had been stunned by flying debris, sending him immediately to the rear. Eighteen year old Sergeant Ned Parsons and Corporal Newell T. Dutton, carrying the flags of the regiment, rushed past the rim of the Crater and planted their flags in the smoking fissure of the demolished fort. (Dutton also later claimed that these were the first flags planted in the Crater, suggesting they arrived ahead of Ledlie's men.) Just as the tandem flags surmounted the Crater, Ned Parsons "whirled around with a terrible wound in his thighs and hip, and the Stars and Stripes fluttered to the ground for the third time in ... [that] regiment's history." It was quickly retrieved by a man from Parson's hometown who hurried on into the pit. Sergeant Charles J. Simons, the first of his regiment, and by many other accounts the very first Federal soldier into the Crater, was soon among the very first captured. Simons told his captors that Grant was coming with over 50,000 men. He indicated to them that "If he doesn't get in, you can take me safely to your rear; if he does get in, I'll take you safely to our rear." The Rebels agreed to this straightforward proposition. Soon, the rest of the regiment appeared and Simons exclaimed, "Now is your time, boys; just drop your guns and come with me!" whereupon Simons, rather than remaining a prisoner, led them to the Union rear.[10]

Lieutenant J.J. Chase, of the 32nd Maine, reported that upon reaching the advanced rifle pits and the Crater some of his men tumbled and others jumped into the hole. He also asserted that his regiment was one of the first into the abyss, with Adjutant Hayes being the first officer in to the Crater. Another soldier of the 32nd Maine indicated that when he got over the rim, "there were but two colors that I saw planted there, the 31st and 32nd Maine." Colonel Bartlett, when he reached the fort, grasped Colonel Wentworth's hand and said, "I am glad to shake hands with the only officer who had led his men in." Looking back toward the Federal lines, there was a "winnow of dead and dying" men from the 32nd on the path to the Crater. The Confederates, upon their recovery from the blast, quickly began to throw shells and a heavy barrage of musketry into their ranks. Thus, the men were exposed to almost certain death in any attempt to leave the Crater in order to return to the Federal lines.

The regiments in the Crater had absolutely no intention of staying put, however. Wentworth gave the order "Forward, Thirty-second Maine" and pointed up the steep side of the Crater. Although men could be seen constantly dropping from the top, the regiment hesitatingly moved forward. Finding no one to hold the colors, Lieutenant Chase mounted the fort and held them himself. Before it was firmly planted, the staff was shot in two and the flag was literally cut to pieces. As Wentworth emerged from the Crater, he was hit with the same round which had passed through Sergeant Eaton. Consequently, the men took shelter in a trench just outside the fort, mixing with the 9th New Hampshire, and returned the Confederate's fire, firing their first shots of the battle. From this point, the men observed other Confederates forming in the ravine, as if for a charge.[11]

Meanwhile, other portions of the 9th New Hampshire moved through the Crater, up the other side, and into a wide traverse constructed for taking artillery in and out of the fort. Corporal George Wakefield and two fellow soldiers jumped over the trench, where they found a huddle of half-dressed Rebels too stunned to resist. As they herded the prisoners back toward the Union lines, a picket line of the Eighteenth Corps began firing into the Confederate prisoners, driving them back on their captors. The Rebels, finding themselves caught between two fires, retrieved some fallen rifles and began swinging them at their captors. Following a brief struggle, the prisoners escaped. Private Leander C. Barnes of Company B took as a prisoner a young Rebel "whose hair had been dark before the explosion, but when we took him out it had turned white from fright."[12]

The lead wing of the brigade, still led by Colonel White, soon came upon the partially abandoned Confederate trench to the immediate north of the Crater. The ground in that immediate vicinity was cut up with small sheltered pits, traverses and covered ways soon filled with Confederate defenders, who kept up a severe fire from these sites and from a line of pits in the ravine where McMaster had ordered the remnants of Elliott's brigade to re-form and defend. Lieutenant Powell, Ledlie's judge advocate, later observed the tremendous difficulty the Federal troops had in traversing the terrain, "owing to the peculiar character of the enemy's works, which were not single, but complex and involuted and filled with pits, traverses, and bomb-proofs, forming a labyrinth as difficult of passage as the crater itself. This broke up the brigade, which, meeting the severe fire of canister, also fell back into the crater, which was then full to suffocation."[13]

The men turned sharply and swept down the Confederate line for a considerable distance and were immediately successful in capturing a second line for approximately 200 yards to the north. In the process, they forced Elliott's brigade back considerably, until it reached a second line formed in the covered way.[14] The men were unable to negotiate the intricate works beyond the initial Confederate trenches. At the same time, they were also stung by a heavy storm of Confederate canister from Wright's Battery, and heavy rifle fire from Elliott's men, and they were thus reluctantly forced to give way. Although pushed back, the Confederates had all recovered and opened with a scalding fire themselves. Potter would later claim

Charge of the Second Division, Ninth Army Corps, into the Crater (*Harper's Weekly*).

that the opposition was as severe as he had ever seen. After rather severe hand-to-hand fighting, the Rebels had the upper hand, given the familiar terrain and their defensive fire. It was soon impossible for the Federals to drive them beyond where they held Ledlie's troops. On top of all of these difficulties, White's men were still further impaired by having become intermingled with the portions of Bartlett's men who were attempting to form and move out of the Crater on the right.[15]

The fierce opposition White's men initially encountered in the form of a heavy hail of bullets and several counterattacks was the work of a portion of the 17th South Carolina, which was still occupying their works north of the Crater. They were, however, spread dangerously thin after Colonel Smith's sudden departure into the ravine. This rather fragile line finally faltered when hit by White's men, causing Colonel McAfee to move to the right to bolster the 17th and also to send the 49th North Carolina under Lieutenant Colonel John Fleming rapidly to their aid at a double-quick. The 49th ran toward that portion of the 17th South Carolina, urging them to hold on, assuring the men that "We are coming!" The Tarheels rushed into the endangered works and began unleashing a feverish fire into White's men, as well as that portion of the first division which had emerged from the Crater. The men fired and then accepted another loaded musket from those in the rear in order to keep up a rapid fire. The officers in the rear exhorted their men with cries of "Hold them back, boys! Hold them back!" shouted to the men that they were fighting for their lives and everything they held dear in life. Elliott's men were soon forcefully pressed back upon the 49th; and one of its members observed how "nobly ... most heroically, did those South Carolinians contest every inch of the ground. Color after color was placed upon the works from which our men were driven until twelve stands wave defiance in our faces. Beyond the brow and hidden by it from us, six more flaunted before our astonished boys, thus making eighteen in all."[16]

As Elliott's men backed up toward where the 49th North Carolina then stood firm and resolute, Colonel Fleming quickly ordered his men into the ditch running perpendicular to the main trench, telling them to stop the Federals who were pouring around inside the works and coming down their right flank. The remainder of the regiment then poured a galling fire into the Federals who were rushing over the works and down on the Rebels. The men in the front ranks fired round after round as loaded muskets were rapidly passed forward, while the officers in the rear paced feverishly with their sabers drawn, shouting words of encouragement. Crates of ammunition were brought up and the cartridge tins were strewn within easy reach along the parapets. In the melee, Colonel Fleming fell, shot through the head and killed instantly. However, the fierce killing machine had done its work. White's men had been checked and caused reluctantly to be laid low. Then the very frightening sharpshooting commenced on both sides. Owing to the advantageous position of a portion of the 49th in the aftermath, they were able to fire right into the ditch packed full of Federals.[17]

White's force took this fire full in the face. In addition to this formidable defense by the Carolinians, White's men were being shredded in the enfilading fire from Wright's Battery, hidden in the woods across the ravine to their right, as well as from the single, but remarkably effective, gun from Davidson's Battery on the left. By then, at least a dozen Confederate mortars had also begun to rain shells around and into the Crater. White was now obliged to swing his line around to adjust for the angle made by the 49th North Carolina, a portion of which had swung back into one of the covered ways. Clearly, White's momentum was spent, having made, at best, 200 yards down the Confederate line north of the Crater. White sent word back to General Griffin reporting his position and inquiring as to why the first division had not advanced: "General. We have taken the enemy's works and hold them. How are our lines doing on the right and left?"

He was already well beyond Ledlie's division, whose flank his force was to protect according to orders; his exposed flanks were suffering, and their ammunition was running low. Griffin responded by writing on the back of White's message: "We hold the fort, and are all right. Hold what you have gained. First division is now advancing. All looks well as far as we have gone."[18] Griffin did not include in his response that the Federal infantry to his right was still totally inert as far as an advance was concerned. Nor did he explain to the embattled White that he was at that time actually the right flank of the army's advance. Further, he did not include, because he was then unaware that Burnside's order to Ledlie to move out of the Crater had reached him at the bombproof hospital where he had closeted himself, and that upon receiving these orders, Ledlie still chose to remain there, sending a staff officer forward instead to spur his disorganized and demoralized division forward. And so White's troops valiantly attempted to maintain the ground they had earned with their blood, in the complete and undoubted anticipation that help was on the way, while continuing to take heavy casualties in the process.[19]

While Ledlie's men were struggling in and around the Crater and halting, and Potter's oncoming division was moving along to the right, a frustrated General Meade began a series of inquiries and orders to Burnside. At 5:40 A.M., he asked Burnside, "What news from your assaulting column? Please report frequently." Burnside promptly replied that his men had "the enemy's first line and occupy the breach. I shall endeavor to push forward to the crest as rapidly as possible." At 5:40 A.M., Meade, through chief of staff Humphreys, sent the following message:

> The commanding general learns that your troops are halting at the works where the mine exploded. He directs that all your troops be pushed forward to the crest at once. Call on General Ord to move forward his troops at once.

Then, growing increasingly frustrated at the continued failure of the assaulting force to move on toward Cemetery Hill, Meade telegraphed Burnside at 6:00 A.M.:

> Prisoners taken say there is no line in their rear, and that their men were falling back when ours advanced; that none of their troops have returned from the James. Our chance is now; push your men forward at all hazards (white and black) and don't lose time in making formations, but rush for the crest.

Burnside promptly replied to this last order that he had "given orders to all his division commanders to push everything in at once."[20]

Griffin had by then brought up the remainder of his brigade to support Colonel White's advance. His arrival on the scene with the remainder of his men confirmed that his left was terribly entangled with Ledlie's men. The Crater itself was full of dismembered units and various officers giving contradictory commands to hopelessly mixed clumps of soldiers from disparate units. Consequently, next to nothing was happening, and there was absolutely no advance and not much hope of one. Men were literally falling on their hands and knees, and bodies were so thick on the ground that it was difficult for a man to walk. When a man was shot, he fell and rolled to the bottom of the abyss.

Having received Burnside's verbal order to "carry the hill in front of the mine" instead of to the right, according to the plan, Potter immediately communicated this revised order to his brigade commanders. He then "gave such orders as were necessary to alter the disposition of the troops, and endeavored to push [his] ... column forward." Griffin communicated the change in orders to his subordinates and immediately began an attempt to carry them out. He leaped atop the trenches and waved his sword frantically, "practically begging his regiments to come out and take it." He then was able to coax out a very thin skirmish line, and to his right more of his men inched toward the hill; but "just then the defenders opened up with additional artillery" and "the indecisive Union front lost what little temerity it had had." Most of Griffin's skirmish line was subsequently mowed down, and Griffin himself was hit by two spent bullets. The "scattered blue uniforms faded back into a cloud that still lingered over the crater...." [21]

Burnside's orders to Potter and his other division commanders were precipitated by Meade's 5:40 A.M. telegraph that all his troops "be pushed forward to the crest at once." Lieutenant Colonel Charles G. Loring, Burnside's assistant inspector general, had written his commander a dispatch reflecting the utter reluctance of Ledlie's men to advance beyond the Crater. Loring had, by Burnside's order, followed Colonel Marshall's men in their assault and was then present with them in the Crater. The communiqué stated that "Ledlie's division has occupied the crater without opposition. But his men are crowding down in it, and he cannot get them forward." Loring entrusted the dispatch to a courier who was unaware that Burnside had changed his headquarters for the assault to Fort Morton or that General Meade was utilizing Burnside's permanent headquarters for the day. Thus, the dispatch intended for Burnside was delivered instead to Meade, which precipitated his rather abrupt order of 5:40 to his perplexed corps commander to "push your men forward at all hazards and don't lose time in making formations, but rush for the crest."[22]

Potter was aware that Griffin's brigade had lost heavily in the assault and had been thrown into confusion after having been mixed with the disorganized units of the first division. Interpreting the latest directive as a radical change of plans, he therefore directed Griffin to move forward without any reference to other troops and to attack the enemy frontally. As the first division was unlikely to advance in coordination with his own, Potter had his men proceed on their own, but in so doing "they were compelled to pass through the confused ranks of the First Division, and consequently became themselves broken and confused." As the fire from the Rebel defenders by this time was so hot, it was impossible for Griffin to re-form his ranks. In spite of the immense difficulties he was experiencing, Griffin did manage to get three or four regiments across and beyond the line of enemy works, and "was getting them into pretty good shape." Convinced that he needed a diversion to distract the Rebel's attention from Griffin's forward movement, Potter gave Colonel Zenas R. Bliss, commander of the first brigade, orders to send two regiments to support Griffin's advance, and to then take the remainder of his brigade and attack farther to the right of the Crater. He arranged that the two regiments going in support of Griffin's brigade should pass through the Crater, then turn to the right and sweep down the right of the enemy's works. Potter also gave Bliss a warning to be wary of Confederate fire against his right flank.[23]

Griffin had sent word that there was room for three regiments in addition to his own in the advancing front. Thus Bliss advanced with the 4th Rhode Island—which had just joined the brigade on July 16 after serving as the garrison troops at the Point Lookout, Maryland, prison camp—with Lieutenant Colonel Martin P. Buffum in the lead. As Corporal George H. Allen of Company B later recalled, the regiment had spent the prior night in their rifle pits:

> ...thinking of home and all that was dear to us, and of the bloody work that we must soon undertake, wondering how many of us would, ere the setting of the next day's sun, have passed away in the roar and smoke of battle and bidden farewell to earth; and we looked upon each other's faces and whispered messages to be left with those who were likely to be kept out of the fight, as if indeed we were about to part with them for the last time. And well were those looks cast, and well those messages given for many of our comrades who returned not again.... [The explosion caused] shrieks of the doomed garrison, the roar and rush of the huge guns and timber down from the great black clouds of smoke that were curling and unfolding over our heads, and the mingled noise and shock of the explosion, struck terror into the hearts of the bravest of our troops, and for a moment not a man stirred out of his tracks, not an eye was taken off that awful spectacle."

Then the cry "Forward, Fourth Rhode Island" was heard, and the unit started up the hill. Next in line was the 45th Pennsylvania, under the command of Captain Theodore Gregg. Bliss had ordered Gregg to leave part of his regiment deployed as skirmishers and to move the rest to the edge of the woods and form on the right of the 4th Rhode Island. As the unit massed in front of the mine, it contained only 110 men and eleven officers. Following the 45th was the 58th Massachusetts, that morning under the command of Captain Charles E. Churchhill as a result of the commanding officer, Captain E.S. Horton, being indisposed. The original plan was for Bliss to swing these regiments obliquely to the right. However, given Burnside's revised order, Potter had them face to the front and march through the covered way by the left flank.

As this lead element of the first brigade came up to the front, it was discovered that some of Griffin's brigade, primarily the 6th New Hampshire, had not yet left the Union lines. Consequently, Bliss's men were

Col. Zenas R. Bliss (National Archives).

required to wait for the 6th New Hampshire to move out. The 6th had earlier requested orders to move forward in order to "take a hand in the fight," but were told to remain where they were for the time being, while Confederate artillery played havoc on their position. As Captain Lyman Jackman of the 6th and Colonel Bliss were sitting with some barrels filled with dirt, a shell landed near them. They decided to move just before a second round came in, killing two men outright and wounding several others. Griffin then sent word that the 6th could move forward into the open field halfway between the two lines. There the regiment became a fine target for Confederate cannon fire on two sides. The unit stayed in the hot field, with the temperature reaching 105 degrees, for the rest of the battle, retiring only when the shattered holdouts of the Union ranks staggered back to their lines at 4:00 P.M. and receiving fire from front, right and left, with no protection save what dirt they could throw up with their tin cups.[24]

As the 4th Rhode Island moved out, it heard cries to cease fire, that they were firing on their own men. This, however, proved to be a ruse; the battle-wise Federals had experienced this before in the cornfield at Antietam. Thus, they charged across the open field to the Crater, where they encountered Bartlett's men emerging from the right side. No one seemed to be in charge in this area as Griffin endeavored to extricate his men from the mass of entangled troops. George Allen of the 4th noticed that Burnside's instincts regarding his men had proven to be correct. They were reverting to their "old habit of sheltering themselves" by stopping and digging in at the first opportunity. Officers were vainly attempting to get their men to move on, leaping on the parapets and grabbing their colors. But the men kept "bleeding back to the hole again" under the intense Confederate fire. The 4th was forced to lie down on the outside of the pit and immediately started suffering casualties.

The 45th Pennsylvania under Captain Gregg was ordered to follow the 4th Rhode Island and they marched by the left flank through the covered way, then went double-quick across the open field to the destroyed fort, all the while exposed to severe fire from grape, canister and musketry. The regiment arrived to find the same scene, with the Crater's slopes covered with the dead, dying and wounded of the first and second divisions. There Gregg gave the order to "face by the right flank" in order to march in line of battle. Upon arriving at the Crater's edge, he then faced his men again by the left flank and marched in single file around and to the rear of the Crater.

The 58th Massachusetts, under Captain Churchill, initially moved out in good order behind the 45th Pennsylvania, but in moving through the covered way they became confusingly intermixed with the men of another division. The main portion kept moving to the fort amid severe artillery and musketry fire, encountering the disorganized mass of men and hopeless debris and confusion at the site of the explosion. "In doing this the right and left wings of the regiment became separated." Captain Churchill went to see where the balance of his regiment had gone. Unfortunately, he found that "they had been ordered by another officer to file to the right of said fort, which split the regiment in two."[25]

By this time, Bliss had sent only three of his regiments forward, the remainder being held on the Federal front lines as the Crater was so crowded and he realized that "there was no more need of troops in front." The 7th Rhode Island, assigned to the division as engineers, was ordered under the hill in reserve. Bliss later reported that he had actually ordered the 58th Massachusetts, supported by the 4th Rhode Island and the 45th Pennsylvania, to move to the right down the Confederate lines, "with the understanding that as soon as [he] ... saw the flag move [he] ...would order the New York regiments to charge across between the two lines, and if they carried the rebel lines to connect with the other regiments of the brigade and hold the line." As no charge was made after he had twice ordered one to commence, Bliss sent in his brigade inspector, Captain E.T. Raymond of the 36th Massachusetts, with orders to move out immediately.[26]

As soon as he saw the colors of the 58th Massachusetts commence to move, Bliss sent the 51st New York and the 2nd New York Mounted Rifles, then functioning as a dismounted unit, and together they crossed the field without difficulty, and commenced hitting the flank of the 24th and 49th North Carolina to the right of Elliott's men. Bliss then watched as the 4th Rhode Island, the 45th Pennsylvania and half of the 58th Massachusetts, instead of charging to the right in support of the New York regiments as he had directed, charged obliquely to the right toward Cemetery Hill. This movement left a dangerous gap between the right of these three regiments and the left of the New York regiments. The reason for this was that Griffin had not been informed of Bliss's intentions, so he had countermanded Bliss's first two orders to move and then countermanded the third, thereby causing the gap to occur. As Private Frederick Cushman of the 58th recalled the dilemma, Bliss's three regiments near Griffin had been given orders from Griffin and General Bartlett to charge upon a Confederate battery about a fourth of a mile in the rear of the Crater. It was then learned that some of the first brigade's other regiments were bearing to the right in the direction of another Confederate battery (which turned out to be Wright's), neatly positioned in the woods. There was thus a considerable misunderstanding as to which battery the left wing of Bliss's brigade was intended to capture. The result was hesitation and confusion. Bliss's brigade, therefore, remained not only separated but actually poised to move in opposite directions under orders from various leaders, some of whom were not even with their division. The confusion was so great that Captain Gregg later told the Court of Inquiry that "I received so many orders from so many different commanders at that time that I did not know which to obey."[27]

Griffin's revised objective after receiving Potter's new orders was the Jerusalem Plank Road, approximately 500 yards in the rear of the Crater. While the Confederate fire, both artillery and musketry, was quite intense by this time, the ground was still held only by the remnants of the Confederate force blown up in the explosion under Colonel Smith, the North Carolina regiments and Flanner's battery of North Carolina artillery. Thus, Bartlett ordered Captain Gregg to charge across the plain and secure the buildings on the plank road, including the Gee house, to be used by sharpshooters against the Confederate batteries along that road. Unbeknownst to Bartlett, Generals Lee, Beauregard and Johnson were at the time observing the struggle from that very house. As Griffin readied his brigade, plus the three regiments of Bliss's, for this assault to the west, he was raked by intense fire from Smith's Carolinians and by the canister from Wright's Battery in the woods high to his right. As the men started out for the high ground in front of Jerusalem Plank Road, they were soon hit by the Ellet and Brander batteries to the northwest, and Flanner's in front of them, in addition to the continuing devastating fire from Wright's guns. The ensuing charge was a gallant one, under murderous fire of grape and canister from the enemy artillery brought to bear from every direction, "yet the little band kept on, and the Forty-fifth Pennsylvania [by a rather fanciful account] had nearly reached the house on the top of the hill,[28] when the line wavered, and, for want of support, obliged to fall back to the covered way leading to work previously taken," which they held with several other regiments of the second brigade. Colonel Buffum called for the 4th Rhode Island to "Keep your eye on the colors" and "Forward the Fourth," and the regiment advanced on a run toward the crest through what a number of the regiment later ascribed as "the hottest fire we ever experienced. But in spite of all the officers' exertions, the regiments back in the crater ... would not follow them." After gaining approximately one hundred yards, the 4th lay down and awaited support from the rest of the brigade. Corporal George H. Allen of Company B later described their situation, "[v]olley after volley sweeps over us, and in a moment the enemy has trained their guns and mortars upon the spot where we lie. We are digging our noses into the ground, to escape the fire."

Simultaneously, the 58th also charged some distance under heavy fire. Still the men worked their way over the traverses and bombproofs just recently vacated by the Confederates. The 45th Pennsylvania later alleged that they almost reached the crest, but the troops to their left were unable to support them further. Then, Flanner's North Carolina Battery came tearing up the Jerusalem Plank Road at breakneck speed, wheeled onto the hilltop, and opened up on the advancing Federals. The resultant "hail of canister was unbearable."[29]

The fighting was "the hottest work we have ever seen," Sergeant Burnham of the 9th New Hampshire commented. The Confederates seemed to, instead of replying to the Federal barrage, have "reserved their fire for our advance, and now commenced pouring in a withering fire of case and canister that compelled our men to seek protection in the trenches and the ruins of the fort." The hail of canister became unbearable. Frederick Cushman of the 58th Massachusetts later reflected on the situation:

> The order to charge was obeyed promptly and without a murmur. Advancing with the rest of our brigade into the open field, it was discovered that some of the regiments were bearing to the right.... The enemy kept up its incessant firing; the line of battle wavered and finally broke, the men filing off into the fort; and into the saps and trenches which led from it. Again the order came to charge upon the battery across the field. The charge was made; but fruitlessly, the men returning to the fort and filing every portion of it to overflowing.

A round struck a lieutenant of the 45th Pennsylvania in the cheek, destroying his eye and much of his face. One of the unit's captains ministered to the wounded officer, binding his gross wound with his handkerchief and sending him to the Federal rear. When released from a Confederate prison months later, the astonished captain learned that this severely injured lieutenant had somehow survived. Corporals Allen and Frank Tompkins of the 4th Rhode Island found themselves fighting for the same shell hole in the merciless hail of Confederate artillery shells and lead. "Get out of this hole, its mine" they each yelled as they grappled for position. The matter was settled when a canister round dealt Tompkins a glancing blow in the side, whereupon he yelled, "I'm wounded" Allen immediately told him, "Get to the rear then, where you belong," as he nestled deeper in the hole. At last, the noble effort to take the crest ground to a halt, and no more ground could be gained against the withering fire without support from the Federals behind the works. Griffin's men had gained barely one hundred yards beyond the Crater, but they could not even hold on to this purchase, which had been paid for with so many lives.

The 45th Pennsylvania retreated into a traverse extending one hundred feet to the rear that was about four feet wide and three feet deep, with the excavated dirt piled up on the sides. From this traverse branched two more traverses, one to the right for about forty feet from the outer edge and the other about twenty feet from the outer end toward the left. The 45th fell into this second traverse after its unsuccessful charge, mixing with other regiments, including the 58th Massachusetts. There, they were in very close quarters with the Rebels. Captain R.G. Richards of the 45th encountered a Confederate major pointing a revolver at him and insisting that he surrender. As the encounter escalated, Captain Gregg suddenly appeared and grabbed for the Confederate's gun, finally compelling him and his two men to surrender.[30] Gregg took charge of the prisoners and ordered Richards to remain there in command within fifty feet of the Confederates who were laying down that withering fire. Richards and his men dug in, anticipating that reinforcements would soon rescue them from their dire straits.

While this action was transpiring near the Crater, Bliss's two New York regiments well off to the right made considerable progress in clearing the Confederate trenches containing Ransom's men in the direction of Wright's battery. The 51st New York had considerable success fighting its way to the right against Ransom's flank, with the 2nd Mounted New York Rifles working in tandem on the Union side of the line. The 2nd captured the front line of Rebel rifle pits, which it held until 3:30 P.M. that day. These two units captured almost 300 yards of the Confederate line north of the Crater, thus becoming a significant threat to Wright's Battery on the knoll above the ravine. Over time, however, the gap between the two units and the main body of their brigade left them highly vulnerable. This gap "should have been filled by ... [Bliss's] regiments ordered to charge down the line to the right, but subsequently sent against the hill" instead. The fire into the ranks of the New Yorkers was so intense that, unfortunately, there were just not enough troops to seize and hold so lengthy a prize of trench works without support.

Following a terrifying artillery barrage, the 51st was forced to fall back rapidly. The command soon devolved upon Major George Whitman, brother of the famous poet Walt Whitman, when a solid shot struck Major John G. Wright in the side. Shortly thereafter, Major Whitman himself became a casualty. Soon, these two New York regiments were severely cut up by the heavy doses of canister and fell short of capturing the guns of Wright's Battery by twenty yards or more. However, they could then get no farther due to a lack of support, "its progress being impeded by slashed timber, while an increasing fire of canister was poured into the men. They fell back to the enemy traverses and intrenchments."

The unit found that it was enfiladed on both flanks by small arms fire as well. While so stalled, Lieutenant William T. Ackerman of Company F was still able to make life difficult for his Rebel foes in the artillery battery as he: "kept one of the guns from doing us harm by shooting every man down that got in front of it to load it. I kept several of my men loading rifles while I fired them and I did not stop till the rebs were on their works." Eventually, both New York regiments were required to fall back for lack of support.[31] Griffin's men had by now been extricated from the terrible confusion near the Crater and began moving forward slowly, under hot fire, cautiously moving the whole second division around the destroyed fort. However, while Griffin was still valiantly but tenuously holding his advanced position past the Crater, the New York regiments were simultaneously falling back.

Third division commander Brigadier General Orlando B. Willcox was born in Michigan in 1823 and graduated from West Point in 1847. He served in the army for ten years, his tenure including participation in the Mexican War, as well as time fighting the Seminoles in Florida. Upon the war's inception, he left a law practice in Detroit and in May of 1861 was appointed colonel of the 1st Michigan Volunteer Infantry. He was taken prisoner leading his unit at First Manassas and spent over a year in a Rebel prison. Upon his release he was soon promoted to brigadier and commanded a division of Burnside's Ninth Corps at Antietam, Fredericksburg and Knoxville. On July 30, his division was relieved by the 18th Corps and formed close to Ledlie's left and rear, with Brigadier General John Frederick Hartranft's first brigade in the front line. Colonel William Humphrey's second brigade occupied a part of the second line of the rifle pits and the covered way leading to Hartranft's brigade.

Willcox's orders were to move down, clear the enemy's works on the left, then move up toward the Jerusalem Plank Road and take a position thereon. At 5:00 A.M.,[32] Hartranft followed Ledlie's advance with his brigade consisting of the 27th Michigan, under Lieutenant Colonel William B. Wright, the 37th Wisconsin, under Colonel Samuel Harriman, the 109th New York under Captain Edwin Evans and the 13th Ohio Volunteer Cavalry (Dismounted) under Colonel Noah H. Hixon, and passed the Federal front lines in column of battalions: "Moving fast and paying little attention to the murderous fire pouring in on them, the 1st brigade hit the Confederate line to the left of the Crater and penetrated beyond. They smashed into a rebel battery and managed to sweep across the enemy line to their left."

As Hartranft's men moved out, the column mistakenly obliqued to the right, so that instead of taking the line to the left of the Crater, it hit just to the left, adjacent to the Crater itself, in piecemeal fashion, in that portion of the fort which had not been demolished. Had the lead elements of the brigade moved in a more orderly fashion against the more open portion of the Confederate line between Baxter Road and the Crater, the brigade would undoubtedly have enjoyed more success. As it was, however, the first three regiments, like Griffin's before them, became entangled with the first division, which had come to a halt in the Crater. As a result, Hartranft could not move forward despite the efforts of his able commanders. He endeavored to push the lead three regiments to the left as far as possible, into the undamaged portion of the fort. However, regimental organization was broken by the irregularity of the surface, the mass of troops and the enfilading fire from the Confederate artillery on the right and the left of the Crater.

Once Ledlie's men halted in the Crater, the route forward was soon so congested that two regiments of Hartranft's brigade were forced to remain exposed on the rear slope of the Crater, while the remaining two, the 8th Michigan under Lieutenant Colonel Ralph Ely and the 51st Pennsylvania under Colonel William J. Bolton, were left waiting in the rear of the Federal works for a space to move forward. Hartranft's halt resulted in forcing the units behind him also to a stop, precipitating a traffic jam for the remainder of Willcox's division, and leaving some of them strung back into the covered way in the rear. Hartranft and Willcox later reported that his lead regiments recovered two partially covered guns in the fort and soon had them operational, enabling them to be used effectively against the Confederate rifle pits to the left

and in the assaults which the Rebels later made on the Crater (ironically, the same two guns that the 14th New York Heavy Artillery claimed to have captured and rendered in operational). Hartranft had orders to wait for Ledlie to advance, so he waited with his regiments strung out from the left of the Crater all the way back to the Federal lines.[33]

Hartranft was born in 1830 in Montgomery County, Pennsylvania, and graduated from Union College. He was a civil engineer on the railroads and later practiced law. When the war started he organized the 51st Pennsylvania, and, like Willcox, he was in the Ninth Corps for several years. He was made a brigadier for his gallantry at Spotsylvania. Many years following the war's end, he was retroactively awarded the Medal of Honor for his gallantry at First Manassas.

The confusion and crowding in the Crater had become quite disastrous and the congestion was holding up the forward progress of the entire corps. Colonel Loring had attempted to alert Burnside to this problem in the message that ended up in Meade's possession by mistake. Powell was then sent by Marshall at about that time to inform Ledlie of the problem, and to urge something be done

BG Orlando B. Willcox (Library of Congress).

to the right and left of the Crater, indicating that "every man who got into the trenches to the right or left of it used them as a means to escape to the Crater, and the enemy was reoccupying them as fast as our men left." When Willcox later saw what was occurring and the resultant effects on his division, he did not push the remaining regiments of Hartranft's brigade forward, but instead reported to Burnside that no more troops could assault the breach and recommended instead attacks on the right and left of the Crater.

In this chaos, every additional regiment that marched into the breach only increased the crowding and confusion, and interfered the more with the officers in reforming for another advance. Unfortunately, Meade's response to this intelligence was to order Burnside to have "all your troops be pushed forward to the crest at once," which had been sent at 5:40 A.M. Ledlie thus sent Powell back with orders for his brigades to press immediately for Cemetery Hill in blind obedience to the orders, with no personal knowledge of the matter or the condition of his troops in the Crater.[34] Willcox, in turn, sent word to Hartranft to advance regardless of whether or not Ledlie's division advanced from the Crater. However, Hartranft soon sent word back that such movement was impossible, despite valiant efforts to move forward. The situation had deteriorated to the point where the ensuing confusion was so great "that when orders came to advance and take the opposite crest, the commands could not be got in hand."

Willcox, after receiving Burnside's order to move directly on Cemetery Hill, interpreted the command literally. He indicated that his "idea was to carry out the spirit of what was understood the day before, and my plan was to throw the whole division on the left into line, so that the right would rest on the Jerusalem plank road; and that would have completely protected the flank of the First Division." He therefore ordered Hartranft to send at least one regiment to the left to clean out the Confederate flank as far as possible and then advance to give his brigade more room south of the Crater, so that the remainder of the brigade could come up with room to maneuver. In compliance, the 27th Michigan started down the trench line, but its commander, Colonel William B. Wright was soon severely wounded. The regiment was met with a solid wall of flame, and was soon thrown into great confusion as their ranks were raked by the fire. The enemy, protected by their traverses, had such an extensive line of fire from their pits that the 27th could not make much headway, even with the support of the captured gun firing down the left from the fort. And so, before Willcox could move on Cemetery Hill, the Rebels began concentrating so much firepower on them that his units could not move any farther. The 27th Michigan was hit very hard, and struggled to gain ground: "From the Lake Superior copper ranges, where the 27th was recruited, to the farms and villages of Jackson, Ingham, Muskegon, and Genesee, the evil genie of the Crater left the mark of his hand in blood on the lintels of hundreds of Michigan homes."

BG John F. Hartranft (National Archives).

By this time, the opportunity for success had

seemingly passed. Soon Hartranft's brigade was once again crowding back into the short length of trenches that they had previously taken south of the Crater. The Confederates causing this carnage belonged to the 26th and 59th Virginia regiments, which Colonel Goode had sent northward to plug the breach. There they were joined by the 23rd South Carolina and the remnants of the 22nd taking up positions in traverses perpendicular to the 27th Michigan's flank. Having already wreaked havoc with the first division on the left of the Crater, they were ideally positioned to prevent the Federals from gaining much ground south of the Crater as well.[35]

Colonel William Humphrey, in command of the second brigade of the third division, moved his troops to the covered way leading to the right of Roemer's battery well before daybreak on the 30th. He had orders to hold his command there until Hartranft's brigade had moved forward and then to mass in the space left by the first brigade. As soon as that advance commenced at 5:15 A.M., Humphrey had formed his brigade in column of battalions on the ground just cleared by the first brigade. However, the whole of the first brigade did not immediately move out of the Federal pits, as it was larger than the first, and thus Humphrey could not follow the prescribed plan. He requested permission to form his brigade in line behind the Federal works and this line was formed with its right opposite to the left of the Rebel line then held by Hartranft's men, with its left resting on the road. Humphrey lined up the brigade in no-man's-land in line of battle to the left of the Crater. On the extreme right he placed the 1st Michigan Sharpshooters under Captain Elmer C. Dicey, then to its left the 2nd Michigan, Humphrey's own regiment, under Captain John L. Young, and the 20th Michigan under Lieutenant Colonel Byron M. Cutcheon. Then to the left of the Michiganders were the 46th New York under Captain Alphons Serviere and the 50th Pennsylvania under Lieutenant Colonel Edward Overton, Jr. Then, in order to support the vulnerable left flank of his attacking force, Humphrey backed up the 46th New York and the 50th Pennsylvania with the 60th Ohio under Major Martin P. Avery and the 24th New York Cavalry (Dismounted) under Lieutenant Colonel Walter C. Newberry. The 1st Michigan Sharpshooters was comprised in part of one hundred Native Americans, primarily Ottawa, Ojibwa (Chippewa) and Ottawa-Ojibwa Indians from the state's Lower Peninsula.

These Indians, mostly in Company K, became the most famous Indian unit in the Union army east of the Mississippi. Like other sharpshooter units, the 1st Michigan was an elite organization. In addition to daily competitive rifle shooting, the sharpshooters honed their marksmanship by hitting targets placed at a distance of 600 yards, a difficult feat even with today's precise weapons.

> Equally important, the drill instructors cultivated a feeling of invincibility, that the sharpshooters could not be defeated. Armed with new Sharps NM 1859 breechloaders, they could fire ten shots a minute without changing position, a decided advantage during periods of heavy fighting. Besides their physical appearance, the Indians of the 1st Michigan were set apart from the other units in the Army of the Potomac by their 'battle flag.'

A rather startled soldier of the 20th New York once wrote home that the Indians' most unusual standard was a "large live Eagle perched on a pole some six feet long on a little platform." From Spotsylvania to the Crater, under the leadership of Colonel Charles V. DeLand, the Indian sharpshooters were used in numerous human wave frontal assaults and took heavy casualties in nearly every engagement once Grant took command in 1864.[36]

William Humphrey was born in 1828 in Michigan and joined the 2nd Michigan as a captain in April 1861, and was promoted to major in June 1862. On May 1, 1863, he was promoted to colonel of the 2nd Michigan. After participating in all the major battle of the Ninth Corps, he was twice wounded at Spotsylvania Court House. In June 1864, he was appointed commander of the second brigade of the third division, Ninth Corps. After his role in the Battle of the Crater, he continued as brigade commander of the second brigade. Then, on September 30, 1864, Humphrey was summoned to Grant's headquarters, where he was to be assigned command of the first division in the Eighteenth Corps until a general officer could be identified for permanent command. Instead, Humphrey tendered his resignation and was mustered out of the army that same day, with General Hartranft taking temporary command of the brigade. Humphrey's brigade saw him for the last time that morning as they passed in front of the Gurney house as he was leaving for City Point and home. "Many in the brigade had no idea he was leaving until this moment ..." and they missed him dearly in times to come.[37]

The 2nd Michigan Volunteers, commanded at that time by Captain John L. Young, was a veteran unit, having organized in 1861. It took part in First Manassas and the Peninsular Campaign in 1862 and was engaged in numerous battles on the western theater. The unit had the rather unusual distinction for two years of having a female fighting in its ranks, one Sarah Emma Edmonds, disguised as Private Franklin Thompson. The unit came east and joined the Overland Campaign on May 5, 1864. The 20th Michigan, another veteran unit, commanded by Lieutenant Colonel Byron M. Cutcheon, was recruited in July 1862 and attached to the 9th Corps in September 1862, immediately after the Antietam engagement. After serving in many battles in the West, it too, came east and joined the Overland Campaign in May 1864. By July 30, it contained almost as few men as the 1st Michigan.

At 8:00 A.M., these three Michigan regiments on the right of the line charged across the field and moved by the right flank at double quick, taking the pits in their front "The Michiganders were sent off on the left oblique behind Hartranft for the purpose of supporting him and their orders were to clear out the rebel trenches, particularly the laterals, which gave the enemy well-protected positions from which they were delivering a devastating flank fire."

Willcox especially wanted Humphrey's men to silence the sole but deadly effective gun of Davidson's Battery on the left, and to disperse Goode's refused left. The men went in with a cheer, climbing over their breastworks and through three lines of abatis. Once in no-man's-land, they went forward at a run. A veritable "tornado of bullets greeted us," recalled Lieutenant Colonel Cutcheon. "Many times I felt the breath of bullets on my face, and once it seemed to burn."[38] "Theirs was the deepest penetration made that day," at least according to regimental historian Frank Woodford. Upon reaching the enemy works, Colonel Cutcheon of the 20th Michigan ordered the Confederates out of the trenches, when a Rebel lieutenant became reluctant to move. Cutcheon raised his sword as if to strike and the reluctant Rebel hurried out of the trench, only to be hit by a bullet from his own side as he jumped. The wounded officer asked to be taken to safety, but Cutcheon was unable to get his own men out, and so he gave the man a drink of water and a rubber blanket to ward off the intense sun and left the wounded lieutenant. He never saw him again.

The 1st Michigan Sharpshooters immediately

Col. William Humphrey (USAMH).

took thirty prisoners, and then, together with the 20th Michigan, cleared a small "flanker" of Confederates, capturing another twenty men. The 1st Michigan pulled apart the Rebel abatis under heavy fire and reached the left flank of the enemy fort, where they immediately took cover with the 2nd Michigan on their left. Behind the 2nd and to its left was the 20th Michigan, which hit the Confederate line and forced the surrender of thirty more Confederates. The Michigan units were supported by the 46th New York and the 50th Pennsylvania. To strengthen the vulnerable left flank, Humphrey backed up the left two units with the larger 60th Ohio and the 24th New York Cavalry (Dismounted).[39]

As Humphrey's brigade pressed forward at the double quick, the stranded 23rd and 22nd South Carolina regiments pivoted to face the new attack, along with the single operating gun in Davidson's Battery. The remainder of Goode's Brigade fired obliquely into Humphrey's left. Thus exposed to the flanking artillery fire, canister began to tear huge holes in the Federals' ranks. The 20th Michigan lost 25 percent of it men just getting to the Rebel trenches. The Confederates were also rallying in large numbers in a swale between the Crater and Cemetery Hill, protected by the contours of the land from Federal artillery. "And to add insult to injury, their riflemen in the trenches had clean shots at the backs of the Michigan soldiers who had pressed beyond them. Willcox's entire division now was under galling fire from the front, rear, and left...." "Still the Michiganders held on, trading death for death in

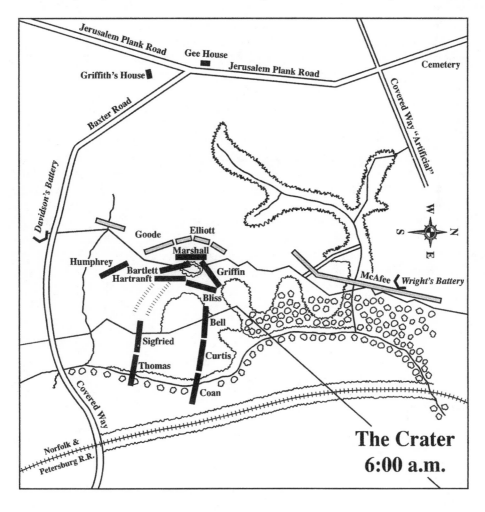

heaping measure, until the 46th New York, having had enough of the slaughter, panicked and broke."

The 46th New York, upon clearing its own lines, had lost contact with the 20th Michigan on its right. In their panic, they stampeded over the 50th Pennsylvania and the two other units of the second brigade's left flank, falling back to the road on their left, and ultimately back to their own lines. "Their disgraceful retreat threw two remaining regiments of the Second Brigade into temporary disorder and separated them from the line of battle," reported Willcox after the battle. Humphrey reported that "had it not been for the causeless breaking of the Forty-sixth New York there is no doubt but the whole line would have been carried and the troops occupying it captured, and the achievement of the object for which we set out in the morning rendered more than probable."[40]

Captain Alphons Seviere, commander of the 46th New York, later somewhat defensively claimed that the regiment on his right moved very rapidly past their breastworks in a right oblique and the connection was thereby lost. He allowed that after charging about one hundred yards in the face of that galling musketry fire and "seeing the impossibility of taking the fort, my right wing ... being disconnected, no support coming from the rear, and a number of my men falling dead or wounded at every step forward, I, fearing that a panic might seize upon my men, gave orders to retire to the road" where the 50th Pennsylvania on his left had already retired.[41]

These occurrences left the six Michigan regiments in the two brigades unsupported and totally exposed to the fury of a potential Confederate counterattack. The three Michigan regiments of Humphrey's brigade succeeded in clearing about one hundred yards of the entrenchments, despite the disintegration on their left, and sent its fifty prisoners back to the Federal lines. Once Humphrey's men took the trenches to the left of the Crater, the two captured guns manned by Sergeant Stanley and some of Hartranft's men in the Crater were turned toward a new threat.[42]

At this point, three full divisions of Burnside's Ninth Corps were engaged and inextricably held up in the Crater and its outlying trenches. The Crater itself was a mass of disorganized humanity, and it was so crowded only those at the rim facing out could fight. Two of his division commanders and his inspector general had urged Burnside not to send in anymore troops, but rather to make another attack at a different part of the line. However, Meade had specifically ordered him to engage all his troops (white and black), and to push forward to Cemetery Hill at all hazards. Burnside still had one division uncommitted — Ferrero's fourth division. Given the pressures upon him, he was about to severely compound what was already a situation which had all the makings of a major disaster.

CHAPTER 12

The Federal Advance Is Halted

Ferrero's fourth division massed on the open hillside below the ruins of the Taylor house, near one of the covered ways leading to the forward trenches. With them as a reserve was the second division of the Tenth Corps, under Brigadier General John W. Turner, temporarily assigned to the Eighteenth Corps. Sergeant Joseph H. Payne of the 27th USCT presided over an impromptu religious service at the site. He related that "[o]ur prayer meeting was short but not without good and lasting impressions being made upon the hearts and minds of many." The men had been up before daybreak preparing for the day's work. Colonel Henry Goddard Thomas joined his staff in a soldier's breakfast—"two pieces of hard-tack with a slice of raw, fat salt pork between—not a dainty meal, but solid provender to fight on." The men of the fourth division had a grand view of the explosion of the mine and then began an anxious wait as the three white divisions advanced to the demolished fort and became mired in the Crater. During this time, the black troops made ready. Chaplin Garland White, of the 28th USCT, himself an ex-slave, was besieged by men requesting him to write loved ones for them and begging him "when pay-day comes, if it ever does come, [to] send what money is due [to their home]." As the black troops prepared to enter the covered way, squads of wounded Union soldiers and Confederate prisoners began to trickle back through their ranks in a steady stream.

At about 5:45 A.M., as Thomas' men lay on their arms awaiting orders to go forward, Thomas heard a quiet voice from behind asking, "Who commands this brigade?" Turning as he responded "I do," he found that he was face to face with General Grant, accompanied only by Colonel Horace Porter, his aide-de-camp and a single orderly. "'Well, said the general, slowly and thoughtfully, as if communing with himself rather than addressing a subordinate, 'why are you not in?'" Thomas quickly responded that his orders were to follow the first brigade, which was still in front of his position:

> Feeling that golden opportunities might be slipping away from ... [them], ... [Thomas] added, "will you give me the order to go now?" After a moment's hesitation he [Grant] answered, in the same slow and ruminating manner, "No, you may keep the orders you have." Then, turning his horse's head, he rode away at a walk.[1]

In another fifteen minutes, at 6:00 A.M., one of Ferrero's aides gave Thomas the order and they moved into the covered way, following Lieutenant Colonel Joshua K. Sigfried's brigade. There they laid for another hour or more, listening to the ever-increasing sounds of the battle. At first, the men sat down, resting against the walls of the covered way. Before long, however, they were forced to stand in order to make room "for the constantly increasing throng of wounded who were being brought past ... [them] to the rear." Some of these wounded were bantering with Thomas' men, bragging that their wounds were "'good for a thirty days' sick leave.'" Others were either silent, with pinched faces betraying their attempts to suppress groans, while the rest were "moaning or bellowing like wild beasts." The men of the fourth division had to stand for an hour viewing this endless procession of wounded men, which was definitely a hindrance to the maintenance of good morale. General Thomas expressed the sentiments of all the men in his command when he described the wait: "There could be no greater strain on the nerves. Every moment changed the condition from that of a forlorn hope to one of forlorn hopelessness. Unable to strike a blow, we were sickened with the contemplation of revolting forms of death and mutilation."[2]

Communications between Burnside and Meade became even more tense that morning following the difficulties in springing the mine. Around 5:40 A.M., Meade received the message from Colonel Loring, intended for Burnside, contained in a sealed envelope, describing Ledlie's division being held up in the Crater. Meade shared the contents with Grant and his chief of staff, Andrew Humphreys; he also sent it on to Burnside. Soon thereafter, he issued the order at 6:00 A.M. for Burnside to "push your men forward at all hazards (white and black), and don't lose time in making formations, but rush for the crest." Obviously, Meade felt the situation was dire and he wanted to emphasize that to Burnside. Burnside quickly informed him that he had given orders to all his division commanders to "push everything in at once." Still unsatisfied with the progress, Meade then, at 6:05 A.M. telegraphed Burnside again through Humphreys, indicating that "The commanding general wishes to know what is going on on your left, and whether it would be an advantage for Warren's supporting force to go in at once."

Meade received Burnside's response to the question at 6:20 A.M. In it Burnside replied that "If General Warren's supporting force can be concentrated just now, ready to go in at the proper time, it would be well. I will designate to you when it ought to move. There is scarcely room for it now, in our immediate front."[3] Burnside was, indeed, quite concerned with the congestion on his front at this time. All three of his divisions had reported that the Crater was overcrowded and had advised that no more troops be brought in there, but rather that an advance be made at another location on the Confederate line.

Meade issued his reply to Burnside's telegram at 6:50 A.M. It was a very strong rebuke from that thoroughly frustrated army commander, who was not happy with the status of an advance which seemed to be getting away from them before his eyes:

> Warren's force has been concentrated and ready to move since 3:30 A.M. My object in inquiring was to ascertain if you could judge of the practicability of his advancing without waiting for your column. What is the delay in your column moving? Every minute is most precious, as the enemy undoubtedly are concentrating to meet you on the crest, and if you give them enough you cannot expect to succeed. There is no object to be gained in occupying the enemy's line; it cannot be held under their artillery fire without much labor in turning it. The great point is to secure the crest at once, and at all hazards.[4]

Meade was essentially indicating to Burnside to mind his own business and do a better job of that. This exchange was quite similar to the "I am in charge" missive of July 3, when Meade took great umbrage at the wording of a Burnside response to one of his questions, seeking to temporarily command troops of other corps in an assault.

While this tense exchange was taking place between Burnside and his commanding officer, his subordinates were also receiving news from the front. Lieutenant William H. Powell, first division judge advocate and aide-de-camp of General Ledlie, had gone forward with the advance under Ledlie's orders, and had then left the Crater at General Marshall's request to inform Ledlie of the difficulties his brigade had encountered in that pit. After learning Marshall's reasons for not being able to further advance, Ledlie directed Powell to return and inform Marshall and Bartlett "that it was General Burnside's order for them to move forward immediately." Prior to Bliss' advance, Powell left the Crater yet again to urge Ledlie to "have something done to the right and left of the crater." Again he was ordered to go back and inform the brigade commanders to "get their men out and press forward to Cemetery Hill." A rather perturbed Powell later recalled that "[t]his talk and these orders, coming from a commander sitting in a bomb-proof inside the Union lines, were disgusting. I returned again to the crater and delivered the orders, which I knew beforehand could not possibly be obeyed; and I told General Ledlie so before I left him."[5]

Leander Cogswell, General Griffin's inspector general, was also in the Crater that morning. Sometime after 7:00 A.M., on Griffin's orders, Cogswell carried a report to General Potter describing the impossible congestion at the Crater and the difficulties in re-forming men and advancing. Cogswell found Potter at Fort Morton, along with a number of other senior officers.[6] Potter relayed this message to Burnside, who reiterated the order to "Push forward to the crest at once!" Potter immediately took some straw colored silk paper from his pocket, "and using his hat for a support, wrote the order, and ... [Cogswell] carried the same to General Griffin, who, in connection with General Hartranft, proceeded to put the order into execution as far as it was in their power to do so."[7]

Lieutenant Colonel Loring, the Ninth Corps' assistant inspector general, also had a ringside seat for the early action that day. He volunteered to go in with the first division and accompanied Bartlett's brigade into the Crater. After observing the overcrowding and utter disorganization in the Crater, Loring trekked back to report to Ledlie the dire condition that his division was in, with the hope that he could rectify it. He then reported to Burnside on the state of affairs, and thereafter positioned himself on the front line, near Ledlie's bombproof. Just before 7:30 A.M., Ferrero's division was again ordered to advance. Ferrero had by then closeted himself with Ledlie in the hospital bombproof of the 27th Michigan, where, according to Surgeon H.E. Smith, he was also fortifying himself with medicinal rum. Burnside's aide had come to the bombproof two times before with orders for him to advance. On each occasion, Ferrero would advise the aide that he could not go forward until the other troops were out of the way. Ledlie would then send an aide to order his troops out of the way, without himself physically leaving the bombproof. Leander Cogswell observed the two in their safe lair, "sitting as unconcernedly as though nothing were taking place," as he made his way back to the Crater to deliver Potter's orders for his brigade commanders to advance again.

Ferrero was near Loring when he received the third, imperative order from Burnside to push ahead regardless of other units and to lead his division into the Crater, pass the white troops, which had for the most part halted by then, and push for the top of Cemetery Hill at all hazards. Based on recent reports from his staff, Ferrero did not believe it prudent to move his division in, "as there were three divisions of white troops already huddled together there." Loring later related that Burnside's latest order "struck me as being so unfortunate that I took the liberty to countermand it on the spot." Ferrero refused to wait, however, indicating he had "a positive order from General Burnside." Loring responded to this superior officer in his own words that he was "the senior staff-officer present, and that, in General Burnside's name, I would countermand the order until I could go up and inform General Burnside of the state of affairs." Loring then proceeded to find Burnside while Ferrero waited.[8]

With three of his divisions now engaged and the last ready to go in, and knowing that a definite problem existed in the Crater, Burnside realized that he needed to see for himself the true status of affairs and to obtain an answer to Meade's recent question. Major General Warren, commander of the Fifth Corps, had just then arrived at Fort Morton to meet personally with Burnside, who was at the time concluding a conversation with General Ord. Warren related his concern that the battery to the south (left) of the Crater needed to be taken out before further advances were attempted. Burnside suggested that the two of them journey to the front together to observe the state of affairs in and around the Crater firsthand.[9] Burnside climbed down from the embrasure where he had been attempting to observe the progress of his attack through the smoke and dust and proceeded with Warren down the length of Potter's covered way.[10] En route, they encountered the crowded regiments of Brigadier General John W. Turner, commanding the Tenth Corps under Ord's orders, as well as those of Ferrero's two brigades of black troops. The conditions were so crowded that the generals were required to proceed on foot and with next to no staff. While negotiating the covered way, Burnside also encountered Colonel Loring, who had been searching for him after his encounter with General Ferrero. Loring had informed his superior "that this colored division could not be expected to pass the lines of the old troops; that it was impossible to expect green troops to succeed where old troops had failed before them; and furthermore that, instead of accomplishing any good result, they would only throw into confusion the white troops that were already in that line and holding it."[11]

Contrary to Burnside's normal habit with staff officers, he did not reply by stating his reasons for disagreeing with them, but rather simply repeated his previous order.[12] Loring was told that the order to advance came directly from Meade and was not discretionary, and thus he went back to the fourth division and changed their orders to stand down, indicating the previous order to carry forward at all hazards was preemptory. When Burnside and Warren arrived at the extreme front, they observed from an earthen mound to the left side of the covered way Griffin's shattered lines flopping like a flag in the wind, with one regiment advancing while another fell back, only to attempt to advance again. The Confederate artillery was obviously a great concern due to their accuracy and devastating effect on the Union assault. Griffin's men in particular were being shredded by the enfilading fire from Rebel cannon on the right and left.

Confident that they knew what was needed, the two worked their way back through the covered way to their respective commands. With Burnside's approval, Warren wrote Meade that the one gun battery to their left needed to be extinguished, which would thereupon allow the crest to be taken. Burnside indicated to Warren his opinion on how the Fifth Corps should become engaged: "I think your plan would be to strike across by the fort which enfiladed our lines," in order to take out the battery in question (Davidson's). In response, a somewhat reluctant Warren indicated that he would go back and explain to Meade the circumstances, and, "if possible, to get him to come to the front and look for himself" from the Ninth Corps' vantage point. Warren observed that all the approaches leading down to the Crater were filled with Burnside's men still slowly moving down and "there was no chance for me to get at the battery, except to go over the open field." Warren claimed that he therefore determined to put Ayers' division in at once and attempt to take the gun, and he returned to his headquarters to put this plan into effect.[13] When he got back to his headquarters, Warren telegraphed that Meade should come himself to observe the situation from the Ninth Corps vantage point. Since Warren had agreed to report this information to Meade, Burnside made the decision that it was unnecessary for him also to respond directly to Meade's earlier telegraph.[14]

When Burnside returned from his inspection tour, he was immediately confronted by the brutally sarcastic message from his boss. The visit to the front demonstrated that one of the major impediments to the advance was the effectiveness of the single gun of Davidson's battery. Had the pioneers taken the axe to the intervening pine trees, the Federal artillery most likely would have been able to silence the gun. Warren testified weeks later at the court of inquiry about his alleged willingness to advance on the left upon Burnside's say-so. However, even if Warren was genuine in this sentiment, Burnside had no orders giving him specific authority over other corps, and Meade's jealous reminder of July 3 had implied he would never enjoy such control.[15] Thus, Burnside declined to act without consulting army headquarters.

Meanwhile, Meade grew progressively more impatient with the lack of information from the front. General Parke, the Ninth Corps' chief of staff, might well have comforted the army commander with frequent informative missives as he was known to do, but Parke had taken ill once again. In his place, Burnside had appointed Julius White only the night before. During the critical hours of the attack, White sent but one communication to Grant and sent not one to Meade, the commander of the Army of the Potomac. Thus, when Warren and Burnside returned to Fort Morton, Burnside found yet another sarcastic message from his immediate superior, answering his suggestion about Warren's participation by indicating he had been ready for over three hours and again emphasizing the need for haste in the attack. Burnside soon answered the latest telegraph message, which Meade received at 7:20 A.M. In it, Burnside indicated that "I am doing all in my power to push the troops forward, and, if possible, we will carry the crest. It is hard work, but we hope to accomplish it. I am fully alive to the importance of it."[16]

Unfortunately, a very frustrated Meade could not let this self-serving explanation go unanswered. It was not that Burnside had failed to achieve his objectives for the attack; Meade knew that he was having difficulty. From his own intelligence and Loring's message, it was clear to Meade that Burnside's men were huddled in the Crater and that there was some obstacle impeding their advance, whether real or perceived. Regardless of what it was, Burnside was failing to report crucial information; indeed, he had not even attempted to take the crest. To Meade, the impediment faced by Burnside's corps was crucial — if the crest could not be taken, then the troops had to be withdrawn. Thus, at 7:30 A.M., Meade sent Burnside the following message:

> What do you mean by hard work to take the crest? I understand not a man has advanced beyond the enemy's line which you occupied immediately after exploding the mine. Do you mean to say your officers and men will not obey your orders to advance? If not, what is the obstacle? I wish to know the truth and desire an immediate answer.[17]

Meade's message was sent by courier and not by telegraph. The courier, Captain Jay, arrived at Fort Morton and approached Burnside, handing him the message, and indicated that "General Meade desires me to say that this is for you personally."

That last statement was imprudent and, while Meade later claimed that he meant nothing by it, it severely rankled Burnside. As Meade wished, an immediate answer was what he received from the equally frustrated Burnside. Burnside was growing increasingly sensitive to the prodding of his new commander and former subordinate, for whom, in his mind, he had done everything to achieve an accommodation. He reared indignantly at this perceived assault on his veracity and responded within five minutes:

> Your dispatch by Captain Jay received. The main body of General Potter's division is beyond the crater. I do not mean to say that my officers and men will not obey my orders to advance. I mean to say that it is very hard to advance to the crest. I have never in any report said any-

thing different from what I conceived to be the truth. Were it not insubordinate I would say that the latter remark of your note was unofficerlike and ungentlemanly.

Respectfully, yours,

A.E. Burnside
Major-General[18]

Regardless of the disclaimer, Burnside's remarks were, indeed, insubordinate, though perhaps defensible. Meade, rather ominously, requested a copy of the message that had caused the eruption on Burnside's part, indicating that he had not kept a duplicate, as he had intended for it to be confidential. Meade indicated that his subordinate's reply "requires I should have a copy." The breach between these two senior officers was ever-widening, and would ultimately lead to disaster for one of them.[19]

Meade later justified his language by saying that he concluded there was some reason for the delay which had not been officially reported. He considered it "natural" that Burnside would be "indisposed" to make it known, as long as he still harbored hopes of overcoming the difficulties. For Meade, as commander of the army, it was a matter of the utmost importance, because "it was my intention during the assault, and before it, that if we could not carry the crest promptly by a *coup de main*, to withdraw the troops as quickly and safely as possible." In short, Meade claimed that he bore no animosity toward Burnside in sending this missive. Burnside later contended Meade intended to imply that he had not made truthful statements. Regarding what he referred to as "unfortunate correspondence," Burnside, with time to reflect, later indicated that, "at the time I wrote the offensive dispatch ... General Meade intended to imply that I had not made truthful reports, but I am now satisfied that he did not so intend."[20]

While Meade was communicating with Burnside regarding sending Warren's corps into the action, he was simultaneously having independent contact with Warren himself. At 5:50 A.M., he inquired as to the size of enemy force on Warren's front, and ordered that "[i]f there is apparently an opportunity to carry their works take advantage of it and push forward your troops." Warren's response was equivocal, indicating he would watch for an opportunity but that it was difficult to assess the Confederate strength in front of him. Fifteen minutes later, Warren reported that the Confederates had engaged his force and that none of the enemy had left his front. The Federal signal station began seeing Confederates moving north toward the breach in their lines. Meade saw this as an opportunity, for if troops were being marshaled for the Crater from the Confederate right, then their line had to be weakened at some point down the line. Thus Meade's chief of staff telegraphed Warren at 6:30 A.M. that "[t]he signal officer reports that none of the enemy's troops are visible in their works near the lead-works. The commanding general wishes if it is practicable that you make an attack in that direction. Prisoners say there are but three divisions in the works, and but one line of intrenchments, thinly filled with their troops."

Warren replied ten minutes later, stating that he had massed the large portion of his troops on his right but had sent a brigade and a half under General Crawford to "do whatever he can on the left." He asked if Meade wished for him to advance another division to the left for the attack, noting that there was still a heavy battery (Davidson's) in his front behind the Confederate front line. Meade suggested an attack on the Confederate flank "near the lead-works with that part of your force nearest it."[21]

After Warren returned from his reconnoitering at the front lines with Burnside, and before he could put Ayers' division in on the left to capture Davidson's battery as he had previously committed to Burnside, he received a 7:30 A.M. telegraph informing him that Meade

Ninth Corps military telegraph operators (Library of Congress).

would "await General Crawford's reconnaissance before determining whether you should send Ayers also in that direction." At 7:50 A.M. Warren telegraphed Meade:

> I have just returned from the scene of General Burnside's operations. In my opinion, the battery of one or two guns to the left of General Burnside should be taken before attempting to seize the crest. It seems to me it can be done, as we shall take the infantry fire quite obliquely. This done the advance upon the main hill will not be difficult. I think it would pay you to go to General Burnside's position. You can see in a moment, and it is easy to communicate with me as by telegraph. It will be some time before we can hear from Crawford.

Warren soon heard from Crawford, who did not "discover any particular advantage" that would aid an assault by his division. Thus, at 8:00 A.M., he communicated Crawford's report to Meade that "the lead-works are over a mile from the angle of my picket-line. I do not think an attack upon the enemy's works at or near that point at all practicable with the force I can spare," although he felt that he could make a demonstration. Warren added regarding Crawford's offensive capabilities that "so far that I do not think it well to want anything more he can do, and I renew my suggestion that you take a look at things from General Burnside's headquarters, and direct me either to go in with Burnside or go around to my left with Ayers' division and I do the other thing."

Meade responded through Humphreys forty-five minutes later, directing Warren to go in with Burnside and take the battery in question, indicating that the movement to the left "need not be carried further than reconnaissance to see in what force the enemy is holding his right." By this point, however, it was too late. Warren sent Meade a message at 9:15 A.M., relating that just before receiving his 8:45 directive, it appeared that the enemy had driven

Burnside's troops from the lines to the left of the Crater and, if true, he, Warren was "no more able to take the battery now than I was this time yesterday. All our advantages are lost. I await further instructions, and am trying to get at the condition of affairs for certainty." Meade obliged by promptly suspending Warren's attack. He never ventured to Burnside's headquarters, or to the front, for that matter.[22]

Similarly, at 6:00 A.M., Meade advised Major General Hancock through Humphreys that he might be called upon to move his Second Corps forward "at any moment, and wishes you to have your troops well up to the front prepared to move. Do the enemy lines in front of Mott's division appear to be thinly occupied, and is there any chance to push forward there?" Hancock responded immediately, indicating it was impossible to judge the strength in front of Mott's division at that time, and later indicated that he had "sent out to have General Mott's line examined as far as practicable to see how strong the enemy appear to hold their line." Again at 7:00 A.M., Meade asserted that prisoner interrogations indicated a weakness in the Confederate lines and that a considerable portion had been abandoned. He speculated that if Burnside and Ord gained the crest, the Confederate line could not hold, given that they would be exposed front and rear. He then directed that if "the enemy are in force and prepared you will have to await developments, but if you have reason to believe their condition is such that an effort to dislodge them would be successful I would like to have it made. Burnside now occupies their line, but he has not pushed up to the crest, though he reports he is about doing so." To Meade's disappointment, Hancock immediately responded:

> Report from the Second Brigade, of General Mott's division, shows that the enemy are there in some strength, having two batteries which they fire seldom, owing to the close proximity of our riflemen. The commanding officer of the brigade says he can see every man who leaves his front to their right, and none have left since daylight. He is using mortars effectively. I will report any change of troops.

W.S. HANCOCK
Major-General[23]

At 9:00 A.M., Hancock supported his prior assessment of his situation by reporting that Mott's men had put hats on their ramrods, "which elicited quite a spirited volley." Thus, he was convinced the Confederates remained on his front in full force. No help would voluntarily come from the Second Corps to the beleaguered Ninth Corps.[24]

Major General O.C. Ord, following Meade's orders of July 29, had placed the first and third divisions of his Eighteenth Corps in the trenches on Burnside's front, thus relieving portions of his command as trench guards, enabling them to move forward for the morning's assault. He had also assigned Brigadier General John W. Turner's second division of the Tenth Corps to his command for the operation. Ord then ordered Turner and Brigadier General Adelbert Ames' second division of the Eighteenth Corps to the rear of Burnside's corps as reserve supports, in positions previously selected by him. Ord beforehand had his staff obtain suggestions for the locations from Burnside. His commanders had instructions to await orders to be sent as soon as the result of the assault could determine exactly where support might be needed. Ames' division was placed behind Turner's in the rear of a strip of woods behind the fourteen gun battery at Fort Morton. Turner thereafter withdrew from the trenches and moved his division to a point in the rear, where he was to mass at a point where a road led to the woods, and await Ledlie's troops to pass. He then moved to the opening of the covered way on the right of the fourteen gun battery which led to the Federal front lines through which all the Union troops had to pass.

There were actually two covered ways to the front, one on either side of the 14 gun bat-

tery. The fourth division then occupied the one to the left of the battery. Turner was to follow the Ninth Corps in the assault and support it through the right covered way. At about
6:00 A.M., Burnside indicated to Ord that Turner should move in order to support the right
of his advance. However, Turner immediately discovered that his unit was ahead of a portion of Potter's division and he was therefore required to make way and await their departure before he could reach the front lines. When the mine was finally sprung, Turner, "feeling
the importance of being close at hand," moved the head of his column about one hundred
yards distant down the covered way and halted there for a half hour, awaiting further orders
and the development of the attack. Each of Burnside's divisions had to follow one another.
Ord learned later that the only way to the front was through this long (a third of a mile) covered way to the breach in the works. He later expressed his concern that the space was too
narrow for an army to pass. Thus, the movement was very slow and involved frequent delays.
In addition, the wounded from the three engaged divisions had to be brought back through
this same covered way.[25]

John Wesley Turner was born in Saratoga, New York, in 1833, and moved to Chicago
when he was ten years old. At eighteen years of age, he received an appointment to West Point
and graduated as a second lieutenant in 1855. He thereafter served garrison duties in several
outposts in the West, and fought against the Seminoles in Florida. He was Ben Butler's chief
commissary officer in New Orleans early in the war and was thereafter made chief of staff
and then chief of artillery of the Department of the South in 1863. He later directed the
assaults against both Forts Sumner and Wagner. Turner received an order dated 6:30 A.M. to
"move forward on crest of hill to the right of Potter, near or on Jerusalem plank road." The
order obviously anticipated that Burnside's men had advanced sufficiently to allow the Tenth
Corps out of the trenches, as its point of egress was the same as the previous assaulting column's debouchment. However, this had actually not yet occurred; the subject advance was
in total confusion, massed in and around the Crater. Unless these troops could be gotten forward, sending in more would only add to the confusion and cause additional loss of life. In
order to ascertain whether he could be of assistance to the men in the Crater, and evaluate
whether his men could subsist therein, Turner went personally through the Federal lines and
into the Crater and examined for himself the area then held by the Ninth Corps. In so doing,
he became the only division commander to make an appearance in the Crater that day. He
later reported that "every point that could give cover to a man was occupied. There was no
movement toward Cemetery Hill! The troops were all in confusion and lying down."[26]

While in the Crater, he clearly observed the overcrowding and tremendous suffering
already occurring in that terrible pit. He then hurried back and made plans for his own
advance. He soon learned Meade had ordered Ord and Warren to attack on either side of the
Ninth Corps. Turner's troops would have to proceed down the covered way and thus had
"only a two-file front, and in some places only a single file." He followed as close as possible
to Potter's rear, and still it was 7:00 A.M. before his men arrived where the assaulting column
passed through the Federal lines.[27]

Turner reported to Ord that the only place he could get out of the Federal lines was
opposite the Crater, and that he would put in his column as soon as he could. However,
Turner reported that due to the topography, it was impossible to charge directly towards
Cemetery Hill. Rather, he indicated he would be forced to go in "by head of column and
develop to the right." Ames simultaneously reported that, as the covered way was the only
means to the front and it was then occupied by Turner, it was "impossible for [his] men to
move until he gets out of my way." Ord sent this response to Meade, and went to the front
to investigate for himself.[28] Ord thereafter communicated this situation to Meade at 8:00 A.M.

and directed Turner not to put his men into the Crater or the trench adjoining it, but rather to push for the right.[29]

While Meade was feuding with Burnside and attempting to bring in his other corps according to his plan, the three divisions of the Ninth Corps were seriously engaged, with little or no support from any of Meade's other corps. Things were definitely not proceeding according to the plan. Once Bartlett reached the Crater, he and Marshall jointly decided that a further advance should be made and sought permission from General Ledlie to carry the works to the Crater's right and the right rear (both apparently still perceiving that their orders directed them not to proceed past the Crater). Given that the main covered way leading to Cemetery Hill was filled with Confederates, Marshall and Bartlett had determined to attack it obliquely. The 2nd Pennsylvania Provisional, the 21st Massachusetts and the 100th Pennsylvania were to swing up their left and align with Colonel Robinson, while the 14th New York Heavy Artillery was to file over the traverse at the end of the covered way and form a second line for this detachment. These four combined movements brought on considerable fire from both the flank and also the rear. The 14th New York Heavy Artillery made a dash for the second line of breastworks, where they were met with heavy Confederate resistance. In the contested effort, many of the "heavies" got so close to their Southern foes that rifles were clubbed, and Sergeant James S. Hill of Company C was successful in taking a Rebel regimental battle flag by force."[30] However, the fire was so intense on all sides that the men were ultimately forced back to the fort and the Crater. The recaptured cannon were turned on the advancing Confederates and were able to halt their movement. The 14th New York Heavy Artillery performed so well in this task that when General Hartranft came upon the scene, he called for "Three cheers for the 14th!"[31]

The first division now was in a most precarious position. It was attempting to hold the same line of intrenchments as the Confederates, starting from the point where the right of the division rested and extending from there to the right. The men had hastily constructed traverses to shield them from a "terrible and incessant flank fire, which at the same time afforded ... [the] sharpshooters an excellent opportunity for picking off" the artillerymen in the Confederate batteries on their flank. The heat that day was becoming intense. Despite numerous attempts to move forward, the Confederates drove Ledlie's men back on each of their attempts to move on Cemetery Hill. The intended support for such charges did not arrive, or was too feeble to act as support for an advance by Ledlie's men. Given the intricate nature of the Confederate positions behind and on the flanks of the Crater, most of the fighting could not be accomplished by a mass movement of troops, but rather required individual, hand-to-hand fighting. Major Van Buren came upon Marshall and Bartlett soon after 7:00 A.M. with Burnside's order to advance on Cemetery Hill. Marshall conveyed to him that, given their experience thus far, he did not think he could advance from his current position with the enemy on his flanks, and he wanted to await the advance of the fourth division. Van Buren went down the line to the right about three hundred yards in his estimation to where the line crooked.

BG John W. Turner (Library of Congress).

On the other side of this angle was the enemy in the same line, and a "sharp firing was going on." At this point the 3rd Maryland was holding the division's extreme right, occupying the cross traverse which enfiladed the Federal line. They were detailed to cover the flank of the 2nd Provisional Pennsylvania, which had become heavily enfiladed. "From there the Spencer rifles in that regiment did great execution upon the enemy and demonstrated the advantages of an organized corps of sharpshooters."[32] Marshall's position was that he could not at the time charge with the enemy on his flank, as they would then be free to fire into his rear. Van Buren informed Marshall that the order was imperative and the charge had to be made. He then assisted Marshall in once again re-forming his men for the intended charge.[33]

In the meantime, the second division was having its own difficulties in advancing beyond the Crater and its ancillary works. Given Burnside's preemptory order, the regiments on Griffin's right had their objective suddenly changed to Flanner's battery at the Gee house, and they charged nearly directly up the hill (the 45th Pennsylvania under Captain Gregg reaching nearly to the house on top of the hill, at least according to General Potter's later report, which was somewhat questionable).[34] Gregg reported that as they advanced "the enemy opened with batteries stationed at several different points on the right and left flanks and in front, accompanied by a heavy fire of musketry from the rifle pits." However, being totally unsupported, they were unable to maintain their position and fell back to a ditch or covered way leading to the works the Federals had taken, which they held in conjunction with the regiments of the second brigade.[35]

According to Captain Sumner Shearman of Company A, the few of the 4th Rhode Islanders who were able to be pulled together from the confusion of the Crater followed Colonel Buffum and the color bearer beyond the enemy works toward Cemetery Hill, but they soon encountered such "a hurricane of shot and shell that [it] was impossible to face it, and we were driven back again into the shelter of the enemy's works." Some who did not make it back were calling out for help *in extremis*. Lieutenant W. Field heard the cries and leaped up on the edge of the works, shouting, "Who will follow me?" A dozen voices responded, "I," and "[w]ith sword uplifted, he advanced one step and ... [fell] dead." Corporal George Allen of the 4th remembered that one of his advancing comrades, Bob Hamilton's "little yellow dog ... [came] into the fight with him, and is jumping around, yelling and barking, as if fully alive to the importance of the situation. Suddenly a yip and a yell tells us the dog is hit. Bob drops his rifle, grabs and hurriedly examines the dog. A ball has skipped across his back and burnt off the hair, that is all."

But on that note, the offensive fight had gone out of the 4th and they fell back to the captured works. General Griffin reported that "the terrible fire of musketry from every direction, with grape and canister from our front, rendered the formation of lines from such confused masses lying in pits an impossibility; and notwithstanding the gallant conduct of both officers and men, every attempt failed."[36] Colonel Wentworth of the 32nd Maine was shot twice in the failed assault, though he continued to cheer on his men. The last valiant attempt of Griffin's men to advance on Cemetery Hill had extinguished itself in the hail of Confederate gunfire and canister, with the men seeking shelter in the Crater and behind traverses and covered ways. Henry Pleasants, observing this failed attempt to reach the objective, reported that his miners "began to groan and swear, and the volume of their protest made a respectable second to that of the Union Artillery fire."[37]

As the Federals attempted in vain to reach the Gee house, they were cut apart by heavy fire, especially from Flanner's battery, which was then loading double canister for even more devastating effect. Private Cushman of the 58th Massachusetts with Bliss's brigade said of this desperate charge:

[My regiment was] ordered to charge upon a battery which was in position a quarter of a mile in rear of the fort we had mined. The ground over which we were to charge was an open field. Fully in range of the enemy's fire, both musketry and artillery, it was easy to be seen that the task assigned us to perform was replete with difficulty and danger. It even savored of impossibility; yet the order to charge was obeyed promptly and without a murmur. Advancing with the rest of our brigade into the open field, it was discovered that some of the regiments were bearing to the right in the direction of another battery positioned in the woods. There was evidently a misunderstanding as to which battery it was intended to capture. This caused hesitation and confusion. The enemy kept up its incessant firing; the line of battle wavered, and finally broke, the men filing off into the fort, and into the saps and trenches that led from it. Again the order came to charge upon the battery across the field. The charge was made; but fruitlessly, the men returning to the fort and filling every portion of it to overflowing.[38]

The 51st New York of the second division found itself in a very delicate situation. The Confederates had enfiladed them on both flanks and were pouring in a severe cross fire of canister. On Major Wright's orders, Captain George Washington Whitman jumped up and sang out for his men to "follow me" and "the way they tumbled over them breastworks wasent Slow..." he later recalled in a letter to his mother on August 9. Together with the 2nd New York Mounted Rifles on the Union side of the Confederate trenches, the regiment was successful in reducing the fire from McAfee's North Carolinians for a while. However, the gap which existed between these two regiments and the remainder of their second division made their position quite precarious.[39] Meanwhile, the three advanced regiments of Humphrey's second brigade, third division, consisting of the 1st Michigan Sharpshooters along with the 2nd and 20th Michigan, were hotly engaged to the left of the Crater. The 1st Michigan, positioned to the left of the undamaged portion of the fort, was assisting with the firing of the captured guns, and attempting to hold down the ever-increasing fire of the Rebel defenders in their close proximity. The other two regiments, after the initial success in gaining about one hundred yards of the main trench line, were grudgingly giving ground under the relentless fire from Davidson's battery and the Confederate infantry in the area. A patchwork of South Carolina and Virginia troops caused insurmountable problems for the Union troops moving left of the Crater. "Wise's Brigade threw bullets too thick and fast for them," bragged a soldier from the 26th Virginia later, forcing the blue-clad troops back toward the Crater.

The artillery created an unbelievable noise. One of the soldier-participants later wrote:

My head actually aches with the infernal constant racket that the musketry and 350 cannon keep up. Just imagine, when each gun can be fired five times a minute, making about 1,750 shots a minute, add the report of 1,750 shells exploding in the air; some of them weighing 200 pounds—all this is independent of the firing of the rebels' artillery—and then you can judge why my head aches.

The fire from the unrelenting Confederate artillery on three sides continued practically the whole time; contrary to the reports of some, it never diminished during the entire battle. As Colonel Loring later reflected, the "enemy kept up a very steady and heavy fire of artillery from both the left and right, raking the whole of the ground from our line to the crater of the mine; and further, that from the hill in front of the crater they kept up a steady stream of shrapnell and canister."[40]

The 13th Ohio Cavalry Volunteers (Dismounted) had, at General Hartranft's orders, worked its way out of the Crater into the left trench line and fought with the Confederate defenders in fierce, hand-to-hand combat. Sergeant Howard Aston indicated that "the air seemed thick with missiles, and men were dropping all around." However, the fire from the traverses on their left proved to be too severe, and they were soon forced back toward the Crater. As the 13th Ohio retreated toward the Crater, its color sergeant was shot and the regimental colors captured. Nathaniel McL. Gwynne broke free from the retreating ranks and seized the colors from their Rebel captor. In returning with his prize, the arm with which he was supporting the flag was shot away, almost torn from its socket. Still Gwynne persevered and retrieved the colors and moved toward his unit, and was soon shot again in the leg. Regardless of the wounds, he moved on in, and, upon handing the flag to his comrades, fell unconscious. Gwynne had actually been instructed not to accompany the unit into this battle at all, as he actually had not been mustered into the regiment due to his being only fifteen years old at the time. Gwynne would not hear of this, however, and went along, saying, "But that's not what I'm here for!" Afterwards, Gwynne was placed on the muster rolls of the unit, with his muster date appearing as the time of his original application for enlistment in Cincinnati early that spring. He was subsequently awarded the Medal of Honor for his bravery that day.[41]

By now, the three divisions of the Ninth Corps had come to a standstill due to the congestion of troops and the concomitant confusion and resultant intermingling of troops. The Confederates were putting up a significant defense after the initial shock of the explosion. By now, the Federal momentum had already exhausted itself, even though the Federals faced far inferior numbers of troops all along the front.[42]

On the beleaguered Confederate side, the shattered remnants of the survivors of the explosion had been fighting a desperate battle with very little support for several hours, after suffering the cruel effects of the explosion. Their scant infantry support was slowly melting away under the increasing volume of Federal troops thrown into the confined area. The only constant support holding things together at that time was Haskell's battalion of artillery, along with Davidson's and Wright's batteries. Three full Union divisions were already engaged, and two others were on line and ready to move into the fray momentarily. To arrest this massive onslaught, there were but three Confederate brigades available. The fighting thus far was so heavy that almost all of Elliott's men in the two companies on the right had been killed, wounded or captured. Despite repeated endeavors of the Union officers, however, the Union could not advance far from the Crater, due to the efficient work of McMaster's men in the ravine. An indication of the intensity of the fighting in this section were the number of "Yankee and Rebel" minie balls found later, which met point to point and were thus fused into an amorphous lump of lead, with the grooves of the butts distinctly preserved. The troops were indeed fighting "with the fury of madmen."[43]

By this time, there were over 9,000 Federal troops committed to the advance, facing approximately 800 of Elliott's Brigade in the vicinity of the Salient. In the ensuing advance, Private Hoke of the 17th South Carolina, Company A, refused to surrender "to a d___d Yankee"; he knocked down four of his antagonists with the butt of his musket and was subsequently bayoneted. The Federals then attacked Company D, which was surrendered by its officer. Its men were all subsequently sent to Elmira.[44] The Federals soon charged the second traverse, and were repulsed by fifteen men of the twenty-seven in Company C that day. Remarkably, only six were left standing at the end of the day's fighting. Samuel Catawba Lowry, of Yorkville, South Carolina, led the men of Company F, 17th South Carolina, into action. All of its officers had been killed, and he was promoted by fate to captaincy in the heat of battle at age nineteen. His faithful black servant found his body immediately after the battle and retrieved it, in addition to Lowry's diary, and successfully got back through the lines in a miracle, given the confusion after the battle and the excitement of the time. The flyleaf of Lowry's diary entreated the reader: "When I am away, guard it with care, if you love me." The men of Elliott's Brigade had to fight the Union forces virtually alone for almost four hours until help finally arrived from Lee. It was only a matter of time, due to attrition, before the weakened Confederate lines would have given way without such additional assistance.[45]

Over in the area where Willcox had charged to the left of the Crater, the advancing Federals were being sheltered by the timber in the breastworks and thus came close to getting back the Confederate works in subsequent charges. However, the Rebels were able to pour such a fire that the blue-clad soldiers were again forced to fall back. They then re-formed and came on again for the last time. Meanwhile, the 49th North Carolina moved more to the left to guard against any flanking charge of the Union. More men were killed with a bayonet and clubbed by guns "than in any other engagement during the war," according to many participants. The Federals charged again against the breastworks held by the 49th North Carolina, and advanced upon Wright's battery. However, while they got close, there was such a heavy fire poured into them that they could not go any further. The 49th then held this position until 2:00 P.M., when it joined with Mahone's troops in the final assault on the Crater.[46]

At 7:00 A.M., a courier returned from the Confederate right of the Crater indicating that Captain Shedd had informed him that half of his men were gone in the explosion and that the Federals had driven him and the 23rd South Carolina from its breastworks, but that they had since recovered the whole line and would be able to hold it. The Federals, having been repulsed twice in that sector, thereafter ceased to make serious efforts there, as it was out of the line of Cemetery Hill. McMaster went to check on the detachment he had dispatched into the ravine; as he entered the trench, he was knocked off his feet by the moving crowd of Rebels and temporarily lost his pipe. One of the men stopped to retrieve it, as McMaster later recalled, one soldier exclaiming, "'Hold on, men, the colonel can't fight without his pipe!' He picked up the bowl of … [his] pipe and restored it to [him]." McMaster then saw a small space of vacant trench and observed two muskets protruding where the Federal soldiers were trying to shoot around the bend and down the trench line without exposing themselves. He concluded it was not a safe place for the commander. The 17th South Carolina had pressed down the trench nearly seventy-five yards simultaneously with the time Potter made his last charge of the day, which resulted in McMaster deemed "the most terrific musketry I think I heard that day." The Federals had spread their line down to near the branch that took in the part of the right wing of Ransom's brigade.

While the remains of Elliott's infantrymen struggled to keep the Federal troops from advancing beyond the break at the Crater, the Confederate artillery continued a blistering assault on the Federal troops advancing into the breach created by Pleasant's mine. Flanner's battery had opened with its six guns, doubled charged with canister, and poured a deadly fire into the ranks of any Federal unit attempting to advance from the confines of the Crater. The intense fire broke the Federal lines and they unceremoniously fled back to the Crater. The Federal artillery thereafter concentrated on Flanner's position for two hours; nonetheless, the North Carolina artillerymen stood and repulsed every advance of the enemy, holding them in check without infantry support until Beauregard finally arrived with troops commanded by Mahone. Not less than fifty shells a minute were hurled at the battery, and but for the protection afforded by the sides of the road, they would have been "swept off the face of the earth." The Federals pressed "steadily forward, when [the Confederate] … guns were double charged with canister, and deadly fire poured into their ranks." Their lines were then broken, and they fled to the works and there remained until our infantry, composed of the brigade of Mahone, Girardey, "(one of Mahone's staff) and Saunders, all under the command of Mahone, arrived and were placed in position preparatory to making the final charge that resulted in the recapture of the works about two o'clock of the day"[47]:

The artillery arm received full credit for having prevented a major catastrophe at the Crater and high on the list of officers commended was John Haskell. Divisional commander, General B.R. Johnson, praised him for his 'prompt and efficient co-operation' and General Pendleton, chief of artillery of the Army of Northern Virginia, noted in his report: 'Major Haskell, with conspicuous gallantry, taking personal charge of 12-pounders, moved them forward to the trenches within 50 yards of the Crater, so as to render their fire particularly accurate and destructive.'[48]

The 23 year-old John Haskell, who lost an arm at Gaines' Mill, had worked effectively to position his sixteen gun battery. After positioning Flanner at the Gee house, and having moved left to "speak a word of cheery commendation to [James] Lamkin of his battalion, who was already arranging the swarming masses of the enemy with his Virginia battery of eight-inch mortars," he took personal charge of two 12-pounder mortars and moved forward into the trenches within fifty yards of the Crater, achieving particularly accurate fire. To this was added the intense firepower of Wright's battery on the right and the guns of Major Gibbs on the left bearing on all Federal approaches.

Interestingly enough, the Federals had never used mortars in the field until the Petersburg campaign. Porter Alexander had ordered the Confederate mortars to be constructed in Richmond in early June, and they arrived at the front on June 24. They were only twelve-pounders, but they were light and convenient and at close range enabled the Rebels to hold their own with less loss than might have otherwise been expected. The Confederate artillery was by 7:30 A.M. applying an almost insurmountable barrage on three sides, and any attempt to move toward Cemetery Hill was most likely to fall to an intense barrage from this artillery in a horseshoe surrounding the Crater that thoroughly protected the route toward Petersburg.[49] Soon, Abbot's Reserve Artillery regiment brought into use some sixty mortars ranging from 24-pounder Coehorns to ten-inch Seacoast mortars. These weapons caused the Confederates to keep their trenches fully manned but offered no protection against the dropping shells.

The right of the Confederate army at Petersburg was spread quite thin, given the absence of the majority of the army still positioned north of the James to defend Richmond against Grant's diversion. Johnson's division was focused entirely on filling in the breach caused by the explosion at Elliott's Salient. Johnson had sent Colonel J. Thomas Goode's brigade to its left to assist in containing the breach. As a consequence, Brigadier General Alfred H. Colquitt's Georgia Brigade was stretched to the north in order to cover the ground Goode was forced to abandon. The only troops on the scene beyond Colquitt's brigade were the five brigades of Brigadier General William Mahone's division of A.P. Hill's III Corps, which at the time was still officially commanded by Richard Anderson and consisted of the Old Dominion or Virginia Brigade, commanded by Colonel David Weisiger, Wilcox's brigade of Alabamians, then under the command of Colonel John C.C. Sanders, Wright's brigade of Georgians under Colonel Matthew R. Hall, the Florida Brigade under General Joseph Finegan, and the Mississippi Brigade under Brigadier General Nathaniel H. Harris. At the time, Mahone's division was centered around the Willcox farm, located on a prolongation of Adams Street in Petersburg with its left at Rives' Salient, and from there extending westward about one mile in the direction of the Weldon Railroad, thus placing them in front of Warren's Fifth Corps. Its farthest regiment to the right, the 16th Virginia, however, was over a mile away to the west of the breastworks beyond the Willcox farm.[50]

General Lee had deduced that Grant's main assault would fall upon Petersburg and therefore issued orders on the night of July 29 for the "city's defenders to be ready to move at a moment's warning." Lieutenant P.M. Vance of Company F (Bibbs' Grays) of the 11th

Alabama in Wilcox's Brigade recalled being in charge of the picket line on the 29th of July. General Lee rode up and dismounted in full view of the Federal pickets, approached Vance, and asked:

> Lieutenant, have you noticed any unusual movement of the enemy? Bringing my sword to a salute, I replied: "I have not. Lookout, General do you see that tree? There is a sharpshooter in the top of it!" At that moment I saw a puff of smoke, heard the whiz of a bullet and the discharge of the gun, and the missile ended the life of a picket just relieved as he lay in his tent. Gen. Lee stepped down from the embankment, remounted his horse, and rode away. We were expecting something unusual to happen, it having been rumored that Gen. Grant was preparing to blow us up.

Colonel John Marshall Martin, commander of the 9th Florida of Finegan's Brigade, remarked in a letter to his wife that the troops were instructed to be in line ready for action, as the enemy would attack at three o'clock, "[i]n obedience to which we put ourselves in as early as possible." At 2:00 A.M., a general warning was sent down the trenches. Mahone later disputed the notion that his unit was under orders to be "in readiness to move at a moment's notice," as most commentators had subsequently related. Rather, he contended that an order had been issued merely to "be under arms at day-light." Regardless of this discrepancy in the record, the men were definitely to be in a state of readiness around the time set for the springing of the mine.[51]

William Mahone was born in Southampton County, Virginia, in 1826 of Irish roots going back to America's colonial period. Both of his grandfathers were soldiers in the War of 1812, and his father had been a militia commander in the Nat Turner insurrection. Mahone had graduated from the Virginia Military Institute in 1847 and taught briefly at Rappahanock Military Institute in Caroline County, Virginia. Thereafter, he was a civil engineer, and at age thirty-three was president and general supervisor of the Norfolk and Petersburg Railroad line. When the war intervened, he promptly offered his services to Virginia and was made lieutenant colonel and then colonel of the 6th Virginia Regiment. He was soon promoted to brigadier general, in November 1861. After being heavily engaged in the Seven Days battle, he was subsequently severely injured at Second Manassas. The wound prevented his participation in the Maryland campaign, where his brigade distinguished itself in the action. Mahone actively lobbied for promotion in the winter of 1862–63 and had the requisite political and military backing, including that of General Lee. Unfortunately, however, General Lee also pointed out that there was no command then available for a new major general.[52]

Mahone had his difficulties at Gettysburg. On July 2, he refused to participate in the attack on Cemetery Ridge when ordered into the conflict. This was just one of many blunders committed by Lee's generals that day, which doomed the general assault of the Army of Northern Virginia, and perhaps ultimately cost them the battle. The next day, Mahone's brigade was overlooked when manpower was desperately needed for the assault. The following year, in the Wilderness, he commanded a combined attack on the flank and rear of Grant's advance, which rolled back Hancock's command in confusion, presenting an apparent victory for the Rebels until Longstreet fell severely wounded, quite similar to Stonewall Jackson the year before in the same area. When his division commander, Richard Anderson, was chosen to fill Longstreet's position, Mahone was subsequently given command of Anderson's old division. Longstreet and A.P. Hill both recommended his promotion to major general at that time. Soon thereafter, at North Anna, as a division commander without official rank, he distinguished himself by repulsing Warren's corps.

Mahone's "appearance arrested attention. Very small in height and frame, he seemed a mere atom with little flesh," according to staff officer Moxley Sorrel. John Sergeant Wise remembered Mahone, 120 pounds at the very most and somewhere between five feet and five feet, five inches, as "the sauciest-looking little manikin imaginable" and "the oddest and daintiest little specimen" that he ever saw. Given his stature, or rather the lack thereof, he was referred to as "Little Billy." His health was quite delicate and it seemed likely any inflicted wound might be a serious impediment to his condition. When informed of his wounding at Second Manassas, an attempt was made to soften the blow to his wife by describing the injury as a "flesh wound." She knew better, however. "The General hasn't any flesh," she exclaimed. Dyspepsia confined him to a diet of tea, crackers, eggs and fresh milk. So dependent was he on milk that he brought an Alderney cow with him on campaign. Whether from poor digestion or otherwise, he was extremely irritable, even tyrannical, some close to him contended. He was a bundle of nervous energy, and subordinates always gave him a wide berth in view of his hair-trigger temper. His wardrobe could be described as "comfort above convention." He often wore a linen duster so long it covered his sword. At other occasions, he wore a plaited brown linen jacket, buttoned to trousers of a similar material, "like a boy's," complemented by a large Panama hat of beautiful texture, making him look "decidedly comfortable." He wore his hair long; his eyes were blue beneath bushy eyebrows, separated by a dainty, straight nose, below which flowed a drooping brown mustache and long beard that reached his chest.[53]

With his elevation to command of a division, Little Billy came into his own. Cool, courageous and able, he "was emerging as one of the army's premier combat officers," and "was by nature filled for generalship as few men are, and none knew this better than the men of his command ... they always felt a moral certainty that they were properly being led or placed, either to inflict the most damage on the enemy or to have the enemy inflict the least damage on them." Douglas Freeman commented that, while Mahone had been, at best, an average brigade commander, the experience of two plus years of fighting and the additional responsibility of a division had turned him into an elite commander under Lee in the last year of the war. On the morning of that fateful charge to the Crater, a member of his old brigade remarked that "there was not a man in the brigade, knowing that General Mahone was present, who did not feel we ... would be put in when and where the most effective service could be rendered."[54]

BG William Mahone (National Archives).

Mahone was near the middle of his division when he heard the terrific explosion at 4:44 A.M. Soon thereafter, he encountered a hatless and shoeless soldier from the breach who excitedly exclaimed to him that "He-l has busted." Lieutenant Colonel William H. Stewart, commander of the 61st Virginia heard the rumbling and saw the mountain of smoke, which aroused the whole camp. Then two hundred cannon roared "as if every lanyard had been pulled by the same hand." General Robert E. Lee and his staff heard the distant explosion at Violet Bank, Lee's headquarters to the north of the Appomattox near the Richmond-Petersburg turnpike. Details of the explosion and the breach reached Lee through Colonel

Samuel B. Paul, of Beauregard's staff, who was sleeping in his Petersburg home at the time of the blast. He immediately rode to notify Beauregard, who then sent Paul on to inform Lee. Lee was just about to sit down to breakfast when the report was conveyed to him at 6:10.[55] Lee saw the critical nature of the assault and immediately dispatched one of his aides, Colonel Charles Venable, to ride quickly to the right and bring up two brigades from General Mahone's division to the Blandford cemetery, "for time was too precious to observe military etiquette and send the orders through Hill."

General A.P. Hill himself had leaped from his cot at III Corps headquarters to glimpse the rising column of smoke and dust. Dressing quickly, he mounted Champ, his iron gray, and told his chief of staff, Lieutenant Colonel William H. Palmer, "I am going to Mahone's division; I will take his troops—all that can be spared—to the point of the explosion." He ordered Palmer to wait at headquarters for reports and then galloped toward Mahone, four miles to the right of the Salient. While Hill had bitterly resented Stonewall Jackson transmitting orders directly to his subordinates in the Light Division, when informed of Lee's action, he never questioned Lee's propriety in an emergency to send orders directly to Mahone in this circumstance. Hill galloped to the right with plans to organize an attacking column and ordered his artillery chief, Lieutenant Colonel William Pegram, to accompany Mahone's force; soon the light battery of Captains Thomas A. Brander and Thomas Ellett were rattling through Petersburg at a sharp trot "with cannoniers mounted, the swell, severe face of their boy-colonel lit up with that glow which to his men meant hotly-impending fight." Then the "shirt-sleeved Hill, paying no attention to bullets whistling through the air, and too concerned to rely on couriers, galloped ... to hasten Mahone's two brigades to the front."[56]

Colonel Venable sped on his assigned mission and found General Mahone's men encamped at the Willcox farm, near Lieutenant Run, and by then already standing to their arms. Venable encountered Mahone at his headquarters at the Branch house, just west of the Willcox farm, and conveyed Lee's orders to send two brigades to throw back the enemy penetration. Mahone's division was fanned out in an arc before Warren's Fifth Corps, an average of two miles away from the Crater. Mahone, having been chief engineer of the Norfolk and Petersburg Railroad prior to the war, was better acquainted with the terrain than any other commander in the field. He soon sent Captain Tom Bernard, his courier, to inform the Virginia and Georgia brigades of his division as to the critical role they would soon be playing in the deadly contest. These two brigades were chosen based upon their positions as being the farthest on the right, thus making their departure from the front lines less likely for the Federal forces to detect. Captain Bernard soon "came sweeping up the lines on his white charger to the headquarters of Brigadier General D.A. Weisiger" to convey Mahone's marching orders.

Lieutenant Colonel William H. Stewart, commander of the 61st Virginia, was then encamped with his regiment in a graveyard on the Willcox farm in a tent with scarcely enough room for two people when he heard the rumbling of the mine explosion. "The fiery crests of the battlements shone out for miles to our left," Stewart observed, "and the nitrous vapors rose in huge billows from each line of battle, and sweeping together formed one vast range of gloom."[57] Then the drums commenced rolling off the signals, which were followed by "'fall in' and hurried roll calls." The men were given the startling news that they were required to drive back the Federals, who were then close to the gates of Petersburg. While Mahone's men were already standing to arms, "the Federals, from their lofty look-outs," were busily interchanging signals, so as to cover such a length of front without exciting observation required great caution. However, Mahone was able to achieve such deception by having his men go one by one, as if going for water, and thus Warren never detected that the Confederates had left his front. In point of fact, he reported just the opposite to Meade around 8:00 A.M., providing the excuse as to why his corps could not participate in an all out assault of the breach at the Crater. Warren continued thereafter to report to Meade that not a man on the Confederate lines had left his front.[58]

After dispatching Venable to Mahone's headquarters, Lee soon thereafter rode alone to A.P. Hill's headquarters, and learned from Colonel Palmer that Hill had just recently rushed off to the right in order to bring up Mahone's troops himself. Lee then decided to ride on to hurry the men of Mahone's brigades, and, by a short route to the left of Halifax Street and along Lieutenant Run, he hurried with Palmer toward Mahone's location but soon encountered Mahone's men on their roundabout march to the site of the breach. "Lee turned at once, rode out into the open, and when he reached a point whence the break in the lines was clearly visible, he drew rein, took out his glasses and surveyed it carefully." He asked Palmer how many flags he could discern. Palmer looked through his glasses and replied "Eleven," which would indicate the presence of at least three brigades. Lee then wheeled Traveler around and rode back toward Mahone's column as Wright and Weisiger started down Lieutenant Run, and proceeded to Rives' Salient, where he met up with A.P. Hill. After Venable informed him of Mahone's movement, he then rode immediately back to General Bushrod Johnson's headquarters at Blandford Heights and there found General Beauregard, who had previously been at the Gee house some 500 yards in rear of the Crater.

Together, Lee and Beauregard then rode back to the Gee house, close to Haskell's battery of guns, to observe the impending clash of their forces with the Federal onslaught. From this location's second floor windows, Lee and Beauregard had a view of the whole field. At Lee's presence at the front, "all men took heart when they descried the grave and gracious face, and 'Traveler' stepping proudly, as if conscious that he bore upon his back the weight of a nation." Porter Alexander remarked that he did not know any battle where so much was at risk and where the commanding general occupied a point of such danger. The area in front of the Gee house was the point aimed at by all the Federal charges under their personal view, as well as the musketry fire from the Crater, and it was about the center of convergence of the eighty siege guns and eighty field guns especially placed for the attack.[59] Lee also learned that the majority of Elliott's brigade was holding on in the ditches and traverses on the left side of the Union breach and the rest, supported by Wise's brigade, which held the sector on the right from which they could fire into the Crater and cover the field leading up to it, were holding on to the right. One cannon from Davidson's battery barred the Federals, while the battery on the left (Wright's) rained grapeshot and canister into the Crater at almost point blank range.[60]

Venable's message when he arrived at Mahone's headquarters had been for the general to send two of his brigades to the support of Bushrod Johnson, in command of the line currently in enemy hands. Immediately following Mahone's orders, "the men of Mahone's brigade of Virginians and Wright's brigade of Georgians, began to drop back from their places in the breastworks, one by one, into the cornfield in their rear. They dropped back individually as if going for water so as not to alert the Federal observers in Warren's corps' in the signal towers. Warren continued to report that Mahone's men were there in force long after the vast majority had disappeared from the front. Weisiger's brigade totaled about 800 men; of that group, the 61st Virginia was the largest regiment, with a force not exceeding 200 men. The brigades formed in a ravine created by Lieutenant Run in order to escape detection by Federal signal observers:

> ...not with the discontented bearing of soldiers whose discipline alone carries them to what they feel to be a scene of fruitless sacrifice, but with the glad alacrity and aggressive ardor of men impatient for battle, and who, from long knowledge of war, are conscious that Fortune has placed within their grasp an opportunity which, by the magic touch of veteran steel, may be transformed to "swift-winged victory."

The troops moved out with the Virginia Brigade in front concealed in the ravine to the east and then north. When they had proceeded approximately one half mile, Mahone ordered a halt in a peach orchard behind the Ragland house near the intersection of the New Road[61] and ordered the men to strip off all extra equipment except for their cartridge boxes and canteens in order to become battle trim and to avoid exhaustion in the extremely hot summer sun. While the men were divesting themselves of excess baggage, Mahone realized he could not bear to deliver his men to another command and thus informed Venable that "I can't send my brigades to General Johnson — I will go with them myself." While the men could not be seen by Federal observers at this point, haphazard Federal artillery fire was still intense and effective on the men at this sheltered area. George W. Ivey of the 12th Virginia remembered the terrific artillery fire, and of being near a sergeant of the 14th Virginia when he was struck with a shell that tore off his leg. Ivey remembers him crying in his agony, "Oh! My poor mother! What will she do?"[62]

Leaving his men to march on, Mahone quickly rode off to report to General Johnson at his headquarters located at the north side of Blandford Heights, where he also believed he would find his own immediate superior, A.P. Hill. He did not find Hill there, but he did encounter General Beauregard. Mahone saluted and reported, "Gen'l I have, by direction of Gen'l Lee, two brigades of my division on the way, near at hand, for the reinforcement of Gen'l Johnson." Beauregard then called for Johnson, whom Mahone did not know personally, and gave the order to Johnson: "Gen'l you had better turn over any out-lying troops you may have to Gen'l Mahone and let him make the attack," to which Johnson cheerfully replied in the affirmative. Johnson "appeared about ready to take his breakfast," noted Mahone in amazement, who felt Johnson should have been at the front at the breach. Mahone then inquired of Johnson what frontage of line the Federals then occupied. Johnson responded, "The retrenchment cavalier," to which Mahone impatiently replied, "In feet I want to know, Gen'l Johnson, that, as you may imagine, I may determine the face of my attacking force." Johnson then said that it was about one hundred yards wide. Mahone asked Johnson to show him the way to the Crater, and Johnson instead called to "some lieutenant of his staff, and said to him: 'Show Gen'l Mahone the way to the Elliott Salient on Pegram's battery.'" While Mahone was meeting with Beauregard and Johnson, the diligent Colonel Venable had ridden on to find Lee and report on his contact with Mahone. He finally found Lee "sitting with General Hill, among the men in the lines, at a traverse near River [sic] Salient. When I told him of the delivery of the message, and that General Mahone had concluded to lead the two brigades himself, he expressed gratification."[63]

Mahone's columns, after leaving their excess baggage behind the Ragland house, marched along the edge of the hills skirting Lieutenant Run as far as New Road, turning into it about one hundred yards east of the bridge over Lieutenant Run until the road crossed it at the bottom of the ravine, and thence ran westward to within a few yards of the bridge. They then proceeded northward down the ravine on the east side of the run to Hannon's old ice pond, where they finally entered a military footpath leading alongside the pond. At that point, they then filed eastwardly up a ravine along the same military footpath to the Jerusalem Plank Road immediately south of Blandford Cemetery and north of the Crater.

Meanwhile, Mahone and Johnson's designated lieutenant-scout dismounted and traveled down the zigzag covered way, or military footpath, east of Jerusalem Plank Road, following it for about 200 yards, until it emptied into a ravine, or gulch, which there "made a depression to the right quite parallel to the portion of Gen'l Johnson's line," fronting the Crater. The lieutenant, apparently unwilling to proceed further, then informed Mahone that "If you will go up that slope there, you can see the Yankees." Mahone moved quickly up to the high ground behind the Crater:

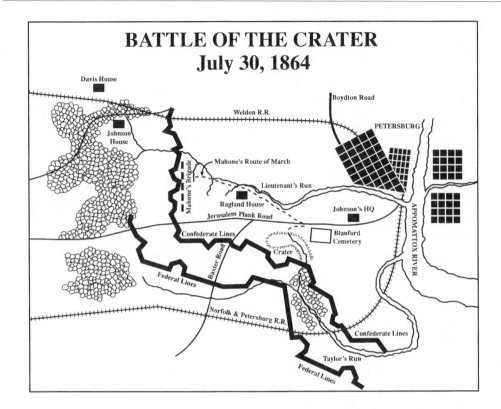

BATTLE OF THE CRATER
July 30, 1864

[There I found myself] suddenly in full view of Gen'l Johnson's "re-trenched cavalier," now crammed with Federal soldiers and thickly studded with Federal flags. For the moment I could scarcely take in the reality, and the very danger to which I was for the moment exposed came to my relief and bade me stand still as the surest course for personal safety, and so I stood where I could keep an eye on the adversary while I directed my own command.

Mahone, after recovering from his surprise at the sheer numbers of the enemy, counted the flags of at least eleven regiments in that single one hundred yard area. If his men were hit by this force while coming up the ravine in columns, they would inevitably be cut to pieces. The only consolation to the highly vulnerable position his comparatively meager force was confronted with was that the Federals appeared to be "greatly disorganized." Mahone's first reaction when he recovered his wits was to send his most trusted courier, Jimmy H. Blakemore, back to his lines for a third brigade — Wilcox's Alabama, a full two miles distant — to be brought up on the same route his other troops had just taken.[64]

Back at the plank road, Mahone's column halted and then countermarched by regiments at 8:10 A.M., thereby placing each of his regiments with its left in front. After then proceeding fifty yards east of the plank road, they subsequently poured in single file at the double quick into the

Capt. Victor Girardey (National Archives).

zigzag covered way, or military road, which Mahone had just traversed on his way to the shallow ravine to their right, running parallel to the Crater and the Confederate trenches, then in the possession of McMaster's reserves:

> There was no cheering, and no gaudy flaunting of uniforms or standards; with them, war's work had become too grim and too real for all that. In weather-worn and ragged clothes, with hats whose brims could shade their eyes for deadly aim, with bodies hardened down by march ... they came, not with earnest look or feelings of mercenaries, but like anxious, earnest men whose souls were in their work, who knew what the crisis was, and who were anxious to perform the task which that crisis demanded.[65]

For the first time that eventful day, a reinforced line of infantry was between the Confederate guns and the Federals, and "the boys at the guns, knowing what reliance could be placed upon Mahone's veterans, took new heart and new courage and pounded away with redoubled energy." Mahone had indicated to Captain Victor Girardey, one of his staff officers, the exact ground on which he desired the Virginia Brigade to form facing the retrenched cavalier. The cavalier was seventy-five feet in the rear of the supporting earthworks of the destroyed fort, with its bank thrown up on the side next to the fortifications. Between the cavalier and the main lines the Confederates had constructed that honeycombed series of bombproofs and traverses. The embankment from the bottom of the ditch was about ten feet and it commanded the outer or main line. The space from the outside of the fortifications to the inner edge of the ditch was more than one hundred feet wide. As the Virginia column approached the ravine along the covered way, at the angles where the Federals could see a moving column, the men were ordered to run quickly by, one man at a time, to conceal the approach of the force and to lessen the danger of passing bullets at these exposed points in the route. As the head of the column of Virginians reached the ravine at around 8:30 A.M., they saw Mahone standing near its mouth, still in the covered way, exchanging words of encouragement with passing soldiers as they filed right into the ravine and slapping some on the shoulder while declaring, "Give 'em hell, boys" and, also to some, according to Lieutenant W.A.S. Taylor of the 61st Virginia, "Give them the bayonet."

Mahone had Weisiger's men file to the right under the direction of Captain Girardey and form a north-south line of battle facing the Crater to the east. As the regiments were passing in front of him, Mahone took their commanders aside and gave them a briefing on the exact situation confronting them. He told them to have each man fix their bayonets and withhold their fire until they closed with the enemy. As Hall's Georgians emerged from the covered way, they were to extend the line farther to the north. The Virginia Brigade moved silently and quickly into line to the right of Smith's detachment of South Carolinians and "formed with that precision dear to every soldier's eye," observed Captain McCabe, "...the Sharpshooters leading, followed by the Sixth, Sixteenth, Sixty-first, Forty-first and Twelfth Virginia—the men of Second Manassas and Crampton's Gap."[66] Still coming at them over the rise were some of Colonel Smith's exhausted detachment of South Carolina refugees from the cavalier trench.[67]

As the men formed in the ravine, they encountered some of Haskell's artillerymen with their mortars in position, and some rudimentary breastworks which looked like they "had been made that morning for temporary shelter by men working with their bayonets." Smith's detachment of the 26th South Carolina and three companies of the 17th had been ordered there and the subject works had actually been thrown up by those men. The Virginians began "guying" these troops for retreating, and in reply the taunted men answered, "Ah, boys, you have hot work ahead—they are negroes, and show no quarter." This was the first word that the troops had that they would be confronting black troops, and the information "infused daring in the men." Colonel John Haskell, there in the ravine, rapidly dropping shell after shell into the Crater, was concerned:

> Notwithstanding this comfortable state of affairs, those of us who had had experience could not imagine it possible that such a state of cowardly incompetency could last long among the enemy, and were trying to resign ourselves to seeing the war end for us right there, when suddenly we saw, coming up the covered way at double-quick, men who showed that they were veterans. To our immense relief we found it was Mahone's Division, and that he was with them. There was no better division and no better commander. Everything changed at once.

Mahone sent for Haskell and questioned him about the situation, and soon directed him to keep up the impressive artillery and mortar fire. He also ordered him to advance some light mortars which could be carried by the men to a point nearer the Crater with protection provided by his infantrymen.[68]

Mahone's men made it almost to the point of the breach without being detected. Presumably, Warren still believed he was confronting Mahone's entire division on his front. But Captain Jedediah Paine, atop a signal tower behind the Ninth Corps lines, was able to detect the head of the Confederate brigade crossing the Jerusalem Plank Road where the covered way bisected the road and count its battle flags. Paine sent a dispatch to Burnside, advising of the fresh troops, and deducing correctly that they originated from the Confederate right. However, precious time transpired before Paine's courier reached Burnside's headquarters, and the intelligence was thus unfortunately too late to be of use to the Union units which were renewing their assault toward Cemetery Hill.

As the 800 men of the Virginia Brigade lay in line with their fixed bayonets gleaming, the Crater and the cavalier trench was crammed full of the enemy. Colonel Stewart counted at least seven flags in front of his 61st Virginia regiment alone. To Private Richard B. Davis, a sharpshooter of the 12th Virginia, the flags in the Crater were as "as thick as cornstalks in a row." "The whole face of the earth, including the ditch which our men formerly occupied, fairly teemed with the enemy." The Federals' "silken banners proudly floating on the breezes, supported by countless bayonets glistening in the sunlight, might on an ordinary occasion have daunted our little band and made them forfeit a trial at arms, but they were desperate and determined."

Mahone had cautioned the men "to reserve their fire and not to shoot until they reached the brink of the ditch, and then after delivering one volley to use the bayonet." This directive was capable of execution in part because Mahone had previously fined anyone who threw away their bayonets, "so his division, unique in the army at the time, was fully equipped with this rarely used weapon. They marched in parades with fixed bayonets." As Thomas H. Cross of Company A, 16th Virginia, remarked years later:

> The order was passed in that subdued tone which denotes a stern purpose to "fix bayonets," and by those to whom the thought had occurred an extra turn was taken on the little screw which holds the bayonet-shank on the gun. The thought of having his bayonet "unshipped" flashed across the writer's mind, and his right hand instinctively sought his cartridge-box and the possibility was provided against.

The fight was personal to many in the Virginia Brigade. Word had by now reached them that the Yankees had broken through and captured some of the lines near Bradford Cemetery. Many of the ranks of the 12th Virginia and other Virginia regiments were from Petersburg, and many had homes within range of the Union cannonade. Add to this was the news they were facing black troops for the first time in the war, as well as the fact that the killing and maiming of hundreds of their compatriots by means of the mine was deemed by most to be uncivilized and cowardly, and it is little wonder that these troops were motivated as they awaited orders to advance. Colonel Stewart later recalled that "[o]ur comrades had been slaughtered in a most inhuman and brutal manner, and black slaves were trampling over their mangled and bleeding forms. Revenge must have fired every heart and strung every arm with nerves of steel for the herculean task of blood."[69]

Mahone desperately wanted to bring Wright's Georgia Brigade into line so that his counterattack would have as great a force as possible, given the numbers of Federals in the Crater and its adjoining works. Thus, the "Georgians tramped across the sunburnt grass behind the Virginians" in quick order. The head of the brigade had left the mouth of the covered way and was filing up the depression to take its place on the right of the Virginia Brigade. Mahone hoped for the time to have it properly formed, in order to extend his line far enough to cover the entire length of the captured works. As Mahone awaited the alignment of his two brigades in the ravine into a line of battle, the 61st North Carolina of Clingman's Brigade of Hoke's division marched south from its position north of Gracie's Salient, to reinforce the troops engaged at the breach, arriving at the same time as Mahone's brigades, and proceeded to form in the ravine with them.

The troops were thus all in place for the denouement of this bloody and fateful battle. After four hours of struggle in the Crater and adjoining works, Ferrero's men were finally going in. To combat this, Confederate reinforcements had finally arrived at the point of the breach, although they were still greatly outnumbered. What would play out in the next hour, from 9:00 am to 10:00 A.M., would determine who would ultimately be victorious that day.

CHAPTER 13

Into the Valley of Death

As Ferrero's black troops continued apprehensively to await further orders to advance in the suffocating covered way, the wounded and maimed of the first three divisions continued to stream back from the front through those close quarters for well over an hour. The men were certainly confused by the last minute changes in choreography, after weeks of strenuous training to lead the charge. Similarly, they were certainly shaken by the screaming, mutilated men being paraded past them through the covered way to hospitals in the rear. Colonel Thomas later recalled that as the men watched this endless procession, "[e]very moment changed the condition from that of a forlorn hope to one of forlorn hopelessness." While the anxious men contemplated their fate at the prospects of an advance into the living hell to their front, many of the untested black soldiers approached Garland H. White, chaplain of the 28th USCT, himself an escaped slave who had become a Methodist minister. Wishing to go into battle prepared, they entreated him: "I want you, brother White, to write to my father and mother ... that George (Thomas, John, or Peter, as we call each other out here) died like a man; and when pay-day comes, if it ever does come, send what money is due to my wife, and tell her to raise Salley and Mary in the fear of the Lord!"[1]

Sergeant John H. Offer of the 30th USCT, a preacher from Maryland's eastern shore, likewise comforted the men with this advice:

> Now, men; this am g'wine to be a gret fight. If we take Petersburg, most likely we take Richmond, and 'stroy Lee's army, an' close de wah. Eb'ry man had orter liff up his soul in pra'r for a strong heart. Oh! member de poor color'd man ober dere in bondage. Oh! member Gineral Grant and Gineral Burnside, and Gineral Meade, an' all the gret Ginerals is right ober yonder watching ye, and any skulker is g'wine to get a prod of dis bayonet. You heah me![2]

After procrastinating for some time due to the lateness of the hour and the overcrowding in the Crater, and then, upon finally ordering the men in, only then to be countermanded by Colonel Loring, Ferrero finally received peremptory orders from Burnside to push ahead, regardless of any interference from other divisions ahead of him. Ferrero reluctantly left his comfortable bunker and advanced to the covered way, where his men had been waiting for what seemed to them like an eternity. As the men were finally moved forward at about 7:30 A.M., they became somewhat disorganized moving toward the front, as there was little room for an effective attack formation.[3]

As they moved forward, the troops encountered General John Turner returning from the Crater on a reconnaissance visit preliminary to his scheduled assault in support of the

LOOK HERE,   AND   HERE.

GEN. VAN SKULKO, OF THE POTOMAC ARMY, AT THE BATTLE OF JULY 30.

Where Gen. Grant intended him to be—   AND   *Where he really was, all the time.*

"General Van Skulko" (Davis —*Death in the Trenches*).

Ninth Corps. Colonel Joshua K. Sigfried's first brigade had been chosen to lead Ferrero's division into the fray. They finally moved forward down the same covered way from which Ledlie's men had surged two and one half hours earlier, with the 30th USCT under Colonel Delevan Bates in the lead. Following the 30th were the 43rd USCT under Lieutenant Colonel H. Seymour Hall, the 27th USCT under Lieutenant Colonel Charles J. Wright and the 39th USCT under Colonel Ozora Stearns. There was one final delay as Sigfried requested permission from his commander to deploy in a line of battle rather than to advance in column, a request which was summarily denied by Ferrero. The brigade halted in a meadow where

Humphrey's men, unable to advance due to the congestion at the Crater, had come to a standstill. As they reached the forward entrenchments, they, too, were required to use sandbag stairways to negotiate the head high front trenches.

As the men started forward, it seemed as though they were "going to a camp meeting or to a 1st of August dinner."[4] "Gathering his sword and scabbard up in his arms," Joshua Sigfried "turned to ... [Major Oliver Bosbyshell] 'Come on, Bosby!' And, leaping the Union parapets, followed by his staff and the black regiments of his brigade, bore down upon the crater." He intoned to his men "Attention, battalion! Fix bayonets!" Following a sharp rattling of steel came the final order: "Trail arms! Forward, March!" As the men surged through the covered way to the break in the lines, they encountered a white sergeant who was being carried to the rear with his leg shot off who cried out to the black troops, "Now go in with a will, boys. There's enough of you to eat 'em all up." A sergeant in one of the advanced USCT regiments replied for all his comrades: "Dat may be all so, boss; but the fac' is, we habn't got jes de bes' kind ob an appetite for 'em dis mornin."[5]

The officers soon learned that it would be nearly impossible to advance toward Cemetery Hill in any orderly fashion. Compact divisional squares "had to be turned into strung-out, four abreast columns that were then jammed into the two covered ways leading from the staging area to the Union front line." The men first had to negotiate those same Federal breastworks that had caused the white divisions difficulty, which caused critical delays as the men ramped up two sets of sandbag stairways, then struggled with the remaining abatis and obstacles thrown up by the explosion with which their predecessors had been forced to contend. Then, with fixed bayonets, the 30th started across the open field. By then the time was approaching 8:00 A.M. Once in the open, the 30th USCT then went forward by the left flank, with battalions side-by-side, four men at a time skipping up the passageway toward the Crater. "The appearance of the regimental colors seemed to be the signal for the enemy's batteries," recalled Delevan Bates, "and it was volley after volley of canister and shrapnel they gave us." Lieutenant Freeman S. Bowley said that "We went on the run for about 100 yards to the crater.... I remember seeing a lot of dead white soldiers lying on the slope that we ran over." As they moved further onward, the men of the 30th were confronted with a stretcher conveying the mortally wounded Colonel Jacob Gould of the 59th Massachusetts back to the Federal lines. As the eager troops surged forward, the Rebel batteries raked them in a vicious cross fire of grape and canister. An observer from the 6th USCT later wrote of his impressions that day: "Never in all my experience did I see artillery do such awful execution as was done that morning in the ranks of those black men by a Confederate battery that stood in an apple orchard. It looked as if one side of hell had opened, and fire and brimstone were belching forth."

Lieut. Col. Joshua K. Sigfried (Gould — *The Forty-Eighth Pennsylvania*).

Captain Albert Rogall of the 27th USCT described the Confederate fire in their front as they advanced as "tearing the ground in our midst." Major Bosbyshell observed, "How grandly ... [Sigfried's] brigade charged over the cleared ground between the lines, raked by minie ball, shot and shell as no single spot had ever been raked before!" Josiah Jones of the 6th New Hampshire observed that "[a]t that time there was an artillery duel going on; the shell, grape, and canister made dismal music over their heads, and they went into this vortex of death with artillery and musketry fire from front and flank." Men started dropping like leaves due to this intense Rebel barrage. Soon the 30th USCT's flag was down, its color sergeant staining the stars and stripes with red blood: "A grape-shot had torn his head in pieces. A corporal quickly caught up the colors, but the color lance was shattered by a shot." Bowley recalled the "rushing, hurtling sound of grape-shot in close proximity; and ... heard a smashing sound, and a file of four men were swept away from ... [his] very side. [He] ... yelled to the men, and the gap was instantly closed."

The canister cut a huge swath in Lieutenant Freeman Bowley's company, but the men quickly closed ranks and went on. Bowley recounted that "[t]he fire at that point was so hot that no one wanted to stay there long." "No troops entered the fight under more severe a fire, nor did any march steadier or behaved with greater coolness," than the fourth division that day, according to Oliver Bosbyshell. Behind the 30th rushed the rest of the brigade, the 43rd, then the 39th, and finally the 27th USCT As the 43rd USCT passed in front of Ferrero, the general cried out, "Here comes the Forty-third; let's give them three cheers!" and took off his hat and waved it above his head and personally led the cheering. On they rushed through that terrible killing field at the double quick. Lieutenant James H. Clark of the 115th New York of the Tenth Corps witnessed the brigade's advance and commented: "Noble fellows! Grandly they cross the field; they are under a withering fire, but still rush on regardless of fallen comrades, and the storm of pitiless lead and relentless grape that pours upon them from three sides, and gain the works with a ringing cheer." Unfortunately, by the time the troops approached the Crater, all formation was lost in the rush to get across that dreadful cross fire.[6]

As Sigfried's brigade approached the Crater, there appeared to be no place to go, with the scattered remnants of three full divisions milling around in mass confusion and disorder. Sigfried was determined to keeping out of this cul-de-sac of teeming humanity as best he could. With Colonel Delevan Bates leading the 30th USCT, the regiment veered away from the Crater. However, the intense rifle fire focused on them at that point, together with the mass of disorganized white units, forced some of the regiment into the pit. General Bartlett sent an aide to direct the men to the left, and ultimately went himself to attempt to ward off the further disorder that would be caused by the onrush of the black troops. However, the efforts failed and the black soldiers rushed into the Crater and into the first division. General Turner witnessed the disorganization, which only added "confusion to the confusion which already exist[ed]." "The men literally came falling right over into the crater on their hands and knees," recalled Turner. "They were so thick in there that a man could not walk." Colonel Marshall was at that time in the process of re-forming his men for another attempt at the Confederates in his front, which was "knocked all to pieces" by Sigfried's men, according to Major Van Buren.

Knowing Ferrero's men were advancing on the Crater, Marshall commented, "Here is Ferrero. Hadn't we better hold on to what we have got, till we see what the Egyptians can do for us?" Bates led the majority of his men through the Crater, "gamely pushing out a ragged battle line a short distance northwest of the hole." He called out to Captain David E. Proctor, in charge of the leading company, to "[p]ush down the line." On they rushed through Ledlie's massed men and out the other side where the men formed a rough line of battle. The rest of Sigfried's brigade followed the 30th USCT across the field and up to the Crater. Captain Matthew R. Mitchell recalled "the 27th marching in double quick up that approach to the crater and through it, stepping over our dead and wounded" as they advanced.[7]

Closely behind the 30th was the 43rd USTC. As it attempted to push through the smoking pit, Lieutenant Colonel Hall saw that the milling mass inside would make it virtually impossible to follow the 30th. Apparently, as the 30th had rushed through, it startled the current occupants of the Crater, who were by then milling around so haphazardly that the remainder of Sigfried's men could not negotiate the hazard without becoming totally disorganized. In back of the front Confederate lines were impenetrable abatis, in front of chevaux de frise fastened with strong wire. Hall, in front of his regiment, found a narrow space at the foot of the outer slope of the intrenchments, beyond which the abatis had been knocked down. Hall thus took this partially sheltered route, leaving Adjutant James O'Brien at the Crater to close up the companies and direct them forward, and led his men "along the front of the enemy's intrenchments, so close that some of ... [his] officers and men were wounded by the bayonets, others burned by the powder flashes of the foe." O'Brien mounted the debris in the Crater and sent his troops onward while becoming "a shining mark for the bullets of the enemy" and soon was hit with a bullet in the left shoulder.[8] Hall later reflected on the moment: "I saw at once the utter hopelessness of passing the enemy's lines through and over the mass of soldiers in the yawning gulf. Without an instant's pause, the Forty-third followed my lead to our right around on the crest of the Crater's rim till near the enemy's main line of intrenchments on our right," then fully manned by the Rebels.

As the black troops were moving by the left flank around the edge of the Crater, the file closers, on account of the narrowness of the covered way, were compelled to pass through the mass of white men inside the Crater. One such file closer was a massively built black man, "a powerful and well-formed sergeant" who was stripped to the waist, "his coal-black skin shining like polished ebony in the strong sunlight." As he passed up the slope to merge on the Confederate side, he encountered one of his own company comrades, "evidently with the intention of remaining inside the crater, out of the way of the bullets." The sergeant accosted the man with "None ob yo' d__n skulkin,' now," while at the same time he seized the culprit in one hand and, lifting him up in his powerful grasp by the waistband of his trousers, threw him to the crest of the Crater, then threw him over onto the Confederate side and quickly followed him back into the fray. As the 30th and 43rd USCT moved on past the first line of Confederate intrenchments, the remainder of the brigade, consisting of the 27th and 39th USCT was left behind, unable to work its way past the milling chaos in and around the Crater. They would soon find a significant role to play in this tragedy, however.[9]

Bates attempted to lead his regiment toward the Confederates and finally encountered the labyrinth of traverses and bomb-proofs inside the main line. Some of these traverses were filled with the remnants of Griffin's nearly stalled assault, whose men were then holding the rearmost earthworks. However, in the dense smoke the blacks could not distinguish friend from foe. Coming to the main trenches, they spotted a crowd of soldiers on the other side. The line of black troops charged into the men in the trenches "and waving their flags, cried out to us to surrender, according to a white Union soldier, and then began firing down at us." The 9th New Hampshire, just returning from its latest unsuccessful assault toward Cemetery Hill was severely hit, and along with several other regiments all but disintegrated by the heavy volleys.

Finally, Captain Andrew Jackson Hough, commander of the 9th New Hampshire, leaped onto the parapet after grabbing the United States flag from Corporal Brown, its current color bearer, and waved the banner in their faces in a desperate attempt to identify his men. The black troops at long last "realized their mistake and hopped down among their fellow, overcrowded Federal troops, landing among the labyrinthine Confederate works," thereby crowding the works too densely for anyone to move. Indeed, Captain Willard D. Tripp of the 29th

Massachusetts reported that the colored division marched into the works and the position held by his regiment and the area "was filled so full of them that it was quite impossible to move or be in any manner effective." As Captain Hough rejoined his regiment, his adjutant, Lieutenant Brown, cautioned him against such impetuous actions. Hough, however, simply "laughed at him, and said there would be no bullet for him that day," which soon proved to be a mistaken prophesy.[10]

Bates then turned his column to the right until it was beyond the bulk of Griffin's brigade of white troops, and moved along the top embankment of the Confederate parapet. His troops were able to utilize the top due to the fact that the Tenth Corps under Brigadier General John Turner had by this time advanced to the north and were keeping McAfee's North Carolinians quite occupied on his right. Sigfried's right nearly connected with the 51st New York of the second division near the ravine, partly covering the troops of the second division, who had "charged up the hill and fallen back into the covered way." They had run into the entrenchments of the 17th South Carolina: "Like panthers they tore into the Confederate infantrymen." The Rebel trenches were quickly taken in fierce hand-to-hand combat and, though the cost was considerable, "the combat spirit of the Negro troops was now honed to razor's edge and they were eager to go in.... Now they sweep everything before them. Prisoners are taken," exclaimed Lieutenant Clark of the 115th New York, "... and are forced to run the fearful gauntlet of fire." Meanwhile, the 43rd USCT charged the Confederate troops in their immediate front, taking 250 prisoners and a stand of colors, as well as recovering a National flag taken earlier from one of the white regiments and recovered by Lieutenant Robert W. Armstrong. In hand-to-hand combat, the men killed a number of the surrendered Rebels "in spite of the efforts of their officers to restrain them." Captain Albert D. Wright, of Company G, found himself in advance of his regiment down the Confederate trench works and began firing his pistol "alongside of every gun I could reach, as they moved them over to fire at our men." Six of his company had followed him, and, recognizing their plight, Wright implored them, "We cannot go back; they will kill us! If we lie here they will capture us, and they say they will take no nigger prisoners or white officers with them. Let's jump in."

The Confederates were surprised, and "the colored men killed everyone within reach, instantly." This created a panic and Wright and his men then turned to the right with his men "yelling like fiends and bayoneting everyone they could reach." The Confederates near the Crater were obliged to fall back to the next trench. The breastworks were thus cleared out for the whole length of the regiment, as the Confederates mistook their rush for a charge by the very large force of troops they knew to be in the Crater. Wright captured the flag attributed to his regiment in his almost single-handed charge and personally captured five prisoners. As they rounded an angle at the head of the ravine, the Confederates could see how small the force that had intimidated them actually was, and they immediately opened a galling fire on the men of the 43rd. Wright worked his way through the passage in the abatis and went into the enemy works with some members of Companies F and G and there "saw a Rebel color sticking above a rifle-pit in rear of the line ... [they had] charged, jumped up on the mound of earth, aimed his empty pistol down at the color guard, and demanded their surrender." Some of his men soon appeared behind him, "and the Rebels prayed to be protected from the 'niggers.'"

"From where we were," Wright recalled, "I could see into Petersburg, there being no other works or men between ourselves and that city." While packing sandbags to protect his band of troops in the rifle pit, Wright was severely wounded in the arm and retired to a field hospital. As he left the field of combat, he took satisfaction in seeing the rest of his regiment crawling through the Confederate abatis and flowing into the rifle pits to safety.[11] As Wright retired with his captured prize, he was confronted by a Federal colonel near the Crater who attempted to take the banner by force. However, the colonel desisted when confronted by a number of the men from the 43rd. Not one company of white troops followed them, "and although their ranks were necessarily broken by the obstacle," the blacks "charged under a deadly fire of artillery and musketry which reached them from all sides at once."[12]

The 43rd finally linked up with the 30th USCT on the outside of slope of the Crater in the cleared second line of works. For all the crowding, crossfire and confusion, the inexperienced blacks had moved out gallantly, and strode across the open furlong toward the shallow cavalier trench held by the last survivors of the morning's holocaust. "Their steady advance put the lie to Meade's doubt that they could not have done this endeavor under even less adversity," and in a few minutes the "battered but determined black line pried the defenders from the cavalier trench." It appeared, at least, as though the day was about to be won. The two regiments were soon joined by the remaining two regiments of the brigade following their own deadly passage through no-man's-land and the disorderly crowd in the pit. The Rebel works in this part of the line were "a perfect honeycomb of bomb proofs, trenches, covered ways, sleeping holes, and little alleys running in every direction, and in each hole there appeared one or more rebel soldiers, some verbally asserting their readiness to 'kill the niggers' when they came in view and some praying for mercy," according to Delevan Bates. The blacks by now were supported by some disjointed fragments of the white troops who had been fighting in this area for hours. However, the large portion of Griffin's men was still reeling from the disruption of having Sigfried's brigade fire into them and then crash through their ranks screaming wildly. Thus, the officers of neither Griffin's nor Bliss's brigades were able to mount organized support to Sigfried's advance. Additionally, the white troops had been under fire so long that many commanders were dead or wounded and had not been properly replaced.[13]

Bates later recalled being instructed by a staff officer looking for Sigfried that "Col. Bates, a charge must be made on Cemetery Hill at once." These two regiments, the 30th and 43rd USCT, surged forward through the cross fire and frontal defenses in the cavalier trench held by the detachment of McMaster's men from the 17th South Carolina and portions of the 26th, while the remainder of Elliott's Brigade applied effective fire from the right and left. As a portion of the cavalier trench was soon enfiladed by the onrushing black men in blue, McMaster's men were forced to fall back to another cross ditch approximately one hundred feet to the rear. Seeing their enemy falling back from their assault, the blacks began yelling, "No Quarters, remember Fort Pillow" as they dove into the trenches and proceeded to take prisoners and in a number of cases slaughtered their unarmed charges.[14] This slogan and their initial brutal actions would prove to be a deadly problem for the black men a short time thereafter.[15]

One Confederate captain refused to surrender and implored his men to "Kill 'em! Shoot 'em! Kill the damned niggers!" His exhortations were quickly quieted with the bayonet. "'Surrender! Surrender! Surrender!' was heard on every side, and those who defiantly refused were given the cold steel without mercy." Lieutenant Clark of the 115th New York recalled the activities as the black soldiers rushed through the trenches and traverses, sweeping everything before them:

> Prisoners are taken, and are forced to run the fearful gauntlet of fire. A fellow comrade said he saw a colored soldier in an agony of frenzy, bayonet a rebel prisoner and his own captain justly shot him dead. Others placed wounded comrades in blankets and shelter tents, and compel the chivalry at the point of the bayonet to carry them from the field.
> The colored troops are greatly elated at their success, and wildly mass and crowd together regardless of all order or position.[16]

The intensity of the black units' fighting spirit was also recounted by Lieutenant James W. Steele of the 43rd USCT:

> I know something about the prisoners, for there was a half determination on the part of a good many of the black soldiers to kill them as fast as they came to them. They were thinking of Fort Pillow, and small blame to them. The first batch I saw had been driven together just in front of the line of earthworks we had taken and occupied. I climbed over and rushed out there to save them from a group of men of my own company, who in two minutes would have bayoneted the last poor devil of them.[17]

When the second brigade came on, Lieutenant William Baird of the 23rd USCT similarly reported encountering troops from other units who were stymied by prisoners and the wounded of their own units. As Baird passed by his colonel, there was a wounded black soldier on a stretcher with too few men to successfully carry the litter to the rear. At this time, a Confederate officer was passing to the rear as a prisoner, and Colonel Cleveland J. Campbell ordered the officer to assist in carrying the wounded black Federal to the rear. "The Confederate with an oath said he would not help carry any Negro and started on ... the colonel whipped out his revolver and shot him."[18]

Sigfried's brigade paid a very heavy price for its advance to the cavalier trench and its efforts to clean out the adjacent works in its proximity. Bowley estimated at the time that one half of the brigade had been lost in the assault. Colonel Bates referred to the rate at which his men became casualties by comparing those losses to leaves "in the forest in the gales of Autumn." Given these losses and the complete disintegration of order caused by the efforts to push past the other three divisions and the stalled assault itself, Sigfried ordered the brigade to be re-formed before attempting any further advance, if one was to be so ordered; this process took approximately twenty minutes. While re-forming, an aide from Burnside's staff appeared and asked Bates his intentions for further offensive action, to which Bates responded, "This is as far as my orders go." The staff officer then pointed to a white house in the direction of Petersburg near a Confederate battery (probably Flanner's) and said, "That will be your next objective point; advance at once." Once re-formed, Sigfried's men attempted to advance again toward the Jerusalem Plank Road. However, McMaster's men, while having been grudgingly driven back from their defensive position by the initial assault, were not about to give up any more ground without a struggle to the death. On the black soldiers came, taking a storm of canister and shot from three sides but still standing up quite well. According to some sources, they came closer to the crest than any other unit.[19] Bates recalled that forming a line of battle proved impossible, so "all that I could do was to order an advance to the front, which order was at once complied with by my regiment, and such portions of the other regiments that were near us." Bates sprang forward from the ditch along with about 200 men. Those on the left wing of the regiment could not see him, and it was impossible to hear anything.

As the small band advanced toward Ransom's men and Cemetery Hill,[20] the movement was anticipated by the Confederates, and Colonel Bates was shot in the head, with the bullet traversing his cheekbones. As Bates recalled, "An ounce of lead struck me in front of the right ear, passed above the roof of the mouth, and came out close behind the left ear." As he was being carried off the field his bearers saw a discharge from Davidson's Battery to the right of the crater, which was raking the field with canister, and they immediately dropped to the ground. "Such a shrill, sound as was made by the charge passing about two feet above us," Bates later reflected, "God knows I never want to hear again." Although considered to be mortally wounded, he survived his wound.[21]

Major James C. Leeke was then shot in the chest and began coughing up blood. Sigfried reported that Leeke still was urging his men on, with blood pouring from his mouth. Captain William Henry Seagrave had a leg shattered and a number of other officers quickly fell. Lieutenant Colonel Charles Wright, commanding the 27th USCT, retained command despite having received two serious wounds. Colonel Hall, commanding the 43rd, was shot in the arm, a wound which ultimately required amputation. After turning over command to Captain Jesse Wilkinson and retrieving his saber, which he had dropped when he was hit, Hall was carried to the rear.[22] "Bullets came through all the little alleyways, and found victims in the most unexpected places." Captain Frank Holsinger of the 19th USCT remembered that his unit was still in the Federal works when the wounded Colonel Hall was taken past them. Hall "raised his left hand toward the enemy and said, 'Go in, boys; there is plenty there for all of you.'"[23] At one point, the colors of the 30th USCT were picked up by Private William Gray, who was quickly "struck by a minie ball in the left breast causing almost immediate death." The 43rd USCT had its colors almost entirely cut up by the fire and its staff splintered and broken. The regiment lost all of its officers, requiring the fearless black noncommissioned officers to take command after their officers were borne off the field dead or wounded. The hand-to-hand fighting with bayonets was horribly fierce as the Federals made small flank attacks, jumping over barricades. The aftermath of few battles evidenced as many bayonet wounds as this one. Combined with this close quarters combat was the intense artillery fire on three sides of the Union attack, which devastated the brave, black troops as they attempted to advance on their objective. Additionally, McMaster's detachment gave them volley after volley, leading McMaster to proudly proclaim that the blacks were "welcomed ... to hospitable graves at 9 o'clock A.M."[24]

With this staunch defense by McMaster's men, coupled with the artillery positioned on three sides which produced a galling fire into their midst, further Federal advance there was impossible. Soon it became too dangerous to retreat or advance, forcing the men (black and white alike) to simply hold their place in this extremely hostile environment. One white officer said that "I felt like sitting down & weeping on account of our misfortune."[25] The blacks found themselves largely unsupported by the three divisions that preceded them into the man-made hell. There were many instances of individual bravery among the fourth division that morning. Captain Ervin T. Case of the 9th New Hampshire observed one powerfully built soldier come to the front as McMaster's men were pushing the stalled troops back. The soldier calmly loaded his rifle, and, waiting until the Rebels rallied for another charge, "[d]eliberately stepping over the breastworks that separated us, he shot the foremost rebel, then clubbing his musket he dispatched the two next with its butt, and breaking it at the second blow, with a look of disgust he threw it away and came back amid a shower of bullets, unharmed." Josiah Jones observed the color-bearer of one of the USCT regiments killed, "and their flag go down, but it was lifted from the ground by another who was shot, but again rescued by a third, who carried if forward into the fight."[26]

It took almost half an hour for the four regiments of Sigfried's brigades to clear the advance route sufficiently for Colonel Thomas to lead his second brigade forward. First in that line was the 31st USCT under Lieutenant Colonel W.E.W. Ross, with the 19th USCT bringing up the rear under the command of Lieutenant Colonel Joseph G. Perkins. In between these regiments were the 23rd under Colonel Cleveland J. Campbell, the 28th (a battalion of companies) under Lieutenant Colonel Charles J. Russell and the 29th USCT under Lieutenant Colonel John A. Bross. Initially, Thomas's regiments were moving "left in front," anticipating the requirement to form on the left of the division line beyond the Crater. Seeing Sigfried's difficulties, however, Thomas took his brigade to the right, thus causing them to form with the rear rank in the front line, "an undesirable formation for the best-trained units." This tactical error almost instantly proved inconsequential, however, because Thomas's regiments soon lost all formation in the trench complex to the right of the crater. As Colonel Russell of the 28th called "Fix bayonets; charge bayonets!" the last words exchanged with Chaplain Garland White by many of the men were "Brother White, good-bye. Take care of yourself—for today someone must die, and, if it be me, I hope our people will get the benefit of it." Colonel Russell, in starting forward, told the men he intended to lead them to Petersburg that day. Lieutenant Colonel John Bross of the 29th cried out, "'Forward, 29th' and they advanced on over the mass" of men in the Crater. Turning to Captain Brockway, Bross then said to, "bring forward the colors." As the brigade reached the Crater, and Chaplain White saw the colors waving over the Rebel works, he cried, "Boys, the day is ours, and Petersburg is Sure."[27]

Thomas's brigade moved gallantly on the right over the bombproofs and through the men of the first division. As the second brigade moved and intermingled with Ledlie's and Bliss's men, the impact on Bliss's men in particular was to cause great difficulties. Frederick Cushman of the 58th Massachusetts wrote that "[a]n indescribable scene of confusion immediately followed. Colors which had been planted by our troops, sanguine of success, on the parapet in the early part of the day, were thrown down and trampled under foot in the mud. White men and negroes lay indiscriminately together, piled up three and four deep."[28] As they mounted the rifle pits outside the Crater, the men of Thomas's command encountered a deadly enfilade fire from the Confederate battery on its right as well as a cross fire of musketry which decimated their ranks. Many of the officer corps fell in this initial barrage, as well as hundreds of the men. "While in this work and coming through we were exposed to a heavy cross fire of artillery & musketry," recalled Captain Robert Porter of the 29th USCT. "Here we lost all our line officers." "These black men commanded the admiration and respect of every beholder on the day," one of the Federal participants watching from the breastworks commented. Unfortunately, Thomas never retained full control of his brigade once the advance began.

Two of his regiments were soon bogged down in the confusion of the Crater, while a third, the 19th USCT, became hung up before it ever reached the pit. Once the units halted and became somewhat sheltered from the Rebel fire by its protective walls, many of the men then refused to move forward, and yet they could not return to their own lines through the deadly cross fire on no-man's-land. The Crater acted as "a mighty whirlpool, whose suction drew in and engulfed all who came near it, although there was no music of sirens to entice them there to meet their doom, or council of Circe to guide them beyond."[29] Thomas recalled that the deadly enfilade fire from the battery to their right (Wright's) and a murderous cross fire to the left (Davidson's) greeted them as they mounted the pits. General Thomas indicated that of the first to fall was "the gallant Fessenden of the 23rd Regiment," followed in rapid succession by Ayers and Woodruff of the 31st, Liscomb of the 23rd, Hackhiser of the 28th and Flint and Aiken of the 29th. "Major Rockwood of the Nineteenth then mounted the crest, and fell back dead, with a cheer on his lips. Nor were these all, for at this time hundreds of heroes 'carved in ebony' fell," commanding the respect of many of their fellow Union soldiers that had previously been withheld primarily due to their race. Josiah Jones later recounted that "I had been in the army since 1861, and had seen some hard fighting, and notwithstanding all that has been said to the prejudice of these troops on that occasion, it was a grand sight."[30]

Thomas was successful in getting a portion of his brigade over the men of the first division and over the bombproofs beyond the Crater, extending southward the perimeter battle line begun by Sigfried's troops. With two of his regiments still bogged down in the Crater,

Thomas made his first effort to further advance. He attempted a movement before the white troops on his flanks were ready, however, and it went nowhere. Thomas and two of his staff officers stepped up out of the trench, followed by his white orderlies. The most advantageous point for an initial objective was 800 feet from the Crater, and Thomas's men then leapt from the works and endeavored to make a rush for the crest. "Captain Marshall L. Dempcy and Lieutenant Christopher Pennell, of ... [his] staff, and four white orderlies with the brigade guidon accompanied ... [him], closely followed by Lieutenant-Colonel Ross, leading the 31st regiment." The 28th USCT also attempted to advance with the 31st. The men leaped into a Rebel covered way leading toward Cemetery Hill. Under Charles S. Russell of Boston, the Indiana-recruited unit[31] advanced about fifty yards beyond the Rebel's main line where they were exposed to a fierce fire from the Confederates in their front. The rather disorganized regiment was unable to offer any further resistance and was forced to fall back. The obstacles thrown up by the explosion, the deadly cross fire from the Confederate batteries, and the vast confusion among the three

Col. Henry G. Thomas (Library of Congress).

white divisions milling in the Crater proved to be a very formidable obstacle. Ross was shot with a bullet in the left leg the instant he left the works. The next in line, Captain Wright, was hit by a piece of shell as he bent over the supine Ross, with one of his captains immediately landing on top of him. Captain Robinson then took command and he was also quickly killed.

The bullets "came amongst us like hailstones.... Men were getting killed and wounded on all sides of me," an officer later wrote home. Two of the four orderlies were wounded — one with the flag in his hand, while the other two sought shelter — when Lieutenant Christopher Pennell, the only surviving staff officer, dashed to rescue the guidon, hastening down the line outside of the rifle pits. Lieutenant Bowley of the 30th USCT, from his position on higher ground, saw Pennell start out and knew that he was "doomed." Pennell's audacity was impressive and conspicuous, and therefore quickly attracted the Carolina marksmen that McMaster had reserved against just such a contingency: "With his sword uplifted in his right hand and the banner in his left, he sought to call out the men along the whole line of the parapet. In a moment, a musketry fire was focused upon him individually, whirling him round and round several times before he fell." At first he refused to fall and spun as more missiles struck home, and he "continued to stagger in that ghastly pirouette until he keeled over head foremost, perhaps already dead." His actions were so brave, and he presented such a commanding figure, that, according to Colonel Weld's later testimony, a number of his command were soon shot because, being entirely "spell-bound, they forgot their own shelter in watching this superb boy, who was an only child of an old Massachusetts clergyman ... demonstrate his extraordinary valor in the face of overwhelming odds."[32]

The men of the 31st USCT, along with parts of two other regiments, attempted to follow, but they were unfortunately distracted by Pennell's spectacular death and were thus soon mowed down like grass, with absolutely no hope of reaching the crest. Thomas, therefore, ordered them to scatter and retreat back toward the front-most Confederate trenches. The fire was so heavy that Captain Dempcy and Thomas were the only two officers of those who had left the works for that fateful charge just a few minutes before who were to return unharmed. Fully half of those who began the advance were gone. This marked the end of the second brigade's first attempt to move on Cemetery Hill. The brigade was now back within the honeycombed passages and bomb-proofs; only a short time thereafter, however, came the order to advance again on the crest "at all hazards."

Thomas's command was crowded into the Confederate rifle pits and traverses, which were already full of troops before his arrival, and was sandwiched against the men of the first division. By this point, the men were effectively leaderless and the unit's organization was totally destroyed. "The slaughter was fearful, but some way I got up to the position but was not safe. After I got there bullets came in amongst us like hailstones," one of Thomas's young lieutenants wrote afterwards. At this juncture, Thomas had a conference with Major Van Buren, conveying a message for Burnside that "unless a movement simultaneous with mine was made to the right to stop the enfilading fire, I thought not a man would live to reach the crest; but that I would try another charge in about ten minutes, and I hoped to be supported." Thomas knew such an attack would be suicidal under the fierce enemy flanking fire. Still hoping for support, he sent word to Burnside soliciting such a supporting attack on the flanks. Unfortunately, however, rather than support, all Thomas received was a further order from Ferrero to the effect that "Colonels Sigfried and Thomas, if you have not already done so, you will immediately proceed to take the crest in your front."

In response to the directive, a somewhat despondent Thomas then ordered the commanders of 23rd, 28th and 29th USCT to assemble their commands together as much as possible and to separate themselves from the other divisions, for they had by this point become entirely mixed up with the white troops and each other to the point where the ability to organize was next to impossible. The 31st USCT was so shattered and diminished and largely devoid of officers by this point that Thomas sought to get the remains of the regiment out of the way of his charging column as much as possible. The 19th USCT was still in the rear and unable to move up to the rest of the brigade. Its flanks rested on the line and its own line ran to the right of the Crater. There it ultimately remained, unable to participate in the advance, but exposed enough to have very heavy casualties inflicted upon it. About one hundred of its dispirited men eventually drifted into the Crater and participated in its defense.[33]

Major Van Buren, Burnside's aide-de-camp, met with both Sigfried and Thomas at this time and gave them instructions for a final charge of the whole division, with Sigfried's brigade on the right and Thomas's on the left. Marshall's and Bartlett's brigades were to form in the rear of Ferrero's men and support their advance. The fourth division's last assault on Cemetery Hill then went forward with three of Thomas's regiments, an attack which was inevitably doomed without significant support, for which the optimistic Thomas still felt hopeful. In the lead was Lieutenant Colonel John Bross of the 29th USCT, the brother of William Bross, the lieutenant governor of Ohio, who had vowed to "show the world today that the colored troops are soldiers." Bross may have had some premonitions concerning his role in the current mission the previous night while preparing for his unit's role in the advance. His fellow officers talked of his "seeming somewhat anxious and agitated; but he at once controlled himself, and joined cheerfully in conversation, talking over the coming struggle." He had previously confided to his pastor regarding his considerably more precarious position as a leader of colored troops: "If need be, I am willing to be offered." The morning of the attack, he meticulously dressed himself in his full uniform, apparently as an inspiration to his troops. The futility and suicidal nature of this charge without support of the other corps was well known to many of the men involved. "Our generals had pushed us into this slaughter pen," Lieutenant Robert Beecham of the 23rd USCT related, "and then deserted us." Beecham related that as the blacks of the three regiments formed for the second attack, they were "as ready to face the enemy and meet death ... as the bravest and best soldiers that ever lived."

Griffin's men had not yet recovered from the disruption caused by the friendly fire from the blacks and the disorganization precipitated by their crash through their ranks. As a consequence, neither Griffin nor Bliss's brigade was of much assistance in this latest advance. Added to this was the fact that the white troops had been in action so long by this time that many regimental commanders were dead or severely wounded, and their replacements were not in place or did not even know their status. Still, some disjoined fragments of white regiments moved out with Bross's new assault. Bross, seeing his men begin to falter in the face of the withering fire, seized the colors (the last five bearers having fallen in the first few minutes), and, waving the colors zealously "amid the storm of shot, shell and canister" and running forward, he yelled "Forward, my brave boys" and was the first to make the leap "into the valley of death below."[34]

While the Ninth Corps was engaged in a fight to the death with the remnants of Elliott's Brigade and the sparse reinforcements from McAfee's brigade, General Jonathan W. Turner was trying desperately to decipher General Ord's confusing orders to get his "Flying Division" engaged in the battle. Turner had received his orders from General Ord at 6:30 A.M. to "Follow Potter's division and move out to the right." In response to the orders, Turner reported that Burnside's troops currently filled the trenches in his front, occupying the Crater and blocking the way forward. Accordingly, Ord wrote out a dispatch intended for General Meade indicating that Burnside's troops "fill our trenches in his front, occupying the crater, and that the Confederates still held their trenches to the right and left." He therefore asked, "Shall I order the divisions (two) of the Eighteenth Corps to try and charge the enemy's trenches over the heads of the men?" Ord first submitted this dispatch to Burnside, who requested that he wait a few minutes and "he would have the way cleared." Shortly thereafter, Ord received Meade's order indicating that "you will at once move forward your corps rapidly to the crest of the hill, independently of General Burnside's troops, and make a lodgment there, reporting the results as soon as obtained."[35]

Ord forwarded this on to Turner and General Ames of the Eighteenth Corps. Turner was required to take his division down Potter's covered way, which was so constricted that he could proceed only by a two file front, and at some places, a single file, which caused the movement to be quite slow. When the head of his column finally reached the point where the assaulting forces passed through the Federal lines, it was already 7:00 A.M. Turner jumped up on the parapet to determine the state of affairs in front of him. The Crater, only seventy-five yards away at that point, was full of disorganized troops milling about and lying down seeking shelter. The ground in between was being ravaged by a severe cross fire from the Confederate artillery. Turner had assumed the Ninth Corps would penetrate the Rebel line there and roll it up to the right and left, allowing his division to move out and cover the right flank of the assaulting column. However, as the enemy still held its line to within seventy-five yards of the Crater itself, the only open point of attack was directly opposite the Crater itself, already filled to overflowing, with no apparent forward movement at the time.

Turner then received another order from Ord to move out rapidly to the right and cover Potter's advance on his right flank. He later recalled that "[i]t was evident to my mind that General Ord did not understand the topography of the country and the condition of affairs as they were at that moment. It was impossible to move out to the right." Turner immediately responded to this order that "[t]he only place I can get out of the lines is opposite the crater. It is already full of men who cannot develop. I shall put in my column as soon as I can. It is impossible, by reason of the topography, to charge in the manner you indicate. I must go in by head of column and develop to the right."[36] Ord's order evidently anticipated that the Ninth Corps had moved sufficiently to allow the Tenth Corps to advance to where the assaulting column debouched. Soon thereafter, however, General Ames likewise replied that "the covered way is the only way of getting to the front. General Turner occupies the road, and it is impossible for me to move until he gets out of my way."[37]

Ord's thinking was that the enemy line would be rolled up to the right by the Ninth Corps, and Turner would then go to the right over the Federal lines for some 400 yards. However, given the current state of affairs, Turner would have had to mount the parapet exposed to enemy fire directly opposite him, push through the Federal abatis, cross the open space under a devastating cross fire, negotiate the Rebel abatis and then mount the Confederate line where it had been deemed impregnable for the past two months. Thus, the only plausible location to achieve such a movement was by the Crater and by rolling the lines up right and left; and yet there were already too many men in the Crater already. Ord later freely admitted that he "had not seen the ground, and supposed all this time that there were several places of exit and the ground tolerably free from obstructions."[38] He was equally unaware that the two covered ways were still filled with the Ninth Corps troops, with the fourth division totally occupying the left covered way. Upon reflection after the battle, he considered the obstructions "insurmountable." Given that the Confederates still held the line within seventy-five yards on the right of the Crater, any attempt to get out of the Federal lines elsewhere would have been futile.[39]

Turner had personally been to the Crater to examine the ground, an examination that quickly confirmed his prior judgment. It was full of disorganized men seeking shelter. He found that "they were lying all around and every point that would give cover to a man was occupied." Turner was informed that an attempt to move out toward Cemetery Hill had already been attempted and failed. While he was questioning an officer in the pit, the fourth division appeared at the crest and began piling in and through as best they could. Turner exclaimed, "What are these men sent in here for? It is only adding confusion to the confusion which already exists!" Men were falling in on their hands and knees, and there were so many of them that "a man could not walk." Fearing he would be trapped there himself, Turner decide to leave post haste. He called to an officer he presumed was in command: "If you can get these troops beyond this line so that I can get out, I will move my division right out and cover your right flank!" Then he proceeded back to his division to prepare for such an alternative.[40]

When Turner returned from the Crater, he found General Ord had arrived at the location where his men were then massing. He immediately informed Ord that "unless a movement is made out of the crater toward Cemetery hill, it is murder to send more men in there. That colored division should never have been sent there; but there is a furor there, and perhaps they may move off sufficiently for me to pass my division out."[41]

Turner still subscribed to the belief that the Ninth Corps could move out of the Crater enough for him to send his division out from the debouchment. Ord told him to do so if he could reasonably accomplish it and pledged "all the aid in ... [his] power...." Soon thereafter, Turner thought that the Ninth Corps had started to make a rush toward Cemetery Hill, and he immediately ordered his leading brigade, having massed by regiments, to charge to the right of the Crater. Turner formed his command in massed column of regiments, left in front, thus bringing the 169th New York to the head of the division. This was performed under the cover of the advance line of the Union works. By this time, the colored troops had almost, but not totally, advanced into the Crater. By then, its lead regiments had passed to the right of it perhaps fifty yards and were all lying down, principally on the Federal side of the Confederate lines and in it, and were trying to cover themselves as best they could. Ord directed Turner not to go into the Crater or the trenches already filled with Union troops, but rather to make a charge to the right where the enemy was massing. Turner thus decided to throw his whole three brigades in north of the Crater, and directed a portion of his troops to pass over the parapets to the right, as the ground in front of the area of exit was occupied by the other troops and there was no room after they got out for them to be of service without moving for a considerable distance by the flank to the right or left.[42]

Turner instructed Colonel Lewis Bell to attempt to take the trenches north of the Crater, so as to sweep the enemy lines where Bliss's two New York regiments had advanced and had only recently been repulsed. The son of Governor Samuel Bell of New Hampshire, Louis Bell was born in 1837 and graduated from Brown University at eighteen. A lawyer by profession, he joined the 1st New Hampshire as a captain, and in August 1861 was appointed lieutenant colonel of the 4th New Hampshire and subsequently its colonel in March 1862. He subsequently led a brigade in the siege of Forts Wagner and Sumner.[43] The twenty-seven year old Bell's third brigade went in first, parallel and to the right of Ferrero's assault, with Lieutenant Colonel Nathan J. Johnson shouting, "Battalion, right face-file left-march!" and the 115th New York leading the brigade forward. It was quickly followed by Lieutenant Colonel William B. Coan's second brigade, which slid even farther to the right. Finally, Colonel N. Martin Curtis's first brigade went into the Union works, alongside a couple of the overlooked regiments of Zenas Bliss's brigade of the second division, there to mass and be held in readiness for any exigency. Soon after Turner's division moved out, Grant met up with Ord and directed him to inform Burnside to send no more men into the Crater or the Confederate trenches already filled with Union troops, but rather to send intrenching tools and work to hold all his that men had gained.[44]

The area Turner's men had to traverse to reach their objective fell off down into a swampy or bottom area in front of the Federal entrenchments. There were bushes and trees in front of the division, and the men could not see anything in that direction for thirty or forty yards off. The Confederates would thus be able to form there, entirely screened and in such position as to be in the flank and, in a measure, in the rear of those going from the Federal works to the Crater. As Turner's men went in, Coan's brigade of New York and Pennsylvania regiments moved to the north of Bell's third brigade. At the same time, Colonel Curtis's New Yorkers went to its southern flank. Lieutenant James H. Clark, of Company H, 115th New York of the third brigade, later remembered:

> How well all who were engaged remember the scenes enacted on that eventful and bloody day; the swaths of lead; crushed and mangled limbs; the deadly pallor on a thousand noble cheeks; the bravery, daring and inspiring devotion of the soldiery, and the awful roar and tempest of battle on the green hill-sides of Petersburg.[45]

Suddenly, progress was impeded and the road blocked with the flow of the wounded being dragged to the rear. A wounded captain was carried by on a stretcher and exhorted the troops to "Go quick boys. Go quick! It's your only salvation!" Clark observed "[h]ow fast the shells go screaming over us, and how the grape tears up the ground." Turner quickly identified where he wanted the 115th New York and, flashing his sword and glancing at the men, exclaimed, "'Come on my brave boys,' and they go on; some on to death, and some on to the rebel works." As the 115th advanced, they watched some of the fourth division move beyond the

Crater, rushing onward despite the relentless grape that poured down upon them from three sides and sweeping everything before them. On Bell's brigade went, with the 115th New York still leading the way. Lieutenant Francisco of Company K and Sergeant Fellows, the "iron hearted color sergeant," were among the first of the men over the works. "Forward, hundred and fifteenth!" rang all along the line. The regiment and the whole brigade swept forward "with a deafening yell."

Soon the color bearer unfurled "'the dear old flag,' and with fire flashing from his eyes, tells the boys to come on" recall Lieutenant Clark, "then calmly pointing to the works we were to carry, he flew away." The ground was covered with the dead and wounded: "The grim banners of death floated here and there, yet the invincible columns pressed furiously on, and at last took the position by storm." The men each "dreamed that he would stem the tide of battle. And that some other poor fellow would fall. We left the ground colored with killed and wounded. The grim banners of death floated here and there, yet the invincible columns press furiously on, and at last took the position by storm."

In the Crater lay the naked corpses of the South Carolina troops, along with a large body of Union troops, lying in line of battle, seemingly awaiting the command to move forward. Soon, however, they realized that all these Union troops were dead: they were lying "not singly or scattering, but in long rows; in whole companies." Clark observed that the whole ground was "blue with Union dead...." As the 115th climbed over the trenches, it received "a storm of bullets as thick as hail" that forced the troops to lower their heads as they advanced, "as if facing a storm." As they advanced beyond the first set of trenches, Clark was hit in the right thigh by a minie ball. The brigade proceeded, and took the next trench, holding it under a galling fire, which "poured in from every part of the semi-circular line." As the 115th New York moved on through the Rebel works, they took over the third line, with the black troops in the first two lines north of the Crater. The 13th Indiana, after losing over 200 men when their enlistments expired, was consolidated into three companies armed with repeating rifles to act as sharpshooters. Adjutant Lentz of the 13th Indiana described how "the enemy had also been driven from a second line, which was a short distance from the first line, and the space between the two was occupied by the colored troops in column." They found the Confederates in the same line with them, "on our right and left, and they engage us on either flank with infantry, at the same time sweeping our lines with a cross fire of grape."[46]

The 169th New York succeeded in holding its position "though the charge as a whole was not successful...." As Turner gave the command to forward, the regiments dashed over the Federal works and quick-timed across the ground between the lines. Upon reaching the Rebel defenses, further progress was impeded by the mass of men in front who now occupied the enemy pits. The 169th held its position while enfiladed by a fierce fire from the Confederate batteries to their right. The men in front occupied the Confederate rifle pits. The 4th New Hampshire charged with the brigade in the second

Col. Louis Bell (USAMHI).

line. The object was to break the Confederate lines in the middle of the "horseshoe" and thus flank the two wings. The third assaulting party behind the Tenth Corps did not engage, which, in bugler Elias Bryant's opinion, lost the battle that day. Captain Joseph M. Clough by then was the acting colonel and commanded the regiment. "As we climbed over the works already taken we were received with a storm of bullets as thick as hail. We ran with our heads down, as if facing a storm."[47]

To the right of the third brigade lay the second brigade, commanded by Lieutenant Colonel William B. Coan, with the 97th Pennsylvania on its left flank. The brigade had formed in the rear of Curtis' first brigade. Coan had come up through the ranks with the 48th New York, becoming its colonel, and was in charge of a brigade by the end of the war. Before the formation was accomplished, Brigadier General Joseph B. Carr, commander of the third division, Eighteenth Corps, had ordered the 47th New York Volunteers and a part of the 97th Pennsylvania to move to the right without Coan's knowledge or that of Major Isaiah Price, its commander,

Lt. Col. William B. Coan (Palmer — *History of the Forty-Eighth Regiment New York Volunteers*).

who was leading the regiment. Carr simply ordered Lieutenant Eachus of Company C and others to take a different direction than that by which the right of the regiment had proceeded. These "detached" companies were sent on a charge of the Confederate rifle pits to the right flank of the advance. While the detachment accomplished its objective, it was with a high cost in lives and its colors were almost captured.

Soon thereafter, Colonel Coan moved the rest of his brigade to the right in the same direction taken by the 47th New York and the detachment of the 97th Pennsylvania taken from its left. Pursuant to orders from General Turner, Coan soon moved the rest of the brigade to the right, and immediately ordered the 48th New York Volunteers to move across the creek bottom and take a position under cover in a belt of woods on the side of the ravine. The 48th New York had been organized by the Reverend James H. Perry, who had been born in 1811 in Ulster County, New York. He graduated from West Point and had a role in the independence of Texas from Mexico. He then became a minister, but upon the outbreak of the war, he recruited the 48th New York and acted as its first commander. Given his religious status, and the fact that a significant number of the original recruits were from seminaries, the regiment became known as "Perry's Saints" or "The Fighting Parson's Regiment." Immediately after the 48th New York was positioned, Coan ordered the 76th Pennsylvania and Companies A, D, F, and I of the 97th Pennsylvania to also move forward, with the 97th on the left of the 48th New York, and the 76th to form in its rear. Turner then called for Coan to move his entire brigade into the belt of woods on the slope of the ravine. Coan ordered Price to advance the 97th Pennsylvania to a point indicated on the right, then to move as far as possible to the right from there. The battle was raging and the men were now falling rapidly.[48]

The 97th, then consisting of Companies A, D, F and I, moving "by the flank at double

Burnside's corps charging the Confederate position on the right of their line of defense (*Harper's Weekly*).

quick, [and while] exposed to a brisk fire ... advanced across a meadow, following the bed of a creek; reached the wood with but little loss, formed by company into line upon the run, then ascended the bank on the top of which was a line of rebel rifle pits from which the enemy had retired to a second line a few yards further on." The regiment then moved along the ditch until it reached a point beyond which an enfilading fire of Confederates, who occupied the prolongation of the same line, prevented any further progress. In response to orders from Coan, Major Price left Captain Mendenhall of Company D in charge and moved to the find the remaining companies of his regiment with a view of bringing them to the part of the field occupied by the right of the regiment. Price eventually found the remainder of the 97th and began moving them back to rejoin his command. Once the rest of the regiments were up, Coan moved along the line personally to reconnoiter his command's position. There he found about one hundred men of the 2nd New York (Dismounted) Cavalry in front of his center occupying small rifle pits in front of the Confederate main work. The detachment of the 97th Pennsylvania was to the left of the 2nd New York's main position. Here it suffered heavy losses, including most of its color guard and nearly the colors themselves.

The distance by the flank through the narrow defiles of approaches under enemy fire, by which the ravine was enfiladed by Confederate fire from the right and left, caused considerable delay before the troops reached a position from which they could charge upon the enemy's line.[49] The formation of the ground in this area gave Ransom's men the opportunity to shoot for effect and the companies on the right of the brigade were eager to get into the fight, and consequently pressed up the trench in the space which Colonel Smith's regiment occupied. With the 17th South Carolina, they poured a fire into Turner's troops and the blacks. Meanwhile, the 48th New York was also finding the position extremely precarious. James Nichols of the 48th New York, the "Fighting Parson's Regiment," later reflected that the disaster "was one of the most serious that our army had suffered for a month." Its losses were heavy, including its commander, Major Samuel M. Swartwout, one of the brigade's oldest and most beloved officers, who was killed leading the regiment across the creek bottom to the woods. While Coan's brigade did not reach the main Confederate works, it did attain a position in the undergrowth at a short distance in front of it, from which it was able to keep up a sharp fire that diverted the Rebel fire from Bell's brigade, which Turner was planning to use in yet another charge.[50]

The first brigade of the Tenth Corps, under Colonel N. Martin Curtis, started through the covered way at 7:30 A.M., leading to the right and the line in rear of the destroyed fort.

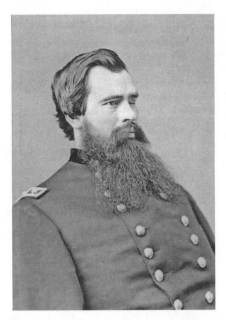

Col. Newton Martin Curtis (Library of Congress).

Newton Martin Curtis was born in DePeyster, New York, in 1835. He enlisted as a captain in the 16th New York Regiment in May 1861. By October 1862, he was a lieutenant colonel with the 142nd New York and became its colonel in 1863. He was brevetted a brigadier general in October 1864 and a major general in March 1865.[51] A great part of this journey was required to be made in single file, as the road was continuously obstructed with stragglers and groups of men returning with wounded in blankets. Curtis ordered up the 3rd New York and extended the brigade's line to the right. He was then ordered to form the brigade in column, by battalion, in the rear of the Federal advanced earthworks, and there to await further orders. Unfortunately, just as Colonel Curtis cried out "Forward the Third," the entire line north of the Crater began to suffer a severe setback — one from which they would not recover that day.[52]

The 7th Rhode Island of the second division under Lieutenant Colonel Percy Daniels had been left standing at the assigned rendezvous point in a depression around the entrance to the mine, awaiting the left of its division to pass. Then, before the men could move forward, Bell's brigade of Turner's division followed so closely on the heels of Potter's men that the 7th was absolutely sidetracked at about 7:30 A.M. Colonel Daniels went in with Colonel Bell in his charge to ascertain where the 7th, acting as engineers, would be most needed. The regiment's function that day was to supply tools (three per man) to the pioneer groups of both of Potter's brigades. The regiment finally followed the division to the left of the ravine and remained there, just in back of the forward Federal works.[53]

Now the entire Ninth Corps was fully engaged in a desperate struggle to seize Cemetery Hill, or more accurately, as events quickly unfolded, in a struggle for survival. Additionally, Jonathan Turner had committed his division to the cause, and it was heavily engaged to the right of Burnside's men. Thus, by 9:00 A.M., there were approximately 18,000[54] Union troops fighting in or around the Crater or actively supporting the effort. Burnside was still confident of support from the Fifth Corps to his left, and the Second Corps to his right, as well as two divisions of the Eighteenth Corps which were to follow Turner. Thus, over 40,000 more troops were ready, at least on paper, to assist Burnside's efforts to obtain Cemetery Hill. However, his difficulties were just beginning!

CHAPTER 14

"Forward, and with Cold Steel"

Weisiger's Virginia Brigade quickly began to set up in the ravine as it came out of the natural covered way. Colonel McMaster had reported to Mahone regarding the position of Smith's detachment of Carolinians behind the Crater, and suggested to him that forming on his left was the "only practicable place from which to make a charge...." McMaster recalled Mahone "quietly listening and stroking his long beard" and then quietly adopting his suggestion. Mahone, standing by a traverse to which his horse was tied, directed Colonel David Weisiger to move up the ravine and "[f]orm your brigade for the attack and inform me when you are ready." Weiseger promptly moved up and placed his brigade along the slope of the hill, with its left resting some distance from the traverse. The 12th Virginia had been on the right of the brigade on its hasty march to the front, but in taking position after its reverse march on the Jerusalem Plank Road, it found itself on the extreme left, followed by the 41st, 61st, 16th and, finally, the ninety-five men comprising the 6th Virginia on the right. Along with the 6th Virginia was the battalion of the brigade's sharpshooters, whose presence there was purely accidental. Their usual placement involved day service on the front lines, where they performed picket and skirmish duty. The night before, however, the right wing of the 6th Virginia relieved the sharpshooters, and thus, when the Virginia Brigade hastily formed for its march in the morning, there was no time to send out pickets, and the sharpshooter battalion went along with the balance of the 6th in place of the 6th's own right wing, and thus occupied the extreme right of the brigade in the line of battle.[1]

Once his regiment took its assigned position, Captain James E. Phillips of Company G, of the 12th Virginia, saw the works north of the Crater filled with thousands of Union troops and personally observed twenty-one flags. The sight "gave ... [him] no hope of ever getting away alive."[2] A stunned private of the 12th Virginia felt that the flags appeared almost thick as cornstalks in a row. He observed that "[t]he whole face of the earth, including the ditch which our men formerly occupied, fairly teemed with the enemy." Another soldier recalled observing that the silken banners floating in the breeze, "supported by countless bayonets glistening in the sunlight, might on an ordinary occasion have daunted our little band and made them forfeit a trial at arms; but they were desperate and determined, and reckoned not the hosts that confronted them."[3]

As the Virginians filed past Mahone, he met with each regimental commander in turn and instructed them to move up the ravine. Colonel George T. Rogers, commanding the 6th Virginia, recalled Mahone's orders to "halt your right front, and give the order softly that no shot is to be fired until after the men are in the broken trenches. Fix your bayonets, and await the order to forward. Let your men understand that it is only 'forward,' and with cold steel."

Lieutenant W.A.S. Taylor, adjutant of the 61st Virginia, heard Mahone at the mouth of the gully where the covered way led shouting, "Give them the bayonet!" As the men formed on the slope of the ravine, Weisiger also ordered his commanders to have the men fix bayonets and lie down.[4] Colonel Rogers offered that "such orders were not often given. They were not often necessary. We looked around and saw that there must be no failure." There was no second Confederate line, as the Federals had thought, between the Virginians and Petersburg. If this thin line broke and the Rebels failed to retake and reestablish the broken line, the Federals "could march without strong check to the capture of the city."[5] Thomas H. Cross of Company A, 16th Virginia, recalled:

> The order was passed in that subdued tone which denotes a stern tone which denotes a stern purpose to "fix bayonets," and by those to whom the thought had occurred an extra turn was taken on the little screw which holds the bayonet-shank on the gun. The thought of having his bayonet "un-shipped" flashed across ... [his] mind, and his right hand instinctively sought his cartridge-box and the possibility was provided against."[6]

David Addison Weisiger was born in 1818 in Chesterfield County, Virginia, and served honorably in the Mexican War as a second lieutenant. He then entered into business in Petersburg. A captain in the Virginia militia, he was the officer of the day at the hanging of John Brown in 1859. He was a major of the 4th Virginia Battalion in Norfolk at the war's inception and then colonel of the 12th Virginia in May 1861, following in William Mahone's footsteps. He succeeded Mahone as brigade commander in the III Corps following the Wilderness and was considered a competent soldier and an able leader, who, despite having personal issues with Mahone, performed admirably in the field. He was considered by many to be "an impetuous, dashing man, among the bravest of the brave." On the day of the battle, he was the oldest colonel in the Confederate army.[7]

After having his aide-de-camp, Captain Drury A. Hinton, give instructions to all regimental commanders along the line to instruct their men to reserve fire until the enemy was reached, Weisiger had Hinton inform Mahone that his Virginia Brigade was prepared to move. Mahone responded by telling him that Weisiger was to "wait for orders from [either] me or Capt. Girardey." Mahone was still intent upon having the Georgia Brigade in line before the attack commenced, in order for his front to cover the full extent of works occupied by the Federals.

Captain Richard W. Jones of the 12th Virginia, who had rushed to his regiment at the explosion from spending the night with friends in Petersburg, had just returned from a meeting of regimental commanders where Mahone had ordered the Georgia Brigade to move rapidly into position on the right of the Virginia Brigade. Mahone then addressed his commanders with a stirring message:

> The enemy have our works. The line of men which we have here is the only barrier to the enemy's occupying the city of Petersburg. There is nothing to resist his advance. Upon us devolves the duty of driving him from his strong position in our front and re-establishing the Confederate lines. We must carry his position immediately by assaulting it. If we don't carry it by the first attack we will renew the attack as long as there is a man of us left or until the works are ours. Much depends upon prompt, vigorous, simultaneous movements.

Jones indicated that the words and the address "were given with such peculiar emphasis and under such impressive circumstances that the sentiments were indelibly inscribed on ... [his] mind." Back with his own regiment as the men awaited word to advance, Jones stepped forward and addressed them:

Men, you are called upon to charge and recapture our works, now in the hands of the enemy. They are only about one hundred yards distant.[8] The enemy can fire but one volley before the works are reached. At the command "forward" every man is expected to rise and move forward at a double quick and with a yell. Every man is expected to do his duty.[9]

It was by now approaching 9:00 A.M.

Soon after Captain Hinton reached the right of the line and relayed Mahone's orders to Weisiger, Captain Girardey came up to where Weisiger and Hinton were standing in conversation. As they conferred, "a magnificent looking Federal officer [later identified as Lieutenant Colonel Bross] stepped out from the occupied works, and grabbing a flag, called upon his men to form a line preparatory to a charge, which order appeared to be very indifferently obeyed." Here and there a man would jump out from the works, but the great mass of the men in the trenches failed to respond. The colonel was using all means to induce the regiment to charge from the broken line he held on the heights in his front. It was hard to encourage the black soldiers out of the sheltered trenches, which presented a double line of ditches at least four feet deep and just as wide, capped by heavy, thick sandbags. However, this colonel was so energetic that Mahone worried that he might get them to charge, as he seized the colors and sprang over the protecting ditch "and by every gesticulation showed the way to the front — and perhaps to victory."

Approximately 200 blacks from three separate regiments were eventually assembled and "with a thin little cheer they came on in a ragged line." This caused the men on the right of Mahone's line to commence firing despite Mahone's prohibition. Standing as he waved the flag, exposed to a sudden gale of fire, Colonel Bross's fate was inevitable, and he was cut down as some of his men answered his call to charge.[10] Lieutenant Fred A. Chapman, who was beside Bross when he was hit, later wrote the colonel's wife describing the regiment's passing the outer Confederate works and rushing up the hill over the dead and dying from both sides until the hail of enemy fire caused it to halt:

I will remember how he looked, standing in the midst, his countenance lighted up with steadfast hope and an almost superhuman courage, he cried out, "Forward, 29th," and we moved on over the mass. The men were falling thick and fast, and soon my turn came. Lying on the field, I felt the auspicious moment had passed. His form was ever a prominent mark. Turning to Captain Brockway, he said, "bring forward the colors." Then seizing them in his own hand he cried, "Follow me, my men." But it was in vain.

Col. David Weisiger (USAMHI).

After ordering a quick retreat, Bross had then attempted to rescue the colors. "The fatal ball came, and he fell, but the legacy of his bright example and the memory of his noble deeds remain. The intense sorrow and grief of that night I will not attempt to portray."[11] Colonel Weld of the 56th Massachusetts later remarked, regarding the officers of these black units whom his observed attempting their final assault, "I have never seen greater bravery shown than that displayed by a large number of these officers of the colored division. Although almost certain death to mount this parapet, they showed no shrinking or hesitation."[12]

Given this Federal activity, Weisiger anxiously suggested to Girardey, "had I not better go in now?" Girardey, however, responded in the negative, indicating that "Gen. Mahone desires to annex Wright's [Georgia] brigade on to you and send you in together." As the men conferred, a private of the 61st Virginia was able to attract his colonel's attention to the movement. Weisiger simultaneously observed Bross's actions and told Girardey that the charge really needed to commence at once, without waiting for the Georgia Brigade, and indicated that "if we do not move forward promptly all would be lost." Weisiger later claimed Girardey agreed with him and Weisiger requested that he report to Mahone the circumstances and that he should be ordered forward. Girardey, who had previously been on the staff of Wright's Georgia Brigade, was an able battlefield commander who had taken control of his brigade in a skirmish during the retreat from Gettysburg.

Nonetheless, he ran back to the left of the formation posthaste to alert Mahone of the impending Federal assault. When he was about eighty feet from his commander, he shouted to Mahone, "General, they are coming!" Mahone clearly did not want to stand and take the volleys in an open field from perhaps two or three lines of battle. Thus his quick response, ignoring the failure of the Georgia Brigade to finish forming, called back to Girardey, was, "Tell Weisiger to forward." Without reporting back to Weisiger or issuing preparatory orders himself, the young staff officer drew his sword, waved his hat and yelled at the top of his voice, "Forward! Charge!"[13] Thus the Virginia Brigade were ordered to make the fearful charge "unprotected or unsupported by the flanks, and the boys answered to the low-toned command."[14]

"At the Gee house, Lee knew that Mahone was forming, and he must have watched with anxious eyes [as] the gray regiments spread themselves along the ravine; but still more anxiously must he have looked to the occupied line to see if the Federals would advance before the Confederates were ready for them." The line was about 150 yards in length as it started. As they moved out, the sharpshooters obliqued to their right toward the Crater. Before it was halfway there, the line had lengthened another 100 to 200 feet. There was no spectacle more impressive than this column of veterans, "every man of whom appreciated the vital importance of getting to the works and closing with the enemy in the quickest possible time — every man feeling that to halt or falter for a moment on the way was fatal." As the line of attack came over the hill, Private George Bernard of Company E, the "Petersburg Riflemen" of the 12th Virginia, cast his eyes to the right. His impression of the rapid but steady and beautiful movement of 800 men remained a vivid memory for the rest of his life, as "our fine Virginia regiments, their five battle flags, borne by as many gallant color-bearers, floating in the bright sunlight of that July morning, and the battalion of sharpshooters double-quicked across the field they were unconsciously making famous."[15]

As the troops sprang to their feet, their right side, where Girardey and Weisiger were both situated, advanced first, and the 200 yard long, twenty foot deep line went screaming toward the Crater until in full view of both armies. "Looking up the line I saw that the right of the column had begun to charge," Orderly Sergeant J. Edward Whitehorne of Company F, 12th Virginia, recalled. "Instantly we sprang to our feet and moved forward at the double quick." The line sprang up "and ran the hill, every man for himself, muskets in every position of trail, and 'right shoulder shift,' every man tugging for himself." The line of battle consisted from left to right of the 49th and 25th North Carolina regiments and the 26th and part of the 17th South Carolina regiments under Colonel Smith. Next in line was Mahone's old Virginia Brigade, then under Weisiger, consisting of the 12th, 41st, 61st, 16th and the 6th Virginia, along with the brigade's sharpshooters, in that order, along with the 48th Georgia and about one half of another regiment of the Georgia Brigade.[16]

The 61st North Carolina from Clingman's Brigade had just arrived as the advance began and fell in immediately behind the Virginia Brigade. It was soon apparent that the bulk of the Georgia Brigade had not advanced with the rest. Thus, the total front of attack was far too short to cover the entire portion of the Confederate line held by the Federals. The men unconsciously obliqued to the left as they advanced; as a result, when they approached the second line, their right was perhaps one hundred yards to the left of the Crater. Observers noted that the flanks of the line were slightly advanced as the men advanced at trail arms, moving in perfect alignment up the hill, making the formation to be curved like the blade of a scythe. A Federal soldier in the Crater observed at the time that "Looking to the front I saw a splendid line of gray coming up the ravine on the run. Their left was nearly up to the bomb-proofs, and their line extended off into the smoke as far as we could see. They were coming, and coming with a rush. We all saw that they were going straight for the Second brigade [Thomas's brigade of the fourth division]."[17]

"As Lee saw the valiant gray line spring from the ground at the very instant they started their charge, he must have had some of the [same] exhilaration he had felt that day at Fredericksburg when he ... [expressed to] Longstreet [that] 'it was well war was so terrible as they would grow too fond of it.'" Captain McCabe shared Lee's elation:

> The whole line sprang along the crest, and there burst from more than eight hundred warlike voices the fierce yell which no man has yet heard unmoved.... Storms of case shot from the right mingled with the tempest of bullets which smote upon them from the front, yet there was no answering volley for these were veterans ... and even in the tumult the men did not forget their orders.

The men proceeded onward, with bayonets fixed and arms at a trail, reserving their fire as they had been ordered. "It was a glorious sight to see that line of veterans with their tattered uniforms, as it swept across the open field, in the face of tremendous fire, that was thinning its ranks at every step and every man appreciating the vital importance of getting to the works and closing with the enemy as quick as possible." The sight of the oncoming gray line proved just as awesome to the men in blue.[18] George Allen of the 4th Rhode Island in Potter's division recalled that "[t]he field in front of us is thick with the rebel gray. On they came. With sleeves rolled up and rifle at trail, crouching like a tiger to spring upon its prey, they resolutely advance, and with a rush pierce our line and turn back our right."[19]

Private George Bernard recalled that, just before the order to advance, Emmet Butts, a young lawyer friend of his, was positioned on his right. His proper place would have been on the left, so Bernard, having "a superstitious belief that the safest place for a man in battle is generally his proper place," asked Butts to change places. Butts graciously replied in the affirmative. Immediately upon reaching the works, Butts fell with a minie ball through his forehead. Richard B. Davis, together with James A. Farley and Sergeant Marcellus W. Harrison of Company E, 12th Virginia, were both serving as sharpshooters in the brigade on the right of the 16th Virginia. While lying in wait, Farley had pointed out to Davis a United States flag which seemed to have been planted in the ditch nearest them, and exclaimed, "Dick, when we start, go for the flag!" As they charged, the two of them headed for the flag. Marcellus Harrison was shot in the face as he approached within three feet of the ditch and died instantly. Farley was never seen again, undoubtedly an unknown casualty of the battle.[20]

On and on the fearless gray line rushed, three columns deep in their charge, with "officers in front, with uncovered heads and waving hats, and grandly and beautifully swept onward over the intervening space with muskets at trail." As they moved forward, the line was "cheered by their comrades who were holding the works on each side of the crater." No shot was fired until the men were atop the ditch, as Mahone had ordered. Once there, Lieutenant Colonel

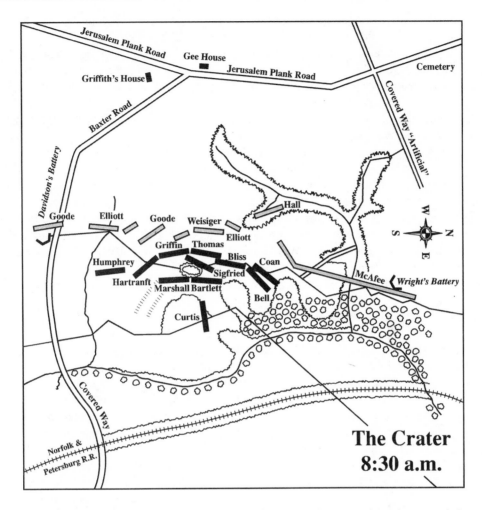

The Crater
8:30 a.m.

Stewart of the 61st Virginia counted seven Federal colors in his immediate front, and shouted to his men, "We must have those flags, boys!" As the men went forward, they were hit with a devastating volley from the rifles of all of the regiments in the trenches, particularly to their immediate right from the Crater itself. Captain John W. Wallace of Company C, 61st Virginia, was hit in the thigh and lay on his back, but refused to allow his men to carry him from the field until the battle was over. Rather, he cheered his men while waving his hat, urging them to "Go on; go forward." Storms of case shot from the right mingled with the tempest of bullets which poured into them from the front, and yet was there no answering volley, for these were battle-hardened veterans whose impetuosity had long since been controlled to a finer temper by the stern code of discipline, and even in this bloody confusion the men did not forget their orders. "Still pressing forward with steady fury, while the enemy, appalled by the inexorable advance, gave ground, they reached the ditch of the inner works."

Sergeant Eli Miney of Company K, 26th South Carolina, was struck in the arm by a ball, which caused him to drop his musket. Still he advanced with Weisiger's line, until he was subsequently hit in the other arm. Yet still, he "kept up with the line, seized a gun from the ground on arriving at the Crater, and did manful work with it." As the men closed with the occupied trenches, these rushing Rebels could clearly hear the admonition of Federal officers advising "No quarter," uttered from the occupied trenches of the fourth division. Such battle cries were soon to be regretted by those in the ranks of the issuers. As the cavalier trench was reached by the bold survivors of the Virginia Brigade, they gave the Federals their first volley, and the black defenders fell back immediately, and "the work of the bayonet began" in earnest. In the wake of the extremely brave charge, a keenly observant Robert E. Lee remarked, "That must have been Mahone's old brigade." When he was informed that his observation was correct, he remarked, "I thought so."[21] This onslaught of the Virginians, who took extremely heavy casualties in their counterattack, proved to be too much for the blacks, who were too disorganized as a result of their recent combat and the act of rushing headlong through their own comrades to withstand this well-organized attack.

The men in the tattered gray line, as they swept down upon their foe, soon found the internal reserves to intensify their fierce charge as they discovered that many of the Federal soldiers they faced were black. Captain George Whitman[22] of the 51st New York described it as "one of the boldest and most desperate things I ever saw." As the Rebels approached within ten feet of the trenches, a Southern participant observed that "the air is filled with oaths, shouts, curses, shrieks, and groans. We are wild; we are crazy; we force them back; we fire in their faces; we beat them with the rifle breech." When the Confederates reach within ten yards of the ditch of the inner works, one volley crashed in unison from the whole line of these disciplined Federal veterans. Almost all the Federals had obeyed the order not to fire their guns until the Confederates reached the works. There, the Confederates hit a mixture of Griffin's, Thomas's, Bliss's and Sigfried's commands—both black and white.

As the gray line approached, the severe raking it took demolished its alignment to the point that it "would disgrace a West Point man, but it glorified Virginia's soldiers. They arrived irregularly at the pits and trenches." After a moderate fusillade, they jumped into the trenches pell mell. Their bayonets were leveled "like the rusted lances of so many jousting knights." They pitched themselves down the slope at a dead run, "their collective roar of rage punctured by the pounding of their feet, and they hardly paused when they emptied their muskets at point blank range before flinging themselves into the cavalier trench." Then, clutching their empty guns and redoubling their intense battle cry, the men leaped over the retrenched cavalier and down the line, and then the truly dreadful work of the bayonet began.

The men instinctively began clubbing and stabbing everything and anything clad in blue. After clearly hearing the shouts of "no quarter" as they advanced on their foe, the Virginia soldiers asked for none in return, and the "bayonet [was] plied with such irresistible vigor as insured success in the shortest space of time. Men fell dead in heaps, and human gore ran in streams that made the very earth mire beneath the tread of the victorious soldiers." The rear ditch soon being theirs, the Virginians hurled their foes from the front line up the very mouth of the Crater itself. As this gray line approached the trenches, the blacks in the front line rapidly began to falter.[23]

Weisiger's Virginians were even more sensitive on this issue of confronting black foes than was the average Confederate soldier. A great many of these men had relatives who were slain or had aided in the suppression of Nat Turner's Rebellion of 1831, only forty miles down the Jerusalem Plank Road in Southampton County. Most had gone to war viewing Lincoln's call for 75,000 volunteers as a much larger version of John Brown's forlorn raid at Harpers Ferry (consequently, also an insurrection of slaves). Almost half of the brigade's men were from the immediate Petersburg area and saw themselves as standing between their relatives and friends in Petersburg and utter havoc of the same sort that Nat Turner had loosed on their kin years before.

The Confederate soldiers later related to having "ferociously reacted not only to what seemed a cheating kind of warfare, represented by the tunnel-bomb, but even more to the insult of being attacked in their Virginia by uniformed Nat Turners." Thus, being made to fight these black soldiers served to infuriate the Virginians all the more. "To most Confederate, the North's employment of black troops was nothing short of infamous, and at the Crater no quarter was given." This was most probably the first time the Virginians were confronted with former slaves in arms on the field of battle. A field officer of the 61st Virginia expressed the feelings that day quite well: "Our comrades had been slaughtered in the most inhuman and brutal manner, and black slaves were trampling over their mangled and bleeding forms. Revenge must have fired every heart and strung every arm with nerves of steel for the herculean task of blood."[24]

Major William H. Etheredge, commanding the 41st Virginia, later explained that the black troops "could not tolerate the Rebel yell" and the bayonet, and thus many quickly broke for the rear. Next in line behind them were the white troops; so great was their desire to keep the blacks in front of them as a sort of forward breastwork, Etheredge subsequently reported, that they lost sight of the Confederates until they were only a short distance from them and every shot from the gray line thus made its mark, "as they were as thick in the breastworks as they could stand, and it was impossible to miss a man." The hand to hand combat which soon followed was fierce and extremely gory, causing the disputed ditch to literally run with blood. The slaughter was so great and the dead were piled up so quickly that Etheredge and Lieutenant Colonel Stewart, commander of the 61st Virginia, "had to make a detail to pile the dead on the side of the ditch to make room so that he could reinforce to the right and left as the occasion might require."

Etheredge described this hand to hand fighting as being so intense that "our men would drive the bayonet into one man, pull it out, turn the butt and knock the brains out of another, and so on until the ditch ran with blood of the dead and dying." The Southerners' gunstocks and bayonets soon bore "nappy hair in clogged blood" from the heads of the Confederates' recent assailants. As Etheredge, one of the first Virginians to leap into the ditch alighted, a Federal soldier fired through a nearby traverse and killed the first sergeant of Company D, who came in at Etheredge's side. Etheredge caught up with two Federals who quickly rose and stood before him. The man who had just killed the first sergeant "stooped down and picked up a musket evidently with the intention of killing ... [him]." Etheredge thus quickly took hold of the other two Federals and kept them so close in front of him that it was impossible for the third to kill him without injuring his comrades. Then the other men of the regiment jumped into the ditch "like frogs." Peter Gibbs of Company E stepped one pace to the right of Etheredge and killed the third Federal "as quickly as you could wink your eye." The other two were promptly made the brigade's first prisoners.[25]

The ferocious hand to hand combat around the Crater was widespread and awesome in its intensity and brutality. William C. Smith of the 12th Virginia indicated that one of the first of his regiment to reach the ditch was Sergeant Emmett Richardson, "a tall, strong, athletic fellow, who, after discharging his gun, did terrible work with the bayonet and with the butt of his gun. No less than five of the enemy fell beneath the terrible strokes of this powerful man." Here, also, Captain Seagrave of the 30th USCT, his knee severely mangled by a bullet so that he unable to retreat, still refused to surrender and continued fighting with his sword and revolver. He killed at least six Rebels before he was ultimately shot and subsequently bayoneted in seven separate places. A Confederate officer who witnessed his gallant fight, as a tribute to his bravery, sent two Yankee prisoners to carry Seagrave's body to the rear after the fight.[26]

The Rebels were in a frenzy and the subsequent slaughter in the trenches was terrible. "The soldiers were excited; they were reckless; they burst the negroes' skulls with the butts of their guns like eggshells. The officers tried to prevent it, but they were powerless." Many of the wounded attempted to crawl out from under the piles of the dead; they then ran out on the Confederate side and made their way down the little rivulet that ran from the spring above through the works, "filled up with water and then died like flies." Artillerist Lieutenant Colonel William Pegram later wrote his wife on August 1 that "I never saw such a sight as I saw on that portion of the line for a good distance in the trenches, the Yankees, white & black, principally the latter, were piled two and three or four deep" at that point.[27]

Lieutenant Freeman Bowley, believed to the contrary that it was the white troops who broke first, and he quickly observed the whole Federal line to his left going back slowly at first and then breaking and rushing over the breastworks toward the Union line or running down the traverse towards the Crater.[28] Bowley confessed, however, that the blacks, while having been brave in their charge, were, as a body, "wholly unmanageable, and totally demoralized in their defeat." Bowley, with a dozen men from his company of the 30th USCT, went down the traverse and into the Crater. His small unit was among the last to reach it, and the rifles of the trapped Union troops were then flashing in their faces as they jumped in, with the Confederates not more than twenty yards behind them. An enfilading fire was rapidly emanating from the traverse from which Bowley had just retreated. General Bartlett therefore ordered the troops to construct a protective breastwork by throwing up lumps of clay, but it was very slow going. Finally, in desperation, the bodies of white and black dead were utilized to build up the barrier in the trench in order to prevent the oncoming Confederates from using it as an avenue into the Crater.[29]

The black soldiers, particularly Thomas's men in the front lines, were hit very hard, and the majority of their officers fell in the first few minutes, thereby leaving the inexperienced blacks without leaders; thus many quickly gave way to the rear. To escape the gray-clad demons, the fugitives jumped from one traverse to another, rapidly crowding back on the white troops of Griffin's command. Private Henry Van Leuvenigh Bird, of the 12th Virginia, however, reported that many of the blacks initially remained in place and "fought like bulldogs and died like soldiers. Their cry of 'No quarter' was met with the stern cry of 'amen.'" Soon thereafter, many of the Federals threw down their arms to surrender, but in many cases were not allowed to do so. The trenches were eventually won all the way on the Confederate right up to the Crater. However, this hard won territory still had to be cleared foot by foot, through hand-to-hand combat, and by the utilization of the bayonet. "To think of it makes me recoil even now," Colonel Rogers, then commander of the 6th Virginia, wrote years later. Soon the trenches were filled with the dead; in many places they lay in vast heaps, "and there was literally no place on the ground for feet." A number of the Virginians had been wounded by the blacks in the close quarter fighting, and this situation enraged the rebel men all the more. Later, John Wise, the son of former Virginia governor and then Brigadier General Wise, at the time serving on his father's staff, was appalled at the conduct of his fellow Virginians toward their black foe:[30] "Our men, inflamed to relentless vengeance by their presence, disregarded the rules of warfare which restrained them in battle with their own race, and brained and butchered the blacks until the slaughtering was sickening."

George Bernard later wrote that his "heart sickened at deeds I saw done.... I have never seen such slaughter on any battle field" as the Confederates beat and shot at blacks, and "as the latter, terror-stricken, rushed away from them." Bernard related that "I saw one negro running down the trench towards the place where several of us stood and a Confederate fired at the poor creature seemingly heedless of the fact his bullet might have pierced his victim and struck some of the many Confederates immediately in its range." Bernard also witnessed a black noncommissioned officer standing in the ditch begging for his life before two Confederates, one striking him with a steel ramrod, the other holding a gun in his hand while trying to get off a shot. The second Confederate fired, but the bullet did not seem to cause serious injury to the black captive, who still continued to plead for his life. Ignoring the pleas, the Rebel soldier reloaded, placed the muzzle of the gun against the black soldier's stomach and fired again. "It was a brutal, horrible act," Bernard declared, "and those of us who witnessed it from our position in the trench a few feet away could but exclaim: 'That is too bad! It is shocking!'"[31]

Bernard himself had his own encounter with his black foe as soon as he jumped into the trench. After loading his gun, at his feet was a black soldier who immediately began to beg him not to kill him, imploring, "'Master, don't kill me! Master, don't kill me! I'll be your slave as long as I live. Don't kill me!' he most piteously cried, whilst I was rapidly loading my gun," no doubt expecting that the bullet was for him. Instead, Bernard proceeded to address him: "Old man, I do not intend to kill you, but you deserve to be killed." The black man thereupon began to fan a poor wounded Confederate soldier, one of Elliott's men buried in the breastworks at the explosion, who was then *in extremis.* Apparently he must have felt his attention to the helpless Confederate would serve to protect him against other incoming Rebel soldiers.[32]

Another such encounter was related to Colonel Porter Alexander by Colonel Frank Huger, who had been recognized by one of the blacks in the trench as he entered it. He immediately heard a voice call out "Mass Frank," and recognized a barber who had once shaved him in Norfolk some four years earlier. This frightened and seriously wounded black soldier cried out, "Please, Mass Frank, can I have some old greasy water what they been washing dishes in? I don't want no good water, just old greasy water they are going to throw away." Huger immediately gave the man a drink, "but his wound was one for which nothing could be done." Many of the defeated blacks tried any device which might keep them alive as they implored for their lives. "One old cornfield chap exclaimed, 'My God, massa, I never pinted a gun at a white man in all my life; dem nasty, stinking Yankees fotch us here, and we didn't want to come fus!'" Other captured blacks to a man indicated they had been forced to take up arms and "that they had been most cruelly treated, and worked hard by the Yankees." Many begged to be turned over to their former masters.[33]

Colonel Pegram later related yet another incident during a temporary lull in the fighting following the recapture of the Confederates' first position of the line and before the taking of the second, when he was thus in the midst of the fighting and there witnessed a duel between a black soldier and a Confederate: "I suppose the Confederate told the negro he was going to kill him, after he had surrendered. This made the negro desperate, & he grabbed up a musket & they fought quite desperately for a little while with bayonets until a bystander shot the negro dead." Pegram found justification for such actions on the Virginians' part, indicating that while "[i]t seems cruel to murder them in cold blood, but I think the men [who] did it had very good cause for doing so." He recalled that Mahone had related to him an incident where a Confederate had a bayonet run through his cheek, "which instead of making him throw down his musket & run to the rear, as men usually do when they are wounded, exasperated him so much that he killed the negroe, although in that condition. I have always that I wished the enemy would bring some negroes against this army. I am convinced, since Saturday's fight, that it had a splendid effect on our men."

According to Private Henry Biggs, son of a former North Carolina senator, General Mahone soon "grew sick of the slaughter going on and begged his men to stop killing the negroes, and I suppose on the strength of that they captured 150 negroes." Another soldier contended that all the blacks would have been slaughtered if not for Mahone, "who beg our men to Spare them." Biggs confessed that he would not have taken any of them, "especially after they shouted 'No quarter' which they did when they mounted the breastworks." Mahone's ordinance officer also indicated that "the slaughter was frightful, and the work of vengeance may have exceeded the proper limit." Dorsey Binion of the 48th Georgia, one of the few Georgia Brigade units which went into the breach with the Virginians, likewise reported becoming enraged at the blacks' cries of "no quarter," and indicated that "we did not show much quarter but slayed them. Some few negroes went to the rear as we could not kill them as fast as they passed us."[34]

This is not to say that the Federals did not give as well as they received in many instances. Bernard later recalled jumping from traverse to traverse while trying to get to the Confederate rear and meeting several unarmed, terrified negroes begging for mercy. As he approached the main ditch he spotted a young Confederate of Elliott's brigade, really just a boy, running down the length of the ditch. As Bernard entered the main trench, he found it unfortunately filled with Yankees, both white and black. He immediately spotted the same youth to his left leaning with his back against the breastwork and a large black soldier looming over him with musket in hand, about to bayonet him. The youth struggled desperately to keep the weapon at bay. Bernard advanced and lunged with his bayonet at the black's side. Instead of entering his body, however, the bayonet struck upon his hip bone. The black immediately dropped his rifle and seized Bernard's, and a struggle to the death quickly ensued. As the two men thus were scuffling, a Federal lieutenant pointed a pistol at Bernard's face and ordered him to surrender. Bernard refused and the officer fired, but his pistol malfunctioned. He quickly reloaded and fired again, but at such close range that Bernard was able to knock the pistol out of position and the bullet missed its mark. Before he could shoot again, some of the Richmond Grays of the 12th Virginia entered the ditch, converged on the Federal and quickly bayoneted the Federals. Meanwhile, the young man Bernard had just fortuitously rescued picked up a large army pistol and with the butt end knocked the black antagonist a blow that felled him.

Bernard then advanced down the main ditch, whereupon he soon encountered an officer with a uniform exactly like that worn by Federal officers. The man was running after a mob of Yankees crowding toward the Crater, some crying out, "We surrender!" and waving white handkerchiefs. Many others in the same mob, however, were shooting back at the pursuing Confederates. Bernard raised his gun to shoot the officer as he ran from him; however, just then the officer shouted to the Federal mob still firing back, "Stop shooting, if you wish to surrender!" Bernard held his fire at this. Just as the officer turned, Bernard discovered it was one of General Beauregard's staff officers dressed in his fatigue uniform. When Bernard informed him of his close encounter with death, the officer indicated he would not have been at fault, "as it was [a] very imprudent thing in him to go into action dressed as he was." Soon thereafter, in this ditch, Emmet Butts fell directly at Bernard's side, so close that Bernard would "never forget the sound of the ball which pierced his forehead and killed him [Butts] instantly" just after he had exclaimed, "I got him!" referring to a Yankee he had just fired upon.[35]

Everywhere, the leaderless black soldiers, particularly Colonel Thomas's men, were quickly driven back, and the Confederates soon were again in possession of the cavalier trench. Griffin's men, situated beyond the Crater, were quickly swept back with the rest. A Federal officer later wrote that "[t]he stampede, once begun, was not arrested at the Crater, at least only in part, but continued back to our lines, carrying along hundreds upon hundreds, both black and white." These hapless men "recognized the coming of the Day of Wrath, & turned & fled." The Confederates then jumped out of the trench they had just taken to pursue the retreating Federals. The blacks, to date unaccustomed to close quarters fighting and astonished at the Rebel's ferocity, quickly began to panic. Suddenly, "the whole body broke, went over the breastworks toward the Union line, or ran down the trenches toward the crater." Many threw down their arms in their haste in order to evade the enraged men in gray. As the panic-stricken blacks fled, Wise's brigade quickly poured a raking fire into the blue mass from its left regiments, while Wright's and Davidson's batteries provided a devastating cross fire of canister. Similarly, the 56th North Carolina of Ransom's Brigade, which had aided greatly in holding the Federals in check while Mahone formed, subsequently delivered a devastating fire to any and all Yankees who even attempted to start to the rear from the north or west side of the Crater.

Many of these fleeing masses attempted to make a stand in the various traverses and bombproofs behind the Confederate forward lines. In so doing, they flung themselves into traverses that were filled with the white Federal troops they had disrupted on their advance only some few minutes before. Again and again, their officers tried to rally them, but "words or blows were useless. They were victims of an uncontrollable terror, and human agency could not stop them." An officer of the Tenth Corps, which was soon overrun by the fleeing blacks, indicated at the time that "We used our sabers freely on the cowards but could not stop them and were all driven back."

The blacks did not stop at the innermost captured breastworks, "but only communicated the alarm to those sheltering themselves there, & not only did the whole mob stampede back to the Federal lines, but they took with them the greater part of two white divisions, one of the 9th Corps & one of the 18th." Major General Humphreys later wrote that Mahone drove the blacks quickly back in confusion, "the whole division rising from the ground & running in wild disorder back to out intrenchments, carrying with them many of Potter's troops, both of Turner's brigades & most of the men lying around & in rear of the crater." By 8:45 A.M., Ferrero's men and their white comrades were in full retreat in a crazed disorder and, "like lemmings diving senselessly to their death in the sea, jumped into the crater, forcing the soldiers already in it further up against the steep walls of the pit and touching off a terrific frenzy of shoving and pushing and cursing for space to fight."[36]

George Allen, of the 4th Rhode Island, adequately typified the disgust of the white soldiers still in the field describing the black flight: "But here they come back, rushing pell-mell over into our midst, knocking us down, shouting, panic-struck, and — with some noble exceptions — they fly to the rear." In their flight, the blacks fled wide-eyed into the lines of white troops behind them, still disorganized from the rush through their works only moments earlier, which disrupted what little unity remained. The white troops found themselves unwillingly carried to the rear as though by a surf. Many of the blacks ran with their bayonets before them, thus unknowingly wounding their white comrades and knocking them over, trampling them underfoot as they jumped into the overcrowded trenches to avoid the gray surge, plunging into the pits with fixed bayonets in "frightful confusion," and finally broke for the Federal lines. Private Clements of the 9th New Hampshire commented regarding the black soldiers:

> The rebels gave it to them so hot that they broke and came back, jumping and tumbling into the trench where we were already as thick as we could stand. They had their bayonets fixed, and one of them would have run me through if I had not warded off his gun with my own. As it was, his bayonet drew blood in my abdomen, and the scar is there now.[37]

Again and again "their officers tried to rally them. Words and blows were useless. They were victims of an uncontrollable terror, and human agency could not stop them." This stampede, crowding the Crater and the pits already filled with white troops to capacity, rendered "confusion worse confounded." The black soldiers, being exposed to the extent of half of their bodies where they were then standing, in order to escape the Rebel fire soon jumped over onto Griffin's men. Corporal Newell Dutton described the resultant chaos as "a mass of worms crawling over each other." The men in Griffin's remaining forces had no sooner recovered from the rout of Ferrero's division before Mahone's men came right down on them, resulting in a vicious, hand-to-hand encounter. Men were bayoneted, crushed and trampled; at the same time, the Confederates came up at the head of the traverse and commenced to pour a fire down on Griffin's men. When the black soldiers rushed through Griffin's men, the Virginians demanded surrender, which was instead unfortunately met with a volley "right in their faces and at very short range," causing them to momentarily fall back. The Rebels finally pressed so closely that the Federals, who could hardly move in these trenches, started to run for the Crater. Newell Dutton himself "jumped onto the top of the ground at the side of the traverse, and ran along with ... [the 9th New Hampshire's] colors, and finally made... [his] way into the crater, which was packed full with men from different regiments." As he settled into his new shelter, Dutton encountered a lieutenant from the 9th New Hampshire who had bravely managed to bring off the national colors in a very similar fashion.[38]

Griffin's current position quickly became totally untenable. Twelve or more pairs of Confederate colors danced on his line in the midst of the fierce fighting. The color sergeant of the 32nd Maine was soon wounded and captured, along with his flag. Similarly, the color sergeant of the 11th New Hampshire was quickly engaged in a losing battle with a corporal of the 6th Virginia, who succeeded in taking his flag, which by then was reduced to shreds. A corporal of the 61st Virginia then wrestled for the flag of the 31st Maine, which was also torn to pieces in the fight before being taken. One Confederate who thought he had captured the highly sought-after national flag of the 21st Massachusetts was set upon by Sergeant Leander Wilkins of the 9th New Hampshire, "a brawny farmboy from New Hampshire's northern neck." Wilkins tore the staff away and charged into the middle ranks of his regiment with his prize.[39]

Griffin's men then started backing methodically toward the Crater. Sergeant James Lathe, his own company all but disintegrated, gave up commanding and became an impromptu sharpshooter in the withdrawal. Lathe picked off five Confederates in the short period of time, encouraged by an officer who found himself without a command. As Lathe finally reluctantly retreated into the Crater himself, a bullet tore through his right hand, tearing the middle and right fingers back nearly to the top of the wrist. He soon encountered Lieutenant John Sampson of Company E, who quickly tied a handkerchief around the ruined hand and told Lathe to run for it back to their lines. Turning away from Sampson, Lathe ran for the Federal lines. Captain Andrew Jackson Hough, commanding the 9th New Hampshire, who had bravely exposed himself earlier to ward off the black soldiers' mistaken attack on his regiment's position, was rather belatedly able to fulfill his prediction of invincibility. Shortly after the retreat into the Crater, one of his own men fumbled the hammer on his rifle while reloading it, and the weapon discharged, blowing a gruesome chunk out of the back of Hough's head.[40] As luck would hae it, he was down but not out! Command of the 9th quickly fell under the control of Captain John B. Cooper, who at the time was still awaiting a response to his resignation.[41]

The Confederates sealed off the trenches north of the Crater and captured many of the men that Griffin had not long before led in the assault. The brigade's fugitives sought refuge in the myriad of traverses, jamming in so tightly one officer complained that he could not raise his hands from his sides. As the Federals were forced to surrender, "[h]undreds of prisoners trudged toward the plank road, passing at least once through the fire of their own artillery, and the enemy filled the trenches as they trooped out of them, working that much closer to the Crater itself."[42]

Further to the north, Mahone's counterattack caused even more chaos in what had already become a disastrous mess. Bartlett's brigade had suffered greatly in its futile attempts to advance. The 57th Massachusetts had already lost two commanders, Major Prescott and Captain Dresser, who had quickly succeeded him. Command then devolved upon Captain George H. Howe, a staff officer of the brigade, who made a gallant attempt to confront the Confederates. He mounted the extreme outer edge of the Crater in the face of the enemy, then advanced in force, waving his sword for the regiment to follow, but soon fell back almost instantly, shot through the heart. At about this same time, Lieutenants Barton and Anderson of the regiment were both wounded, leaving only one officer standing, the newly commissioned Lieutenant Doty. The Rebels succeeded in obtaining a lodgment within a few feet of these Federals, so near that they could almost reach each other with their respective bayonets. Whites and blacks were squeezed so tightly in the confined space that there was hardly any standing room. Many of those killed still remained in a standing position thereafter until they were jostled to the ground. The dead were thereupon trodden upon and the wounded were trampled to death. Lieutenant Anderson of the 57th Massachusetts described the scene as "one seething cauldron of struggling, dying men."

Added to this were the multitude of shells exploding in the midst of the men while the musketry stormed at close range, creating a simply murderous situation. Anderson was reminded of Tennyson's famous refrain regarding the famed Light Brigade:

> Cannon to right of them,
> Cannon to left of them,
> Cannon behind them
> Volley'd and thunder'd.

Reflecting on this slaughter, and conversely upon the overwhelming number of Federal troops in place behind their lines ready to move, Anderson commented, "How often we turned and looked anxiously towards our lines only to be disappointed." Unfortunately, he concluded that they "were left in the shambles for the slaughter that was steadily increasing." Most of the men in a position to return fire had run out of ammunition and gathered cartridges from the dead and dying, while others threw bottles, stones and debris. "The close-range fighting was virulent and unmerciful, and blood ran down in streams in the hard, brown clay [and] formed pools in which the men slipped, and it got on everything."[43]

Colonel Stephen Minot Weld, commander of the 56th Massachusetts, in nominal command of the right wing of Bartlett's brigade, had by the time of Mahone's first counterattack lost what little semblance of order he had previously maintained over his scattered troops. The advance of the fourth division through his command had totally disintegrated its quite tenuous formation. When the blacks subsequently reversed and stampeded back through those still disorganized ranks, disaster then was assured. Weld recalled that the Confederates drove "the negroes over heels into us, trampling everyone down, and adding still more to the confusion." Once the blacks flung themselves back into the trenches, the men there were trapped like fish in a barrel, and the Confederates poured a barrage of musketry and cannon fire into their exposed ranks.

Weld was unable even to raise his arms from his side due to the sheer numbers in that confined space. His men were soon mingled in a confused mass with the black troops, where he observed a Confederate flag hanging over the parapet about four feet away. Soon thereafter, the muzzles of a multitude of rifles spewed fire into the huddled masses. Lieutenant George Barton of the 57th Massachusetts recalled how the blacks "broke & ran like a flock of sheep, & black at that falling back upon our trenches, they completely jammed us up into a

heap so that there was no room to fight." Barton later reflected on the situation and concluded that "This war must be *fought out* by *white men* & we might as well make up our
minds to the first at last to say it." A number of Weld's force was quickly cut off and surrounded. Weld took refuge in a bombproof and was taken prisoner. A black soldier was by
his side as they emerged and a Rebel soon shouted, "Shoot the nigger, but don't kill the white
man." and the black was quickly shot down right by Weld's side. As Weld was marched to
the Confederate rear as a prisoner, he spotted another black soldier ahead of him. Three Virginians rushed up to him in succession and shot him. "It was altogether the most miserable
and meanest experience I ever had in my life," Weld said years later.[44] Of the nine regiments
in Weld's brigade, he was the only regimental commander left alive at day's end, the rest having all been killed or mortally wounded.[45]

Still further to the north of the Crater, Sigfried's black troops had disrupted the impending attempts of Colonel Louis Bell to neutralize McAfee's North Carolinians. The blacks held
the first two lines and the white troops of Bell's brigade, together with some scattered blacks,
the third. James Clark of the 115th New York watched as the Confederates came on in a "beautiful line." As the oncoming gray mass did not display any arms in their hands, the Federal
officers concluded that the Rebels were coming in as prisoners. But "[s]uddenly the sneak-
ing rebels bring their guns in view, and give us a crushing volley. We give them a volley in
return. The colored troops in our front for the same reason become panic stricken, and blindly
hurl themselves back on our bayonets; and a wild scene of confusion ensues."

The first line of black troops bowled into Bell's men inadvertently, stabbing and injuring many whites with their bayonets and carrying them away, thereby providing McAfee's
troops an uninhibited field of fire that further accelerated the rout of black and white alike.
General Carr of the Eighteenth Corps had reported that at about 8:30 A.M., while Turner was
still forming, there was an attempt made by the troops on the right to charge the rifle pits.
He consequently took command of a part of Turner's troops in order to fill the gap in the
line and then charged the rifle pits in front, about 200 yards to the right of the Crater. As
Carr stepped toward the covered way leading to the front, he estimated that at least "2,000
men came back" in total disorder. Carr was immediately "lifted from ... [his] feet by the rushing mass, and carried along with it ten or fifteen yards in the covered way." As Mahone's men
charged, the startled blacks of Sigfried's brigade suddenly gave up all semblance of an offensive and began to flee. Brigadier General R.B. Ayres of the Fifth Corps observed the counterattack, and saw the blacks coming back "like a sandslide." He reported that the mass of
Union troops were swept back "like a breath of air, and are cut badly on the backward track."
Hermon Clarke of the 117th New York Volunteers of Curtis's brigade, still in reserve, described
how "the rebs gave one volley and a yell, and such a skedaddle you never heard of! They [the
black troops] ran over us and never stopped until the provost guard halted them. The whole
9th Corps was routed, and our division held the enemy two hours."

General Turner himself related the sight:

> [t]he troops in vast numbers come rushing back, and immediately my whole first brigade
> came back, and then my second brigade on my right, and everything was swept back in and
> around the Crater, and probably all but about one-third of the original number stampeded
> back right into our lines. After some exertion I rallied my men of the First and Second
> brigades after they got into our lines, while my Third brigade held the line.[46]

Sergeant Elias Bryant, of the 4th New Hampshire, by then down with a wound, heard a great
noise and almost immediately observed the blacks coming right back over the works in utter
confusion. Officers were waving their swords and shouting, "Halt!" but to no avail. Some Federal officers gave orders to their men to bayonet the retreating, frightened men and "many

utterly stricken with terror ran into them and were wounded." Bryant himself sat up on his stretcher "and shouted to them to halt at the top of … [his] voice and swung… [his] hands … in frustration."[47] Orders were also given by some officers to fire on the retreating mob, "but nothing succeeded in stopping them." The fugitives crowded into the covered way until it was packed solidly full. As a consequence, the stretcher bearing Bryant to the rear had to be carried outside, exposed to Confederate fire.

Bell later wrote that "[w]e used our sabers freely on the cowards but could not stop them and all were driven back — pell-mell." In the ensuing blind panic, most of Bell's brigade was swept back toward the Federal lines by the stampede. Bell later contended that had his command "not been run over and confused by the mob of panic-stricken negroes I could have held the position I occupied against any force then visible," although it would have taken severe loss due to the sharp, enfilading fire" from the flanks. Some blacks were impaled on bayonets, but they still swept away the line in front of them, rushing over it to the rear. Company H of the 115th New York, with the regiment's colors, together with some others of the regiment, was able to stem the tide of confusion and remained in place, single-handed and alone to contest the ground. The flag of the 115th still floated from the works and the brave boys surrounded it with a cordon of bayonets. Soon, however, Colonel Sammons feared the flag would be lost if it remained there, and he thus rushed forward to insure its protection, when a Rebel, seeing the movement, shot him in the leg.[48]

As it was madness to remain there unprotected, the remnants of the regiment were then ordered back and thereafter reached the Federal line under a dreadful fire of lead. Charlie Fellows, the brave color bearer, twice had the staff cut off in his hands in the retreat, with balls and grape tearing through the banner. The flag was later found to have sustained nine fresh wounds, and, for the fourth time, the staff was shot into pieces. Captain Smith calmly told the men to fight "as long as there is hope," while the Confederates continued to swarm around them. Captain Percy Daniels, commanding the 7th Rhode Island, the acting engineers of the second division, had bravely sought to obtain permission for Bell's men to take the next battery, some 500 rods from the Crater. Percy personally scouted the battery, reaching the ditch which protected it just as Mahone's men came up and shouted, "Come in, here, Billy!" Instead, Daniels ran back and reached the Federal rifle pits, some thirty to forty yards in the rear of the woods. Some of the Federals in the pits were hit as Daniels came in.[49]

Coan's second brigade, situated still further to the Federal right, found itself unduly exposed as Mahone's counterattack soon began driving back the advance forces. Isaiah Price of the 97th Pennsylvania had finally found his detached companies and was therefore attempting to bring them to the right, just in the rear of Turner's two brigades, which were lying against the slope of the hill in column by regiments closed en masse, when a sudden movement by a heavy force of Confederates on the left flank exposed the position to capture. The troops came rushing down the hill, breaking through the ranks of Price's men, "sweeping all in confusion across the meadow in the rear." Price followed in order to rally his men, which he was able to accomplish behind the earthworks, where the line was re-formed. Turner then ordered Price to occupy the line of entrenchments to the left of his regiment until further orders. His small detachment thus remained in this position until the close of the engagement, exposed to a heavy flank fire of musketry and shell from the Confederate works.

Meanwhile, the right of the 97th continued to hold its own position, repelling successive attempts to charge and retake the line. Along with the 48th New York, these two regiments, then under the command of Captain Taylor, remained under cover on the hillside near the brigade's right. There the regiments stayed for hours, helping to prevent the Rebels from flanking Bartlett's position in the Crater from the rear and cutting him off from the main force, until Coan ordered the detachment to rejoin the rest of the brigade. Coan's losses in the process were quite dreadful. They were considered "one of the most serious that our army had suffered for months." Major Samuel M. Swartwout was killed, "one of the oldest and the best of all the officers who had been connected with the regiment." The brigade did not end up moving into the Crater, but it was so placed that it suffered "a most terrible fire through those hours." Turner's men stood firmly for three more hours under severe fire of musketry and artillery in this "isolated and perilous position."[50]

Colonel N. Martin Curtis's first brigade soon followed the second and third into the conflict. Before it could get fully into position on the front, however, the tide of battle had turned as a result of Mahone's counterattack, who threw in his men "with determination of recovering the ground we had lost." When the panic started, Curtis was still in reserve in a skirt of woods under a knoll in back of the Federal lines. As the Confederates came up, it appeared they were attempting to surrender, and thus an order thus was given to cease fire. Unfortunately, the Rebels then halted and poured a well-directed fire into Turner's troops. Once Mahone attacked, "an unaccountable panic occurred, which threw the assailants into utter confusion, and converted the hoped for success of yesterday into mortifying disaster." The blacks of the fourth division, according to William Hyde, upon "seeing half a dozen lines advancing against them, had become panic-stricken [and] dropped their arms and fled without dealing a blow, embarrassing the white troops around and behind them and in the end ensu[r]ing for us a defeat."

Curtis did attempt to stop some of the black fugitives at the point of the bayonet as well as to hold the captured works which were in imminent danger. Only the 112th New York Volunteers and the 142nd New York were actually in position at the front when the stampede ran through Coan's men. The 3rd New York and the 117th New York were still in the covered way, and were given orders to stop the stragglers. These units admirably attempted to stop the retreating mass, forcing these men into the works with fixed bayonets and holding them there

Battle of the Crater (courtesy John Elder/The Westmoreland Club).

until they were able to contribute to the defense of that portion of the line. "We did what we could to arrest it but were too feeble." Colonel Smith went with the right wing of the 112th, crowded through and was in good position on the left of the passageway.

Meanwhile, Captain Ludwick had command of the left wing of the regiment. The track through the knoll was jammed with the fugitives when the regiment was ordered to advance; those in front were pushed on by the dense mass from behind. Seeing that it was useless to attempt to push through, Ludwick leapt from the trench to the top of the knoll and shouted for the men to follow him and started for the line he was to occupy. The brigade was now in full view of the Confederates, who were pouring lead and canister into the dense mass of men crowded there. Chaplain William L. Hyde of the 112th New York related that the Confederates then "turned their attention to the heroes, who amid this wild fright, were resolutely rushing to rescue our works from the pursuing foe."[51]

The 3rd New York was still on the way to the front through the deep trench whose sides rose to seven or eight feet in height. Their forward progress was brought to a complete halt by the "terror-stricken darkies, who came surging over with a force which seemed almost irresistible. They insisted that the rebels were close on their heels and would gobble us all up — that their strength was twice our own," Sergeant Edward King Wightman of the 3rd New York, who had earned two degrees from New York University before the war later wrote home. Knowing they were needed at the front, but unable to get the blacks to return to the fight, the men of the 3rd New York "hoisted up our color bearer and then, helping each other up, rushed over the parapet with a great volley of musket balls and, trotting down a little hill, formed under the cover of the N & P [Norfolk & Petersburg] Railroad," Wightman continued. Another two hundred yards brought the regiment to where the brigade was formed for the charge.[52]

William Hyde of the 112th New York Volunteers, in a letter of August 1, 1864, discussed Mahone's counterattack and its impact on his unit: "One man told me that a huge nigger came tumbling over him and almost broke his neck! In our endeavoring to hold the position till the line could be reformed, our Regiment suffered some casualties...." The officers of the 112th New York attempted to halt the retreat of the totally panic-stricken blacks, who were sweeping everything before them in their wild flight. In the panic, white and black became inextricably intermingled. The blacks crashed through Curtis's brigade, and then met General Ferrero himself, throwing him back in their irresistible tide "grabbing and clutching like a cat on a fence on a windy day." The blacks yelled and groaned in despair and "when we barred their progress to leap and scramble up the sides of the trench, they did their prettiest to jump out of our empty barrel. You might form an idea of the performance of some of the poor nigs on the extraordinary occasion," Wightman declared. The brigade moved another 200 yards and had just taken its position when an order to advance was countermanded and it was quickly forced to retreat under heavy fire into the trenches.

The unfortunate blacks had more to worry about than the vengeance of the Southerners bearing down on them. The white troops who were overrun by the fourth division, a good many of them for the second time that morning, began to express a hatred of these black reinforcements which was "unexcelled by the southerners." Private James Barnes, a Canadian youth in the 9th New Hampshire, heard someone yell, "Give the black devils a dose, and then take the bayonet to the rebel!" George Kilmer of the 14th New York Heavy Artillery later recalled that some of his comrades "declared that they would never follow 'niggers' or be caught in their company, and started back to our own lines, but were promptly driven forward." Driven back from their unsanctioned retreat, when the USCT line broke, the men who distrusted the blacks vented their feelings freely. As they came back into the Crater with the

Rebels on their heels, the black soldiers were confronted with "a worse fate than death on the charge. It was believed among the whites that the enemy would give no quarter to negroes, or to whites taken with them, and so to be shut up with blacks in the Crater was equal to a doom of death." Therefore, some of the panicky white soldiers bayoneted their black comrades at arms as they fell back into the Crater, in order to preserve themselves from Confederate vengeance. "Men boasted in my presence," asserted Kilmer, "that blacks had been thus disposed of, particularly when the Confederates came up." Such sentiments pervaded the 9th New Hampshire also. "Lieutenant George Emery told a correspondent several weeks later that "the men was bound not to be taken prisoner among them niggers." Elsewhere, officers ordered their men to charge bayonets on the frightened blacks rushing back stricken in terror, thereby wounding a great many. John S. Majors of the 13th Indiana of Bell's brigade wrote his wife, Carrie, on August 7, 1864, describing the panic-stricken blacks running "rite over our second line of battle. Our white soldiers could not stop them. So our Regiment had to kill a grate many of them."[53]

Weisiger's force was able to retake all the occupied works north of the Crater, and had advanced to within fifty feet of the pit itself. It had covered a front the length of its advancing line, so that once it veered left, it did not include the Crater in its reach. In so doing, the Virginians had suffered severe losses, were totally spent and had insufficient numbers to mount further assaults on the Crater by itself. Additionally, the numerically superior Federal force now largely trapped in the Crater was still able to lay down a devastating enfilading fire on these Confederates in the trenches to the north. The advance, therefore, came to a complete halt without the Crater itself being taken. Approximately three-fourths of the cavalier trench in the rear of the Crater was retaken, along with all the entrenchments on the north of it. South of the Crater, the Federals still held fifty feet of a traverse up to the junction of the main line and the Crater.

Mahone was also conscious of the fact that the hold he currently possessed was tenuous, and thus was already formulating the advance of the Georgia Brigade, which he had done all in his power to have sent in combination with the Virginians. As he planned this next assault, Mahone asked Colonel John Haskell if he could not get closer to the enemy with his Eprouvette mortars in order to further demoralize them. Haskell moved a section of his mortar battery under Captain James Lamkin forward from its position in the Jerusalem Plank Road, placing the pieces amongst the men of the 16th Virginia. Mahone felt that by getting much closer, Haskell "could amuse himself till one o'clock, and perhaps no such opportunity had ever occurred or would likely occur for the effective employment of these juvenile implements of death." Haskell later related that "I advanced the mortars along the line, took two of them into the trenches we had recaptured. The enemy were again so close that we could hear them calling, so we began throwing shells with squibs for charges, and every few minutes numbers would dash into our lines crying for quarter."

The mortars were now within yards of the Crater's rim. Using a powder charge cut to one and a half ounces, the little Eprouvette or Coehorn mortars would throw the shell barely fifty feet in the air. Haskell recalled that the shells with the light charges "would rise so slowly as to look as if they could not get to the enemy," which was by then so close he could hear the Union soldiers cry out when the shells fell among them. Haskell's handiwork added greatly to the horror, for now, "without intermission, the storm of fire beat upon the hapless men imprisoned within" that horrid pit. The scene became not unlike Dante's "nine-circled Hell," as mortars on the right and left and now in front caused shells to fall at regular intervals on the huddled blue masses. From right and left, the missiles fell at regular intervals with graceful curves and deadly accuracy and burst among the helpless masses in the pit. Howard Aston described his experiences inside the Crater as the mortar battery "got our range beautifully, and every few minutes dropped shells into the crater":

> Some burst over our heads, and the fragments would fly in every direction. Others would bury themselves in the loose earth, then, perhaps burst, carrying with them the body of some poor fellow into the air, or shattering an arm or a leg. It was no unusual thing during the last two hours I was in the crater to see the body of a man blown to pieces. I know that I saw arms and legs twenty feet in the air.

Aston recounted that "the boys who worked those mortars got the range *admirably* (for them — but not for us)." The screams, groans and explosions which threw up human limbs made the scene one of awful carnage. The deadly mortars were "hurling destruction every minute, if not every second," leaving no place to retreat, and no place for shelter. Dead men were tumbling to the bottom of the pit by the dozens, "piling up like cordwood." Sheets of blood washed down the sides, "pooling in ghastly puddles around the mounting stack of bodies." It was believed to have been one of Haskell's shells which shattered General Bartlett's artificial leg around this time. Another Federal in the trenches who recoiled from Haskell's barrage later remarked in horror at the weapons' effectiveness—"dismembered bodies, legs, arms, and heads strewed the ground in every direction, and this horrible butchery explains why men's clothes were covered with blood and fragments of human flesh and brains to a degree never seen in any other battle of the war."[54]

Moving the mortars that close to the Crater proved to be dangerous, however, as the traverses were still full of straggling Yankees. As Haskell himself was rounding a curve in the trench with a borrowed pistol, he was confronted by a white Federal officer and two black soldiers. The officer called for the blacks to fire, and at the same time raised his own pistol. Haskell jumped back, firing as he did so, and called for his men behind him to charge. "They dashed around the corner and got fifteen or twenty negro soldiers, who were close behind the white man I had fired at. I found him lying on his face, shot through the head." The officer was found to be a colonel of a black regiment, but, like many of the officers of the colored regiments, he bore no insignia of rank. Haskell reflected that he never saw the white soldiers wear insignia of rank in a fight, as "they had learned that our men did not readily give quarter to officers of negro regiments, so they preferred, when caught, to pass themselves as privates of white regiments."[55]

In addition to bringing up Haskell's mortars to demoralize the Yankees in the Crater, Mahone, who was in the trenches within minutes of the attack, also set out sharpshooters to the right to train their guns on the pit and its environs, "the vast rim of which frowned down upon the lower line occupied by his troops." Thus, "[w]hile this deadly work of the Coehorns was going on, sharp-shooters dispatched back into the pit, either dead or wounded, every man who attempted to scale its sides and get away...." The Virginians, Captain McCabe later wrote, viewing the ease with which the mortars were lobbed into the pit, and to preserve their precious ammunition, "with the imitative ingenuity of soldiers, gleefully gathered up the countless muskets with bayonets fixed, which had been abandoned by the enemy, and propelled them with such nice skill that they came down upon Ledlie's men "like the rain of the Norman arrows at Hastings." Often these javelins would be sent back by the Yankees in the Crater. Other Confederates who ran out of ammunition resorted to throwing chunks of iron, rocks and other debris into the Crater as the best tactic within their means "to hasten the completion of the work all were anxious to close out."[56]

As bloody and gruesome as this counterattack was, the whole process had lasted only twenty minutes or less, with some eyewitnesses placing the total elapsed time at not more than ten minutes. In these few minutes, however, the floor of the whole trench was strewn with the dead bodies of blacks, "in some places in such numbers that it was difficult to make one's way along the trench without stepping upon them." In an incredibly brief time, the whole of the advance line north of the Crater was retaken, with the Federals in headlong flight.

Mahone's men were not isolated from the devastating effects of their gallant charge into history that day, however. The Virginia Brigade suffered dreadfully for its heroic charge. To their considerable disadvantage that fearful morning, the Virginians had never grown accustomed to the advantages of earthworks in battle. Thus, in comparison to their Northern foe, they could be considered to be more reckless in the attack. The 6th Virginia brought ninety-five men to bear that fateful day when it appeared over the rise, after having left half its number on the picket line at Willcox Farm. A total of eighty-five fell that morning, leaving only ten to report for duty the next morning. Old Company F of Norfolk (the "Dandies") of the 6th Virginia carried in twelve men, all of whom were killed or wounded. The Sharpshooters sent in eighty men, and had sixteen report for duty the next morning. Among the slain was its commander, Captain William Broadbent, who was the first to leap over the works. His body was found mercilessly savaged, his skull broken and "almost every square inch of his body ... perforated with a bayonet stab." He was mourned as "a simple captain, of whom we may say, as was said of Ridge: 'No man died that day with more glory, yet many died and there was much glory.'"[57] Lieutenant Colonel William Stewart of the 61st Virginia reflected on the morning's butcher's bill: "In that supreme moment, when exulting over a great victory, how great I shall leave for others to judge, as our eyes fell upon the bleeding comrades around us, our hearts sickened within, for more than half our members lay dead, dying, wounded and writhing in agony around us." Nearly one half of the 61st Virginia fell in that short time frame. The 12th Virginia had eighteen killed and twenty-four wounded, which amounted to ten percent of those engaged. Colonel Weisiger was himself quickly wounded in what he claimed was a mortal injury, and he had to be carried from the field.[58]

Command of the brigade was turned over to Colonel George Thomas Rogers of the 6th Virginia, as Weisiger believed himself to be *in extremis.* Soon thereafter, Rogers himself was temporarily captured, but was rescued by his fellow Virginians. Leaving the field, Weisiger was leaning on a private, working his way back toward the Gee house, at which point he ran into General Beauregard. The chivalrous Creole bowed low "in a style as moribund as his cause," and informed Weisiger, "Colonel, you have covered yourselves with glory." Five members of the 61st Virginia were placed on the Confederate Roll of Honor for their heroism that day. The 61st Virginia captured five flags, including the 57th Massachusetts, the Stars and Stripes, a regimental standard of the 31st Maine and a portion of the staff and fringe of another regiment.

The battle flag of the 12th Virginia was relatively new and had been used little to date. The old one was badly torn and was put away for safekeeping. Though the new flag of the 12th had been in battle on several occasions, it had never been touched by a bullet. After the day's fighting, an examination was performed on the flag and at least seventy-five shots were found to have passed through the new banner, and another nine shots had struck its staff. The staff was so badly shattered that it had to be reinforced with a ramrod during the battle. Mahone then gave the regiment a staff from a U.S. flag captured by his brigade that day, a staff still in use when the unit surrendered at Appomattox eight months later. In all, Weisiger's Brigade alone sent back fifteen Federal flags to the Confederate War Department in Richmond as trophies of their victory. Meanwhile, the regimental flag of the 6th Virginia was captured by Corporal Frank Hogan of Company A, 45th Pennsylvania who received a Medal of Honor for his actions in capturing the flag that day. Hogan himself had nothing but praise for the gallantry of the 6th Virginia after the war.[59]

A study of the psychological makeup of these Civil War soldiers which might account for some of the savage treatment manifested in this battle is beyond the scope of this book. Needless to say, such brutality, although the exception to the rule, can be found in any of the wars in which the United States has participated. Moreover, the brutality was by no means limited to one side of the fighting. However, with certainty, much of what was precipitated that day owed its origin at least partially to the battle of Fort Pillow, as well as the deep-seated Southern prejudices against blacks, and, more particularly, black soldiers.

Fort Pillow, some forty miles above Memphis, Tennessee, on a bluff overlooking the Mississippi, had been in Federal hands for two years. It was garrisoned by some 557 troops, half of them former slaves. On April 12, 1864, troops under Nathan Bedford Forrest surrounded the fort and demanded its surrender. Its commander refused the terms, while the Federal inhabitants, black and white alike, began "taunting the rebels gleefully and profanely from the parapets throughout the cease-fire." The subsequent assault was brief and furious. Clearly, in numerous instances, no quarter was shown to the Federals attempting to surrender, particularly the black soldiers. Of the total Federal force, 63 percent were casualties, and two-thirds of these — 221 — were killed. A more telling factor, however, was the fact that only fifty-eight blacks were marched out of the fort as prisoners, representing just 20 percent of the black force, while 168 whites, or 60 percent of the total white force, survived.

Within six days, a subcommittee of the Joint Committee on the Conduct of the War heard testimony and in short order concluded the Rebels had engaged in "indiscriminate slaughter." The credibility of the Joint Committee "was seriously questioned by many sources, North and South," however. At Lincoln's request, General Grant wired Sherman that "[i]f our men have been murdered after capture, retaliation must be resorted to promptly." Sherman began an investigation, but made no such recommendation for retaliation, proof enough for many that none was justified, for, "with Sherman in charge, retaliation would have been as prompt as Grant could have desired."[60] Many authorities see the massacre otherwise, contending that if it had been premeditated, there would have been no survivors, as no prisoners would have been taken.

There were allegations that the black troops ignored orders to surrender, in large part prompted by their white officers. Forrest himself accused the North of convincing the black soldiers that they could expect no quarter from Forrest's troops, and this, according to Forrest, "caused them to fight more desperately." Factually, Forrest did capture and turn over many black prisoners to the Confederate authorities.[61] Regardless of any premeditation or the exact circumstances leading up to the incident, many historians believe the action of the Rebels did more to hurt the Southern cause than help it, and eventually aided in an ultimate Federal victory. It also helped put a nail in the coffin of any chance of assistance for the South on Great Britain's part (very slim by then in any event).[62]

Regardless of the relative merits of these arguments, Fort Pillow certainly solidified Northern support for the United States Colored Troops and hardened the attitude toward the Confederates within the black units. "They fought with a little more vigor, and they also decided that wartime atrocities was something 'at which two can play,' so wrote Brig. Gen. August Chettain" at the time:

> At times they fought under the black flag, which warned the Confederates that they would neither take prisoners nor ask for any mercy for themselves; in other engagements, they acted without warning. An officer in the USCT wrote his wife that some troops in his regiment trapped ten Confederates and gunned down five of them. Had it not been for Ft Pillow, those

5 men might be alive now. Remember Ft Pillow is getting to be the feeling if not the word. It looks hard but we cannot blame these men much.

Reaction in the Union army was widespread and intense. In Louisiana, a company of blacks instructed their men to "Remember Fort Pillow" and executed seventeen unarmed prisoners. A Wisconsin soldier in Sherman's army in Georgia wrote his fiancée about charging upon the Confederate works at Resaca in May 1864, where "twenty-three of the rebs surrendered but the boys asked them if they remembered Fort Pillow and killed them. Where there is no officer with us, we take no prisoners.... We want revenge and will have it."[63] George Templeton Strong, in his now famous diary, wrote on July 1, 1864:

> Grant's staff indicate black troops fight well, "and take no prisoners." Don't know how it is— we have made no enquiry—somehow they give the Provost Marshall nothing to do. I suppose they have to kill their prisoners before they can take them. When they go into action, they yell "Fort Pillow!" But it is queer they don't take any prisoners, though they fight so well. Very queer, indeed.

Captain Charles Francis Adams of the 1st Massachusetts Cavalry, the grandson of President John Quincy Adams, wrote to his father on June 19, 1864:

> The cruelty of Fort Pillow is reacting on the rebels, for now they dread the darkies more than the white troops; for they know that if they will fight the rebels cannot expect quarter. Of course, our black troops are not subject to any of the rules of civilized warfare. If they murder prisoners, as I hear they did, it is to be lamented and stopped, but they can hardly be blamed [referring to the fighting before Petersburg in June, 1864].[64]

Many clear examples do exist of Union atrocities and maltreatment of Confederates based upon animosities related to Fort Pillow. After the Wilderness battle, Austin Fenn of the 10th Vermont wrote home:

> I saw Burnsides Negro Soldiers that day [May 8] and they looked 5 times as well as I ever supposed Nigger soldiers could look.... They had in Big letters on their flag remember Fort Pillow, no quarter when they came on to A wounded reb they knocked his brains out with the butts of their Guns that is the way Johnnys are getting their pay.[65]

The first atrocities committed in the Petersburg siege actually occurred on June 15 when Brigadier General Edward Hinck's black troops of the Eighteenth Corps bayoneted Southern prisoners captured in that day's successful assault on the Dimmock Line until white units intervened to protect the Confederates. That same day, Burnside's fourth division attacked Confederate batteries along the Confederate line, where at least one unarmed Confederate was killed by USCT soldiers, who, according to Hermon Clarke of the 117th New York, "came up to him ... and ran his bayonet through his heart. Our boys turned on the Niggers and kept them back." Such actions, often performed with the complicity of their white officers, "represented the reverse side of the Fort Pillow coin."[66]

Captain William Morgan of the 11th Virginia was captured May 21, 1864, at the North Anna. As he was marched to the rear as a prisoner, he encountered black regiments; "[t]hese were the first negro troops we had ever seen. One of them remarked as we passed by, 'They ought to have gin'em (us) Fort Pillow. If we had catch'em we would have gin'em Fort Pillow.'" Chaplain Enoch Miller attributed the atrocities committed by black soldiers in killing unarmed prisoners, without condoning them, to the fact that "'some of the men who had been slaves' would remember old grievances and 'seek to avenge them on such occasions.'"[67] Many Northerners seemed to believe such "retaliation" was justified. Nurse Cordelia Handcock of the first division, Second Corps wrote her sister on June 20, 1864: "I walked out with Mrs. Husbands and talked with an intelligent Colored Sergeant. He said they intended to show the Rebels no quarter. I encouraged them very strongly and retired to my tent."[68]

Sometimes the black troops would act without warning, as when a USCT officer wrote that his regiment had trapped ten Confederates and gunned down five of them following their surrender: "'Remember Ft Pillow' is getting to be the feeling if not the word.'" White officers often exhorted their black troops to "Remember Fort Pillow" and executed prisoners they captured without mercy. Many white USCT officers often overlooked such retaliation on the part of their men. "In fact, the problem of blacks executing Confederates became so widespread that black chaplain Henry M. Turner complained publicly about these atrocities."

When the fourth division advanced on July 30, the thin line of Confederate defenders clearly heard the blacks shouting at the top of their voices, "No quarter to the Rebels! No quarter to the Rebels!" and the blacks proceeded to butcher every man they found alive in the works. The Confederates would never forget that charge which was accompanied by the "dreaded shout, 'No quarter' from the negro troops [that] rang in our ears for days afterwards.... To be captured by the negro troops meant death not only to ourselves but, it appeared, to the helpless women and children in Petersburg." Even Confederates who were taken prisoner faced death from their black foe. Lieutenant James W. Steele of the 43rd USCT said:

> There was a half determination on the part of a good many of the black soldiers to kill them [their prisoners] as fast as they came to them. They were thinking of Fort Pillow, and small blame to them. The first batch I saw had been driven together just in front of the line of earthworks we had taken and occupied. I climbed over and rushed out there to save them from the group of men of my own company, who in two minutes would have bayoneted the last poor devil of them.

Thus, the savagery of the fighting grew largely out of the use of emotionally charged battle cries such as "Remember Poison Springs"[69] and "Remember Fort Pillow." Most often, no action was taken against atrocities, and so the troops on both sides inferred that they had tacit approval for the use of the "black flag."[70]

As previously discussed, there existed an overwhelming prejudice against blacks generally, and an increased, intense prejudice against black soldiers. The editors of the *Richmond Examiner* concluded for themselves that Grant diabolically wished to taunt and humiliate the defenders of Petersburg by using black soldiers against them. When the first black troops were raised by the Union, the Confederate Congress had passed a law providing for the execution of the white officers of black units taken prisoner, following a military trial, on the grounds that leading such black men was included in the capital crime of inciting a slave revolt. Such sentences were never formally invoked by the Southern army, however, although Southern white soldiers would never accept blacks as legitimate foes. They considered the act of having to fight blacks to be a violation of all the rules of warfare, as well as of the sacred rights of humanity. Thus, the Emancipation Proclamation did much to help unite the white South against the blacks. Private Smith of the 51st Illinois watched black troops charge the Confederate lines at Nashville at a time when the Rebels were at the point of wavering. As the blacks entered the fight, however, the Confederates went into a "frenzy" at their approach. They fought "like demons, slaughtering the poor blacks fearfully." The Southerners, observed Smith, "gave up with a very bad grace," in being taken prisoner. Smith felt it was considered a disgrace to be captured by men who were perhaps their former property.

While Fort Pillow is usually cited as the epitome of the Confederates' virulent hatred of black troops and reaction to the Union's use of black soldiers, there are many more commonplace examples, such as the general reaction in the trenches around Petersburg as the siege took hold. A Pennsylvania regiment, for example, found it advisable when on picket in the forward trenches, to call over that "the 2nd Pa was back again." An informal truce would be maintained while the white troops were on picket; otherwise, the Confederates kept up a constant fire. A soldier of the 2nd Pennsylvania wrote his mother that "they hate a niger worse than they hate a copperhead Snake." A lieutenant of the 9th Alabama captured at Gettysburg, when he learned that prisoner exchanges which would have provided for his freedom had been suspended indefinitely because the Confederates refused to exchange black captives, replied "I hope there may never be another exchange."[71]

Prejudice and racism were by no means limited to the Southern ranks during the war. Unfortunately, the vast majority of Northerners considered blacks to be an inferior race, albeit a majority of them undoubtedly believed in the blacks' right to freedom from slavery. At the time, there still existed considerable legal disabilities in the North affecting blacks' ability to vote, to serve in the militia, to receive an adequate education, and to marry whites, among a multitude of other barriers and social taboos. "Almost all northerners held blacks in contempt as members of an inferior race and believed that any association with them degraded the white race. It was in this atmosphere that the experiment of black enlistment began." Blacks were often stereotyped as ignorant, lazy and unable to prepare for the future. These prejudices led most Union soldiers to oppose the enlistment of blacks, for they felt deeply it was "a white man's war."

Many opponents feared that any relaxation in this discrimination would open up claims to full citizenship. Charles Willis, a lieutenant of the 7th Illinois Cavalry, expressed a not uncommon feeling, that "[t]his matter of slavery is an awful sin and I'm satisfied debases the governing race, but if we have to keep these negroes in the country, I say keep them as slaves." Many felt slavery was a necessary evil to protect and discipline blacks. Colonel Charles Wainwright, who played a key role in the Federal artillery barrage which accompanied the assault on July 30, once wrote that "blacks represented the antithesis of all admirable human qualities." When the famed 54th Massachusetts under Colonel Robert Gould Shaw planned to pass through New York City on its way to the front, its chief of police telegraphed Massachusetts Governor John A. Andrew that he would not be able to protect the regiment against mob violence.[72] New York City was later the scene of one of the most infamous examples of Northern prejudice during the draft riots of 1863, when at least eleven blacks were lynched from lampposts or otherwise severely beaten, and many others were killed by white rioters over their anger and frustration with new military drafts to further prosecute the war, as well as over local labor issues. The official death toll there was 119, with over one thousand injured. Many placed the death toll much higher.[73] The *New York Times* wrote during the war that blacks were good in great disaster, "not having the moral stamina to see long the horrible affects on the human body which shell or round shot produce." Most Federal officers believed blacks were "wild and undisciplined in battle," and having dash and courage, cannot be beaten in a charge.[74] Blacks were originally preferred as storming parties or shock troops to punch holes in the Confederate lines. "Permitting them to storm the enemy works and destroy everything in their path utilized what whites perceived as the greatest fighting quality of blacks, their innate savagery, to its fullest potential." [75]

These undisguised prejudices manifested themselves in a variety of ways among the common soldiers of the Union. Blacks endured a variety of insults and hardships at the hands of their white comrades. A Massachusetts officer expressed to a newspaper correspondent that blacks should not be allowed to fight "because the Rebels hate us for making them soldiers." A private added that he looked on them "as a lower order of beings than ourselves.... The old prejudice remained. We were not willing to deal fairly. We asked the negro to help fight our battles, but we were willing to pay him only half a soldier's wages, as if we feared this simple act of justice might be construed as an acknowledgement of his social as well as civil equality." Hermon Clarke of the 117th New York typified the attitude of many Union soldiers when he wrote his brother on July 23, 1863, from Bermuda Hundred about his sergeant's capturing a "darkie" near Hanover Court House and "keeping" him. The black contraband "blacks boots, brings water, and eats the extra rations. He makes fun for the camp. Co. D sergeants are the only ones that sport a nigger!"[76]

After the battle, a prevalent impression among the Union soldiers was that the day was lost due to the poor performance of the black soldiers, whose "all ... pent-up prejudice flew." William Day of the 49th North Carolina went to the spring behind the Confederate lines after the battle to wash the powder smoke from his hands and face. There he encountered a Rhode Island soldier who indicated that he was a prisoner and asked the way to Petersburg. The soldier said he knew it was a mistake when they sent the black soldiers in to fight, as "white men fighting white men is different from white men fighting negroes." Lieutenant George Edward Barton of the 57th Massachusetts wrote his family on August 3 from the first division field hospital: "I trust the Colored troops did not win many laurels in this last Charge in fact the entire failure of the undertaking is laid upon their shoulders." Barton's opinion, while not accurate, was shared by the majority of the first division, if not the whole Army of the Potomac.

Another soldier wrote his family that "you ought to have seen the niggers run back we had to fix Baonetts to stop them. I think if they would have left them out weed a gained a victory." William L. Hyde of the 112th New York reflected in a letter to his family that "[t]his recruiting new Regiments & enlisting almost solely negro soldiers will prove in the long run very disastrous." Colonel Charles B. Wainwright, Fifth Corps chief of artillery, noted in his diary that Colonel Charles S. Russell, commanding the 28th USCT on July 30, commented after the assault that his men, after charging admirably, soon lost heart, and to a man "yelled and groaned most hideously, which tended to demoralize the others." Wainwright postulated that "[a]s both the traits are natural to the negro character, I have no doubt of his correctness." Captain Levi C. Brackett, an aide-de-camp to Orlando Willcox, wrote the general's wife on August 4: "What a lamentable sight to see the Negroes come back like a flock of black sheep. But what a grand sight it was to see our little band of white troops permit the colored troops to pass by — and then repulse the charge. I only counted four white men that returned with the blacks."

Even members of Meade's staff displayed thoughtless humor at the black soldiers' expense. Colonel Theodore Lyman spoke of a black trooper who was separated from his unit and was later found at City Point. He told of advancing to the front under "Ginral Pharo" and "[p]resently I see some of our boys a-runnin' back. 'Ho, ho,' sey I, 'run is you word, is it?' So I jes separates myself from my gun and I re-tires to dis spot." Many of the Northern newspapers, such as the *New York Times* and the *New York Herald*, were quick to reinforce the Union soldiers' view that the defeat was due to poor performance on the part of the black division. Chaplain Garland White of the 28th USCT responded to these editorials in a letter, stressing that one should "[l]eave no ground for a set of cowards at home, like Bennet and other foul-hearted buzzards, to attribute the loss that day to the arms of the colored troops. None of these troops, white or colored, are responsible for the actions of the Generals."

However, perhaps nothing could serve as a better example of the white Union soldier's racial prejudice than the fact that many actually shot and bayoneted their fellow black comrades when they broke and fled back to the Union held positions, and thought nothing of doing so. Even after the battle, there were many examples of this systemic discrimination which manifested itself in the disparate treatment afforded the black participants in the failed assault. Local Petersburg physician John Herbert Claiborne was chief of all Confederate military general hospitals during the Petersburg siege. Given the overwhelming number of wounded following the battle, Claiborne approached five Union surgeons, who were themselves prisoners, and asked if they would like to take a hand at surgery to relieve the backlog of treatment for the Union wounded. They readily assented to the request. The wounded, mostly blacks, were brought in and laid upon the grass in front of the hospital in preparation for examination and treatment. The following day, Claiborne was urgently informed by local attorney George Bolling, who lived near the hospital, that he had better look into matters at the hospital. Upon arriving at the hospital, Claiborne found 150 wounded black soldiers lying on the ground, mostly naked and with all conceivable types of wounds and mutilations, "shrieking, praying, and cursing in their agony and delirium, their wounds undressed and festering under a summer sun. My first thought was, 'Is this Christian civilization.'"

Claiborne found the five surgeons lounging in front of their quarters, doing nothing at

The Old Blandford Church at the time of the battle (Library of Congress).

all, despite very heated entreaties from the Southern surgeon in charge of treating the blacks. Claiborne, "pointing to the scene of horror," asked what this meant, and was informed by the Union surgeons they were "sick and tired, and disgusted, and that they were not in duty bound to do any work." Noting that they should have expressed that sentiment to him the day before, Claiborne sent for Lee's provost marshal to dispatch guards for the men. The Union surgeons inquired as to the implications of Claiborne's actions, and were informed that they were to be bound for Andersonville the next day. After the Union surgeons pleaded for another opportunity, Claiborne relented and by the next morning, everything was in "ship-shape order."[77] The obvious, prevalent prejudice against black soldiers in the Union army was indeed an insurmountable fact.

Meanwhile, quite apart from this discussion of racial prejudices, a disorganized mass of white and black soldiers held on for dear life in the Crater, with no further thought of advancing on their military objective, but rather merely hoping against hope for ammunition, food and water, and the scant prayer for reinforcements or rescue before it was too late.

CHAPTER 15

A Veritable "Slaughter Pen"

As the Ninth Corps struggled for its life after having been brutally forced back into the Crater, and the Tenth Corps on its right was being battered and pushed back in fierce fighting, yet another struggle was playing out between Burnside and his immediate superior — a struggle which ultimately would lead to disaster for one of them. Meade, in the catbird seat given his rank, intended to avoid any possibility of being the one to come up short in the end. After receiving reports of the inability of the Fifth and Eighteenth corps to actively become involved as ordered, Captain W.W. Sanders, Meade's aid at Burnside's headquarters, informed Meade that Griffin's movement had been checked. Meade telegraphed Burnside at 8:00 A.M. inquiring as to the current morale of his troops. He also related that General Ord had indicated that "he cannot move until you get out of the way. Can't you let him pass out on your right, and let him try what he can do?"

Then, from 8:00 A.M. until 8:45 A.M., Meade received several encouraging messages indicating some progress was being made in the efforts to take Cemetery Hill. Colonel Comstock of Grant's staff, also embedded with Burnside that day, wrote a message at 8:00 A.M. indicating that "a brigade more of our men have moved up to the crater, and then filed off to the right, along the enemy's line. They are still moving to the right." At 8:45 A.M., Captain Sanders telegraphed Meade again regarding the Federal troops' utilization of the captured gun in the undemolished portion of the fort against the Confederates. He further reported: "Have not heard anything from the attack made from the left of mine. One set of colors just sent in captured by the negroes." This positive news undoubtedly prompted Meade at 8:45 to order Warren to

> "go in with Burnside," and to take the "two-gun battery [Davidson's]. The movement on the left need not be carried further than reconnaissance to see in what force the enemy is holding his right. The cavalry are ordered to move up on your left, and to keep up connection."

By 9:00 A.M., however, hope seemed to dwindle as further setbacks by the embattled Ninth Corps were realized and reported. Burnside dispatched Meade at that time, seeking the support he believed he was to expect from his adjoining corps:

> General Meade:
>
> Many of the Ninth and Eighteenth Corps are retiring before the enemy. I think now is the time to put in the Fifth Corps promptly.
>
> A.E. BURNSIDE
Major-General

At the same time, Captain Sanders wired Meade from Burnside's headquarters that the "attack made on the right of mine has been repulsed. A great many men are coming to the rear." In response to Meade's order to advance, Warren dispatched Meade at 9:15:

> The enemy drove ... [Burnside's] troops out of the place and I think now hold it. I can find no one who knows for certainty or seems willing to admit it, but I think I saw a rebel battle-flag in it just now, and shots coming from it this way. I am, therefore, if this [be] true, no more able to take the battery now than I was this time yesterday. All our advantages are lost.

Meade later indicated that Burnside's 9:00 A.M. message "was the first information I had received that there was any collision with the enemy, or that there was any enemy present." Were this true, it would speak volumes for Meade's leadership abilities and military acumen. The very statement is rather astonishing.[1]

To the suggestions that he did not keep Meade adequately informed about events as they transpired that day, Burnside later defended himself quite ably. He also indicated his view on the frequency of dispatches, opining that he could "[r]eadily conceive General Meade's anxiety which would induce him to write frequent dispatches, but in my rule of conduct with my officers I have rather cultivated the idea that frequent dispatches, unless they are well authenticated, are not desirable, particularly dispatches with reference to the condition of the troops and calls for re-enforcements."

Burnside correctly pointed out that Captain W.W. Sanders, a member of Meade's staff, was stationed at his headquarters at Fort Morton that day. He had been the "means of communication" between the two generals on June 18, and Burnside indicated that he was pleased with his presence there that day. He claimed that he attempted to "give at all important points (I do not mean in minutia) to General Meade by telegraph and to Captain Sanders by word, all information of which I was possessed." Burnside thoroughly believed that he had supplied every answer to Meade's inquiries either in person, or by virtue of Captain Sanders, who remained present at his headquarters throughout the Federal advance that day. Sanders was near him constantly, Burnside contended, and "knows that I never failed to give an aide-de-camp, situated as he is, every possible information, heard all my conversation with my aides-de-camp, and I think [Sanders] had free access to every dispatch and report that reached me from the front or from my division commanders." Burnside indicated that Sanders also confirmed this in the presence of General Humphreys, Meade's chief of staff. Burnside was further certain that at least three written dispatches and one verbal one were sent to Meade by Sanders following the springing of the mine.[2]

Despite the foreboding nature of the dispatches arriving at his headquarters, Meade held off closing the curtain on the entire operation for some time in the forlorn hope that a victory was still within his army's grasp. This was a considerable leap of faith for the man who had been so skeptical of the enterprise at its inception and who later claimed that he was ready to abort the battle the instant it appeared the troops could not advance beyond the Crater. The impetus for the delay in such action on Meade's part appeared to be a dispatch from a signal officer of the Fifth Corps indicating that Ferrero's men had captured a brigade of Rebels with four of their colors. Meade immediately suspended any orders for withdrawal until such intelligence could be verified.[3]

While Ferrero's fourth division and Turner's men methodically made their way into the fray, Grant continued his observations at the front, alone but for his aide, Colonel Horace Porter. He personally observed the utter confusion of the attacking units as a constant flow of wounded streamed back through the ranks of those reinforcements struggling to move forward. As the sun rose higher in the July sky, the heat became insufferable:

The general wore his blue blouse and a pair of blue trousers—in fact, the uniform of a private soldier, except [for] the shoulder-straps. None of the men seemed to recognize him, and they were no respecters of persons as they shoved and crowded to the front. They little thought that the plainly dressed man who was elbowing his way past them so energetically, and whose face was covered with dust and streaked with perspiration, was the chief who had led them successfully from the Wilderness to Petersburg.[4]

Henry Pleasants, watching the charge of the black division from the Union rifle pits through the breach created by his handiwork, observed two figures completely ignoring the heavy Rebel fire sweeping the entire hillside, and was on the verge of shouting to them when he recognized the commanding general in his private's uniform and with the broad-brimmed hat and no sword, squinting anxiously and chomping on a cigar. He thought to himself, *What kind of battle is this*, with "brigadiers hiding in bombproofs and the Commanding General of the US Army sauntering nonchalantly along the front, under fire!" By 9:00 A.M., Grant's personal inspection had thoroughly convinced him that further assaults were useless. "Scarcely a word was spoken in passing over the distance crossed. Sometimes the gait was a fast walk, sometimes a dog-trot," recalled Horace Porter regarding the Grant's personal reconnaissance. Grant quickly sought out Burnside and finally found him in a small forward fieldwork overlooking the front, and as Grant emerged from outside the breastworks he at once exclaimed in utter frustration to an astonished Burnside, "There is now no chance of success. These troops must be immediately withdrawn. It is slaughter to leave them here."[5] Grant then made his way back to where his horse was waiting and proceeded on to consult with Meade.

Meade had already informed Grant that in his opinion there was no further prospect of success in the assault and that the time had now passed for the coup de main to continue. A decision on withdrawing, however, had been temporarily suspended by the inaccurate news from the signal officer that Ferrero's division had captured a Confederate brigade and four sets of colors. When Meade found that the signal officer's previous report had been a misinterpretation of unfolding events, he again broached the issue of whether the attack should be called off, as it appeared fruitless to waste any more men in a continuation of the offensive. Meade by then had fashioned an order for withdrawal, but had postponed the inevitable in hopes of a miracle. Thus, after hearing from Ord himself that the signal officer's report was completely inaccurate, and that Ferrero's men had broken and fled, Meade once again "referred the subject to the lieutenant-general and again gave him ... [his] opinion that as it was then about 9:25 it was unnecessary to make any other efforts and an unnecessary sacrifice of life," and that in his opinion the troops could be withdrawn without difficulty, as opposed to waiting and consequently having more difficulty withdrawing them at a later time.

Grant gave his assent, and the order was therefore given to withdraw all the engaged troops. Without delay, Meade sent a series of directions to his subordinate commanders calling off the attack at 9:25 A.M., the first to Warren, thereby countermanding the earlier order to take Davidson's battery, and then to Hancock, informing him that offensive operations had been suspended, and to hold his troops in place. Burnside's orders, sent at 9:30 A.M. and issued through Humphreys, were much less decisive, however. They read:

> The major-general commanding has heard that the result of your attack has been a repulse, and directs that, if in your judgment nothing further can be effected, you withdraw to your own line, taking every precaution to get the men back safely.[6]

No sooner had Meade issued these orders to Burnside leaving him with discretion to continue than word came to Grant from Lieutenant Colonel Comstock, his aide-de-camp, indicating that "I cannot see that we have advanced beyond the enemy's line in the vicinity of the mine. From here it looks as if the enemy were holding a line between that point and the crest." Warren soon thereafter reported that the Confederates "have reoccupied all the line we drove them from except a small area around the crater, which a small force of ours still holds." This was all the impetus Meade needed to firm up his resolve regarding what he really needed to be done. Therefore, at 9:45 A.M., Humphreys wired Burnside a new directive that "The major-general [commanding] directs that you withdraw to your own intrenchments." Simultaneously, Meade wrote Warren that "All offensive operations are suspended. You can resume your original position with your command."[7]

Burnside was astonished by the order, as he was far from ready to concede defeat, although thoroughly frustrated at the manner in which Meade had directed the assault. While having witnessed the repulse of Ferrero's assault, he felt strongly that the introduction of Warren's corps at this critical juncture could turn the tide. Given the report from his signal tower that the Confederates had stripped their right almost bare to reinforce the Crater, as witnessed by Mahone's recent presence in the area, Warren could theoretically have found an almost clear path forward on the left of the Crater. In fact, given the severely weakened Confederate line, an attack by Warren could well have succeeded; and this was the rationale for Burnside's request that Warren be sent in at that time. But Meade, never one to lend full support to the attack or to anything personally recommended by Burnside, had by then decided the day was lost.[8] Burnside later related his belief that with the called-for assistance:

> [w]e could hold the position which we occupied, if we could not gain more ground. In fact I was under the impression at the time that we were gaining ground in the direction of the enemy's rifle-pits, to the right and left, and I felt that if troops were put in on our left flank that then we would have been enabled to establish ourselves on the enemy's line, which, of course, would have made our position secure. However that is simply a matter of opinion, upon which the commanding general had to decide. I also felt that if we could gain no more ground we could run our lines at an angle to the crater and establish a salient upon the enemy's lines, which would be of material advantage to us in future operations, particularly in making him vacate that part of the line which is now opposite my front, and, in fact, as I had not given up all hopes of carrying the crest even, if a positive and decided effort were made by all the troops.

Burnside thus felt compelled to forcefully plead with Meade in person to retract his withdrawal order. Accompanied by Ord, he turned his horse for his field headquarters and surged into a full gallop, with Ord struggling to keep up with him, while leaving General White in charge at Fort Morton. On the way, Burnside undoubtedly had visions of déjà vu regarding his role at Antietam, when a solid push by his reinforced troops would have broken the Confederate resistance, but at the critical juncture, his requested support was withheld. Unfortunately, still smarting from Meade's earlier telegraph, which to him seemed to question his veracity,[9] and cognizant of the fact that, while having been thwarted at every turn in the proper execution of the operation, he would still be its ultimate scapegoat, Burnside did not have sufficient time to cool down before confronting his superior.

Meade and Grant were both at Burnside's Harrison Creek headquarters when Burnside and Ord arrived: "Burnside leaped from his lathered gelding and confronted Meade with words unmixed, his ample forehead ablaze with indignation.... This was one of his rare rages, and staff eyebrows climbed as he thundered at Meade over the order to withdraw. The past months of sarcasm and condescension had finally brought him to full boil." Burnside was at most times "the personification of amiability," Horace Porter remarked, but that day "the scene between them was decidedly peppery, and went far toward confirming one's belief in the wealth and flexibility of the English language as a medium of personal dispute." One of

Meade's staff referred to Burnside's language as "extremely insubordinate." Burnside argued that the assault could still succeed if it were properly continued, which included promptly bringing Warren's corps into the action. He argued that, if allowed to remain, his troops could take the crest by nightfall. General Meade remained unconvinced, however, and indicated that he, Burnside, had been fighting from 5:30 A.M. until 10:00 A.M. without success, and had, in fact, been driven out of the works he had been occupying. Meade further indicated that Burnside had not raised any reasons to show that he could still actually take the crest.[10] In an attempt to give Burnside's position fair consideration, Meade then turned to Ord and asked his thoughts on the current situation and whether the crest could be carried. Ord responded "very positively that it was entirely out of the question."[11]

Ord later amplified his answer by stating that he felt that Burnside's men, together with Turner's division, were insufficient to carry the crest in their current state. They had been repulsed, disorganized and crowded into the enemy trenches and the Crater, and "under the circumstances we could not carry it with all our troops at that point of attack." Burnside firmly disagreed. Ord later expanded upon the reasoning for his opinion:

> I supposed he meant that he could take it with the force he had, consisting of his own corps and my reserves, though he said something about it was time then for the Fifth Corps to move up. The remark was made by General Burnside with a view of persisting in the attack which he had commenced, and it had been my opinion, ever since I was near enough to see what was going on in the crater, that the sooner we withdrew our troops, when we got into such a bad position, the better, and any persistence in the attack at that point I looked upon as very improper.

Burnside was quite exercised at the time over Ord's remarks to Meade and immediately gave his own opinion:

> None of General Ord's troops were in the enemy's line, and he would have no trouble in withdrawing; that none but the troops of the Ninth Corps were in the line, and I thought that my opinion on the subject would probably be a proper one to be received; and I stated that I did not think that we had fought long enough that day; that I felt that the crest could still be carried if a decided effort were made to carry it.

Meade then referred the matter to Grant and it was soon decided that "no further attempt should be made to take the crest, but that the men should be withdrawn whenever that could be done with security."

Burnside, once outside of headquarters, verbally attacked Ord for his failure to back him up in front of Meade, indicating that Ord had 15,000 men "concentrated on one point. It is strange if you cannot do something with them." Ord responded with equal venom that he could not move his men, as he was currently being "held by the throat," seemingly unaware, in Burnside's view, that his forces were no longer blocked and that only a "single, small regiment stood in the way of his [Ord's] assault on Burnside's right."[12] Burnside then turned on General Grant's observer, Colonel Comstock, who was known to have publicly ridiculed Burnside freely in the past, and who was now concerned that some of his injudicious comments "might have made their way back to their subject." Comstock attempted to calm him, but Burnside was seething at this point and told him "to go back to Grant's camp and never return; if the lieutenant general had need of a spy at Ninth Corps headquarters, he could send someone else." Apparently, by this time, Burnside's anger and frustration were beyond his ability to control, and this fateful confrontation at Harrison's Creek went a long way toward sealing his ultimate fate.[13]

Burnside cooled down sufficiently to send the discouraging results of his meeting on to General White at Fort Morton: "I have no discretion in the matter. The order is peremptory to withdraw. It may be best to intrench where we are for the present, but we must withdraw as soon as practicable and prudent." White telegraphed back with advice that they could hold the Crater permanently by incorporating it into the Union trench system. The topography made this foolhardy, however, and when Meade refused, Burnside did not press the point. He did ask, and was quickly granted permission, to postpone his withdrawal until dark, when the Confederate cross fire might have subsided. White sent Burnside's dispatch on to the division commanders, instructing them in turn to consult with their commanders in the field as to the "proper time of evacuation."

Both Potter and Willcox read the dispatch and sent it on for endorsement to the general officers in the Crater, those being Hartranft, Griffin and Bartlett. None of Burnside's division commanders actually signed the order. Burnside sent for the commanders to meet with him at Fort Morton, as he felt it imperative to have a perfect understanding as to the method and timing of a withdrawal. Meade had provided absolutely no dispositions for assistance from the other corps in that effort. There was absolutely no chance of diversionary attacks to cover the withdrawal or to otherwise occupy the Confederates except for keeping up a fire on their entrenched lines. After discussion, it was mutually agreed that the optimum method for evacuation was to dig a trench or a series of trenches from the Federal main line to the Crater, thereby providing the troops' protection as they withdrew. Unfortunately, Burnside's order to withdraw and his request for input from the generals in the Crater did not reach the fiery cauldron until 12:30 P.M., when the dust and sun had long since emptied every canteen.[14]

With all the important decisions seemingly having been fully made, Grant and Meade saw no further reason to remain on the tactical front. Meade decided there was nothing more that could be accomplished, having determined there were enough troops on hand at the front to defend themselves against any counterattacks, and that Burnside and Ord could insure that their troops were pulled out as safely as possible. He indicated that he would, however, remain in telegraphic communication with the front, and thus he expected to be continuously informed "of anything that should occur."[15] Meade was unaware of any difficulty in the manner of removing the Ninth Corps troops and later wondered why they had not been so removed, presuming that "our men were [actually] in the crater...." At about the same time, Grant also departed to his City Point headquarters, and, in essence, had washed his hands of the whole affair.

Mahone's hold on the recaptured Confederate works was a tenuous one, however, given the limited number of Confederate troops engaged. Additionally, his assault had failed to retake the Crater itself and the undemolished redoubt to the left of the pit. To ensure that his foothold would remain permanent, Mahone definitely had to bring more troops into action, and very soon. Thus, he called upon Lieutenant Colonel Matthew R. Hall, then in command of Wright's Georgia Brigade, to move Willcox's troops out of the trenches south of the Crater, in addition to retaking the pit itself. By this time, Hall's men had all arrived in the ravine, and its commanders had been briefed by Mahone himself. Thus, it fell upon the Georgians, in Mahone's words, to "clean up the job and to restore the full integrity of our line and to remove absolutely the peril to which Gen'l Lee's Army had been fearfully exposed by the success of the mine."

At 10:00 A.M., an hour after the Virginia Brigade had charged, Hall's Georgians were ordered forward from the same ravine from which their Virginia comrades had recently begun their assault. Their mission was to retake the fifty yards of captured Confederate works to the right of the Virginia Brigade and south of the Crater.[16]

Wright's brigade that day was made up of the 3rd Georgia under Lieutenant Colonel Claiborne Snead, the 22nd Georgia under Colonel George H. Jones, the 48th Georgia under Lieutenant Colonel Reuben W. Carswell and the 64th Georgia under Colonel John W. Evans.[17] Also, part of the brigade at the time was the 10th Georgia Battalion and the 2nd Georgia Battalion, although these units did not move out with Mahone on his march that morning, as the 10th Georgia Battalion was engaged on picket duty in the Confederate trenches back at their front lines. The brigade was led that morning by Lieutenant Colonel Matthew R. Hall from Augusta.[18] The unit had been positioned over two miles to the right of the Crater at the time of the explosion, and followed the Virginia Brigade on its journey to the front. Colonel Hall had until recently been the temporary commander of the 48th Georgia, which had captured the colors of the 87th Pennsylvania on June 22, 1864.

The 3rd Georgia, otherwise known as the "old Third" in Anderson's Division, was one of the historic old regiments in Georgia, by then needing "no laudation, as its gallant deeds are entwined around the hearts of its grateful people." It was formed early in 1861 and marched out of Augusta on May 1, 1861, with Wright as its colonel (who was later to take command of the Georgia Brigade). The regiment fought in all the major battles in Virginia, Maryland and Pennsylvania. The 48th Georgia was also a veteran regiment, having been organized in March of 1862 in Effingham, and it also participated in all the major battles of the Army of Northern Virginia, along with the 3rd Georgia. The 22nd Georgia, commanded by Colonel George H. Jones, was likewise a veteran unit, having been mustered in on September 1861 at Big Shanty, and also participated in the major battles of the Army of Northern Virginia. The 64th Georgia was organized in the spring of 1863 and fought in Florida, including the battle of Olustee in February 1864. It was then transferred to Petersburg in May, where it was originally a part of Wise's Brigade, and then Johnson's old Tennessee Brigade, before being inherited by Mahone.[19] Being the youngest regiment in the brigade, and having been spared much of the heavy fighting to date that its fellow units had endured, it had an effective strength of 388 men that morning, far greater than the others. The 48th Georgia had previously gone in on the right of Mahone's brigade with the Virginians in their charge. "The bullets whistled by us here faster than any man in the brigade ever heard before, and it was certainly one of the most sanguinary fights on record." The regiment occupied the works to the right of Mahone's immediate right, and kept up a continuous fire on the enemy until the whole line was re-established. In its front the "dead lay thicker than ... [had ever] been seen on any battle-field of this war."[20]

In the respite between the attack of the Virginia Brigade and that of the Georgia Brigade, the Federal troops in and around the Crater were about to undergo yet another serious test. By this point, they had largely cleared out from the trenches everywhere, unbeknownst to Mahone. The entire Ninth Corps was by now trapped either in the Crater itself or in the undemolished portion of the redoubt where Hartranft, who was in the process of marshalling both his and Humphrey's brigades, had established himself. Several thousand Federal soldiers were now trapped in a front less than a hundred yards wide and in a very poor position to defend themselves. Whatever scant organization they had experienced was by then altogether makeshift. To most of those in the Crater and its environs, the charge of the Virginia Brigade, followed by the massing of the Georgians, spelt the beginning of the end, regardless of Burnside's positive protestations back at headquarters.

Mahone hurried back to the Georgia Brigade from the line recently retaken by the Virginians[21] and explained the situation and how its men must make a move to retake that part of the Confederate works south of the Crater, on the right of the Virginia Brigade,[22] and "tidy things up." When the charge was to be executed, the Virginians were instructed to keep down and to fire rapidly in their front to cover the new assault. Every man had been supplied with several guns— his own and others found lying in the trenches in huge quantities. Shortly after 10:00 A.M., the Georgians formed, the command to forward was quietly given, and the troops started in "as gallantly as any men could." The command was promptly obeyed and the 64th Georgia under the command of Captain Thomas J. Pritchett immediately acted with great gallantry in the lead, as "emergency demanded the most desperate remedies, and most faithfully did the Sixty-fourth administer them." The brigade came out of the protection of the swale, and immediately found itself met with a steady stream of lead and iron.

General Hartranft had employed every man who could fight in line in the undemolished portion of the fort, and Sergeant Wesley Stanley of the 14th New York Heavy Artillery oversaw the loading of both captured guns with captured Confederate canister. In the Crater itself, Potter's men dug footholds along the rim to afford a secure firing position. Howard Aston recalled the Georgians' charge from his position in the center of the Crater. As the force approached close to the rim to the left of its center, he "fired to the right oblique into the Georgians." A Federal artillery officer who also observed the charge of the Georgia Brigade remarked that "[t]he canister, pieces of shell and other missles [sic] striking the slope (over which this charge was made) produced an effect upon it similar to the heavy drops of rain in a thunder shower falling upon a placid sheet of water." Their flank was thus exposed to this intense defensive fire, causing devastating losses among the advancing Georgians. Sergeant Stanley unloaded bucket after bucket of canister, "doing yeoman service on this last day of his life." Major Etheredge observed from his position on the Confederate line that "by the time the enemy had filled the breastworks as full of men as they could stand together, and as soon as the Georgians got near enough the enemy opened fire, and they fell like autumn leaves."

Under this terrific and deadly fire, wrought by the "heroic hundred riflemen who decorated the lip of the Crater," the Georgians began to swerve too far to the left, away from the intended target. Gordon McCabe observed that "so closely was every inch of the ground searched by artillery, so biting was the fire of musketry, that, obliquing to their left, they sought cover behind the cavalier-trench won by the Virginia brigade — many officers and men testifying by their blood how gallantly the venture had been essayed." Among those killed was Colonel John W. Evans of the 64th Georgia, although he was not in actual command that day. Seeing the line beginning to stagger under the withering fire which poured into the ranks of the regiment, Evans "sprang upon the breastworks, and waving his hat over his head shouted, in tones which rang distinctly over the tumult of battle: 'Remember, boys, you are Georgians,' and at that moment received the shot through his generous, noble heart, which almost instantly terminated the mortal existence of as gallant and amiable a man as ever lived or died." Hall's men were required to take cover in the traverses and bombproofs that had impeded their forward progress. Eventually, they were also driven out of these shelters, taking cover partially behind the ranks of the Virginia Brigade. A small portion of the Georgians rushed into Hartranft's fort with their hands in the air. A few others retreated back to the edge of the swale.[23] In such manner ended the first effort of the Georgians to retake the Crater.

As Mahone's first countercharge had gained momentum, the Federal troops were rapidly forced out of the forward trenches, and, while giving ground very grudgingly in many cases, they were soon forced to seek refuge in the Crater, which on first impression appeared like a safe, protected enclave. Little did they know what they were about to experience over the next several hours, as Mahone pressed up to the pit's very rim. With Davidson's Battery and Mahone's sharpshooters operating at full potential, those in the bloody pit soon found they were virtual prisoners there, as it was almost certain death to attempt a retreat back to the Federal lines.

General Hartranft, positioned in the undestroyed portion of the redoubt, and Generals

Bartlett and Griffin, in the Crater itself, held the remaining ground with fragments of four broken divisions. While Meade had suspended the assault and ordered the evacuation of the Crater and its environs by 9:30 A.M., the intense Confederate cross fire, combined with Mahone's storm of lead from the front and augmented by Haskell's efficient mortars, kept all but the really panic-stricken from attempting to retreat to the Federal lines. The Union forces in the Crater were quickly running out of ammunition after five hours of continuous fighting, and many began to gather cartridges from the dead, while others threw stones, bottles and other debris.

The two sides were so near in some places that many were cut by broken glass, bruised by rocks and stabbed by bayonets. Close-range fighting was virulent and unmerciful, and blood ran down in streams in the hard, brown clay, forming pools in which the men slipped. In many places, the Crater was a scene of unparalleled horror. In some areas, the panic-stricken soldiers were so tightly packed that they could not move or even raise their arms to defend themselves. Sergeant George Wakefield of the 9th New Hampshire recalled running the gauntlet to retrieve fresh supplies of cartridges: "My clothes were literally covered with bloody debris, and called forth many comments from the troops in the rear, but I quickly secured my cartridges and returned to the crater."

In the Crater, the first counterattack by the Virginians had finally been beaten back. The respite that followed gave Griffin's men time to consider flight, and they decided first to get into the Crater for protection and to assess their next move. Unfortunately, they did not realize how accurate Haskell's mortars were or how little coverage the pit actually afforded them. All seven of Griffin's regimental commanders had been killed, wounded or captured by this time, and few of their apparent successors were aware of their elevation, adding immensely to the confusion. Despite vastly inferior numbers, Mahone's men north and south of the Crater were in good order, "thus proving far more powerful despite their vastly inferior numbers," and the musketry and canister kept the Federals pinned on three sides. The Confederates threw up a barricade following the 20th Michigan's withdrawal into the Crater in order to prevent any further Yankee resurgence. The fort was now completely sealed off and the final work had begun. When the Georgians charged, Hartranft was able to blunt their charge before they could do serious damage to the Federals' confined position. "Sheets of blood were washing down the clay sides of the pit, pooling in ghostly puddles around the mounting stack of bodies." Only a few men at a time could gain footholds to fire out of the Crater with considerable effort before sliding down to reload.[24] However, the ultimate result was assured once Meade determined that a withdrawal was necessary.

By 11:00 A.M., the 51st Pennsylvania had taken back its old position in the Federal works. General Willcox, who had stockpiled a number of cases of cartridges within 200 yards of his front lines, detailed the 51st to transport this ammunition to the men in the beleaguered pit. The regiment's men divided into teams of four and piled as many cartridges as possible into the center of a shelter half. Picking up the shelter half by its corners, they raced through the fusillade of lead and steel which was no-man's-land. In this fashion, some 10,000 rounds of ammunition were ultimately delivered to Hartranft, although at a cost of a number of the brave men of the 51st. Some of these men were killed by Haskell's exploding mortar shells fully loaded with lead balls the size of Harpers Ferry musket shells, which exploded one hundred yards from the earth, throwing out the balls in all directions. Colonel William J. Bolton, the unit's commander, was hit in the face by one such blast and carried off the field dead.

The regiment's men clung to the hope that the tide of battle would still turn back in their favor. They could not believe that they had been abandoned in the pit, "in this mouth of an infernal Golgotha, to continue such a hopeless struggle alone," and they did not give up hope, but as they viewed a large enemy force now massing, they were left to wonder: "[c]ould it be that 50,000 men would remain idle to their brutal slaughter?" For an hour after they entered the Crater, they believed that one gallant and determined assault from the main line would have carried the day, as the Rebel force was still weak in comparison, and thus they prayed for such a movement.[25]

At 11:00 A.M., Mahone ordered the Georgians to have another go at retaking the Crater as well as the undemolished fort to its south manned by Hartranft's improvised command. The Georgians' second assault met with no more success than its first, however, and they were again repulsed, having been met by "such a withering fire of shell and shot that they again recoiled with heavy loss." In the two charges, the 48th Georgia had forty-eight men killed and wounded. Its battle flag was pierced by 103 bullets, and its staff was cut in two on three separate occasions in the action. The 64th Georgia lost nine officers killed on the field, and seventy-nine men killed or wounded, most of them mortally.[26] While Mahone had not accomplished all that he had set out to, he could now realize that the Confederates were "masters of the situation." Utilizing two of his brigades, Mahone had immobilized three Federal corps. He was still eager to remove any doubt, however, before the Federals could heavily reinforce their troops.

The Ninth Corps was cowering leaderless in and around the Crater, Ord's men were driven back to the main Federal lines, and on the left, Warren's corps had never been able to mount an attack, largely due to the impression that Mahone was still in its front. The two brigades presented "an enfilading fire into the crater, and they made it very lively for us," Sergeant Howard Aston of the 13th Ohio Cavalry indicated. Added to this favorable situation, Mahone also had one more brigade yet to throw at the entrapped Yankees. Additionally, Wise's Brigade on the south side had pushed right up to the very rim of the Crater. Now the enemies were huddled on either side of the same embankment, and took to spearing each other by lofting abandoned fixed bayonets over the crest. Colonel McMasters later referred to this period as the "laziest fight I ever saw; we longed for hand grenades." The men were so close that they threw ignited artillery shells at the Federals packed in a dense mass in the Crater. Major Haskell, of course, kept up his incessant lobbing of mortar shells into the pit with deadly accuracy.[27]

The Federal assaulting forces had been cleared from the trenches everywhere. They were in a very poor position to defend themselves and suffered from a total lack of organization. To the left of the Crater, Hartranft had assumed the role as acting division commander. Sergeant Wesley Stanley of the 14th New York Heavy Artillery served as his chief of artillery, albeit with a total force of only two Confederate Napoleons, and was instrumental in fending off the two charges of the Georgia Brigade. In the Crater itself, General Simon Griffin had assumed the role of de facto commander of all other scattered commands in the Crater. William Bartlett, the only other general officer, was by this time totally incapacitated, his artificial cork leg having been totally destroyed as a result of Haskell's exploding mortar shells. He was thus unable to move and had to sit or lie immobile on the pit's floor among the dead and dying, "nonchalantly chomping a cigar, unable to aid them."

Hartranft had called for the 20th Michigan to come back into the undemolished fort to assist in stemming the current Federal rout caused by Mahone's initial counterassault. In obedience to this order, the regiment passed along the main trench and into the left of the fort. Before moving north, Sergeant Urie had experienced trouble holding the 20th Michigan's banner aloft, as "[i]t was continually struck by enemy slugs." The 20th, being Willcox's left-most regiment, was the last Union force in the works south of the Crater to move into the redoubt. As they moved to the right pursuant to Hartranft's orders, they found their fellow Michiganders, the 1st Michigan Sharpshooters, as well as the 2nd Michigan, already in the remaining ramparts where they had also just recently entered. The Crater was now solidly packed with a disorganized mob of men "who were as much concerned with avoiding being trampled by their own comrades as they were with what the enemy was doing." Here the 20th assisted in stemming the Federal stampede and in repulsing a number of Confederate assaults. It remained there until 2:00 P.M. that day. The Crater itself had by then become "a veritable 'slaughter pen,'" packed as it was with the disorganized portions of four separate divisions.[28]

At around 10:30 A.M., in between the Georgians' two charges, Major General Johnson finally made an appearance in the ravine where Mahone's troops had formed and sent for him. From 4:44 A.M. until well after 10:00 A.M., Johnson had never crossed the Jerusalem Plank Road, leaving the fighting entirely to his brigadiers. Earlier, he had not even thought it important to alert Lee of the threat posed by the initial Federal assault. Consequently, it was 6:00 A.M. before Lee was informed of the danger.

Bushrod Rust Johnson, born in Ohio to an abolitionist Quaker family, graduated from West Point in 1841, in the same class with Generals Sherman, Thomas and Ewell. He served in various frontier posts prior to the Mexican War, where he fought at Palo Alto, Resaca de la Palma and Monterrey. During the war, however, he was forced to resign due to his participation in an alleged profiteering scheme. Thereafter, Johnson followed a career in education, ultimately becoming superintendent of the Military College of Nashville in 1855. Despite being strongly antislavery, he decided to remain with his adopted state of Tennessee when war came. Perhaps the lingering embarrassment of his forced resignation from the U.S. army also had something to do with that decision. Johnson was soon was involved with the early planning of defensive operations in Tennessee.

Placed in command of Fort Donelson on the Cumberland and promoted to brigadier, Johnson was able to escape when the fort ultimately fell to Grant's forces. He then commanded a brigade at Perryville and Murfreesboro, as well as the division at Chickamauga that split Rosecrans' force, thus insuring a Southern victory. Johnson was then attached to I Corps in the Army of Northern Virginia under General James Longstreet, ultimately moving back to Virginia with him. In May of 1864, he was promoted to major general. As such, he was one of the few generals of the Confederacy to serve in both major armies, that being the Army of the Tennessee and the Army of Northern Virginia. Johnson was not well respected by the troops he commanded at Petersburg, however, which included Elliott's South Carolinians, Gracie's Alabamians and Wise's Virginians. John Sergeant Wise referred to his remaining in his headquarters as the Rebel forces desperately attempted to hold on after the explosion of the mine as "vegetating, without any friendly intercourse with his command or communicating with it save through official channels." He was seldom, if ever, seen in the trenches and was barely known on sight by the men. When Lee reached his headquarters that fateful day, Johnson was totally ignorant of the details regarding the disaster, or of any of the dispositions to repair it, regardless of the fact that it was his own division which had been directly impacted.

Regardless of Johnson's lack of competence or courage, Mahone immediately worked out a plan with him to retake the remainder of the Confederate line still occupied by the Federals. It was agreed that Johnson's troops south of the Crater would drive at the left of the Union position occupying the remaining fifty feet between them and the traverse. Additionally, Colquitt's brigade would lay down a thick cross fire behind them. Mahone would then send in the Alabama Brigade against the Crater from the southwest. From this angle of attack, the last of Mahone's brigades on the scene could avoid the traverses which had proved so difficult to negotiate in the previous charges. Additionally, the flanking fire of Goode's (Wise's) Brigade would likewise hinder Sergeant Stanley's gun crews in the undamaged portion of the fort, whose captured Napoleons had been raining canister on the prior assaults. This coverage would greatly enhance the chances of success for the Alabamians.

Simultaneously, the Virginia Brigade, as well as McAfee's Brigade, were to lay down a galling fire to discourage any retreat from the Crater, thereby enhancing the chances of not only retaking the original Confederate lines, but also capturing most of Burnside's men still languishing in the Crater. The time for the next coordinated, final assault was set for 2:00 P.M.,[29] by which time the arrival of the Alabama Brigade could be insured. While these plans awaited fruition, the Confederates continued to cover no-man's-land with a heavy rifle fire, in order to prevent the Federals from leaving their self-imposed prison. Additionally, Haskell's mortars advanced ever closer, raining the Crater with accurate mayhem from their continually exploding shells of destruction. This effect was enhanced even further by the Confederate artillery posted along the Jerusalem Plank Road and Wright's and Davidson's batteries from the flanks.[30]

MG Bushrod R. Johnson (USAMHI).

The 45th Pennsylvania sent a note wrapped in a stone requesting picks and shovels and threw it toward the undestroyed fort, as it was impossible for them to actually reach it. They set to work with bayonets for picks and tin cups for shovels and in short order had constructed an earthen barricade across a traverse opening into the Crater, thus partially protecting themselves in the event of another charge. The soil at that location consisted of "a clayish substance and very hard," according to Captain R.G. Richards, "which we dug out of the side of the traverse." The men worked hard and "were well nigh exhausted by the continual exertions under the heat of the burning sun, and almost famished from thirst." Strong men wept, and yet stood determined, Spartan-like, at the post of duty.

Across the traverse at the junction of a branch deviating to the right, the bodies of fifteen to twenty Federals were literally piled up in a heap directly in line with the branch traverse to their left filled with Rebel troops. Here the men had faltered as they attempted to advance over the parapet of the demolished fort. A few of the Union troops attempted to climb to the edge and organize a defense, but the odds were heavily against them. The walls were so steep that it was impossible to climb unless the men dug in with their heels and inched their way backwards, which many did.

General Bartlett did everything in his power to rally the men, but the effort unfortunately proved to be impossible, as they were worn out, famished and thirsty. White and black fought bravely together — but with no division commanders within eighty yards of the captured works, no brigade commanders there outside of the Crater and no formation on any kind to resist the charge, it was in all vain. In spite of these travails, however, "the Union mass in the Crater held on ... [despite] the effort to push them out of their manmade hole." During this time, they seemed to be without anyone managing them, "and finally they fell back to the rear out of the way of the volley of canister and musketry that was plowing through the ranks." It was practically every man for himself. "The enemy was sweeping the ground over which ... [they] must pass to escape, with a terrible fire on both artillery and musketry. In the crater, which was one hundred feet or more in diameter, was the most sheltered place to be found." There was no means of getting food or water to the huddled masses in and about the Crater and they were beginning to suffer after many hours of fighting. Burnside had determined that it was probably best to leave the men in the Crater until nightfall. This assessment proved to be ill-conceived, however. By the time Burnside finally did call for a daylight retreat, the Crater was a living hell.[31]

Haskell's mortar battery, now almost up to the edge of the Crater itself, was hurling its deadly payload down on the next to helpless Federals inside every few moments. The Crater and the space separating it from the Federal lines became the focus upon which the ever-increasing Confederate fire was concentrated. The Confederate field artillery was intensified until many believed it became as terrible as any endured in the whole campaign, at least by those who experienced it. At the same time, the Federal artillery had subsided to a trickle. Captain Lyman Jackman of the 6th New Hampshire observed that the Confederate bombs continued to fall, "exploding, and tearing the men to pieces in a most horrible manner." The Federals quickly learned to watch for the deadly payloads upon hearing the hollow thud of the mortars just beyond the pit. A beleaguered Jackman explained how they gained knowledge in "dodging bombs" by learning through experience to note the detonation of mortars trained upon them, and then quickly looking "into the sky directly over our heads. Presently we would discover a small black spot at the instant the bomb reached its height, and keeping our eyes on it, we could follow it in its descent, discover its direction, and guess, within a few feet, where it would strike."

Usually, a man could dodge just in time, but, still, some were hit, in spite of "dodging," because of their inaccurate calculations, while the wounded or those not watching were often torn to pieces in a most horrible manner. Some mortar shells would shriek overhead; others would bury themselves in the ground and burst, "carrying with them the body of a man blown to pieces. I know that I saw arms and legs twenty feet in air," explained Sergeant Aston of the 13th Ohio Cavalry. Other shells would burst overhead, showering men with fragments. At other times, a shell "would come crashing down among us," Aston explained, and "there would be a crash, a cloud of smoke and dust and the flesh and blood of some comrade would splatter over those nearby. Shell, grape and musket balls swept the crest and the field between the crater and our breastworks, so that three out of every four who tried to run the gauntlet to our lines were struck down." Dismembered bodies, legs, arms, and heads "strewed the ground in every direction and this horrible butchery explains why the men's clothes were covered with blood and fragments of human flesh and brains to a degree never seen in any other battle of the war."

Private Ethan Morehead of the 100th Pennsylvania, then trapped in the Crater, later wrote home that his lieutenant, Richard Craven, had been "blown all to pieces" in this manner. Scores of the dead and wounded could not even fall to the ground, "and their blood, brains, and bone fragments splattered the living men near them." Those slain who eventually did fall to the ground were often stomped beyond recognition by the shoes and boots of their terrorized comrades, and sometimes even the injured were trampled to death. The incessant roar could not quite overpower the screaming of the men who were trapped in this horrid pit. By this point, the Confederates outside the Crater were also running low on ammunition, thus they again threw fixed bayonets like spears, harpooning many Yankees in the pit, and still others continued to throw bottles and rocks.[32]

"It was one seething cauldron of struggling, dying men," explained Lieutenant John

Anderson of the 57th Massachusetts. He could not believe that they had "been entirely abandoned in this dark pit, in the mouth of an infernal Golgotha, to continue such a hopeless struggle alone." Thousands of men were trapped with no water or ammunition: "Soldiers extended their tongues to dampen their parched lips until they seemed to hang from their mouths like those of thirsty dogs, and yet they were kept waiting in this almost boiling cauldron, suffering with thirst and worn out with their all-night preparations and their fearful morning's work." What just hours before had given so much promise of success "was fast sinking behind ... a black cloud of horrible disaster."

There were no means of getting food or water to the men to ease their suffering. All had gone in without equipment, save their weapons and canteens, long since drained dry. The sun and the intense heat caused waves of moisture produced by the exhalation from this mass which rose above the Crater in perceptible, horizontal layers.[33] The men appeared to be completely whipped, and the dead and dying were soon stacked like cordwood — eight deep in some places. Many tied rags to their bayonets to fan themselves and beat away flies which gathered at the blood feast. "There was no order; confusion reigned supreme." The intense rays of the sun "converged like burning glass into this airless hole." General Potter himself later reported that "[m]ost of the men were so exhausted that it was physically impossible to get any work out of them, and their suffering from thirst was very great, it being impossible to get any water at all." By noon, the Crater was a veritable slaughter pen packed with the disorganized remnants of four full divisions.

The sun continued to blaze down from a cloudless sky and the heat was intense. "The cries of the wounded were heart-rending. Officers and men on both sides stopped their ears, and turned away heartsick at the sight." "It was an exhibition of the horrible features of war which, once seen, is forever remembered." Men were fainting from the heat. Sergeant Aston, in speaking of this unbearable heat, indicated that his tongue was swollen and his lips cracked from a combination of the heat and the powder they were exposed to from biting the cartridges. His gun got so hot that he was forced to stop firing and, once, it went off prematurely due to its heat just as he was loading it. The discharge burnt off his eyebrows and lashes. Lieutenant Bowley reported that the men in his vicinity of the pit "were dropping thick and fast," most of them shot through the head. Every man that was shot rolled down the steep sides to the bottom, and in places they were piled up three and four deep. The cries of the wounded, pressed down under the dead, were piteous in the extreme.[34]

Despite these extremely onerous conditions, the Union mass in the Crater held on. The fighting became a fury of smoke and deafening noise from the rifle discharges and artillery shells, some hurled by hand. Lieutenant Anderson of the 57th Massachusetts observed that in places the Confederate battle flags were within seven feet of his regimental banner. He reported that during Mahone's charges, "several times the rebs charged right up to the bank, and some of them jumped over among our men, and went at it hand to hand." Men fell every second, almost all shot in the head, and slid down the wall of the Crater. Major George Randall, acting aide to General Ledlie,[35] had to physically force some men up to the edge of the redoubt. "Some would not fight & could not be drove to take a part in the action," Randall bitterly wrote afterward of the battle. Others tried to escape, but had to crawl over the lip of the Crater in full view of the Confederates to do so, which proved almost suicidal.

The blacks trapped in the Crater kept up a heavy fire, and aided greatly in repelling Mahone's subsequent charges. R.G. Richards of the 45th Pennsylvania saw a black soldier stand on a human pile of bodies and fire his musket; then while he was hurriedly reloading, he was shot in the face. Still loading, he was shot in the back of the head, and yet continued loading until a third shot laid him prostrate on the pile, all in the space of a few seconds. Only a few men, no more than one hundred at one time, could cling with toeholds to the steep wall of the Crater at the top of their bastion. The men clung from the elbows and toes and delivered their fire. To reload the muzzle-loaded arms, they had to turn away from the wall and place their backs against it, thus exposing themselves.[36]

The 1st Michigan Sharpshooters, along with the others in the Crater, kept up a slow, deliberate fire on the Confederate foe, while conserving their ammunition, by then in very short supply. While many soldiers balked at going up to the Crater's rim, the American Indians of the regiment showed great coolness in taking these precarious positions. "They would fire at a Johnny & than drop down. Would then peek over the works and try to see the effect of their shot," commented a Federal comrade. A number of these Native Americans who were shot at the edge of the Crater lay dying at the bottom of the pit. These Michiganders, consisting mainly of Chippewas (Ojibwa), had been joined by some Senecas of the 14th New York Heavy Artillery, and some others from the 37th Wisconsin Volunteer Infantry, in the defense of the Crater.[37] From their exposed positions, they were considered "sitting ducks" for the regrouped Rebels. With the Indians virtually surrounded late in the day, and with little ammunition, Freeman Bowley of the 30th USCT later described their valor. As conditions continued to deteriorate, some of the mortally wounded Indians drew their blouses over their faces, and "chanted a death song and died four of them in one group" a long way from "the cool air and giant whispering pines of Michigan's north country." Their brave deaths, according to historian Frank Woodford, inspired many others to safety that day. John Claiborne, the Confederate surgeon who had the unfortunate experience with the Union surgeon-prisoners at the field hospital, also encountered some of these wounded Indians in his hospital the very next morning.[38]

The Confederate artillery and musketry had located an excellent target at a point where a traverse on the north side opened into the Crater, the other end of which was then filled with Rebels up to within twenty yards of the Crater itself. Through this opening, they were able to rain devastation across the entire mass of Union troops in the Crater. This new threat caused immense panic, with the rather helpless Yankees milling about until General Bartlett ordered the black soldiers to construct a breastwork across the opening. The blacks who were physically located near the opening built a barricade of lumps of clay and other debris in the absence of lumber and proper excavating implements. They made very slow progress, however, while canister continued to pour in on the beleaguered soldiers. Someone finally called out, "Put in the dead men," and a large number of the dead, white and black, Union and Confederate, were piled into the trench. This made a partial shelter, concluded Lieutenant Bowley, which temporarily halted the Confederate advance in that sector. Sergeant Aston of the 13th Ohio observed two Federal flags flying, with their staffs stuck in the earth on the crest of the Crater near the traverse. He counted twenty-one blacks shot within a one hour period at that position: "They would crawl up under the flags and barely get their heads above the crest when they would come tumbling back and roll down among the heaps of dead and wounded below."[39]

Sergeant Aston recalled seeing a tall, handsome, light-haired young man standing close to him as the shells continued to rain in amid the devastation; the man was very deliberate in his shooting, in addition to being very accurate. Of course, by this point the firing was at point blank range, with the Confederates heavily concentrated about their beloved flags. Another light-haired boy less than eighteen years of age also stood close to Aston for over an hour. Whenever this boy fired his weapon, the barrel was positioned directly over Aston's shoulder. Aston related that "I had just fired, when I saw his barrel close to my head, and at the same instant I felt the wind of a bullet and the burning of my ear, heard a dull thud, and the poor boy fell with his head against my feet, his blood gushing over them from a death wound in his forehead." No one seemed to know the youth, as the troops were by then so intermingled, so "I pulled his cap over his face, and turned my attention to the enemy." Another lad of seventeen, Corporal George Wakefield of the 9th New Hampshire, who, despite his young age was already a veteran of two years, described a scene around him of the multitude of "dismembered bodies, and the stray arms, legs, and heads of his comrades, a sight that could and did unnerve many a soldier older than [he]." Young Wakefield had survived three wounds up to that point. Blood was everywhere, trickling down the sides of the crater in streamlets, and in many places there were ponds of it as large as an ordinary wash basin. He managed to survive the Crater fight, and returned unscathed "remarking only on the solid layer of blood, flesh, and brains that covered his uniform."[40]

Even after the second repulse of the Georgians, the trapped Federals began to view their predicament as hopeless. Many of the officers invited the men to "look out for yourselves, and [to] get back to your lines if you can." A member of the 9th New Hampshire recalled that this admonition signified that they were free to leave "whenever we felt like running the gauntlet, which we could see was a terrible one." However, many of the brave defenders, trapped in this earthen Alamo, still responded, "We'll whip 'em yet," and went on dodging mortar shells and scrounging for cartridges among their dead companions. Some of their bravery may have been attributed to the trail of death behind them which awaited any attempt to escape that fearful pit. A Confederate officer speculated that the men "remained in the Crater more from fear of running the gauntlet to their own lines than from any hope of holding their position." Any man who attempted to leave the Crater or its environs was quickly hit by the canister from the Confederate battery on Baxter road and the sharpshooters in Mahone's lines. Occasionally men would run this fearful gauntlet, lurching up from the wreckage of four full divisions "into that solid level sheet of lead and iron, sprinting toward the Union trenches without so much as a backward glance. Something like half of them made it,"[41] and "a lot of them were winged on the way." Troops swarmed out of the pit in squads to escape the horror, losing fearfully on the way back: "Some, running a few yards, dropped themselves to the ground, taking advantage of every hillock and furrow that the surface afforded; then rolling their bodies over the ground to another place of shelter, or making a short run, in this way succeeded in running the fearful gauntlet."[42]

Rarely did anyone in the Crater encounter anyone they actually knew, so thoroughly confused were the units by then. Lieutenant John Sampson of the 9th New Hampshire, who had earlier given first aid to the injured Sergeant Lathe of his unit, paced in the rear of the pit alone, apparently having encountered none of his regiment save Lathe, whom he had already sent to the rear. Around noon, he finally encountered his first sergeant, Franklin Burnham. Sampson doubted there was much hope to the escape attempt, but still gave Burnham, who had a reputation for leading a charmed life, the opportunity to save himself if he could. Burnham climbed up on the Crater's rear rim near a clay boulder which was the size of a house, where he intended to hide. However, he found that he was immediately in the Confederate sharpshooters' sights, necessitating a quick decision to run for it. He successfully made it to the Federal lines with dust thrown up from the bullets acting as a screen. Witnessing Burnham's successful flight, Sampson "sheathed his sword, gathered up the trailing scabbard, and bolted out of the crater. A few paces into the open he was struck by a couple of pieces of shot and fell, stone dead."

Upon entering the pit, Sergeant Newell Dutton, who had bravely carried his 9th New Hampshire colors into the Crater with him, soon encountered Lieutenant Isaac Leonard Harlow of Company H, who had himself saved the regiment's stand of National colors. The two managed to negotiate the confusion in the pit back to its edge, and they lay there for some time behind a large clump of earth and debris which afforded some protection. After a serious debate on what to do next, the pair decided to make a run for it, and waited until they "saw what looked to be a favorable opportunity, and then started, in company with several others." The two reached the Federal lines safely, behind a cloud of dust created by the broadsides from the Confederate batteries, although just as Sergeant Dutton passed over his breastworks a bullet struck the flag, passing through its tassel.

At 12:30 P.M., General Bartlett himself deemed further resistance useless and simply murder. He gave instructions to those who wished to take the risk of getting back to the main Federal lines. Bartlett reasoned that he, given his incapacitated condition, would undoubtedly be forced to surrender. Lieutenant John Anderson, although by that time disabled with a shattered arm, took the risk along with others of the 57th Massachusetts and successfully ran the gauntlet: "The ground was being ploughed up with shot and shell while a perfect tornado of musket balls swept across with deadly effect. It was passing under a cloud of smoke and 'pillar of fire,' the ground was strewn with the dead and dying over which we had to leap. Others were attempting to make their way out, and men were falling at every step."[43]

As the Federals trapped in the Crater struggled for their lives against their Confederate foes, they were also losing a second battle due to the excessive heat that day. The temperature was over one hundred degrees, and the men had gone into the battle with only their arms and canteens, which had long been drained dry. The men were exposed to the effects of a broiling sun without food or drink, so that very soon "many were completely overcome and used up," according to Colonel Cutcheon of the 20th Michigan. The cries of the wounded were heartrending. They would call out "Water!" and then shriek it out again. "The sun gave out his fiercest rays, and flesh could not be allowed to remain uncovered" without serious consequences. General Griffin also remarked that the "day was excessively hot, and while we lay there in the burning sand awaiting the action asked for, it was sickening to see the suffering of the wounded and the destruction caused by the enemy's incessant fire."

In this tragic setting, a soldier covered in dirt and gore approached Griffin and asked permission to go for water. There was a cool, clean spring directly behind the 9th New Hampshire's old campsite behind the forward lines. While Griffin reasoned that any man who was fortunate enough to survive the deadly dash across the perilous field to their rear would never willingly come back into that hell hole by doubling his risk and exposure in the process, he was still "willing to let the man run for his life if he dared." He thus told him to go, and then, almost as an afterthought, ordered the soldier to take as many canteens as he could carry, not really expecting to ever see him again. The soldier departed with a dozen canteens bouncing and rattling at his side. Subsequently, a number of other exhausted soldiers also sought to go for water in order to alleviate the suffering of their thirsty, suffering comrades. Again, Griffin felt glad to give them "a chance to run for their lives, though not expecting human nature to be equal to the ordeal of passing twice through the almost certain death of that terrible cross-fire for the sake of alleviating the suffering of comrades." Soldier after soldier subsequently came to him with the same request, and upon receiving the same response, would "speed way across that field of death — some to pass safely over, and some to fall by the way."

After enduring the sheer agony of the Crater for what seemed an inestimable amount of time, Griffin was surprised to make out a solitary, shadowy figure in the storm of lead and steel in no-man's-land, running toward the hell hole, instead of remaining in sanctuary behind Federal lines. The oncoming soldier seemed to be laboring under a heavy burden. As the figure got closer, it proved to be the first man who had requested to go to the rear for water, coming back into "that apocalyptic cavern with a dozen filled canteens for his prostrated brothers-in-arms. Here was true material for a medal if ever there was any, but Griffin had neglected to get the man's name." Recounting the deed, General Griffin exclaimed "What cheers greeted him as he came in! What blessings were called down upon him by those wounded men for that cooling water!" Then still others began to be sighted also running the gauntlet back into the horrific conditions which were the Crater. A number were killed on the parapet, and some died in their attempt to dodge the brutal cross fire. Yet, in time, Griffin believed that, remarkably, all the men who sought permission to leave either made it back or died in the attempt to do so. "It was one of the noblest and bravest acts I ever saw during the whole war," Griffin later remarked. General Bartlett sought the name of the first water carrier and promised a commission for him "if we get out of this," which, unfortunately, was not in the cards that day.[44]

At around noon, General Bartlett, then unable to move freely due to the shattering of his artificial leg, but still remaining "cool, calm and courageous, with an unlit cigar in his mouth," ordered Captain Theodore Gregg of the 45th Pennsylvania to act as field officer of the day and gave orders to rally every soldier in the defense of the Crater. Bartlett had witnessed an earlier struggle between Gregg and a Rebel officer who had rushed him and ordered him to surrender while simultaneously bringing his revolver to his head. At the time, Gregg had charge of a number of Confederate prisoners on the slope of the Crater. Josiah Jones of the 6th New Hampshire observed "[w]ith a quick movement of his arm, ... knocked away the hand of the rebel officer, at the same time drawing his sword with the other, and running him through. The officer, impaled with the sword, fell back on the other side of the breastwork." In Gregg's own words, "I succeeded in taking his revolver from him, and after a sharp struggle left him dead on the spot." Bartlett presented Gregg with his sword, saying to him, "Captain, you are more worthy to wear it than I am." After the war, Gregg returned this sword to Bartlett, which had been presented to him by his old 57th Massachusetts regiment. Bartlett had by then been forced to sit helplessly among the dead and dying in the floor of the pit, knowing there would be no escape for him that day. "If the rebels who inevitably took the place did not kill him, he was bound for Libby Prison. That was the best he could hope for."[45]

By 11:00 A.M., every straight-thinking officer at Fort Morton knew that the day was lost. Withdrawal, however, was far from an easy undertaking. The danger was an immense hazard for an entire army because of the disorganization within the Crater and the lethal cross fire behind it, which had the potential of turning a withdrawal into a stampede that could affect the uncommitted divisions in the Union works. General Potter had started across the field to consult with his two brigadiers, Griffin and Bliss, on accomplishing such a withdrawal. But when he was within eighty yards of the redoubt, one of Burnside's orderlies caught up to him and brought an order to report to Burnside's headquarters immediately. Potter therefore had an aide go to his brigadiers with instructions to withdraw. This was as close as any Ninth Corps division commander came to the front that day!

At 12:30 P.M., the order came from Burnside that the troops should withdraw to the Federal lines, but with officers using their best judgment on the time and manner of withdrawing. The officers had decided the risk was too great until it was dark. The men in the Crater had already been in the area for eight hours and were at the end of human endurance. The crowded mass could not defend itself due to the overcrowded front and, in any case, had very little ammunition and water, and most of the men had not eaten since the previous night. The avenue of escape now seemed just about sealed off to anyone whose speed was impaired. Men like Private Herman A. Clement, who had already been gored by a USCT bayonet, and had since taken a bullet in the thigh, had no chance of making a dash for his freedom, along with many others.

Burnside had requested General White to have the corps' commanders endorse his order to retire. However, no division commander ever signed the actual order, as it had gone instead to the acting division leaders in the Crater. A brave staff officer appeared with a scrap of paper folded to the size of a *carte-de-viste* and delivered it first to General Hartranft. This order represented Burnside's announcement of Meade's withdrawal order. Hartranft immediately endorsed it, adding a request for artillery support on his left to subdue a battery (presumably Davidson's) that was raking the ground his men would have to cross with canister. The order was next taken to Bartlett, who scribbled something about the men being a perfectly uncontrollable rabble who could never withdraw in good order. Hartranft then added yet another endorsement, indicating that if the troops on the right and left could make a diversionary attack, the trapped men in the Crater could make a run for it en masse. Griffin agreed that one headlong rush under cover of a diversion was the only reasonable hope. An aide then rushed back to Burnside's headquarters with the endorsed order. Somewhere en route, "a little piece of gore splashed on the order, and ... dried there when Burnside's assistant adjutant general filed it for posterity." Up to this point, the fighting had been brutal and hard. "After Burnside's order to withdraw reached the men holding the breach ... however, the combat descended into animal savagery, pointless killing, and racial genocide." One soldier remarked that the "carnage became terrible past description."[46]

The Crater's leaders, including Griffin, Hartranft, Lieutenant Colonel Cutcheon and Major Grant, among others, gathered in the undemolished fort. Just outside the fort was Colonel Marshall, who was in charge of Ledlie's remaining men. The regiments were so mixed and confused by that point that almost no plans could be made. All of Griffin's seven commanders were dead or wounded, and he was unsure as to who had assumed command of his regiments, "and probably most of those men did not know they had succeeded to such positions." Hartranft and Griffin finally agreed that a daylight retreat would be feasible only if the troops on either side made a diversionary assault. This could only refer to the Second and Fifth corps, as the Ninth Corps was entirely engaged. Of course, Burnside had no authority over those troops, and Meade had already effectively ruled them out of the equation by his actions. Burnside's men would get no assistance from their fellow soldiers. Regardless of such support, Griffin and Hartranft then proceeded to run "like madmen," attempting to broadcast their plan for withdrawal. With all semblance of organization totally disintegrated, they were forced to rely on passing the word from man to man. Lieutenant Powell went back on his own initiative to confer yet again with Ledlie, and argued for trenches to be dug forward toward the Crater in order to provide cover for the men when they attempted their mass breakout. Powell claimed that at the time, the idea was "looked upon with disfavor," and no digging implements could be found in any case.[47]

At around 1:30 P.M., Lieutenant Colonel Cutcheon volunteered to run the gauntlet and return to the Federal lines in order to obtain water, tools, sandbags and ammunition, and also to seek to have the gun which was enfilading them on the left (presumably Davidson's) silenced. By that time, the Federal batteries had ceased to fire at all. Hartranft willingly approved the mission. Unfortunately, when he reached the Federal lines, Cutcheon could not find a single brigade or division commander near the front, which required him to walk all the way back to Fort Morton. Like Powell, Cutcheon found that no picks, shovels or sandbags were readily available to assist the trapped men in digging out of their predicament from the Crater.[48] Simultaneously, General Willcox, sensing that any rush back through dead-man's land would be devastating for the trapped men without some form of protection, had on his own initiative commenced work on three covered ways toward the Crater. At his request, black troops from Colonel Guy V. Henry's brigade of the Eighteenth Corps and many of Ferrero's men, who had by then returned to the Federal lines after Mahone's initial countercharge, began digging the trenches. In addition, the 35th Massachusetts was also involved in the project, as its role that day called on it to be the acting engineers of the first division.

In desperation, the trapped, suffering troops in the Crater began to dig back toward the trenches to meet them, "flailing away at the clay with bayonets and scooping it up in their bare hands, making pitiful progress." However, the Confederates had the range and plugged bullets into their effort "so thick and fast that no one could work on it." Similarly, the work of the 35th Massachusetts was unfortunately also coming to naught. The farther the men proceeded with their excavation, the more the Federal soldiers in between the lines quickly sought refuge in the newly built trenches to escape the fury of the Confederate canister and musketry. One of the supervising officers told his men to bury those Federals who refused to leave the confines of these newly dug trenches. However, the effort was hapless in any event, in view of the distances that had to be traversed and the devastation which rained down on the excavation parties. Thus, after the parties had been reinforced several times to no avail, the work finally had to be abandoned.[49]

There were still those who believed that a further advance might yet be attempted from the right of the Crater to save the day. Burnside himself was still of the opinion, after the repulse of the black troops, that further advances could be made toward Cemetery Hill to prolong the fight. The Rebels had not followed up on their advantage and some in and around the Crater expected that they could yet go again, or at the very least hold what they had initially taken, according to Captain Charles J. Mills, assistant adjutant of the first division. Potter had made some preparations to connect the disorganized line and entrench it. Colonel Marshall had placed Colonel Robinson in command of forces in his area and had directed that as soon as the men were again organized, word should be sent to Ledlie that another advance against the works on their right should be made and a fire kept up towards their right. Robinson thereafter sent a report to Ledlie, through Lieutenant Randall, to the effect that "there were four hundred and fifty men of the Second Brigade formed and ready to go forward, and that he proposed to attack to the right of the old position, and to secure that flank from which all the trouble had come."

A similar report was forwarded by Colonel Barnes regarding the men he had rallied from the first brigade. Potter himself was of the opinion that the day might yet be saved if such an attack could be shifted to the right on the side of the ravine, and proposed Bliss's brigade for the task. By so doing, he believed such a force could burst through the Rebel line and take out Wright's Battery, which was then applying such a destructive fire on the Union flank, while at the same time, some of his force would charge from the right flank of the slope. When Potter read the dispatch requiring the movement, he indicated to Henry Pleasants that he was going to report to Burnside in person to argue for the alternative decision. When he entered the log and sod structure serving as Burnside's command post, he received word from Burnside himself that Meade had given the order for withdrawal, and, unfortunately, that was it. Randall reportedly brought back word that the men were not to advance, but rather were to withdraw. In the meantime, Lieutenant S.W. Pierce reported that B and E companies of the 38th Wisconsin in Hartranft's brigade had actually charged single-handedly toward the Confederates until ordered to halt.[50]

While the men in the Crater were subsequently ordered to withdraw, the issue remained how and when. Hartranft, Griffin and Bartlett had decided the best chance of survival for the majority of the trapped, suffering troops was to await construction of the proposed covered ways, or in the alternative, the advent of nightfall. Captain Charles H. Houghton, Company l, 14th New York Heavy Artillery, had struggled back to the undemolished section of the redoubt after the repulse of the black troops to where he had left Sergeant Stanly in charge of the two captured Napoleons. While he was passing through a narrow passage, General Hartranft, who had preceded him, called out for Houghton to drop down, as Confederate sharpshooters were picking off everyone who passed that particular point standing up. Houghton was also present when Hartranft, Griffin and Bartlett made their decision to remain until conditions were more favorable for a safe withdrawal.

Looking over the current conditions in the Crater, as well as the area between the lines, then strewn with the bodies of the fallen, the hot rays of the blistering July sun beating down on them, Houghton, however, became convinced that any further delay would only add to the death toll, or insure that those remaining would at best be prisoners by nightfall. Houghton reported that "[t]he sun was pouring its fiercest head down upon us and our suffering wounded. No air was stirring within the crater. It was a sickening sight: men were dead and dying all around us; blood was streaming down the sides of the crater in pools for a time before being absorbed by the hard, red clay."

The generals collectively attempted to dissuade Houghton from this course of action, "predicting sure death to any one crossing that field, which was swept by both artillery and infantry fire of the enemy from both directions and was so thickly strewn with killed and wounded, both white and black, that one disposed to be so inhuman might have reached the works without stepping on the ground." Corporal Bigelow, who served as Houghton's orderly that day, was asked what he preferred to do, and he responded that he would follow his commander whichever way he chose. The two thus passed the embrasure overlooking the Federal line in order to make preparations, and were confronted by Colonel Marshall, who also asked what they intended to do. When so informed, he, too, pronounced the mission certain death. Houghton replied that "it would be sure death or starvation in Confederate prisons to remain and that ... [once safely behind Federal lines] I could release all of them by opening fire so that the smoke would obscure the field and all could come out."[51]

Houghton thus picked out a target where he could see his regimental flag "floating in the slight sultry breeze, indicating its direction," which was favorable to his plan. He then gave the word that they would be off on the explosion of the next shell, keeping a little apart from each other — and they did so, passing a shower of bullets. Safely reaching his own lines after a harrowing journey through no-man's-land, he then promptly ordered his men to lay down a furious fire on the Confederate line, in order to cover the withdrawal of those still in the Crater.[52] It was almost 2:00 P.M., and those remaining in the Crater were unaware that they were very rapidly running out of options.[53]

CHAPTER 16

"A Sad Day's Work, and Nothing Gained"

Wilcox's Alabama Brigade was the third of the five brigades comprising Mahone's division occupying the breastworks around the Willcox farm to the right of Petersburg called into the day's fight. About 10:00 A.M. that morning, orders were delivered by R.R. Henry of Mahone's staff to its commander, Colonel John C.C. Sanders, to move his brigade up to the ravine in front of the Crater. The men had been expecting the courier, as they were next in line and could hear the progress of the battle, and word had been passed down to them that the Salient had not yet been retaken. Sanders had been sitting on the gallery of a house when the explosion occurred, whereupon he galloped to the works and took a position in the rear center of the brigade near a company of the Washington Artillery.

The brigade was then quietly withdrawn from the works, leaving only a few skirmishers (one man every twenty paces) commanded by Major J.M. Crow of the 9th Alabama to occupy the space. Utilizing the same route employed by Mahone's other two brigades that had preceded them, the Alabamians arrived first at Blandford Cemetery, then entered the zigzag covered way, filing through singly to avoid enemy fire, and eventually came out in the ravine opposite the Crater at about 11:00 A.M. As soon as the brigade emerged from the covered way into the swale running parallel with the works, they were met by a wounded General Weisiger, then being evacuated to the rear. Sanders and his staff abandoned their horses and hastily met with Weisiger. Soon thereafter, they were met by Mahone himself arriving on foot, accompanied by General Johnson.[1]

John Colwell Calhoun Sanders was born in Tuscaloosa, Alabama, in 1840. He was a student at the University of Alabama when he enlisted in the 11th Alabama in June of 1861, and quickly moved up the ranks to captain. He was subsequently wounded at Frazier's Farm in the Seven Days' Battle, returning to duty in August 1862. Thereafter, he led the 11th Alabama at Second Manassas, Antietam, Fredericksburg, Chancellorsville and Gettysburg. He was promoted to colonel after Antietam and was again wounded in the knee at Gettysburg. He returned to active duty in the spring of 1864, and took temporary command of Wright's brigade,[2] then commanded by Abner M. Perrin, following that officer's death at Spotsylvania. In his new capacity, Sanders assisted in the recovery of the Mule Shoe in that critical battle. His bravery in that engagement earned him his brigadier's star that same month, whereupon, at twenty-four years of age, he was given command of Wilcox's Alabama Brigade, making him truly a "boy general."[3]

Cadmus Wilcox's brigade of Alabamians had seen heavy fighting since the start of the war, sustaining grievous losses from Seven Pines through the Wilderness and Spotsylvania. It bore the brunt of Sedgwick's assault at Salem Church in 1863 with a devastating loss of 557 casualties that one day, but still succeeded in protecting Lee's scattered army at Chancellorsville, enabling Lee to consolidate his victory there. It excelled at Gettysburg despite heavy losses on the third day in supporting Pickett's charge. Due to losses in prior battles, by July 1864, many regiments were now commanded by captains, and companies by sergeants, with some companies so depleted that they were required to be consolidated into other units. As the Alabama Brigade formed for their desperate charge that morning, there were only 632 men in the ranks, spread over five regiments, down from its initial complement of 5,000. The 8th Alabama was under the command of Captain M.W. Mordecai, while the 9th was commanded by Colonel Joseph Horace King, and the 10th by Captain W.L. Brewster. The 11th Alabama was led into battle that day by Lieutenant Colonel George E. Tayloe and the 14th Alabama by Captain Elias Folk. The Brigade was eager to have a go at the Yankees, whom they held in utter contempt for perpetrating such a cowardly act on their fellow soldiers.[4]

The brigade was comprised totally of battle-hardened veteran regiments which had seen more than their share of fighting. The 8th Alabama was organized in Richmond in June 1861 and fought in all the major engagements of the Army of Northern Virginia. The 9th Alabama was also organized in Richmond in May of 1861. It did not reach Manassas due to a railroad accident, was held in reserve at Seven Pines, and was not actively engaged at Second Manassas. Thereafter, however, it was always in the thick of the fighting, beginning at Salem Church, where it bore the brunt of Sedgwick's assault, with very heavy casualties. It had fifty-eight killed at Gettysburg, and lost heavily in the Overland Campaign. The 10th Alabama was organized at Montgomery in June of 1861, and originally commanded by Kirby Smith. It was heavily engaged in the Seven Days' Battle and experienced severe losses in these various engagements. At Antietam, it suffered casualties of over 50 percent and also sustained the shock of Sedgwick's assault at Salem Church, suffering 120 casualties out of 400 engaged. At Gettysburg, it lost 175 out of 450 men, and another 110 in the 1864 battles leading up to the siege at Petersburg. The 11th Alabama was also enlisted in June of 1861 at Lynchburg, Virginia, with 972 men. Like its fellow regiments, it lost heavily in the major battles leading up to Petersburg, including a total of 117 men at Salem Church. The 14th Alabama was organized at Auburn, Alabama, in August 1861, and was almost annihilated at Frazier's Farm and Malvern Hill, losing nearly all of its officers in repeatedly charging Federal positions, suffering 335 casualties in the process.[5]

Sanders had sent Captain George Clark, his assistant adjutant general, ahead to look over the ground where the brigade was to mass and commence its charge. There, not far from the lip of the Crater, Clark met with Colonels W.H. Stewart and George Rogers of the Virginia Brigade. Clark felt the Virginians had done magnificent work in heroically holding their positions, but he also felt that the Georgia Brigade had failed in not car-

Col. John C.C. Sanders (*Miller's Photographic History*).

rying the trenches that had been assigned to them.[6] The Alabama Brigade was at that time resting just east of a little branch, or marsh, under the hill. When he returned, Clark was then ordered to pass along the line, count the men, and inform them, as well as the regimental commanders, that the attack would begin at 1:00 P.M.[7] The brigade went into position in the works to the south, or right, of the traverse behind the Crater.

By the time the Alabamians had arrived, many Confederates were already falling victim to the intense heat. There was no shade or water in the ravine, and the men had been exposed for hours in the scorching heat, which caused strong men to faint and required them to be carried to the rear. Further attacks had been postponed to arrange cooperation from Colquitt on the right and Wise on the left. Mahone, finally arriving on foot, met the brigade and explained the situation to its officers and gave them their orders for the fight.[8] He advised that the brigades of the Virginians and Georgians had successfully advanced and taken the works on the left of the fort, "but that the fort was still in possession of the enemy, as was also a part of the works on the right of it, and that ... the Alabama brigade ... was expected to storm and capture the fort, as ... [it was] the last of the reserves." There was no time to call on assistance from north of the James.

Mahone directed that Sanders should move his men up the ravine as far as they could walk unseen and then lie down on the ground until the Rebel artillery in the rear could draw

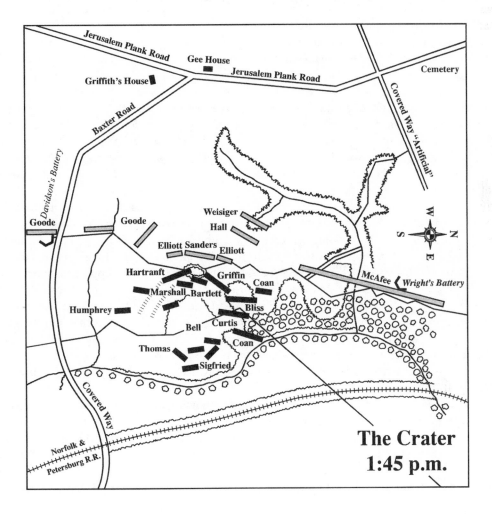

**The Crater
1:45 p.m.**

the fire of the Union artillery posted on a ridge beyond their main line and covering the fort. He explained that the object of the countercharge was to recover the rifle pits on the right, as well as the Crater itself. This would require a right oblique after starting forward, so as to cover the points of attack. The brigade was instructed to stay low as it moved up the grade and when the enemy came into view, to rush toward them and not stop until it had reached the Crater. Once this was accomplished, the Confederate artillery would cease firing; they were then to rise up and move at trail arms with guns loaded and bayonets fixed. The men were instructed not to yell or fire their guns until they drew the fire of the Union troops in the fort, and then to charge at a "double quick" for the walls of the fort which had not been destroyed. From there, they would be protected from the Federal artillery, and could fire unmolested into the horde of troops in the Crater below. Mahone informed his officers that he had ordered the Confederates occupying the line on either side to provide a covering fire into the enemy when they showed themselves above the top of the fort or along their main line, thereby shielding the men as much as possible from their fire. Unlike the Georgia Brigade, the Alabamians' attack would commence from the less broken ground to the southwest of the Union position.[9]

As the time for the attack approached, Mahone strode between the lines, reminding the men that there were blacks in the Crater who had sworn to give no quarter, in an effort to energize them for the bloody work ahead.[10] He also pointed out the Gee house to the west, and stated that Marse Robert himself would be watching them on their impending attack. They were told they had to be successful "if the day was to be saved." Sanders had previously told Clark to inform the men "that Gen. Lee had notified him that there were no other troops at hand to recapture the works, and if this brigade did not succeed in the first attempt, they would be formed again and renew the assault, and that if it was necessary, he (Gen. Lee) would lead them." The men knew that they "were making General Lee's last play on the checkerboard of war, as ... [they] were the last reserves." As ordered, Captain Clark thus informed the men that Lee was prepared to lead the charge himself if the men failed in the first attempt, which emphasized to all 632 men the importance of their mission. One of the Alabamians responded, "If the old man comes down here, we will tie him to a sapling while we make the fight."

The synchronized attack was to begin at 2:00 P.M.[11] with a signal from two guns from the batteries in the rear. Mahone emphasized "that every man must be ready to rise and go forward at the signal, slowly at first, and then at a double quick as soon as ... [they ascended] the hill—that ...[the] object was to recapture the rifle pits on ...[their] right as well as the crater, and for this purpose the brigade would be compelled to right oblique after starting as to cover the points of attack—no man was to fire a shot until ...[they] reached the works, and arms must be carried at a right shoulder shift," to ensure that nobody would succumb to the overpowering urge to stop and fire in self-defense. Mahone advised Sanders that if the brigade paused in the open field to fire they would never survive the intense volume of fire from the Federals. Thus, they were to await the signal to emerge from cover, and then oblique to the right to ensure the charge would cover the extent of the Crater itself as well as the rifle pits to its south.

After the officers returned to their regiments following Mahone's briefing and ordered their men to load and fix bayonets, the brigade immediately moved up the ravine as ordered. As they started out, Captain John C. Featherston of the 9th Alabama reported that a soldier "worse disfigured by dirt, powder and smoke than any I had before seen, came up to my side and said 'Captain, can I go into this charge with you?'" Featherston replied, "Yes. Who are you?" The man identified himself and stated that he had been with one of the South Carolina regiments blown up in the explosion and he thus wanted to get even with the Yankees. He requested that Featherston take his name to inform his officers if he were killed in the assault. Captain Featherston informed the soldier that he had no time for writing. He later lamented, however, that he did not record the soldier's name and regiment, for he was truly a "rough diamond." The soldier went on into the charge with them, but history did not record whether or not he survived, as Featherston never saw him again.[12] As the men raised their heads in front of the Crater, they could see the enemy and its many flags. They knew the odds were greatly against them, but as Captain Clark pointed out, "it was not ours to ask the reason why, only ours to do and die," quoting Tennyson's line about an almost identical number of troops in the famous Light Brigade who charged against insurmountable odds. Sanders then had Clark inform the men that the attack would begin at 1:00 P.M.[13] with the firing of two signal guns.[14]

Meanwhile, in the horrible pit, the "thunderous tempo subsided," evidence for the embattled Federals of a calm before the storm. "The men in the pit paused in their furious activity to listen to that ominous silence." A few men continued to break for the rear, as all sensed what was soon coming. "A handful of weary, blood-spattered men clawed their way up the front wall of the crater with loaded rifles, perching at the rim, hanging on with their toes and elbows, waiting."[15]

As Sanders' men lay flat on the ground 200 yards in front of the Crater, the Confederate artillery in the rear opened on their Federal counterparts in order to draw their fire, thereby allowing the Alabamians to charge without the murderous effects of hostile artillery fire. However, according to Captain Featherston, the Yankees seemed to comprehend the objective of this action and failed to respond accordingly. Finally, at 2:00 P.M., as the prearranged two gun signal boomed, Sanders gave the order "Forward" and the brigade went in with the 9th Alabama advancing on the right. The Alabamians were supported by the 61st North Carolina of Hoke's division and the 17th South Carolina under Major Culp on their right. Further to the right, Johnson was to advance with the 23rd South Carolina and the remaining five companies of the shattered 22nd South Carolina under Captain Shedd. His object was to divide the attention of the Federals trapped in the Crater between Mahone's charge and his own. To free up troops, the 21st South Carolina from Hagood's brigade of Hoke's division had occupied a position on the right of Baxter Road when Johnson moved his troops to the left.

The Rebel guns ceased as the men in gray advanced as directed, in quick time, at trail arms and with bayonets fixed, "the yip-yip-yip of the rebel yell drifting like an eerie taunt before it." In a short distance the Alabamians came into view of the Yankees, both infantry and artillery, and this presented "one of the most awfully grand and cruel spectacles of that terrible war." The brigade of 632 men was charging into an open field filled with 5,000 of the enemy and supported by a huge park of artillery. Featherston continued:

> When we came within range, we saw the flash of the sunlight on the enemy's guns as they were leveled above the walls of the wrecked fort. Then came a stream of fire and the awful roar of battle. This volley seemed to awaken the demons of hell, and appeared to be the signal for everybody within range to commence firing.

They raised the Rebel yell and sprinted to get under the walls of the fort before the Union artillery could open up, "but in this ... [they] were unsuccessful." One of the South Carolinians in the assault observed that "[t]he Yankee cannon seemed literally to tear up the ground under the very feet of the brigade. The heavy guns joined in the awful din, and the air seemed literally filled with missiles." The first shots went over the men's heads and did no damage.

However, as the men reached the works, many were soon struck down and the gaps in the line became apparent. The artillery began to open huge gaps in the ranks, as the air seemed to be literally filled with missiles. Captain Featherston commented that they went literally "into the mouth of hell." Yet steadily, straight ahead they moved. "When a soldier was shot down, the order was passed along the line, 'Close up, men'; and I never saw a prettier line kept on drill," commented Featherston. "It was as handsome a charge as was ever made on a field and could not have been excelled by the 'Guard' at Waterloo under Ney."[16]

As Mahone's last hope advanced, Lee watched from the Gee house, his view sometimes obscured by the dense smoke, "and saw them reach the second line, from which the enemy had fled." They waited there only long enough to catch their breath and were about to dash under the walls of the Crater before the artillery could open up, but this exercise was unsuccessful. The Virginias, Georgians and South Carolinians and the Confederate artillery commenced firing from the flanks on either side, as well as at the Federal main line. On the Alabamians went, "into the mouth of hell." Knowing they had to reach the rim of the Crater or all was lost, the Alabama men stopped at nothing, though many fell in the process. Sanders' men quickly mounted the inner line and forced the enemy backward to the outer line and the Crater. In one of the strangest scenes of the assault, a dog which had attached itself to the general staff "went with them in the charge. When they raised a yell, as they neared the crater, the dog, either braving, or in blissful ignorance of the danger ran along before the rapidly advancing line, and dashed over into the crater barking most fiercely. But he soon came out with a 'flea in his ear' and ran off yelping and limping."

As the Alabamians neared the wall, they first encountered Captain Richardson's detachment of the 45th Pennsylvania, which surrendered when further resistance became pointless. One of the soldiers of the 45th had earlier captured a flag of the 6th Virginia and "bore it in triumph as a trophy of one of the bloodiest conflicts of the war," as was able to escape. The color bearer of the 45th also got away after a hand-to-hand fight "and succeeded in defending ... [their colors] against all comers." When Sanders' men finally reached the wall, he had them drop to the ground so as to get the men in order and let them catch their breath. As they waited just outside the Crater, the Alabamians could hear the Yankee officers on the other side encouraging their confused, trapped men, to "Remember Fort Pillow." The men collected a great number of abandoned muskets with bayonets affixed lying on the ground around the fort. Captain Featherston himself recalled the large number of abandoned muskets with bayonets lying on the ground around the front:

> Our men began pitching them over the embankment, bayonet foremost, trying to harpoon the men inside, and both sides threw over cannon balls and fragments of shell and earth, which by the impact of the explosion had been pressed as hard as brick. Everybody seemed to be shooting at the fort and doubtless many were killed by their friends. I know some of the Yankees were undoubtedly so killed.[17]

Inside the Crater, a large portion of the Yankees were not able to see the charge of the Alabama troops, but could distinctly hear their fearful cry, and "the dreaded sound made their blood run cold." General Griffin recalled that he did not see the Alabamians until they suddenly appeared in "a good line of battle" on the rising ground in their immediate front. Captain McCabe later noted in his journal that the Alabamians should be quite proud to know that "a brave enemy said this," about their movement.[18] Some of the white Union soldiers then quickly turned panic-stricken on their black comrades, shooting them down or bayoneting them for fear the screaming Rebels would take no white man prisoner if he were found with the black soldiers. One Federal officer who survived the horror noted that "the men was bound not to be taken prisoner among them niggers." Major John Haskell encountered a Yankee who had grabbed his musket and, "shouting out that he would kill the 'damned niggers,' had dashed out the brains of a colored soldier." A black prisoner later identified the man to Colonel Haskell as his captain and the dead black man as a member of his company. Haskell told this Yankee officer that he deserved death, and his orderly quickly so dispatched him.

Along the rim of the Crater, bolder men kept up the fight. As the Alabamians began scaling the sides of the Crater under the covering fire of their comrades, General Bartlett soon observed a Confederate flag appearing over the parapet only six feet from his own guidon. The Alabamians tipped their rifles over the edge to fire, or sometimes jumped up for a quick shot, causing brave defenders to respond in kind. As the bayonet-tipped muskets were hurled into the Crater, the cartridge poor Yankees collected them and threw them back. Generals Griffin and Hartranft could rally only a handful among the thousands of commingled soldiers; only a motley rear guard of approximately 150 men could be mustered to hold back the Confederates entering the breach. Given the withdrawal of Warren and Ord's corps, the Confederates were able to give their full attention and firepower to the trapped blue mass in the Crater, as they soon surrounded it on three sides. By now, even the Michigan sharpshooters had been silenced.[19] There was now nothing left in between the forces but the edge of earth thrown up by the explosion. Giving up all hope of awaiting nightfall to retreat, Griffin and Hartranft sent their staffs through the mass with orders to withdraw on a prearranged signal, which would be the opening of all Union artillery on the Confederate lines north and south of the Crater.[20]

The divergent fragments of Mahone's command drew around the Crater at about 2:00 P.M., "encircling it like hands around a throat," and fired a devastating volley into the cringing survivors and dove into them, stabbing wildly as they advanced. Undaunted by the disparity in numbers, the Rebels "commenced scaling the sides of the fort." Meanwhile, the Federals kept up a vicious fight around the rim, so it "seemed like a second Vesuvius belching forth its fire." The explosion of the two separate magazines had divided the Crater into two distinct compartments separated by a narrow ridge of clay. Captain Houghton of the 14th New York Heavy Artillery noted that the "bottom, sides and nearly all parts of the crater were strewn with dead, dying and wounded soldiers, causing pools of blood to be found at the bottom." The Alabamians soon entered into the larger chamber of the Crater, followed by some of their comrades from other brigades. In this larger chamber, Lieutenant Bowley of the 30th USCT waited with a black sergeant, the only other survivor of his company. The men seemed utterly apathetic and indifferent, Bowley noted. "The killing of a comrade by their very sides would not raise them in the least." A voice heard on the other side of the compartment exclaimed, "Every man get his gun loaded, give one spring and go right over; they are out of ammunition, they won't fight." This was soon followed by the command "Forward 41st!"

Soon Bowley, with his revolver loaded and cocked, spied a large Rebel officer, later identified as Major William Etheredge of the 41st Virginia. As Etheredge jumped into the ditch he yelled, "Kill the man in front of me," which order was instantly fulfilled by his men. Then, almost instantly, a Rebel sergeant pointed his rifle at Bowley and cried out for the trapped Yanks to surrender. Most around Bowley complied immediately. However, the Confederates soon began shooting and bayoneting the black prisoners, including Bowley's sergeant. These actions caused the blacks to take back their arms and continue with the brutal hand-to-hand fighting, with the blacks rushing the Confederates as they "bayoneted, clubbed their guns, and, for a moment, drove everything before them."[21]

Colonel J.H. King ordered the men near him to put their hats on their bayonets, and when the Federals riddled them with bullets, to immediately spring over the walls and into the destroyed fort. At the same time, Sanders ordered Lieutenant P.M. Vance of the 11th Alabama, Company F, to take his company and go over the embankment that had been formed by the explosion. Vance's men climbed to the top of the embankment. Lieutenant Harkness of Company C stood by Vance's side waving the colors and shouting to the men to "Come on!" Then the fearful hand-to-hand fighting began for them. When the Federals fired, the Alabamians sprang over the top and down into the Crater. One soldier recalled that "This day was the jubilee of fiends in human shape, and without soul." The Federals shrank back and the Alabamians became enraged as they first encountered the black soldiers mingled in with whites in the fort — at the blacks for being there and at the whites for having them there. "Men were brained by butts of guns, and run through with bayonets, and fists and feet."[22]

Two lieutenants of the 11th Alabama flung themselves into the Crater and quickly found themselves face to face with their black adversaries. Lieutenant Vance was shot through the leg as he leaped into the pit. There he quickly encountered the black soldier who had just shot him. As the soldier drew his large spring-back knife to finish him off, Vance, fainting from the loss of blood and unable to wield his sword, caught the soldier in a desperate bear hug until some of his men could come to the rescue. Vance later explained that he "grasped the negro's hand, holding it fast and making an effort with ... [his] right hand to run ... [his] sword through him ... but could not do so due to the smallness of the pit." Soon his men bayoneted and clubbed the black soldier to death. His men then made a litter of blankets and carried Vance from the field. Captain W.L. Fagan of the 8th Alabama indicated that the combat in the Crater, unlike other battles, was "a series of deeds of daring, of bloody hand-to-hand fighting, where the survivor could count with a certainty the men he had slain." Fagan related that the men "stood face to face at the crater. Often, a bayonet thrust was given before the minie ball went crashing through the body." Fagan himself saw severe fighting from Williamsburg to Appomattox, but witnessed only two other bayonet wounds in all that time. Colonel Sanders found himself in a duel with a black trooper, and, fortunately, both proved to be bad marksmen. Adjutant Fonville of the 14th Alabama and Lieutenant John W. Cole of the 11th were both killed by black soldiers as they rushed into this quadrant of the Crater.[23]

Not all the black soldiers had stampeded; many were mingled with the white troops and put up a fierce struggle. Given to believe that the Confederates would show them no quarter, the blacks, together with many of the whites near them, fought with unparalleled desperation. Mahone's men were greeted with "defiant yells" while their ranks were mowed down by withering fire. "Encouraged, threatened, emulating the white troops, the black men fought with desperation," according to many of those at the scene. In the melee, some Confederates "recognized their slaves at the crater. Captain J ____, of the Forty-first Virginia, gave the military salute to 'Ben' and 'Bob,' whom he had left hoeing corn down in Dinwiddie." Another former slave, upon recognizing his "young master" in the fight, threw down his musket, rushed to the young man and threw his arms around his neck exclaiming:

> "[y]ou haven't hurt my young massa." At that instant, another Federal soldier, "not so mercifully disposed," fired at the Alabamian, but the ball instead of hitting the object aimed at, took effect in the body of the repentant slave who threw his arms of protection around his "young mass," inflicting a severe wound upon him. Master and slave came safely off the field together, and the wound of the latter was properly attended.

Many blacks fought with a level of obstinacy that was quite surprising and held their ground until the fighting was at close quarters. One black soldier stood up "at a distance of

30 paces, and had a regular duel with the Sergeant Major of our reg't; a fearless, high-spirited young Southern blood, armed only with a pocket 6 shooter," Charles Trueheart, Assistant Surgeon of the 8th Alabama later wrote his brother.

> He fired at the negro five or six times; the negro the mean while loading and shooting at him as fast as he could. At last he plugged the Sgt. in the forehead. Fortunately his head was as thick as his heart was brave, and the ball glanced upwards inflicting not even a fracture of the skull. The negro is said to have been shot by [one] of our men on the spot.

Another Rebel officer ordered a captured black soldier to fire on his retreating comrades, which he did, "going through the manual of arms from beginning to end, and down to the minutest detail. The officer made him fire at them thus six or seven times, and then started him to the rear," as a prisoner.[24]

The animus against the black soldiers was so great that, in many instances, blacks who threw down their arms in surrender were not allowed to do so by the Alabamians, being told that they had arms and must fight, and some Confederates continued to shoot them down. Another black attempted to raise a white flag, but it was instantly pulled down by a Federal officer. One soldier, describing the brutal butchering with bayonets and the butts of guns, stated that he heard "that the officers had liked to have never stopped our boys from butchering them. Just what they deserved, every one of them." Major Haskell observed the final thrust:

> Nothing in the war could have exceeded the horrors that followed. No quarter was given, and from what seemed a long time, fearful butchery was carried on. There was little firing, the men being too crowded together, but they stabbed with their bayonets and clubbed with their muskets until utterly exhausted, with fresh men coming in at every moment. Some of the white men were spared but very few negroes.

Within a few minutes, the whole floor of the pit was strewn with the dead bodies of the blacks, in some places in such numbers that it was difficult to make one's way along the floor without stepping on them. In many places, the bodies were by then three and four deep. Both sides seemed to assume there would be no quarter given by the other, and so the fighting continued. Major Matthew Love of the 25th North Carolina wrote home:

> Such Slaughter I have never witnessed upon any battle field any where Their men were principally negroes and we shot them down until we got near enough and then run them through with the Bayonet.... we was not very particular whether we captured or killed them the only thing we did not like to be pestered berring [burying] the Heathens.

Private Dorsey Binion of the 48th Georgia wrote home almost apologetically that "some few negroes went to the rear as we could not kill them as fast as they past us." Another Rebel soldier observed "How the negroe's skulls cracked under the blows. Some of them ran over on our side and started for the rear, while others made a dash for their own lines, and a great many of them made their escape." After acknowledging the bravery of the black soldiers who "fought us till the veary [*sic*] last," John Lewis of the 61st North Carolina of Hoke's division was satisfied that "we kild asite of nigers." Private W.C. McClellan of the 9th Alabama said that all the blacks "would have ben killed had it not been for gen[eral] Mahone who beg our men to Spare them." McClellan saw Mahone confront one Alabama soldier who had just killed several blacks, ordering him, "For God's sake stop." The soldier replied "Well gen[eral] let me kill one more," whereupon he took out his knife and slit a prisoner's throat. Another Confederate soldier, Private Noble John Brooks of Cobb's Legion Cavalry indicated that, finally, "Gen. Mahone with drawn saber and awful thrusts caused then to desist from their barbarous work." A soldier of the Alabama Brigade reported that "[j]ust before the job was completed General Mahone sent orders to us not to kill quite all of them. I don't know how many were left, but there were thousands of them killed." One lieutenant in the Alabama Brigade wrote that the "troops that our Brigade fought were principally negroes and the slaughter was immense: *heart sickening*." Private Brooks went on to observe "Oh! the horrors of war. Oh! the depravity of the human heart; that would cause men to cry out 'no quarters' in battle, or not to show any when asked for." Major Haskell, himself no bastion of racial equality, when attacked in the Crater by a black soldier whom he quickly subdued, spared the man and sent him to the rear when he begged for his life.[25]

The melee went on far longer than anyone anticipated, with only the rim of the Crater separating the combatants. Meanwhile, Generals Hartranft and Griffin were together in the Crater pondering their fate. No longer was there a thought of holding out until dark. While the generals had requested artillery support to cover their withdrawal, when the Alabamians charged, they concluded there "was no use in holding it any longer." They had passed the word for the men to retire just as the Alabama men struck. Hartranft explained:

> When they saw the assaulting column within probably 100 feet of the works, I passed the word as well as it could be passed, for everybody to retire, and I left myself at that time. General Griffin and myself were together at that time. The order to retire we had indorsed to the effect that we thought we could not withdraw the troops that were there on account of the enfilading fire over the ground between our rifle-pits and the crater without losing a great portion of them, that ground being enfiladed with artillery and infantry fire.

Griffin, who had been ready to lead his men into the half-completed covered way and adjoining saps, estimated the Confederate charge encompassed only 600 men versus literally thousands of Federals in the Crater. However, there was neither cohesion nor determination left among the embattled troops: "The shell-shocked survivors of Griffin's brigade fled pell-mell over the corpse-littered slope behind the crater, swirling away in a hopeless hodgepodge with other divisions. They threw down their rifles and ran with their hands before them, wide-eyed."

Hartranft and Griffin spread the word just as the Alabamians were coming up "yipping their eerie staccato chorus of the Rebel Yell and tilting toward the gaping rupture in their works, spun to a frenzy by tales of the black soldiers the hated Yankees had armed against them." Hartranft himself appeared trapped, and the Confederates targeted him and his aides, killing two of his orderlies. However, he was much more willing to be killed than captured with the resultant dire fate of languishing at Andersonville. The generals had discussed the choice of remaining and thus becoming prisoners, or certain death in retreat, and they chose the latter.

Near General Hartranft, Howard Aston of the 13th Ohio Cavalry finally came to realize his predicament. Aston related to the others that "They'll get us this time if we don't get out. Let's start together." Aston and his men made it and went to a stream flowing red with the blood from the wounded. The retreat quickly became a rout and the pursuing Confederates often fired at such close range so many times that many had powder burns on their bodies. The Rebel artillery provided a killing cross fire all along the line of withdrawal, causing the fleeing Federals to fall at every step. "The ground was being ploughed up with shot and shell while a perfect tornado of musket balls swept across with deadly effect," observed a Federal soldier at Fort Morton. While it was next to impossible to remain in the Crater, "to retire was to run the gauntlet of almost certain death." The space between the abyss and Burnside's breastworks was swept by a cross fire from the enemy's artillery and infantry. The trapped men were left with an outrageous dilemma — to remain in the Crater meant "certain destruction," thus a deadly retreat was their only alternative if they valued their freedom. Federal cannon still remained silent, giving no covering fire to the exposed comrades. One Federal officer exclaimed that "[i]t was mass murder." "Those who made it back quickly jumped into their trenches and breathed with relief at having run the gauntlet safely. They were exhausted, filthy, hungry, thirsty, and shamed, but they were glad to be alive."[26]

As the Alabamians made their way up to the tip of the Crater and then began descending into its depths, fragments of other regiments also came forward and entered the bloody pit. The 41st Virginia was one of the earliest non–Alabama regiments to enter. Soon Carolinians, both North and South, began pouring into the Crater, along with some regiments of the Georgia Brigade. Among the troops that went in were the 25th and 26th North Carolina, having assisted in fully recapturing the entire Salient, according to Lieutenant Thomas F. Roulhac of the 49th North Carolina.[27] Major William S. Grady, who led the 25th North Carolina that day, was mortally wounded in the last charge, a charge which resulted in the taking of the Crater.[28]

As the Alabama Brigade dashed forward in its final assault, Griffin was already leading "his" men into the half-finished covered way. Thus, as the Alabamians approached the pit, "[t]he shell-shocked survivors of Griffin's brigade fled pell-mell over the corpse-littered slope behind the crater, swirling away in a hopeless hodgepodge with other divisions." The Alabamians had not yet entered the smaller compartment when General Hartranft turned his back and started for the rear, calling on everyone to follow him. Griffin, making his own decision to make a run for the Federal lines rather that face imminent capture, "stopped for a moment, took a survey of the surroundings, then stepped off briskly toward ... [the Federal] lines." The men expected to see him fall at any time, for the Confederate eyes were all upon him and many hostile guns were leveled upon him. However, due largely to the promised covering fire of Captain Houghton from the Federal front, he came off safely, "to the thankful joy of us all," said one member of the 6th New Hampshire, "for General Griffin was the favorite with the men of the Sixth."

An unknown author testified to being close to General Hartranft near the end inside the Crater when a fourteen inch shell exploded, killing an officer of the 20th Michigan Volunteers and wounding the unknown author, with flesh and blood spattering all over General Hartranft. The unknown author remembered Hartranft advising him not to "try to go to the rear for you will never reach our lines." However, the unknown author did so anyway and safely made it, thanks to a one inch thick bundle of papers tucked in his shirt, which stopped a minie ball which would otherwise have torn through his body. Hartranft gave the final order to withdraw from his sector of the Crater, and the withdrawal was performed "in much haste and disorder." Shortly thereafter, Hartranft himself was able to lead the men near him out under cover of the Federal artillery and Captain Houghton's covering fire at about 2:30 P.M. Houghton later wrote that "I ordered my men to open fire on the enemy's line. They replied by a furious fire, and soon the smoke settled over the field, and under cover of that fire all the general officers but Bartlett escaped. Bartlett and Colonel Marshall were captured."[29]

All the remaining, bewildered Federals could do was to press into the smaller chamber of the pit. The killing in that quarter of the Crater therefore continued unabated, with each side believing no quarter would be given; consequently, those unable or unwilling to run remained in the pit desperately fighting for their lives, but with the Confederates definitely getting the better of it. Soon the Confederate batteries were ordered to cease fire and Mahone called for volunteers to assault the Crater. However, so many Alabamians volunteered themselves for this dangerous service "that the ordinary system of detail was used." Finally, Lieutenant Morgan Smith Cleveland, Adjutant of the 8th Alabama, standing in the Crater "in the midst of the horrid carnage, with almost bursting heart ... said to a Federal colonel who was near him, 'Why in the hell don't you fellows surrender?' and he put the accent on the cuss word. The Yankee replied quickly, 'Why in the hell don't you let us?'" Finally, Lieutenant Kibby of the 4th Rhode Island tied his white handkerchief to his sword and when he held it up, the killing quickly subsided around him. Even after this, a few more blacks were shot or bayoneted by the angry Confederates until an officer of the Alabama Brigade stopped the violence by shouting, "Hold on there; they have surrendered."[30]

By now, almost as many wounded and dead as active men occupied the Crater. Concerned that the wounded might be left unattended, many Federal officers urged their men to give up. Finally, they agreed, and it was over in all areas of the pit. As the Rebels came in and plunged their bayonets into the wounded, many blacks rearmed themselves. A Confederate officer ordered the men back and called in to the blacks that those who surrendered would be spared and if they resisted, all would be killed. He assured them that upon surrender, they would be treated as prisoners of war. The Federal officers advised them to lay down their arms.[31] However, during this standoff, before the assault could be formed, a white handkerchief was raised inside the pit and after a brief pause, "a motley mass of prisoners poured over the side and ran for their lives to the rear."[32]

As the mopping up continued by the Alabama troops, Lieutenant Cleveland assisted a Federal captain who was obviously mortally wounded and suffering intensely. Near him was "a burly, wounded negro. The ... [wounded captain declared] that he would die. The negro, raising himself on his elbow, cried out: 'Thank God. You killed my brother when we charged, because he was afraid and ran. Now the rebels have killed you.' Death soon ended the suffering of one and the hatred of the other."[33]

General Bartlett, reclining on his clay throne, received a note from General Griffin at 2:00 P.M. to the effect that the Crater and the entire Rebel works were to be abandoned, "and that he had better get out of the crater and save himself." Benjamin Spear of Company K of the 57th Massachusetts was near Bartlett when the alarm went up: "Here they come!" Bartlett asked to be lifted up in order to see what was transpiring. As soon as his head rose above a log serving as part of the Crater's fortifications, he was immediately struck by a bullet which cut a long furrow over his scalp. He fell back stunned but revived in time to witness the disaster. He then ordered Captain Gregg to make every man do his duty and give him the name of any officer who refused to rally the men. Gregg had requested Bartlett to leave and go for the Federal lines, but Bartlett said it was impossible and that he would therefore hold the fort to the last.[34]

Knowing he would not get out, Bartlett left a message with Griffin for his family and friends. Bartlett himself had desired to surrender the Crater earlier, when the first Rebels arrived inside, but the worries of "no quarter" harbored by both sides kept all fighting for their lives, especially the blacks. Bartlett felt that further resistance was useless and "meant simply murder," and had thus issued permission allowing all those who desired to run the gauntlet to do so. Colonel Marshall then reentered the Crater to "assist General Bartlett," while Lieutenant Colonel Robinson was sent to report back to Ledlie regarding the proposed attack to the right. "At last, to save further slaughter, there being no hope of our being rescued," General Bartlett later wrote, "we gave it up."

Bartlett later wrote from a Confederate prison that it was "impossible to withdraw without sacrificing all the men, so I held on as long as possible in hopes of reinforcements." When Bartlett surrendered, his shattered artificial leg produced quite a sensation among the Confederates when the Union prisoners were eventually brought out of the Crater. Captain Clark remembered encountering Bartlett on crutches made out of two abandoned muskets, muzzles down and butts under the arms, with fragments of the cork leg dangling. He remarked to Bartlett that he must have nerves of steel, as he had one leg shot away. One of the Alabamians remarked, "By God! There's a plucky Yankee! One leg shot off & look at him hoofing it along on the stump!" Bartlett smiled and explained that he had lost the leg two years before at Williamsburg, and that the shattered leg was indeed cork. Another soldier then proclaimed, "General, you are a fraud. I thought that was a good leg when I shot it." One of the Alabama officers ordered two of the black prisoners to move Bartlett, but he protested, according to Featherston, and was thereupon given white assistance. General Mahone, soon coming upon the scene, gave Bartlett his horse to ride out.[35] Even after Bartlett ordered the surrender, however, some blacks continued to resist and were shot.[36]

A great number of troops still in the Crater were left to their own devices to make it back to the Federal lines through the heavy cross fire of the Confederate batteries and the small arms fire from the Rebel troops now surrounding the Crater as the Rebels moved into the pit. Thousands of troops scurried across the open ground to their own trenches, albeit with heavy casualties. Wright's guns were rapidly leveling the fleeing masses in front of the Crater. The slaughter was terrific, and more men were probably killed in the retreat than in the advance. "The masses of terrified troops—the wreckage of Burnside's whole corps—stampeded in a pounding, mindless horde, most of them made safe from the murderous enfilade by the unintentioned sacrifice of the unfortunate few who skirted the fringes of the herd, and whose bodies absorbed the bullets." "No one remained behind save those who could not rise and those who chose to cover the retreat of their comrades. A thin company of riflemen clung to the lip of the works to slow Mahone's six-hundred-or-so Alabamians, before whom fled ten times their number."[37]

The 4th Rhode Island and the 45th Pennsylvania held their positions outside of the Crater, fighting hand to hand until ordered out of the ditch. The 51st New York, whose right had rested on the fourth division, was compelled to fall back when the rest of the division did, and the 48th New York and 97th Pennsylvania were soon ordered back to the Federal lines. Captain Whitman later explained that he tried to keep his men from falling back, but after Captain Sims was killed there was just no use attempting to rally the men until they were behind their own works.[38] The 2nd New York Mounted Rifles on the right of the ravine "held this line within twenty yards of the rebel fort, at the old barn, until ordered back to the trenches by ... Colonel Zenus Bliss ... at 4 P.M." General Willcox lost some of his bravest, who stayed fighting to the last in this last assault of the Rebels.

The order to withdraw could not be fully accomplished before the troops remaining in the fort were required to surrender. When the last of the troops were ordered to retire "each man for himself," few, if any, of the Ninth Corps who were not disabled remained to be captured, choosing instead to run the gauntlet of fire across open field once a "miniature hell." As the Rebels bore down on those men of the 45th left in the Crater, someone shot the color bearer of the 6th Virginia and Corporal Franklin Hogan of the 45th took the flag, "tore it off the staff and rolled it up and put it in the bosom of ... [his] shirt." In the final charge, the 45th Pennsylvania went back to the Federal works as best they could. The unit's major ordered the color bearer to take the flag and go to the rear and invited all who desired to likewise go, as the works were going to be surrendered.[39]

The Confederates surrounded the Crater and fired a devastating volley into the cringing survivors and then dove in among them. White flags soon sprang up, and handkerchiefs dangled from sword tips and ramrods. Lieutenant George H. Drew and Sergeant Major Franklin Foster of the 9th New Hampshire soon surrendered. Herman A. Clements loped in advance of many fugitives despite the fact that he had a bayonet wound in his belly and a bullet in his knee, and he and the others never looked back — "they dared not."[40] By 3:00 P.M., according to Colonel Cutcheon, he could still see three Michigan flags of the second brigade standing on the edge of the Crater, 150 yards away, including thirty men of the 20th Michigan. The First Michigan Sharpshooters' regimental banner, as well as the state colors given to the regiment by Mrs. Austin Blair, still flew in the face of the onrushing Rebel forces. Color bearer Sergeant Urie faithfully and bravely kept it aloft until the very end. It and two others were subsequently captured when the men surrendered, they being unable or unwilling to run back.

Some of the Sharpshooters, including Privates Sidney Haight, Antoine Scott and Charles Thatcher, covered the retreat of their comrades as best they could. Haight and Scott were conspicuous in front of the fort, bravely firing on the surging Rebels. Scott, of Company K, was one of the last to leave the fort. They stood in the open and kept up a brisk fire. "Only at the end, when all was falling apart, did they leave the fort, running the 'gauntlet of shot and shell' to their own lines." Thatcher, Haight, Scott and DePuyall were all cited for the Medal of Honor that day. Unfortunately, Thatcher did not make it back and was taken prisoner. Haight, the last Sharpshooter to leave the fort, fired his last shot and immediately a Rebel officer with an uplifted sword demanded his surrender. Haight lunged and rammed his bayonet into the Confederate. He then turned and bolted for the Federal lines. On the way, he lost his cap and felt several minie balls tear through his jacket and another in the heel of his shoe.

Of the thirty men still remaining of the 20th Michigan at around 2:30 P.M., ten made their escape and the remainder was taken prisoner, including the color guard. Colonel Cutcheon believed that the 20th and the 2nd Michigan were the last two units to display their colors in the Crater. Rather than surrender those colors, Alexander Bush and Frank Phillips, two of the color bearers of the 20th, cut up one of the standards and buried the pieces in the dirt at the bottom of the bloody pit. The other was captured by Private John M. Critcher of the 9th Alabama. Sergeant John H. Deaton of the 8th Alabama then succeeded in taking the colors of the 2nd Michigan. These brave Federal soldiers were some of the last men to successfully pull out of the Crater.[41]

Most of Turner's "Flying Division" of the Tenth Corps had moved back to a defensive position following the retreat of Ferrero's fourth division, and thus escaped being trapped between the lines and sharing the plight of their Ninth Corps compatriots. Once Colonels Bell and Coan succeeded in arresting the headlong flight caused by the blacks' stampede in their front, Turner's men then remained back in their lines until finally being ordered to retire during the afternoon. They were replaced by troops of Carr's division of the Eighteenth Corps, except for some troops of the 115th New York, who remained in the trenches for another twenty-four hours as there were no troops to relieve them. A few units, such as the 48th New York State Volunteers and the 97th Pennsylvania Volunteers of Coan's brigade remained forward for one hour before being ordered back to their lines. As the 169th New York of Bell's brigade withdrew under fire, Major Colvin, then in command of the regiment, personally brought off the regimental colors after the color bearer was wounded.

In the forward trenches were a large number of severely wounded men. James Clark of the 115th New York recalled one "grey-haired old man, bordering on three score years and ten, ... [lying] down the hill, his white locks red with blood." Some of the wounded in front of the Crater called out to be killed, indicative of the state of their misery. They cried out for water, but could not be reached, and "none but God in heaven ... [could] save them." A nearby sergeant vowed that "'We'll fight 'em till we die, won't we boys?' he said, and then swooned away." As they lay among the dead and dying, some of whom could not be identified as black or white due to being begrimed with powder burns, the men of the Tenth Corps' second division sipped coffee which had just arrived. Eventually, these men were relieved and moved further to the right—"Free from fire! How good it sounds."

Edward King Wrightman of the 3rd New York of Curtis's first brigade wrote to his brother on August 1, 1864, that when he got back to the rear, he found he was the only man left of Company H (which going into the fight had only four privates, two sergeants and one lieutenant). The men of Turner's division, after the rout of the blacks, watched helplessly as the Ninth Corps, both white and black, "were decimated by a re-formed enemy line and forced to flee from the crater" under extremely adverse circumstances. Turner's men lost a total of 323 men during the fight that day. His division was soon relieved from duty with the Eighteenth Corps and ordered to rejoin the Tenth Corps again at Bermuda Hundred.[42]

As the battered, exhausted and disorganized men of the Ninth Corps attempted to work their way back to their lines amid the devastating cross fire of canister and musketry from three sides, they were totally defeated and their morale was close to nonexistent. Some regiments had suffered staggering losses. A total of 654 casualties was inflicted on the first division. The 14th New York Heavy Artillery, one of the first units into the Crater, and one of the last to leave, lost 126 men and six officers (one officer killed, two wounded and three captured). Among the fallen was Sergeant James Hill of Company C, who had captured the colors of a Virginia regiment of Mahone's division.[43] He, along with Adjutant C.H. VanBrakle, presented the captured banner to General Ledlie in his bombproof, and then bravely returned to the Crater to continue the fight with his unit. Hill was later posthumously awarded the Medal of Honor, which was presented to his company for him by General Meade, and was simultaneously commissioned a lieutenant. Captain Houghton of the 14th was also awarded the Medal of Honor for his conspicuous bravery in the Crater covering fire.

The fiasco devastated morale. Private Alfred A. Saunders of Company K wrote his family on September 10 that they should give the Johnnies independence and "settle the thing right off for I don't believe in such warfare as this." Saunders' brother-in-law, Charles H. Austin, was among the seventy-eight missing members of the 14th New York Heavy Artillery that day. Saunders continued: "I kind of want father to put in a Vote for Maclelan for my sake...."[44] The 100th Pennsylvania, the "Roundheads," lost a total of sixty-four men, including twenty-two killed. When the regiment was inspected days after the battle, it "did not seem larger than a full company. Some of the companies came out of this commanded by a corporal." However, what probably hurt morale the most was the fact that the Roundheads had lost both their old state flag and the one given to them at Camp Copeland. The state flag had "inscribed on it the name of every battle the regiment had ever been in."[45]

The 57th Massachusetts was next to wiped out; six of its seven officers were casualties and forty-five of its ninety-one men suffered the same fate. Lieutenant Albert Doty was now in command of the forty-six remaining, battle fatigued soldiers. Some were so furious that they openly wept in frustration and rage, unable to comprehend why no one would come to their aid, why there was little or no covering fire from their own artillery, and why their commander remained back in a safe bombproof, "full of John Barleycorn." The regiment's flag, color guard and most of the left wing were captured. John Anderson later wrote that "[i]n the loss of the colors our pride had been humiliated, yet we felt a consciousness that the brave men who were with the Fifty-Seventh that day had done all, under the circumstances, that brave men could do." Few of their captured comrades survived the suffering and privations of prison life.[46]

Potter's second division suffered 832 casualties, including eighty officers. Amidst the fog of war, after witnessing firsthand the debacle of the Crater's fall and the bloody, battered and disorganized remnants of his command straggling back to the Federal lines, Potter believed his division was all but destroyed. In a somber communiqué to Burnside at 2:30 P.M. that day, he reported:

> The Ninth and Eleventh New Hampshire, Seventeenth Vermont, and Thirty-first and Thirty-second Maine, are reported to be captured almost entirely. Also the Fifty-eighth Massachusetts and Second New York Mounted Rifles, and Second Maryland Volunteers, are almost entirely captured, besides several hundred of killed and wounded left upon the field. The line from which we advanced this morning in so weak that it is in great danger. I beg leave to call the attention of the commanding general to the fact that my division is reported as nearly annihilated and cannot therefore possibly reoccupy the position from which it advanced this morning.

While later morning reports would indicate his dire news was considerably overstated, he was not far off the mark, as most of his regiments had indeed been deeply depleted and probably were unable to defend the length of the trenches formerly assigned to them. The 9th New Hampshire lost ninety-two men, or roughly one half of the total regiment engaged. While its national colors fell three times in the fray, they, along with the regimental colors, were safely carried to the rear. Sergeant Lathe, with his mangled hand, heard at the hospital that only five of the twenty-three in his already depleted company that he led into battle that morning had returned to the bivouac that evening (although Lathe later counted eleven more in the hospital with him). As the gray-clad troops surrounded the earthen Alamo and the fighting finally ceased, "[t]he survivors peeled off their cartridge boxes and stumbled into a ragged column pointed toward the coveted Jerusalem Plank Road."

Among those of the 9th New Hampshire to surrender were Lieutenant George Drew and Sergeant Major Franklin Foster, along with twenty-two others. An equal number of its men lay dead or wounded in between the lines. The regiment was led out by Captain Cooper, the last captain in the regiment; four of its companies were now commanded by sergeants.[47] The 45th Pennsylvania fared about the same in the butcher's bill that day. Captain Theodore Gregg reported charging the Rebels that morning with 110 men, and he had forty-four report back to the bivouac that night. Among the casualties were two captains and three lieutenants. As the unit retreated, Captain Fessler and Lieutenant Cheeseman were credited with their noble efforts to rally the blacks and others while retreating back across the front line. Captain R.G. Richards of Company G later recalled the instant when the Rebels finally broke through. Declaring that further resistance was impossible and would result in useless sacrifice of lives, Richards, upon being confronted with a gun to his chest and being ordered to surrender, reluctantly did so with all the others.[48]

The 32nd Maine was severely decimated — out of sixteen officers, only three escaped unharmed. Adjutant C.L. Hayes wrote in his diary that night: "I have made my evening report; five officers wounded, eight missing, and eight men killed, thirty-one wounded, and seventy-six missing. A sorry day's work for us, and nothing gained."

Hayes related that, following the battle, there were eighty-five men in the regiment, "including cooks, present sick, and extra duty men," of the 150 who went into the action that morning. Henry Houston was ordered to carry off the unit's commander, Colonel Mark Wentworth, who had been wounded twice in the side during the assault. After he had secured the colonel's safety, and was about to return to the Crater, he heard that the Federal forces were repulsed and driven out back over the Federal front lines, and that the 32nd Maine had been cut to pieces. The men of the 58th Massachusetts, under Captain Charles E. Churchill, who did not retreat, surrendered to the Rebels or were cut down attempting to flee. The regiment lost a total 114 casualties out of 200 men and officers, eighty-three of whom were captured or missing. Only twenty-eight tired soldiers reported back to the unit's bivouac that night. The last of Potter's units to withdraw in the retreat was the 2nd New York Mounted Rifles, after lying on the right of the ravine within twenty yards of the Confederate battery (Wright's).

After a large portion of the 58th Massachusetts was taken prisoner, the Confederates outflanked the 4th Rhode Island, which was anchored to the Federal left. The colors went down and three unsuccessful attempts were made to raise them, with the flag catching the wounded men's blood in its folds. Word finally arrived to the regiment: "Colonel Buffum, take your regiment to the rear. We can get no support. The day is lost." As the men in this quadrant hastily left the dreaded pit, a wounded officer being borne past the men cried out, "Every man of the Fourth Rhode Island deserves promotion!" However, given the prevailing conditions at the time, many preferred to stay on the line and surrender as prisoners rather than risk crossing the shot-swept plain. As the men who survived finally did reach friendly lines, they looked back and witnessed the Rebels sweeping over the Crater taking everyone prisoner. The 4th Rhode Island had gone into battle with 200 men and lost eighty-three in the contest. George Allen reflected on the despair felt by the men at their plight, and their terrible look: "Faces and hands are black with powder, clothes and equipments pierced and cut by Minie-balls, and torn and begrimed with blood and dirt, rifles black and bloody." At 4:00 P.M., as the last unit out of the Crater finally returned to the Federal trenches with colors flying high, the men were warned to lower them or risk a shelling. They ignored the advice and quite soon a mortar hit within three feet of them, wounding a number of them severely.[49]

Willcox's Third Division lost a total of 659 men, which was the highest ratio of killed among Burnside's three white divisions. Among the division's last units to retire from the Crater was the 37th Wisconsin under Colonel Samuel Harriman. This unit lost 145 men, including thirty-four killed, a casualty rate of 57 percent.[50] Only ninety-five men remained to answer their names at roll call that evening out of a complement of 250 which had entered in the assault that morning, according to the regiment's historian (an additional ten men were later added to the rolls). Some of the 1st Michigan Sharpshooters, including Privates Sidney Haight, Antoine Scott and Charles Thatcher, covered the retreat of their comrades as best they could. "Only at the end, when all was falling apart, did they consent to leave the fort, running the 'gauntlet of shot and shell' to their own lines." These three, as well as Private DePuyall, were all cited for the Medal of Honor that day. The Sharpshooters' flag was thoroughly riddled with bullets, and "hung in the still, heavy air." A Rebel sergeant, J.W. Connelly of the 22nd South Carolina, snatched the banner from Sergeant Urie and walked off with it to the Rebel rear. The 1st Michigan thus lost its state colors and had forty-five casualties out of one hundred men engaged. The 20th Michigan and 2nd Michigan were also among the last regiments to leave the bloody pit. The 20th incurred fifty-three casualties, including Lieutenant Barnard and the color guard, who were all taken prisoner; it lost seventeen out of twenty-two officers. Color Sergeant Alexander Bush unfortunately did not get the order to withdraw.[51] Most of these men were captured by the 9th Alabama as they assailed the bloody pit. The 20th's colors were not seen again until after the close of the war, when they were recaptured with the fall of Richmond. Lieutenant Colonel Cutcheon, who ably led the unit throughout the fight, was brevetted a brigadier for his actions in the Crater that day.[52]

The Fourth Division, although it entered the fray some three plus hours after the assault began, still suffered mightily for a number of reasons. First, they entered the contest after the Confederates had totally recovered from the initial shock of the explosion and the concomitant Federal bombardment, as opposed to the conditions experienced earlier by the white divisions. Secondly, they found themselves in the advanced lines just as Mahone's counterattack was initiated, and thus they absorbed the initial shock of that horrific charge. Thirdly, there were incidents of intentional assaults by white Federal troops as the blacks fell back into the already crowded trenches when they broke under Mahone's assault, and yet again when the Confederates closed in on the huddled mass crowded inside the Crater. Finally, there is no doubt that many Rebels dealt much more severely with the black troops, including numerous incidents of brutal atrocities. These factors likely account for the elevated casualty rates.

Colonel Henry Thomas noted that the fourth division was not only cut to pieces four times in charges, but then once again in the repulse. When the enemy retook its former lines, those left in the Crater were cut off. Many who attempted to dash back to the Federal lines quickly fell in the attempt. Thomas reported losing thirty-six officers and 877 men as casualties.[53] Hardest hit of any of the black regiments was the 23rd USTC, which took a total of 310 casualties, including eleven of its eighteen officers. The 31st USCT had but two officers return to its camp that night. It was widely reported that the 29th, under Lieutenant Colonel Bross, went into the charge that morning with 450 men, with but 128 exiting the battle, its casualties including 150 killed, 100 wounded, and from seventy to eighty taken as prisoners.[54] Sigfried's first brigade lost a total of 555 men, including fifty-four killed. In addition, there was a total of 333 wounded and 168 missing or captured. The 43rd USCT charged that morning with 346 officers and men. Lieutenant Colonel H. Seymour Hall later reported that only 200 retired at the last moment, with forty-one killed and 104 wounded.[55]

There are many assertions that the fourth division suffered disproportionately higher casualties than the other three divisions. Of course, one must first agree as to the gross statistics in order to perform the calculations necessary to test the accuracy of this assertion. As demonstrated by the foregoing accounts of the losses sustained by the black units, there are many discrepancies in the accuracy of the numbers actually reported. For example, John David Smith, in his work *Black Soldiers in Blue*, contends that of the 4,500 [*sic*] soldiers in the fourth division, 1,327 were wounded and 426 died. He reports that the three white divisions sustained 2,471 casualties, including 227 deaths. Michael Barton, in *Civil War Soldier*, reports that the blacks suffered 40 percent of the fatalities and 35 percent of the total casualties, despite the preponderance of white troops engaged. Noah Trudeau contends that the total number of black fatalities amounted to 436 (almost the total number for the whole Ninth Corps as reported in the Official Records).[56]

In attempting to reconcile some of this conflicting data, it is first necessary to reach common ground on the total troop strength and aggregate casualty statistics. One first needs to determine the actual relative troops strengths of the white and black divisions in the Ninth Corps on July 30, 1864. Contrary to subsequent inflated numbers, Burnside put the total strength of his three white divisions as of July 20 at a total of 9,023 men. By July 30, that number would be approximately 8,723 men.[57] The effective strength of the Fourth Division on July 30 was 4,300 (Trudeau had placed the number at 4,500).[58] While there are many varying figures for the casualties from the Crater battle, the Official Records reports a total of 472 killed, 1,644 wounded, and 1,356 missing or captured from the Ninth Corps, or a total loss of 3,472.[59] Of these, the three white divisions' casualties were 263; 947; and 935, respectively, for a total of 2,145 (including three in its artillery brigade).[60] Utilizing these figures, the following statistics can be extrapolated:

	White	*Black*
Killed	56%	44%
Wounded	58%	42%
Captured/Missing	69%	31%
Total Casualties	62%	38%

Thus, the percentage of the Ninth Corps killed or wounded was indeed disproportionately high for the black Fourth Division, thereby substantiating, in part, the specter of racial prejudice in the Confederate actions on retaking the Crater, a fact already established even in Southern writings on the subject as well as in first hand accounts. If, as many historians contend, many of these blacks listed as missing or captured were actually among the unidentified dead on the field, these "killed" percentages would be considerably higher. Trudeau claims only 180 blacks were taken prisoner, of which only seven survived their prison experience.[61] He also asserts pension records would establish that the total fatalities among blacks was actually closer to 436 men.[62] Obviously, this would increase the disparity of fatalities based upon race. Glatthaar professes that blacks suffered 35 percent of all casualties that day. Their total percentage of the Ninth Corps was 33 percent, very close to their percentage of the Ninth Corps' population.[63]

The Confederate forces, while victorious, did not escape a high-priced butcher's bill, although their total payment was not nearly as high as their enemy's, despite the huge disparity in numbers, as well as the cataclysmic explosion in their ranks upon the opening of the battle. The total casualty list of Mahone's three brigades was 588 men. Weisiger's Brigade had ninety-four killed, 159 wounded and fourteen missing. Wright's Georgia Brigade suffered seventy killed, 139 wounded and twenty-two missing. The Alabama Brigade had a total of eighty-nine casualties. In Johnson's Army of Southern Virginia and North Carolina, which lost a total of 891 men, Elliott's brigade alone had 125 killed, 224 wounded and 351 missing or captured. Wise's Virginia Brigade had twenty-five killed and eighty-six wounded; Ransom's North Carolina Brigade suffered fourteen killed, sixty wounded and eight missing or captured. Colquitt's Georgia Brigade had a total of thirty-one casualties. Clingman's North Carolina Brigade had thirty-nine casualties. Pegram's battery suffered twenty-two killed and eight missing, with the total artillery losses placed at sixty men. Thus, the total Confederate losses from the conflict in which they were taken totally off guard was approximately 1,650.

However, certain units were nonetheless devastated, such as the 17th, 18th and 22nd South Carolina, all severely depleted by the demolition of Elliott's Salient and the subsequent attack of the Ninth Corps. In Mahone's subsequent counterassault, the 6th Virginia, already at half strength, suffered twenty-three killed and forty-three wounded and fourteen captured, for a total loss of eighty. "These were certainly the highest losses, percentage wise, of any unit fighting that day. When the remnants of that devastated regiment finally arrived back at camp, the picket line saw "only about fifteen of the 95 they had left behind returning." Robert C. Mobry wrote two days later that "it pains me to say that my company was almost entirely swept away; it carried in the Fight Twenty one muskets & three commissioned officers, came out with two men & one officer.... I hear there are only Ten privates left in the entire Regt." One of the companies, Company F of Norfolk, lost every last man. The Sharpshooters carried in eighty men and lost sixty-four, including their commander, William Broadbent, who was pierced by eleven bayonet wounds.

Private Walter B. Wellons of Company H captured the colors of the 11th New Hampshire, and had his name placed on the Roll of Honor as a result.[64] The 61st Virginia captured five of the seven banners they had previously spied in their front as they prepared to move against the Crater, including the 57th Massachusetts, the 31st Maine, one national color and two unknown regiments.[65] In all, a total of at least twenty-five stands of colors were captured by the Confederates that day, including nineteen alone by Mahone's soldiers.[66] Private Patrick Sweeny, Company A of the 59th Virginia, voluntarily joined in the last charge at 2:00 P.M. and successfully captured the colors of the 20th Michigan, and, although he was wounded, brought them off along with a Sharps rifle. Private Henry Moore, also of the 59th Virginia, captured a stand of colors. In the last charge that day, Sergeant J.W. Connelly of Company F, 22nd South Carolina, captured the colors of the 1st Michigan Sharpshooters, which he subsequently delivered in person to General Beauregard.[67]

The battle was over soon after 2:30 P.M. and the job of rounding up prisoners and reestablishing the Confederate line began. As quickly as it could be done, the Confederates ran an earthwork around the edge of the Crater and the line was reestablished. At 3:25 P.M., Lee reported to the War Department in Richmond that "We have retaken the salient and driven the enemy back to his lines with loss." Lee also issued a message regarding the defense and subsequent counterattack to the effect that "[e]very man in it has today made himself a hero." Mahone was soon elevated to permanent command of the division he previously had been temporarily commanding and was promoted to major general.[68] Colonel Weisiger and Captain Girardey were both promoted to brigadier.[69]

A.P. Hill issued the following General Order No. 17 on August 4, 1864:

> Anderson's Division, commanded by Brig. Gen. Mahone, so distinguished itself by its success during the present campaign as to merit the special mention of the corps commander, and he tenders to the division, its officers, and the men his thanks for the gallantry displayed by them whether attacking or attacked. Thirty-one stands of color, fifteen pieces of artillery, and 4000 prisoners are the proud mementoes which signalize its valor and entitle it to the admiration and gratitude of our country.

Captain Featherston wrote his wife that at the surrender, they raised the Confederate flag upon the ramparts and sent a number of the Federal colors to the rear in triumph: "Then a shout ran out along our lines from one end to the other. It is said that General Lee, who was looking on, when he saw we were successful pulled off his hat and waived it, and said: 'Well done.'"

Throughout the night, Mahone's ambulance corps was employed in removing the wounded. The work of burying the dead found in the floor of the Crater and adjoining trenches soon began. Spades were brought in and the earth was thrown from the sides of the excavation until the bodies were covered to a sufficient depth. To assist in the process, a detail of two men from every company was identified to help bury the dead. The Federals, due to the time constraints, were buried where they fell, "in one indiscriminate heap in the pit of the Crater." Black prisoners were conscripted to assist in this work. Confederate dead were placed in a grave one hundred feet in the rear of the Crater. One black prisoner, eager to bury the fallen corpses, grabbed one of George Bernard's sleeping companions by the ankle and placed him in a grave "when the adjutant, not then ready to be buried, awoke, to the great consternation of the poor prisoner, who thought he was handling a genuine corpse."[70]

While the battle ended, the grief and dying continued on the devastated battlefield and adjoining works. Captain H.A. Chambers of the 49th North Carolina related how he and his friend Captain Edwin V. "Spec" Harris congratulated each other for having made it through the heavy fighting totally unharmed. Harris was then moving back toward his company on the extreme left of the regiment, chatting gaily with Major James Davis, when they reached an exposed position on the line. A ball missed Davis, and as he turned to warn the rest of the party, Harris reeled, the ball passing through his neck. "The blood spouted from his neck in a stream as large as one's finger, and gushed from his mouth." Harris could not speak, but was, however, cognizant of his condition, and stepped up to Major Davis and "passed his left hand through the major's arm to support himself from falling and extended his right to tell the major farewell, while he gave him a look ... [which] seemed to say 'I am killed; I know you cannot help me; do not forget me; good by!' " Harris then "tottered to Lieutenant Crawford, of his company, shook hands with him, gave him the same look," then fainted from loss of blood and ceased breathing. "Thus it was that poor 'Spec' ... died." Chambers related his profound sorrow, saying, "He was my best, my most intimate, friend in the regiment." Sergeant Andrew McWilliams, of Captain Featherston's Company F, 9th Alabama, who was in the process of reconstructing the Confederate line that afternoon, was shot in the mouth, the ball not touching his lips as it entered, as he was apparently barking orders at the time, the ball exiting the top of his head. McWilliams fell on the embankment with his head hanging over the fort. He was taken down, and that night was carried out and buried behind the Crater.

C.W. Trueheart, assistant surgeon of the 8th Alabama, later wrote his brother Henry regarding the battlefield after the fighting ceased, indicating that in many places, one could not walk without stepping on the "carcasses lying one two or even three deep." While traversing the devastation, he wrote:

> I saw a boy bending over the dead body of a confederate, taking the contents of his pocket, and as I naturally supposed, ro[b]bing the dead. I ordered him in harsh terms to stop it at once. The fellow turned his face towards me revealing a countenance, the very picture of distress, and with tears streaming down his sunburnt face, and a voice tremulous with emotion, he said "This, Sir, is my brother and I wish to save the valuables about his person."

Surgeon Trueheart related that at another place he saw "an old graybearded man bending and weeping over the mangled corpse of his son, a lad of 16 or 17." Sergeant Samuel Catawba Lowry, who had been killed at age nineteen while leading Company F of the 17th South Carolina in Mahone's first charge, was found after the fighting by his black servant, who rescued his diary and carried him from the field. Lowry's family then met the train bearing his body to his hometown, accompanied by his faithful dog, Major. Seeming to sense the gravity of the tragedy, poor Major was found dead the next morning outside the door of the room where his master had spent his last night under that familiar roof.

One miraculous event did transpire in the aftermath of the fighting, as a lone Confederate emerged from under the debris and dirt of the Crater, like Lazarus from the dead: "His clothes were saturated with red mud made of red dirt and sweat. He was bareheaded and his hair was matted with the same red mud, and his face was covered with it, except here and there were streaks washed clean by perspiration. But his eyes showed happiness to their very bottom." He was from Elliott's Brigade and had been buried and rendered unconscious by the explosion at 4:44 A.M. When he awoke from his concussion, he discovered that he was totally entombed by the debris. He worked throughout the whole day with his fingers, and finally "emerged from what he feared would be his grave and was happy."[71]

Back in the Federal lines, the mood was especially somber in the wake of the unmitigated disaster. On a day that started with such high hopes, there was nothing left from which the exhausted soldiers could take solace. A Federal officer back from the front replied to a fellow officer who had not been engaged in the fight that "They have whipped us like hell." As Adjutant Hayes of the 32nd Maine put it, "A sorry day's work for us, and nothing gained." A dark, heavy mood hung over the entire army.

> The lack of sympathy, unity of council, and concert of action among the leaders, as evidenced by the almost entire neglect to render any support to the Ninth Corps ... only served to increase and intensify these feelings, so naturally following the heels of defeat and disaster.

Lyman Jackman of the 6th New Hampshire lamented that the soldiers' "hearts were all very sad that night at the loss of so many brave fellows, with so little to show for the heavy cost." Such feelings were not limited to the common soldier, either. Those officers and generals who were in the midst of the fight shared the gloom at this devastating defeat and meaningless sacrifice. Outside General Griffin's headquarters tent, as the sun began to set that bitter day, "the brigade band showed up with its incongruously clean uniforms and full ranks, carrying armloads of shiny brass instruments. The bandmaster waved his baton and the first few notes of a patriotic air blotted over the anguished landscape. Griffin emerged and muttered to them, and the sulking musicians went away." To add insult to injury for the desolate Federal soldiers, during the long night following the defeat, many Confederates began shooting abandoned ramrods at them for the sheer fun of hearing them whiz. One Federal finally called out, "Great God! Johnnie, you are throwing turkey spits and stringing us together over here. Stop it."[72]

Once the fighting died down and the surrender was accepted, the job of marshalling Federal prisoners to the rear began. As soon as the defeated Yankees dropped their arms as their safety was guaranteed, they were forced to remove their sword belts and cartridge boxes at bayonet point. Then many of Mahone's men proceeded to exchange their recently perforated hats for those of the Union soldiers. Particularly prized by the Rebels were the black hats of certain Federal regiments and even their ordinary blue forage caps. When captured, Colonel Weld was quickly told to "Come out of that hat, you Yank!" His captor then asked him "what do you 'uns come down here to fight we 'uns for?"

General Mahone noted that once the white flags were raised over the Crater, the Federals, "like swallows out of a chimney, came pouring over the crest, and in passing to our rear over the dreadful slope were hurried on — many to the grave — by the mistaken fire from the guns of the Federal batteries that had previously so fearfully blistered all the ground in our rear." In their eagerness to get beyond the conflict in the Crater, the Federal prisoners went across an open field along the same route over which Mahone's men had charged. Federal artillery, observing them go to the rear under a flag of truce, still thought the movement comprised Confederates being repulsed and therefore opened fire on them, killing and wounding quite a number. One unfortunate Federal prisoner who had his arm shot off by Federal artillery fire while being marched to the rear exclaimed that "I could bear it better if my own men had not done it."

Additionally, Federal cavalry, seeing this movement to the rear, also thought that it indicated Confederates retreating and opened fire on the prisoners, killing some and wounding a number of Confederates and some Federals in the process. As they were marched away ultimately to dreadful conditions in Southern prisons, one of the Federals from Potter's division remarked that "Referring to this *fiasco*, I will only add that when we were marched off the field to the rebel rear, and learned that our available force of three army corps out numbered the enemy engaged in a ratio of at least six to one, our chagrin and humiliation was complete."[73]

The number of blacks taken prisoner has never been firmly established. Some Confederate soldiers claim that the total taken numbered as many as 500. Others place that number at 180, while still others contend none were taken. Dr. Claiborne counted 150 black prisoners wounded in hospitals alone, and the next day's parade of prisoners through Petersburg certainly belied the notion that only thirty-six were alive as prisoners, as Colonel Thomas had reported. Mahone reported a total of 1,101 prisoners, without attribution of race. Lee reported to Richmond the capture of a total of 929 prisoners. The *Richmond Dispatch* placed the number at 513, including 150 black prisoners. W.J. Andrews of the 23rd South Carolina reported that "We carried away 500 prisoners (black and white) together with a few Indians from the West." Featherston reported the prisoner count at 1,200 to 1,500, while Freeman Bowley of the 30th USCT put that number at 1,901 missing or captured.[74] Whatever the number, the blacks were frantic with fear after seeing the end of Mahone's charge. As they came into the Confederate lines through the devastating friendly fire of their own artillery, they fell to their knees, eyes rolling in terror, exclaiming, "Fur God sake, Marster, doan' kill me. Spar' me, Marster, and I'll wuk fur you as long as I lib." Many alleged that they were impressed into service and that they "never pinted a gun at a white man in my life; dem nasty, stinking Yankees fotch us here, and we didn't want to come fus!"

John Sergeant Wise related how a number of Virginians were thus reconciled with their former slaves, all of whom claimed they were not volunteers, but had been impressed into service against their will. Those who reclaimed slaves felt safe that "his man" would never again volunteer upon either side in any war. A Rebel sergeant had advised Lieutenant Bowley to go to the right where he would find a covered way taking him to the Confederate rear, as opposed to traversing the open field, "as you'uns people is shelling right smart." Bowley was the last prisoner to leave the field. All the captured black soldiers who could walk were sent to the Confederate rear; many of the severely wounded never got out. When he got to the covered way, Bowley found that it was full of Confederates, mainly from South Carolina units, and he was thus forced to traverse the open field despite the prior warning, where many Federal prisoners were being killed by their own artillery.[75]

The black soldiers taken prisoner were considered to be the lucky ones. Private Isaac Gaskins of the 29th USCT was one of these so-called lucky ones. After being made prisoner, he was shot by a Rebel and his cartridge box was carried away. The man called him "a damned nigger" and indicated that if he had known he was a nigger he would not have taken him prisoner, as "he did not recognize any damn negro as a prisoner of war and that ... [he] would never get back to ... [his] brother Yankees alive." The black troops lucky enough to be captured alive were corralled up in a ravine. Lieutenant Bowley was sent to the rear past the second line of Confederate defenses composed of the South Carolina troops, where he was divested of his haversack and watch. Those officers of the U.S. Colored Troops who were taken prisoner faced a certain dilemma. Under official, published Confederate government policy, captured white officers leading black troops could be charged with inciting insurrection of slaves, a capital offense. This policy, while having been promulgated, had never been put into practice. Still, it gave white officers room for pause in readily identifying themselves as officers of USCT units. Numerous officers thus refused to acknowledge their service in the USCT. Major William Miller Owen recalled that many USCT officers tore off their shoulder straps so that they would not be recognized as officers of such units. Often, however, the fresh marks on their sun-burned jackets were enough to give them away. A Major Bob W. of A.P. Hill's corps nearly scared the life out of many of them by "standing them apart from the Negroes and impressing the fact upon them that they were to swing instanter. How they begged, and, without exception, said they had been forced in; they could not avoid commanding the blacks, and all that."

Some, however, "had consciences that would not let them lie, or they were too proud of service alongside black soldiers to conceal it from anyone." To their credit, the black soldiers who witnessed this scene never betrayed any of their less than courageous officers when they denied their true service. One disgusted officer, after hearing of his fellow officers deny their service by giving false information, when his turn eventually came, proudly declared that he was "Lemuel D. Dobbs, Nineteenth Niggers, by God!" Despite his proud declaration, Dobbs received no worse treatment than any officer who surrendered after the battle. When confronted with the same decision, Lieutenant Bowley debated whether he should issue the same denial as some of the other officers had done: "Should I do the same? I thought of the black men who had rallied with me in the Crater, and who had died to the last man. Then I told my comrades that I should face the music, and if I died, I should die without denying the

brave fellows we had left behind in that trap of death." After this, several other officers followed suit. Both Bowley and Charles B. Sanders identified themselves as "Thirtieth United
States Colored Infantry, and saw the words "Negro officer" written after their names. Often
in these circumstances, Confederate officers intervened to prevent any mistreatment of officers
of the black units. When Lieutenant Joseph K. Nelson surrendered and identified his unit as
the USCT, a Rebel soldier shoved a revolver in his face, but an officer immediately interceded
to prevent any mistreatment.[76]

Union prisoners generally fared worse than their Confederate counterparts in prison,[77]
due primarily to the lack of supplies available to the Confederates and especially the extreme
short handedness of the divisions around the Crater on July 30. The animosity toward black
soldiers taken prisoner, as well as toward whites who were perceived as agitators, made matters worse. No food was distributed to the prisoners that evening and, even worse, no water.
Additionally, they were not provided with blankets or tent shelters. All the prisoners were
crowded into a stone-littered field to sleep, and by then they were crazy with thirst and hunger.
There, many officers were robbed of their possessions by their Confederate guards, who largely
consisted of local reserves or militia. The next day, the prisoners were marched into Petersburg in a formation designed to amuse the population as well as humiliate the prisoners.

Senior officers were placed at the head of the column, four abreast, followed by four
blacks. Then four more officers followed, and then four more blacks, until the supply of
officers was exhausted, and finally the supply of black soldiers. Lieutenant Randall of the 1st
Michigan Sharpshooters assisted General Bartlett on his journey into Petersburg. Randall was
stripped of his field glasses, hat, pocket knife and money. Lieutenant Bowley wrote that "my
first impression of the Confederacy did not improve with a more intimate acquaintance"
(which included seven months in prison before he was finally freed). About 200 blacks were
in the march, according to Bowley. Prisoners who still retained personal possessions were
quickly disrobed of hats, boots, socks, blouses and swords. William Baird of the 23rd USCT
reported "they left me with a shirt and a pair of pants and this constituted my wardrobe from
that date ... up to and including the 17th day of February 1865." The parade was "much after
the style of a circus." As they walked through the streets, they were assaulted by a volley of
abuse from the city's men, women and children "that exceeded anything of the kind I ever
heard." Some of the blacks were hardly able to walk and the whites were ordered to support
them. The officers of the 43rd USCT reported taunts of "See the white and nigger equality
soldiers!" and "Yanks and niggers sleep in the same bed!" General Bartlett was apparently not
called upon to be a participant in this circus, and Colonels Marshall and Weld as well were
allowed to march solely with the white troops.[78]

While the Federal prisoners were in Petersburg, it was discovered that many of the blacks
were from eastern Virginia, and were thus formerly owned by the men they were fighting. A
notice was thus posted permitting the rightful owners to reclaim their "property." The blacks
were actually delighted at this prospect of being treated as slaves at this point, rather than
being put to death or being sent to a Confederate military prison. John Sergeant Wise recalled
a wounded soldier of his brigade who was given ten days furlough in Petersburg. Upon spot-
ting a notice to owners that they might reclaim their slaves from the prisoner population, and
thinking that he might find one or more of his father's slaves, he went down to Poplar Lawn,
where the prisoners were camped under guard. While searching at that site, "an attractive,
smiling young darkey caught his eye and said, 'Boss, fur God sake, claim me fur yo' nigger.'"
The Rebel declared that he did not know the black man, who then replied, "I knows it, sah,
but ef I says I belongs to you, who gwine to dispute it, if you don't?" The young Rebel replied
that he would sell the man the next day, to which the black replied, "I don't keer ef you does

sell me, sah.... Dat's a heap better den goin' to a Confederick prison pen." "Done!" said the Confederate. "When I come back here, you speak to me and call me 'Mars Ben,' and I'll attend to the rest."

The white soldier soon returned accompanied by the officer in charge, and was greeted by the black soldier: "How you do, Mars Ben?" After cursing him for his ingratitude, Ben claimed the black man as his own. He then took him to Richmond and sold him for $5,000 in Confederate currency. "Mars Ben" had a great furlough with the $5,000 and returned to duty with a new suit of clothes. The black man ended up back on a plantation instead of a Confederate prison and a year later was thus a free citizen. Wise encountered Ben years later and asked if he ever thought about the black he sold back into slavery after the Crater fight. Ben professed that he prayed for forgiveness many a night, but did not want "to expose himself before his friends and neighbors," however.

Some of the captured black soldiers encountered prejudice from an unlikely source. Major John Haskell spotted a home guard soldier marching a captured black soldier back toward the front. Suspecting the worst, Haskell stopped the Rebel and learned that he intended to summarily execute the black, and the man refused to turn back when he was so ordered. Fortunately, some more Confederates appeared who recognized Haskell and made the man obey, and they took the Rebel soldier to the guardhouse and the black was sent to Haskell's camp. Walking behind the two when Haskell encountered them was a young black of eighteen to twenty years of age whom Haskell recognized as the body servant of Colonel Stephen Elliott. Haskell told the boy to accompany him and he "would see that he went back to his master at the hospital." As they walked along, the young man kept up a constant grumbling and, when confronted, exclaimed that Haskell "ought to have let that white man kill that Yankee negro." A shocked Haskell demanded to know why he felt that way, and the boy informed him it was so he might get his clothes. Haskell thereafter encountered about forty to fifty wounded black soldiers lying by the spring that ran from the ravine. They were utterly miserable, and their pleas for water appeared to delight a group of local blacks, termed by Haskell as "camp negroes and colored loafers," who made fun of their suffering and refused them any assistance. Upon discovering that the wounded blacks were there upon orders of a captured Yankee surgeon who claimed that there was no room at the hospital, Haskell sent for his body-servant, who was quite influential with the other camp servants. He asked his servant to gather the other servants and take the wounded to the hospital. Unfortunately, his servant refused, saying that a "slave though he was, he would die first." Upon approaching the others, Haskell found they were all of the same mind. Haskell finally had his assistant surgeon undertake the task and got the men to a hospital.[79]

The prisoners laid on the ground in Petersburg again on Sunday night, and then, according to William Baird, in the morning some were relocated to a small island in the Appomattox River where they remained until August 3 without anything to eat. Others had been placed on a train on August 1. The first stop for most to the prisoners was Danville, Virginia. From there, they were moved to Richmond and then to various Southern prisons. General Bartlett and Colonel Weld ended up in Columbia, South Carolina, where they were housed in the Richland Jail. There they were surrounded by friends and relatives of the 22nd South Carolina regiment, which had been blown up in the mine's explosion, who were most anxious to learn the fate of their loved ones. Lieutenant Bowley was sent to Camp Asylum in the Columbia Military Prison complex. Others were left in prison in Danville.[80] Sergeant Rodney Long of the 29th USCT spent seven months there, where he claimed to have suffered terribly. Isaac Gaskins was also sent there, and he later claimed that of the 180 black soldiers imprisoned there, only seven survived prison life.[81]

Burnside was no doubt staggered by reports emanating from his commanders regarding the status of the Ninth Corps troops. After being overruled in his attempt to reignite the assault, he then discovered that his plan for an orderly, covered withdrawal of his men that night would not be possible. Potter's 2:30 P.M. report, which suggested that his division had been almost totally destroyed, must have cut Burnside to the quick. Paralysis by depression was undoubtedly setting in as he was forced to admit that the attack had been a complete disaster, that his corps had been severely damaged, and that his own military career was indeed in shambles. Ledlie's and Potter's divisions were entirely devastated; portions of Willcox's division remained effective for duty, primarily because they had been quickly routed in Humphrey's early morning assault and had returned to the lines and been re-formed. Wilcox moved into the trenches left vacant by Ord's withdrawal, which saved Burnside from the humiliation of having to request that his entire corps be relieved. Meade had announced the return of the remainder of the Confederate army from north of the James, and cautioned Burnside to strengthen his line of works, where the obstacles had been removed, and warned him to marshal his reserves against a possible counterattack that evening.

Burnside was still smarting from the morning's dispatch, which he felt had impugned his integrity; he was, in fact, smoldering like a cauldron of heated emotions ready to blow. Then further fuel was added to the mix. At 7:40 P.M. that evening, General Humphreys sent the following on Meade's behalf:

> The major-general commanding desires to know whether you still hold the crater, and, if so, whether you will be able to withdraw your troops from it safely to-night, and also to bring off the wounded. The commanding general wishes to know how many wounded are probably lying there. It will be recollected that on a former occasion General Beauregard declined to enter into any arrangement for the succor of the wounded and the burial of the dead lying under both fires, hence the necessity of immediate and active efforts for their removal in the present case.

This proved too much for Burnside to swallow. He later admitted to having summarily thrown the message away and indicated to his staff officer that he

> would not answer such a message; that if General Meade felt disposed to cease offensive operations on the right and left, and leave us to get out of the crater as best we could, and had taken no little interest in the matter as not to know late in the evening that we had been driven from the crater before two o'clock, I certainly would not give him the information, and I believed he knew all about it.

With the passage of time, Burnside had the opportunity to cool down, and later admitted to the Joint Committee on the Conduct of the War that his action was insubordinate, "for which no excuse can be offered; but it had no effect upon the result." The failure to elicit a response greatly irritated the prickly Meade, however, who then forwarded a further inquiry late that night. At 10:35 P.M., Humphreys telegraphed that "The major-general commanding desires to know whether you have any wounded left on the field and directs me to say that he is awaiting your reply to the dispatch of 7:40 P.M." True to his earlier word, Burnside would not respond to this further inquiry. Thus, if Meade is to be believed, he retired for the night "without knowing whether his troops were in the crater, or whether they were not."[82]

Burnside was correct; Meade had to have had a rather good idea of exactly what had transpired. He had heard of the Federal wounded lying between the lines; Ord himself had appealed for him to do something to help. Rumors were circulating that Burnside had been thoroughly repulsed. Yet Meade did nothing to ascertain the exact status of the assault except to send dispatches. It is easy to speculate that his own actions were calculated to place Burnside in an even worse light, and that he was, in fact, less that anxious for a response from his frustrated subordinate, already on weak ground for his prior dispatches and emotional outbursts, in addition to the failure of the day's mission, much of which he attributed to Meade's interference. Meade seemed most intent on "making a record," rather than displaying genuine concern for the fate of the men of the Ninth Corps. Burnside by then clearly believed that Meade was taunting him. Then again at 8:40 A.M. in the morning of the 31st, Humphreys queried Burnside on Meade's behest:

> The major-general commanding directs me to call your attention to the fact that you have made no report to him upon the condition of affairs in your front since he left your headquarters yesterday, and that you have made no reply to the two special communications upon the subject sent you last night at 7:40 and at 10:40. I am also directed to inquire as to the cause of these omissions.

Burnside finally responded in part at 9:00 A.M., indicating difficulty in compiling an accurate report due to the fact that the "rumors are very numerous and exaggerated." He promised to send a report by messenger, adding his own taunt: "The order to retreat caused great confusion, and we have lost largely in prisoners." Burnside was heavily occupied by then in efforts to arrange a truce to alleviate the suffering and bring in his wounded, as well as in efforts to relieve Ord's troops under orders from Meade. In the afternoon, he did supply Meade with a count of his effective strength, which he placed at about "10,000 men," and sought relief from having to relieve Cutler's division in Warren's line in addition to Ord's men. Finally, at 6:40 P.M., Burnside communicated the loss of his corps at 4,500, "the great proportion of which was made after the brigade commanders in the crater were made aware of the order to withdraw," again reminding Meade exactly where he felt the blame belonged.

It did not take Meade long to respond to that reference. At 7:20 P.M., Humphreys wrote:

> Your dispatch relative to the loss in your corps yesterday is received. The commanding general requests that you will explain the meaning of the latter part of the dispatch, and again reminds you that he has received no report from you of what occurred after 11 A.M. yesterday.

A little more than an hour later, Meade again inquired when he could "expect the return of casualties in your command in the engagement of yesterday." While acknowledging the prior dispatch as to aggregate casualties, he wanted to be furnished with "a statement showing the killed, wounded, and missing, distinguishing under each head between the officers and enlisted men."[83]

Burnside responded after 9:20 P.M. to Humphreys' 7:20 P.M. dispatch with a rather scathing analysis of his attitude on the withdrawal orders and lack of support from Meade:

> Your dispatch of 7:20 P.M. received. Just before the order for withdrawal was sent in to the brigade commanders in the crater the enemy made an attack upon our forces there and were repulsed with very severe loss to the assaulting column. The order for withdrawal, leaving the time and manner of the execution thereof to the brigade commanders on the spot, was then sent in, and while they were making arrangements to carry out the order the enemy advanced another column of attack. The officers knowing they were not to be supported by other troops, and that a withdrawal was determined, ordered the men to retire at once to our old line. It was in this withdrawal and consequent upon it that our chief loss was made. In view of the want of confidence in their situation, and the certainty of no support consequent upon the receipt of such an order, of whose moral effects the general commanding cannot be ignorant, I am at a loss to know why the latter part of my dispatch requires explanation.[84]

Burnside had modified considerably his original, even more acerbic draft, which had stated in part, "Please say to the Cmdg. Genl. that the latter part of my dispatch means just what it says and inasmuch it is very distinct the requiring of an explanation seems to be superfluous. He knew the state of affairs by my written and verbal reports when he ordered a withdrawal and he knows that state of affairs now." There is no question as to Burnside's firmly held belief that Meade's order precipitated the hasty, disorganized and bloody retirement from the Crater. Desirous of having the final word on this subject, however, Meade fired back within minutes that "the order for withdrawal did not authorize or justify its being done in the manner in which, judging from your brief report, it appears to have been executed, and that the matter should be inquired into by a court." Meade asserted that the time and manner of withdrawal were left to brigade commanders "on the spot." He also wanted to know why no division commander was present, "by whom the withdrawal could have been conducted."[85] The stage was firmly set for a scapegoat to take the fall for this disaster, and it was not going to be George Meade. Sadly, in his righteous indignation, even though his role in the affair was indeed far from admirable, Ambrose Burnside had greatly assisted in his own demise.

CHAPTER 17

"Such a Lot of Fools Did Not Deserve to Succeed"

Despite General Potter's complaints, few of the Federal wounded had been brought off the field by nightfall. The ratio of wounded to dead left by the retreating Union soldiers was unusually small, testifying to the savagery of the fighting and the atrocities committed. Still, many wounded men in blue lay in the small pockets, trenches and shell holes between the lines. Nothing could be done to alleviate their suffering or even to administer water to those literally dying of thirst in the intense heat. Those less seriously wounded crawled about and administered to the needs of the rest as best they could. A very few lucky ones even managed to crawl back to their own lines. When nightfall finally arrived, the most that could be done for those suffering soldiers was to throw out canteens of water. As night descended, the battlefield displayed its unusual horrors. The wounded moaned, screamed and pleaded for help and water, and many for a quick, merciful death. The sharpshooters on both sides remained extremely vigilant, expecting hostile activities to be renewed the next moment. Their firing was so severe that none desired to approach the wounded even as night fell.

Added to this horrific scene, the Confederates continued to fire abandoned ramrods into the Federal lines, much to the demoralized blue troops' consternation. This new feature in warfare excited a great amount of merriment among the Rebel troops. "The sound of the ramrod singing through the air 'is peculiar.'" Many of the wounded black soldiers crawled close to the Rebel lines and "were driven back out by tossing among them bunches of cartridges with a slow match attached, that they might more easily become victims of rebel hatred."[1] The black troops had been paid just before the assault, and the Confederates took great delight in removing the money from their dead and wounded within the lines. As they went about this ghoulish work, they exhorted their Federal counterparts to "Send them in on another charge when they get their money."[2]

The Confederates stayed occupied burying the dead from both sides found lying in the Crater and its adjoining trenches. They employed squads of black prisoners as burial details for the task, and these squads worked throughout the night interring the multitude of casualties from the day's heavy fighting. Those in the Crater were covered over where they fell with earth from both sides of the excavation. Many of the Confederate dead were carried back to Blandford Cemetery for burial. The Federal dead in the Crater were buried simply by hastily shoveling the broken and loose dirt in upon the bodies. Colonel Rogers noticed one

The dead lying on the field at the conclusion of the battle (*Harper's Weekly*).

Federal lying on his stomach with his face to the side. The man did not move at all while the earth rose around him. His tongue hung from his mouth and the flies buzzed about his head. Finally, fear of being buried alive overtook the dread of the enemy, and he rose up and shook away the earth from his body, finding he had no wound but one which passed through his jaw, severing his tongue. He was soon sent to the rear as a prisoner. A black barber from New York made so terrible an outcry that Rogers asked him why he continued with his ravings. He replied he was badly wounded by a piece of shell which shattered his thigh and was thus in great pain and could not control his cries. Like a number of the black soldiers faced with this situation, he related that he was in the army against his will, and was drafted and obliged to take up his musket; he said, "I ain't fired a shot to-day, Massa. I prays don't kill me." Rogers told him no harm would come to him, and when the firing slackened he would be removed with the wounded to the Confederate rear. After the conversation, the man then patiently waited until aid came.[3]

The details were still hard at work as the sun rose over the Crater the next morning. Private Andrews of the 23rd South Carolina recalled coming upon a scene of a dead black and a Confederate, both "on their knees, with their guns clenched in their hands, their bayonets thrust through their bodies ... their backs against a clay wall, both stiff in death." More than one exhausted, sleeping Confederate awoke as he was being carried to the grave by the unsuspecting work details. The extreme heat had already caused purification and the bodies strewn about on the field, and especially the blood-soaked earth underfoot in the trenches, emanated such a nauseating smell that Colonel Stewart of the 61st Virginia confessed that he "was forced to abandon ... [his] supper although ... [he] had not tasted a morsel of food since the previous night." The men around the Crater that night slept over "those who slept the sleep that knows no waking."[4]

The next morning the sun brought on another fiercely hot, oppressive atmosphere, which added to the suffering of the wounded, already frantic with hunger and thirst in addition to the suffering associated with their unattended wounds. Henry Matrau of the 6th Wisconsin observed that "[t]hey could only get a truce of 15 minutes to put shades over the poor fellows to keep off the glaring sun & had to leave them there lying on the ground. The Johnnies gave them water, we could see them." The wounded stuck up pieces of tent and blankets on their rifles to escape the broiling heat and blistering rays of the sun. The sharpshooters on both sides made the best of the situation by blasting away at any activity that showed itself in the opposing lines, making it impossible to bring any of the wounded back. "Water! Water! Water!" groaned the wounded as they motioned to friends for aid. "Poor fellows: they are only a few yards from us," Lieutenant James H. Clark of the 115th New York exclaimed, "but it is death to any man who undertakes their rescue, and none but God in heaven can save them." He recalled the horrible scene:

> The soldiers who were badly wounded, lay exposed to the fire of friend and foe alike. One moves painfully towards our works an inch at a time, but the heartless rebels give him a volley of bullets for his pains. Another unable to move, piteously begs to be saved, and motions to some friends, imploring with his hand. The brave fellows' hearts are melted with pity, and they risk their own lives and crawl out to get their comrade. After long and painful exertions their efforts are crowned with complete success; their friend is safe.[5]

The sun was merciless and the stench intolerable. George Whitman of the 51st New York wrote home:

> One of the worst things of the whole affair was, that quite a number of out wounded lay between the rebel lines and ours, and there the poor creatures had to lay in the sun, until the afternoon of the next day, when the rebs allowed us to send out a flag of truce to give them some water, but they wouldent allow any of them to be removed until the second day after the fight when a ceecession [*sic*] of hostilities was agreed to for three or four hours.[6]

Regardless of these conditions, permission to bury the dead between the lines was still refused.

Many brave Confederates nonetheless went among the wounded with canteens of water, and when a flag of truce was not flying, the braves ones would jump the works, wave their canteens and, despite the unrelenting fire, creep up to a Union soldier who was crying in agony. "At such times, all firing of sharp shooters in that direction would cease." These acts certainly testified to the fact that many Confederates possessed compassion for their fellow human beings, regardless of the color of their skin.

On and off throughout July 31, informal truce flags flew over the battlefield. At such times, the works on both sides swarmed with the opposing armies. Howard Aston of the 13th Ohio Cavalry saw on two occasions a number of women and children dressed in white among the Confederates on their lines. After a time, the flags would come down and one side would call out, "Hunt your hole, Johnnies," and the other side would cry, "Hunt your holes, Yanks," and heads would disappear and the shooting would commence again. While Aston was deeply angered at the "inhumanity" of the Confederates in not allowing the Federals to remove their wounded who were suffering the "tortures of hell," he rationalized that from childhood on up, they were taught that the black man was only fit to be a slave and when confronted with these men as uniformed adversaries, they were deeply enraged.

Colonel Stewart vividly recalled that Sunday, with "thousands" of the Federal dead still lying on the field, putrefying under the scorching rays of the sun. He specifically recalled:

A negro between the lines, who had both legs blown off, crawled to the outside of our works, stuck three muskets in the ground, and threw a small piece of tent cloth over them to shelter his head from the hot sunshine. Some of our men managed to shove a cup of water to him, which he drank, and immediately commenced frothing at the mouth, and died in a very short time afterwards. He [had] lived in this condition for nearly twenty-four hours.

George Bernard recalled asking himself at breakfast that Sunday, *Are we to eat in this horrible place, the air filled with offensive odors from the presence of hundreds of bodies still unburied, many of them within a radius of a few feet from us? Yes, or starve.* The meal, hardtack and fried pickled pork, with no coffee, was not enjoyed by the men. Stewart talked about abandoning his meal after the trenches "exhaled such a nauseating smell." That same morning, across the Appomattox, Generals Lee and Hill sat next to each other as Reverend General William N. Pendleton conducted a Sunday morning prayer service. The "[c]oncentration during the service was broken by a small dog, which took turns rubbing itself against Lee and Hill — to the delight of both officers."[7]

Burnside reported to Meade's assistant adjutant general at 9:00 A.M. on the 31st that "[n]early 100 wounded are lying between the lines in our front, which possibly could be brought in by a flag of truce." Soon thereafter, Burnside telegraphed Meade himself the following:

> GENERAL: I have the honor to request that a flag of truce be sent out for the purpose of making arrangements for assisting the wounded and burying the dead left on the field of battle. The number of wounded left between the lines and beyond the first lines of the enemy has been exaggerated by rumor. There are not believed to amount to over 100 in all. Of these there are but few between the lines, the greater part being beyond the first line of the enemy's works.

Meade promptly replied, and included a letter addressed to General Lee "asking for a cessation of hostilities sufficiently long to enable us to bring off our wounded and dead." However, Meade cautioned Burnside that "if an informal arrangement for this purpose can be entered into it will not be necessary to forward the communication to General Lee." Responding to Burnside's further inquiry as to whether the communication to Lee was to be forwarded sealed, Meade responded in the affirmative at 11:30 A.M., and again emphasized that "it would not be necessary for it to go to General Lee if the officer taking it to the enemy's line could make an informal arrangement with the officer receiving it for the recovery of our wounded and dead." Apparently, Meade wished to avoid any admission of defeat, which would be implied with a formal flag of truce.

At noon, therefore, Burnside attempted the informal arrangements Meade desired. A sole Yankee in a clean white shirt jumped atop the Federal works holding the flag and was promptly followed by two "elegantly uniformed officers." Major P.M. Lydig of Burnside's staff, accompanied by Colonel Cutcheon, displayed the flag of truce, that being a piece of cloth about a yard square on a new staff, as they advanced beyond their lines, whereupon the firing ceased and the two went toward the Crater. In the Rebel lines, General Sanders asked those near him if they had a white handkerchief, and all replied "no." A private in the line then said to his comrades, "Boys, some of you take off your shirt and hand it to the General," whereupon another from the 9th Alabama quickly replied, "Never do that; they will think we have raised the black flag."

Sanders finally located a handkerchief, which he and Captain George Clark tied to a ramrod, and went out to meet the Yankee delegation, conversing halfway across the field, or about forty yards between the lines. After a brief discussion, the Federals handed Clark a paper and withdrew. Clark informed Sanders that they were requesting a truce to bury their dead and remove their wounded. Sanders promptly forwarded the communication to Beauregard's headquarters, as he was unwilling to accede to such a truce without approval from higher up the chain of command.[8]

Sometime later, the requested truce was formally denied, as it had come from Burnside, and thus "not being in accordance with the usages and civilities of war ... [as such], it was promptly returned with information that when ever a like request came from the General commanding the Army of the Potomac to the General commanding the army of Northern Virginia it would be entertained." The Union delegation soon returned with the appropriate letter from Meade, being the one which had been prepared earlier that morning, but which was not delivered due to Meade's stubbornness. It was promptly taken to Lee's headquarters; Lee however, forwarded it to Beauregard, in whose department the Crater lay. Unfortunately, by this time it was too late in the day to remove all the dead and wounded from the field before dark. Rather than extend a truce into the night, or break it into two separate sessions, Beauregard put off its commencement until 5:00 A.M. the next morning, August 1, when a four hour truce would begin.

Meanwhile, Burnside reported the initial delay to Meade at 6:30 P.M., indicating that it was "impossible to say when an answer would be given," and that the flag of truce "still continues." Meade was greatly disturbed by this news and directed Burnside to "at once withdraw the flag of truce," indicating that he "did not anticipate that the flag would be kept out longer than might be necessary to effect an arrangement for the recovery of the wounded or to deliver the letter for General Lee to the officer sent to receive it." Thus, while the Union truce initiative was attempted several times that day, no resolution was obtained, and "so the wounded lying between the lines had to be left another long night in their terrible suffering with unattended wounds and exposure to the constant fire of the skirmishers." Meade's reluctance to seek a formal truce was largely responsible for this undue suffering among the wounded of the Ninth Corps. While the truce was temporarily in effect, "soldiers of both sides mounted their works, and indulged in a free and unmolested survey of their surroundings, a privilege they had not enjoyed since their arrival on that ground."

Sergeant Thomas Bowen wrote his mother on August 1, 1864, regarding the wounded lying under the burning sun on the hot sand. Standing on a hill on the 31st, Bowen wrote of observing "hundreds of poor fellows squirming & rolling around on that open fields." One black soldier, with both legs broken above the knee, "by lying on his back & using his elbows managed to reach ... [the Federal] line. He was all night getting over about twenty rods." The wounded lay all day on the 31st on the field in the fierce, blazing sun, screaming for relief. Charles Elliott recalled walking under the flag of truce that day over two or three acres of battlefield "and it was a piteous sight of the horrors of war." Hundreds of Federals were lying slain by bullets and shells, "their bodies swelling from the heat of the sun to immense size and they were filled with maggots and flies. The stench was unbearable."[9]

Burnside's reluctance to withdraw the flag of truce while the issue was being resolved did bear some meaningful fruit for the suffering wounded that day. While none could be removed from between the lines while the issue was pending, the Confederates did allow water and whiskey to the wounded while the flag was flying. Additionally, a number of civilians from Petersburg were observed bringing aid and comfort to the wounded Federals, regardless of color. An officer of the 9th New Hampshire went with the second truce delegation and recognized Lieutenant Sampson's body in the dust east of the Crater, where his run for his life had ended. By nightfall on the 31st, however, the ranks of the wounded were down to a handful of sunburned men, left to endure yet another long night, many unable to raise the canteens of water, afforded them too late, to their mouths.[10]

The terms of the truce, once finally resolved, called for a cessation of hostilities to begin

The Crater in 1865 (USAMHI).

at 5:00 A.M. and to continue until 9:00 A.M. The wounded were allowed to be removed, and the dead were to be interred in ditches to be dug halfway between the lines. Thus, at promptly 5:00 A.M. on August 1, a white flag was planted between the lines, and with a cessation of hostilities all along the line, the work of burying the dead and retrieving the few wounded remaining alive began in earnest. A New Hampshire soldier commented on what a "beautiful Sabbath Morning ... it was."[11] However, the weather was excessively hot, "which added much to the suffering of the wounded, and hastened the end for many who had lain for two days between the lines with no treatment for their wounds and without shade or water." Under the flag of truce, the 35th Massachusetts and one of the black regiments were assigned to act as the burial detachment. A detail of the 12th Virginia emerged from the other side to assist the Union soldiers in carrying off the wounded and burying the dead. With them came a considerable number of black prisoners to perform some of the more distasteful work.

The scene which confronted these men was one they would never forget. Over two days of intense heat had bloated and blackened the bodies so that the only way to distinguish white from black was by their hair. Colonel Thomas observed that there was no distinction of color on the battlefield, as all had turned a purplish black. Many had literally exploded from the pent-up gases, with their viscera protruding out of their gaping abdomens. Others were mutilated and torn apart from the incessant mortar and small arms fire; many were covered in maggots and flies. Still others were trampled beyond recognition. The Reverend Henry E. Whipple, who served with the U.S. Christian Commission, went in with the burial party. He was "aghast at the butchery. Blackened, bloated caricatures of men covered with flies exerted an unimaginable horror on the landscape." Some of the men searched the putrid dead for identification, then wrapped those few in blankets, and pinned their names to the shrouds. However, many of the bodies were so swollen and decomposed that no one wished to touch them, and thus they were relegated to the grave anonymously.

The ghastly scene of the dead was difficult to fathom even for these veteran fighters. Private William Guerrant of Otey's Battery wrote of going "to the pit":

> In the field in the rear of the works and the ground thrown up by the explosion were the Yankees and negroes stranded in every position, naked, swollen, black, dusty.... In the mound I noticed our dead crushed by the masses of earth thrown on them. Near the top of the mound was one poor fellow sitting up as if he had fallen asleep and merely sunk unconsciously with his gun in his hand. He had evidently crawled up to get a better shot at the Yankees.

An officer of the 32nd Maine mirrored Colonel Thomas's observations in describing the horrors of the scene: "Men were swollen out of all human shape, and whites could not be told from blacks, except by their hair. So much were they swollen that their clothes were burst, and their waist-bands would not reach half-way around their bodies; and the stench was awful." Not a shot was heard along the entire line. The *Richmond Dispatch* on August 3 reported that "[f]or five hours the work of burying the dead went vigorously forward. The Yankees brought details of negroes, and we carried their negro prisoners out under guard to help them in their work. Over 700 Yankee whites and negroes were buried." Burnside later reported burying 220 men found between the lines, and about twenty wounded were brought in to the Federal lines.[12]

Major Claudius Grant of the 20th Michigan observed that the dead were laid out in rows. "'With no services,' coffinless and shroudless our gallant brothers were buried, intoned Reverend Whipple." A South Carolina captain told Chaplin Jones of the 20th Michigan that "At any rate we piled your damned niggers up for you." The white men were placed in one long trench, and the blacks in another, placed on top of one another crosswise until all were disposed of and the terrible sight was shut away from view. Thus, "[m]any an anxious wife who learned that her husband was reported missing heard no more from him, and when the Confederacy's prisoners were all released eight months later they had to give up what shreds of hope they may have saved." Some few bodies that were recognizable, mainly officers, and which could be lifted without falling apart were carried to the Federal lines where their names were transferred to wooden markers. Howard Aston noted that the members of the 13th Ohio Volunteer Cavalry could be discerned by their cavalry jackets, but they were still buried without marking their graves. Sergeant Charles Greenwell of Company B, 29th USCT, identified and helped bury his friend Henry Heighton, who had written his wife just days earlier to "[r]emember me ... that my return may be safe to the bosom of loved ones and that I may be kept in the path of duty and not be led astray by the many snares that beset the path of the soldier in the field."

The burial pits were four feet deep. Bodies were rolled in, and in some cases shoveled onto stretchers and dumped into the trenches until within two to three inches of the top, and then covered with loose dirt. Private Welborn J. Andrews of the 23rd South Carolina observed green flies without number that "buzzed audibly all around us and added to the hideousness of the scene. Every attempt to eat or even open one's mouth caused nausea ..." and the soldiers could not get the stench out of their nostrils for days. Private Andrews recalled that "[t]he hills were whitened with lime to enable us to remain on duty there." The Yankees wanted to utilize a rounded ridge over the burial trenches, but that request was denied by Mahone, who observed that they might be utilized as a breastwork for an advancing column, and thus ordered them leveled even with the ground. The work was so difficult, and there were so many Federal dead on the field, that an extension of the truce for one hour was requested and quickly granted.[13]

By the time the Federals were able to remove their wounded only about a dozen were found still to be alive. The blacks who lay in the exposed field for thirty-six hours bore their suffering much better than their white counterparts, according to Charles Trueheart, who wrote his brother Henry that "[s]carce a groan escaped them; or nothing more [than] occasionally one of them would ask in a most objectly submissive tone, 'Master. Please give me a little water; I am nigh dead for want of it.'"[14]

Before the flag of truce, not a human could be seen above ground within cannon range. After it was raised, however, "men like magic sprung up out of the ground, numbering tens of thousands; and the ramparts on both sides were lined with rows of men." William Stewart commented on how the troops "swarmed together like bees, mingling as neighbors and talking as sociably as life long friends. It was surely an impressive scene to witness two armies, which had been fighting out of the earth and came together in such a friendly manner over the burial of the dead." Featherston described how the two armies seemed to rise out of the ground and faced each other and the earth seemed to be peopled with men, "like an illustration of Cadmus sowing the dragon's teeth." Major William Miller Owen of the Washington Artillery described the scene:

> I went down to the flag of truce, and there met [a party of high-ranking Union commanders].... These officers were very courteous and chatty, and brought out buckets of lemonade and other refreshments in profusion. They were desirous of getting a glimpse of some of our generals, and had pointed out to them Gen. Bushrod Johnson, clad in a linen duster and a straw hat; and A.P. Hill, in a gray flannel shirt, standing upon the edge of the crater. They were anxious to see Gen Lee, but "Uncle Robert" didn't gratify them.

The men "swapped tobacco for coffee, chatted, and returned to their lines to resume the war." Both sides came over their works and, upon meeting in the center, "mingled, chatted, and exchanged courtesies as though they had not sought in desperate effort to take each other's lives but an hour before." While this camaraderie flourished, one Confederate leapt to the parapet and shouted, "Let's all go home!" "Whilst the truce lasted the Yankees and the 'Johnny Rebs' in countless numbers flocked to the neutral grounds and spent the time in chatting and sight-seeing. The stench, however, was quite strong, and it required a good nose and a better stomach to carry one through the ordeal."

Ham Chamberlayne wrote to Martha Burwell Chamberlayne on August 3, 1864, that, during the truce, he walked among the Yankees "considerably," and that the "Yank Officers [were] very fine." Colonel Theodore Lyman spoke of venturing to the Taylor house ruins (next to Fort Morton) early that morning and then moving down the covered way. The advance parapet was crawling with troops "looking silently at the scene of the late struggle." From a distance of 350 feet he could view the Crater, and "shapeless masses of hard clay, all tumbled on top of each other." On the ridge stood crowds of Rebel soldiers in slouched hats and "ghostly grey uniforms. Really they looked like malevolent spirits, towering to an unnatural height against the sky." As Lyman went to the enemy lines, he wrote, "I can never again see anything more horrible than this glacis before the mine. It did not take long to satisfy our curiosity, and we returned to camp."[15]

As Major Owen had reported, the Union officers brought buckets of lemonade with ice and other refreshments as both sides introduced themselves; they were curious to place faces with the names of those they had never met. During the removal of the dead, the Confederates brought out a brass band and posted it in the front lines of the works. J.R. Holibough of

Pennsylvania reported that "for two hours the bands of the two sides played alternatively, the Federals playing National airs and the Confederates playing Southern airs." The officers and men of both armies mingled there, "when we were caring for the dead, or sat upon the breast-works on our left and right and engaged in friendly conversation." The Confederates on that part of the line that could be seen from Fort Morton "mounted on their works, enjoying a freedom which was the envy of the Ninth Corps men, and which was, no doubt, equally so for their immediate opponents." It was a strange sight to witness the two armies commingling together between the lines; one Federal officer felt that "in some cases there was too much intimacy. I could not have approached the creatures whilst immediately before my eyes were hundreds of black soldiers, no doubt the majority of them having once owned masters in happy Virginia homes."[16]

John Featherston characterized General Potter, who gave him a canteen which Featherston sampled and "found in it nothing objectionable," as "exceedingly polite and affable." Potter also gave Featherston a good cigar and together they "smoked 'the pipe of peace.'" They discussed Saturday's battle and Potter indicated that they had lost over 5,000 men. Featherston then inquired about the "handsome Yankee General in the crowd, and Potter indicated that it was General Ferrero, who commanded "the negro troops." Captain Featherston indicated to Potter that he had acquired some of Ferrero's papers, which had been captured in the Crater, and displayed them to Potter. The Federal general suggested that he "call ... [Ferrero] up and introduce him, and we will show him the papers and guy him." Featherston, however, replied that "we down South were not in the habit of recognizing as our social equals those who associate with negroes." At Potter's request, Featherston gave the papers to him.

Potter then asked him to point out the Confederate generals then standing on the embankment of the wrecked fort, which he proceeded to do. None of the Confederate generals, with the exception of Colonel Sanders, who was in charge of the truce, chose to mingle with the other side. Featherston did point out General Harris of Mississippi, along with A.P. Hill and Mahone. Mahone was dressed "in little boy fashion" in a suit made of tent cloth "with a roundabout jacket." He was observed by Potter as being very slight in stature, not much over one hundred pounds; Potter laughingly remarked to Featherston, "Not much man but a big general." Potter also noted Sanders, "the best looking and best dressed Confederate officer present ... sauntering leisurely about, having a general superintendence over the whole affair." A.P. Hill darted here and there attired in long gauntlets, a slouch hat and round jacket, and watched "silently ... from the top of the earthworks."[17]

As the burial parties sought to recover and inter all of the Federal dead, the men of Captain Hough's company of the 9th New Hampshire searched among the bodies looking for their beloved leader. Once again, they located Lieutenant Sampson's stiffened body, and his friends sent him home to his family. However, despite a thorough search, Captain Hough's body was nowhere to be found. Some of the men in their search may have stumbled upon a shallow but vacant grave on the Crater floor, which the Confederates had dug for Hough out of respect for a gallant foe. However, Captain Hough had refused to die, and was instead carried into Petersburg as a wounded prisoner despite the freshly dug grave in the Crater.

Then, at 10:00 A.M., a signal gun was fired and the armistice was over.[18] The officers "bade each other adieu and returned to their respective lines." One of the Confederate officers present said, "We lifted our hats to the Federal officers, bowed, and each retired to their respective lines, ready to renew hostilities." On the way back to the Federal lines, Colonel Thomas unfortunately took a wrong turn coming back from the Crater. He was marched to the Confederate rear and eventually set free some eighteen hours later. He was in Petersburg during his brief captivity and later informed Lyman of the flower patches and singing canary birds hung in cages before the doors there, and said that in spite of the brutal Federal bombard-ment, "everything looked as if the inhabitants meant to enjoy their property during their lives and hand it down to their children." He also observed that "little damage seemed to have been done by our shells." Thomas told his Confederate captors during his brief visit to Peters-burg that he had carried in 2,200 men and brought out only 800.

Once the truce was over, the sharpshooters on both sides began firing again and busi-ness returned to normal on the front lines. The Confederate command made a standing offer of sixty days' furlough to anyone who would crawl down to within thirty feet of the Yankee works and tie a rope on the twelve-pounders so they could be hauled into the Confederate works. This undertaking was so dangerous, however, that no one would attempt the rescue.[19]

The Confederates were anxious to be rid of the Federals in their midst, because they were then in the process of tunneling their own mine under the Federal works, while continuing their countermining efforts against further Federal mining operation. Lieutenant Colonel William Blackford was in charge of the Confederate engineers in that area, and he kept his men busy prospecting for additional Union mines there. The nauseating gases from the dead in the Crater soon permeated every underground fissure in the area, and, due to the explo-sion, such fissures were very prevalent. Blackford himself was overcome by the gases when he crawled into the tunnel to investigate the problem that his miners were experiencing. He was eventually able to ventilate the countermine enough with fans and improvised ducting for his men eventually to discover the original shaft that Pleasants' men had dug. When they dug into the tunnel to prevent a possible reenactment, gases from the powder and the decom-posing bodies were so strong that some of the men fainted.

Meanwhile, Captain Douglas had deposited a magazine near Gracie's Salient just beyond Burnside's right, in front of the Eighteenth Corps. When the truce ended, Douglas set off four fuses, but, in a replay of Pleasants' earlier miscue, nothing happened. A volunteer went in, "Henry Reese style," and found that three of the fuses had burned out and the fourth was sputtering. The detonation was therefore postponed, and the tunnel was extended further. Eight more barrels of powder were set into the two new chambers. At 6:30 P.M., on August 5, the mine was finally detonated in front of Ord's extreme left, but the effects were quite unspectacular, causing no damage to the Federal trenches. Fortunately for the Rebels, no assault had been planned, and the misplaced explosion did not result further in casualties to either side. In the flurry of artillery fire that followed, however, Colonel Griffin Stedman, com-manding the second brigade of the first division, Eighteenth Corps, was killed by a stray frag-ment of canister.[20]

Regardless of the cordial feelings between the blue and the gray during the truce, its ces-sation quickly resulted in renewed hostilities, of perhaps even greater rancor than before. The Confederates, in particular, appeared to possess an increased animosity for the Federals who were besieging them, in large part due to the twin offenses of the horrific mine explosion and the use of significant numbers of black troops against them. Phoebe Yates Levy Pember, matron of Chimbarazo Hospital in Richmond, had observed how the Confederates previ-ously had borne a great deal of respect for their Northern adversaries. After the explosion of the mine, however, she observed that such considerations seemed to abruptly change. Mahone's wounded men reached the hospital "cussing and snarling at the Yankees," and proudly displaying their muskets with the bloody hair of their adversaries still imbedded in them. In Matron Pember's words, following the explosion, they had "craved foes worthier of their steel, not caring to rust it in the black cloud that issued from the crater." [21]

The aftershock of this disaster was strongly felt and widespread. The Army of the Potomac, generally, and especially the Ninth Corps, were considerably demoralized. The mood seemed to permeate into every fabric of society. Benjamin S. Schreck, in a letter of August 3, wrote, "Our force was repulsed there on Sunday. Petersburg has been recaptured by them, so far as it was lost. It looks dark for our country." Captain Robert Goldwaite Carter wrote home in a letter on August 3 that "Sherman lost colors and guns on the 22nd; Grant lost enough on the 30th, and now the rebs are in Pennsylvania. It is time to do something desperate now.... The fates seem to be against the Potomac Army." A member of the 48th Pennsylvania wrote home that "I expected to write to you of one of the most glorious victories that was ever won by this army, but instead of victory I have to write about the greatest shame and disgrace that ever happened to us. The people at home may look at is [*sic*] as nothing but a mere defeat, but I look at it as a disgrace to our corps."

"This was our worst battle," remarked the wounded Sergeant James Lathe, "and looking back now it seems like a horrible dream, which none but those that were in it ever fully realize." Captain Charles Mills, assistant adjutant of the first division, wrote his father on August 2 that he felt the "campaign, so full of promise, is about up. We expect every day to leave here." The following day, Mills wrote his mother that "I felt perfectly heart-broken, and I fear my letter showed it. We do not any of us feel particularly cheerful now, but the reflection that there is nothing to do but bear it.... It is, I fear, a settled fact that we cannot take Petersburg, and the next move is not clear." Horace Porter reported that, afterwards, Grant was quieter than usual for the night after the battle. Thoroughly disgusted, he sadly offered that "[s]uch an opportunity for carrying a fortified line I have never seen, and never expect to see again." He later reported to General Halleck that it was "the saddest affair I have witnessed in the war." Lyman Barton of the 8th Connecticut Volunteers wrote on August 12 to his sister that the fiasco "was the shamefullest thing that I have seen or herd of since I have been out."[22]

The mood of the North, already reeling from the huge losses in the Overland Campaign, took an even sharper turn for the worst following newspaper reports describing the battle and its outcome:

> In the memory of men who lived in Washington during the months of July and August, 1864, those days will appear to be the darkest of the many dark days through which passed the friends and lovers of the Federal Union.... The darkness that settled upon us in the summer of 1864 was the more difficult to be endured because of its unexpectedness. The hopes so buoyantly entertained by our people when Grant opened his campaign in Virginia had been dashed. No joyful tidings came from the army now; a deadly calm prevailed where had so lately resounded the shouts of victory. In every department of the Government there was a manifest feeling of discouragement. In the field of national politics confusion reigned.

The failure at the Crater was one of a series of events contributing to the malaise, in addition to Early's presence in Maryland, which caused considerable pressure on Washington, as well as Lincoln's recent call for another 500,000 troops.[23] August 1864 was considered the cruelest month of the year for the Union and the president, with the military outlook turning "even darker just before the month opened. When an elaborate effort to take Petersburg ... resulted in what Grant himself admitted as a 'stupendous failure'" gold went to its highest notch compared to Federal greenbacks, $2.90 to one of gold, making the price of gold $300, its highest during the whole war. Using a financial thermometer as a guide, William Stewart opined that "the Confederate States were nearer to independence on the day of the Crater than at any other time during the great war between the Northern nation and the Southern republic." Salmon Chase had peremptorily resigned as secretary of the treasury, with his last official words being that "nothing could save the finances but a series of military successes of undoubted magnitude." Additionally, the "uneasy whispers in Washington of another draft gave new suggestions to popular discontent."

The Confederate Congress had published an address on recent military events and reaffirmed the South's resolve, while deprecating the North's continuance of the war. These declarations were seized upon eagerly by Northern journalists, many of whom "insisted that no time should be lost in determining whether they might not possibly signify a willingness on the part of the South to make peace on the basis of new constitutional guaranties." The *New York Herald* went so far as to advise that an embassy should be sent to the Confederacy "to see if this dreadful war cannot be ended in a mutually satisfactory treaty of peace."[24]

Support for Grant's military endeavors suffered greatly. The *New York Herald* declared that the great plan to scatter and destroy Lee's Army of Northern Virginia was "an utter and disastrous failure." In Washington, the *Intelligencer* declared:

> [a]fter a loss of more than five thousand men, the army has made no advance towards the capture of that city, which is itself only an outpost of the city of Richmond. The delay in springing the mine, the want of concert and promptitude in following up the explosion with a dash by our assaulting column, and the inaptitude which ordered that this assaulting column should be selected from the least trustworthy and homogeneous corps in the army, are a sufficient explanation perhaps of this calamity.

The *New York Times* wrote in even more explicit terms:

> Under the most favorable circumstances, with the rebel force reduced by two great detachments, we failed to carry their lines. Will they not conclude that the twenty-five thousand men that held Grant in check are sufficient to garrison the works of Petersburg? Will they not conclude that, if they were able thus to hold their own with the force of from eighteen to twenty thousand men sent to the north side of the James River neutralized, this force is available for active operations elsewhere?[25]

Some newspapers reminded readers of Sevastopol, which had been assaulted unsuccessfully many times, while others argued that the time had come to draw troops back to protect the "loyal territory," rather than pursue the defeat of the Confederacy. While the conclusions regarding the ability to suppress the rebellion or the security of the Union itself were open to debate in the North, one conclusion seemed universal. The high hopes for a relatively expeditious end to the war, which were so exalted as spring came to the nation in 1864, were thoroughly and completely dashed. The fiasco on July 30 served to confirm to the Union's high command the original conclusion that a costly, protracted siege would be necessary to defeat Lee's army. Grant became firmly committed to a lengthy war of attrition, whereby Lee would either be forced to come out and fight or face the prospect of complete strangulation. Regis de Trobriand wrote later that "the unfortunate affair ... closed the series of direct attacks against Petersburg. They had cost us more than twenty thousand men. It was full time to adopt a ... method ... exclusively directed against the communications remaining open between the city and the South." The campaign thus narrowed down to a continuous effort to turn the Confederate right and cut off Lee's communications. An attack on Richmond from the north side would be attended with frightening loss of life. To Private Charles Smith of the 1st Connecticut Heavy Artillery, who wrote his wife on August 1 that "nearly all of our heavy batteries were ordered to the rear or somewhere else that same night," the agenda of the war seemed to have completely and abruptly changed.[26]

The mood on the Confederate side was predictably the exact opposite, with the prevailing feeling being of increased confidence due to the relative ease with which the enemy was dispatched. The troops felt a righteous indignation at Grant for exploding the mine and for sending black troops into the assault. "Never was the Army of Northern Virginia more defiant in its bearing—never more confident in the genius of its leaders." Deserters poured into the Rebel lines, bringing reports of the demoralization of the Army of the Potomac. "Most officers and men in the Army of Northern Virginia, adding the Crater to the list of their victories so far in 1864, had their faith in Lee and themselves strengthened." They felt that they would successfully frustrate whatever plans Grant might have in store for them in the future. The battle certainly became a great rallying point for the future. As one Confederate officer put it: "The world has not forgotten Thermopylae — neither will it forget the battle of the crater."[27]

A Federal soldier wrote after the battle that "no battle fought during the war was so discredible to the Union arms as this, and yet in none were the troops actually engaged less deserving of censure." Many described the battle as a "most disgraceful one on their part." Men gathered in several camps and "discussed angrily and discontentedly the responsibility of yesterday's disaster." Regardless of the men's general feelings of having performed admirably, with a disaster of such proportions fingers were going to be pointed and blame assessed, however undeserving of blame some participants might have been. While there was a lot of blame to go around, it certainly was quite unjustified to focus on the common soldier in this aborted assault. Yet, that is where the onus was placed.

Among the soldiers themselves, once their initial complaints against their individual leaders were voiced, the focus seemed to be placed upon the newest element in the mix — the fourth division's black soldiers. Charles Smith, who served with the 1st Connecticut Heavy Artillery, wrote his wife on August 1 that the "[s]ad disaster has completely discouraged the white troops in Burnside's Corps and they say (both officers and men) that they will never fight again as long as the nigger troops are with them." Many were not that surprised when the recriminations began; the black troops often got the blame. General Willcox, for example, praised the second and third divisions afterward, but indicated Ledlie's and Ferrero's men "acted badly." The Crater became an excuse among the ranks to damn the blacks as soldiers. George F. Cram of the 105th Illinois wrote his mother after the battle: "What a pity! When so near the most brilliant victory ever known." He continued that "the abolitionists may talk as they please, but I tell you that colored troops cannot be depended on and that evidently caused this great defeat."

This ill feeling extended to the press also. The *Daily Union* in Manchester, New Hampshire, for example, actually "chuckled at the defeat of the 'Niggers.'"[28] A New York cavalryman north of the James wrote a friend on August 3: "There hasn't any big bouts happened since I wrote you here, but at Petersburg they have had a stunner and would have done something if it hadn't have been for the nigger troops, but it was too warm for them and they took the back track, leaving a gap open and the Johnnies rushed in and the troops that was on the right and left of it had to fall back to keep from being flanked, you see." Another disgruntled soldier in the Ninth Corps unfairly said, "Put the niggers out of our corps as I do not want to be in the corps they are."[29]

If many soldiers in the Union ranks and journalists away from the front blamed the disaster on the blacks, the same opinion was not shared by those in high authority. Meade opined in his report on the battle that the "colored troops" were not open to more criticism for their conduct than the other troops engaged. Burnside believed the black division broke only when so high a proportion of their officers went down that they could not maintain their position. "They certainly moved forward as gallantly under the first fire and until their ranks were broken as any troops I ever saw in action." Burnside also commented that "[n]o raw troops could have been expected to have behaved better." Grant later admitted to the Joint Committee in December 1864 that if Burnside had been allowed to proceed with his original plan with the black troops in front, the assault "would have been a success."[30] Charles Francis Adams, the grandson of President John Quincy Adams, observed the battle and later gave his impressions of the failure in a letter to his father on August 5: "Those who dislike blacks blame it on them. However, they ... [in Adam's view] seemed ... to have behaved as well or as badly as the rest of the troops and suffered more severely. This division, too, never had really been under fire before, and it was "a rough breaking in for green troops of any color." Secretary of War Edwin M. Stanton was later quoted as saying that "the hardest fighting was done by the black troops."[31]

Once their original recriminations based upon prejudice were voiced, many of the rank and file then had time to reflect on the real reasons for the failure. On more thoughtful reflection, many, if not most, tended to place the lion's share of the blame on mismanagement in the assault after the explosion of the mine. Chaplin White of the 28th USCT wrote that "None of the troops, white or colored, are responsible for the action of the Generals. I hold that there can be no higher sin in the entire world than to blame innocent people for the consequences for which they are not responsible." An insightful Lyman Barton of the 8th Connecticut Volunteers wrote his sister on August 12 that there was "jealousy" between the generals which caused the problem: "One afraid that he will do something that the other will get praise for or give the other a chance to do some thing more than he could do." He opined that if the generals would only work together the war would have been brought to a close a long time ago. Colonel Stephen Weld wrote that the battle "was a most disgraceful failure — discreditable to the officers and the men of the 9th Corps, but chiefly to Generals Burnside and Ledlie."

Allen Albert of the 45th Pennsylvania observed:

> Never did men fight with more courage and desperation, but somewhere, not with the rank and file, nor with the regimental officers on our side, lay the responsibility for the disaster. It was then, as it is now when we can calmly consider the situation, evident that a splendid victory was within our grasp, but lost because of mismanagement and for want of competent leadership. Are we not justified in believing that had General Burnside's plan of battle been approved, the results would have been different.

However, "backbiting, pettiness, foolishness, and other foibles of the Federal commanders [were considered to have] buried the chance to win." A final word on the battle was the assessment of Colonel Charles Wainwright who later wrote of his superiors: "Surely such a lot of fools did not deserve to succeed."[32]

On August 1, in his request for an estimate of the army's losses in this "miserable failure" from Meade, Grant indicated that he thought "there will have to be an investigation of the matter." Burnside's stock was certainly at an all time low at Grant's and Meade's headquarters. Captain Lawson Harrill of the 11th Alabama later asked a "prominent" member of Grant's staff what he thought ought to have been done with Burnside for the failure, and the staff officer replied without hesitation, "He ought to have been shot." Meade, in fact, needed little impetus for initiating an inquiry, as he was most anxious to clear himself of any blame therein or from being a target after the fiasco. Therefore, that same day, Meade by Special Orders No. 205, ordered a board of officers to convene the next day "to examine into and report the facts and circumstances attending the unsuccessful assault on the enemy's position in front of Petersburg on the morning of July 30, 1864. The board will also report whether in their judgment any party or parties are censurable for the failure of the troops to carry into successful execution the orders issued for the occasion."

Meade chose Major General Winfield Hancock, Brigadier General Romeyn B. Ayers, Brigadier General Nelson A. Miles and Colonel Edward Schriver to comprise the board. The selection was curious in that all of these officers were from the Army of the Potomac, and all were friends of Meade. Additionally, the officers were far from impartial as to the abilities of Ambrose Burnside.[33] Hancock had previously expressed a lack of confidence in the Ninth

Corps' commander. Ayers had already opined by then that the failure was a result of Burnside's improper deployment of troops. In fact, he went on to so testify at the court of inquiry on which he served as a member of the court.[34] Additionally, Hancock, Miles and Ayers had all led troops in the very battle for which they were then to assess blame. Last, but not least, Colonel Schriver was Meade's own inspector general. Given the general distaste for the Ninth Corps and the individual prejudices of these officers, their appointment not only assured Meade's exoneration, but also signaled that Burnside was in great difficulty well before any evidence was heard.[35]

The board got off to a very rough start the next day, however, when it was discovered that it did not have the legal authority to proceed. Under the Articles of War, only the president of the United States could properly convene such a tribunal except on a demand of the accused, and none had been identified in the case. Meade therefore requested that Grant refer the matter to President Lincoln "with a request that he either confirm the powers given to the Board or constitute them into a court of inquiry. I am clearly of the opinion the interest of the army and of the country are involved in having an investigation. I am desirous that my conduct, as well as that of all others concerned, should be thoroughly examined."

Meade asked Grant to use his influence with the president "to confer upon the Board the necessary authority." Grant quickly complied with Meade's request and that same afternoon forwarded to General Halleck the following dispatch:

> I have the honor to request that the President may direct a court of inquiry, to assemble without delay at such place as the presiding officer may appoint, to examine into and report upon the facts and circumstances attending the unsuccessful assault on the enemy's position in front of Petersburg on the morning of July 30, 1864, and also to report whether, in their judgment, any officer or officers are censurable[36] for the failure of the troops to carry into successful execution the orders issued for the occasion, and I would suggest the following detail: Maj. Gen. W.S. Hancock, Brig. Gen. R.B. Ayers, Brig. Gen. N.A. Miles, Volunteer service; Col. E. Schriver, inspector-general and recorder.
>
> U.S. GRANT,
> Lieutenant-General.

The president wasted little time in acceding to his general's request, and Special Orders No. 258 soon declared the following:

> By direction of the President, a Court of Inquiry will convene in front of Petersburg ... to examine into and report upon the facts and circumstances attending the unsuccessful assault on the enemy's position on the 30th of July, 1864. The Court will report their opinion whether any officer or officers are answerable for the want of success of said assault, and, if so, the name or names of such officer or officers.

All of Meade's choices for the membership of the board were confirmed in the order.[37]

Burnside was far from opposed to a thorough investigation as a vehicle for clearing his name from what he believed were the unfair machinations of General Meade. However, he was shocked when he learned of the board's composition. He promptly wrote Secretary of War Edwin Stanton on August 6, submitting that the board "should be composed of officers who do not belong to this army." He felt strongly that he was due an investigation, but he would not press his claim in any degree adverse to Meade, and was willing to "await the verdict of time." He believed, on the other hand, that "if an investigation is to be had, I feel that I have a right to ask that it be made by officers not in this army and not selected by General Meade." Such a demand was not at all uncommon, as unassigned officers, or those from other armies would normally compose such a board to insure impartiality. Burnside also accurately pointed out that all the officers constituting the subject court held command in supporting columns which were not brought into action that day, and that the court's judge-advocate was a member of Meade's staff. Lincoln, through Secretary Stanton, essentially advised Burnside not to worry, as "he does not see any evil can result to you" from the board's composition. Stanton reasoned that "[t]he action of the Board of Inquiry will be merely to collect facts for his [the President's] information." Stanton closed by indicating that Lincoln directed him to assure Burnside "that you may feel entire confidence in his fairness and justice."[38]

Meade remained quite occupied pursuing legal proceedings that first week of August. On August 3, he forwarded a series of charges and specifications to General Grant regarding Burnside, indicating that he was "compelled from a sense of duty" to do so, and requested that Burnside be relieved from duty with the Army of the Potomac. The rationale for the detailed charges which Meade forwarded to Grant evidenced a great deal of ill will toward Burnside. As supporting documents, Meade reiterated the series of dispatches which resulted in "no satisfactory information, but was answered by a personal insult," as well as the lack of responses to his inquiry regarding the corps' losses at the end of the day. Burnside had already attempted to resolve this situation through a personal meeting with Grant, and felt he had adequately done so. Meade contended the statement of facts was "of itself sufficient to justify my application for General Burnside being relieved, and to convince the lieutenant-general commanding that I cannot be, and ought not to be, held responsible for the handling of this army where such an extraordinary course is adopted by a subordinate officer."

Meade indicated to Grant that he omitted charges and specifications for neglect of duty and disobedience of orders in the conduct of the assault, although believing that Burnside's actions were "open to criticism, if not grave censure," as such conduct was to be taken up by the court of inquiry.

The accompanying charges and specifications were as follows:

Charge I — Disobedience of orders

That Burnside failed to:
— advise Meade of the operation's progress, despite orders to do so;
— advise Meade of the operation's progress or to make any report from 11:00 A.M. on July 30 and 9 A.M. on July 31, despite being ordered to do so;
— advise Meade regarding whether the Crater was still in Federal possession and the ability to withdraw and bring off the wounded, although specifically ordered to do so by telegraph at 7:40 P.M. on the 30th;
— give information in response to Meade's telegraph of 10:35 P.M. of the 30th, or to reply thereto;
— relieve the troops of the Eighteenth Corps as ordered.

Charge II — Conduct prejudicial to good order and military discipline

That Burnside:
— responded to a 7:30 A.M. inquiry as to whether his "officers and men will not obey your orders to advance," by including in his response "Were it not insubordinate, I would say that the latter remark of your note was unofficer-like and ungentlemanly."

Meade provided Burnside with a copy of the charges and specifications the same day, and included a note informing him that he had also asked that Burnside be relieved from duty. Burnside mentioned these charges in his letter to Stanton, who responded that "[n]o charge or even imputations have reached him [the president] or the Department in respect to you." One reason Stanton may not have been aware of the charges is that Grant apparently did not see fit to allow them to move forward. One source indicated that Grant deemed them "too frivolous for notice."[39]

Colonel Henry Pleasants was at the very end of an emotional rope resulting from the immense frustration of constructing the mine despite seemingly insurmountable roadblocks, and then watching his tremendous efforts go for naught in the debacle of the failed assault. He thus put in for a leave of absence immediately after the battle. Burnside called him to a meeting on August 1, at which Pleasants later reported that his commander "looked years older, and sick, but he acknowledged his visitor's salute with a cordial greeting and sat erect, his brusque, bluff manner slowly returning." Burnside told Pleasants that he wanted to talk privately and personally with him. He first congratulated Pleasants for "the perfect success of ... [his] project," telling him that it "was not ... [his] fault that it failed to accomplish what we had hoped for." During a long conversation that followed, Burnside freely admitted his share of the blame for the fiasco by allowing Ledlie to command the first division, for not obtaining order out of the chaos, and for determining the order of battle by drawing lots.

Burnside reached into a chest and produced a bottle of brandy and two glasses. He then unburdened himself as to his difficulties with General Meade, of how Meade had deluged him with dispatches, hour after hour throughout the battle, and how he finally was stung into retaliating with a caustic message which he now felt was certain to be construed as insubordination. He was beside himself with anxiety, and told Pleasants that Meade would probably prefer charges against him and would undoubtedly require testimony of all the officers concerned with the mine and the subsequent disaster. He also confessed that he was exhausted and sick, and that he would like to apply himself for a leave of absence to collect his senses and to get some needed rest. No doubt, Burnside needed a sympathetic ear from another officer intimately involved in the operation, and he probably desired to sound Pleasants out regarding his potential testimony, assuming a court martial was to proceed.[40]

General Meade later called Pleasants to his own headquarters three miles from the Ninth Corps salient. There Pleasants was ushered into an "atmosphere of cold formality that contrasted strongly with the lesser headquarters he had [just] visited." Meade's headquarters, he observed, exhibited a pervading sense of neatness and precision, which gave the impression that the "very grass blades under the General's feet were combed regularly each morning." Meade rose when Pleasants arrived, acknowledged his salute and held out his hand, which Pleasants took diffidently. Meade, who towered above him, was "a great, bearded, imposing figure in his faultlessly tailored uniform." Meade immediately congratulated Pleasants on the success of his project, indicating that the mine was entirely satisfactory from a military standpoint. As this praise was uttered, Pleasants remembered the issue of the theodolite, the delay in supplying the gun powder, the short pieces of fuse, and the "scores" of ways this man had seemingly "sought to frustrate and embarrass him."

Pleasants indicated his intention to apply immediately for a leave of absence, and Meade gave his approval, indicating that he did not feel Pleasants' presence was needed at the court of inquiry. Meade also issued General Orders No. 32 on August 3, acknowledging the valuable services of Lieutenant Colonel Pleasants and the officers and men of his command. Pleasants, however, considered the gesture "belated," if not disingenuous. Meade was undoubtedly relieved by Pleasants' absence, considering his abysmal treatment of him the prior month. With the investigation commencing in days, it was probably just as well from Meade's standpoint for this fiery and embittered young man to be miles away from the proceedings. Meade, too, had his agenda with regard to the upcoming legal proceeding.[41]

Others were concerned with the upcoming court of inquiry, most specifically as to how they might be perceived. Orlando Willcox wrote his wife on August 8:

> As I expected, the public wrath & clamor about the failure grows worse every day — judging from the papers. And gross falsehoods & unjust criticisms that are furnished in order to gratify the shameful public taste are worse than all. As the public is disappointed & mad, every

contemptible scribbler attempts to invent if he cannot find something new to censure & somebody else to blame. It is so undignified & babyish to whine over every disaster in the war &
expose our nakedness without shame to the eyes of the world.

He indicated Burnside would bear his share of the blame notwithstanding his good intentions, and he did not believe the whole truth would ever come out. He further believed that
"humble commanders like myself need not hope to escape. If my division would not advance,
why did I not bring down a section of artillery & blow them out of the crater with grape &
canister — as a certain division commander of the old Army of the Potomac is reported to
have said he would have done. That is the kind of talk we hear." Willcox went on to indicate
that the court of inquiry would "settle things," but probably not to his liking or that of many
in the Ninth Corps: "I hope a thorough examination will be made, & if any of us were at fault,
let us bear the brunt like brave men who have tried their best. Meantime, the immaculate,
patriotic, self-sacrificing, heroic public will eat their cent per cent [sic] while they curse that
infernal blunder & those blundering generals at Petersburg."[42]

The court of inquiry officially commenced on August 6. A circular was distributed to
certain officers indicating they were free to attend all sessions "should you desire to do so."
In all, the court met for at least portions of sixteen different days, and heard the testimony
of thirty-two witnesses. However, the proceedings were quite carefully orchestrated to produce what seemed to be a predetermined outcome. Given the composition of the board, this
was to be expected, and confirmed Burnside's worst fears, which he had previously expressed
to Secretary Stanton. Meade was the first to testify on August 8, and, through his carefully
prepared testimony and exhibits, he made a compelling case for his complete exoneration for
having done all that was within his power to achieve a success for the assault. The list of witnesses seemed to be carefully calculated to exonerate Meade and make a strong case for mismanagement on the part of Burnside and certain of his subordinates. There is no question
that Burnside and some of his subordinates deserved criticism and some, perhaps, censure.
However, the proceedings carefully steered clear of Meade's involvement in the preparation,
and his conscious refusal to appear at the front. Burnside's lack of preparation for clearing
the Federal parapets, as well as the failure to clear the abatis and the trees in front of the Confederate batteries, was emphasized by the judge advocate's questioning of witness after witness.

Burnside himself was later able to force Meade to modify his statements regarding Burnside's failure to report, and made a strong point that it was Meade himself who later ordered
a withdrawal at 9:00 A.M. when Warren's front was clear of Confederate infantry.[43] Burnside
then testified as to the monumental difficulties he faced in constructing the mine without any
assistance from Meade or his staff. He then detailed the reasoning behind choosing the fourth
division to lead the assault, and attempted to reflect favorably on why he later chose the drawing of lots to decide the advance division once Meade vetoed his plan for the order of battle.
He also strenuously complained of the failure of Warren to engage the enemy on his left, when
it would have proven extremely advantageous. When questioned about the preparations he
had made to the Federal parapets, he admitted he had required little to be done, due to the
danger involved, the fear of communicating his intentions to the Rebels, and, in any case,
because the obstructions were already riddled beyond effectiveness. He estimated that at most
five minutes might have been lost moving the first division forward, which estimate was later
corroborated by General Willcox, who indicated that the infantry obstructions were actually
"no obstacle whatever."[44]

Major Van Buren, aide-de-camp on Burnside's staff, kept a detailed notebook during the
inquiry, where he jotted down the correspondence Meade submitted, while doodling on the

back pages during the boring portions of testimony of the first two days. When Burnside made his first appearance late on the second day, Van Buren informed him that some of Meade's submitted dispatches pertained to their hostile exchange following the battle, which greatly upset Burnside. Burnside strongly objected to the admission of any such dispatches or testimony subsequent to 2:00 P.M. on the 30th, the time when the troops were withdrawn and the assault was over, and requested that it be "erased from the record, and [that] no such evidence admitted in the future." His logic was that the court was limited to reporting on the "facts and circumstances attending to the unsuccessful assault on the enemy's position on the 30th of July, 1864," and whatever occurred subsequent to the withdrawal had no possible relation to the success or want of success of the assault, and was therefore not within the purview of the court. He also related that the subsequent occurrences were likewise the subject of charges against him to be tried later by another venue, and should thus not be investigated by the subject court.

Following Burnside's formal objection to such evidence, Van Buren scribbled the words "Schriver cross" in his notebook, referring to the judge advocate. Meade made his own objection to Burnside's request, indicating that, since his conduct was also the subject of the investigation, it was necessary for him to demonstrate that he was not responsible for the manner of the withdrawal or the circumstances attending it. He also argued that the dispatches had no bearing on the charges preferred against Burnside, as those related to disobedience, and not his management of the affairs of the 30th. Meade argued the charges were "a foreign matter," and stood on their own merits, with no direct connection to the proceedings. Finally, he argued that the subject dispatches were official documents and their use in his vindication would have no bearing against Burnside, should he be tried on charges of disobedience of orders. The court then deliberated and found that "the proper time for objection to the reception of evidence is when it is offered, and before accepted." It indicated that notice had been given to all persons who were believed to be interested in the investigation, including Burnside, to be present at the hearing "if they so willed." Deciding the evidence had a bearing on the conduct of individuals other than Burnside, the court thus determined that it had a duty "to examine into all the circumstances of the assault, the subsequent withdrawal of the troops, and everything connected therewith." It thus ruled that the proffered evidence could be considered.[45]

It became reasonably clear exactly where the case was headed by the nature of the questions asked by the board itself. Almost every witness was questioned about the obstacles in front of the Federal works, which Burnside had been ordered to take down, as well as the leveling of the parapets and the equipment available to reduce the Confederate works. Additionally, three engineers were called for their opinions on this matter. Several artillerymen were called to discuss the impact of the trees which Burnside made a conscious decision to leave in place until the explosion, despite clear orders to remove them.[46] Additionally, the issue of inadequate egress from the Federal line as it affected the movement of troops toward the Crater, requiring many to approach by the flank and thereby become exposed to heavy fire once the Rebels recovered from the initial shock, also became a focus of the inquiry. Most witnesses were also asked their opinion on the reasons for the assault's failure. The respective responses were varied, with at least ten different reasons, probably the most common being the troops having to advance by the flank instead of line of battle, a formation caused by debouching almost entirely from the two covered ways, with severely limited openings in the Federal breastworks.[47]

Interestingly, a number of witnesses commented on the lack of one commander with overall responsibility for the assault as being a primary cause of the failure thereof. General

Warren stated this quite precisely, despite Meade's attempt to sway his answers that "some one person having general command should have been there to have seen and directed all at once." General Ames, when asked for the causes of the failure of the assault, also indicated that "the trouble was ... [that there was] no one person at the front who was responsible, in consequence of which there was no unity of action." Captain F.U. Farquhar, an engineer on Ord's staff, indicated that if one person of authority had been present at the front, the assault would have been successful. When asked if there was any necessity for the presence of an officer with a "more general command than the commander of the troops making the assault and the commanders of the supports and reserves," General Ord indicated that he considered Burnside "had a right to give me orders," and that he, Ord, would "be bound to obey any instructions that he might give."

Early on, Colonel Schriver attempted in his questioning to suggest that Burnside, as the "senior officer present," was "responsible for putting in at the proper time the troops designated as supports." Burnside, reflecting upon Meade's former tirades when he believed that Burnside was attempting to exert any control over the other corps, responded honestly that he "never dreamed of having any authority whatever to order in the troops of any other corps." When Schriver honed in on the specific issue, by asking if Burnside did not consider he was responsible for anything further than his own corps, Burnside responded: "No, sir; except as to make such suggestions as I thought were proper. I did not think that I had any general command that day. In fact, I had no authority to order in any other troops than my own corps, General Meade having specially reserved that right to himself." Clearly, he was thoroughly accurate in this assertion![48]

Curiously, Burnside was never asked if he failed to level his parapets because he feared for the success of the operation. He himself offered no such reasoning. Had he chosen to do so, he could have cited Meade's worried order of 5:00 P.M. on the 30th, directing him to strengthen the works where he might have torn them down, when a Rebel counterattack was feared. Equally strange, General Ledlie was allowed to take a leave of absence due to "physical disability" on August 4. Thus, he was never examined as to whether his men had moved by the flank simply because he had failed to instruct his brigade commanders to do otherwise. His brigade commanders themselves were both in Confederate prison during the hearings and could not offer their own opinions.

Burnside himself departed on a twenty day leave of absence on August 13, which had been granted by General Grant, after testifying for three days. Before he left on leave, he had visited Grant and explained his injudicious letter written to Meade that suggested Meade's tone had been "unofficerlike and ungentlemanly." Burnside, after consulting with several friendly officers, came to believe that Meade's intentions in the 8:00 A.M. dispatch had not been intended as accusing him of being less than truthful. Burnside left Grant's presence strongly believing that if he was to retract the word of his response, any unfavorable ramifications would be forgotten. However, when he returned to his headquarters that same day, he was nonetheless confronted with the pending though inactive charges against him based in part on that same letter, and the assertion that he should be relieved of command. Burnside then left the Army of the Potomac on leave, never to return to it.[49]

The court of inquiry did not meet every day. In fact, halfway through the investigation, from August 23 to August 25, Winfield Scott Hancock led his corps into a fight at Ream's Station, "from which it fled in ignominious rout, every bit as shameful as anything that happened at the Crater." Given Hancock's and Miles' status, this defeat went uninvestigated, while the Crater inquiry resumed four days later. On September 1, Grant sent a telegraph to Burnside indicating that, under the current circumstances, "he does not deem it best to return you to the command of your corps at present, but that he will not relieve you from it unless to assign you to some other command. He therefore desires you to remain at Providence or such other place as you may select until further orders from him."

The court of inquiry finally delivered its findings on September 9 after sixteen days of testimony and 32 witnesses. The causes for the failure of the operation were found to be:

1. The injudicious formation of the troops in going forward, the movement being mainly by flank instead of extended front. General Meade's order indicated that columns of assault should be employed to take Cemetery Hill, and that proper passages should be prepared for those columns. It is the opinion of the Court that there were no proper columns of assault. The troops should have been formed in the open ground in front of the point of attack parallel to the line of the enemy's works. The evidence shows that one or more columns might have passed over at and to the left of the crater without any previous preparation of the ground.

2. The halting of the troops in the crater instead of going forward to the crest when there was no fire of any consequence from the enemy.

3. No proper employment of engineer officers and working parties, and of materials and tool for their use, in the Ninth Corps.

4. That some parts of the assaulting column were not properly led.

5. The want of a competent common head at the scene of the assault to direct affairs as occurrences should demand.

The court then found that if the foregoing causes had not occurred, failure might still have resulted from "the failure to have prepared in season proper and adequate debouches through the Ninth Corps lines for troops, and especially for field artillery, as ordered by Major-General Meade." Predictably, General Burnside was the focus of this failure. The court found that he failed to obey the orders of General Meade in not giving such formation to his assaulting column to insure a reasonable prospect of success, and also that he did not prepare his parapets and abatis for the passage of the columns of assault. He was also faulted for not employing his engineer officers to lead the assaulting columns with working parties, and for not causing proper materials to be provided necessary for crowning the crest when the assaulting columns arrived there. Finally, the court found that Burnside neglected to execute Meade's orders with respect to the prompt advance of Ledlie's troops from the Crater to the crest, or alternatively, to have them fall back and give room for other troops "more willing and equal to the task," instead of delaying until the opportunity passed away, thereby allowing the Rebels to recover from their surprise and concentrate their fire on the advancing troops.[50]

Moreover, the court found that Brigadier General Ledlie failed to push forward his division promptly, thus blocking the avenue designed by orders or the passage of troops ordered to follow up and support his assault. No one reported to Burnside that his troops could not be driven forward, which the court found was a clear neglect of duty on the part of General Ledlie, as such a timely report might have enabled Burnside to have made other arrangements for prosecuting the assault before the action became too late. Rather than lead his division, Ledlie spent most of his time in a bombproof where it was impossible to see anything of the movement of troops going into battle.

General Ferrero was also cited for not having all his troops formed, ready for the attack at the prescribed time, for not going forward with them in the attack, and for being in a bombproof "habitually," where he could not see the operation of his troops. By his own order issued while in the bombproof, he displayed that he did not even know the position of the two brigades of his division or whether they had taken Cemetery Hill.

Colonel Zenas Bliss was cited for remaining behind with the only one of his regiments which did not go forward according to orders and occupying a position where he could not properly command a brigade which constituted a portion of an assaulting column, and where he could not see what was transpiring.

Finally, General Orlando Willcox was found not to have made appropriate efforts "commensurate with the occasion to carry out General Burnside's order to advance to Cemetery Hill," and that "more energy might have been exercised by Brigadier-General Willcox to cause his troops to go forward to that point."

Without focusing on Meade by name or position, the court did find that orders should have been given "assigning one officer to the command of all troops intended to engage in the assault when the commanding general was not present in person to witness the operations." There was, however, no reference to Burnside's prophetic July 3 appeal to "say when and how the other two corps shall come in to my support." The court members showed their superior officer extreme lenience as compared to the opprobrium they attached to Ledlie, Ferrero and Bliss for similar omissions, or for that matter, for the refusal to invest Burnside with authority to put in supporting troops at the appropriate time, as he saw fit.[51] One historian of the Ninth Corps, after reviewing the court's findings, said that the "fairest conclusion to be reached is, that its 'opinion' is of little authority."[52]

Clearly, the officers on the court of inquiry were operating under a bias which prevented them from impartially finding the true cause of the fiasco. Their primary finding was quite weak in that sufficient openings had been made in the parapets to pass through at least a company at a time, which could quickly have been combined into regimental or brigade formations. (Obviously, however, it would have eased the situation considerably had more openings been made in the parapets.) Some would maintain the battle was actually lost on July 29, when Meade denied Burnside's plan to put the fresh, black troops in the lead, as well as his plan employing divergent flank guards, which threw Burnside back on his battle-weary white divisions. Unfortunately, the bravest of the three white divisions by then "lay dead on too many battlefields this side of the Rapidan," while those who survived had a habit of keeping their heads down, as Burnside had accurately predicted. Grant himself later concluded that had the black division been placed in front, pursuant to Burnside's plan, "it would have been a success." However, he stuck to his initial support of Meade's objection to the plan, given the political implications surrounding such a failure.[53]

Those officers cited by the court for poor performance associated with the assault's failure were stigmatized by the findings. Burnside, despite retaining his rank and active status, was never again assigned to active duty. General Ledlie was relieved of command on August 6 and placed on sick leave, and Brigadier General Julius White was subsequently assigned to his command. After having been away for four months, Ledlie returned to the Army of the Potomac on December 8. Meade immediately wrote Grant, requesting that he be permanently relieved of duty in the army. Grant informed Meade that he had recommended that Ledlie be mustered out of the service, and told Meade to order him home to await further orders, "and communicate to him the fact that he cannot have here again another command." Ledlie resigned his commission in January 1865. Orlando Willcox might well have been considered Burnside's logical successor at one time. Instead, he continued to command his division until the end of the war. One of the most senior brigadiers at that time, he never advanced beyond that grade until being brevetted at the end of the year. Zenas Bliss was granted sick leave until October 1864. Therefore, he was made president of a board of examination until the end of the war and, although a West Point graduate, was not promoted.[54] Curiously, Ferrero retained his position in the army, although he, along with his division, was transferred to the Army of the James, and was, in fact, promoted to brevet major general in December 1864 for "bravery and meritorious service."

After Grant informed Burnside not to return to his corps for the time being, Burnside patiently awaited further word from his home in Providence, Rhode Island. Toward the end of September, Grant ordered Burnside to return his staff officers to duty with the corps. By then Burnside undoubtedly had to be feeling quite insecure over these signals. Then in November, he asked Grant for permission to visit the army. Grant curtly responded, "You are authorized to visit headquarters." After visiting with General Parke, who had succeeded to his command, Burnside went to pay a call on General Grant, but missed him when his train failed to depart on schedule, and Grant had left on his way to New Jersey to spend time with his family. Burnside then followed Grant to Fort Monroe and Baltimore, but missed him at each location, finally returning to Washington without having seen him.

Desiring to "earn his salary" with some type of command, Burnside visited the president before going home and offered to resign his commission. He complained that the court of inquiry and his inactivity had put him under a cloud. Lincoln refused to accept his resignation and "begged his indulgence." Burnside visited Lincoln again in December to discuss the upcoming attack on Wilmington, which had been his own brainchild. That assignment ultimately went, however, to Benjamin Butler for political reasons. Again in January, he visited Lincoln, who promised him that a command was forthcoming. Grant had apparently agreed to place him in temporary command of the Middle Department; however, Secretary Stanton instead gave that position to an obscure brigadier. Burnside finally mailed in his final resignation to Lincoln on the day that the president was assassinated, indicating that he would be happy to visit Washington for a farewell audience. Instead, four days later, he joined Grant, Andrew Johnson and other dignitaries at Lincoln's Washington funeral. President Johnson had accepted Burnside's resignation that very day, retroactive to April 15, 1865.[55] Thus ended the military career of Ambrose Burnside, clearly a tragic, if not blameless, scapegoat of the disastrous Battle of the Crater. The overwhelming majority of the men of the Ninth Corps continued to believe that George Meade had personally destroyed their beloved leader's military career.

The findings of the court of inquiry turned out not to be the last words on the fiasco and its causes. On the motion of a political friend of Burnside, Senator Henry Anthony, Congress in its infinite wisdom decided to investigate the debacle on its own, and on December 15, 1864, it gave the assignment to the notorious Joint Committee on the Conduct of the War. The committee first interviewed Burnside in Washington on December 17, and then proceeded down to Petersburg to conduct its own, impartial investigation, unimpeded by a military chain of command. While far from one-sided, the joint committee appeared much friendlier to Burnside than the board had been. Unlike the "stacked deck" set up by Meade, this venue had no vested interest in finding him responsible. The committee heard from fewer witnesses than the court of inquiry, but nonetheless produced several significant individuals overlooked by the court. It was soon clear that the joint committee was approaching its inquiry from a different vantage point. It devoted many questions to the role played by Meade in changing the plans for the assault, his failure to insure that the mine's construction was properly supplied, his role in the total lack of support the Ninth Corps received during the assault, and the extent of his ability to oversee the assault from his headquarters. Meade did his best to justify his many decisions and establish his total blamelessness. Edward Ferrero's questioning did much to rehabilitate Burnside. He agreed that the debouchment was adequate, that the abatis could not safely be removed before the explosion, and that the Fifth Corps should have been ordered in to support the assault on the left. Grant, while supporting Meade's decisions, did confess that, knowing in advance Burnside had selected the "worst commander in his corps" to lead the assault, he should have stepped in and prevented it from happening, "but did nothing in regard to it." He went on to indicate that this was "the only thing I blame myself for."[56]

Very damaging testimony relative to Meade was produced from one of the key participants in the operation of the 30th who was never called as a witness by the court of inquiry. Lieutenant Colonel Henry Pleasants testified before the joint committee back in Washington on January 15, 1865. The joint committee delved into his curious absence from the long list of witnesses at the former proceeding, and Pleasants responded that he was on an authorized leave of absence "to attend to private business." He admitted he did not want to go before the former board, believing that as a career officer, "no good would come of it; it would only make me enemies, and I thought it better, as long as I remained in the army, that I should not go before the board. Therefore, I made application for a leave of absence," leave that was subsequently granted by General Meade.

Upon further questioning on the matter, Pleasants said he felt his testimony "might be injurious to some of the general officers," and since the failure of the operation could not be remedied, "no good would come of it if I did testify, and it might have the means of losing me some friends and making me some enemies." Indeed, his subsequent testimony did prove injurious to at least one general officer — General Meade. The joint committee focused many of its questions on the preparation of the mine, and obtained from Colonel Pleasants his feelings of the total failure of Meade's headquarters to supply him with needed equipment, starting with the tools and necessary lumber for the excavation, and its failure to allow him to utilize the theodolite which was readily available at headquarters. He related Burnside's efforts to obtain an old fashioned theodolite in Washington when he was denied use of the army's instrument. The questioning then turned to the fuses used to detonate the mine. Pleasants indicated that he was supplied with common blasting fuses, instead of the more sophisticated fuse he had specifically designated for the task at hand. Moreover, this inadequate fuse was then cut into pieces, some no more than ten feet long, to which he raised great objections, to no avail. The fuse required a length of ninety feet, and thus had to be spliced in many places, which resulted in its failing to detonate the mine when first lit, thus resulting in a delay of over one hour. Pleasants' testimony certainly cast Meade's role in the mine's preparation, and his mental disposition generally, in a very different and unfavorable light.

Charles G. Loring, assistant inspector general of the Ninth Corps, yet another witness missing from the court of inquiry, testified that he had informed Burnside that "the white troops of his corps were not in a fit condition to make the assault," as many had been in close proximity to the enemy lines for six straight weeks, and it was "impossible that they should have the same spirit as fresh troops." Loring also testified that he was with General Ledlie near the front line just before the assault, and that when Ledlie's men went in, "it was not with the formation that General Burnside had desired, nor with exactly the same object." He believed that the intended plan had been changed by Meade's headquarters. He also indicated that despite his advising Burnside not to put the fourth division into the Crater due to the overcrowding, Burnside still gave the order, displaying to Loring his written orders from Meade in essence ordering him to throw in all his troops and push for Cemetery Hill. Burnside told him "he could not have done otherwise than he did," given Meade's clear order.[57]

The joint committee concluded its hearings on January 17, 1865, and deliberated on the accumulated evidence for another two weeks. In early February, Chairman Ben Wade published the committee's independent report and findings. Contrary to the court of inquiry, the committee's main culprit in the disaster was clearly General Meade, whom they cited for forcing Burnside to change his plan of attack and substitute another division for his fresh, trained fourth division. This they found to be the "first and great cause of disaster." They found it reasonable to suppose "the immediate commander of a corps is better acquainted with the condition and efficiency of particular divisions of his corps than a general further removed from them." Had Meade left the plans alone, with Ferrero's division to lead the attack, and with regiments turning right and left to sweep up the flank threat from the Rebel lines immediately, the plan should have worked. Grant had so much as admitted this in his own prior testimony. The congressmen also blasted Meade for his failure to supply Colonel Pleasants with the necessary tools and materials to construct the mine. It was not just a lack of faith in the success of the enterprise, but a lack of faith "accompanied by an entire failure to furnish the assistance and implements necessary to the success of the undertaking within a reasonable time."

They found that the enterprise could have been accomplished in one-third to one-fourth the time with Meade's proper assistance. The failure of the first detonation was placed upon inadequate fuses, although the delay was not seen as contributing to the failure of the operation. Meade was likewise faulted for ordering a withdrawal and ceasing offensive operations on the right and left of Burnside's position, which left the Confederates free "to make such dispositions as they chose against the force of General Burnside." The congressmen also found that the issue of the leveling of the parapets and removal of obstructions so as to afford a sufficient debouche for the assaulting troops, which had been so heavily relied upon at the court of inquiry as a cause of the failure, was not an issue at all, given the huge number of troops that ultimately passed from the lines into the enemy works.[58]

Grant himself was held up to critical scrutiny to some degree. He had previously testified that the failure of the assault was due at least partially to the troops being sent in unaccompanied by any of the division commanders. The joint committee questioned how effective a division commander would have been in any event to overcome the confusion and disorientation into which the troops were thrown from the other causes they found. They cited the fact that no one else brought up the fact (and certainly confessed they did not direct significant attention to it). Burnside certainly did not escape completely blameless, however. The committee found fault with the manner in which he had finally selected the leading division, advising that using chance for such an important mission "does not commend itself to the judgment of your committee." Given the circumstances of Meade's interference, however, his malfeasance seemed to be downplayed by the report, and the choice of Ledlie's division was not indicative of poor judgment.

The joint committee's conclusions, following their findings, were that:

> The cause of the disastrous result of the assault of the 30th of July last is mainly attributable to the fact that the plans and suggestions of the general who had devoted his attention for so long a time to the subject, who had carried out to a successful completion the project of mining the enemy's works, and who had carefully selected and drilled his troops for the purpose of securing whatever advantages might be attainable from the explosion of the mine, should have been so entirely disregarded by a general who had evinced no faith in the successful prosecution of that work, had aided it by no countenance or open approval, and had assumed the entire direction and control only when it was completed, and the time had come for reaping any advantages that might be derived from it.

How much more scathing an indictment of Meade, and a vindication of Burnside could have been possible in these findings?[59]

Unfortunately, the findings of the joint committee, coming as late as they did, were of no assistance to Burnside in salvaging his military career, if this had ever been possible. Within two months, he had resigned, retroactive to April 15, 1865, without ever having been given another command. These findings went a long way toward rehabilitating his standing in history, however, and precluded his being considered the solitary scapegoat of the failure, as the court of inquiry had so designated.

Epilogue

"A Perfect Success, Except It Did Not Succeed"

A Confederate officer once proclaimed of the fighting at the Crater that "I have always claimed that ... [it] was one of the most desperate, bloody and fearful battles for the number engaged in the fight of any in the war." "Thus ended an operation conceived with rare ingenuity," Horace Porter later stated in describing the conclusion of the affair, "prepared with unusual forethought, and executed up to the moment of the final assault with consummate skill, and which yet resulted in absolute failure from sheer incapacity on the part of subordinates." The affair was viewed by the Federal troops as a "humiliating, disgraceful failure, which filled the North with mourning." George Templeton Strong, one of those soldiers, described the day as "more spectacular than important, but it was an episode which caused discouragement at the North, and elation at the South."[1]

The Union losses amounted to at least 504 killed, 1,881 wounded and 1,413 captured, for a total of 3,798 casualties, 3,475 of these from the Ninth Corps alone, and 323 from Turner's division, the Tenth Corps. Ferrero's Fourth Division suffered the greatest number of casualties, 1,327 over all; of this number, 209 men were killed, a number greater than any other division and accounting for almost one half of the Ninth Corps dead. Colonel Thomas reported that his Second Brigade had lost thirty-six officers and 877 men, amounting to 40 percent of its total complement. (The Official Records reflected a total of 772 men lost.) These figures substantiate that the Fourth Division was either exposed to the greatest force of the Confederate counteroffensive, or was the least likely to be given quarter by the Confederates. The losses were unusually heavy in Burnside's other divisions as well. Most of the regimental leadership of the first division had fallen in the assault, with all but one of Bartlett's regimental commanders being casualties. The 9th New Hampshire lost over one half of its men. Captain Hough, its commander, was left for dead; however, he survived and was taken to a hospital in Petersburg and his grave was unfilled. Both the first and second brigade commanders of the leading, first division were ultimately captured by the Confederates. The Federals had used at least eighty-one of 144 cannon in the engagement and had shot 3,823 rounds, amounting to over seventy-five tons of ordnance. The Confederate used twenty-five cannon and fired approximately 1,600 rounds of ammunition.[2]

What caused this assault, conceived with such "rare ingenuity," to fail so miserably? The answers are numerous and readily discernable. From a strategic point of view, the primary

335

reason for its failure had to be the first division's headlong plunge into the Crater, followed by its halting therein and its subsequent refusal to be driven forward. It was upwards of an hour before the Confederate artillery was effective in punishing the advancing Federal troops. For a good twenty to thirty minutes, there was also little or no infantry opposition to the advance. Yet the first division would not go forward. It could seemingly have advanced on to Cemetery Hill with ease had it progressed straight on through the Crater, or, more realistically, around it. The reasons why it did not were several:

1. Its two brigade commanders had been given orders from General Ledlie which they interpreted as requiring them to stop at the Crater;

2. the men, as Burnside had predicted, had a strong propensity to seek shelter and dig in at the first opportunity;

3. the initial debouchement, through narrow, confined openings, caused all order to be broken, resulting in disjoined, confused commands;

4. the gapping hole itself was extremely difficult to negotiate one's way through once inside, and finally;

5. troops from other divisions piled into the rear of the first division in the overcrowded staging area and added greatly to the confusion.

Then, when additional divisions moved out, they became intermingled with the first division, and total chaos reigned, aggravating an already serious situation. When the fourth division was finally sent in, it was far too late to be effectively utilized in the overcrowded area where so many men were already engaged with the Confederates. Added to this, committing Turner's division made matters even worse. They should not have been dispatched. Instead, what was needed, as Burnside pointed out, was a diversion from the flanks, most particularly from the left, with the Fifth Corps, going into the undermanned section of the Rebel trenches south of the Crater, thereby relieving Confederate pressure on Burnside's men. It was sheer madness to continue sending troops into the Crater, where confusion reigned. Instead, the works on both sides of the Crater should have been simultaneously assaulted, which could easily have been accomplished with the vast numbers available to Meade.

There may have been no greater error in the history of the war than the decision which plunged so many troops through such a "bung hole." Further, once it was determined that a withdrawal was necessary, all support from the flanks was withdrawn immediately, as the Rebel forces on the right and left were left entirely unoccupied and thus could concentrate on the masses in the Crater and the Federal withdrawal from there. As Burnside later stressed in his own defense, "It could hardly have been expected that the withdrawal could have been made without disaster, after all offensive operations had ceased on the right and left, and the supporting force withdrawn from the rear."[3]

There were a number of individuals to whom blame can be assessed for the fiasco at the Crater. Given the results, no Federal commander involved therein can escape completely unscathed. Certainly George Meade must take top honors for the assault's failure in spite of his next to complete exoneration by a court of inquiry, comprised of officers under his command influence, in addition to being his friends. His last-minute decision to require one of the three worn-out white divisions to lead the charge, countermanding Burnside's decision to lead with Ferrero's fourth division, which had trained for the event, had attached to it all the makings for a disaster from its very inception. In so doing, regardless of how pure his motives were, Meade ignored the warning of the man who knew his troops' tendencies to seek a shelter at the first opportunity, a prediction which came to pass as soon as those troops reached the Crater, with disastrous consequences. As the joint committee subsequently found, a corps commander is better acquainted with the condition and efficiency of his corps than a general further removed from them. This last minute change in the division assigned to lead the assault also left little time for the ultimate commander of that lead division to make adequate preparations for the advance, which resulted in confused orders, causing both his brigade commanders to believe they were not to advance beyond the Crater, but rather to simply make way for the divisions behind them to spearhead the assault on to Cemetery Hill.

Despite Meade's arguments to the contrary, he, in effect, also changed the tactical order of attack from Burnside's original plan. Instead of moving regiments to the right and left of the Crater in order to drive the Confederates from their forward lines, thereby removing the danger of flank attacks on the advancing Federal columns, Meade directed that all advancing troops should push at once for the crest of Cemetery Hill. The Rebel lines to the right and left could easily have been rolled up if hit immediately after the explosion of the mine. This change in the tactical plan added to the horrific confusion and crowding in the Crater and its immediate environs, and made it next to impossible for subsequent troops to drive the Confederates from the front lines on either side of the pit as the battle progressed.

The poisonous atmosphere and almost total lack of harmony between Burnside and his commander certainly also played a role in the disaster, given Meade's apparent distrust and distaste for his subordinate, as well as the stilted communication between the two men as the battle disintegrated. Responsibility for this atmosphere must be attributed to Meade as the man in charge. He certainly demonstrated a total lack of respect for Burnside, and permitted an atmosphere for his staff to do likewise. His fragile ego prevented allowing Burnside to undertake any initiative beyond his corps's involvement in the battle, which resulted in a total failure of any coordinated efforts from the other corps of the Army of the Potomac hierarchy, again with disastrous results. Burnside had attempted to placate Meade, and had willingly allowed himself to be subordinated to him in the Army of the Potomac, despite his seniority in rank. Meade would have none of it, though, and would not hesitate to advise against anything Burnside suggested, or to treat him in a condescending and humiliating manner. When a trusting, respected relationship was essential toward a commander leading such a significant assault, Meade placed next to no worth in Burnside's handling of the advance, and made no attempt to support him.[4]

Once the Ninth Corps was bogged down in and around the Crater, Meade had the ability to send in the Fifth and the Second Corps as a diversionary measure to relieve the pressure on that concentrated area, thereby allowing the troops to breakout and continue their advance on Cemetery Hill. Corporal George Allen of the 4th Rhode Island was quite passionate in his criticism of Meade's leadership in this regard, pointing out the four heavy lines of battle, including the Second, Fifth, Tenth[5] and Eighteenth Corps, which lay "waiting and anxious," to support the Ninth Corps, or at least give them a chance to retreat. With the exception of a division of the Tenth, and one of the Eighteenth Corps, Allen bitterly observed, "not a man was allowed to go to our assistance." The Ninth Corps was "in a box" and Meade knew it, according to Allen, and it appeared to the rank and file that "he was perfectly willing we should stay there. Four thousand of them did, and we hope he was gratified," Allen bitterly asserted. Meade certainly should have taken a firmer stand with Warren and Hancock regarding their ability to come to Burnside's aid at this critical juncture, especially when Burnside asked for and desperately needed assistance.

The rank and file of the army certainly believed more should have been done in this regard. As Lyman Barton related to his sister, Mary Barton, after the battle, it was "jealousy between the Generals" that resulted in mismanagement and failure. He related that the Confederates had but three divisions in place:

[and] we had 4 Corps ... and had possession of their works at one time and I will not say could not hold them for we could if they had done as they had aught to they sent in 2 or three Divisions and carried the works and then let them be drove back when we had 13 more Divisions laying back in reserve doing nothing, would it not of been better to sent in one half of us and carried their works and drove them across the Appomatox.[6]

Many of the officers engaged in the attack agreed that a vigorous assault from the Fifth Corps would have relieved the troops in the Crater from the severe crossfire, thereby allowing forward movement on their part. Meade readily accepted Warren's assertion that no Confederate troops had left his front, when, in fact, they were spread exceedingly thin there due to the departure of three of Mahone's five brigades.[7]

Finally, Meade can also be severely faulted for his failure either to be at the front in person or to have appointed some individual with overall responsibility to give necessary commands on the spot. It was clearly evident that Burnside did not possess such authority; Meade had made that pointedly clear to him. The other corps commanders, including Warren and Ord, felt that there were certainly moments when such a supreme authority was needed to decide at once on a course of action. Warren was clearly directionless and lacked a willingness to commit his corps at a time when such an action arguably could have saved the day. Testimony at the court of inquiry suggested that the assaulting troops, to have been completely successful, "only wanted some person present to tell them what to do afterwards." The troops "wanted ... handling," and "had the troops been pushed forward properly ... there would have been no difficulty in the place being carried."

Lieutenant John Sergeant Wise later wrote that a Stonewall Jackson or a Phil Sheridan "would never have frittered away an opportunity so glorious by directing subordinates from a distant position of safety."[8] The presence of Meade or an empowered surrogate was desperately needed at the front. The lack of either caused a total lack of coordination among the several corps, and a missed opportunity to have cleared the logjam around the Crater, thereby allowing the assault to continue its advance on to the objective. Finally, while not a cause of the assault's failure, Meade's decision at 9:45 A.M. to withdraw all support on the right and left of the embattled Ninth Corps and, almost incomprehensively, to call off Federal supporting artillery fire, gave the Rebel infantry a free fire zone on the trapped men in the Crater. The Confederates were able to increase the use of their heavy guns exclusively on the trapped men and their escape route. This situation made it next to impossible to achieve any semblance of an orderly retreat from the Crater and caused the majority of the Federal casualties that day.

Ambrose Burnside must also be held accountable for the dimensions of the fiasco, however sincere and properly motivated he was in directing the assault. Regardless of the intensity of his feelings associated with his original plan and his distain for sending in the thoroughly spent white troops, he should never have resorted to a lottery to identify the lead division for the assault. This decision definitely displayed a lack of proper leadership, which spelled serious trouble for the assault before it ever commenced. He did not want Ledlie present at the final briefing, relenting only when pressed by General Willcox. While there remains some doubt as to his knowledge of Ledlie's incompetence, given the lengths that Ledlie's staff went to shelter him, obviously Burnside did not place a high value on his leadership or advice. To have thus given Ledlie the responsibility for this critical undertaking displayed unforgivably bad judgment. Additionally, Burnside's orders to his division commanders, while clear, were not sufficiently direct as to their execution. By his inclusion of a series of "if possibles" to their orders, far too much latitude was allowed his subordinates in their decision-making process. Thus, in the end, Ledlie's orders to his brigade commanders resulted in a contradiction of those given by Meade and Burnside. Burnside must share the blame for this breakdown in communication, together with its disastrous consequences.

When things began to disintegrate soon after the explosion, there was a great need for a commander to direct the assault and salvage victory from the confusion. The subordinate commanders attempted to carry out orders issued prior to the commencement of the action, while the very first attack resulted in conditions absolutely necessitating a change of those plans. While Meade can properly be criticized for being too far removed from the action, the same criticism holds true for Burnside. Like Meade, he was not there to direct Ledlie and his other division commanders when they desperately needed such direction. If Burnside had once shown himself at the head of his command, the troops might have followed him to the objective, however disorganized they were, and he could still have carried his advantage in numbers to its legitimate results.[9] Mahone himself later indicated there was plenty of time between the explosion and the arrival of his troops where "there was nothing on the Confederate side to prevent the orderly projection of any column through the breach which had been effected, cutting the Confederate army in twain."

An energetic commander with well-led troops should have been able to get through the gap onto the high ground beyond in that time frame. With the lead troops confused about the objective and their role in it, and the troops following behind needlessly crowding into the Crater, the presence of Burnside at the front may well have been enough to sort out the confusion, bring order to the chaos, and set the troops on to their objective before the Confederates recovered and consolidated their forces. Even later in the action, his immediate presence might have brought some order to the scattered attacks, and would certainly have assisted in an orderly withdrawal. Burnside can also be faulted for his failure to properly prepare the advance routes and debouche points and to remove natural and military obstructions. The joint committee, however, considered his failure in this regard inconsequential, as a sufficient number of troops had advanced on the Crater. Regardless of these considerations, the lack of openings in the lines and the absence of sufficient egress held up the troops and resulted in confusion and disorganization as they advanced. Utilizing but two covered ways held up vital supporting troops and resulted in an advance by the right flank for many, as opposed to an attack in line of battle, all with adverse consequences on the achievement of the objective. Similarly, failing to clear the trees to the north masked Wright's battery from the Federal artillery, which had disastrous effects on the advancing troops. Burnside had his reasons for refraining from obeying the order to clear them prior to the explosion. However, insufficient planning and inadequate execution following the explosion hindered their removal in time to prevent the problems which occurred.[10]

Little explanation is needed for General Ledlie's failures that fateful day. He was solely responsible for the ineffective communication of orders that resulted in both Bartlett and Marshall believing that their orders were to halt at the Crater and act as support for the columns behind them, with the resultant tragic consequences. He then compounded his malfeasance by remaining safely ensconced in a bombproof under the influence of alcohol while his hapless troops advanced and confusion reigned. Regardless of reports of their reluctance to advance from the Crater and the terrible confusion which had overtaken the advance, Ledlie still chose to remain in his safe haven instead of going to the front, and arguably into the Crater itself, actively to command his men. His condemnation by the court of inquiry was well justified.

In dispensing criticism of the leadership of the rest of Burnside's commanders, one must note that the remaining division commanders themselves were not at the front to actually lead the troops and keep them advancing forward.[11] Grant later noted that "had he been a division commander ... [he] would have been at the front giving personal directions on the spot." He believed the men would have performed had they "been properly led and skillfully handled." Further, General Bartlett misinterpreted Ledlie's orders regarding the direction in which he was to lead his men, resulting in the intermingling of his brigade with Marshall's. Such a mistake is hard to fathom, as it came from an experienced, field grade officer and Harvard student. Finally, General Ferrero, when his division was belatedly ordered into the fray, chose to join Ledlie in his bombproof, sampling "Dutch courage" instead of supervising his men, who were soon being butchered in the chaos.[12]

General Warren cannot escape some blame for his nonfeasance in the affair. Granted, he was not in a position to independently commit his Fifth Corps to the attack on the left in support of Burnside's troops. However, his lack of enthusiasm for such an action certainly did not give Meade an incentive for committing the Fifth Corps to the action. Additionally, Warren was totally unaware that Mahone had stripped three of his five brigades from his front, thus presenting an extremely weakened front that was vulnerable to an attack, the knowledge of which would have greatly relieved the pressure on the Ninth Corps to his right.

Grant himself cannot go uncensured on several accounts. While arguably Ledlie's drunkenness and incompetence may have escaped Burnside's knowledge due to the protectiveness of Ledlie's staff, the one person who definitely knew of those failings was the man responsible for assigning Ledlie to the Ninth Corps and the Army of the Potomac — Ulysses S. Grant himself. While knowing that Ledlie was "the worst commander in the Ninth Corps," and that he had been chosen to lead this critical assault by chance, Grant, by his own admission, neglected to do anything about the situation, with the obvious tragic consequences. Grant also should have realized that the massive pit situated directly in front of the troops, the natural result of the mine's explosion, would cause considerable problems in troop movement in and around the Crater, thereby breaking up all formations. His position of authority, and prior successes, however, insulated him from any criticism at the time.

Major Charles F. Adams of the 1st Massachusetts Cavalry[13] delivered a fitting eulogy to the tragic battle when he stated that it "was agreed that the thing was a perfect success, except that it did not succeed." John Sergeant Wise succeeded in trumping this characterization with his comment that, "in the whole history of war, no enterprise so auspiciously begun ever resulted in a conclusion more lame and impotent." The Battle of the Crater was such a confusing one that contemporary accounts differ widely in regard to the details. In many respects, it was a fight similar to the Wilderness, where many times an overview is all that can readily be pieced together given the chaos brought on by conditions inherent to the engagement. Thus, portraying a concise and clear picture of events is difficult, if not impossible. However, the mistakes that led to the bedlam are ascertainable. This present work has been an attempt to bring some order to the chaos in order to present an accurate picture of the events which led up to, and which occurred during, the battle.[14]

The war and the killing would continue for almost nine more months, resulting in perhaps 80,000 more deaths, in some significant part due to the failure of the Federal assault on July 30.[15] Grant's attempt at frontal assaults on Lee's army was over. From then on, the Army of the Potomac fought a war of strangulation, cutting communications and needed supplies in its relentless attempt to force Lee out of the trenches. This was finally accomplished on April 3, 1865, when Lee finally abandoned Petersburg, and thus Richmond, beginning the long and painful retreat to Appomattox Court House and his surrender six days later on Palm Sunday, April 9, 1865. The surrender resulted in a slow chain reaction that over the next eleven weeks resulted in the surrender of all Confederate forces in the field.

Meanwhile, the scenery of the battle around the Crater remained a grotesque scene from hell for months to come. Partially covered bodies would frequently open the earth as pent-up gases escaped from them. Subsequent storms washed loose covering earth down, and for months, actually "until the end of the war, long rows of bleached skeletons marked this field of awful slaughter."[16]

Appendix A

Organization of Opposing Forces

UNION FORCES — JULY 30, 1864

United States Army / Lieutenant General Ulysses S. Grant Commander-in-Chief

Adjutant General and Chief of Staff — Brigadier General John A. Rawlins
Asst. Adjutant General — Lieutenant Colonel Theodore S. Bowers
Asst. Adjutant General — Captain Ely S. Parker
Asst. Inspector General — Lieutenant Colonel William L. Duff
Asst. Quartermaster — Captain Henry W. Janes
Aide-de-Camp — Colonel Horace Porter
Aide-de-Camp — Colonel Orville E. Babcock
Aide-de-Camp — Colonel Cyrus B. Comstock
Aide-de-Camp — Lieutenant Colonel Frederick T. Dent
Aide-de-Camp — Major Peter T. Hudson
Chief Commissary — Lieutenant Colonel Michael R. Morgan
Chief Quartermaster — Brigadier General Rufus Ingalls
Military Secretary — Lieutenant Colonel Adam Badeau
Military Secretary — Lieutenant Colonel William R. Rowley

Army of the Potomac / Major General George G. Meade Commanding

Chief of Staff — Andrew A. Humphreys
Chief of Artillery — Brigadier General Henry J. Hunt
Chief Engineer — Major James C. Duane
Volunteer Engineer Brigade — Brigadier General Henry W. Benham
Battalion U.S. Engineers — Captain George H. Mendell
Guards and Orderlies — Captain Daniel P. Mann
Provost Guard — Brigadier General Marsena R. Patrick
Signal Corps — Captain Benjamin F. Fisher

343

Ninth Army Corps / Major General Ambrose E. Burnside Commanding

Chief of Staff— Brigadier General Julius White
Asst. Inspector General— Lieutenant Colonel Charles G. Loring
Aide-de-Camp— Major James L. Van Buren
Escort— 3rd New Jersey Cavalry (Cos. A & E)— Lieutenant John S. Hough
Provost Guard— 8th United States Inf.— Captain Milton Cogswell

FIRST DIVISION

Brigadier General James H. Ledlie

FIRST BRIGADE

Brigadier General William Francis Bartlett (C)
Lieutenant Colonel Joseph H. Barnes

21st Massachusetts— Captain William H. Clark (MW)
29th Massachusetts— Lieutenant Colonel Joseph H. Barnes
Captain Willard D. Tripp
56th Massachusetts— Colonel Stephen M. Weld (C)
Captain Charles D. Lamb
57th Massachusetts— Major Albert Prescott (K)
Captain Edson A. Dresser (K)
Captain George H. Howe (K)
Lieutenant Albert Doty
59th Massachusetts— Colonel Jacob Parker Gould (MW)
Lieutenant Colonel John Hodges, Jr. (K)
Captain Ezra Palmer Gould
100th Pennsylvania— Major Thomas Jefferson Hamilton (MW&C)
Captain Walter Oliver (K)
Captain Joseph H. Pentecost

SECOND BRIGADE

Colonel Elisha G. Marshall (C)
Lieutenant Colonel Gilbert P. Robinson

3rd Maryland Battalion—	Lieutenant Colonel Gilbert P. Robinson
	Captain David J. Weaver
14th New York Heavy Artillery—	Major Charles Chipman (organized into two battalions)
	Captain Lorenzo I. Jones
	Captain Charles H. Houghton
179th New York—	Major John Barton (K)
	Captain Albert A. Terrill
2nd Pennsylvania Provisional Heavy Artillery—	Lieutenant Colonel Benjamin Griffin Barney (W)
	Captain James W. Haig

Acting Engineers
35th Massachusetts—   Captain Clifton Aurelius Blanchard

SECOND DIVISION
Brigadier General Robert B. Potter

FIRST BRIGADE
Colonel Zenas R. Bliss

36th Massachusetts—	Captain Thaddeus L. Barker
58th Massachusetts—	Captain Charles E. Churchill
2nd New York Mounted Rifles—	Colonel John Fisk
51st New York—	Major John G. Wright (W)
	Captain George Washington Whitman
45th Pennsylvania—	Captain Theodore Gregg
48th Pennsylvania—	Lieutenant Colonel Henry Pleasants
4th Rhode Island—	Lieutenant Colonel Martin P. Buffum (C)
	Major James T.P. Bucklin

SECOND BRIGADE
Brigadier General Simon G. Griffin

31st Maine—	Lieutenant Colonel Daniel White (WC)
	Captain James Dean
32nd Maine—	Colonel Mark F. Wentworth (W)
	Captain Joseph B. Hammond
2nd Maryland—	Lieutenant Colonel Henry Howard, Jr. (MW)
	Captain James H. Wilson
6th New Hampshire—	Captain Samuel G. Goodwin (K)
	Captain Robert L. Ela (W)
9th New Hampshire—	Captain Andrew J. Hough (WC)
	Captain John B. Cooper
11th New Hampshire—	Captain Arthur C. Locke
17th Vermont—	Lieutenant Colonel Charles Cummings

Acting Engineers
7th Rhode Island—	Lieutenant Colonel Percy Daniels

THIRD DIVISION
Brigadier General Orlando B. Wilcox

FIRST BRIGADE
Brigadier General John Hartranft

8th Michigan—	Lieutenant Colonel Ralph Ely
	Major Horatio Belcher
27th Michigan (1st & 2nd Cos. Sharpshooters attached)—	Lieutenant Colonel William B. Wright (W)
	Captain Edward S. Leadbeater
109th New York—	Colonel Isaac S. Catlin (W)
	Lieutenant Colonel Philo B. Stilson (W)
	Captain Edwin Evans

13th Ohio Dismounted Cavalry—Lieutenant Colonel Noah H. Hixon
51st Pennsylvania—   Colonel William J. Bolton (W)
                                   Major Lane S. Hart
37th Wisconsin—   Colonel Samuel Harriman
38th Wisconsin (5 Cos.)—   Capt. Newton S. Ferris (MW)
                                   Lieutenant Colonel Colwert K. Pier*

*On detail at Headquarters

SECOND BRIGADE
Colonel William Humphrey

1st Michigan Sharpshooters—   Captain Elmer C. Dicey (C)
2nd Michigan—   Captain John L. Young (K)
                                   Captain Ebenezer C. Tullock
20th Michigan—   Lieutenant Colonel Byron M. Cutcheon
24th New York Cavalry (Dismounted)—Lieutenant Colonel Walter C. Newberry
46th New York—   Captain Alphons Serviere
60th Ohio (9th & 10th Cos.
  Sharpshooters attached)—   Major Martin P. Avery
50th Pennsylvania—   Lieutenant Colonel Edward Overton, Jr.

Acting Engineers
17th Michigan—   Colonel Constant Luce

FOURTH DIVISION
Brigadier General Edward Ferrero

FIRST BRIGADE
Lieutenant Colonel Joshua K. Sigfried

27th USCT—   Lieutenant Colonel Charles J. Wright (W)
30th USCT—   Colonel Delevan Bates (W)
              Lieutenant Colonel Hiram A. Oakman
39th USCT—   Colonel Ozora P. Stearns
43rd USCT—   Lieutenant Colonel H. Seymour Hall (W)
              Captain Jesse Wilkinson

SECOND BRIGADE
Colonel Henry Goddard Thomas

19th USCT—Lieutenant Colonel Joseph G. Perkins
23rd USCT—Colonel Cleveland J. Campbell
28th USCT—Colonel Charles S. Russell
29th USCT—Lieutenant Colonel John A. Bross (K)
          Major T. Jefferson Brown
31st USCT—Captain Thomas Wright

ARTILLERY BRIGADE
Lieutenant Colonel J. Albert Monroe

Maine Light, 2nd Battery (B)—Captain Albert F. Thomas
Maine Light, 3rd Battery (C)—Captain Ezekiel R. Mayo

Maine Light, 7th Battery (G) — Captain Adelbert B. Twitchell
Massachusetts Light, 11th Battery — Captain Edward J. Jones
Massachusetts Light, 14th Battery — Captain Joseph W. B. Wright
New York Light, 19th Battery — Captain Edward W. Rogers
New York Light, 27th Battery — Captain John B. Eaton
New York Light, 34th Battery — Captain Jacob Roemer
Independent Pennsylvania, Battery (D) — Captain George W. Durell
Vermont Light, 3rd Battery — Captain Romeo H. Start
Mortar Battery (2nd Penn. Prov. H.A.) — Captain Benjamin F. Smiley

FIFTH CORPS ARTILLERY

Colonel Charles S. Wainwright

Massachusetts Light, 3rd Battery (C) — Lieutenant Aaron F. Wolcott
Massachusetts Light, 5th Battery (E) — Captain Charles A. Phillips
Massachusetts Light, 9th Battery — Captain John Bigelow
1st New York Light, Battery (B) — Captain Robert E. Rogers
1st New York Light, Battery (C) — Captain Almont Barnes
1st New York Light, Battery (D) — Captain George B. Winslow
1st New York Light, Battery (E) — Lieutenant James B. Hazelton
1st New York Light, Battery (H) — Captain Charles E. Mink
1st New York Light, Battery (L) — Lieutenant Charles Anderson
New York Light, 15th Battery — Captain Patrick Hart
1st Pennsylvania, Battery (B) — Captain James H. Cooper
4th United States, Battery (B) — Lieutenant James Stewart
5th United States, Battery (D) — Lieutenant William E. Van Reed

SIXTH CORPS ARTILLERY

Captain William Hexamer
1st New Jersey Light, Battery A

Maine Light, 4th Battery (D) — Lieutenant Charles W. White
New York Light, 3rd Battery — Captain William A. Harn
1st Ohio, Battery (H) — Captain Stephen W. Dorsey
1st Rhode Island Light, Battery (C) — Captain William B. Rhodes

Army of the James / Major General Benjamin Butler Commanding

SIEGE ARTILLERY

Colonel Henry L. Abbot

1st Connecticut Heavy Artillery — Colonel Henry L. Abbot
Company A — Captain Edward A. Gillett
Company B — Captain Albert F. Booker
Company M — Captain Franklin A. Pratt

Eighteenth Army Corps / Major General Edward O.C. Ord Commanding

TENTH ARMY CORPS
(Attached to Eighteenth Corps)

SECOND DIVISION
Brigadier General John W. Turner

First Brigade
Colonel N. Martin Curtis

3rd New York — Captain George W. Warren
112th New York — Lieutenant Colonel John F. Smith
117th New York — Lieutenant Colonel Rufus Daggett
142nd New York — Lieutenant Colonel Albert M. Barney

Second Brigade
Lieutenant Colonel William B. Coan

47th New York — Captain Charles A. Moore
48th New York — Major Samuel M. Swartwout (K)
                Captain Joseph Taylor
76th Pennsylvania — Major William S. Diller
97th Pennsylvania — Captain Isaiah Price

Third Brigade
Colonel Louis Bell

13th Indiana (3 Cos.) — Lieutenant Samuel M. Zent
9th Maine — Captain Robert J. Gray
4th New Hampshire — Captain Joseph M. Clough (W)
                    Captain Frank W. Parker
115th New York — Lieutenant Colonel Nathan J. Johnson
169th New York — Major James A. Colvin

CONFEDERATE FORCES — JULY 30, 1864

Army of Northern Virginia / General Robert E. Lee Commanding

Aide-de-Camp & Asst. Military Secretary — Major Charles Marshall
Aide-de-Camp & Asst. Adjutant General — Colonel Walter H. Taylor
Aide-de-Camp & Asst. Inspector General — Major Charles S. Venable
Chief of Artillery — Brigadier General William N. Pendleton
Judge Advocate General — Major Henry E. Young

Chief Commissary — Lieutenant Colonel Robert G. Cole
Chief Engineer — Colonel Walter Husted Stevens
Chief of Ordnance — Lieutenant Colonel Briscoe G. Baldwin
Chief Quartermaster — Lieutenant Colonel James L. Corley
Medical Director — Surgeon Lafayette Guild
Military Sec. & Act. Chief of Artillery — Colonel Armistead L. Long

Third Corps / Major General Ambrose P. Hill Commanding

RICHARD ANDERSON'S DIVISION
Brigadier General William Mahone

MAHONE'S (VA.) BRIGADE
Colonel David Weisiger (W)
Colonel George Thomas Rogers

6th Virginia — Colonel George Thomas Rogers
　　　　　　　Lieutenant Colonel Henry W. Williamson (W)
12th Virginia — Captain Richard W. Jones
16th Virginia — Lieutenant Colonel Richard Owen Whitehead
41st Virginia — Major William H. Etheridge
61st Virginia — Lieutenant Colonel William H. Stewart

WILCOX'S (ALA.) BRIGADE
Colonel John C.C. Sanders

8th Alabama — Captain M.W. Mordecai
9th Alabama — Colonel J. Horace King
10th Alabama — Captain W. L. Brewster
11th Alabama — Lieutenant Colonel George E. Tayloe
14th Alabama — Captain Elias Folk (K)

WRIGHT'S (GA.) BRIGADE
Lieutenant Colonel Matthew R. Hall

3rd Georgia — Lieutenant Colonel Claiborne Snead
22nd Georgia — Colonel George H. Jones
48th Georgia — Lieutenant Colonel Rueben W. Carswell
64th Georgia — Captain Thomas J. Pritchett
　　　　　　　Colonel John W. Evans (W)*
*Not in command

ARTILLERY
Brigadier General William N. Pendleton

FIRST CORPS
Lieutenant Colonel Frank Huger

HASKELL'S BATTALION
Major John C. Haskell

Branch (N.C.) Battery — Captain Henry G. Flanner
Nelson (Va.) Battery — Captain James N. Lamkin

13TH BATTALION VIRGINIA LIGHT ARTILLERY
Major Wade Hampton Gibbs (W)

Company A, Otey Battery — Captain David Norvell Walker
Company B, Ringgold Battery — Captain Crispin Dickenson
Company C, Davidson's Battery — Lieutenant John H. Chamberlayne
Mortar Battery (manned by Otey & Ringgold Batteries) — Lieutenant Jack Langhorne

THIRD CORPS
Colonel Reuben Lindsay Walker

PEGRAM'S BATTALION
Lieutenant Colonel William J. Pegram

Crenshaw's (Va.) Battery — Captain Thomas Ellet
Letcher's (Va.) Light Artillery — Captain Thomas A. Brander

Department of North Carolina and Southern Virginia
Lieutenant General Pierre G.T. Beauregard / Commanding

JOHNSON'S DIVISION
Major General Bushrod R. Johnson

RANSOM'S BRIGADE
Colonel Lee M. McAfee

24th North Carolina — Colonel William John Clarke
25th North Carolina — Major William Simmons Grady (MW)
35th North Carolina — Colonel James Theodore Johnson
49th North Carolina — Lieutenant Colonel John A. Flemming (K)
                          Lieutenant Colonel James Taylor Davis

ELLIOTT'S (S.C.) BRIGADE
Brigadier General Stephen Elliott (W)
Colonel Fitz William McMaster

17th South Carolina — Colonel Fitz William McMaster
                          Major John R. Culp
18th South Carolina — Captain R.H. Glenn
22nd South Carolina — Colonel David G. Flemming (K)
                          Captain James Nelson Shedd
23rd South Carolina — Captain E.R. White (W)
26th South Carolina — Colonel Alexander D. Smith

WISE'S (VA.) BRIGADE
Colonel J. Thomas Goode

26th Virginia — Captain Napoleon B. Street
34th Virginia — Major John R. Bagby
46th Virginia — Captain George Norris
59th Virginia — Captain Henry Wood (W)

HOKE'S DIVISION
Major General Robert F. Hoke

CLINGMAN'S (GA.) BRIGADE
(assigned temporarily to Johnson)

Brigadier General Thomas L. Clingman

61st North Carolina — Colonel James Dillard Radcliffe

COLQUITT'S (GA.) BRIGADE
(assigned temporarily to Johnson)

Brigadier General Alfred H. Colquitt

6th Georgia — Colonel John T. Lofton
19th Georgia — Colonel James H. Neal
23rd Georgia — Colonel James H. Huggins
27th Georgia — Major Hezekiah Bussey
28th Georgia — Captain John A. Johnson

Casualties of the Battle of the Crater

UNION

Ninth Corps

FIRST DIVISION

FIRST BRIGADE

	Killed	Wounded	Missing/Captured	Total
Staff	—	–	2	2
21st Massachusetts	2	14	7	23
29th Massachusetts	2	7	6	15
56th Massachusetts	4	21	25	50
57th Massachusetts	4	16	31	51
59th Massachusetts	6	19	49	74
100th Pennsylvania	10	28	30	68
Total	28	105	150	283

SECOND BRIGADE

	Killed	Wounded	Missing/Captured	Total
3rd Maryland Battalion	3	7	16	26
14th New York Heavy Arty	10	44	78	132
179th New York	5	20	31	56
2nd Penn. Provisional Heavy	9	35	72	116
Total	27	106	197	330
35th Massachusetts (Acting Engineers)	10	28	3	41
Division Total	65	239	350	654

SECOND DIVISION

FIRST BRIGADE

	Killed	Wounded	Missing/Captured	Total
36th Massachusetts	1	1	—	2
58th Massachusetts	4	24	86	114
2nd New York Mounted	10	31	7	48
51st New York	10	21	2	33
45th Pennsylvania	5	22	39	66
48th Pennsylvania	–	1	—	1
4th Rhode Island	7	51	25	83
Total	37	151	159	347

SECOND BRIGADE

	Killed	Wounded	Missing/Captured	Total
2nd Maryland	5	20	38	63
31st Maine	9	26	51	86
32nd Maine	9	29	62	100
6th New Hampshire	6	35	1	42
9th New Hampshire	9	35	30	74
11th New Hampshire	9	32	22	63
17th Vermont	8	22	23	53
Total	55	199	227	481
7th Rhode Island (Acting Engineers)	—	4	—	4
Division Total	92	354	386	832

THIRD DIVISION

FIRST BRIGADE

	Killed	Wounded	Missing/Captured	Total
Staff	1	–	–	1
8th Michigan	1	15	–	16
27th Michigan	11	51	23	85
109th New York	11	24	18	53
13th Ohio Cavalry	17	59	7	83
51st Pennsylvania	4	23	3	30
37th Wisconsin	34	59	52	145
38th Wisconsin	9	12	8	29
Total	88	243	111	442

SECOND BRIGADE

	Killed	Wounded	Missing/Captured	Total
1st Michigan Sharpshooters	2	14	29	45
2nd Michigan	6	15	38	59

	Killed	Wounded	Missing/Captured	Total
20th Michigan	5	22	20	47
24th New York Cavalry	–	9	–	9
46th New York	3	21	–	24
60th Ohio	1	9	–	10
50th Pennsylvania	1	20	1	22
Total	18	110	88	216
17th Michigan (Acting Engineers)	–	1	–	1
Division Total	106	354	199	659

FOURTH DIVISION

FIRST BRIGADE

	Killed	Wounded	Missing/Captured	Total
27th U.S. Colored Troops	9	46	20	75
30th U.S. Colored Troops	18	104	78	200
39th U.S. Colored Troops	13	97	47	157
43rd U.S. Colored Troops	14	86	23	123
Total	54	333	168	555

SECOND BRIGADE

	Killed	Wounded	Missing/Captured	Total
19th U.S. Colored Troops	22	87	6	115
23rd U.S. Colored Troops	74	115	121	310
28th U.S. Colored Troops	11	64	13	88
29th U.S. Colored Troops	21	56	47	124
31st U.S. Colored Troops	27	42	66	135
Total	155	364	253	772
Division Total	209	697	421	1,327

ARTILLERY*

	Killed	Wounded	Missing/Captured	Total
Maine Light, 7th Battery G	1	–	–	1
New York Light, 19th Battery	–	1	–	1
Pennsylvania Light, Battery D	–	1	–	1
Total	1	2	–	3
Ninth Corps Total	473	1,646	1,356	3,475

*Remainder had no casualties

Tenth Corps

SECOND DIVISION

	Killed	Wounded	Missing/Captured	Total
Staff	–	1	–	1

FIRST BRIGADE

	Killed	Wounded	Missing/Captured	Total
3rd New York	–	2	–	2
112th New York	1	13	–	14
117th New York	–	2	—	2
142nd New York	2	12	–	14
Total	3	29	—	32

SECOND BRIGADE

	Killed	Wounded	Missing/Captured	Total
47th New York	1	13	2	16
48th New York	6	21	3	30
76th Pennsylvania	3	40	9	52
97th Pennsylvania	4	29	5	38
Total	14	103	19	136

THIRD BRIGADE

	Killed	Wounded	Missing/Captured	Total
13th Indiana	–	11	6	17
9th Maine	4	30	13	47
4th New Hampshire	6	35	5	46
115th New York	2	18	5	25
169th New York	2	8	9	19
Total	14	102	38	154
Division Total	31	235	57	323

RECAPITULATION

	Killed	Wounded	Missing/Captured	Total
Ninth Corps	473	1,646	1,356	3,475
Tenth Corps	31	235	57	323
Grand Total	504	1,881	1,413	3,798

CONFEDERATE

Army of Northern Virginia

A.P. HILL'S THIRD CORPS

	Killed	Wounded	Missing/Captured	Total
Mahone's Division — Staff	–	1	–	1
Sander's (Ala.) Brigade	N/A	N/A	N/A	89
Wright's (Ga.) Brigade	70	139	22	231
Weisiger's (Va.) Brigade	94	159	14	267
Total	164+	299+	36+	588+

JOHNSON'S DIVISION

	Killed	Wounded	Missing/Captured	Total
Ransom's (N.C.) Brigade	14	60	8	82
Wise's (Va.) Brigade	25	86	–	111
Elliott's (S.C.) Brigade	125	224	351	700
Colquitt's (Ga.) Brigade**	4	27	—	31
Total	178	397	359	924

HOKE'S DIVISION

	Killed	Wounded	Missing/Captured	Total
Clingman's Brigade	4	35	–	39

ARTILLERY

	Killed	Wounded	Missing/Captured	Total
Pegram's Battery	22	–	8	30
Others	N/A	N/A	N/A	30
Grand Total	358+	731+	403+	1,611+

**From Hoke's Division

Medal of Honor Recipients and Confederate Roll of Honor Recipients

Medal of Honor

NINTH CORPS

Bates, Delevan, Colonel, Commander, 30th United States Colored Troops. Gallantry in action, where he fell at the head of his regiment. Awarded June 22, 1891.

Catlin, Isaac S., Commander, 109th New York Infantry. Wounded attempting to rally troops and wounded a second time while attempting to return, resulting in amputation of his leg. Awarded January 13, 1899.

Cohn, Abraham, Sergeant Major, 6th New Hampshire Infantry. Advanced bravely on the enemy line under severe fire (also for actions at Wilderness). Awarded August 24, 1865.

Davidson, Andrew, First Lieutenant, Co. H, 30th United States Colored Troops. Gallantry in assisting in rallying and saving remnants of the command when most of the regiment's officers were casualties. Awarded October 17, 1892.

DePuy, Charles H., First Sergeant, Co. H, 1st Michigan Sharpshooters. Assisted General Bartlett in working the abandoned guns in the Crater. Awarded July 30, 1896.

Dodd, Robert F., Private, Co. E, 27th Michigan Infantry. Voluntarily assisted in carrying off wounded from the ground in front of the Crater under heavy fire. Awarded July 27, 1896.

Dorsey, Decatur, Sergeant, Co. B, 39th United States Colored Troops. Planted the colors on the enemy's works in advance of his regiment. Rallied the men when they were driven back to the Union works. Awarded November 8, 1865.

Gwynne, Nathaniel, Private, Co. H. 13th Ohio Cavalry (Dismounted). Lost arm retrieving regimental colors. Only 15 years of age, was not mustered into the unit at the time of the incident. Awarded January 27, 1865.

Haight, Sidney, Corporal, Co. E, 1st Michigan Sharpshooters. Remained in the Crater instead of retreating with the rest of the troops, continuing to fire on the advancing enemy. Awarded July 31, 1896.

Hill, James, Sergeant, Co. C, 14th New York Heavy Artillery. Captured enemy flag, shot enemy officer who was attempting to rally his troops. Awarded December 1, 1864.

Hogan, Frank, Corporal, Co. A, 45th Pennsylvania Infantry. Captured flag from the 6th Virginia Infantry. Awarded October 1, 1864.

Homan, Conrad, Color Sergeant, Co. A, 29th Massachusetts Infantry. Fought his way through the enemy lines with the regimental colors when the rest of the color guard was killed. Awarded June 3, 1869.

Houghton, Charles H., Captain, Co. L, 14th New York Heavy Artillery. Conspicuous gallantry and repeated exposure to enemy fire; wounded three times and lost leg (also for actions at Fort Stedman). Awarded March 25, 1865.

Knight, Charles H., Corporal, Co. I, 9th New Hampshire Infantry. In the company of a sergeant, was the first to enter the Crater; while wounded took several prisoners back to Federal lines. Awarded July 27, 1896.

Mathews, William H., Sergeant, Co. E, 2nd Maryland Infantry. Came upon the 17th South Carolina regiment. Killed one and took three prisoners. Awarded July 10, 1892, under the name of Henry Sivel.

McAlwee, Benjamin F., Sergeant, Co. D, 3rd Maryland Infantry. Picked up a shell with burning fuse; threw it over parapet. Awarded April 4, 1898.

Schneider, George, Sergeant, Co. A, 3rd Maryland Infantry. Seized colors and planted them in enemy works. Awarded July 27, 1896.

Simons, Charles J., Sergeant, Co. A, 9th New Hampshire Infantry. Among first into Crater; captured a number of prisoners, was himself captured, but escaped. Awarded July 27, 1896.

Swift, Harlan J., Lieutenant, Co. H, 2nd New York Mounted Rifles. Advanced on enemy and compelled surrender and returned with four prisoners, returning them to the Federal lines. Awarded July 20, 1897.

Thatcher, Charles M., Private, Co. B, 1st Michigan Sharpshooters. Continued firing from the Crater and continued until captured by advancing enemy. Awarded July 31, 1896.

Welsh, James, Private, Co. E, 4th Rhode Island Infantry. Bore off the regimental colors after the color sergeant was wounded, thus saving them from capture. Awarded June 3, 1905.

Wilkins, Leander A., Sergeant, Co. H, 9th New Hampshire Infantry. Recapture of colors of the 21st Massachusetts. Awarded December 1, 1864.

Wright, Albert D., Captain, Co. G, 43rd United Sates Colored Troops. Captured colors and color guard and then was severely wounded. Awarded May 1, 1893.

EIGHTEENTH CORPS

Jamison, Walter, Sergeant, Co. B, 139th New York Infantry. While his regiment was not engaged, he went between the lines and carried a wounded officer back to the Union lines. Award April 5, 1898.

Confederate Roll of Honor

Barnes, David, Private, Co. G, 16th Virginia Infantry. Captured Union Stars and Stripes.

Billsoly, Julius J., Lieutenant, Co. D, 61st Virginia Infantry. Captured Union Stars and Stripes.

Butler, Solomon V., Corporal, Co. D, 16th Virginia Infantry. Captured colors of the 28th USCT.

Critcher, John M., Private, Co. K, 9th Alabama Infantry. Captured colors of the 20th Michigan Infantry.

Deaton, John E., Sergeant, Co. E, 8th Alabama Infantry. Captured the colors of the 2nd Michigan Infantry.

Foreman, John Edgar, Private, Co. E, 61st Virginia Infantry. Captured portion of staff and fringe of unknown regiment.

Goodwin, Joseph B., Lieutenant, Co. F, 16th Virginia Infantry. Captured Union Stars and Stripes.

Harrison, William H., Corporal, Co. A, 61st Virginia Infantry. Captured colors of the 31st Maine Infantry.

Herndon, Furney I., Corporal, Co. F, 3rd Georgia Infantry. Captured colors of the 58th Massachusetts Infantry.

Howell, Peter F., Sergeant, Co. G, 61st Virginia Infantry. Captured colors of unknown regiment.

Keeton, James N., Private, Co. G, 11th Alabama Infantry. Captured guidon, Union Stars and Stripes of unknown regiment.

Kilby, Leroy Richardson, Captain, Co. B, 16th Virginia Infantry. Captured colors of the 100th Pennsylvania Infantry.

Lane, W.F., Private, Co. G, 16th Virginia Infantry. Captured Union Stars and Stripes.

Miles, John W., Private, Co. D, 41st Virginia Infantry. Captured unknown regimental guidon.

Sadler, A.J., Private, Co. F, 16th Virginia Infantry. Captured colors of the 58th Massachusetts Infantry.

Tucker, Lemuel, Private, Co. B, 41st Virginia Infantry. Captured portion of a Union flag and staff.

Wellons, Walter B., Private, Co. H, 6th Virginia Infantry. Captured the 11th New Hampshire Infantry colors.

Whitehead, Richard Owen, Lieutenant Colonel, Commanding, 16th Virginia Infantry. Captured Union Stars and Stripes.

Wilson, St. Julien, Lieutenant, Co. C, 61st Virginia Infantry. Captured colors of the 57th Massachusetts Infantry.

Others Who Captured Colors

Connelly, J.W., Sergeant, Co. F, 22nd South Carolina Infantry. Captured the colors of the 1st Michigan Sharpshooters.

Moore, Henry, Private, Co. A, 59th Virginia Infantry. Captured a stand of colors of unknown regiment.

Sweeney, Patrick, Private, Co. A, 59th Virginia Infantry. Captured two colors of the 20th Michigan Infantry, and brought them out though wounded.

Appendix D

Union Officers Killed
or Mortally Wounded

Ninth Corps

FIRST DIVISION

First Brigade

Captain William H. Clark	21st Massachusetts
Major Albert Prescott	57th Massachusetts
Captain Edson T. Dresser	57th Massachusetts
Captain George H. Howe	57th Massachusetts
Colonel J. Parker Gould	59th Massachusetts
Lieutenant Colonel John Hodges, Jr.	59th Massachusetts
Captain Lewis E. Munroe	59th Massachusetts
Major Thomas J. Hamilton	100th Pennsylvania
Captain Walter C. Oliver	100th Pennsylvania
Lieutenant Richard P. Craven	100th Pennsylvania
Lieutenant Samuel G. Leasure	100th Pennsylvania

Second Brigade

Lieutenant Ezra T. Hartly	14th New York Heavy Artillery
Major John Barton	179th New York
Captain Allen T. Farwell	179th New York
Lieutenant Baker L. Saxton	179th New York

Acting Engineers

Lieutenant Samuel G. Berry	35th Massachusetts

SECOND DIVISION

First Brigade

Lieutenant Clement C. Granett	58th Massachusetts

Captain Samuel H. Sims	51st New York
Lieutenant John K. Knowles	4th Rhode Island
Lieutenant George W. Field	4th Rhode Island

SECOND BRIGADE

Captain Almon H. Gushee	31st Maine
Lieutenant Byron C. Gilmore	31st Maine
Lieutenant John G. Thompson	31st Maine
Lieutenant John G. Whitten	31st Maine
Lieutenant William B. Allyn	31st Maine
Lieutenant Colonel Henry Howard	2nd Maryland
Lieutenant R. Wilson Register	2nd Maryland
Captain William K. Crossfield	6th New Hampshire
Lieutenant George E. Upton	6th New Hampshire
Lieutenant Jon C. Sampson	9th New Hampshire
Major William B. Reynolds	17th Vermont
Lieutenant George Hicks	17th Vermont
Lieutenant Leonard P. Bingham	17th Vermont
Lieutenant William E. Martin	17th Vermont
Lieutenant Henry B. Needham	17th Vermont
Lieutenant John R. Converse	17th Vermont

THIRD DIVISION

FIRST BRIGADE

Lieutenant Nathan J. Griswold	109th New York
Lieutenant Clayton G. Jewell	13th Ohio Cavalry (Dismounted)
Lieutenant Isaac W. Short	13th Ohio Cavalry (Dismounted)
Lieutenant Allen H. Filman	51st Pennsylvania
Captain Allen A. Burnett	37th Wisconsin
Captain Frank A. Cole	37th Wisconsin
Captain Newton S. Ferris	38th Wisconsin

SECOND BRIGADE

Captain John L. Young	2nd Michigan
Lieutenant John G. Buck	2nd Michigan
Lieutenant Austin Gibbons	24th New York Cavalry (Dismounted)

FOURTH DIVISION

FIRST BRIGADE

Captain John Cartwright	27th USCT
Captain Alfred W. Pinney	27th USCT
Lieutenant Amos Richardson	27th USCT
Lieutenant Seymour A. Cornell	27th USCT
Major James C. Leeke	30th USCT
Lieutenant James T. Hayman	43rd USCT

Second Brigade

Major Theodore H. Rackwood	19th USCT
Lieutenant Christopher Pennel	19th USCT
Captain Adam C. Liscomb	23rd USCT
Captain Zelotes Fessenden	23rd USCT
Lieutenant Charles W. Perigree	23rd USCT
Captain John C. Hackniser	28th USCT
Lieutenant James C. Grant	28th USCT
Lieutenant Colonel John A. Bross	29th USCT
Captain Hector H. Aiken	29th USCT
Captain Richard K. Woodruff	31st USCT
Lieutenant William H. Ayers	31st USCT
Lieutenant James T. Hayman	31st USCT

Tenth Corps

SECOND DIVISION

First Brigade

Captain William P. Johnson, Jr.	142nd New York

Second Brigade

Major Samuel M. Swartwout	48th New York
Lieutenant Jeremiah O'Brien	48th New York
Lieutenant Daniel McVey	76th Pennsylvania
Lieutenant Levi L. Marsh	97th Pennsylvania

Third Brigade

Lieutenant Edwin T. Clifford	9th Maine
Captain Augustus D. Vaughn	169th New York

Chapter Notes

Chapter 1

1. Bruce Catton, *A Stillness at Appomattox* (Garden City, NY: Doubleday, 1954), 39.

2. Andrew Humphreys, *The Virginia Campaign of '64 and '65* (New York: Scribner's, 1916), 12; Shelby Foote, *The Civil War: A Narrative*, 3 vols. (Alexandria, VA: Random House 1974), 3: 134–36; Henry Steele Commager, ed., *The Blue and the Gray*, 2 vols. (Indianapolis: Bobbs-Merrill, 1950), 1: 32–35; Gordon C. Rhea, *The Battle of the Wilderness, May 5–6, 1864* (Baton Rouge: Louisiana State University Press, 1994), 52–55.

3. Rhea, *Wilderness*, 55.

4. Carl Sandburg, *Abraham Lincoln: The War Years*, 4 vols. (New York: Harcourt, Brace, 1939), 3: 45–46.

5. Noah Andre Trudeau, *Bloody Roads South: The Wilderness to Cold Harbor, May–June 1864* (Boston: Brown, 1989), 118; William Marvel, *Burnside* (Chapel Hill: University of North Carolina Press, 1991), 35

6. Anderson succeeded to command of the I Corps when Longstreet was wounded on May 6th.

7. Trudeau, *Bloody Roads*, 164–65.

8. Ibid., 225.

9. James M. McPherson, *Battle Cry of Freedom: The Civil War Era* (New York: Oxford University Press, 1988), 724; Foote, 3: 264.

10. Ulysses S. Grant, *Personal Memoirs of U.S. Grant*, 2 vols. (New York: Century, 1885-86), 2: 130–32. Ord could not get along with Sigel and requested to be relieved, a request granted on April 17. His force was subsequently consolidated into Crook's and Sigel's.

11. William C. Davis, *The Battle of New Market* (Garden City, NY: Doubleday, 1975), 26; Foote, 3: 247; Don Lowry, *No Turning Back: The Beginning*

of the End of the Civil War, March–June 1864 (New York: Hippocrene Books, 1992), 120.

12. Davis, *Battle of New Market*, 119; Lowry, *No Turning Back*, 369.

13. Gordon C. Rhea, *To the North Anna River, Grant and Lee, May 13–25, 1864* (Baton Rouge: Louisiana State University Press, 2000), 341; Lowry, *No Turning Back*, 336–38.

14. Foote, 3: 274–75.

15. Horace Porter, *Campaigning with Grant* (Bloomington: Indiana University Press,1961), 146; Rhea, *To the North Anna*, 358–59; Lowry, *No Turning Back*, 427.

16. Ernest B. Furgurson, *Not War But Murder: Cold Harbor 1864* (New York: Alfred A. Knopf, 2000), 134–35; Gordon C. Rhea, *Cold Harbor, Grant and Lee, May 26–June 3, 1864* (Baton Rouge: Louisiana State University Press, 2002), 312, 314–15; Porter, *Campaigning with Grant*, 174–75; Trudeau, *Bloody Roads South*, 279–80.

17. Trudeau, *Bloody Roads*, 280–81.

18. Catton, *A Stillness at Appomattox*, 163; Robert Underwood Johnson and Clarence Clough Buell, eds., *Battles and Leaders of the Civil War*, 4 vols. (New York: A.S. Barnes, 1956), 4: 142, Furgurson, 150; *War of the Rebellion: A Compilation of the Official Records of the Union and Confederate Armies*, 128 vols. (Washington, D.C: Government Printing Office, 1880–1901) [Series I unless otherwise indicated], Vol. 36, Part I, Series I, 1032, 1059 (hereinafter cited as *OR* __) ; Foote, 3: 292.

19. Foote, 3: 290.

20. Lowry, *No Turning Back*, 454; Furgurson, 178.

21. He had already sent Wade Hampton and two divisions of cavalry on June 3 to intercept Sheridan, who was headed to the Shenandoah.

22. *OR* 36 (3), 897; Furgurson, 230–31.

23. Foote, 3: 316–17; Trudeau, *Bloody Roads*, 321–22; Furgurson, 349–50.

Chapter 2

1. Catton, *A Stillness at Appomattox*, 177–78.

2. Jeff Kinard, *The Battle of the Crater*, Abilene, TX: McWhiney Foundation Press, 1998), 13; Noah Andre Trudeau, *The Last Citadel: Petersburg, Virginia, June 1864–April 1865* (Boston: Little, Brown, 1991), 6.

3. The preceding January the British, under Brigadier General Benedict Arnold, the American traitor, assaulted and burned much of Richmond.

4. James G. Scott and Edward A. Wyatt IV, *Petersburg's Story, A History* (Petersburg, VA: Deitz Press, 1960), 28–30.

5. The Blandford Cemetery also features a shaft placed over the grave of Captain McRae in 1857 known as the Cockade Monument, honoring the Petersburg men who fought and died during the War of 1812.

6. Scott, *Petersburg Story*, 126–28.

7. Horn, John, *The Petersburg Campaign, June 1864–April 1865* (Cambridge: Da Capo Press, 2003), 11–12; Trudeau, *Last Citadel*, 5–6; Richard Wayne Lykes, *Campaign for Petersburg* (Washington, DC: National Park Service, 1970), 7.

8. Scott, *Petersburg Story*, 92–94.

9. Ibid., 167.

10. Trudeau, *Last Citadel*, xiii.

11. Scott, *Petersburg Story*, 167; Trudeau, *Last Citadel*, 6–7.

12. Trudeau, *Last Citadel*, xiii.

13. Lykes, 9–10.

14. William Glenn Robertson, *Back Door to Richmond: The Bermuda Hundred Campaign, April–June 1864* (New-

ark: University of Delaware Press, 1987), 239.

15. Robertson, *Back Door*, 240; R.E. Colston, "Repelling the First Assault on Petersburg," in *Battles and Leaders*, 534–35; Horn, 41–42; Scott, *Petersburg Story*, 177–79; Trudeau, *Last Citadel*, 4.

16. The militia had been encamped at the head of Washington Street since Butler's appearance.

17. Trudeau, *The Last Citadel*, 8–9; Scott, *Petersburg Story*, 178; Horn, 41–43; Colston, 535.

18. Scott, *Petersburg Story*, 179–81; Trudeau, *Last Citadel*, 10–12; Horn, 42–45, Colston, 535.

19. Horn, 45–46; Trudeau, *Last Citadel*, 11–12; Scott, *Petersburg Story*, 180–81; Robertson, *Back Door*, 240.

20. Lowry, Don, *No Turning Back*, 464, 505; Trudeau, *Last Citadel*, 16–17; Foote, 3: 313.

21. Catton, *A Stillness at Appomattox*, 180.

22. Clifford Dowdey and Louis H. Manarin, *The Wartime Papers of Robert E. Lee* (Boston: Little, Brown, 1961), 782–83; Trudeau, *The Last Citadel*, 21–22; Catton, *A Stillness at Appomattox*, 180–81; Furgurson, 250–51; Foote, 3: 315–17; Horn, 49–51.

23. Foote, 3: 315–16; Catton, *A Stillness at Appomattox*, 181; Lowry, *No Turning Back*, 511.

24. Porter Alexander, *Fighting for the Confederacy* (Chapel Hill: University of North Carolina Press, 1989), 420.

25. Trudeau, *Last Citadel*, 25; Lowry, *No Turning Back*, 513–14; Foote, 3: 428; Porter, *Campaigning with Grant*, 199–200.

26. Robertson, *Back Door to Richmond*, 240; Catton, *A Stillness at Appomattox*, 184.

27. Foote, 3: 314–15; Catton, *A Stillness At Appomattox*, 184–85; Lowry, *No Turning Back*, 512.

28. Robertson, 240; Catton, *A Stillness at Appomattox*, 184–85; Foote, 3: 429; Horn, 52–53; Trudeau, *Last Citadel*, 32–33.

29. Foote, 3: 316–17; Trudeau, *Last Citadel*, 24.

30. Trudeau, *Last Citadel*, 36–37; Horn, 53–55; Foote, 3: 429.

31. This force included the 26th, 34th and 46th Virginia, the 64th Georgia and the 23rd South Carolina, Archer's militia, Battle and Wood's battalions, Sturdivant's battery and Dearing's cavalry.

32. Pierre G.T. Beauregard, "Four Days of Battle at Petersburg," in *Battles and Leaders*, 4: 540; Robertson, *Back Door*, 241; Lowry, *No Turning Back*, 512; Trudeau, *Last Citadel*, 36; Horn, 53; Scott, *Petersburg Story*, 184; Foote, 3: 433.

33. Beauregard argued this was not

reinforcement from Lee, despite Jefferson Davis' assertion to the contrary. Hoke's division, indeed, was never a part of the Army of Northern Virginia, as it was sent north to reinforce it after the battle of Drewrey's Bluff.

34. Lowry, *No Turning Back*, 513; Robertson, 241; Dowdey and Manarin, 777–78.

35. Trudeau, *Last Citadel*, 39; Foote, 3: 433.

36. Humphreys, *Virginia Campaign*, 206–10; Horn, 59–60, 69–70; Catton, *A Stillness at Appomattox*, 189; Foote, 3: 431–32; Trudeau, *Last Citadel*, 41; Furgurson, 252–53. Later "racial" atrocities attributable to the Confederates in late July of the same year were thus not the first incidents in the Petersburg fighting.

37. Foote, 3: 432–33; Robertson, 241; Catton, *A Stillness at Appomattox*, 189–90; Horn, 57–59; Scott, *Petersburg Story*, 184.

38. Trudeau, *Last Citadel*, 42–43; Robertson, *Back Door*, 241; Foote, 3: 434–36; Horn, 59–60; Beauregard, *Battles and Leaders*, 541.

39. Clifford Dowdey, *Lee's Last Campaign: The Story of Lee and His Men against Grant 1864* (New York: Bonanza Books, 1950), 335–36; Foote, 3: 434–35. Beauregard, *Battles and Leaders*, 4: 541.

40. Robertson, 241; Catton, *A Stillness at Appomattox*, 192; Foote, 3: 433.

41. Dowdey, *Last Campaign*, 36–37; Foote, 3: 435; Catton, *A Stillness at Appomattox*, 193–94.

42. Scott, *Petersburg Story*, 183–84; Horn, 58; Alexander, *Fighting*, 425.

43. Beauregard said after the war that "Petersburg at that hour was clearly at the mercy of the Federal commander, who had all but captured it, and only failed of final success because he could not realize the fact of the unparalleled disparity between the two contending forces." Beauregard, *Battles and Leaders*, 4: 541.

44. Trudeau, *Last Citadel*, 41.

45. Foote, 3: 436; Trudeau, *Last Citadel*, 43.

46. Trudeau, *The Last Citadel*, 44–45.

47. OR 40 (3) 86; Catton, *A Stillness at Appomattox*, 192.

48. Beauregard, *Battles and Leaders*, 4: 541; Horn, 60.

49. OR 40 (1), 306; Horn, 61–62; Foote, 3: 436.

50. Beauregard, *Battles and Leaders*, 4: 541; Trudeau, *Last Citadel*, 36.

51. Catton, *A Stillness at Appomattox*, 192; Horn, 61.

52. Alexander, *Fighting*, 427; Scott, 184; Beauregard, *Battles and Leaders*, 4: 541.

53. Trudeau, *Last Citadel*. 47; Scott, *Petersburg Story*, 184; Horn, 62.

54. Had Warren brushed the skirmishers aside that night, continued on and attacked from the south the next morning, Beauregard later indicated that he would have "been compelled to evacuate Petersburg without much resistance" (Foote, 3: 436).

55. Catton, *A Stillness at Appomattox*, 194–95; Trudeau, *The Last Citadel*, 48–49; Foote, 3: 436.

56. Horn, 62.

57. Henry Pleasants, *The Tragedy of the Crater* (Boston: Christopher Publishing House, 1938, repr. Eastern National Park & Monument Association, 1975), 23–27.

58. OR 40(1), 307, 318, 532, 535.

59. The primary fort across from Elliott's Salient, which eventually contained a fourteen gun battery, and was the site of Burnside's headquarters on July 30, had been named for this valiant officer.

60. Marvel, *Burnside*, 386–87.

61. Lykes, 7; Foote, 3: 438; Horn, 63–64; Don Lowry, *Fate of the Country: The Civil War from June to September 1864* (New York: Hippocrene Books 1992), 61–62.

62. Trudeau, *Last Citadel*, 49–50; Horn, 62–63; Scott, *Petersburg Story*, 185.

63. Beauregard, *Battles and Leaders*, 542; Scott, *Petersburg Story*, 186; Trudeau, *Last Citadel*, 51; Alexander, *Fighting*, 429; Lowry, *Fate of the Country*, 54; Foote, 3: 439.

64. Early had made contact with Hunter that day, however, and would not be in a position to move on Petersburg for some time.

65. Thomas Howe, *Wasted Valor, June 15–18, 1864* (Lynchburg, VA: H.E. Howard, 1988), 102; Beauregard, *Battles and Leaders*, 4: 542–44; Foote, 3: 438–49; Lowry, *Fate of the Country*, 54, 56; Horn, 65. Porter Alexander indicated that it was difficult to see why Lee was so slow to believe that Grant had moved on to Petersburg; certainly Beauregard kept him well informed. Alexander speculates that Lee "underestimated the enemy's facilities for crossing, & over estimated the time that would be required for them to do it" (Alexander, *Fighting*, 429). Of course, Lee also knew that one wrong move on his part would place the capital in a completely untenable position. Alexander, and Beauregard, for that matter, leave out much in the translation. Lee was tasked with protecting the capital while continuing to seek out Grant and divine his next move. He was quite perplexed to learn Beauregard had unilaterally withdrawn from Bermuda Hundred. The War Department had failed him completely, with central control seeming to have totally vanished. Lee was immediately faced with attempting to re-

lieve the Federals' hold on the lines between Petersburg and Richmond, while still uncertain as to Grant's position. When Beauregard asked for reinforcements at 9:45 A.M. on the 16th without identifying exactly who was on his front, he was seeking two divisions at a time when Lee knew nothing of what was actually happening at Petersburg. Lee asked for additional information from Beauregard on several occasions and received no adequate response. Beauregard, in his rendition of events, rearranges the exchange regarding requests for support. Thus, despite Beauregard's arguments, Lee was still uncertain of Grant's movements. When pressed on the issue, Beauregard stated he had no information of Grant's having crossed the James, although Hancock and Smith were on his front. All the while, one third of Lee's remaining army was fighting in his department to clear up the mess he had suddenly left at Bermuda Hundred (however justified the decision).

66. Dowdey, *Last Campaign*, 340–41; Scott, *Petersburg Story*, 186; Alexander, *Fighting*, 431; Foote, 3: 439–40; Lowry, *Fate of the Country*, 63; Howe, 115; Hassler, 215.

67. Foote, 3: 439; Catton, *A Stillness at Appomattox*, 196–97; Beauregard, *Battles and Leaders*, 544; Alexander, *Fighting*, 4: 431; Horn, 65–66.

68. Catton, *A Stillness at Appomattox*, 197; Foote, 3: 440; Lowry, *Fate of the Country*, 65–66.

69. Howe, 132; Lowry, *Fate of the Country*, 69; Catton, *A Stillness at Appomattox*, 197–98; Foote, 3: 440–41.

70. Foote, 3: 441; Porter, *Campaigning with Grant*, 210; Catton, *A Stillness at Appomattox*, 199; Horn, 68; Alexander, *Fighting*, 432; Beauregard, *Battles and Leaders*, 4: 544, Scott, *Petersburg Story*, 187.

71. Confederate losses were put at about 4,700, according to Porter Alexander. Alexander, *Fighting*, 433.

72. Foote, 3: 441.

73. Alexander, *Fighting*, 433.

74. William Thomas Venner, *The Iron Brigade's 19th Indiana Regiment* (Shippensburg, PA: Burd Street Press, 1998), 259; Lykes, 16; Hassler, 215; Scott, 188. However, before settling for a strategy of gradual approaches, Grant envisioned one final, grand movement to envelope Petersburg. He thus prescribed a massive raid on the local rail lines still remaining in Confederate hands. A force of two cavalry divisions under Brigadier Generals James H. Wilson and August Kautz set forth on June 22 to achieve this end, with their primary targets being two railroad bridges over the Appomattox and Roanoke rivers west of the city. In order to keep the Confederates occupied, Sheri-

dan's cavalry was to engage Major General Wade Hampton's cavalry force and keep it north of the Appomattox, while the Second and Sixth corps moved southwest to the Weldon Railroad in order to prevent Lee from moving against the Federal cavalry movement and to insure an open approach for the raiding forces' return. However, the Federals were hit fast and hard by Mahone's division of A.P. Hill's III Corps, and were unable to remain in control of their objective. In the end, Mahone's three brigades inflicted a stinging defeat on three full Federal divisions of the two corps. Meanwhile, Rooney Lee's cavalry harassed the Wilson-Kautz forces, and kept them from achieving their primary objectives. Hampton shook free of Sheridan and almost trapped the entire Federal cavalry force as it attempted to reenter its own lines. Finally, he was able to slip away, and he got back to the Federal lines on July 2, having lost 1,445 men and 16 guns, while inflicting only 300 casualties on the Confederates. The destruction to the rail lines which the raid caused was repaired in a short time.

Chapter 3

1. Michael Cavanaugh and William Marvel, *The Battle of the Crater: "The Horrible Pit," June 25–Aug. 6, 1864* (Lynchburg, VA: H.E. Howard, 1989), 2; George R. Agassiz, ed., *Meade's Headquarters, 1863–1865: Letters of Colonel Theodore Lyman* (Boston: Atlantic Monthly Press, 1922), 164–68; Marvel, *Burnside*, 389.

2. Cavanaugh, *Battle of the Crater*, 3–4; Foote, 3: 437; Horn, 64.

3. OR 40 (1), 572–73; Marvel, *Burnside*, 388–89; Lowry, *Fate of the Country*, 54–55.

4. Marvel, *Burnside*, 389–90.

5. Marvel, *Burnside*, 383, 386–90; Agassiz, *Meade's Headquarters*, 148; OR 40 (2), 168.

6. Catton, *A Stillness at Appomattox*, 218.

7. Powell, William H., "The Tragedy of the Crater," *The Century Illustrated Monthly Magazine* 34 (May–Oct. 1887): 760–61; Marvel, *Burnside*, 390; Cavanaugh, *Battle of the Crater*, 4.

8. Byron M. Cutcheon, *The Story of the Twentieth Michigan Infantry* (Lansing, MI: Robert Smith Printing, 1904), 137; H.A. Chambers, "The Bloody Crater," *Confederate Veteran* 31, no. 1 (1923): 174; John Cannan, *The Crater: Burnside's Assault on the Confederate Trenches, July 30, 1864* (Cambridge: Da Capo Press, 2002), 17–18.

9. Freeman Bowley, "The Peters-

burg Mine," in 60 *MOLLUS* (Wilmington, NC: Broadfoot Publishing, 1995), 27; Warren Wilkinson, *Mother, May You Never See the Sights I Have Seen: The Fifty-Seventh Massachusetts Veteran Volunteers in the Army of the Potomac, 1864–1865* (New York: Quill-William Morrow, 1990), 241.

10. John Anderson, *The Fifty-Seventh Regiment of Massachusetts Volunteers* (Boston: E.B. Stillings, 1896), 168; Chambers, "Bloody Crater," 174; Cutcheon, 138; Humphreys, *The Virginia Campaign*, 250.

11. Chambers, "Bloody Crater," 174; Horace Burbank, "The Battle of the Crater," The 16 *MOLLUS* (Portland: Thurston Print, 1898), 1: 283–84; Scott, *Petersburg Story*, 192; Henry Goddard Thomas, "The Colored Troops at Petersburg," *The Century Illustrated Monthly Magazine* 34 (May–Oct. 1887), 777.

12. B.F. Phillips, "Wilcox's Alabamians in Virginia," *Confederate Veteran* 15, no. 11 (Nov. 1907): 490; Cutcheon, 138.

13. William A. Day, "Battle of the Crater," *Confederate Veteran* 11, no. 8 (1903): 355; Stewart, William H., "The Charge of the Crater," *Southern Historical Society Papers* (Richmond, 1897), 41; OR 40 (1), 778.

14. Robert Barnhill, "A View on the Crater Battle," *Confederate Veteran* 33, no. 1 (1925): 176; the Rev. J. William Jones, *Army of Northern Virginia Memorial Volume* (Richmond: J.W. Randolph & English, 1880), 148; Alexander, *Fighting*, 442; Day, "Battle of the Crater," 355; Chambers, "Bloody Crater," 174.

15. Edward A. Pollard, *The Lost Cause: Southern History of the War* (New York: Fairfax Press, 1990), 334.

16. Alexander, *Fighting*, 442.

17. Day, "Battle of the Crater," 335; Barnwell, 177; OR 40 (1), 788.

18. Barnwell, 177; Dr. J.B. Stinson, "Mistook Each Other for an Enemy," *Confederate Veteran* 2, no. 6 (June 1894): 187.

19. Barnwell, 177.

20. Wilkinson, *Mother, May You*, 231.

21. Another source, W.A. Day, indicated Wright had six guns at this location.

22. Alexander, *Fighting*, 443, 450–451.

23. Alexander, *Fighting*, 443; W.P. Robinson, "Artillery In the Battle of the Crater," *Confederate Veteran* 19 (1911): 165.

24. OR 40 (1), 789. Davidson's battery was 373 yards from the Salient; Otey's battery was 473 yards from the Salient; and Ringgold's was posted on a salient angle, 573 yards on the right and south of the Salient. Robinson, 165.

25. Marvel, *Burnside*, 397.

26. James Madison Aubrey, *The Thirty-Sixth Wisconsin Volunteer Infantry* (Milwaukee, 1900), 104; Humphreys, *Virginia Campaign*, 284; OR 40 (1), 284, 278–80, 283–84; Edward G. Longacre, *The Man Behind the Guns: A Biography of General Henry J. Hunt, Commander of Artillery, Army of the Potomac* (Cambridge, MA: Da Capo Press, 2003), 98, 108, 201–05.

27. Longacre, *The Man Behind the Guns*, 205.

28. Longacre, *The Man Behind the Guns*, 205–06; Scott, *Petersburg Story*, 218.

29. Cavanaugh, *Battle of the Crater*, 1, 3.

30. Trudeau, *The Last Citadel*, xiii.

31. The Northern newspapers published a report that the Confederate soldiers kept up a heavy fire in the area due to the presence of black troops in the rear of the Ninth Corps position. "As a matter of fact, the men in the front trenches of the whole Ninth Corps line had been ordered to expend one hundred rounds of ammunition per man each day" (Freeman Bowley, "The Petersburg Mine," 60 *MOLLUS* (Wilmington: Broadfoot Publishing, 1995), 28). This obviously caused retaliatory fire from the Rebels. Additionally, due to the closeness of the lines at this point, and to prevent reinforcements to the Salient and detection of the Union excavations, the Union fire was much more intense here than anywhere else on the whole line.

32. Alexander, *Fighting*, 435; Commager, *The Blue and the Gray*, 1016.

33. Colonel Harold B Simpson, *Hood's Texas Brigade in Reunion and Memory* (Dallas: Alcor Publishing, 1983), 425.

34. Aubrey, 110–111.

35. John Sergeant Wise, *The End of an Era* (Cambridge, MA: Houghton Mifflin, Riverside Press, 1899), 346–48; Pleasants, *Tragedy of the Crater*, 31; Jarrot's Hotel, *A Guide to the Fortifications and Battlefields around Petersburg* (Petersburg, VA: Jarrot's Hotel, 1866), 12; Douglas Southall Freeman, *R.E. Lee: A Biography* (New York: Scribner's, 1934), 463; Catton, *A Stillness at Appomattox*, 201.

36. John D. Billings, *Hardtack and Coffee: Soldier's Life in the Civil War* (Philadelphia: Thompson Publishing, 1888), 380–85; Catton, *A Stillness at Appomattox*, 202.

37. Billings, *Hardtack*, 57–60; Catton, *A Stillness at Appomattox*, 202–03.

38. W.P. Robinson, "Artillery In the Battle of the Crater," *Confederate Veteran* 19 (1911): 165; Wise, *End of an Era*, 347–48.

39. Richard Wheeler, *On Fields of Fury: From the Wilderness to the Crater,*

An Eyewitness History (New York: HarperCollins, 1991), 277; Wise, *End of an Era*, 348.

40. Robert Goldwaite Carter, *Four Brothers in Blue* (Austin: University of Texas Press, 1978), 472.

41. Daniel N. Rolph, *My Brother's Keeper: Union and Confederate Soldiers' Acts of Mercy during the Civil War* (Mechanicsburg: Stackpole Books, 2002), 12–13; Bell Irvin Wiley, *The Common Soldier in the Civil War: The Life of Johnny Reb* (New York: Grosset & Dunlap, 1943), 80; Wise, *End of an Era*, 348–49.

42. Wise, *End of an Era*, 350–51, OR 40 (1), 782, 784, 786; Billings, *Hardtack*, 57–58.

43. Catton, *A Stillness at Appomattox*, 219; Allen D. Albert, ed., *History of the Forty-fifth Regiment, Pennsylvania Veteran Volunteer Infantry, 1861–1865* (Williamsport: Grit Publishing, 1912), 149.

44. Clifford Dowdey, *Lee*, 493–94; Cavanaugh, *Battle of the Crater*, 7.

45. M.W. Venable, "In the Trenches at Petersburg," *Confederate Veteran* 34, no. 2 (February 1926): 60; Alexander, *Fighting*, 444. One reason for a lack of information on their use is the fact that sap rollers soon ceased to be popularly used by the Union forces after July.

46. Alexander, *Fighting*, 451.

47. Ibid., 452.

48. Henrietta Stratton Jaquette, ed., *South after Gettysburg: Letters of Cordelia Handcock from the Army of the Potomac* (New York: Thomas Y. Crowell, 1937), 137.

49. Carter, 470.

50. Dowdey, *Lee*, 493.

51. George T. Stevens, *Three Years in the Sixth Corp* (Albany, NY: S.R. Gray Publishers, 1866), 366–67.

52. Jaquette, 124–25.

53. Abijah P Marvin, *History of Worcester in the War of the Rebellion* (Worcester, MA: Abijah P. Marvin, 1880), 253.

54. Albert, *History of the Forty-Fifth Regiment Pennsylvania*, 144; David Lane, *A Soldier's Diary: The Story of a Volunteer, 1862–1865* (Jackson, MI: 1905), 177; Cutcheon, 137; Catton, *A Stillness at Appomattox*, 201; Augustus C. Brown, *The Diary of a Line Officer* (New York 1906), 91.

55. Dowdey, *Lee*, 494–95.

56. Ibid., 495.

57. Ibid., 494.

58. Ibid., 495–96.

59. Ibid., 496.

60. Ibid., 496–97.

61. Sandburg, 3: 124–25.

Chapter 4

1. Newberry, 115–16; Commager,

The Blue and the Gray, 1017; Bowley, "Petersburg Mine," 28; Catton, *A Stillness at Appomattox*, 212.

2. Shearman, 389; Burbank, 283; Stevenson, 2; OR 40 (1), 572.

3. Davis, *Death in Trenches*, 67; Burbank, 283; Trudeau, *Like Men of War*, 230; Sherman, 389; Newberry, 114.

4. Catton, *A Stillness at Appomattox*, 220.

5. Oliver Christian Bosbyshell, *The 48th in the War: Being a Narrative of the Campaigns of the 48th Regiment Infantry, Pennsylvania Veteran Volunteers during the War of the Rebellion* (Philadelphia, PA: Avil Publishing, 1895), 163; Catton, *A Stillness at Appomattox*, 220; Pleasants, *Tragedy of the Crater*, 14–20, 22–26; Lowry, *Fate of the Country*, 51. Pleasants died in 1880 at age 47 of a brain tumor (eight months before medical science perfected a procedure that could have prolonged his life). He resumed his mining career after the war, and then, as a law officer, was active in suppressing the Molly Maguires.

6. Catton, *A Stillness at Appomattox*, 220; Kinard, 25.

7. Wilkinson, *Mother, May You*, 231; Wheeler, *Fields of Fury*, 272, 274; Bosbyshell, 164–165; Cannan, 18–19. Cavanaugh reports that Potter came up with the mining proposition independently around June 19, and Pleasants corroborated this plan. This is contrary to the reports of most other sources.

8. The exact location for the mine can thus be attributed to McKibben.

9. OR 40 (2), 396–97; Pleasants, *Tragedy of the Crater*, 35–36; Bosbyshell, 164–165.

10. OR 40 (1), 58; Catton, *A Stillness at Appomattox*, 221; Pleasants, *Tragedy of the Crater*, 32–33; Trudeau, *Like Men of War*, 230.

11. *Report of the Joint Committee on the Conduct of the War on the Attack on Petersburg* (Washington, DC: Government Printing Office, 1865), 113 (hereinafter, *JCCW*); Wilkinson, *Mother, May You*, 232; Trudeau, *Like Men of War*, 230; Catton, *A Stillness at Appomattox*, 222.

12. Catton, *A Stillness at Appomattox*, 222; Pleasants, *Tragedy of the Crater*, 37; Bosbyshell, 165; *JCCW*, 112–13; OR 40 (1), 58.

13. Michael B. Ballard, *Vicksburg: The Campaign that Opened the Mississippi* (Chapel Hill: University of North Carolina Press, 2004), 368–70; Wilkinson, *Mother, May You*, 231–32; Burbank, 284.

14. Raleigh C. Taylor, "War Underground: The Petersburg Mine," *The Regional Review* (National Park Service) 5, no. 1 (1940): 30.

15. Catton, *A Stillness at Appomattox*, 222; Newberry, 114; Allan Nevins and Milton Halsey Thomas, eds., *The Diary of George Templeton Strong: The Civil War 1861–1865* (New York: Octagon Books, 1974), 3: 441.

16. Burbank, 284.

17. Lowry, *Fate of the Country*, 102; Nevins and Thomas, *Diary of Strong*, 441.

18. Horn, 99–100; *JCCW*, 10, 156. Meade later testified that he never considered the location of the mine a "proper one" (OR 40 (1), 58).

19. Humphreys, *Virginia Campaign*, 230–35; Wilkinson, *Mother, May You*, 231; Wheeler, *Fields of Fury*, 274; Catton, *A Stillness at Appomattox*, 222.

20. Trudeau, *Like Men of War*, 230; Catton, *A Stillness at Appomattox*, 222–23; Cavanaugh, *Battle of the Crater*, 5–6; Foote, 3: 532; Wheeler, *Fields of Fury*, 272.

21. Some men reported that the imbibing ended soon after it began, when several of the men became inebriated after consuming a number of days' worth of stockpiled allotments (Trudeau, *Last Citadel*, 102). Other sources claim the process continued throughout the construction.

22. Marvel, *Burnside*, 391; Pleasants, *Tragedy of the Crater*, 37.

23. Pleasants, *Tragedy of the Crater*, 55; Scott, *Petersburg Story*, 195; Newberry, 115; Cavanaugh, *Battle of the Crater*, 5; Wheeler, *Fields of Fury*, 276.

24. Powell, "Tragedy of the Crater," 762; Davis, *Death in Trenches*, 68; Marvel, *Burnside*, 391; Trudeau, *Like Men of War*, 230; Cavanaugh, *Battle of the Crater*, 6.

25. Trudeau, *The Last Citadel*, 102.

26. Trudeau, "Chaos in the Crater," *Civil War Times* 43, no. 3 (August 2004): 31; Foote, 3: 532; Cavanaugh, *Battle of the Crater*, 6; Wheeler, *Fields of Fury*, 276; Joseph Gould, *The Story of the Forty-Eighth: A Record of the Campaigns of the Forty-Eighth Pennsylvania Volunteer Infantry during the Four Eventful Years of Its Service in the War for the Preservation of the Union* (Philadelphia: Regimental Association, Alfred M. Slocum, 1908), 212.

27. Pleasants. *Tragedy of the Crater*, 42.

28. Wheeler, *Fields of Fury*, 276.

29. Powell, "Tragedy of the Crater," 761–62; Pleasants, *Tragedy of the Crater*, 43; Bosbyshell, 166–67; Marvel, *Burnside*, 391–92; Wheeler, *Fields of Fury*, 276; Burbank, 284.

30. Powell, "Tragedy of the Crater," 762; Pleasants, *Tragedy of the Crater*, 42–45; Wheeler, *Fields of Fury*, 274; Commager, *The Blue and the Gray*, 1017–18; William H. Powell, "The Battle of the Petersburg Crater," *Battles*

and Leaders, 4: 545; OR 40 (1), 558; *JCCW*, 113.

31. The theodolite was the predecessor of the modern transit.

32. Wheeler, *Fields of Fury*, 274; Wilkinson, 232–33; Catton, *A Stillness at Appomattox*, 223; *JCCW*, 113.

33. Wheeler, *Fields of Fury*, 276.

34. Anderson, *Fifty-Seventh Regiment*, 164.

35. Anderson, *Fifty-Seventh Regiment*,169–70; Cavanaugh, *Battle of the Crater*, 5.

36. OR 21 (1), 128; OR 19 (2), 314; Cavanaugh, *Battle of the Crater*, 5.

37. Pleasants, *Tragedy of the Crater*, 46; Horn, 97; Scott, *Petersburg Story*, 195; Marvel, *Burnside*, 392; OR 40 (1), 557; Bosbyshell, 167–68.

38. Trudeau, *Last Citadel*, 105.

39. Pleasants, *Tragedy of the Crater*, 43; OR 40 (1), 557; William McFeely, *Grant: A Biography* (New York: W.W. Norton, 1981); Wilkinson, *Mother, May You*, 232; Trudeau, "Chaos," 29.

40. Burnside admitted before the Congressional Committee that his wording was, perhaps, "unfortunate" and "capable of misconstruction, whether intentional or otherwise" (Pleasants, *Tragedy of the Crater*, 49–50).

41. OR 40 (2), 608–09, 629–30; Pleasants, *Tragedy of the Crater*, 49–54; Horn, 97; Marvel, *Burnside*, 392. Henry Pleasants, Jr., believed that it was incredulous that Meade could have taken offense at Burnside's letter, and that there was a "precariously placed chip resting on the two-star epaulet." He believed it may have been fortunate for Meade that these letters were not forwarded to Grant, as by military regulations they should have been.

42. Pleasants, *Tragedy of the Crater*, 38–39.

43. Ibid., 40–41.

44. Horn, 101; OR 40 (1), 286–88; Longacre, *The Man Behind the Guns*, 205.

45. Albert, *History of the Forty-Fifth*, 143.

46. Ried Mitchell, *The Vacant Chair: The Northern Soldier Leaves Home* (New York: Oxford University Press, 1993), 84.

47. George H. Allen, *Forty-Six Months with the Fourth R.I. Volunteers in the War of 1861 to 1865* (Providence, RI: J.A. & R.A. Reid, 1887), 281–82; Cavanaugh, *Battle of the Crater*, 9–10.

48. Bosbyshell, 168–69; OR 40 (2), 300–01.

49. OR 40 (1), 557; Commager, *The Blue and the Gray*, 1017; Pleasants, *Tragedy of the Crater*, 46–47; Wilkinson, *Mother, May You*, 232–33; Walter C. Newberry, "The Petersburg Mine," 12 *MOLLUS* (Chicago, 1899), 116; Catton, *A Stillness at Appomattox*, 225;

Scott, *Petersburg Story*, 194; Davis, 68; Bosbyshell, 169; Lowry, *Fate of the Country*, 268–69; *JCCW*, 113.

50. OR 40 (1), 136, 138; Pleasants, *Tragedy of the Crater*, 64; Horn, 103; Cavanaugh, *Battle of the Crater*, 12.

51. There was a running debate over the adequacy of the charge, which was one-third less than that which Pleasants had prescribed. Some men suggested that the engineers' suggestions were appropriate, and that a smaller charge would actually be more effective (Catton, *A Stillness at Appomattox*, 225). Burnside felt strongly that "the greater the explosion the greater the crater radius, and less inclination would be given the sides of the crater," thereby allowing for an easier passage of troops in and out of the resultant pit (OR 40, Part I, Series I, 59). Major Lyman, an acquaintance of Major Duane and fellow staff member at Meade's headquarters, wrote that "Duane had sent for the mining records before Sebastopol and got me to read them to learn the proper charge; for, what with malaria, and sunstroke, and quinine, whiskey, and arsenic, he can hardly see, but clings to duty to the last! Finding nothing there, he said the book was a humbug, and determined on 8000 lbs." (Agazziz, 196n). Thus, Duane's recommendation may not have been a well-reasoned, expert one, based on careful analysis. In point of fact, Duane was quite ill with malaria at the time. Lyman's journal refers to Duane as not being able to use his eyes in August. By November, Lyman indicated Duane was "Better, but not well." He lamented "Poor Major Duane! He can't do much but talk and tell stories, for he is quite miserable and is not fit for duty" (Agassiz, 196n, 223, 257, 260–61, 289).

52. OR 40, Part II, Series I, 300–01; Pleasants, *Tragedy of the Crater*, 58, 63, 65; Marvel, *Burnside*, 393–94.

53. Trudeau, *Last Citadel*, 106.

54. *JCCW*, 10, 156; OR 40 (1), 557; Pleasants, *Tragedy of the Crater*, 63–65; Burbank, 284; Catton, *A Stillness at Appomattox*, 225; Wilkinson, *Mother, May You*, 233; Horn, 105; Cavanaugh, *Battle of the Crater*, 13; Marvel, *Burnside*, 394; Davis, *Death in Trenches*, 72; Kinard, 36.

55. Alexander, *Fighting*, 445.

56. Alexander, *Fighting*, 445–46; Davis, 68; Scott, *Petersburg Story*, 195.

57. Alexander, *Fighting*, 446.

58. The authorities differ as to the timing of the countermining's commencement around Elliott's Salient. Some suggest Douglas started his efforts a week before Alexander reported his suspicions to Venable (Cavanaugh, *Battle of the Crater*, 11). Others suggest the operation got un-

derway on July 10. Still others place the timing as late as July 15 (Davis, *Death in Trenches*, 68).

59. Horn, 97; Cavanaugh, *Battle of the Crater*, 11; Kinard, 32–34; Wheeler, *Fields of Fury*, 276.

60. Venable, "In the Trenches," 59; OR 40 (3), 771, 790, 807.

61. Venable, "In the Trenches," 60.

62. Cavanaugh, *Battle of the Crater*, 11; Kinard, 32–34.

63. Cavanaugh, *Battle of the Crater*, 11; Scott, *Petersburg Story*, 196; William Woods Hassler, *A.P. Hill: Lee's Forgotten General* (Chapel Hill: University of North Carolina Press, 1962), 219; John C. Featherstone, "And Then A.P. Hill Came Up," *Southern Historical Society Papers* (Richmond) 33 (Jan.–Dec. 1905), 2; John C. Featherstone, *Confederate Veteran* 14, no. 1 (Jan. 1906): 107.

64. Wilkinson, *Mother, May You*, 239.

65. Wise, *End of an Era*, 352.

66. Ibid., 351.

67. John M. Taylor, "The Crater," in *With My Face to the Enemy: Perspectives on the Civil War*, ed. Robert Cowley (New York: Putnam's, 2001), 464.

68. Cavanaugh, *Battle of the Crater*, 10.

69. Pleasants, *Tragedy of the Crater*, 63.

70. Catton, *A Stillness at Appomattox*, 225; Foote, 3: 534; Wilkinson, *Mother, May You*, 233.

71. Wilkinson, *Mother, May You* 233.

72. Freeman, *R.E. Lee*, 464; Scott, *Petersburg Story*, 196.

73. Wilkinson, *Mother, May You*, 239.

74. Scott, *Petersburg Story*, 196.

75. Wise, *The End of an Era*, 352.

76. Simpson, *Hood's Texas Brigade*, 426.

77. Elizabeth Fry Page, "If You Love Me," *Confederate Veteran Magazine* 35, no. 4 (April 1927): 134. Lowry fell four hours after the explosion on July 30 while leading his men into action. He had been promoted to captaincy at age nineteen when all the officers of his company were killed following the explosion in Elliott's Salient.

78. Kinard, 34; Wilkinson, *Mother, May You*, 233.

79. Wheeler, 276.

80. Wilkinson, *Mother, May You*, 233; Wheeler, *Fields of Fury*, 276; Foote, 3: 534.

81. Wheeler, 276.

82. Alexander, *Fighting*, 450; Humphreys, *Virginia Campaign*, 251.

83. OR 40 (3), 813, 816, 819–20.

84. Alexander, *Fighting*, 450.

85. Barnwell, 177; Wise, *The End of an Era*, 352; Scott, *Petersburg Story*, 195; Davis, 69. Alexander's analysis

claims there was no gorge trench, nor were there artillery or mortars concentrated on the approaches to the Salient. Alexander, *Fighting*, 450.

86. Alexander, *Fighting*, 443, 450; Davis, *Death in Trenches*, 69; Barnwell, 177.

Chapter 5

1. Horn, 97, 102; Humphreys, *Virginia Campaign*, 250.

2. Foote, 3: 531; Humphreys, *Virginia Campaign*, 250.

3. Wheeler, *Fields of Fury*, 277; Catton, *A Stillness at Appomattox*, 236; Lowry, *Fate of the Country*, 269; Cavanaugh, *Battle of the Crater*, 28; Scott, *Petersburg Story*, 196; Wise, *End of an Era*, 354; Horn, 104.

4. Powell, 762.

5. James I. Robertson, Jr., *Civil War Virginia: Battleground for a Nation* (Charlottesville: University Press of Virginia, 1991), 164–65; Horn 101, 103.

6. Catton, *Grant Takes Command—1863–65*, (Garden City, NY: Doubleday, 1968), 320; Lowry, *Fate of the Country*, 245–46.

7. Horn, 103–04; Sandburg, 145–46.

8. Horn, 104; Davis, *Death in Trenches*, 70.

9. Powell, "Battle of the Petersburg Crater," 546; Humphreys, *Virginia Campaign*, 247; Taylor, "The Crater," 465.

10. Douglas Southall Freeman, *Lee's Lieutenants: A Study In Command* (New York: Scribner's, 1944) 3: 542; OR 40 (1), 762.

11. Grant, *Memoirs*, 2: 310; Catton, *A Stillness at Appomattox*, 236; Humphreys, *Virginia Campaign*, 247–48.

12. Cavanaugh, *Battle of the Crater*, 28; OR 40 (1), 308–09; Alexander, *Fighting*, 452–53; Foote, 3: 533; Taylor, "The Crater," 465.

13. OR 40 (1), 330; General Theodore F. Rodenbough, "Sheridan's Trevilian Raid," *Battles and Leaders*, ed., Johnson and Buell, 4: 236.

14. OR 40 (1), 308–09; Regis De Trobriand, *Four Years with the Army of the Potomac* (Boston: Ticknor, 1889), 604–05; Cavanaugh, *Battle of the Crater*, 29.

15. OR 40 (1), 759; Alexander, *Fighting*, 452; Cavanaugh, *Battle of the Crater*, 29.

16. Humphreys, *Virginia Campaign*, 247–48; OR 40 (1), 308–09; OR 40 (3), 808; Catton, *A Stillness at Appomattox*, 236.

17. OR 40 (1), 309.

18. Four Mile Creek and Bailey's Creek converged and flowed into the

James at the tip of Jones' Neck. The mouth of the combined creek, together with the hydrology of the river's loop, caused a deepwater area ideal for the docking and loading of vessels—hence the name, Deep Bottom.

19. Cavanaugh, *Battle of the Crater*, 29–30; Humphreys, *Virginia Campaign*, 247–48.

20. Cavanaugh, *Battle of the Crater*, 30; Humphreys, *Virginia Campaign*, 243; OR 40 (1), 692; Trudeau, *Last Citadel*, 146.

21. Humphreys, *Virginia Campaign*, 252; OR 40 (1), 762, 805–06; Hassler, 218–19; Stevenson, 3; "Deep Bottom and the Crater," www.members.aol.com/siege1864/crater.html.

22. Humphreys and Wise both later contended that all of Wilcox's division left Petersburg, leaving only 13,000 men in defense of the city.

23. Freeman, *Lee's Lieutenants*, 3: 542; Hassler, 219; Humphreys, *Virginia Campaign*, 252; Scott, *Petersburg Story*, 196; Rodenbough, 236.

24. Freeman, *Lee's Lieutenants*, 3: 542; George A. Bruce, *The Twentieth Regiment of Massachusetts Volunteer Infantry 1861–1865* (Boston: Houghton Mifflin, 1906), 413; Catton, *A Stillness At Appomattox*, 236.

25. D. Augustus Dickert, *History of Kershaw's Brigade with Complete Roll of Companies, Biographical Sketches, Incidents, Anecdotes, etc.* (Newberry, SC: Elbert H. Aull, 1899), 390; Cavanaugh, *Battle of the Crater*, 30; OR 40 (1), 308–09; Horn, 105–06.

26. OR 40, Part I, Series I, 310; 330, 391–92, 692, 759, 800, 805–06; Freeman, *Lee's Lieutenants*, 3: 542; Cavanaugh, *Battle of the Crater*, 31; Humphreys, *Virginia Campaign*, 249; Horn, 106.

27. OR 40, Part I, Series I, 310; Cavanaugh, *Battle of the Crater*, 31–32; Bruce, 413; Humphreys, *Virginia Campaign*, 249.

28. Alexander, *Fighting*, 453; Cavanaugh, *Battle of the Crater*, 32; OR 40 (1), 310; Rodenbough, 236; Davis, *Death in Trenches*, 70; Horn, 107; OR 40 (3), 809.

29. John Gibbon, *Personal Recollections of the Civil War* (Dayton: Morningside Bookshop, 1978), 248–49; OR 40, Part I, Series I, 310–11; Cavanaugh, *Battle of the Crater*, 34.

30. OR 40, Part I, Series I, 310–11.

31. Frances A. Walker, *History of the Second Army Corps of the Army of the Potomac* (New York: Scribner's, 1886), 566; OR 40 (1), 311.

32. OR 40 (1), 759, 762; Rodenbough, 236; Cavanaugh, *Battle of the Crater*, 35–36.

33. OR 40 (1), 693; Davis, 70.

34. OR 40 (1), 2, 134, 388–89, 762; Wise, *End of an Era*, 354; Marvel, *Burnside*, 395.

35. Humphreys, *Virginia Campaign*, 253, 258; Horn, 108–09.

36. OR 40 (1), 312.

37. Freeman, *Lee's Lieutenants*, 3: 542; Foote, 3: 533: Horn, 107.

38. OR 40 (1), 311, 331, 369, 392, 759; Alexander, *Fighting*, 454; Trudeau, *Last Citadel*, 100; Horn, 105.

Chapter 6

1. OR 40 (1), 58.

2. OR 40 (1), 58–59, 161; OR 40 (2), 629–30; Marvel, *Burnside*, 392.

3. Such displays of ego and independence were simply not part of Burnside's nature. When their roles had been reversed, Burnside promoted Meade to command of the Fifth Corps after Fredericksburg, in spite of considerable staff resistance. When Meade had been subjected to criticism for the Mine Run campaign, Burnside wrote him a note of encouragement, indicating his willingness to serve under him in command of a corps. Burnside had also voluntarily placed himself under Meade's command that May, although he was senior in rank, having once held Meade's current position. However, Meade was irritable, disagreeable, condescending and petty, especially to those whom he held in low regard, such as Burnside. While he did not dislike Burnside more than his other corps commanders, he did not value his intelligence and capacity for command (Cannon, 44).

4. OR 40(1), 161; Marvel, *Burnside*, 392; Cavanaugh, *Battle of the Crater*, 16; Cannon, 44.

5. Marvel, *Burnside*, 2–6, 10–36, 41–96, 99–159; James M. McPherson, *Antietam* (New York: Oxford University Press, 2002), 13, 17, 80; Joseph P. Cullen, "The Very Beau Ideal of a Soldier: A Personality Profile of Ambrose E. Burnside, *Civil War Times* 16, no. 5 (August 1977): 4–8; John G. Waugh, *The Class of 1846* (New York: Warner Books, 1994), 57.

6. Phillip Thomas Tucker, *Burnside's Bridge* (Mechanicsburg: Stackpole Books, 2000), 40–152; McPherson, *Antietam*, 125–30; Cullen, "*Beau Ideal*," 9–10.

7. Doris Kearns Goodwin, *Team of Rivals: The Political Genius of Abraham Lincoln* (New York: Simon and Schuster, 2005), 486 (from Fanny Seward's diary entry of January 1, 1863).

8. John Wesley Hollensed, Letters to Family, *McCain Library and Achieves*, University of Southern Mississippi, Hattiesburg, MS; Cullen, "*Beau Ideal*," 10, 38–42; Marvel, *Burnside*, 175–95; George C. Rable, *Fredericksburg! Fredericksburg!* (Chapel Hill: University of North Carolina Press, 2002), 227–28,

266, 288–90; Edward J. Stackpole, *The Fredericksburg Campaign* (New York: Bonanza Books, 1957), 134–35, 209–16.

9. Marvel, *Burnside*, 218–25, 277–85, 340–42.

10. Cannan, 36; Marvel, *Burnside*, 392.

11. OR 40 (1), 130–31; Davis, 67.

12. OR 40 (1), 130–31; Cannan, 38–39.

13. OR 40 (1), 132.

14. Humphreys, *Virginia Campaign*, 251; Horn, 105; Cannan, 40: OR 40 (1), 474–76.

15. OR 40 (1), 133; Humphreys, *Virginia Campaign*, 250–51.

16. Lowry, *Fate of the Country*, 269; Pleasants, *Tragedy of the Crater*, 55; OR 40 (1), 58.

17. OR 40 (1), 59; Trudeau, *Like Men of War*, 231; Horn, 101.

18. OR 40 (1), 136; Albert, 149; Pleasants, *Tragedy of the Crater*, 55; Davis, *Death in Trenches*, 72.

19. Albert, 149; Horn, 105.

20. Marvel, *Burnside*, 392–94; Albert, 149.

21. Thomas, "Colored Troops," 777.

22. Allen, *Forty-Six Months*, 282; Hondon B. Hargrove, *Black Union Soldiers in the Civil War* (Jefferson, NC: McFarland, 1988), 184; Bowley, "Petersburg Mine," 28; John M. Taylor, *Grinding, Relentless War* (Leesburg, VA: PRI-MEDIA Enthusiast Publications, 2004), 54–55; Charles Carlton Coffin, *Four Years of Fighting, Personal Observation with the Army and Navy from the First Battle of Bull Run to the Fall of Richmond* (New York: Arno & The New York Times, 1970), 377–78; Albert, 149; Wilkinson, *Mother, May You*, 233–34; Marvel, *Burnside*, 393–94; Trudeau, *Like Men of War*, 231; Scott, *Petersburg Story*, 197; Commager, *The Blue and the Gray*, 1018; Anderson, *Fifty-Seventh Regiment*, 170.

23. JCCW, 91.

24. Marvel, *Burnside*, 329–30; Kinard, 39; Cannan, 29; Ezra J. Warner, *Generals in Blue* (Baton Rouge: Louisiana State University Press, 1964), 150–51; Tucker, 114, 136–37.

25. Hargrove, 184; Thomas, "Colored Troops," 777; Albert, 149.

26. Hargrove, 180; Thomas Wentworth Higginson, *Army Life in a Black Regiment* (East Lansing: Michigan State University Press, 1960), 1; Dudley Taylor Cornish, *The Sable Arm: Black Troops in the Union Army, 1861–1865* (Lawrence: University of Kansas Press, 1987), 132–33; Marvel, *Burnside*, 347–48; Horn, 69.

27. Hargrove, 180.

28. Cannan, 29; Thomas, "Colored Troops," 777; Cavanaugh, *Battle of the Crater*, 17; Wilkinson, *Mother, May You*, 234; Cornish, 273.

29. Trudeau, *Like Men of War*, 229; Marvel, *Burnside*, 393; Cannan, 30; Cavanaugh, *Battle of the Crater*, 17.

30. McFeely, *Grant*, 178; Cavanaugh, *Battle of the Crater*, 17.

31. David W. Blight, ed., *When This Cruel War Is Over: The Civil War Letters of Charles Henry Brewster* (Amherst: University of Massachusetts Press, 1992), 316; Agassiz, 102; OR 40 (3), 320.

32. Jackson, 144.

33. Trudeau, *Like Men of War*, 228.

34. Campanion H. Seymour Hall, "Mine Run to Petersburg," War Talks in Kansas, *MOLLUS* (Wilmington, NC: Broadfoot Publishing, 1992); Thomas, "Colored Troops," 777; Scott, *Petersburg Story*, 58; Powell, "Tragedy of the Crater,"763.

35. Bowley, "Petersburg Mine," 28.

36. Hall, 221: Anderson, 170.

37. Hall, 220–21.

38. OR 40 (3), 304–05, 320–21; Marvel, *Burnside*, 393.

39. Thomas, "Colored Troops," 777; Cornish, 273; Carl G. Hodges and Helene H. Levene, eds., *Illinois Negro Historymakers* (Chicago: Illinois Emancipation Centennial Commission, 1964), 25; Robert Paul Jordan, *The Civil War* (Washington, DC: National Geographic 1969), 196.

40. Pleasants, *Tragedy of the Crater*, 61.

41. Wilkinson, *Mother, May You*, 234.

42. Jordan, *Civil War*, 191.

43. Albert, 149.

44. Bosbyshell, 174; Wilkinson, *Mother, May You*, 234; Albert, 149; Trudeau, *Like Men of War*, 231.

45. Marvel, *Burnside*, 393; Hall, 221; Thomas, "Colored Troops," 777; Pleasants, *Tragedy of the Crater*, 62; John David Smith, ed., *Black Soldiers in Blue: African American Troops in the Civil War Era* (Chapel Hill: University of North Carolina 2002), 58; Cornish, 274.

46. Thomas, "Colored Troops," 778; Cornish, 274; Coffin, *Four Years of Fighting*,377.

47. OR 40 (1), 60.

48. Ethan Rafuse, *George Gordon Meade and the War in the East* (Abilene, TX: McWhiney Foundation Press, McMurry University, 1968), 139; OR 40 (3), 266; Davis, *Death in Trenches*, 74.

49. Wilkinson, *Mother, May You*, 235; Wheeler, *Fields of Fury*, 280. Shelby Foote refers to this line of thinking as "racism in reverse." Foote, 3: 534.

50. Burnside later substantiated that in the period from June 20th to July 29th alone, the three white divisions had suffered 1,150 casualties, which was over 12 percent of his force. In the

fight for Petersburg on the 17th and 18th of June, these three divisions had lost a total of 2,903 men.

51. OR 40 (1), 60–61; Marvel, *Burnside*, 394; Cannan, 45, Horn, 104–05.

52. Marvel, *Burnside*, 394; Horn, 108; Cannan, 45; Cornish, 274.

53. Cannan, 47.

54. McFeely, 178; Wheeler, *Fields of Fury*, 280.

55. Wheeler, *Fields of Fury*, 280.

56. William A. Frassanito, *Grant and Lee The Virginia Campaigns 1864–1865* (New York: Scribner's, 1983), 284.

57. OR 40 (1), 61.

58. Ferrero was in Washington when this meeting took place, and was already well-versed on the current plan. Ledlie arrived after the meeting started (Hall, 222; *JCCW*, 17).

59. JCCW, 117; Marvel, *Burnside*, 394.

60. At some point later that day, a written confirmation reached Burnside's headquarters from Major General A.A. Humphreys, chief of staff of the Army of the Potomac, which bore a date and time of 10:15 A.M., July 29, 1864. It indicated that "I am instructed to say that the major-general commanding submitted to the lieutenant-general commanding the armies your proposition to form the leading columns of assault of the black troops, and that he, as well as the major-general commanding, does not approve the proposition, but directs that those columns be formed of the white troops" (OR 40, Series I, Part I, 137).

61. OR 40 (1), 61–62; Allen, *Forty-Six Months*, 282; Davis, *Death in Trenches*, 74; *JCCW*, 17, 42, 98, 125; Marvel, *Burnside*, 394; Cannan, 46–47; Scott, *Petersburg Story*, 182.

62. Allen, 282.

63. Davis, *Death in Trenches*, 74; Cannan, 47.

64. There is no explanation as to Ledlie's initial absence from the meeting. Wilkinson suggests it was because Burnside "was fed up with his ineptitude, but General Willcox was of the decided opinion that he should be briefed regardless, and at Willcox's suggestion, Burnside relented and called the commander of the 1st Division into the council" (Wilkinson, *Mother, May You*, 237).

65. While Potter did not volunteer his division at that critical meeting, he later expressed his belief that Burnside should, nonetheless, have chosen him to lead: "My division expected and was anxious to have the advance, because they knew the ground, had an interest in the work, were in the best condition, and known to be the best division of the Corps." Henry C. Potter, "General Robert B. Potter and the Assault at the Petersburg Crater," *The Century* (The Century Company, 35, no. 3: 481).

66. Hall, 222; OR 40 (1), 61–62; *JCCW*, 15–18; Marvel, *Burnside*, 395; Wilkinson, *Mother, May You*, 237; William Marvel, "And Fire Shall Devour Them: The 9th New Hampshire in the Crater," *A Journal of the American Civil War* 2, no. 2 (Campbell, CA: Regimental Studies, 1992), 118.

67. Potter contended that all of the commanders argued for the lead, and Burnside devised the lottery to avoid favoritism and the "appearance of partiality for a very dear personal friend which would not improbably have been said to have influenced him had he chosen General Potter." Potter, "General Robert B. Potter," 481.

68. OR 40 (1), 61; Marvel, *Burnside*, 395; Wilkinson, *Mother, May You*, 237; Cavanaugh, *Battle of the Crater*, 23. Wilkinson suggests that Burnside performed this lottery with three blades of grass from outside his tent. Wilkinson, *Mother, May You*, 237.

69. Wheeler, *Fields of Fury*, 280.

70. *New York Times*, August 16, 1882; Billy Ellis, *Tithes of Blood: A Confederate Soldier's Story* (Murfreesboro, TN: Southern Heritage Press, 1997), 164; Kinard, 41.

71. Grady McWhiney and Jack Jay Jenkins, "The Union's Worst General: James H. Ledlie," *Civil War Times* 14, no. 3 (June 1975): 30–33.

72. Ellis, *Tithes*, 164–65.

73. McWhiney, "Union's Worst General," 30–33.

74. Ibid., 35–36.

75. Grant, *Memoirs*, 2: 313; Cannan, 50; Lowry, *Fate of the Country*, 270; Horn, 108. After the war, Ledlie became an engineer for the Central Pacific Railroad. He built the Nevada Central line from Austin to Battle Mountain, Nevada, and had a siding named after him near the Reese Valley. Ledlie was in Battle Mountain the day that President Grant came to town on his triumphant speaking tour. No doubt Ledlie remained out of sight. *New York Times*, August 16, 1882; Battle Mountain Nevada, History and Description, www.nevadaweb.com.

76. Lowry, *Fate of the Country*, 270.

77. OR 40 (1), 47; Rafuse, 139–42.

78. OR 40 (1), 61–62, 165; Marvel, "And Fire Shall Devour Them," 121; Anderson, 169; Rafuse, 139–42; Davis, *Death in Trenches*, 75; Humphreys, *Virginia Campaign*, 254.

79. OR 40 (1), 45, 134–35.

80. Jones, *Army of Northern Virginia*, 120; Coffin, 379; OR 40 (1), 61–62; Anderson, 169.

81. OR 40 (1), Taylor, "The Crater," 55; Albert, 149–51; Scott, *Petersburg Story*, 182; Powell, "Tragedy," 764.

82. Cavanaugh, *Battle of the Crater*, 23.

83. Trudeau, *Like Men of War*, 235, *JCCW*, 90, 98.

84. Wilkinson, *Mother, May You*, 238; Marvel, *Burnside*, 396–97.

85. Wilkinson, *Mother, May You*, 238; Anderson, 202.

86. OR 40 (1), 62, 158–59.

87. Anderson, 175.

88. Marvel, *Burnside*, 396; Cannan, 51.

89. Davis, *Death in Trenches*, 74; Marvel, *Burnside*, 396; Anderson, 202.

90. OR 29 (1), 531; OR 40 (1), 352, 369; OR 40 (2), 609; OR 40 (3), 99, 364, 610; OR 51 (1), 1169; Scott, *Petersburg Story*, 182; Thomas, "Colored Troops," 777.

Chapter 7

1. Anderson, *Fifty-Seventh Regiment*, 175–76.

2. Wilkinson, *Mother, May You*, 240.

3. Powell, "Battle of the Crater," 549; Marvel, *Burnside*, 395–97.

4. Marvel, *Burnside*, 396.

5. Charles H. Houghton, "In the Crater," *Battles and Leaders*, ed. Johnson and Buell (New York: Castle Books, 1956), 4: 561; Cannan, 51–52.

6. OR 40 (1), 538, Powell, "Battle of the Crater," 549; Lowry, *The Fate of the Country*, 270.

7. Others placed the movement at about 10:00 P.M.

8. Wilkinson, *Mother, May You*, 242–43.

9. Other accounts of the order of battle had the second and third lines reversed. While not a critical issue, this writer has decided to attribute the accounts of Captain Charles H. Houghton and Lieutenant Colonel Gilbert Robinson of the 3rd Maryland with the accurate order of battle (OR 40, Part I, Series I, 541; Shaw, *A History of the 14th Regiment*, 27–28; Charles H. Houghton, "In the Crater," *Battles and Leaders*, ed. Johnson and Buell, 4: 561. See, however, Anderson and Wilkinson for accounts of a different order of battle. Major Charles Chipman commanded the 14th New York Heavy Artillery throughout July, 1864, had been reassigned from commanding the 29th Massachusetts when there was a lack of field grade officers in the former unit. However, due to an illness, he did not participate in the assault on July 30. He returned to command immediately thereafter and was killed by a mortar shell on August 7, 1864 (Letter dated August 1, 1864 from Charles Chipman to his wife, Papers of Charles Chipman, U.S. Army Military History Institute, Carlisle, PA; OR 42 (2), 80–

81. On August 18, 1964, Major George M. Randall was placed in command. Randall was a lieutenant and aide-de-camp to Ledlie on July 30, as a member of the 4th U.S. Infantry (OR 40 (1), 534).

10. Anderson, *Fifty-Seventh Regiment*, 175–76, 205–06; OR 40, Part I, Series I, 535, 541; Wilkinson, 241–42; Powell, "Battle of the Crater," 550; Lowry, *The Fate of the Country*, 270.

11. Wilkinson, *Mother, May You*, 242–43.

12. It was the 2nd Brigade, 3rd division of the Eighteenth Corps, under Colonel Samuel A. Duncan which lost its way. This brigade consisted of the 2nd U.S. Colored Cavalry (Dismounted), and the 4th, 5th, 6th and 22nd U.S. Colored Troops. Potter reported to Burnside that "I am not sure that this is much of a misfortune, as Duncan's troops were colored troops and I did not get a very favorable account of some of these troops in that corps" (OR 40 (3), 665). While Carr appeared in the order of battle as being in command of the third division, at the court of inquiry he testified as to being in command of the first division and a portion of the colored division known as Hink's division (OR 40 (1), 119, 266).

13. OR 40 (1), 88–89, 91, 549, 567; Marvel, *Burnside*, 396; JCCW, 86; Marvel, "Fire Shall Devour Them," 122.

14. OR 40 (1), 88, 550–51; JCCW, 116; Frederick E. Cushman, *History of the 58th Regt. Massachusetts Volunteers, From the 15th Day of September 1863 to the Close of the Rebellions* (Washington, DC: Gibson Bros., 1865), 140.

15. OR 40 (3), 665; JCCW, 86.

16. Tucker, *Burnside's Bridge*, 116–17, 127, 137; Kinard, 26; Frank Woodford, *Father Abraham's Children: Michigan Episodes in the Civil War* (Detroit: Wayne State University Press, 1961), 191–92.

17. OR 40 (1), 61, 101, 574; JCCW, 86.

18. OR 40 (1), 103, 138, 586, 590.

19. Marvel, *Burnside*, 223, 229, 241, 286, 342, 352–379, 461. Willcox remained in the service after the war and commanded the Department of Arizona. He retired in 1887 as a brigadier general. He died in 1907; the town of Willcox, Arizona, was named for him.

20. Robert Garth Scott, ed., *Forgotten Valor: The Memoirs, Journals, & Civil War Letters of Orlando B. Willcox* (Kent, OH: Kent State University Press, 1999), 555; Thomas, "Colored Troops," 564.

21. Bowley, "Petersburg Mine," 29; OR 40 (1), 595; Hall, 221–22; Cutcheon, 138.

22. Wilkinson, *Mother, May You*, 242; James H. Rickard, "Services with Colored Troops in Burnside's Corps," in *Personal Narratives of Events in the War of the Rebellion, Being Papers Read Before the Rhode Island Soldiers and Sailors Historical Society* 5, no. 1 (Providence, RI 1894): 28; Thomas, "Colored Troops," 777; Hall, 222; Smith, *Black Soldiers in Blue*, 183; William Kreutzer, *Notes and Observations Made During Four Years of Service with the Ninety-Eighth N.Y. Volunteers in the War of 1861* (Philadelphia: Grant, Faires & Rodgers, 1878), 217.

23. Rickard, "Services with Colored Troops," 28–29; Wilkinson, *Mother, May You*, 242; OR 40 (1), 147.

24. JCCW, 86; OR 40 (1), 159, 595; Trudeau, *Like Men of War*, 236.

25. OR 40 (1), 83–84, 698–99, 706–07, 723–24; JCCW, 60–61, 86, 118–19; Stevenson, 2; W.P. Derby, *Bearing Arms in the Twenty-Seventh Massachusetts Regiment of Volunteers Infantry During The Civil War 1861–1865* (Boston: Wright & Potter, 1883), 360.

26. Davis, *Death In Trenches*, 73; OR 40 (1), 61, 77, 134–35, 311, 624–25; Powell, "Battle of the Crater," 773; Lowry, *Fate of the Country*, 270; JCCW, 66.

27. OR 40 (1), 61; OR 40 (3), 480, 612; Cavanaugh, *Battle of the Crater*, 25; Agassiz, 197; JCCW, 19, 52.

28. Edward G. Longacre, *The Man Behind the Guns*, 202, 205; OR 40 (1), 210, 284.

29. One has but to examine Hunt's map accompanying his report on the operation displaying the lines of fire to appreciate the precision of his planning. See Calvin D. Cowles, *The Official Military Atlas of the Civil War* (New York: Arno Press/Crown Publishers, 1978), originally published by the U.S. Government Printing Office, Washington, DC, in 1891, Plate 64.

30. The 2nd Maine battery of four 3-inch guns was on the right of the 1st division; the 19th New York and 11th Massachusetts, with six 12-pounders, was in front of the 2nd Division and to the rear and left of the Old Barn, and to the right of the covered way leading to the mine; the 3rd Vermont and Durell's D, Independent Pennsylvania was in the heavy work on the left of the same covered way and in the rear of the Taylor house; Roemer's 34th New York and Mayo's 3rd Maine was in the work on the knoll to the left of the Petersburg, or Jordan, road, each unit with four 3-inch guns; Twitchell's 7th Maine, one section in front on the line to the left of the ice house, and the other to the left of the Taylor house near the Petersburg road, and one at the right of the house, being two 12-pounders; two Coehorn mortars were in position at the Old Barn.

31. OR 40, Part I, Series I, 484, 599–600, 658, 726–27. This is considerably more than is generally attributed to the numbers participating in the barrage. Grady McWhiney attributes 110 guns and 54 mortars to the barrage, which is the number General Henry Hunt, Chief of Artillery, Army of the Potomac reported. OR 40(1), 280. (See Grady McWhiney, *Attack and Die: Civil War Military Tactics and the Southern Heritage* (Tuscaloosa: University of Alabama Press, 1982), 122.

32. Gould, 215; OR 40 (1), 96; Longacre, *Man Behind the Guns*, 207; Agassiz, 197; Adjutants-General, Connecticut, *Record of Service of Connecticut Men in the Army and Navy of the United States During the War of the Rebellion* (Hartford, CT: Press of the Case, Lockwood & Brainard, 1889), 118; Edgar B. Bennett, *First Connecticut Heavy Artillery: Historical Sketch and Present Addresses of Members* (East Berlin, CT, privately published, 1889), 20; Marcia Reid-Green, ed., *Letters Home, Henry Matrau of the Iron Brigade* (Lincoln: University of Nebraska Press, 1993), 89; Annette Topert, ed., *The Brothers' War: Civil War Letters to Their Loved Ones from the Blue and the Gray* (New York: Times Books, 1988), 209; Stevenson, 5. In total, there were twenty-four 12-pounders and twenty-eight rifled guns, six 4.5 inch siege guns and eleven Coehorn mortars in the works, in addition to the sixteen mortars and six siege guns commanded by Abbot, for a total of ninety-one pieces of ordnance which took part in the bombardment along the Fifth Corps lines (OR 40 (1), 483–84).

33. Stevenson, 3; Humphreys, *Virginia Campaign*, 254; Barnwell, 176.

34. Barnwell, 177; Bagby, Edward, *Edward Bagby of Virginia*, 455; Pleasants, *Tragedy of the Crater*, 87; the Rev. J. William Jones, "The Battle of the Crater," *Southern Historical Society Papers* (Richmond) (January–December 1882): 119–20; OR 40 (1), 787.

35. Warren Wilkinson and Steven E. Woodworth, *A Scythe of Fire: A Civil War Story of the Eighth Georgia Infantry Regiment* (New York: William Morrow, 2002), 294. One has to wonder if Captain Reed read the accounts on how the 18th South Carolina fared that "wild morning."

36. Page, "If You Love Me," 134.

37. Chambers, 174.

38. During a reorganization of the Confederate army in May of 1862, one of Petersburg's infantry companies, Lee's Life Guard, was reconstituted as a battery of artillery. Most of the men comprising the unit came from Mahone's brigade. The battery was known first as Branch's battery and later as Pegram's battery. On July 30, 1864, the

battery was in that fateful position atop the gallery loaded with 8,000 pounds of gunpowder, and many of its members died in the ensuing explosion. By an interesting quirk of fate, Mahone's brigade was a part of the force which eventually recaptured the Crater, where the battery had stood. In so doing, Mahone's men retook the guns of their former comrades in Pegram's battery (Horn, 43).

39. Barnwell, 176–77; H.W. Burton, *The History of Norfolk, Virginia* (Norfolk, VA: Virginia Job Print, 36 and 38, 1879), 89; OR 40 (1), 788.

40. J.C. Coit, "Letter to Fitz William McMaster," August 2, 1879, *Southern Historical Society Papers* (1882): 124–125; Michael Cavanaugh, *The Otey, Ringgold and Davidson, Virginia Artillery* (Lynchburg, VA: H.E. Howard, 1993), 59–61; Barnwell, 177; Robinson, 165–166; Henry G. Flanner, "Flanner's North Carolina Battery at the Battle of the Crater," *Southern Historical Society Papers* (Richmond: Jan.–Jun.1878), 5: 247–248, 257; Peter S. Carmichael, *Lee's Young Artillerist William R.J. Pegram* (Charlottesville: University Press of Virginia, 1995), 129–131; John Cheves Haskell, *The Haskell Memoirs: The Personal Narrative of a Confederate Officer*, Gilbert E. Govan and James W. Livingood, ed. (New York: Putnam's, 1960), 72–73; William W. Chamberlaine, *Memoirs of the Civil War Between the Northern and Southern Sections of the United States of America 1861 to 1865* (Washington, DC: Press of Byron S. Adams, 1912), 106–07; George S. Bernard, ed., *War Talks of Confederate Veterans* (Petersburg, VA: Fenn & Owen Publishers, 1892), 178; Davis, *Death in Trenches*, 86; Alexander, *Fighting*, 441–43, 450–51.

41. Coit, "Letter to McMaster," 124–26; Day, "Battle of Crater," 355; Alexander, *Fighting*, 450–51.

42. Bernard, *War Talks*, 178.

43. E.P. Alexander, "Confederate Artillery Service," *Southern Historical Society Papers* 11 (1883): 111–12.

44. OR 40 (1), 43, 128; Taylor, "The Crater," 56; Humphreys, *Virginia Campaign*, 254; JCCW, 19; Davis, *Death in Trenches*, 74.

45. JCCW, 19.

46. OR 40 (1), 88, 97; JCCW, 35, 39, 83–84, 111; Davis, *Death in Trenches*, 74; Scott, *Forgotten Valor*, 555–56. The extent to which the failure to remove the abatis proved to be detrimental to the success of the operation is debatable. While Grant, Meade and Warren testified that leaving them proved extremely damaging, others had differing opinions. Willcox indicated that actually very little of the Federal abatis was actually even left to be removed, as most had already been shot away in the

previous weeks' fighting. His commanders all later indicated that the abatis was sufficiently cleared away for the passage of the troops. Willcox also felt any prior removal would have excited the enemy pickets, which would have proven very detrimental to the operation. Ferrero also had no issue with the obstructions not being removed beforehand. He later indicated that "Every arrangement was made that it was possible to make under the circumstances, as it was necessary that we should do everything without giving information to the enemy." He felt it was impossible to do more ahead of time, and the troops were able to get across with the "necessary rapidity" required at that moment. Burnside himself felt that any delay caused by the existing abatis, if there indeed was any, was no more than five minutes (JCCW, 19, 22, 106–08; Scott, *Forgotten Valor*, 555–56).

47. Longacre, *Man Behind the Guns*, 207; OR 40 (1), 79, 110, 117; JCCW, 98. Following the explosion, Burnside agreed to provide a detail to Monroe to remove the trees. However, the total force thus assigned was only 80 men. Due to the small size of the detail, only a portion of the trees were ultimately cut down. The guns were thus enabled to be of some service but could never see the flanking guns that caused such a great deal of harm.

48. Davis, *Death in Trenches*, 74; JCCW, 99; OR 40 (1), 97–98; Humphreys, *Virginia Campaign*, 254.

49. OR 40 (1), 88, 108; JCCW, 83; Anderson, 169; Taylor, "The Crater," 56. Duane would later testify that the main cause for Burnside's lack of success was the failure to clear away obstructions in front of his own works and the enemy's lines, as well as attacking in the flank rather than in three columns (which arguably was necessitated by the small opening in the lines resulting from inadequate preparation).

Chapter 8

1. Wilkinson, *Mother, May You*, 243–44.

2. OR 40 (1), 139.

3. Henry Pleasants, Jr., and George H. Straley, *Inferno at Petersburg* (Philadelphia: Chilton Book, 1961), 120–21; OR 40 (1), 139; OR 11 (3), 656; JCCW, 128; Davis, *Death in Trenches*, 75.

4. Scott, *Petersburg Story*, 197; Pleasants, *Inferno*, 122; Davis, *Death in Trenches*, 75.

5. Jones, *Army of Northern Virginia*, 152.

6. James J. Chase, *The Charge At*

Day-Break: Scenes and Incidents at the Battle of the Mine Explosion, Near Petersburg, Va., July 30, 1864 (Lewiston, ME: Journal Office, 1875),16; Pleasants, *Inferno at Petersburg*, 122; JCCW, 108, 129, 153, 163; OR 40, (1), 657; Davis, *Death in Trenches*, 75; Lowry, *Fate of the Country*, 270–71; Shamokin *Daily News*, August 1, 1927; Jones, *Army of Northern Virginia*, 152.

7. JCCW, 19–20.

8. Lowry, *Fate of the Country*, 270–71; Trudeau, *Like Men of War*, 236; Scott, *Petersburg Story*, 197; Gould, 224; Wilkinson, *Mother, May You*, 244.

9. On February 15, 1865, Major General John G. Parke, then acting commander of the Ninth Corps, issued a communication to Colonel George D. Ruggles, assistant adjutant general, recommending Reese for the Medal of Honor for conspicuous gallantry at Petersburg. He was one of sixty-eight enlisted men so deserving of that distinction. Ruggles misplaced the list and it was not recovered until 1896, at which time Reese's recommendation was renewed by the Record and Pension Office of the U.S. Army. Unfortunately, by then Reese had died (on May 3, 1893). Despite several attempts made since then to award the Medal to Reese posthumously, he has yet to receive this well-deserved distinction.

10. Pleasants, *Inferno*, 123–24; Agassiz, 198; Wheeler, *Fields of Fury*, 281; Jones, *Army of Northern Virginia*, 152; JCCW, 19.

11. OR 40 (1), 140; Pleasants, *Inferno*, 123–24; Jones, *Army of Northern Virginia*, 155.

12. Burnside later mistakenly testified that the material supplied was only enough for one fuse, claiming that this fuse material was not furnished "in sufficient quantity to run three or four separate fuzes, as was contemplated by the plan. In fact, we had but material enough to run one line of fuze, and that material came to us in small pieces of from ten to fifteen feet in length, and had to be spliced before it was laid." When questioned about this allegation, Meade indicated that he believed there was enough material for three fuses, but was not certain (JCCW, 23, 40).

13. OR 40 (2), 528; JCCW, 19–20, 35, 40–41, 88, 99; McFeely, 178.

14. JCCW, 114–15.

15. JCCW, 163; OR 40 (1), 47, 62–63, 139–40; Cavanaugh, *Battle of the Crater*, 39.

16. Cutcheon, 139; McFeely, 178; Wise, *End of an Era*, 355; Pleasants, *Inferno*, 124.

17. Hyland C. Kirk, *Heavy Guns and Light: A History of the 4th New York Heavy Artillery* (New York: C.T. Dillingham, 1890), 299; Davis, *Death*

in Trenches, 75. The mushroom cloud of smoke and debris was variously described as being from 100 to 200 feet in height. John J. Pullen referred to the event as "the Hiroshima of the Civil War" (John J. Pullen, *The Twentieth Maine, A Volunteer Regiment in the Civil War* (Philadelphia: J.B. Lippincott, 1957), 217). The cloud was variously described: "looking like the picture of the Iceland geysers," (Agassiz); "the shape of a Prince of Wales' feather, of colossal proportions" (Lieutenant) Solon Wesley Pierce, *Battle Fields and Campfires of the Thirty-Eighth: An Authentic Narrative and Record of the Organization of the Thirty-Eighth Regiment of Wis. Vol. Inf'y and the Part Taken by It in the Late War* (Milwaukee, WI: Daily Wisconsin Printing House, 1866, 36); "an outstretched umbrella" (Oliver Bosbyshell); "a lily-shaped fountain of dark red and yellow fire, with brown spots and streaks in it, in shape like an old ring jet of water, called the 'lily' in the Boston Frog Pond fountain" (Anderson, 206); "like an immense mushroom whose stem seemed to be of fire and its head of smoke" (Wheeler, *Fields of Fury*, 281); the earth "shot up like a volcano" (Carter, 467); the dirt, smoke and flame rose in the air and "curled over like a plume" (Bernard, *War Talks* 167); "like a mountain reversed" (Henry C. Houston, *The Thirty-Second Maine Regiment of Infantry Volunteers* (Portland, ME: Press of Southworth Brothers, 1903), 344).

18. Letter of August 16, 1864, from Lewis Crawford to friend Samuel P., *Lewis Crawford Papers 1864*, Pearce Civil War Collection, Navarro College, Corsicana, Texas.

19. William H. Osborne, *History of the Twenty-Ninth Regiment of Massachusetts Volunteer Infantry in the Late War of the Rebellion* (Boston: Albert J. Wright, 1877), 312; Edwin S. Redkey, *A Grand Army of Black Men: Letters from African-American Soldiers in the Union Army, 1861–1865* (Cambridge: Cambridge University Press, 1992), 111; Pierce, 36; Wheeler, *Fields of Fury*, 281; Derby, 360; Letter of Ethan S. Morehead, www.100thpenn.com (transcribed).

20. Wise, *End of an Era*, 355; F.W. McMaster, "The Battle of the Crater, July 30, 1864," *Southern Historical Society Papers* (Richmond 1882), 10: 125–126.

21. J. Tracy Power, *Lee's Miserables: Life in the Army of Northern Virginia from the Wilderness to Appomattox* (Chapel Hill: University of North Carolina Press, 1998), 136.

22. William P. Hopkins, *The Seventh Regiment Rhode Island Volunteers in the Civil War, 1862–1865* (Providence, RI: Snow & Farnham, Printers, Providence Press, 1903), 200; Alexander, *Fighting* 456.

23. William L Hyde letter dated August 1, 1864, *William L. Hyde Papers*, Pearce Civil War Collection, Navarro College, Corsicana, Texas.

24. Alexander, *Fighting*, 456; Charles Pinckney Elliott, *Elliott's Brigade How It Held the Crater and Saved Petersburg*, William Fitz McMaster Collection (reprint of address before Confederate Veterans of Camp Hampton, Columbia, SC, December 15, 1895), from *William Fitz McMaster Collection* 12; the Rev. J. William Jones, "The Battle of the Crater," *Southern Historical Society Papers* (Richmond: January–December 1882): 10: 153; Wise, *End of an Era*, 356; A.B. Thrash, "Vivid Reminiscences of the Crater," *Confederate Veteran* 14, no. 11 (November 1906): 509.

25. James T. Bacon, "Capt. George B. Lake," *Confederate Veteran* 2, no. 5 (May 1894): 153; De Witt Boyd Stone, ed., *Wandering To Glory: Confederate Veterans Remember Evans' Brigade* (Columbia, SC: University of South Carolina Press, 2002), 185–90; William B. Green letter dated July 3, 1864 (most probably Aug. 3rd), *South Caroliniana Library*, University of South Carolina; Cavanaugh, *Battle of the Crater*, 40. Hood's Texas Brigade had moved July 28 to counter Grant's diversionary move on Richmond. Had they not moved out, they would have shared the fate of Elliott's men at the Salient. After the battle, a great number of Federal prisoners expressed disappointment that the Texas Brigade was not "extinguished" in the explosion. Bill Calhoun of the 4th Texas, the brigade "wag," spoke for the brigade when he said: "Well, boys, hit's a d—d sight more comfortabler ter be stannin' here on good old Virginny *terror firmer* than ter be danglin' heels up an' heads down, over that cussed mine, not knowin' whether you'd strike soft or hard groun' when you lit" (Col. Harold B. Simpson, *Gaines' Mill To Appomattox: Waco & McLennan County in Hood's Texas Brigade* (Waco, TX: Texian Press, 1988), 426–27.

26. Ellis, *Tithes of Blood*, 177–79; Robinson, "Artillery in the Battle of the Crater," 165; Henry R. Howland, "An Anecdote of the Petersburg Crater," *The Century Magazine*, no. 2 (Dec. 1887), 323.

27. Bosbyshell, 175–76.

28. OR 40 (3), 820, Cavanaugh, *Battle of the Crater*, 41.

29. Edward B. Williams, *Rebel Brothers: The Civil War Letters of the Truehearts* (College Station: Texas A & M University Press, 1995), 115; Pierce, 36.

30. Stone, 189; Joshua Hilary Hudson, *Sketches and Remembrances* (Columbia, SC: State Company, 1903), 48; Jones, "The Battle of the Crater," 120; Ellis, *Tithes of Blood*, 179; Davis, *Death in Trenches*, 75; Newberry, 188.

31. Stevenson, 6; Wise, *End of an Era*, 356; Wheeler, *Fields of Fury*, 281.

32. Longacre, *Man Behind the Guns*, 209.

33. The number of Federal guns which participated in this barrage is variously reported as somewhere between 150 and 200 pieces, counting fieldpieces, siege guns and mortars. In actuality, it appears to be more, as previously indicated.

34. Philip Katcher, *Lethal Glory: Dramatic Defeats of the Civil War* (London: Arms and Armour Press, 1995), 174; William Stewart, *Description of the Battle of the Crater* (Norfolk, VA: Landmark Book and Job Office, 1910), 6; Cushman, 14.

35. Unknown Soldier John A. letter dated August 6, 1864, *Pearce Civil War Collection*, Navarro College, Corsicana, Texas; Reid-Green, 89; Pierce, 36; Pollard, 335; Count Regis De Tobriand, "Burnside Fumbles His Chance to Take Petersburg," *The Blue and the Gray*, 1020; Hopkins, 200.

36. Ried-Green, 89; Hopkins, 200.

37. Elliott, *Elliott's Brigade*, 14–15; James H. Clark, *The Iron Hearted Regiment: Being an Account of the Battles, Marches and Gallant Deeds Performed by the 115th Regiment N.Y. Vols.* (Albany, NY: J. Munsell, 1865), 146.

38. Agassiz, 198; Andrew Carroll, ed., *War Letters: Extraordinary Correspondence from American Wars* (New York: Washington Square Press, 2001), 97. Major General Gouverneur K. Warren reported there was not much response by the Confederate artillery in the first fifteen minutes following the explosion: "Their batteries were mainly placed for enfilading any line attacking, and probably reserved their fire until that line approached" (OR 40 (1), 79).

39. Longacre, *Man Behind the Guns*, 208.

40. Bernard, *War Talks*, 167; Davis, *Death in Trenches*, 75; Wilkinson, *Mother, May You*, 245.

41. Katcher, 174; Cannan, 83.

42. Wilkinson, *Mother, May You*, 247.

Chapter 9

1. OR 40 (1), 535–36.

2. *New York Times*, August 4, 1883 (obituary); Rochester *News*, June 23, 2000; Marvel, *Burnside*, 386.

3. Marvel, *Burnside*, 397. Marshall received the highest brevet commission

issued to any officer of his rank for his war service, that of major general of volunteers. He was taken prisoner at the Crater on July 30, 1864, and held at Columbus, Georgia. The war was essentially over when Marshall was released from Confederate prison in April, 1865. He served as commandant of a post in Fort Union, New Mexico, from August 1866 to February 1867, when disabilities forced him to retire. He was often known as a schemer who could ruffle feathers. In 1864, after managing to divert recruits from another regiment to the 14th New York Heavy Artillery, which he was in the process of reorganizing, a historian of that regiment described him as an "evil genius." He died at Canandaigua, New York, on August 3, 1883 (*Rochester News,* June 23, 2000; *New York Times,* August 4, 1883). On June 22, 2000, during the summer solstice, Marshall's grave in Mt. Hope Cemetery, Rochester, New York, was robbed and his skull taken. Satanic symbols were found around the grave (*Rochester News,* June 23, 2000).

4. Lieutenant Colonel Gilbert Robinson later testified that the 14th New York Heavy Artillery was in the second line, followed by the 3rd Maryland and the 179th New York. He ended up in command of the brigade by the battle's end, following Marshall's capture (OR 40, Part I, Series I, 541). See prior chapter.

5. Powell, "Tragedy of the Crater," 766; George L. Kilmer, "The Dash into the Crater," *The Century Illustrated Monthly* 34, (May–Oct. 1887): 774; Agassiz, 199; Stephen M. Weld, *War Diary and Letters of Stephen Minot Weld, 1861–1865,* 2nd ed. (Boston: Massachusetts Historical Society, 1979), 352.

6. Stephen M. Weld, "Petersburg Mine," *Papers of the Military Historical Society of Massachusetts,* 5: 207; Kilmer, 774; OR 40 (1), 114.

7. Kilmer, 774; Stevenson, 7; Pierce, 38; Powell, "Tragedy of the Crater," 766–67; OR 40 (1), 535–36; Anderson, *Fifty-Seventh Regiment,* 205–06.

8. Wilkinson, *Mother, May You,* 247; Powell, "Tragedy of the Crater," 767.

9. Wheeler, *Fields of Fury,* 281; Humphreys, *Virginia Campaign,* 255–56; Wise, *End of an Era,* 357.

10. OR 40 (1), 102–04, 118–19, 128; Wilkinson, *Mother, May You,* 247; Kilmer, 774; Anderson, 207.

11. Burnside had deliberately refused to have the parapets lowered for the assault, as he was ordered by Meade. His engineers had constructed two narrow sandbag stairways, but this was hopelessly inadequate for the

thousands of men struggling to scale the parapets (Kinard, 48–49).

12. Wilkinson, *Mother, May You,* 247; Powell, "Tragedy of the Crater," 767; Gould, 230; Alexander, *Fighting,* 457; Davis, *Death in Trenches,* 75; Cannon, 90; Stevenson, 8; Pleasants, *Inferno,* 125; W. Gordon McCabe, "Defence of Petersburg," *Southern Historical Society Papers* (1876), 2: 284; Charles A. Shaw, *A History of the 14th Regiment N.Y. Heavy Artillery in the Civil War 1863 to 1865* (Mount Kisco, NY: North Westchester Publishing, 1918), 28.

13. de Chanal was a member of the French commission sent to observe the campaign.

14. Agassiz, 199; Pleasants, *Inferno,* 126.

15. Weld, "Petersburg Mine," 207.

16. Wilkinson, *Mother, May You,* 248; Newberry, 118; Katcher, 175; Taylor, "The Crater," 56; *JCCW,* 83; Pleasants, 126.

17. *JCCW,* 22; Anderson, 169; Alexander, *Fighting,* 458; Elliott, "Elliott's Brigade," 15; Pleasants, *Inferno,* 126. One of his main critics, Major James Duane, would later cite this as one of the main reasons for the failure of the assault (*JCCW,* 99).

18. Wilkinson, *Mother, May You,* 247–48; OR 40 (1), 115; Powell, "Tragedy of the Crater," 767.

19. Hargrove, 184; OR 40 (1), 535; W. F. Beyer, ed., *Deeds of Valor: How America's Civil War Heroes Won the Congressional Medal of Honor* (Stamford, CT: Longmeadow Press, 1993), 384; Longacre, *Man Behind the Guns,* 209.

20. Trudeau, *Last Citadel,* 109.

21. Walter Wolcott, *The Military History of Yates County, N.Y.* (Pen Yan, NY: Express Book and Job Printing House, 1895), 99. At least ten minutes were definitely lost from the explosion until the troops of the second brigade advanced into the obstacles of both Federal and Confederate making (McFeely, 178–79).

22. Powell, "Tragedy of the Crater," 763.

23. Weld, *War Diary,* 354.

24. Wilkinson, *Mother, May You,* 248; Anderson, 178; OR 40 (1), 538; *JCCW,* 36; Weld, "Petersburg Mine," 208.

25. Pleasants, *Inferno,* 127; Wilkinson, *Mother, May You,* 249; OR 40 (1), 114, 541.

26. OR 40 (1), 115; Katcher, 175.

27. Kilmer, 774; Powell, "Tragedy of the Crater," 767–68; Wilkinson, *Mother, May You,* 249; Wheeler, *Fields of Fury,* 282; Anderson, 177.

28. There are at least three reasons for the men entering the Crater, in spite of directions to the contrary. It may have been (1) a lack of proper

leadership, (2) the slight resistance encountered thus far and the inherent urge to take cover, (3) simply the common soldier's natural curiosity, or (4) all three!

29. Pierce, 38; Powell, "Tragedy of the Crater," 768; Anderson, 208; Alexander, *Fighting,* 458; Davis, *Death in Trenches,* 76; Taylor, "The Crater," 56; Anderson, 178; Gould, 231; Wise, *End of an Era,* 357; Trudeau, *Last Citadel,* 110; Shaw, 28.

30. Agassiz, 199.

31. *JCCW,* 92, 107; Osborne, 313; Taylor, "The Crater," 56.

32. Wilkinson, *Mother, May You,* 249–50.

33. OR 40, Part I, Series I, 538–39; Wilkinson, *Mother, May You,* 249; Anderson, 208.

34. Weld, *War Diary,* 352–54.

35. Although other units contended otherwise, this appears to be an accurate account.

36. OR 40 (1), 541; Kilmer, 774–75; Beyer, 384–85; Trudeau, *Last Citadel,* 110; Anderson, 208.

37. Katcher, 175; Kilmer, 775; OR 40 (1), 541; Shaw, 28; Gould, 231; Powell, "Tragedy of the Crater," 767–68; Pierce, 38.

38. Shaw, 29; Wilkinson, *Mother, May You,* 250.

39. Stevenson, 8; Wheeler, *Fields of Fury,* 282; Kilmer, 775; Davis, 76–78; Wilkinson, *Mother, May You,* 249–50; OR 40 (1), 541; Anderson, 208. Warren Lee Goss, *Recollections of a Private: A Story of the Army of the Potomac* (New York: T.Y. Crowell, 1890), 335.

40. Stevenson, 8; Wheeler, *Fields of Fury,* 282; Kilmer, 775; Davis, *Death in Trenches,* 76–78.

41. Alexander, *Fighting,* 458; Stevenson, 9; Trudeau, *Last Citadel,* 110–11; *JCCW,* 36; Gould, 231; Anderson, 178, 182.

42. Haskell, *Haskell Memoirs,* 73; Powell, "Tragedy of the Crater," 768.

43. Goss, 334; Anderson, 179–82, 200; Wilkinson, *Mother, May You,* 253; Powell, "Tragedy of the Crater," 768–69; OR 40 (1), 536.

44. Anderson, 204–05.

45. Anderson, 202–205, 212–214; Wilkinson, *Mother, May You,* 240; Albert, 152; Humphreys, *Virginia Campaign,* 255.

46. Powell was quite annoyed with the fact that Ledlie, a politically appointed general, chose to keep some of his politically connected volunteer staff with him, while sending the regular army, career officers off to the fighting.

47. Powell, "Tragedy of the Crater," 769.

48. Gould, 232; Powell, "Tragedy of the Crater," 769; OR 40 (1), 140; Anderson, 215–16; Katcher, 177.

Chapter 10

1. Elliott's brigade lost a total of 667 men that day, accounting for nearly half of all Confederate losses (Stone, 184, 202).

2. Both soon to die in the fighting.

3. Stone, 190, 206–07.

4. Ibid., 190, 205–207; McMaster, "Battle of the Crater," 129; Alexander, *Fighting*, 460; Wilkinson, *Mother, May You*, 252; Gould, 268.

5. McMaster, "Battle of the Crater," 120.

6. The Rev. Silas Pinckney Holbrook Elwell, *Recollections of War Times* (Bamberg, SC : Bamberg Herald Print, 1895), 48; Pleasants, *Tragedy of the Crater*, 91.

7. Davis, *Death in Trenches*, 76; OR 40 (1), 795, 800; Stone, 191; Barnwell, 178.

8. McMaster, "Battle of the Crater," 29.

9. OR 40 (1), 789.

10. In one of the innumerable ironies of the Civil War, Brigadier General Robert Potter, whose division tangled with Elliott's brigade on June 17, and who faced directly across from his salient that fateful day, also was the son of an Episcopal bishop (Marvel, *Burnside*, 397).

11. Haskell, *Haskell Memoirs*, 162; Elliott, *Elliott's Brigade* 37; Stone, 281, n5.

12. Haskell, *Haskell Memoirs*, 74; Elliott, *Elliott's Brigade*, 6.

13. On April 18, 1864, General Evans was driving a buggy on the streets of Charleston when one of the traces gave way, causing the horses to start off at full speed. This action ultimately broke the shaft short off, causing the front of the carriage to crash to the ground. Evans struck his head on the pavement with violent force. Temporary command was given to Brigadier General William S. Walker, who was subsequently captured at Warebottom Church on May 20, 1864, in his first battle in command of the brigade. Command was thereafter given to Elliott, and since by then it was apparent that Evans would not be able to resume command, the appointment was considered a permanent one, and the name of the unit was officially changed to "Elliott's Brigade."

14. Stone, 174–75. After recuperating from his shoulder wound, but without use of that arm, Elliott commanded a brigade on James Island, South Carolina. When Charleston was evacuated in 1865, Elliott joined General Joseph Johnston in North Carolina and was wounded once again at Bentonville. Following Johnston's surrender at Durham, North Carolina, Elliott returned home to Beaufort and was again elected to the state legislature. He died in 1866 of his grievous war wounds (Stone, 281, n. 7, 285, n. 8; Elliott, *Elliott's Brigade*, 8. One of his colleagues wrote upon his death that "In war was never lion rage more fierce; in peace was never lamb more mild than was this young and princely gentleman." Elliott, *Elliott's Brigade*, 6. A former chaplain at Fort Sumner wrote, "My eyes gather moisture as I recall the sympathy and pity he showed for his wounded men, and burn with bitter grief for his yearnings to be at home among his loved ones once more" (Elliott, *Elliott's Brigade*, 32).

15. Haskell, *Haskell Memoirs*, 74; Jones, *Army of Northern Virginia*, 155.

16. Barnwell, 177–78; Bernard, *War Talks*, 89; Stone, 191–92; Chambers, 81; McMaster, "Battle of the Crater," 121; Elwell, 49–50.

17. McMaster, "Battle of the Crater," 129.

18. Ibid.

19. Elwell, 50.

20. Stephen Elliott, Jr., letter to wife, July 14, 1864, *Elliott Family Papers*, South Caroliniana Library, Columbia, SC.

21. Stone, 159, 161–62, 172–75, 246, 248.

22. Edward McCrady, "Heroes of the Old Camden District, South Carolina, 1776–1861," *Southern Historical Society Papers*, 16: 25; Stone, 13, 16, 255–53, 254–55.

23. Pleasants, *Tragedy of the Crater*, 89–90; Stone, 97, 162, 181, 285 f8; Mary Boykin Chesnut, *A Diary from Dixie* (Boston: Houghton Mifflin, 1949), 434; McMaster, "Battle of the Crater," 121; Elwell, 50–51; Bernard, *War Talks*, 153: Barnwell, 178.

24. Pleasants, *Tragedy of the Crater* 90; Stone, 194; McMaster, "Battle of the Crater," 122–23.

25. Thrash, 509; Walter Clark, ed., *Histories of the Several Regiments and Battalions from North Carolina in the Great War 1861–65*, 5 vols. (Goldsboro, NC: Nash Brothers, Book and Job Printers, 1901), 3: 141–43; Cavanaugh, *Battle of the Crater*, 44.

26. OR 40 (1), 790–91; Chambers, 175–76; Day, 355; George Clark, *A Glance Backward, or Some Events in the Past History of My Life* (Houston, TX: Rein, 1914), 27–28.

27. OR 40 (1), 790–91; Freeman, *Lee*, 471; Wise, *End of an Era*, 359; Bagby, 456.

28. Alexander, *Fighting*, 461; Gould, 268; Davis, *Death in Trenches*, 81; Stone, 195; Elwell, 51; W.H. Edwards, *A Condensed History of the Seventeenth Regiment S.C.V.C.S.A.: From Its Organization to the Close of the War* (Columbia, SC: R. L. Bryan, 1908), 46–47.

29. Branch's battalion also included Bradford's (Mississippi) Battery, consisting of four 20-pounder Parrots, and Kelly's (South Carolina), with four 12-pound Napoleons. On July 30, Kelly's battery was detached in North Carolina. Bradford's battery was on the north side of the Appomattox; there it could enfilade Federal lines as far as the Hare house (McMaster, "Battle of the Crater," 124–27).

30. This third battery was not called for during the battle, and so Pegram remained at his headquarters and did not play a role in the action. The battery was placed in the second line near the Jerusalem Plank Road after the battle (Bernard, *War Talks*, 209).

31. Later revised to twenty-two killed and wounded (OR 40 (1), 788).

32. McMaster, "Battle of the Crater," 120, 124–27; Bernard, *War Talks*, 209; Stone, 191; Gould, 269; OR 40 (1), 789.

33. McMaster, "Battle of the Crater," 126–27; Humphreys, *Virginia Campaign*, 256; Gould, 269; OR 40 (1), 789; Jones, *Army of Northern Virginia*, 155, Bernard, *War Talks*, 205. Wright's battery had the only guns in the Confederate lines which could not only enfilade the enemy at close range, but could also fire on the Crater and adjoining works (McMaster, "Battle of the Crater," 120).

34. Cavanaugh, *The Otey, Ringgold and Davidson Virginia Artillery*, 61.

35. Cavanaugh indicated that the battery was equipped with two Napoleons and "two bronze 6-pounders."

36. John Hampden Chamberlayne, *Ham Chamberlayne — Virginian: Letters and Papers of an Artillery Officer in the War for Southern Independence, 1861–1865* (Richmond, VA: Press of the Dietz Printing, 1932), xliv; OR 40 (1), 760, 789; Stone, 191; Jones, *Army of Northern Virginia*, 155; Freeman, *Lee*, 471; Lee Wallace, *A Guide to Virginia Military Organizations* (Lynchburg, VA: H.E. Howard, 1986), 6; Alexander, *Fighting*, 466. The Otey Battery — Company A of the 13th Virginia Light Artillery Battalion was named for Captain George G. Otey, who was killed on October 21, 1862, and not for Lieutenant Otey, a distant relation who disgraced himself that day. Otey was subsequently court-martialed for cowardice in that action. Chamberlayne indicated to his mother on August 19, 1864, that Otey was found guilty and "will probably be shot." He was sentenced to death, and all arrangements had been made to shoot him when he was pardoned by President Davis. Porter Alexander indicated that he was in favor of that action, "for the strain of that position that morning was very severe upon men of little experience in action" (Chamberlayne, 258; Alexander, *Fighting*, 466).

37. Cavanaugh contends that this scenario is highly unlikely, and that Chamberlayne never mentioned this in an August 3, 1864, letter to his mother (Cavanaugh, *The Otey, Ringgold and Davidson Virginia Artillery*, 61). Porter Alexander, in illustrating the placement of artillery at the time of the battle, referred to the position of Davidson's battery as "Chamberlain." See Alexander, *Fighting*, 442–43. Cavanaugh reported in another work that Chamberlayne was present at the Battle of the Crater, however. See Cavanaugh, *Battle of the Crater*, 146.

38. The 34th Virginia had two companies (C and K) that had formerly been artillerymen.

39. Henry R. Pollard, "Edward Bagby of Virginia," *Confederate Veteran Magazine* 27, no. 12 (1919): 456–57.

40. Pollard," Edward Bagby," 453–57; Alfred A. Bagby, *King and Queen County, Virginia* (New York: Meade Publishing, 1908), 153–54.

41. Ned's oldest brother, John, later wrote, "I knew I loved & esteemed him but I did not know until now how well or how worthy he was of my admiration." John Robert Bagby, unfinished letter to his brother, Richard Hugh Bagby, *Bagby Family Papers, 1808–1942*, Mss/B1463c66, Virginia Historical Society, Richmond, VA. John Robert Bagby was the major of the regiment at the time of the battle. Alexander Bagby, his cousin, succeeded to command of Company K when John was promoted to major.

42. John Robert Bagby letter to Richard Bagby, *Bagby Family Papers*; Pollard, 456–57; Robinson, 166; Bernard, *War Talks*, 203; OR 40, Part I, Series I, 792.

43. Robinson, 166; Pollard, "Edward Bagby," 453–54, 456–57; Haskell, *Haskell Memoirs*, 75; Davis, *Death in Trenches*, 78; Gould, 268–69; OR 40 (1), 789: Bernard, *War Talks*, 203–04.

44. Cavanaugh indicated that the battery had three Napoleons and one three-inch rifled piece. Robinson stated otherwise in his article on the battle. See Cavanaugh, *Otey, Ringgold and Davidson Virginia Artillery*, 65; Robinson, 165.

45. Robinson, 166.

46. Robinson, 165–66; Cavanaugh, *Otey, Ringgold and Davidson Virginia Artillery*, 58; John A. Cutchens, *A Famous Command: The Richmond Light Infantry Blues* (Richmond: Garrett & Massie, 1934), 130. In other accounts of the battle, observers claim that Wright's and Flanner's batteries, together with the one gun from Davidson's battery were the only fieldpieces directly engaged in the fight, together with the mortar batteries under Lam-

kin and Langhorne. See, for example, McMaster, "Battle of the Crater," 125.

47. Bernard, *War Talks*, 203, 206–07.

48. Cavanaugh speculates that Lamkin's mortars were "probably all 12-pound Coehorns" (Cavanaugh, *Battle of the Crater*, 147). However, Bushrod Johnson's report differentiates between "Coehorns" and 12-pound Coehorn mortars. See OR 40 (1), 789. Coehorn mortars during the Civil War were found inn two sizes: the 24-pound Coehorn had a tube weighing 164 pounds and an oak bed weighing 131pounds, for a combined weight of 295 pounds, and equipped with handles so a crew of four could readily move it. It had a 5.82-inch caliber and fired a projectile weighing 16.4 pounds. A lighter version of the mortar was the 12-pound Coehorn, which had a tube weighing seventy-five pounds and an oak bed weighing seventy pounds, for a combined weight of 145 pounds. This piece had a 4.62-inch caliber, and fired a projectile weighing 10.2 pounds.

49. Gould, 269–70; OR 40 (1), 789; Flanner, 247–48; Bernard, *War Talks*, 209–10; Jennings Cropper Wise, *The Long Arm of Lee* (Lynchburg, VA: J.P. Bell, 1912), 859.

50. Haskell, *Haskell Memoirs*, 72–73; Jones, *Army of Northern Virginia*, 155; Alexander, *Fighting*, 461; Flanner, 247–48.

51. Haskell, *Haskell Memoirs*, 73–75; Jones, *Army of Northern Virginia*, 155; Gould, 269; McMaster, "Battle of the Crater," 127; OR 40 (1), 760; Freeman, *Lee*, 472.

52. Sir Winston Churchill, Speech before the House of Commons, August 20, 1940.

Chapter 11

1. Lyman Jackman, *History of the Sixth New Hampshire Regiment in the War For the Union* (Concord, NH: Republican Press Association, 1891), 313; JCCW, 85–87; Trudeau, "Chaos," 31; Trudeau, *Last Citadel*, 112; OR 40 (1), 88–89.

2. OR 40 (1), 100.

3. Pleasants, *Inferno*, 129–30.

4. JCCW, 86; Pleasants, *Inferno*, 128–30; Committee of the Regiment, *History of the Thirty-Sixth Regiment Massachusetts Volunteer Infantry, 1862–1865* (Boston: Press of Rockwell and Churchill, 1884), 235; Jones, *Army of Northern Virginia*, 155–56; OR 40 (1), 547, 567.

5. Given other accounts of the assault, this would place the movement as being before Ledlie's advance. Given that Potter later told the Senate Committee that his men did not advance as

ordered, and that he discussed this failure with Pleasants when he came back from the Crater, it is therefore likely Potter's men did not move out until Ledlie had advanced.

6. Pleasants, *Inferno*, 131; Edward Lord, *History of the Ninth New Hampshire Volunteers in the War of the Rebellion* (Earlysville, VA: Old Book Publishing, 1896), 490–500; William Marvel, *Race of the Soil: The Ninth New Hampshire in the Civil War* (Wilmington, NC: Broadfoot Publishing, 1988), 259–60; Leander W. Cogswell, *A History of the Eleventh New Hampshire Regiment Volunteer Infantry in the Rebellion War, 1861–1865* (Concord, NH: Republican Press Association, 1891), 442: Chase, 17–18.

7. Houston, 281–84.

8. Pleasants, *Inferno*, 130; Cogswell, 418; Lord, 499–500; OR 40 (1), 547, 567; Burbank, 288; Chase, 17–18; Lord, 499–500; Marvel, *Race for the Soil*, 261; Houston, 361–62.

9. Pleasants, *Inferno*, 131; Chase, 19, 29–30; Houston, 363.

10. OR 40 (1), 547; Gould, 233–34; Lord, 491–500; Augustus D. Ayling, *Revised Register of the Soldiers and Sailors of New Hampshire in the War of the Rebellion, 1861–1866* (Concord, NH: Ira C. Evans, 1895), 459; Marvel, *Race of the Soil*, 262–63; Jones, *Army of Northern Virginia*, 156; Commager, *The Blue and the Gray*, 1020. Sergeant Simonds was later awarded the Medal of Honor for his actions that day.

11. Chase, 18–22, 30; Burbank, 288; Houston, 364.

12. Lord, 496–97, 504–05; Marvel, *Race for the Soil*, 262.

13. Powell, "Tragedy of the Crater," 769–70.

14. Some accounts have the second division advancing 200 yards beyond the Crater (Houston, 357; Lord, 487). However, this claim is totally unsupported by hard evidence. While such testimony was contained in the court of inquiry, it is erroneous. The only hard evidence as to the results of the advance is from Colonels Thomas and Russell. They both indicate that the charges of their troops were limited to an advance west of the Crater "not exceeding 50 yards" and that they were all driven back by Smith's men in the ravine. The 200 yards was instead "the slow progress made down our line during the four hours' resistance made by Elliott's men and is only 116 yards north of the crater — which is the furthest point reached by the enemy according to the map published by Mr. Bernard in his subsequent book. It was in the trench and not in the rear of the crater, nor in the direction of the crest of Cemetery hill" (Elliott, *Elliott's Brigade*, 22).

15. Bevin Alexander, *Robert E. Lee's Civil War* (Holbrook, MA: Adams Media Corporation, 1998), 289; Humphreys, *Virginia Campaign*, 257; Commager, *The Blue and the Gray*, 1020; Davis, *Death in Trenches*, 78; OR 40 (1), 88–89, 567; Lord, 488; Houston, 357; *JCCW* 87; Cogswell, 418; Jackman, 314–15; Powell, "Tragedy of the Crater," 769–70.

16. Chambers, 176.

17. Day, "Battle of the Crater," 355; Stone, 195–96; Chambers, 176; Cavanaugh, *Battle of the Crater*, 45.

18. White folded this message and placed it in his pocket; he kept it intact through many months in a Confederate prison camp.

19. OR 40 (1), 547, 567; Hunter, Cavanaugh, *Battle of the Crater*, 45–46; Stone, 195–96, 207; Trudeau, *Last Citadel*, 112; Houston, 361; *JCCW*, 87; Cannan, 102–03.

20. OR 40 (1), 140–41.

21. OR 40 (1), 547, 567; Elwell, 53–54; Gould, 234; Marvel, *Race for the Soil*, 264; *JCCW*, 87–88; Hopkins, 205; Jackman, 315; Pleasants, *Inferno at Petersburg*, 133; Lord, 498.

22. *JCCW*, 36–37; OR 40 (1), 141.

23. Committee of the Regiment, 235–36; OR 40 (1), 547, 567; Hopkins, 205; Gould, 234; Cavanaugh, *Battle of the Crater*, 47.

24. Cushman, 14; Allen, 284–285; Albert, 151–152; OR 40 (1), 117, 549; Jackman, 318–321. While Jackman, in his regimental history of the 6th New Hampshire, indicated that the unit remained in the open field between the lines for the whole battle, his account also mentions two of its soldiers who were reported carrying water to the thirsty soldiers trapped in the Crater later that day. Additionally, Sergeant Major Abraham Cohn of the 6th later received the Medal of Honor for "bravely advancing on Confederate line under severe fire." Thus, it does appear that at least some of the unit was significantly involved in the fight. Jackman, 317.

25. Allen, 286–87; OR 40, (1), 117, 551, 553–54, 564; Albert, 375–76; Cushman, 15; McCabe, "Defence of Petersburg," 286.

26. Allen Albert of the 45th Pennsylvania wrote that he also was ordered to march by the left flank and form a line of battle under the cover of the parapet in the rear of the Crater in order to charge in the rear of the line of the Confederate works as a diversion in favor of the rest of Bliss's brigade, which was to charge forward at the moment they saw the colors of the 45th. However, upon receiving contradictory orders from General Bartlett at the Crater to charge a battery in their immediate front, the 45th went into-ward the Jerusalem Plank Road (Albert, 153–54).

27. OR 40 (1), 124, 547, 549–50, 554, 566; Hopkins, 198–201; Cushman, 15–16; Albert, 153–54; Committee of the Regiment, 235–36.

28. The extent of the advance appears to have increased with the passage of time. No unit came close to reaching the Gee house on the Jerusalem Plank Road that day.

29. OR 40 (1), 117–18, 547–48, 551; Allen, 287–88; Marvel, *Race for the Soil*, 264–66; Lord, 498; Jones, *Army of Northern Virginia*, 156–58; Pleasants, *Inferno*, 132–33; Charles A. Cuffel, *Durell's Battery in the Civil War (Independent Battery D, Pennsylvania Volunteer Artillery)* (Philadelphia: Craig, Finley, 1903), 196–97.

30. Lord, 491–92; OR 40 (1), 154–55, 564, 569; Jones, *Army of Northern Virginia*, 156–58; Cushman, 13–16; Albert, 153–54; Anderson, 180; Allen, 288; OR 40 (3), 666. Griffin later contended that his men got 200 yards toward Cemetery Hill. Lieutenant Colonel Russell indicates that the farthest any unit achieved was 50 yards (Elwell, 54).

31. Lord, 498; OR 40 (1), 547–48, 552–53, 791, OR 40 (3), 666; Powell, "Tragedy of the Crater," 770; Committee of the Regiment, 237–38; Gould, 234–35; Hopkins, 201–02, 205; Marvel, *Race for the Soil*, 266; Jerome M. Loving, ed., *Civil War Letters of George Washington Whitman* (Durham, NC: Duke University Press, 1975), 127–28; Shearman, "Battle of the Crater and Experiences of Prison Life," 394; Cutcheon, 141; William T. Ackerson, Diary, *William T. Ackerson Papers*, 1861–1914, Monmouth County Historical Association Library and Archives, Freehold, NJ; Loving, 127–28, 162–63.

32. Others put the advance of Willcox's division closer to 6:00 A.M. See Trudeau, "Chaos In Crater," 31.

33. OR 40 (1), 574–75, 578–79, 582, OR 40 (3), 667; Woodford, 195; Cutcheon, 141; Cannan, 104; Anderson, 180; Gould, 235; Scott, *Forgotten Valor*, 557. These guns were the same ones which the 14th New York Heavy Artillery claimed to have recovered. Hartranft reported that this regiment ultimately manned the guns, and he lauded Sergeant Stanley's performance in manning the guns until his mortal wounding. It is unclear which unit most deserves the honor for recovering the guns. As the 14th New York Heavy Artillery was there first, it is likely its somewhat leaderless men were working on their excavation when Hartranft's men reached the works. See Robert C. Eden, *The Sword And Gun: A History of the 37th Wis. Volunteer Infantry* (Madison, WI: Atwood & Rublee, 1865), 30.

34. Trudeau, "Chaos in the Crater," 30–31.

35. Gould, 234–36; OR 40 (1), 99, 574–75, 579–81; Scott, *Forgotten Valor*, 560; *JCCW*, 77–78; Davis, *Death in Trenches*, 78; Lord, 488; Alexander, *Robert E. Lee's Civil War*, 289; Woodford, 199; Cavanaugh, *Battle of the Crater*, 46.

36. OR 40 (1), 586–87; Woodford, 196; Laurence Hauptman, *Between Two Fires: American Indians in the Civil War* (New York: Free Press Paperbacks, 1995), 125–43; Adjutant General, *Record of Service of Michigan Volunteers in the Civil War 1861–1865* (Kalamazoo, MI: Ihling Bros. & Everland, 1903), 2. Deland was disabled on July 30, 1864, and the regiment was led instead by Captain E.C. Dicey, who was captured in the action (OR 40 (1), 587); Raymond J. Herek, *These Men Have Seen Hard Service: The First Michigan Sharpshooters in the Civil War* (Detroit: Wayne State University Press, 1998), 220.

37. Herek, *These Men Have Seen Hard Service*, 249, 253, 490, ff 88; OR 40 (1), 75, 1137, 1143; Richard J. Sommers, *Richmond Redeemed: The Siege at Petersburg* (Garden City, NY: Doubleday, 1981), 232.

38. Herek, *These Men Have Seen Hard Service*, 221.

39. Woodford, 196–97; OR 40 (1), 574–75, 586–87; Charles Lanman, *The Red Book of Michigan* (Detroit: E.B. Smith, 1871), 377; S. Emma Edmonds, *Papers of Sarah E. Edmonds*, Clark Historical Library, Central Michigan University, Mt. Pleasants; Cavanaugh, *Battle of the Crater*, 51; Deanne Blanton and Lauren M. Cook, *They Fought Like Demons: Women Soldiers in the Civil War* (New York: Vintage Books, 2002), 9, 12, 14–15, 51–52, 75, 98; Herek, *These Men Have Seen Hard Service*, 220–22.

40. OR 40 (1), 586–87, 589–93, OR 40 (3), 667–68; Herek, *These Men Have Seen Hard Service*, 222.

41. OR 40 (1), 592.

42. OR 40 (1), 575, 586–87, 589–93, OR 40 (3), 667–68; Lanman, 377–78; Cavanaugh, *Battle of the Crater*, 51; Woodford, 196; Lewis Crater, *History of the Fiftieth Regiment Penna. Vet. Vols., 1861–65* (Reading, PA: Coleman Printing House, 1884), 69; Gould, 236; Petzold, Herman, *Memoirs Second Michigan Regiment*, (1897), 50.

Chapter 12

1. Thomas, "Colored Troops," 778–79.

2. Bowley, "Petersburg Mine," 29; Trudeau, *Like Men of War*, 238–40; Thomas, "Colored Troops," 778–779; *JCCW*, 122; Cornish, 275.

3. OR 40 (1), 141.

4. Ibid., 141–142.

5. Powell, "Tragedy of the Crater," 768–771.

6. Cogswell states that Grant, Meade and Handcock were all present at Fort Morton when he reported to Potter, and that Meade verbally gave the order to Burnside. At least in Meade's case, this is highly unlikely. There is no indication that Meade was at Burnside's temporary headquarters that day, and their telegraphic exchanges would not have occurred if they were in the same room. Indeed, shortly after this alleged encounter, Gouverneur Warren began urging Meade to visit Burnside's headquarters to familiarize himself with the conditions of the front (OR 40, (1), 451). Grant did visit the front, and could have been present. Back behind the Federal front lines, Cogswell observed Generals Ledlie and Ferrero "in a bomb-proof several rods in rear of the breastworks, sitting as unconcernedly as though nothing were taking place" (Cogswell, 423).

7. JCCW, 26, 92, 108–109; Cannan, 64–65; Powell, "The Tragedy of the Crater," 768–771, Cogswell, 422–423.

8. JCCW, 92–93, 108–109; OR 40 (1), 103, 118–119, OR 40 (3), 608.

9. In Warren's testimony before the court of inquiry, he claimed that the suggestion was his own (OR 40 (1), 80).

10. OR 40 (1), 64, 80–81; Marvel, Burnside, 403.

11. JCCW, 92–93; OR 40 (1), 64.

12. Later that same evening, Burnside showed Loring the written order from Meade directing him to throw all his troops against Cemetery Hill, and he added that "under those instructions he felt that he could not have done otherwise than he did" (JCCW, 93).

13. OR 40 (1), 64, 80.

14. Ibid., 64, 150–151.

15. Meade reiterated the same sentiment earlier that morning with regard to his inquiry regarding Warren's participation. Thus, Burnside was in no position to order another corps into the operation, even if Warren was genuine. Given his correspondence with Meade that morning, it was unlikely Warren was anxious to enter the fray.

16. OR 40 (1), 142.

17. Ibid.

18. JCCW, 164–65; Cavanaugh, Battle of the Crater, 50–51; Marvel, Burnside, 403–04; OR 40 (1), 63–67, 141–43; Cannan, 65–67. Meade later explained to Orlando Willcox that by asking for "the truth," he only meant for Burnside to tell him frankly the true state of affairs, and if it was impossible to advance, for him to just say so in unequivocal terms. However, Meade did not authorize Willcox to communicate his intended meaning to Burnside. Without this clarification from Meade, which Willcox was unable to deliver, Burnside would not withdraw the offending remarks, which later formed one of the charges against him (Scott, Forgotten Valor, 562–63). With the passage of time, however, Burnside became satisfied that Meade did not intend to imply he was untruthful (JCCW, 25).

19. OR 40 (3), 660; Trudeau, Last Citadel, 114; Cavanaugh, Battle of the Crater, 51; Humphreys, Virginia Campaign, 258–59.

20. JCCW, 24–25, 36, 55–56; Trudeau, Last Citadel, 113–15; OR 40(1), 63.

21. OR 40 (1), 149–50.

22. OR 40 (1), 64, 80–81, 149–52, 450–51; JCCW, 81–82. When questioned by the Congressional Committee on the Conduct of the War, Warren indicated that "there was no more reason why I should have attacked the lines on my front on that day than on any day of the preceding forty-two. I had, with more men, failed in my attack before" (JCCW, 82). His corps was never engaged that day (JCCW, 83). His total losses amounted to seven killed and 24 wounded (OR 40 (1), 452–53). General Willcox, however, later testified that he saw no reason why Warren did not move forward that morning (JCCW, 80). Warren had balked about ordering assaults and had openly voiced his opposition to the tactics since Spotsylvania. Meade had even spoken to Grant about relieving him. He was considered stubborn and insubordinate to the point where Colonel Charles Wainwright called him "a very loathsome, profane ungentlemanly & disgusting puppy in power" and considered his actions "a sort of insanity" (Jeffrey D. Wert, The Sword of Lincoln: The Army of the Potomac (New York: Simon and Schuster, 2005), 374.

23. OR 40 (1), 155.

24. JCCW, 76–69; OR 40 (1), 153–155.

25. JCCW, 31, 101–104, 118–120; OR 40 (1), 83, 108, 121, 698–699, 707–708.

26. OR 40 (1), 699.

27. OR 40 (1), 83, 698–699; Davis, Death in Trenches, 80; JCCW, 102; Nathaniel Bartlett Sylvester, History of Rensselaer Co., New York (Philadelphia: Everts & Peck, 1880), 100.

28. Ord believed that if there had been several places to exit rather than just one, his divisions could have attacked the enemy elsewhere and might well have succeeded. He believed hitting the right and left of the Crater at one half mile distances might have succeeded (JCCW, 102–103).

29. JCCW, 102; OR 40 (1), 147–148.

30. Hill was killed later in the action in the Crater. He was awarded the Medal of Honor for his action in capturing the Confederate colors. The Rebel unit was never identified (OR 40 (1), 530, 543); Kilmer, 776.

31. Anderson, 208–210; Wilkinson, 251–252; OR 40 (1), 536–537; JCCW, 92; Katcher, 176–177; Goss, 334; Kilmer, 775; Marvel, Race of the Soil, 266.

32. First Sergeant Barnard A. Strasbaugh, Company A, 3rd Maryland Battalion, in charge of a squad of sharpshooters, there singly captured eight prisoners in one squad and two in another. He was later awarded a Medal of Honor (OR 40 (1), 542).

33. OR 40 (1), 114–15, 536, 541; Goss, 334; Katcher, 176; Pierce, 38; Shaw, 29; JCCW, 92, 96; Anderson, 222.

34. The most any unit progressed to the west of the Crater was fifty to one hundred yards.

35. OR 40 (1), 548–549, 552, 564, OR 40 (3), 666; Marvel, Race of the Soil, 266, Shearman, 395.

36. OR 40 (1), 567. Allen, 288; Shearman, 394–95.

37. Allen, 288; Shearman, 394–395; Jones, Army of Northern Virginia, 158; Wheeler, Fields of Fury, 282; Houston, 364.

38. Cushman, 15.

39. OR 40 (1), 552–553, OR 40 (3), 666–667; Cavanaugh, Battle of the Crater, 50; Loving, 127–28.

40. Thomas H. Parker, History of the 51st Regiment of P.V. and V.V. from Its Organization at Camp Curtin, Harrisburg, Pa., in 1861 to Its Being Mustered Out of the United States Service at Alexandria, Va., July 27, 1865 (Philadelphia: King & Baird, Printers, 1869), 576; JCCW, 95.

41. Howard Aston, History and Roster of the Fourth and Fifth Independent Battalions and the Thirteenth Regiment Ohio Cavalry Volunteers, Their Battles and Skirmishes, Roster of the Dead, Etc. (Columbus., OH: Press of Fred J. Heer, 1902), 99–100; Beyer, 394–396; Bernard, War Talks, 181.

42. OR 40 (1), 587; Jones, Army of Northern Virginia, 158; Trudeau, Last Citadel, 112; Parker, 576; JCCW, 95.

43. Elliott, "Elliott's Brigade," 24; David Hunter, "Fighting With the Fury of Madmen: Tar Heels Describe the Battle of the Crater," www.northststerifles.com/crater.htm; 1–3; Clark, ed., North Carolina Regiments & Battalions, 3: 141–143.

44. Of the 27 captured, 14 survived and two died shortly after their release (Elliott, "Elliott's Brigade," 17).

45. Elliott, "Elliott's Brigade," 16–18; Page, "If You Love Me," 134–135; Stone, 195–196.

46. Day, 356; Jones, Army of North-

ern Virginia, 129; Page, "If You Love Me," 134.

47. Flanner was quite insistent that his battery alone had saved the day at Petersburg, positioned as it was to rake the Federal advance coming out of the Crater toward Cemetery Hill. However, a number of units could justifiably say that they played as significant a role in this defense. Elliott, "Elliott's Brigade," 18–20; Flanner, 248.

48. Jones, *Army of Northern Virginia*, 257, Haskell, 163.

49. George Walsh, *Damage Them All You Can: Robert E. Lee's Army of Northern Virginia* (New York: A Tom Doherty Associates Book, 2002), 394; OR 40 (1), 759–60; Gould, 262; Freeman, *Lee*, 472.

50. Gould, 248; Bernard, *War Talks*, 150, 213–14; Pleasants, *Inferno*, 142; Arnold Blumberg, "Old Dominion Brigade," *America's Civil War* (Leesburg: PRIMEDIA Enthusiast Publications, July, 2004), 23; William Mahone, *The Battle of the Crater* (Petersburg, VA: C.W. Historicals/Franklin Press), 4. Arnold Blumberg indicated that the 16th Virginia was three miles away. Mahone put it at one mile beyond Rives' Salient, or one and three-quarter miles from the breach (Mahone, 4; Blumberg, 28).

51. Hassler, 219; P. M. Vance, "Incidents of the Crater Battle," *Confederate Veteran* 14, no. 1 (1906): 178; John Marshall Martin letter to Sarah Waldo, *John Marshall Martin Papers*, Mss2 M38133 a1, Virginia Historical Society, Richmond, VA; Mahone, 3, Freeman, *Lee's Lieutenants*, 3: 466.

52. *Confederate Military History*, 3: 634–636.

53. Blumberg, 24; Trudeau, *Last Citadel*, 117.

54. Walsh, *Damage Them All You Can*, 391, 395; Bernard, "Battle of the Crater," 37; William D. Henderson, *12th Virginia Infantry* (Lynchburg, VA: H.E. Howard, 1984), 85. Mahone was made major general effective July 30, 1864, for his actions in the Crater. It could be said he defied the standard Peter Principle, for he was a much better division commander than he was at commanding a brigade. By the war's end, he was one of Lee's most conspicuous division commanders. Following the war, he returned to railroad management and became president of two railroad lines that were consolidated into the Atlantic, Mississippi and Ohio Railroad, which he managed until its failure in the financial crisis of 1873. He had served in the Virginia senate during the war, in addition to his field duties. He later was elected to the United States Senate, identified with the Republican Party and carried the

state elections in 1881. He led the Virginia delegation to the Republican convention in 1884, 1888 and 1889. He later was nominated by his party and ran for governor, but lost. In his later years, Mahone lived in Washington, DC. He died on October 8, 1895, and was buried in Blandford Cemetery, which he defended from his Union foes that fateful day in July 30, 1864 (Edward King, "A Ramble Through Virginia: From Bristol to the Sea," *Scribner's Monthly* 7, no. 6 (1874): 650; Kinard, 57.

55. The time was taken from Paul's notebook; he had noted the exact time.

56. Hill biographer William Woods Hassler states that Hill found Mahone at his headquarters before his men moved out, and had a lengthy discussion with him regarding the impending counterattack. Mahone, in his own account of the battle, mentions looking for Hill at Johnson's headquarters, without locating him at the time. Hassler, 220–21; Mahone, 5.

57. William Stewart, *A Pair of Blankets: War-Time History in Letters to the Young People of the South* (New York: Broadway Publishing, 1911), 153; Trudeau, *Last Citadel*, 117; Jones, *Army of Northern Virginia*, 158–159; Pleasants, *Inferno*, 142; McCabe, "Defence of Petersburg," 289; Hassler, 219–221; Wise, *End of an Era*, 361; Scott, *Petersburg Story*, 197; James I. Robertson, Jr., *General A.P. Hill: The Story of a Confederate Warrior* (New York: Random House, 1987), 291.

58. Pleasants, *Tragedy of the Crater*, 91–92; Trudeau, *Last Citadel*, 117; Horn, 112–113; Robertson, *General A.P. Hill*, 291; Cavanaugh, *Battle of the Crater*, 54; Alexander, *Fighting*, 464.

59. In June, John Haskell had requested that Alexander move his unit a short distance to one side given that he had several men killed by Federal sharpshooters. Haskell had one or more men killed by ordinary sniping every day from this position. Alexander had denied the request, however, "as minutes would count in the event of an emergency." Alexander, 464.

60. Burton, *History of Norfolk*, 90–91; Robertson, James, *General A.P. Hill*, 291–292; Alexander, *Fighting*, 464–465; Blumberg, 28; Mahone, 5–6; Stewart, *Pair of Blankets*, 152–154; McCabe, "Defence of Petersburg," 289–290; Jones, *Army of Northern Virginia*, 159; Pleasants, *Tragedy of the Crater*, 91–92; Bernard, *War Talks*, 150–51; Scott, *Petersburg Story*, 198.

61. Later named Graham Road.

62. Henderson, *12th Virginia*, 82–83; Bernard, *War Talks*, 150–151.

63. Bernard, *War Talks*, 150–151, 157; Mahone, 5–6; Jones, *Army of Northern Virginia*, 159; Scott, *Petersburg Story*, 198; McCabe, "The Defence

of Petersburg," 290; Burton, 91; Henderson, *12th Virginia*, 82–83.

64. Burton, 91; Bernard, *War Talks*, 151; Henderson, *12th Virginia*, 82–84; Scott, *Petersburg Story*, 198; Stewart, *Pair of Blankets*, 154–55; Mahone, 6–7; Jones, *The Army of Northern Virginia*, 160; Blumberg, 28.

65. Gould, 248–49; Stewart, *Pair of Blankets*, 152–53; McCabe, "Defence of Petersburg," 291.

66. After the countermarch on the Jerusalem Plank Road, the Virginia Brigade had moved up with the left in front, which accounted for the order of regiments in the ravine when the battle line was formed.

67. McCabe, "Defence of Petersburg," 291; Bernard, *War Talks*, 150–152; OR 40 (3), 652–653, 656.

68. Stewart, *Pair of Blankets*, 9; Bernard, *War Talks*, 152–153; Alexander, *Fighting*, 464–465; Cavanaugh, *Battle of the Crater*, 54–55; McCabe, "Defence of Petersburg," 290; Henderson, 82; Gould, 248–249; Pleasants, *Inferno*, 142–143; Blumberg, 28; Nelson Morehouse Blake, *William Mahone of Virginia: Soldier and Political Insurgent* (Richmond, VA: Garrett & Massie, 1935), 56; Hassler, 221; Haskell, *Haskell Memoirs*, 76.

69. OR 40 (3), 661; Cavanaugh, *Battle of the Crater*, 85; Henderson, 84; Stewart, *Pair of Blankets*, 156; William H. Stewart, *Description of the Battle of the Crater* (Norfolk, VA: Landmark Book and Job Office, 1876), 9–10; George T. Rogers, "The Crater Battle, 30th July, 1864," *Confederate Veteran* 3, no. 1 (1895): 12.

Chapter 13

1. Redkey, 111.

2. Thomas, "Colored Troops," 779; Marvel, *Race of the Soil*, 127; Smith, *Soldiers in Blue*, 183–84; William Baird, *William Baird Memoirs*, Bentley Historical Library, University of Michigan, Ann Arbor, MI, 19–20; Redkey, 111; Stevenson, 15–16.

3. The change in plans dictated by Meade twelve hours before the time for the assault had thus far failed to succeed after three full divisions were fully deployed. Then, after two and a half hours, Ferrero's black division, singled out to lead the charge until the day before, was being ordered in, with no change in Burnside's mission for them. The delay in bringing in the fourth appeared to be a fatal one. "It was the old blunder of Fort Wagner repeated at Petersburg; not that the colored soldiers did not come forward bravely enough; but they were not in position at the proper moment, and the delay was fatal." Delevan Bates

later was at a loss as to why his division was ordered in after so lengthy a delay. He also confessed he did not have "a definite idea of what we were expected to do." He contrasted what occurred with the well-thought-out plan Burnside had devised, and one that the fourth division had trained tirelessly to execute where "[e]very officer and every private knew his place and what he was expected to do." Bates firmly believed that the utilization of the former plan would have insured the army's success that day (Bernard, *War Talks*, 183; Palmer, 161; Stevenson, 11).

4. Then observed by blacks as the day when Great Britain freed its slaves throughout the British Empire in 1833.

5. *JCCW*, 228; Trudeau, *Like Men of War*, 239; Wilkinson, *Mother, May You*, 253–54; OR 40 (1), 596–99; Bosbyshell, 174; Pleasants, *Tragedy of the Crater*, 91; Pleasants, *Inferno*, 135; Joseph T. Wilson, *The Black Phalanx: A History of Negro Soldiers of the United States in the Wars of 1775–1812, 1861–'65* (Salem, NH: Ayer Company Publishers, 1968), 427; Houston, 348; Dudley Taylor Danish, *The Sable Arm: Black Troops in the Union Arm, 1861–1865* (Lawrence: University of Kansas Press, 1987), 274–275; Wheeler, 284; Porter, *Campaigning with Grant*, 268; Thomas, 777–779; Stevenson, 10.

6. Bowley, *Boy Lieutenant*, 94; Hall, 223; Trudeau, *Like Men of War*, 240; *JCCW*, 93; Clark, *Iron Hearted Regiment*, 148. How ironic that Ferrero's men were replaced by Ledlie's for the initial assault to avoid the adverse impact that their potential slaughter might cause in the Union press. Ledlie's men reached the Crater with relatively little resistance, and by the time Ferrero's men were finally called for, no-man's-land was a virtual slaughterhouse, resulting in a much higher casualty rate.

7. Delevan Bates, "A Day with the Colored Troops," *The National Tribune*, January 30, 1980; Freeman S. Bowley, "The Crater," *The National Tribune*, November 6, 1884; Bowley, *Boy Lieutenant*, 94; Trudeau, *Like Men of War*, 240; Goss, 335.

8. Some contemporaneous accounts, such as General Thomas's, had O'Brien shot in the chest or heart. Rumors of his demise were premature, however. Although he suffered a debilitating wound, O'Brien was back on duty before the end of the war, and served in Texas with Hall thereafter (Hall, "Mine Run to Petersburg," 247).

9. Powell, "Tragedy of the Crater," 771; Bates, "A Day with the Colored Troops"; Hall, "Mine Run to Petersburg," 223–24; Wilson, *Black Phalanx*, 416; OR 40, (1), 596.

10. James M. Paradis, *Strike the Blow for Freedom: The 6th United States*

Colored Infantry in the Civil War (Shippensburg, PA : White Mane Books, 1998), 59; Allen, 289; Wilson, *Black Phalanx*, 416–17, 427; Powell, "Tragedy of the Crater," 771; Cavanaugh, *The Battle of the Crater*, 56; Trudeau, *The Last Citadel*, 115–116; Anderson, 180, 211; Bowley, *Boy Lieutenant*, 83–84; Pleasants, *Inferno*, 135; Chambers, H.A., "The Bloody Crater," *Confederate Veteran* 31, no. 1 (1923): 174; Bosbyshell, 174; Gould, 236; Wilkinson, *Mother, May You*, 253–254; Trudeau, *Like Men of War*, 241; Lord, 495–498; Marvel, *Race of the Soil*, 268–269; Marvel, "And Fire Shall Devour Them," 128; *JCCW*, 88, 96–97, 120; OR 40 (1), 540, 554.

11. Captain Albert D. Wright was later awarded a Medal of Honor for his courageous actions that day, which saved so many of his fellow troops (Beyer, 392–93).

12. Hall, "Mine Run to Petersburg," 236.

13. Taylor, "The Crater," 57; Commager, *The Blue and the Gray*, 1020–1021; *JCCW*, 109; Hopkins, 204; Houston, 348; Katcher, 179; Pleasants, *Inferno*, 135; Wilkinson, *Mother, May You*, 254; Hall, 221, 226; Beyer, 392–393; Anderson, 180; Chambers, 175; Powell, "Tragedy of the Crater," 771; Wilson, *Black Phalanx*, 416; Hargrove, 186; Smith, 185; Wheeler, *Fields of Fire*, 284; Freeman Bowley, *Boy Lieutenant*, 83; Marvel, "And Fire Shall Devour Them," 129; Trudeau, *Like Men of War*, 241–42; Cornish, 273–274; OR 40 (1), 548; Cavanaugh, *Battle of the Crater*, 85; Committee of the Regiment, 237.

14. A significant number of Confederate sources refer to the fourth division of the Ninth Corps attacking with "drunken Negroes" or "half-drunken Negroes." This characterization was quite widespread among the Confederate troops who confronted Ferrero's division that fateful day, and who later referred to this characterization when describing the battle in credible publications after the war. The charge was quite commonplace among Southern sources, and appears as accepted fact in many Southern publications. However, there exists little or no evidence that the blacks entered into this extremely decisive engagement under the influence of alcohol. A more plausible rationale for this impression was the cultural differences between the blacks and the Southerners in the Army of Northern Virginia; up to this point, these soldiers had never encountered armed former slaves as their deadly opponents in this long and deadly war.

15. Confederate accounts are close to unanimous that the black troops and their officers charged them with the rallying cry "Remember Fort Pil-

low! No quarter!" or words to that effect. Many reputable Confederates reported hearing the cry themselves. See Pearce, 210. Such behavior would be quite understandable at the time, as an attempt to inspire confidence and ferocity in the untried black troops going into battle. Concomitantly, the slogan, coming from these black faces, was sure to instill righteous indignation, anger and fear of capture on the part of the Southern recipients. Cavanaugh reports that at least one publication attributes Siegfried himself with making such a remark at the time. See *Publications of the Historical Society of Schuylkill County, 1903–1953*, I, 290; Cavanaugh, *Battle of the Crater*, 169–170.

16. Clark, 148; Bernard, *War Talks*, 183; Beyer, 390.

17. Hall, "Mine Run to Petersburg," 238.

18. Wheeler, 284; Stone, 191, 196, 207–208; Horn, 113–114; Trudeau, *Like Men of War*, 241–242; Stevenson, 11; Bowley, *Boy Lieutenant*, 33, 83; Baird, 20–21; Bates, "Day with the Colored Troops"; Davis, *Death in Trenches*, 80–83; Powell, "Tragedy of the Crater," 771–72; Clark, *The Iron Hearted Regiment*, 148; Redkey, 113–114; Roderick J. Heller III and Carolann Ayers Heller, eds., *The Confederacy Is on Her Way Up the Spout: Letters to South Carolina, 1861–1865* (Athens: University of Georgia Press, 1992), 123; Day, "Battle of the Crater," 335.

19. See Marvel, *Race of the Soil*, 269. Some sources reported seeing a single black soldier, with his musket at support arms and seemingly dazed or lost, run straight for the battery on the Jerusalem Plank Road, which was firing canister at a rapid rate. According to Porter Alexander (who was not present that day), this individual ran up to the plank road and jumped into the sunken portion between two guns, whereupon a gunner "drew the trail handspike from his piece & knocked him in the head with it" (Alexander, *Fighting*, 461–462; Gould, 269; Davis, 83).

20. Confederate estimates also claim approximately 200 men advanced on them at this point.

21. On June 22, 1891, Bates was awarded the Medal of Honor for his gallantry that day. Incredibly, Bates found himself back in the trenches at Petersburg a mere eight weeks later, with the experience of July 30 having given him "the star of a brevet-brigadier-general and the command of a brigade through the rest of the war" (Bernard, *War Talks*, 184).

22. Hall was promoted to brevet brigadier general "for gallant and meritorious services in the assault on the enemy's works at the Mine before Pe-

tersburg, Virginia." General Joshua Sigfried later paid tribute to Hall: "No man ever led a regiment under such a severe fire through several divisions of other troops who had preceded them, and who had squatted in a place of shelter" (Hall, "Mine Run to Petersburg," 242).

23. Hall, "Mine Run to Petersburg," 244.

24. Many sources place Bates' wounding at the inception of Mahone's counterattack, which routed all the Federal troops in the area. However, Bates was wounded in the assault "some time" before Mahone advanced (Stevenson, 11). Bates himself confirmed this in a letter to George Bernard in 1891 (Bernard, *War Talks*, 183).

25. It could be argued that some explanation for the disorganization and high losses among the black troops was the difficulty officers had in restraining their men in battle. With inadequate training and a burning desire to prove themselves, the men were quite difficult to control. A lieutenant on the 30th USCT remarked that, although his men "were brave in their charge … as a body, [they were] wholly unmanageable" (Joseph T. Glatthaar, *Forged in Battle: The Civil War Alliance of Black Soldiers and White Officers* (New York: Collier Macmillan, 1990), 154.

26. Jeremiah M. Mickley, *Forty-Third Regiment United States Colored Troops* (Gettysburg: J.E. Wible, 1866), 74–75; Jones, "Battle of the Crater," 119–120; Bates, "A Day with the Colored Troops"; Stone, 207; Powell, "Tragedy of the Crater," 771; Marvel, *Race of the Soil*, 268–69; Jones, *Army of Northern Virginia*, 122; Hargrave, 186; Gould, 236–237; Bowley, 83–85; Stevenson, 11; Wheeler, 284; Trudeau, *Like Men of War*, 242–243; Cannan, 114–115; Michael Barton and Larry Logue, *The Civil War Soldier* (New York: New York University Press, 2002), 235; Lowry, *Fate of the Country*, 276; Ervin T. Case, *Personal Narratives of the Battles of The Rebellion*, no. 10, "Battle of the Mine," *MOLLUS* (Wilmington: Broadfoot Publishing, 1993), 298–99; Bernard, *War Talks*, 183; Beyer, *Deeds of Valor*, 390.

27. Redkey, 111–112; A. Friend, *Memorial of Colonel John A. Bross, Twenty-Ninth U.S. Colored Troops, Who Fell in Leading the Assault on Petersburg July 30, 1864* (Chicago: Tribune Book and Job Office, 1865), 11–19; Goss, 335.

28. Cushman, 15–16.

29. Smith, *Black Soldiers in Blue*, 185–186; Trudeau, *Like Men of War*, 241–42; Thomas, "The Colored Troops At Petersburg," 777–779; Houston, 348; Redkey, 111–112; Cannan, 115–116; Anderson, 180; Horn, 114; Cushman, 16–17; Wilson, *Black Phalanx*, 417, 421.

Chaplain Garland White later paid tribute to the work of the second brigade, which included his 28th USCT, indicating that the first brigade did not stand up to the deadly work as compared to Thomas's brigade. He attributed this to the fact that the first brigade was comprised largely of blacks from slave states, and thus "did not stand up to the work like those from the Free States." He claimed the second brigade charged over the first and carried two lines of rifle pits. Many accounts would dispute his opinion as to the quality of the first brigade's fighting that day, given the success that it had in capturing Confederate rifle pits, the number of prisoners taken, and the capture of enemy colors. It is thus difficult to assert that the second brigade was considered more successful in their efforts that day.

30. James H. Rickard, "Services with Colored Troops," 35; Thomas, "Colored Troops," 779; Goss, 335.

31. An Indiana historical marker commemorating the 28th Regiment was dedicated on July 31, 2004, at the Indiana Soldiers and Sailors Monument (Monument Circle) in Indianapolis, Indiana, where the unit was recruited. This regiment was Indiana's only African American regiment in the Civil War.

32. William Wells Brown, *The Negroes in the American Rebellion* (Miami, FL: Mnemosyne Publishing, 1969), 266–67; Thomas, "Colored Troops," 779; Rickard, "Service with Colored Troops," 36; Cavanaugh, *Battle of the Crater*, 57. Two days later, Thomas attempted to locate Pennell's body for a burial, but the effort was in vain. Pennell was literally shot to pieces and undoubtedly was placed in an unknown grave (Thomas, "Colored Troops," 779). His body lay where thousands of bullets would have reduced it to an unrecognizable pulp.

33. Thomas, "Colored Troops," 779–781; Rickard, 35–37; Trudeau, *Last Citadel*, 116; Smith, *Black Soldiers in Blue*, 60–62; Trudeau, *Like Men of War*, 242; Cannan, 117; OR 40 (1), 598–599; Wilson, *Black Phalanx*, 417.

34. A. Friend, *Memorial of Colonel John A. Bross, Twenty-Ninth U.S. Colored Troops Who Fell in Leading the Assault on Petersburg July 30, 1864*, (Chicago: Privately published), 11–19, 32–34; Trudeau, *Like Men of War*, 243; Thomas, "Colored Troops," 781–82; Powell, "Tragedy of the Crater," 771; OR 40 (1), 598–599; Smith, *Black Soldiers in Blue*, 60, Cavanaugh, *The Battle of the Crater*, 85; Cutcheon, 142–43; Gould, 237; JCCW, 97.

35. OR 40 (1), 147, 707.

36. OR 40 (1), 707.

37. Ibid.

38. Ibid.

39. Ord later testified before the Congressional Committee that troops should have been massed opposite different places of exit and then have gone out as soon as required. But troops were all massed in one place "along by divisions," so that they were all in a column. Using one point with a long covered way caused very slow movements. This was the primary reason the shock of the explosion was not adequately exploited, allowing time for the Confederates to recover. He felt that he could have gotten his troops through on the left of the Crater if they had advanced through the opening by fronts of regiments or even companies. Resistance on the right was much more substantial (OR 40 (1), 86; JCCW, 19–22).

40. JCCW 119–120; OR 40 (1), 696–697.

41. JCCW, 120.

42. OR 40 (1), 121–122, 698–700, 707–708; JCCW, 19, 83–86, 102–104, 121–123.

43. He was later killed in the second expedition against Fort Fisher on January 15, 1865.

44. JCCW, 120–21; OR 40 (1), 77–78, 707–08.

45. Clark, *Iron Hearted Regiment*, 13.

46. William L. Hyde, *History of the One Hundred and Twelfth Regiment N.Y. Volunteers* (Fredonia, NY: W. McKinstry, 1866), 88, 94; J.A. Mowris, *A History of the One Hundred and Seventeenth Regiment, N.Y. Volunteers, (Fourth Oneida), from the Date of Its Organization, August, 1862, Till That of Its Muster Out, June 1865* (Hartford, CT: Case, Lockwood and Company, Printers, 1866), 124; Clark, *Iron Hearted Regiment*, 148–149; George Baker Anderson, *Landmarks of Rensselaer County, New York* (Syracuse, NY: Mason, Publishers, 1877), 121, 175–177.

47. JCCW, 105; Clark, *Iron Hearted Regiment*, 145–150; Anderson, 120–121; Nathaniel Bartlett Sylvester, *History of Rensselaer Co. New York* (Philadelphia: Everts & Peck, 1880), 100–101; Elias A. Bryant, *The Diary of Elias A. Bryant of Francestown, N.H., as Written by him While in his More than Three Years Service in the U.S. Army in the Civil War* (Concord, NH: Rumford Press, 1906), 175–176; Anderson, *Landmarks of Rensselaer County*, 121.

48. Isaiah Price, *History of the Ninety-Seventh Regiment Pennsylvania Infantry during the War of the Rebellion, 1861–65, within the Biographical Sketches of Its Field and Staff Officers and a Complete Record of Each Officer and Enlisted Man*, (Philadelphia: B.&P. Printers, 1875), 309.

49. George Anderson, 120–121; Price, *History of the Ninety-Seventh Regiment*, 299–310; OR 40 (1), 550,

702–703; Palmer, *History of the Forty-Eighth New York State Volunteers*, 163–164; Isaiah Price, *Reunion of the Ninety-Seventh Regiment Pennsylvania Volunteers, October 29th*, MOLLUS (Philadelphia: 1884), 28–29.

50. Palmer, *History of the Forty-Eighth New York*, 162–164; Price, *History of the Ninety-Seventh Regiment*, 308–10; OR 40 (1), 698–699; James M. Nichols, *Perry's Saints, or the Fighting Parson's Regiment in the War of the Rebellion*, (Boston: D. Lothrop, 1886), 250–251; Bryant, *Diary of Elias A. Bryant*, 176–177.

51. Curtis won the Medal of Honor for his gallantry before Fort Fisher in 1865, and later served a number of terms in the United States Congress.

52. OR 40, Part I, Series I, 701; Edward G. Longacre, ed., *From Antietam to Fort Fisher: The Civil War Letters of Edward King Wrightman, 1862–1865* (Rutherford, NJ: Fairleigh Dickenson University Press, 1985), 204; William L. Hyde letter dated August 1, 1864, *William L. Hyde Papers*, Pearce Civil War Collection, Navaro College, Corsicana, TX.

53. OR 40 (1), 566; Hopkins, 199.

54. The July 31 trimonthly reports show 9,555 infantry officers and men as "present for duty equipped" in the Ninth Corps (OR 40 (1), 177). The Ninth Corps reportedly lost 3,475 men in the fighting on the 30th of July. Thus 13,030 infantrymen should have been available for action on the 30th (OR 40 (1), 249). Burnside later claimed only 9,023 "muskets ready for duty" on July 20 (OR 40 (1), 60).

Chapter 14

1. The battalion went in with a total of 104 men, of which 94 were killed or wounded in the subsequent counterattack. Eight of its nine officers were shot through the chest in the fight. The sharpshooters were all equipped with long range, small-bore Enfield rifles and utilized English-made cartridges as opposed to the usual Southern manufactured projectiles. They were also equipped with "two globe-sighted rifles for use on special occasions" (Bernard, *War Talks*, 186); John E. Laughton, "The Sharpshooters of Mahone's Brigade," *Southern Historical Society Papers* (1894), 20: 99, 104.

2. Laughton, 104; Bernard, *War Talks*, 186–187, 198, 217, 224; William H. Stewart, "Carnage at 'The Crater' Near Petersburg," *Confederate Veteran* 1, no. I (1893): 42–3; Henry Van Leuvenigh Bird letter June 30, 1880, *Bird Family Papers*, Mss1 B5325a 32a, Virginia Historical Society, Richmond, VA; Burton, *History of Norfolk*, 92.

3. Blumberg, 29.

4. Henry VanLeuvenigh Bird was a color guard with the 12th Virginia. He claimed in a letter home that most of the men "stood up, very few laid down." He did assert that what he saw from his vantage point might not agree with those who saw it "from some other standpoint" (Bird, *The Bird Family Papers*).

5. Rogers, "The Crater Battle, 30th July, 1864," 12; Bernard, *War Talks*, 153; Elwell, 55.

6. Bernard, *War Talks*, 153.

7. He was subsequently promoted to brigadier effective retroactively to July 30, 1864, for his role in the counterattack and its success. At his death in 1899, he was buried in Blandford Cemetery, the target of the Federal assault that day.

8. The distance was actually 200 yards.

9. Henderson, *12th Virginia*, 82; Bernard, *War Talks*, 154–155, 178, 217; McCabe, "Defence of Petersburg," 291; Blumberg, 28–29.

10. Bernard, *War Talks*, 186, 224; Rogers, "The Crater Battle, 30th July, 1864,"12–13; Cannan, 126: Lowry, 277.

11. Friend, 17, 33–34. Bross, who together with his regiment had joined the Army of the Potomac only in early June, had passed en route through Chicago on May 27 and there related to friends that "we shall remember Fort Pillow, and shall not ask for quarter. I leave a home and friends as dear as can be found on earth; but if it is the will of Providence that I do not return, I ask no nobler epitaph than that I fell for my country, at the head of this black and blue regiment." The men in the ranks adored him, and his fellow officers deeply respected him. Willas A. Bogart wrote Bross's widow that, "although a colored man, a private in the 29th, I found in Colonel Bross a friend, one in whom every member of the regiment placed the utmost confidence, for, and with whom, each one would help defend the country to the end. The 29th; with its leader gone, feels there is no such commander under the sun, to lead it forward and cheer it up. He was loved by every one, because he was a friend to every man." Bross's body could not be retrieved by the retreating men and was subsequently buried on the field by the Confederates when they retook this portion of their line. Of 450 men in the 29th USCT that day, only 128 came out of the battle unscathed (Friend, 11, 17–18, 32–33).

12. Weld, "The Petersburg Mine," 210.

13. There remains an ongoing controversy as to who actually ordered the counterattack. The weight of authority rests with Mahone. Some argue that Girardey took it upon himself to order the charge, pursuant to the authority which Mahone had vested in him, which would then stand for the proposition that it was still done under Mahone's auspices. Weisiger later argued on his own behalf that he took it upon himself to order the charge. He wrote years after the event that "I have never claimed to be the hero of that occasion, but do claim that I gave the order to 'forward!' at the opportune moment, when it was observed that the enemy were preparing for a charge. There was only one of two things to be done — either to be idle and be over-run, or charge with the bayonet." Weisiger suggests Captain Girardey assented to his views, "perceiving the rapidity with which the enemy was forming, and the imminent danger of being overrun before the Georgians could arrive on the field." Weisiger asserts that he requested Girardey to confirm his reasons for doing so and "immediately charged with ... [his] brigade, which, in gallant style, carried the works as far as ... [his] line would cover." Weisiger contended further that Mahone was not even on the field at the time the Virginia Brigade attacked. Unfortunately, Girardey was killed two weeks after the battle, on August 16, and was thus unable to give a firsthand account, which would presumably have put this matter to rest. A number of veterans who served in the brigade came to Mahone's defense immediately following Weisiger's claims, presenting very formidable evidence that Mahone was, indeed, not only present at the time in question, but also responsible for the order to move forward. Captain Charles Ridgelay Goodwin, a volunteer aid on Mahone's staff, observed that Girardey sprang up in front of the men "and, waving his sword, gave the command to forward." The men who heard Girardey presumed that the order came from Mahone and started to run for the works. Colonel George T. Rogers also was convinced Mahone himself ordered the charge. Rogers met Mahone in the trenches and received "timely instructions for the disposition of the men and orders to hold the position, at any hazard and under any loss, until he could bring another brigade to our relief." James Blakemore, one of Mahone's couriers, was no more than two feet from Mahone, standing a short distance from and a little in advance of the left of the line. He heard Mahone give Girardey the order to tell Weisiger to "forward." "Impatient for the fight and knowing his men, Girardey did not want to reach Weisiger, but at once springing in front of the left of the brigade and waving his sword

over his head, he gave the word to charge and led the men to the assault." Henry Van Leuvenigh Bird, a color guard of the 12th Virginia, stated, "We did not know who gave the order to charge, but at the time it was supposed to have come from Gen'l Mahone. We no more thought it necessary to question that than we did to ask who had whipped in the fight nor do I doubt either now." Sergeant Thomas E. Richardson of Company K, 12th Virginia, who was twenty feet from Mahone at the time, recalled that Girardey left Mahone and went to the front to give his command: "I heard no command from Gen. Weisiger. The move commenced from the left of the brigade, immediately where Gen. Mahone was standing." Douglas Freeman, however, contended Weisiger did not wait for Mahone or Girardey, but rather shouted "Forward!" at the same instant Girardey had called to Mahone (Bernard, *War Talks*, 218–221; Bird, Henry Van Leuvenigh Bird, statement of June 30, 1880, *Bird Family Papers*: Freeman, *Lee*, 3: 474; George S. Bernard, "Great Battle of the Crater: The Work of Mahone and Weisiger at the Fight," *Southern Historical Society Papers* (Richmond: 1900), 28: 210–211).

14. Mahone, 7–8; Bernard, *War Talks*, 154, 214, 217–219, 224; Stewart, "Carnage at the Crater Near Petersburg," 41; Rogers, "Crater Battle, 30th July, 1864," 13; McCabe, "Defence of Petersburg," 291.

15. Bernard, *War Talks*, 155; Blumberg, 529; Elwell, 56.

16. Many participants in the Virginia Brigade would argue that the Carolinians did not assemble and advance as a part of their movement. See, e.g., letter of Captain Richard W. Jones, commander of the 12th Virginia, in *War Talks*, 200–201. However, there exists enough concrete evidence to confirm that portions of these North and South Carolina regiments did move out in advance at the time the Virginia Brigade attacked (OR 40 (1), 791).

17. Blumberg, 29; Elwell, 56; Freeman, *Lee*, 3: 474; Bernard, *War Talks*, 155, 180, 200; OR 40 (1), 791; Cavanaugh, *Battle of the Crater*, 88; Taylor, *The Crater*, 57: Wise, *End of an Era*, 364, Elliott, "Elliott's Brigade," 23; McCabe, "Defence of Petersburg," 290.

18. Freeman, *Lee*, 3: 473–74; Bernard, "Battle of the Crater," 155–56; Walsh, *Damage Them All You Can*, 395–96; McCabe, " Defence of Petersburg," 291; Rogers, "The Crater Battle, 30th July, 1864," 13; Elwell, 55–56; Stewart, "Carnage at the Crater," 12–13; Blumberg, 29.

19. Allen, 290.

20. Blumberg, 29; Bernard, *War Talks*, 155, 187.

21. Burton, *History of Norfolk*, 92; Rogers, "The Crater Battle," 13; McCabe, "The Defence of Petersburg," 291; Elwell, 56–57; Bernard, *War Talks*, 190; Freeman, *Lee*, 3: 474–475; Walsh, *Damage Them All You Can*, 396: Stewart, *Description of the Battle of the Crater*, 10; Day, "Battle of the Crater," 356; Stewart, "Carnage at 'The Crater' Near Petersburg," 42.

22. Brother of the contemporary poet Walt Whitman.

23. McCabe, "The Defence of Petersburg," 291–292; Loving, 128; Allen, 289; Stewart, *Description of the Battle of the Crater*, 10; Jones, *Army of Northern Virginia*, 161; James I. Robertson, Jr. ed., *The Civil War Letters of General Robert McAllister* (Baton Rouge: Louisiana State University Press, 1965), 292; Marvel, *Race of the Soil*, 128; Elliott, "Elliott's Brigade," 23.

24. Horn, 114–15; McNeely, 179; Foote, 3: 538; Taylor, "The Crater," 58; Cutcheon, 142–43; Davis, *Death in Trenches*, 83; Robertson, *A.P. Hill*, 294.

25. William H. Etheredge, "Another Story of the Crater Battle," *Confederate Veteran* 15, no. 1 (1907): 167, 205; McNeely, 179; Foote, 3: 538; Bernard, *War Talks*, 192–193.

26. Browley, "The Petersburg Mine," 36.

27. Benjamin Trask, *61st Virginia Infantry* (Lynchburg, VA: H.E. Howard, 1988), 26; Day, 356; Carroll, 99; Trudeau, *Last Citadel*, 119. William R.J. Pegram letter dated August 1, 1864, *Pegram-Johnson-McIntosh Family Papers*, Virginia Historical Society, Richmond, VA.

28. Other officers of the fourth division also contended that it was a white regiment that first broke with the onslaught of Mahone's counterattack. Colonel Sigfried claimed that "as the troops in front were about to make a charge a white color-bearer with his colors crossed the work in retreat" and caused the troops to seek shelter in the Crater, thereby pushing Sigfried's brigade back with them (OR 40 (1), 597). Ferrero later expanded upon this claim, indicating it was a dismounted cavalry regiment from the second division off to the side which broke first and "came back on the double-quick, broke through the ranks of my leading brigade, which of course caused my negroes to break" (*JCCW*, 109; Hopkins, 204).

29. Bowley, "The Petersburg Mine," 36; Stevenson, 13.

30. Earlier in the war, as a cadet at the Virginia Military Institute, Wise was with those cadets when they summarily sent Franz Sigel packing in the valley (Marvel, *Race of the Soil*, 270).

31. J.W. Urwin, ed., *Black Flag Over Dixie: Racial Atrocities and Reprisals in*

the Civil War (Carbondale: Southern Illinois University Press, 2004), 205; Carroll, 99; Marvel, *Race of the Soil*, 270; Bernard, "The Battle of the Crater," 14–15, 20; Cutcheon, 143; Rogers, "Crater Battle, 30th July, 1864," 13.

32. Bernard, *War Talks*, 157. Bernard was later convinced that he had encountered John H. Offer, the chaplain of the 30th USCT who had given the stirring speech to his regiment before they advanced an hour earlier. Lieutenant Freeman Bowley later disputed this speculation, however.

33. Bernard, "The Battle of the Crater," 11–12; Bernard, *War Talks*, 156–157; Alexander, *Fighting*, 462; Williams, *Rebel Brothers*, 115.

34. Leon F. Litwack, *Been in the Storm So Long* (New York: Alfred A. Knopf, 1979), 89; Carroll, 99–100; James M. McPherson, *For Cause and Comrades: Why Men Fought in the Civil War* (New York: Oxford University Press, 1997), 152; William R.J. Pegram letter dated August 1, 1864, *Pegram-Johnson-McIntosh Family Papers*; Carmichael, 130; Randall C. Jimerson, *The Private Civil War: Popular Thought during the Sectional Conflict* (Baton Rouge: Louisiana State University Press, 1998), 114; Robertson, *A.P. Hill*, 293.

35. Bernard, *War Talks*, 190–192.

36. Bowley, "The Petersburg Mine," 35; Burton, 95; Trudeau, *Last Citadel*, 119–20; Cavanaugh, *Battle of the Crater*, 88; Cutcheon, 142–43, Trudeau, *Like Men of War*, 243; OR 40 (1), 567–68, 791; Stewart, "Carnage At the Crater," 42; Alexander, *Fighting*, 465; Wilkinson, *Mother, May You*, 254; Horn, 117; Lord, 502; Clark, *North Carolina Regiments*, 3: 374.

37. Lord, 502; OR 40 (1), 791; Pollard, "Edward Bagby," 456; Allen, 289; Clark, *North Carolina Regiments*, 3: 374; McMaster, "Battle of the Crater," 130.

38. *National Tribune*, November 20, 1902; Bowley, "The Petersburg Mine," 35; Burton, 95; Trudeau, *Last Citadel*, 119–120; Cavanaugh, *Battle of the Crater*, 88; Cutcheon, 142–143, Trudeau, *Like Men of War*, 243; OR 40 (1), 567–568, 791; Stewart, "Carnage at the Crater," 42; Alexander, *Fighting*, 465; Wilkinson, *Mother, May You*, 254; Horn, 117; Lord, 502.

39. Sergeant Wilkins of Company H was awarded the Medal of Honor for his actions, being the *third* one earned by a member of the 9th New Hampshire that fateful day (OR 40 (1), 567). Later, the abandoned staff was found and the regiment was lamenting the loss of their colors when it was discovered that the silken rags were safely within their lines (Marvin, 225).

40. The entire regiment mourned the loss of the gallant Hough, whose

body had to be left where he lay when the unit was soon forced to retreat from the Crater. Two days later under a truce, some of his men went searching for the body. They found a grave which had been dug for Hough by the Confederates, but it had remained empty and Hough was later found to be alive. He was carried into Petersburg and months later was released through a prisoner exchange and subsequently recovered from his wound, although he did not rejoin the army (Lord, 494, 510–12).

41. Dana M. Mangham, "*Oh, for a Touch of the Vanished Hand*" (Murfreesboro, TN: Southern Heritage Press, 2000), 307; Marvel, "And Fire Shall Devour Them," 129–130; Lord, 498–499; OR 40 (1), 567, 754; Rogers, "Crater Battle, 30th July, 1864," 12; Allen, 298; Marvin, 255.

42. Lord, 498–99; Marvel, "And Fire Shall Devour Them," 129–30; Marvel, *Race of the Soil*, 271.

43. Marvel, "And Fire Shall Devour Them," 131.

44. Several authoritative works on the second brigade and its regiments in this conflict point out that Weld surrendered in the Crater at the very end, along with General Bartlett and Colonel Marshall. See, e.g., Wilkinson, *Mother, May You*, 259, for a history of the 57th Massachusetts regiment. Weld's own letters and a paper he delivered to the Military Historical Society of Massachusetts clearly distinguish this error, however. Weld did meet up with Bartlett and Marshall at 4:00 P.M. that day in the Confederate rear as fellow prisoners. However, he had surrendered much earlier that day, given his predicament (Weld, "The Petersburg Mine," 210–211; Weld, *War Diary*, 354).

45. Weld, *War Diary*, 353–55; Weld, "The Petersburg Mine," 210–11; Anderson, 181–82; Wilkinson, *Mother, May You*, 255–58; Cavanaugh, *Battle of the Crater*, 88; Lord, 498–99.

46. Elliott, "Elliott's Brigade," 20; Cavanaugh, *Battle of the Crater*, 89; Harry F. Jackson and Thomas F. O'Donnell, *Back Home in Oneida: Hermon Clarke and His Letters* (Syracuse: Syracuse University Press, 1965), 150–151; Bryant, 178–179; Bernard, "The Battle of the Crater," 31; JCCW, 121–122; Clark, *The Iron-Hearted Regiment*, 148–149; OR 40 (1), 704.

47. Bryant was the company bugler. His colonel criticized him for entering into the engagement, as it was not part of the mission of a bugler to go into the fight, but Bryant felt that "it was to me a duty to go wherever my regiment went" (Bryant, 181).

48. Sammons had just returned to duty the day before the attack from a

sick furlough as the result of a prior injury.

49. OR 40 (1), 699, 704; Clark, *Iron Hearted Regiment*, 151–154; Cavanaugh, *Battle of the Crater*, 89; JCCW, 31; Humphreys, *Virginia Campaign*, 259; Hopkins, 199.

50. Isaiah Price, *History of the Ninety-Seventh Regiment*, 310; Nichols, 250–251; Palmer, *History Of the Forty-Eighth Regiment* 163–164.

51. Hyde, Letter dated August 1, 1864; Hyde, *History of the One Hundred And Twelfth Regiment N. Y. Volunteers*, 88, 92–93; Mowris, *History of the 117th New York Volunteers*, 125–126.

52. Longacre, *From War Letters: Antietam to Fort Fisher*, 204; Hyde, Letter dated August 1, 1864.

53. Kilmer, 776; Bernard, *War Talks*, 169; Wilkinson, *Mother, May You*, 255; Marvel, *Race of the Soil*, 269; Bryant, 178–179; Bert McQueen, *A Civil War Family (A True Story)* (Hagerstown, IN: Exponent Publishers, 1987), 50.

54. Haskell, *Haskell Memoirs*, 73–77; McCabe, "Defence of Petersburg," 292; Wise, *End of an Era*, 365–366; Mahone, 9–10; Bernard, *War Talks*, 182, 205, 216; Jones, *Army of Northern Virginia*, 162; Aston, 103; Trudeau, *Last Citadel*, 121; Marvel, *Race of the Soil*, 272; Alexander, *Fighting*, 467; Dowdey, *Lee*, 497; OR 40 (1), 759–60, 779; Stone, 198.

55. Haskell, *Haskell Memoirs*, 76–77; Cavanaugh, *Battle of the Crater*, 91; Katcher, 180.

56. Bernard, *War Talks*, 216; Mahone, 11; McCabe, "Defence of Petersburg," 292; Stone, 198.

57. Lieutenant Colonel Ridge of the 5th Fusiliers was killed in leading an attack by escalade in the storming of Badajos, Spain, on April 6, 1812, and was immortalized by W.F.P. Napier in his work *History of the War in the Peninsula and in the South of France from the Year 1807 to the Year 1814*, 6 vols. (London: John Murry, 1828–1840).

58. Hassler, 221; Stewart, 11; Bernard, "The Battle of the Crater," 15; Jones, *Army of Northern Virginia*, 162; Bernard, *War Talks*, 187, 225; Etheredge, "Another Story of the Crater Battle," 205; George Clark, "Alabamians in the Crater Battle," *Confederate Veteran Magazine*, 3 (1895), 68; Rogers, "Crater Battle, 30th July, 1864," 12; Cavanaugh, *6th Virginia*, 54; W. R. S., "The Sharpshooters of Mahone's Old Brigade at the Crater," *Southern Historical Society Papers*, XXVIII (Richmond 1900), 308; Stewart, "Description of the Battle of the Crater,"179; Henderson, *12th Virginia*, 84.

59. Trask, 26; Bernard, *War Talks*, 184–85; Burton, 94; Cavanaugh, *6th Virginia*, 53; Power, 138.

60. Foote, 3: 108–112.

61. Hargrave, 175–176.

62. Katcher, 166–68.

63. Glatthaar, *Forged In Battle*, 157; McPherson, *For Cause and Comrades*, 154; William H. Morgan, *Personal Reminiscences of the War of 1861–5: In Camp—in bivouac—on the march—on picket—on the skirmish line—on the battlefield—and in prison* (Freeport, NY: Books For Libraries Press, 1971), 221.

64. Nevins, *Diary of George Templeton Strong*, 463–464; Worthington Chauncy Ford, ed., *A Cycle of Adams Letters 1861–1865*, vol. 3 (Boston: Riverside Press Cambridge, Houghton Mifflin, 1920), 3: 154.

65. Austin Fenn letter dated May 14, 1864, *Austin Fenn Papers*, Pearce Civil War Collection, Navarro College, Corsicana, TX.

66. Morgan, 221; Horn, 70; Trudeau, *Like Men of War*, 225; Jackson, 142.

67. Barton, *The Civil War Soldier*, 241–42; Keith P. Wilson, *Campfires of Freedom: The Camp Life of Black Soldiers during the Civil War*, (Kent, OH: Kent State University Press, 2002), 115.

68. Jayquette, 116.

69. On April 18, 1864, Confederate forces under Brigadier General John Sappington Marmaduke fell upon a wagon train carrying plunder from a large Federal raiding party. Among the 1,100 Federal troops was the First Kansas Colored Troops. Part of Marmaduke's force was made up of Choctow Indians, "who whooped with delight at finding the 1st Kansas (Colored) to their front," as it was well known for its ransack activities in the past, and the troops "unsheathed their knives for bloody work." An unknown soldier later wrote to one Sallie Hearn that "I have seen enough myself to know it is correct our men is determined not to take negro prisoners, and if all of the negroes could have seen what occurred that day, they would stay at home." Southerners already enraged at discovering former slaves confronting them in battle were driven nearly mad at discovering the plunder of the black troops, which included not only foodstuffs, but also bed quilts, as well as women's and children's clothing. They roamed the battlefield shooting the wounded black soldiers, calling out, "Where's the First Nigger now?" Of the 301 Union casualties, 182 were from the First Kansas Colored Infantry and 117 of those were killed (Mark K. Christ, ed., *Getting Used to Being Shot A: The Spence Family Civil War Letters* (Fayetteville: University of Arkansas Press, 2002), 123–125; Foote, 3: 69–70). The vast majority of the deaths that day were attributed to the Choctaws (Foote, 3: 70).

70. Day, "Battle of Crater," 355; Roulhac, 72; Pearce, *Diary of Captain Henry A. Chambers*, 283; William A. Day, *A True History of Company I, 49th Regiment, North Carolina Troops in the Great Civil War Between North and South* (Baltimore, MD: Butternut and Blue, 1997), 80–85; Joseph Addison Waddell, Diary entry of August 2, 1864, *Albert and Shirley Small Special Collections Library*, University of Virginia, Charlottesville; Hall, 238; Stone, 196; Webb Garrison, *A Treasury of Civil War Tales* (Nashville, TN: Rutledge Hill Press, 1988), 209; Hargrave, 195–197.

71. Mitchell, *The Vacant Chair*, 174–175; Cavanaugh, *Battle of the Crater*, 53; Garrison, 205–206; McPherson, *For Cause and Comrades*, 152–153; Steven E. Woodworth, ed., *The Loyal, True, and Brave: America's Civil War Soldiers* (Wilmington: Scholarly Resources, 2002), 175–176: Anderson, 193.

72. When Shaw heard this, he declared, "Give me room to land my regiment, and if it cannot march through New York it is not fit to go into the field." The unit landed with loaded muskets and fixed bayonets with martial music playing and marched down Broadway "turning their menace into an ovation" (Joseph E. Ray, "Our Indebtedness to the Negroes," *New Englander and Yale Review*, no. 51, vol. 236 (November 1889): 356.

73. Many blacks were tortured and killed, and the Colored Orphan Asylum and the Aged Colored Women's Home were attacked, sacked and burned. Thousands of blacks were forced to flee the city (Goodwin, 537).

74. One officer compared the blacks to the Irish Brigade, notorious for its bravery, "although many thought the courage of the Irishmen derived from their ignorance."

75. Jimerson, 88–103; Ray, 356; Joseph T. Glatthar, "Leaving Their Mark on the Battlefield," Barton, 234; Katcher, 179.

76. Redkey, 8; Coffin, *Four Years of Fighting*, 369–70; Jackson, 94.

77. Wilkinson, *Mother, May You*, 262, 266; William L. Hyde letter dated August 1, 1864; Nevins, 447; Unknown Soldier John A. letter, *Pearce Civil War Collection*, Navarro College, Corsicana, TX; John Herbert Claiborne, *Seventy-Five Years in Old Virginia* (New York: Neale Publishing, 1904), 207–209; Agassiz, 212; Redkey, 112; Cornish, 276; Scott, *Forgotten Valor*, 559.

Chapter 15

1. OR 40 (1), 48, 142–144, 151. When confronted with this rather outrageous position at the court of inquiry, Meade admitted to a "discrepancy in testimony" regarding the statement. He felt anyone cognizant of the facts "would know … [h]e never meant to say … [h]e did not know that there was no enemy anywhere." He claimed that he knew that when the Crater "was occupied a number of prisoners were taken," and that "the enemy occupied their lines both on the right and on the left of the position occupied by General Burnside," and that there was "a report of captured colors and that an attack had been made in front of Griffin." He claimed, rather, that at the time, his whole attention was absorbed in the endeavor to have a charge made to the crest, and his "thoughts were all upon that; and when … [he] said this was the intimation … [he] had of there being any enemy in the front … [he] meant any enemy so situated as to prevent a direct assault upon the crest." He also attempted to claim that the sheer volume of dispatches clouded his memory as to the sequence of events, and that the actual stated time of the dispatches may have been totally inaccurate due to "inaccuracies in keeping time on the part of messengers, writers and note takers" (OR 40 (1), 56).

2. OR 40 (1), 63, 67; *JCCW*, 26.

3. OR 40 (1), 57; Cannan, 71–72.

4. Porter, *Campaigning with Grant*, 266.

5. Katcher, 179–181; Pleasants, *Inferno*, 136; Porter, *Campaigning with Grant*, 266–268; Palmer, 163; Trudeau, *Last Citadel*, 116–117; Marvel, *Burnside*, 406.

6. OR 40 (1), 51, 57, 152, 155, Cannan, 71–72.

7. OR 40 (1), 57, 144, 148, 152; Stevenson, 14–15.

8. Many of the rank and file in the Ninth and Eighteenth Corps believed that Meade's animus when it came to Burnside and his poor treatment of the general was caused by jealousy on Meade's part. Private Lyman Barton of the 8th Connecticut indicated that "I think it was jelousey [*sic*] between the Generals one is afraid that he will do something that the other will get praise for or give them a chance to do something more than they can do if they would work to gather…." Others noted that Burnside "Could not show himself along the line but what he was saluted with cheers by all the troops. Gen. Meade could ride the whole day among his men, they scarcely deigning to notice him. Hence the popularity of Burnside was galling to Meade's jealous heart and he desired to see Burnside put down" (Parker, *History of the 51st Regiment of P.V. and V.V.*, 574–575; Lyman A. Barton letter of August 12, 1864, *Barton Family Papers*, Vermont History Center, Vermont Historical Society, Barre, VT).

9. Meade later explained that he did not mean to impugn Burnside's veracity or to suppose "for an instant that he would tell me what was not true." All Meade claimed that he meant was "If you know this, you are naturally reluctant to acknowledge it; and in order to give you an opportunity to do so, I will make my request as urgent and emphatic as possible." (This from a man who approved a plan to excavate a 500 foot tunnel, and refused to furnish shovels to those charged with executing the plan!) Meade claimed that there might have been some difficulty in getting the Ninth Corps forward, "either from the enemy's fire or some imaginary obstacle the troops had to encounter … and began to suppose there was some reason for the delay [in moving on Cemetery Hill] which had not been officially reported. I considered it natural that General Burnside would be indisposed to make it known, so long as he had hopes of overcoming the difficulty." Meade indicated that, as commander, he needed to know the facts, because if the men could not carry the crest promptly by a *coup-de-main*, then they needed to be withdrawn as quickly and safely as possible (*JCCW*, 36, 55). Burnside was livid with the dispatch at the time, but later changed his initial assessment that it questioned his veracity (*JCCW*, 25). Orlando Willcox tried to reconcile these two stubborn individuals before the issue went too far. He wrote his wife on August 8, 1864, that Burnside was as "confident as ever in his old theory of right prevailing in the end, & thinks that his good intentions & honest zeal in the service will finally put to flight all the slanders of his enemies." However, Willcox related that his efforts to reconcile the two had failed: "There were too many points of ill feeling between them. M. has preferred charges against B." Meade had since explained what he meant by his words to Willcox, but he did not authorize Willcox to communicate this to Burnside. Warren went on to say that, for his part, Burnside would not withdraw his offensive remarks without an explanation from Meade, and "it forms now one of the charges against him. I think he is very sorry that he did not take my advice & retract. I did not think I should have allowed the affair to rest, but I found there were so many grudges & charges on other points that the quarrel was bound to come. Those we know are thus reluctant to get involved" (Scott, *Forgotten Valor*, 562–64).

10. Burnside later argued that the reason he did not present specific arguments as to why his men could still take Cemetery Hill was because Meade had asked for none, and his orders were final, in any event (OR 40 (1), 65).

11. Marve, *Burnside*, 405–407; OR 40 (1), 49, 64–65; Cavanaugh, *Battle of the Crater*, 92; JCCW, 57–58; Porter, *Campaigning with Grant*, 267–268; Agassiz, 200–201.

12. While this was true at one time, it was not the case at the time of the argument.

13. OR 40 (1), 49, 65, 87; Porter, 268; Marvel, *Burnside*, 407; Agassiz, 201.

14. OR 40 (1), 65–66; Marvel, *Burnside*, 406–407; Cavanaugh, *Battle of the Crater*, 97; JCCW, 57–58.

15. Meade later testified that he expected to be informed of anything that should occur, and that, despite this impression, he remained in ignorance of any further transactions until 6:00 or 7:00 P.M. that evening (OR 40 (1), 49).

16. Hassler, 221–222; Mahone, 8–9; Davis, *Death in Trenches*, 86–87.

17. The 64th Georgia was technically under the command of Captain Thomas Pritchett on July 30. Colonel John Evans had returned from furlough "one or two days behind his time." The rules of the army required that no officer should take his command "until so permitted by General Lee." Thus, he went into action that day as a mere "volunteer" (James Madison Folsom, *Heroes and Martyrs of Georgia: Georgia's Record in the Revolution of 1861* (Macon, GA: Burke, Boykin, 1864), 102).

18. Colonel Ambrose Ransom Wright, commander of Wright's brigade, was on sick leave for the month of July 1864. He was eventually determined to be unfit for field service and took a command in Augusta, Georgia, for the duration of the war.

19. Folsom, 69–78, 82–92, 94–95, 97–103.

20. Ibid., 76–78, 91, 101–102.

21. Some commentators on the charge of Mahone's division, particularly Weisiger, contended that Mahone was not active in the charge itself, and remained in relative safety in the rear. Such a contention was vigorously rebutted by most of the participants in the action that day, and many sources indicate that Mahone was present with the Virginians within minutes of the brigade's reoccupation of their trenches. Captain W.A.S. Taylor of the 61st Virginia indicated that "In a very few minutes thereafter General Mahone was at that portion of the works occupied by the 61st Virginia, and I heard him remark that "The work is not over,

and that we must retake the balance of the line.'" T.H. Hines of Company B, 16th Virginia stated emphatically that "Mahone was near us in the fight...." When Hines' brother fell by his side in the retaken line, Mahone spoke to him, directing Hines to take his brother back to the surgeons, and gave him directions on finding the way out. W.W. Caldwell of the 12th Virginia also wrote of seeing Mahone in the brigade's forward lines within five minutes after the charge (Claiborne, 236; Bernard, "Great Battle of the Crater," 209–210). Thus, there remains little doubt that Billy Mahone was up front with his beloved Virginians as they reestablished the lines north of the Crater.

22. Cavanaugh, *Battle of the Crater*, 92–93; Lowry, *Fate of the Country*, 278; Davis, *Death in Trenches*, 86; Mahone, 9; Pleasants, *Inferno*, 138.

23. Wheeler, *Fields of Fury*, 285; William H. Etheredge, "Another Story of the Crater Battle," *Southern Historical Society Papers*, vol. 37 (1909): 205–06; Mahone, 9–10; Cavanaugh, *Battle of the Crater*, 93; Gould, 249; Bernard, *War Talks*, 215–216; McCabe, "Defence of Petersburg," 292; Bernard, "Battle of the Crater," 160; Folsom, 102–103; OR 40 (1), 567, 579; Houston, 349; Elliott, "Elliott's Brigade," 23.

24. Marvel, *Race of the Soil*, 271–72; Marvel, "And Fire Shall Devour Them," 132–34.

25. Parker, *History of the 51st Regiment of P.V. and V.V.*, 577; Wilkinson, *Mother, May You*, 256–257; Lord, 501; Horn, 117; OR 40 (1), 575, 579; Anderson, 182; Aston, 103; Scott, *Forgotten Valor*, 553.

26. Bernard, *War Talks*, 162; Elwell, 56; Henderson, 84; Etheredge, " Another Story of the Crater," *Confederate Veteran*, 167; Steward, *Pair of Blankets*, 157; Folsom, 92, 103, Stevenson, 13; OR 40 (1), 792, Blumberg, "Old Dominion Brigade," 29; Bernard, "Battle of the Crater," 16; Stone, 198.

27. Mahone, 10; Davis, *Death in Trenches*, 87–88; Aston, 102–103; Lowry, *Fate of the Country*, 278; Henderson, 84; Cavanaugh, *Battle of the Crater*, 93.

28. Cutcheon, 135–136, 143–144; Woodord, 97; Cavanaugh, *Battle of the Crater*, 93; Herek, 223–24; Marvel, *Race of the Soil*, 272; Scott, *Forgotten Valor*, 261; OR 40 (1), 579.

29. There exists a discrepancy as to the timing of the final charge. Many, such as Bernard, place the time at 1:00 P.M. However, many others assert it was not until 2:00 P.M. The weight of authority rests with an attack which commenced at 2:00 P.M. References to an earlier time may rest with imperfect memory, time changes or some combination thereof. Johnson placed

the charge at 2:00 P.M. in his report (OR 40 (1), 792).

30. Marvel, *Race of the Soil*, 266; Wise, *End of an Era*, 358–359; Elwell, 56; Cavanaugh, *Battle of the Crater*, 93–94; Charles M. Cummings, *Yankee Quaker, Confederate General, The Curious Career of Bushrod Rust Johnson* (Rutherford, NJ: Fairleigh Dickinson University Press, 1971), 22–34; Bernard, *War Talks*, 216; Mahone, 10; OR 40 (1), 792; Marvel, "And Fire Shall Devour Them," 134.

31. Burbank, 289–290; Blumberg, 29; Albert, 155; Woodford, 197–198; OR 40 (1), 555; *Utica Daily Observer*, August 2, 1864, pg. 1; Lord, 491–92; Powell, "Tragedy of the Crater," 772; Gould, 238; Smith, *Black Soldiers In Blue* 60.

32. OR 40 (1), 575; Jackson, 316; Aston, 103–06; Dowdy, *Lee*, 497; Anderson, 182–83; Lord, 489, 501; Wilkinson, *Mother, May You*, 256–57; Albert, 158, Committee of the Regiment, 237, 283.

33. Some placed the temperature at up to 105 degrees Fahrenheit that day (Marvel, *Race of the Soil*, 273). Others claim it was well over 90 degrees (Powell, "Tragedy of the Crater," 772). Sergeant Howard Aston of the 13th Ohio Cavalry claimed that he personally read the thermometer that indicated 110 degrees when he returned to division headquarters that afternoon (Aston, 108).

34. Anderson, 181–182; Alexander, *Fighting*, 459; Wilkinson, *Mother, May You*, 257–258; Katcher, 182; Gross, 335; Mahone, 11; Cutcheon, 143; Coffin, *Four Years of Fighting*, 382; Wheeler, *Fields of Fury*, 285; Marvel, *Race of the Soil*, 273; Powell, "Tragedy of the Crater," 772; Davis, *Death in Trenches*, 86; Newberry, 120.

35. Randall's unit was the 14th New York Heavy Artillery.

36. Herek, 225; Albert, 155–156; Blumberg, 29; Loving, 128; Powell, "Tragedy of the Crater," 772: Gould, 239.

37. There were also some Indians numbered among the USCT troops, as from the whites' perspective, "colored" meant Indians as well as blacks. For example, Private Austin George was a Mashantucket Pequot from southeastern Connecticut and served as a member of the 31st USCT that day (Hauptman, 144).

38. Herek, 226, 232–234; Hauptman, 155; Elwood, 59; Claiborne, 228. The 1st Michigan Sharpshooters used the Sharps NM 1859 breechloaders. Only a handful of their original headcount were left at the inception of the battle (Hauptman, 143). While 155 were listed as available that day, only ninety officers and men went into the

action (Herek, 234). The unit had suffered greatly at Spotsylvania and the Wilderness but never faltered, "sounding the war-whoop with every volley, and their unerring aim quickly taught the rebels they were standing on dangerous ground...."

39. Aston, 104; Albert, 158; Cavanaugh, *Battle of the Crater*, 95; Davis, 86.

40. Aston, 105; Marvel, *Race of the Soil*, 274.

41. Other sources, however, later claimed that only one out of four made it back to the Federal lines through the gauntlet that afternoon (Bernard, *War Talks*, 160).

42. Anderson, 183; Lord, 489, 492; Marvel, *Race of the Soil*, 274–276; Marvel, "And Fire Shall Devour Them," 136; Shearman, 395; Aston, 105; Bernard, *War Talks*, 174.

43. Aston, 105; Bernard, *War Talks*, 174; Anderson, 183; Day, "Battle of the Crater," 356; Coffin, *Four Years of Fighting*, 197; Kreutzer, 218; Lord, 492; Houston, 349; Marvel, "And Fire Shall Devour Them," 136; Marvel, *Race of the Soil*, 274–276; Anderson, 183.

44. Cutcheon, 143; Rogers, "Crater Battle, 30th July, 1864," 13; Jackman, 316–317; Marvel, *Race of the Soil*, 273–76; Wilkinson, *Mother, May You*, 257–258; Bernard, *War Talks*, 160.

45. Albert, 156–57; Marvel, *Race of the Soil*, 273; Cogswell, 442; Goss, 336.

46. Cutcheon, 143; Woodford, 198; Newberry, 120, Humphreys, *Virginia Campaign*, 262; OR 40 (1), 579, OR 40 (3), 663; Marvel, *Race of the Soil*, 273; Kilmer, 776; Albert, 157; Marvel, "And Fire Shall Devour Them," 134–135; Trudeau, "Chaos in the Crater," 32; JCCW, 193; Pierce, 39–40.

47. Shaw, 30; Powell, "Tragedy of the Crater," 771; Marvel, *Race of the Soil*, 273. Burnside, when he met with his other commanders, had endorsed the idea of a trench being dug out to the Crater to afford protection for the beleaguered troops in their attempt to safely traverse no-man's-land. Thus, the idea may have later been abandoned as impractical, either because the exigencies of the situation proved there was not enough time to accomplish such an undertaking, or because the tools to implement such a task were not at hand. However, it is doubtful the "idea" would have been treated with "disfavor."

48. Cutcheon later received a promotion to brevet brigadier general for his brave actions and initiative that day.

49. OR 40 (1), 575, 590; Cutcheon, 143–44; Herek, 225–26; Woodford, 197–98; Katcher, 181; Scott, *Forgotten Valor*, 553; Kilmer, 776; Marvel, *Race of the Soil*, 276; Scott, *Petersburg Story*, 199; Anderson, 211.

50. Gregory A. Coco, ed., *Through Blood and Fire: The Civil War Letters of Major Charles J. Mills, 1862–1865* (Gettysburg, PA: Gregory A. Coco, 1982), 139; Pleasants, *Inferno*, 138.

51. Coco, 139; Committee of the Regiment, 238; Anderson, 211; Pierce, 41.

52. Houghton was awarded the Medal of Honor for his "conspicuous gallantry" that day.

53. Katcher, 181; Shaw, 30–31; Beyer, *Deeds of Valor*, 387.

Chapter 16

1. John C. Featherston, "Graphic Account of the Crater," *Southern Historical Society Papers* 33 (1905): 359; John C. Featherston, "Battle of the Crater as I Saw It," *Confederate Veteran* 14, no. 1 (Nashville January, 1906): 23; Robertson, 293; Mangham, 307; Walsh, *Damage Them All You Can*, 395; Mahone, 7–10; Freeman, *Lee*, 475; Barnwell, 178; Harrill, 57; Wilson, 418; Blumberg, 29.

2. Cadmus Marcellus Wilcox graduated from West Point in 1846, a class which included such notables as George McClellan, Stonewall Jackson, George Gordon, A.P. Hill, George Pickett, John Gibbon and George Stoneman. Ten from that class became Confederate generals and twelve became Union generals, out of a total of thirty-four who participated in the war. Wilcox was commanding a brigade by the time of Second Manassas. Following a very successful record, he was promoted to major general in A.P. Hill's III Corps in January 1864 and thereafter performed admirably in all the major battles in the Overland Campaign (John C. Waugh, *Class of 1846 from West Point to Appomattox: Stonewall Jackson, George McClellan and Their Brothers* (New York: Warner Books, 1994), x.

3. Walsh, *Damage Them All You Can*, 396. Sanders was killed on August 21, 1864, at the Battle of Globe Tavern along the Weldon Railroad when a minie ball severed the femoral artery in both legs, causing him to bleed to death. He was subsequently interred in Hollywood Cemetery in Richmond.

4. Featherston, "Graphic Account of the Crater Battle," 359; Featherston, "Battle of the Crater as I Saw It," 23.

5. Every regiment in the brigade was present and surrendered at Appomattox. The 9th surrendered six officers and seventy men, the 10th ten officers and 208 men. The 11th Alabama surrendered a total of 125 officers and men, while the 14th had but seventy to eighty left at the time.

6. Most observers would agree

that the Georgia Brigade did not carry its objective, despite a noble attempt under a withering fire, thereby requiring the Alabama Brigade to "finish the job." However, some, particularly those from the brigade itself later contended that they had actually obtained their objective. One soldier wrote to the *Augusta Chronicle* and the *Petersburg Express* that the "'portion [of the brigade] which was unmasked' had charged and planted their colors on the works that were their objective. He also contended that this brigade had suffered a higher number of casualties than any other in Mahone's division" (J. Cutler Andrews, *The South Reports the Civil War* (Princeton, NJ: Princeton University Press, 1970), 412).

7. The final charge began at 1:00 P.M., according to Colonel McMaster. Many Federals later placed the retreat at 2:00 P.M., "but this refers to the many who ran back before ... [the Confederates] got the prisoners out of the crater" (McMaster, "Battle of the Crater," 122). As previously discussed, the weight of authority suggests the Alabamians actually commenced their attack at 2:00 P.M.

8. Clark, "Alabamians in the Crater Battle," 68; Mangham, 307; Bernard, *War Talks*, 216; McCabe, 292; Wilson, 419.

9. Featherstone, "Graphic Account of the Crater Battle," 359–361; Robertson, *A.P. Hill*, 293; Pleasants, *Inferno*, 144; Harrill, 58; Featherston, "Battle of the Crater as I Saw It," 23; N.J. Floyd, "Concerning Battle of the Crater," *Confederate Veteran* 16, no. 4 (1911), 159; Freeman, *Lee*, 475.

10. Contrary to some reports, Mahone did not order his men to show no quarter to the black troops, though "Sander's men decided that point" for themselves (Vance, 178).

11. 1:00 P.M. by other accounts, as previously indicated.

12. Featherston, "Incidents of the Battle of the Crater," *Confederate Veteran* 14, no. 108; Clark, "Alabamians in the Crater Battle," 68; Mangham, 307; Pleasants, *Inferno*, 144; Robertson, *A.P. Hill*, 293; Stone, 199, Vance, 178. It was later determined that the soldier was probably Smith Lipscomb of the 18th South Carolina (Stone, 199).

13. In view of other accounts of the action, the time of the assault was most probably 2:00 P.M.

14. Gould, 251; Clark, "Alabamians in the Crater," 69; Mangham, 307; Wilson, 419.

15. Marvel, *Race of the Soil*, 277.

16. Featherston, "Battle of the Crater as I Saw It," 24, Featherston, "Graphic Account of the Crater Battle," 362–363; Clark, "Alabamians in the Crater Battle," 68–69; Gould, 251–252, 270;

Marvel, *Race of the Soil*, 277; Freeman, *Lee*, 3: 476; Mangham, 307; Robertson, *A.P. Hill*, 293; Harrill, 59; Vance, 178; Trudeau, *Last Citadel*, 122; Burton, 94; Stevenson, 14; OR 40 (1), 792.

17. Freeman, *Lee*, 3: 476; Featherston, "The Battle of the Crater," *Confederate Veteran* 34, no. 8 (1926): 24; Williams, *Rebel Brothers* 116; Lewellyn Shaver, *A History of the Sixteenth Alabama Regiment Gracie's Alabama Brigade* (Montgomery: Barret & Brown, 1867), 69; Featherston, "Battle of the Crater as I Saw It," 297; Featherston, "Graphic Account of the Crater Battle," 361–362, 364.

18. William Gordon McCabe, *Commonplace Book: McCabe Family Letters*, Virginia Historical Society, Richmond.

19. Featherston, "Graphic Account of the Crater Battle," 361–362; Kilmer, 775–776; Cavanaugh, *Battle of the Crater*, 98–99; Mangham, 308; Aston, 106; Bowley, "The Crater," Claiborne, 228; Haskell, *Haskell Memoirs*, 78.

20. OR 40 (1), 575, 795; Houghton, 562, Cavanaugh, *Battle of the Crater*, 99.

21. Featherston, "Graphic Account of the Crater Battle," 372; Albert, 158; Cavanaugh, *Battle of the Crater*, 99; Marvel, *Race of the Soil*, 277; Bowley, "The Petersburg Mine," 37–39; Bowley, *A Boy Lieutenant*, 85–86; Bruce A. Suderow, "The Battle of the Crater: the Civil War's Worst Massacre," *Civil War History* 43, no. 3 (1997): 4

22. Featherston, "Battle of the Crater as I Saw It," 297; Alexander, *Robert E. Lee's Civil War*, 290: Mangham, 308; Clark, "Alabamians in the Crater Battle," 68; Robertson, *A.P. Hill*, 293; Harrill, 60; Featherston, "Graphic Account of the Crater Battle," 364; Wilkinson, 258; P.M. Vance, "Incidents in the Crater Battle," *Confederate Veteran* 14, no. 1 (1906), 178; Etheredge, 167. In the years following the battle, a controversy arose among the men of Mahone's division as to the role played by the Alabama Brigade. George T. Rogers, who commanded the 6th Virginia in Mahone's counterattack, wrote an account of that action in 1895. In the course of this commentary, he referred to the work of the Alabamians as a "walkover," given the damage which had already been effected by Mahone's other two brigades, as well as the fact that they provided supporting fire which kept all the Union heads down while the Alabamians charged. Instead, according to George Clark, who was assistant adjutant to General Sanders that day, the number of killed and wounded of that brigade would attest to the opposite. Rather, "[w]ith a handful of men more than treble its numbers were captured, the lines re-established, and what promised at early

dawn the closing victory of the war for the enemy, was turned into disastrous defeat by a few ragged Alabamians." The other two brigades did not go into the crater as the Alabamians did (according to Clark), in one of the "hardest fought fields of the war." Rogers later attempted to amend his characterization, stating that he used the term "comparatively," given the losses suffered by his regiment and brigade (Rogers, "The Crater Battle, 30th July, 1864," 13–14; Clark, "Alabamians in the Crater Battle," 69; George T. Rogers, "Crater Battle: Reply to Mr. Clark," *Confederate Veteran* 3, no. 5 (1895): 137; Harrill, 61).

23. Mangham, 308; Vance, 178; Wilson, 417.

24. Wilson, 417–418; Williams, *Rebel Brothers*, 115–116; J.H. Segars and Charles Kelly, eds., *Black Southerners in the Confederate Armies* (Atlanta: Southern Lion Books, 2001), 125.

25. Power, 138–139; Haskell, *Haskell Memoirs*, 77–78; Trudeau, *Like Men of War*, 246; Mangham, 308; Kevin M. Levin, "The Earth Seemed to Tremble," *America's Civil War* 19, no. 2 (2006): 26; Phillips, "Wilcox's Alabamians in Virginia," 490.

26. Albert, 158–159; Marvel, *Race of the Soil*, 277; Cannan, 138; Parker, *History of the 51st Regiment of P.V. and V.V.*, 576; Ervine T. Case, "Battle of the Mine," *MOLLUS* (Broadfoot Publishing, 1993), 302; Wilkinson, *Mother, May You*, 259; Coffin, *Four Years of Fighting*, 380.

27. One of the members of the 25th North Carolina who was wounded in the neck in the final fighting in the Crater that day was W.P. Inman. The book *Cold Mountain* by Charles Frazier was loosely based upon the journey of Inman following the battle of the Crater. The movie adaptation of this book opened with a dramatic scene over eleven minutes in length depicting the battle in great detail. The movie, directed by Anthony Minghella, was filmed largely in Romania, where approximately 1,000 soldiers of the Romanian army served as the Federal and Confederate soldiers. Unlike their contemporary American counterparts, these men tended to be younger and leaner, almost gaunt, similar to the average soldiers photographed by Matthew Brady during the Civil War. The soldiers were trained in tactics and drill using Hardee's Light Infantry Tactics as a guide to insure accuracy. Minghella used historical and military consultants Brian Pohanka, Michael Kraus and John Bert, along with uniform and accoutrement expertise from famed Civil War artist Don Troiani. A full-size reproduction of the Crater was utilized on the eleven-

week filming of this battle (*Washington Post*, December 24, 2003, C01). See Richard W. Peuser and Trevor K. Plante, "Cold Mountain's Inman: Fact Versus Fiction," *Prologue* (National Archives and Records Administration) 36, no. 2, (Summer 2004): 6–7.

28. Clark, *North Carolina Regiments and Battalions*, 3: 141–43; Garland Ferguson, "Henry Grady's Father in the Battle of the Crater," *Confederate Veteran* 1, no. 11 (1893): 326. George Clark later contended that no units except the Alabama Brigade entered the Crater that day during the battle. Many contemporary authorities disputed this assertion (Clark, "Alabamians in the Crater," 69).

29. Jackman, 322; Kilmer, 776; A.M. Gambone, *Major-General John Frederick Hartranft, Citizen Soldier and Pennsylvania Statesman* (Baltimore: Butternut and Blue, 1995), 107–09; Shaw, 31; Case, 303; Cutcheon, 144; Katcher, 181–82: Gavin, 521.

30. Clark, "Alabamians In the Crater," 69; Mangham, 308; Alexander, *Robert E. Lee's Civil War*, 477; Harrill, 60; Glatthaar, *Forged in Battle*, 156.

31. Bowley, "The Petersburg Mine," 39; Katcher, 182.

32. Mahone, 11; Jones, *The Army of Northern Virginia*, 162; McCabe, 293.

33. Wilson, 425.

34. Gregg had left Bartlett with the intention of procuring water from the Federal lines, but was unable to get back in before the Crater fell.

35. OR 40 (1), 555–56; Albert, 158; Anderson, 183, 188, 211; Houston, 191; Alexander, *Fighting*, 460; Harrill, 60; Cannan, 140; Mahone, 12; Featherston, "Graphic Account of the Crater Battle," 365; Clark, "Alabamians in the Crater," 69; Gould, 253; Jackman, 322.

36. Bowley, "The Petersburg Mine," 39.

37. Marvel, "And Fire Shall Consume Them,"137.

38. Prior to the retreat, Lieutenant William T. Ackerson engaged in sharpshooting at the Confederate battery to their right (probably Wright's), while exposed on the hillside outside the Crater. When the 51st New York moved back, Ackerson tripped on a wire and fell headlong into the ravine. Not being disposed to run the gauntlet from this position, he found himself ministering to the multitude of wounded he encountered in that ravine, as there was a spring from which he was able to afford some comfort to the wounded on that extremely hot day. While he was between the lines, Ackerson also found time to make entries in his journal, providing an extemporaneous account of some of the day's events (William T. Ackerson, Diary, *William T. Ackerson Papers, 1861–1914*, Mon-

mouth County Historical Association Library and Archives, Freehold, NJ).

39. Hogan paid tribute to the men of the 6th Virginia, notwithstanding the loss of their colors, as "men who would charge through a fire like the one we gave them are worthy of the name of soldiers in the full meaning of the term" (Albert, 376).

40. Alexander, *Robert E. Lee's Civil War*, 290; Bernard, *War Talks*, 174; OR 40 (1), 550, 564, 575; Albert, 376; Marvel, *Race of the Soil*, 277.

41. Lanman, 377; Aston, 106–107; Herek, 277–228; OR 40 (1), 553, 589–590, 754 ; Woodford, 197–198; Case, 302; Loving, 127–28.

42. OR 40 (1), 248–49, 699–705; Sylvester, 100; Anderson, *Landmarks of Rensselear County*, 121; Clark, *Iron Hearted Regiment*, 152–155; Palmer, 163–164; William Hyde letter, *William L. Hyde Papers*; JCCW, 102; Longacre, *Antietam to Fort Fisher*, 204, 277–278.

43. The muster roll of the unit for April 1865 reported Hill as having died of disease April 10, 1865, at Danville Prison (Shaw, 31).

44. OR 40 (1), 536–37; Shaw, 31; Private Alfred A. Saunders letter to parents, September 10, 1864, *Civil War Letters of Fannie Austin*, www.free pages.genealogy.rootsweb.com/~snu gaza/Austin/index.html.

45. Stevenson, 18; Ethan S. Morehead letter of August 16, 1864, *Daily Herald*, Old Court House Museum, Vicksburg, MS, www.100thpenn.com. A large portion of the top half of the canton and most of the five upper stripes, including the designation "100th Regt. P.V.," was shot away from the rest of the flag. It fell in the dirt of the Crater and was retrieved by Captain R.L. Kirby of the 16th Virginia. When the 100th's color bearer fell, Lieutenant Richard P. Craven seized what was left of the colors and they were given to Captain James L. McFeeters for safekeeping. When the 100th retreated, McFeeters carried back what remained of the flag, and many in the unit thereby contended that their banner was never captured. After the war, the missing (captured) portion was returned by the War Department and was pieced back together with the remnant held by the State of Pennsylvania.

46. Wilkinson, *Mother, May You*, 260–62; Marvin, 279; Anderson, 184–185, 191–192. A very touching story involves Sergeant Parks of Company A, who was ill on the day of the battle and whose condition deteriorated rapidly thereafter as a prisoner of war. As he lingered in prison dying a slow death, rumors abounded of a prisoner exchange, which he grasped onto "like a drowning man." Finally, a list was published of the names of those to be exchanged and everyone listened breathlessly. Unfortunately, Parks was not called. "Turning sadly away, it seemed as if the last ray of hope had disappeared and he was to be left to a lingering death." Then a comrade, Private Francis M. Harrington of Company K, heard his name called. Aware of Parks' frail condition, and knowing how devastated he would become at the failure to be chosen and that remaining in prison would be a sure death for Parks, Harrington stepped aside and gave his place to him. Parks was later exchanged in his place. Unfortunately, Parks died on September 19, 1864, after reaching Annapolis. Harrington remained in prison until 1865, and by the time he was finally discharged, he was entirely broken in heath (Anderson, 191–192).

47. OR 40 (1), 247, 546–547, OR 40 (3), 666–667; Cavanaugh, *Battle of the Crater*, 102; Marvel, *Race of the Soil*, 277–278; Case, 302; Lord, 507–512; Marvel, "And Fire Shall Devour Them," 138; Cogswell, 512; Marvel, *Burnside*, 408.

48. Albert, 158; OR 40 (1), 555–556.

49. Houston, 360, 365–366; Chase, 27; OR 40 (1), 247, 551; Allen, 289–291; Committee of the Regiment, 239–240.

50. In the charge of the Light Brigade at Balaklava, Lord Cardigan took in 673 men and lost 113 killed and 134 wounded, or a casualty rate of 36.7 percent. William F. Fox, "The Chances of Being Hit in Battle," *Century Magazine* 36, no. 1 (1888): 98. Fox cited the casualty rate of the 37th Wisconsin as 57 percent.

51. Bush received a commission to first lieutenant two days later. However, it was a number of months before he could put on his bars, as he remained in a Confederate prison (Cutcheon, 144; OR 40 (1), 589).

52. OR 40 (1), 247, 574–76, 578–80, 582–83, 586–87, 589–91; Cutcheon, 144; Scott, *Forgotten Valor*, 554; Eden, 32; Fox, "The Chances of Being Hit in Battle," 98; *Ypsilanti True Democrat*, August 12, 1864, 2; Herek, 227.

53. The Return of Casualties for the Crater in the Official Records later recorded the total second brigade losses as 772 (OR 40 (1), 248).

54. These figures of losses totaling about 322 men have been cited by a number of sources. See Smith, *Black Soldiers In Blue*, 61; Friend, 17; Glatthaar, *Forged in Battle*, 150. However, the Returns of Casualties from the *Official Records* reported the regiment's casualties as a total of 124, including 21 killed and 56 wounded. The discrepancy is hard to reconcile (326 versus 128). Obviously, a large number of stragglers must have made their way back to the unit. The number killed could be considerably greater than reported, as some missing could later be identified as dead.

55. Thomas, "Colored Troops," 781–782; OR 40 (1), 248; Hall, 245–247; Friend, 17. The Return of Casualties indicates fourteen killed and eighty-six wounded; another twenty-three were reported captured or missing. Thus, the number of killed could be somewhat greater (OR 40 (1), 248).

56. Smith, *Black Soldiers in Blue*, 61; Trudeau, *Like Men of War*, 247; Glatthaar, *Forged In Battle*, 150.

57. The white troops on the front line were losing approximately 30 men per day due to the continual sharpshooting. Thus on July 30, 1864, the troop strength would be down to approximately 8,723 men. See OR 40 (1), 60.

58. See Thomas, "Colored Troops," 777.

59. Total casualties numbered 3,798, including Turner's division of the Tenth Corps. On August 16, 1864, Meade had placed the total loss at 4,400 men (OR 40 (1), 166).

60. TROOP STRENGTH — NINTH CORPS:

	White	Black	Total
	8,723	4,300	13,023
As a Percentage:	67%	33%	
Killed:	263	209	472
Wounded:	947	697	1,644
Captured/ Missing:	935	421	1,356
Total:	2,145	1,327	3,472*

*plus three casualties in artillery

As a Percentage:

Killed:	56%	44%
Wounded:	58	42
Captured/ Missing:	69	31
Total:	62	38

(OR 40 (1), 247–48); William F. Fox, *Regimental Losses in the American Civil War, 1861–1865* (Albany: Albany Publishing, 1889), ch.6.

61. Statements of only seven black prisoners initially surviving appear to be grossly exaggerated. The 29th USCT alone had thirty-two taken prisoner that day, eighteen of whom died in Confederate camps. Thus, fourteen men of this one unit survived. See Drew E. VanderCreek, "African Americans, Race and Ethnicity in Illinois and the North During the Civil War," in *Illinois During the Civil War Digitization Project* (Dekalb: Northern Illinois University Libraries Digitization Unit, 2002).

62. A similar source puts the number at 423 killed (Suderow, "The Bat-

tle of the Crater," 219–20). This number seems flawed, as he initially cites Confederate claims of taking "only" 200 black soldiers prisoner, and then claims they took only eighty-five black prisoners. Many missing blacks may have been returned to their former owners after the battle, which would also account for the disparity between those missing who were not taken to Confederate prison camps.

63. Trudeau, *Like Men of War*, 247, 249; Glatthaar, *Forged in Battle*, 150.

64. His name was spelled "Nelloms" at the time on the report (Cavanaugh, *6th Virginia*, 53).

65. Suderow, "Confederate Casualties at the Crater," 26–33; Featherstone, "Graphic Account of the Crater Battle," 362; Cavanaugh, *Battle of the Crater*, 129; Blumberg, 29; OR 40 (1), 788, 754, 793; McMaster, "Battle of the Crater," 123; Cavanaugh, *6th Virginia*, 54; Power, 137; Jones, *Army of Northern Virginia*, 163; Burton, 93–94; Trask, 24;

66. The accounting is as follows: 6th Virginia: 1; 16th Virginia: 7; 41st Virginia: 2; 61st Virginia: 5; 8th Alabama: 1; 9th Alabama: 1; 11th Alabama: 1; 3rd Georgia: 1; 23rd South Carolina: 3; 59th Virginia: 2; 22nd South Carolina: 1; (OR 40 (1), 753–755, 791; Power, 137).

67. OR 40 (1), 791–93; Robertson, *A.P. Hill*, 294.

68. When Mahone reportedly spoke of refusing his long-overdue promotion to the permanent rank of major general, A.P. Hill enjoined him, "You cannot think of declining"(Hassler, 223).

69. Girardy's advancement from captain to brigadier marked the only time where this occurred in the Confederate army in the course of the war.

70. Featherston, "Graphic Account of the Crater Battle," 373–374; Davis, *Death in Trenches*, 88; Freeman, *Lee*, 477; Featherston, "Incidents of the Battle of the Crater," 108; Stewart, "The Carnage of the Crater," 86; Bernard, "The Battle of the Crater," 164; OR 40 (1), 752; Mahone, 11–12.

71. Chambers, 177; Pearce, 209–211; Roulhac, 73; Featherston, "Battle of the Crater as I Saw It," 297; Williams, *Rebel Brothers*, 116; Elwell, 59; Page, 134.

72. Houston, 360; Pierce, 41–42; Jackman, 322; Marvel, *Race of the Soil*, 279; Stewart, *Description of the Battle of the Crater*, 15; Wheeler, *Fields of Fury*, 286.

73. Mahone, 11; Stevenson, 13; Featherston, "Graphic Account of the Crater Battle," 364; Gould, 252; Pleasants, *Inferno*, 146; Burbank, 293–294; Weld, *War Diary and Letters*, 355.

74. Robertson, *A.P. Hill*, 294; Tru-

deau, *Like Men of War*, 249; Freeman, *Lee*, 3: 477; OR 40 (1), 753; Welburn J. Andrews, *A Sketch of Co. K, 23rd South Carolina Volunteers, in the Civil War, from 1862–1865* (Richmond, VA: Whittet & Shepperson, 1909), 23; Featherston, "Graphic Account of the Crater Battle," 373; Powell, "Tragedy of the Crater," 773.

75. Wise, *End of an Era*, 369; Bowley, "The Petersburg Mine," 39; Bowley, *A Boy Lieutenant*, 85; Burton, 95; Claiborne, *Seventy-Five Years in Old Virginia*, 208; Cavanaugh, *Battle of the Crater*, 172, ff5.

76. Clark, "Alabamians in the Crater," 69; Trudeau, *Like Men of War*, 247; Wise, *End of an Era*, 368; Sherman, *Battle of the Crater*, 15; Phillips, 490; Bowley, "The Petersburg Mine," 39–40; Cavanaugh, *Battle of the Crater*, 102; Wheeler, *Fields of Fury*, 285; Glatthaar, *Forged in Battle*, 159; Bowley, *Boy Lieutenant*, 85–86; Katcher, 182; Rickard, 29; Barton, *Civil War Soldiers*, 243.

77. But see Michael Horigan, *Elmira: Death Camp of the North* (Mechanicsburg, VA: Stackpole Books, 2002), for a chilling account of appalling, premeditated deprivation on the part of the United States' government regarding its prisoners of war.

78. Weld, *War Diary and Letters*, 358–360; Herek, 228; Cavanaugh, *Battle of the Crater*, 106; Bowley, "The Petersburg Mine," 40; Weld, "The Petersburg Mine," 211–212; *Baird Memoirs*, 20; Trudeau, *Like Men of War*, 247–48; Hall, 231.

79. Wise, *End of an Era*, 369–70; Haskell, *Haskell Memoirs*, 78–80.

80. At that time, enlisted prisoners were generally sent to Danville and officers to Columbia, South Carolina, as Andersonville was already too crowded to receive this many inmates at one time.

81. Baird, *Baird Memoirs*, 20; Bowley, *Boy Lieutenant*, 86; Weld, *War Diary and Letters*, 358–64; Trudeau, *Like Men of War*, 248.

82. OR 40 (1), 145–46, 575–76, OR 40 (3), 664, 666–67; Cannan, 77–78; Cavanaugh, *Battle of the Crater*, 102–03; *JCCW*, 24, 58–60; Marvel, *Burnside*, 408. Meade claimed he was totally ignorant of any further transactions following his departure from Burnside's headquarters at 11:00 A.M. following his order for the withdrawal of all troops from the battlefield. At 6:00 or 7:00 P.M., a "rumor" reached him that there were a number of Federal wounded lying between the Crater and the Federal lines. He indicated that Ord had made an appeal to him for some action to remove these men. He then indicated he was unaware of any difficulty in removing them, and did

not believe there should have been difficulty if Burnside still held the Crater. This prompted his dispatch to Burnside at 7:40 P.M. (*JCCW*, 58).

83. OR 40 (1), 145–146.

84. Ibid., 146.

85. OR 40 (1), 145–47, OR 40 (3), 700–02, 704–05; Marvel, *Burnside*, 409.

Chapter 17

1. Allen, 293; Featherston, "Graphic Account of the Crater Battle," 365; OR 40 (1), 664; Gould, 254–55; Kreutzer, 219; Burton, 95; Case, 306; Clark, *Iron Hearted Regiment*, 152–53.

2. Pullen, 219.

3. Rogers, "The Crater Battle, 30th July, 1864," 13–14.

4. Stone, 201; Gould, 254; Burton, 95; Day, "Battle of the Crater," 356.

5. Clark, *Iron Hearted Regiment*, 152–55, 160.

6. Aston, 108–09; Herek, 229; Featherston, "Graphic Account of the Crater Battle," 366; Case, 306; Loving, 128.

7. Burton, 95; George S. Bernard, "The Battle of the Crater, July 30, 1864," *Southern Historical Society Papers* 18 (January–December 1890): 19–20; Stewart, *Description of the Battle of the Crater*, 15; Houston, 188; Robertson, *A.P. Hill*, 294–295.

8. OR 40 (3), 701–703, 705; Marvel, Burnside, 408; Herek, 229; Gould, 254–55; N.J. Floyd, "Concerning Battle of the Crater," *Confederate Veteran* 16, no. 4 (1908): 159; Featherston, "Battle of the Crater," 298; Featherston, "Graphic Account of the Crater Battle," 366–67; Rickard, 30.

9. Gould, 255; OR 40 (3), 705–706, 821; Rickard, 30, Cavanaugh, *Battle of the Crater*, 104; Cuffel, 199; Carroll, 98; Elliott, "Elliott's Brigade," 26.

10. Bernard, "Battle of the Crater," 20, Marvel, "And Fire Shall Devour Them," 139; Cavanaugh, *Battle of the Crater*, 104.

11. It was actually Monday.

12. R. Lockwood Tower, ed., *Lee's Adjutant: The Wartime Letters of Colonel Walter Herron Taylor 1862–1865* (Columbia: University of South Carolina Press, 1995), 178; Cuffel, 199; Cavanaugh, *The Otey, Ringgold and Davidson Virginia Artillery*, 62; Trudeau, *Last Citadel,* 125; Gould, 256; Featherston, "Graphic Account of the Crater Battle," 165; Robertson, *A.P. Hill*, 295; Richmond *Dispatch*, August 3, 1864; OR 42 (2), 10.

13. Featherston, "Graphic Account of the Crater Battle," 367; Gould, 255; Rickard, 30; Wilkinson, *Mother, May You*, 262–63; Scott, *Petersburg Story*, 199–200; Henderson, 84–85; Feather-

ston, "Battle of the Crater as I Saw It," 26; Day, "Battle of the Crater," 356; Marvel, "And Fire Shall Devour Them," 139; Williams, *Rebel Brothers*, 116; C.W. Owen, *The First Michigan Infantry* (Quincy: Quincy Herald Print, 1903), 27; Allen, 292–293; Stone, 201–202; Bernard, "Battle of the Crater" 20; Robertson, *A.P. Hill*, 295; Stewart, *Pair of Blankets*, 165; Trudeau, *Like Men of War*, 248; Aston, 120; Burton, 95; OR 42 (2), 10–11; Cuffel, 199; Herek, 230–31.

14. Case, 306; *Richmond Dispatch*, August 3, 1864; Wilkinson, *Mother, May You*, 263; Cuffel, 199. Some attributed this stoicism, and the ability better to tolerate the conditions under which they suffered, to the blacks' former status as slaves, where conditions were generally harsher than those experienced by their white counterparts. See, Trudeau, *Like Men of War*, 248.

15. Stewart, *Pair of Blankets*, 165; Wheeler, *Fields of Fury*, 286; Henderson, 84–85; Featherston, "Battle of the Crater," 298; Featherston, "Graphic Account of the Crater Battle," 367; Trudeau, *Last Citadel*, 125; Featherston, "Battle of the Crater as I Saw It," 26; Chamberlayne, *Ham Chamberlayne*, 250; Agassiz, 203–204.

16. Cavanaugh, *The Otey, Ringgold and Davidson Virginia Artillery*, 62; Cuffel, 199–200; Tower, 179.

17. Featherston, "The Battle of the Crater as I Saw It," 26; Featherston, "Graphic Account of the Crater Battle," 367–70; Trudeau, *Last Citadel*, 125; Gould, 256; Robertson, *A.P. Hill*, 295; Featherston, "Battle of the Crater," 298; Trudeau, *Like Men of War*, 248.

18. As previously stated, an extra hour was added to the truce to insure that all burials could be completed.

19. Marvel, *Race of the Soil*, 279; Featherston, "Graphic Account of the Crater Battle," 370; Wheeler, *Fields of Fury*, 286; Herek, 231; Agassiz, 211; Ellwood, 61; Gould, 256; Day, "Battle of the Crater," 356; Scott, *Petersburg Story*, 199–200.

20. OR 42 (2), 63–64, 71, 1162–1163; Cavanaugh, *Battle of the Crater*, 107; W.W. Blackford, *War Years with Jeb Stuart* (New York: Scribner's, 1945), 266–71; Venable, "In the Trenches at Petersburg," 60–61; Derby, 363. The soon to be famous fortified position, Fort Steadman, was named in his honor. He was brevetted a brigadier general for gallantry and meritorious service as he lay dying in a field hospital in the Federal rear (OR 42 (2), 52, 56, 64, 69, 71, 82, 873).

21. Phoebe Yates Pember, *A Southern Woman's Story* (New York: C.W. Carleton, 1879), 105–106; Cavanaugh, *Battle of the Crater*, 105; Lowry, *Fate of the Country*, 279.

22. Carter, *Four Brothers in Blue*, 471–472; Catton, *A Stillness at Appomattox*, 252; *Kittochtinny Historical Society*, Franklin County, PA, Valley of the Shadow Project [etext.virginia.edu/etchin/civilwarlett-browsehead?id+F6084]; Porter, *Campaigning with Grant*, 269; Coco, 140–142; Lowry, *Fate of the Country*, 279; Lyman Barton letter, *Barton Family Papers*, Vermont Historical Society, Barre, VT.

23. Other contributory events may have included the Wade-Davis manifesto, the placement of a new $2 million loan, and Secretary of the Treasury Chase's resignation from the cabinet (Noah Brooks, "Two War-Time Conventions," *The Century Magazine* (March 1895): 729.

24. Brooks, "Two War-Time Conventions," 729; James W. Rawley, *Turning Points of the Civil War* (Lincoln: University of Nebraska Press, 1966), 183; Pollard, *Southern History of the War*, 336–337; William H. Stewart, "A Field of Blood Was the Crater," *Southern Historical Society Papers* 33 (1905): 354; Pollard, *Southern History of the War*, 538; Jones, *Army of Northern Virginia*, 164.

25. On August 6, General Lee and President Jefferson Davis did decide to send additional troops to Jubal Early to counter a threatened Union buildup. By August 14, most of Kershaw's division was positioned near Fort Royal, Virginia, in the Luray Valley (Heller, 124).

26. Stewart, "A Field of Blood Was the Crater," 354; Pollard, *Southern History of the Civil War*, 376–77; Scott, *Petersburg Story*, 200; Pollard, *Southern History of the War*, 538; Jones, *Army of Northern Virginia*, 164; Frassanito, 259; McCabe, "Defence of Petersburg," 295

27. Power, 139–40; McCabe, "Defence of Petersburg," 295; Jones, *Army of Northern Virginia*, 164; Elliott, "Elliott's Brigade," 27; Annette Tapert, ed., *The Brothers' War: Civil War Letters to Their Loved Ones from the Blue and Gray* (New York: Time Books, 1998), 210; Wheeler, *Fields of Fury*, 286.

28. Newspapers were generally equally divided in their opinion, depending upon their political leanings.

29. Newberry, 121; Elliott, "Elliott's Brigade," 27; Hopkins, 202; Tapert, 210; Smith, *Black Soldiers in Blue*, 61; Marvel, *Race of the Soil*, 280; Trudeau, *Like Men of War*, 250.

30. He did go on to support Meade's objection to that plan, however (*JCCW*, 111).

31. OR 40 (1), 166, 528; Smith, *Black Soldiers in Blue*, 61; *JCCW*, 111; Rickard, 30; Ford, 171–172.

32. Lyman Barton letter, *Barton Family Papers*; Trudeau, *Like Men of*

War, 250; Albert, 139; Trudeau, "Chaos in the Crater," 33; Taylor, "The Crater," 58; Weld, "The Petersburg Mine," 219; Allan Nevins, ed., *A Diary of Battle: The Personal Journals of Colonel Charles S. Wainwright, 1861–1865* (New York: Harcourt, Brace & World, 1962), 443.

33. Orlando Willcox, in a letter to his wife on August 8th, exhibited a common feeling among the Ninth Corps veterans that the army "was glad to get a kick at the brave old dog now he is down," reflecting his views that the Ninth Corps was never considered an integral part of the Army of the Potomac (Scott, *Forgotten Valor*, 563).

34. See OR 40 (1), 77–78.

35. OR 40 (1), 17, 134, 171–72; Taylor, "The Crater," 58; Harrill, 61; Marvel, *Burnside*, 409; Ethan Rafuse, *George Gordon Meade and the War in the East* (Abilene: McWhiney Foundation Press, McMurry University, 1968), 142.

36. The word was "answerable" in the original OR 40 (1), 18.

37. OR 40 (1), 18, 42–43, 171–72; Humphreys, (*Virginia Campaign*, 264).

38. OR 40 (1), 531–32; *JCCW*, 25–26; Marvel, *Burnside*, 409–10; Agassiz, *Meade's Headquarters*, 94; Houston, 350.

39. OR 40 (1), 172–76, 531–532; Cogswell, 421; Houston, 351; Taylor, "The Crater," 58.

40. Henry Pleasants, *Inferno*, 148–149.

41. Ibid., 149–51.

42. Scott, *Forgotten Valor*, 562–564. The court of inquiry later found Willcox "answerable for want of success," concluding that more "energy might have been exercised ... to ... cause his troops to go forward" (OR 40 (1), 129; Scott, *Forgotten Valor*, 564).

43. While many might question the degree of his genuineness, Meade wrote his wife on August 10 that "I feel sorry for Burnside, because I really believe that man half the time don't know what he is about, and is hardly responsible for his acts" (Rafuse, 143).

44. OR 40 (1), 43–75, 94, 98; Cavanaugh, *Battle of the Crater*, 109.

45. OR 40 (1), 44, 53–54, 172–76, 531–32; Cogswell, 421; Marvel, *Burnside*, 410; Houston, 351; Taylor, "The Crater," 58. Burnside biographer William Marvel contends the board's decision was illogical in ruling that Burnside should have objected at the time the materials were offered, despite the fact that he was not present. He calls the decision a "technicality." However, given Burnside's knowledge that he was undoubtedly a major focus of the investigation, and that Meade, without question, was out to damage him, it seems logical that he would have been present for Meade's testimony if at all possible. See Marvel, *Burnside*, 410.

46. Some of them, however, reported there was no physical obstacle in the way of a Federal success. See, e.g., OR 40 (1), 123.

47. OR 40 (1), 77–126.

48. OR 40 (1), 71, 80–81, 86, 108, 122.

49. OR 40 (1), 67; OR 42 (2), 44, 155; Cavanaugh, *Battle of the Crater*, 110.

50. OR 40 (1), 127–128.

51. OR 40 (1), 127–129; OR 42 (2), 641; Anderson, 226; Marvel, *Burnside*, 410–411.

52. Houston, 351; OR 40 (1), 127–128.

53. Marvel, *Burnside*, 411–12; *JCCW*, 111; OR 40 (1), 127–128.

54. Both Willcox and Bliss were much later awarded the Medal of Honor, Willcox in 1895 for gallantry at Manassas, and Bliss in 1898 for gallantry at Fredericksburg.

55. Marvel, *Burnside*, 413–418; OR 42 (1), 72; OR 42 (3), 624, 867, 896, 919; Marvel, *Race of the Soil*, 280; Cogswell, 421; Taylor, "The Crater," 58.

56. *JCCW*, 1, 30–76, 105–107, 110–111; Marvel, *Burnside*, 415; Cavanaugh, *Battle of the Crater*, 111.

57. *JCCW*, 91–93, 112–117.

58. *JCCW*, 1–12; Cavanaugh, *Battle of the Crater*, 111; Marvel, *Burnside*, 415.

59. *JCCW*, 11–12; Cavanaugh, *Battle of the Crater*, 111; Houston, 351–55; Hopkins, 208–209. Placing things in political perspective, the Joint Committee was principally composed of Radical Republicans who had adopted

Burnside as a protégé given his avoidance of the McClellan intrigues to the point of alienating McClellan and his faction. The congressmen were thus quite favorable to Burnside, but their bias did not throw them so far from the target as Hancock's court. While they may have looked the other way as to Burnside's loose hand with division commanders, and the fact that he had retained subordinates not measuring up to that sort of discretion, the court of inquiry had missed considerably more than that fact (Marvel, *Burnside*, 415–416).

Epilogue

1. Elwell, 61; Lowry, *Fate of the Country*, 279; Coffin, 381; Nevins, 469.

2. Longacre, 209; Stone, 202. The actual number of Federal guns engaged may have been higher, considering that many were not under the direct control of General Hunt or Colonel Abbot.

3. Scott, *Forgotten Valor*, 556; Wilkinson, *Mother, May You*, 263–64; *JCCW*, 24.

4. Walter Newberry cited one cause of the assault's failure to be Burnside's anomalous position, which allowed him to have his troops occupy an untenable position, thereby subjecting them to heavy losses. He indicated that Meade would not have allowed his other corps commanders such latitude (Newberry, 121). There appears to be little basis for this conclusion, however. Meade reigned Burnside in with

scathing admonitions on several occasions when he felt Burnside was usurping his authority by requesting that he be given authority to direct other troops in the advance. Certainly, Meade gave his other commanders plenty of authority that day to decide whether or not they could support Burnside's corps in the Crater, and acceded to their conclusions that they should not advance.

5. In point of fact, only the second division of the Tenth Corps was actually in place, and it was engaged.

6. Barton, *Barton Family Papers*.

7. Allen, 292; See *JCCW*, 107–108.

8. OR 40 (1), 80, 122; Wise, *End of an Era*, 356–57.

9. Wise, *End of an Era*, 357; Newberry, 121; Wilkinson, *Mother, May You*, 264; Gould, 241.

10. Gould, 241; Lowry, *Fate of the Country*, 279; *JCCW*, 110; Wilkinson, *Mother, May You*, 264.

11. General Potter was at the front for a portion of the action, as was General Turner, though he was not under Burnside's command.

12. *JCCW*, 110; Barnwell, 178.

13. The unit served as provost guard on Meade's staff in the Army of the Potomac.

14. Ford, 174; Wise, *End of an Era*, 357; Wilkinson, *Mother, May You*, 265.

15. Nationwide, not just the Virginia campaign.

16. Allen, 293.

Bibliography

Manuscripts, Letters and Diaries

Duke University, Special Collections Library, Durham, NC

Eugene Verdery, Jr. Papers, 1859–1870: James Paul Verdery letter to sister.
William Mahone. Papers.

East Carolina Manuscript Collection, J.Y. Joyner Library, East Carolina University, Greenville, NC

J.M. Cutchin. "A Soldier's Story," Cutchin Family Collection.
_____. Letter dated January16, 1915, Cutchin Family Collection.

Huntington Library

U.S. Grant to Henry Halleck, August 1, 1864.
U.S. Grant to George Meade, August 1, 1864.

Library of Congress

Hunt, Henry J. Papers.
Wilcox, Cadmus. Papers.

Monmouth County Historical Association Library and Archives

William T. Ackerson Papers, 1861–1914: William T. Ackerson diary.

Museum of the Confederacy, Eleonor S. Brackenbough Library, Richmond, VA

Barksdale, Andrew Sydnor, Cpl. (Halifax Artillery). Letter dated August 1, 1864.
Hawse, Joseph, Sgt. (14th Virginia). Diary.
Hicks, Robert W. Hicks (34th Virginia). Diary.
Mauney, William Andrew, Pvt. (28th North Carolina). Diary.
Stewart, William H. The Charge of the Crater: Personal Statements by Participants.
Trimmer, Theodore, Lt. Col. (41st Alabama). Letter dated May 22, 1864.
Winsmith, John Christopher, Cpt. (1st South Carolina). Letter dated June 22, 1864.

Navarro College, Pearce Civil War Collection, Corsicana, TX

A. [Unknown], John. Letter dated August 16, 1864.
Crawford, Lewis. Papers: Letter dated August 16, 1864.
Fenn, Austin. Papers: Letter dated May 14, 1864.
Hyde, William L. Papers: Letter dated August 1, 1864.

North Carolina Department of Cultural Resources, Raleigh, NC

Letters of Robert C. Mabry (6th Va. Inf.).

Old Courthouse Museum, Vicksburg, MS

Ethan S. Morehead letter transcribed from *Vicksburg Daily Herald*, August 16, 1864 (www.100thpenn.com)

Pennsylvania State Archives, Harrisburg, PA

John F. Hartranft Papers.

Petersburg National Battlefield, Petersburg, VA

Bearss, Edwin C. "Documentation for Troop Movement Maps for the Battle of the Crater, July 30, 1864" (1966).
Bishop, Carter R. "History of the Battle of the Crater."
Campbell, Charles. Diary entries, May 13 to July 22, 1864.
Guy, George W. "A List of Men Blown Up at the Crater Battle" (1937).
Harrison, Thomas. "Route of Mahone's Troops to the Crater Battlefield" (Nov. 1961).
Jackson, C.R. "Report on Artillery Operations in the Battle of the Crater."
Johnson, Bushrod Rust. Report of August 20, 1864. Cat. no. 281.
Morgan, George (48th Pa. Inf.).Letters.
Rich, Alonzo G. Letter dated July 31, 1864.
Russell, William. Diary.
Wallace, Lee A., Jr. "A History of Petersburg National Military Park" (1983).

South Caroliniana Library, University of South Carolina

Alexander, A.N. (Co. F., 22nd SC Inf.) "Twenty-Second South Carolina Infantry" Letter dated July 3, 1864
Elliott, Charles Pickney. "Elliott's Brigade: How It Held the Crater and Saved Petersburg" (reprint of address before Confederate Veterans Camp Hampton, December 15, 1895, Columbia, SC).

Elliott, Stephen, Jr. Letters: Elliott Family Papers.
Green, William B. Letter July 3, 1864 (probably August 3).
McMaster, Fitz William. Papers and Letters. "McMaster's Rejoinder to Brig. Gen. Evans." April 1864.

United States Army Military History Institute, Carlisle Barracks, PA

Bliss, Zena R. Memoirs
Chipman, S. Charles. Papers of Charles Chipman.
Mills, Charles. "Through Blood and Fire." G.A. Coco Collection.
Scroggs, Joseph J. Diary. *Civil War Times Illustrated* Collection.

University of Illinois, Urbana-Champaign, Urbana, IL

James S. Ayers Papers, 1863–1964, 1911–85

University of Michigan, Bentley Historical Library

William Baird Memoirs.

University of Michigan, Clements Library, Ann Arbor, MI

Lieutenant Hilton A. Parker Letters.

University of New Hampshire Library, Durham, NH

Lewis Bell Papers, 1857–1866.

University of North Carolina-Charlotte, Special Collections Library

William Leonidas Faulkner letters to his wife, March 8, 1863–July 23, 1864.

University of Notre Dame, Rare Books and Special Collections, Hesburgh Library

John Mower Jackson Letters.

University of Southern Mississippi, McCain Library and Archives, Hattiesburg, MS

John Wesley Hollensed, Letters to Family.

University of Texas, The Center for American History, Austin, TX

Barclay, H.W. "Reminiscences of H.W. Barclay."
Bliss, Randall Zenas. Papers.
Brady, Thomas Charles. Undated letter, 1864.
Cavaness, I.F. Diary of One Who Wore the Blue.

University of Virginia, Charlottesville, VA (Albert and Shirley Small Special Collections Library)

Claiborne, John H. Letters, 1864–186.
Douglas, Hugh Thomas, CSA. "The Petersburg Crater."
Nelson, Hugh Thomas. Diary, January–September 1864.
Woddell, Joseph Addison. Diary.
Sale, John F. Papers, 1861–1865.
Scott, Alfred Lewis. Memoir of service in the Confederacy (1861–1865).

University of Virginia Library, Charlottesville, VA

Featherston, John. "Battle of the Crater." Lecture delivered at Pottsville, PA, home of the 48th Pennsylvania Volunteers.

Letter to George Strother, March 1864, an account of the Battle of the Crater.

Vermont Historical Center, Vermont Historical Society, Barre, VT

Lyman A. Barton, letter dated August 12, 1864: Barton Family Papers.

Vermont Historical Society Library, Montpelier, VT

Charles Cummings Papers (MS-A28).

Virginia Historical Society, Richmond, VA

Bagby, Edward. Letter: Clark Family Papers, 1815–1938.
Bagby, John Robert. Undated letter: Bagby Family Papers, 1808–1942.
Bird, Henry Van Leuvenigh. Letter: Bird Family Papers.
Chamberlayne, John Hampton. Papers, 1858–1877.
Martin, John Marshall. Letter: John Marshall Martin Papers.
McCabe, William Gordon. Commonplace Book: McCabe Family Letters.
Pegram, William. Letter to his wife, August 1, 1864: Pegram-Johnson-McIntosh Family Papers.

Virginia Polytechnical Institute and State University, Blacksburg, VA

Radcliffe, Col. James. Letter to Martha Choate: Choate Family Papers, Special Collection.
Thomas, Henry Goddard. Letters and Memoirs, 1868–1889.

Virginia State Library, Richmond, VA

David F. Dobie Letters.

Washington and Lee University, James Graham Leyburn Library, Lexington, VA

Alexander Tedford Barclay Papers.

Western Carolina University, Special Collections, Hunter Library, Cullowhee, NC

Captain James M. Cathey. Article.

Newspapers

Charleston (SC) Mercury

August 1, 1864.

Indianapolis Star

April 24, 1915.

New York Times

August 2, 3, 4, 7, 8, 27, 1864; March 3, 6, 7, 15, 1865; August 16, 1882; August 4, 1883.

Olean (NY) Democrat

August 1, 1889.

Pottsville (PA) Republican

January 11–12, 1993.

Richmond Dispatch

August 3, 1864.

Richmond Sentinel

August 10, 26, 1864.

Richmond Whig

May 17, 1864; August 21, 1880.

Rochester (NY) News

June 23, 2000.

Shamokin (PA)Daily News

August 1, 1927.

Utica Daily Observer

August 2, 1864.

Vicksburg Daily Herald

August 4, 1864.

Washington Post

December 24, 2003; June 28, 1905; July 31, 1907; December 24, 2003.

Ypsilanti (MI) True Democrat

August 12, 1864.

Official Compilations

Connecticut Adjutants-General. *Record of Service of Connecticut Men in the Army and Navy of the United States during the War of the Rebellion.* Hartford, CT: Press of the Case, Lockwood & Brainard, 1889.

Michigan Adjutant-General. *Record of Service of Michigan Volunteers in the Civil War, 1861–1865.* Kalamazoo, MI: Ihling Bros. & Everand, Printers, 1905.

United States Congress. *Report of the Joint Committee on the Conduct of the War, Second Session, Thirty-Eighth Congress, Battle of Petersburg.* Washington, DC: Government Printing Office, 1865.

United States War Department. *Atlas to Accompany the Official Records of the Union and Confederate Armies of 1861–1865.* New York, Arno Press/Crown, 1978.

_____. *The 1863 U.S. Infantry Tactics: Infantry of the Line, Light Infantry, and Riflemen.* Washington, DC: Stackpole Books, 2002.

_____. *U.S. Infantry Tactics for the Instruction, Exercise, and Maneuvers of the Soldier, a Company, Line of Skirmishers, and Battalion: For the Use of the Colored Troops of the United States Infantry.* New York: D. Van Nostrand, 1863.

_____. *The War of the Rebellion: A Compilation of the Official Records of the Union and Confederate Armies.* 130 vols. Washington, DC, 1880–1901.

Unit Histories

Albert, Allen D., ed. *History of the Forty-Fifth Regiment Pennsylvania Veteran Volunteer Infantry, 1861–1865.* Williamsport, PA: Grit Publishing, 1912.

Allen, George H. *Forty-Six Months with the Fourth R.I. Volunteers in the War of 1861 to 1865.* Providence, RI: J.A. & R.A. Reid, 1887.

Anderson, John. *The Fifty-Seventh Regiment of Massachusetts Volunteers in the War of the Rebellion, Army of the Potomac.* Boston: E.B. Stillings, 1896.

Andrews, Welburn. J. *A Sketch of Company K., 23rd South Carolina Volunteers, in the Civil War, from 1862–1865.* Richmond: Whittet & Shepperson, 1909.

Aston, Howard. *History and Roster of the Fourth and Fifth Independent Battalions and Thirteenth Regiment Ohio Cavalry Volunteers: Their Battles and Skirmishes, Roster of the Dead, Etc.* Columbus, OH: Press of Fred J. Heer, 1902.

Aubrey, James Madison. *The Thirty-Sixth Wisconsin Volunteer Infantry.* Milwaukee: 1900.

Bartlett, Asa W. *History of the 12th Regiment, New Hampshire Volunteers, in the War of the Rebellion.* Concord, NH: I.C. Evans, 1897.

Bates, Samuel P. *A Brief History of the One Hundredth Regiment (Roundheads).* New Castle, PA: W.H. Thomas, 1884.

Beecher, Herbert W. *History of the 1st Light Battery, Connecticut Volunteers: Personal Records and Reminiscencse: The Story of the Battery from Its Organization to the Present Time.* 2 vols. (New York: A.T. De La Mare Ptg., 1901.

Bennett, Edgar B. *First Connecticut Heavy Artillery: Historical Sketch and Present Addresses of Members.* Hartford, CT: Star Print, 1889.

Billings, John D. *A History of the Tenth Massachusetts Battery of Light Artillery in the War of the Rebellion.* Boston: Hall & Whiting, 1881.

Blumberg, Arnold. "Old Dominion Brigade." *America's Civil War.* Leesburg, VA: Primedia Enthusiast Publications, July 2004.

Bosbyshell, Oliver Christian. *The 48th in the Wars: Being a Narrative of the Campaigns of the 48th Regiment, Infantry, Pennsylvania Veteran Volunteers during the War of the Rebellion.* Philadelphia, PA: Avil Publishing, 1895.

Brown, T.J. "Forty-second Regiment." *Histories of the Several Regiments and Battalions from North Carolina in the Great War, 1861–65.* Edited by Walter Clark. Goldsboro, NC: Nash Brothers, 1901.

Bruce, George A. *The Twentieth Regiment of Massachusetts Volunteers Infantry, 1861–1865.* Boston: Hampton, Mifflin, 1906.

Burrage, Henry S. *History of the Thirty-Sixth Regiment Massachusetts Volunteers, 1862–1865.* Boston: Press of Rockwell and Churchill, 1884.

Camper, Charles, and J.W. Kirkley. *Historical Record of the First Regiment Maryland Infantry, With an Appendix Containing a Register of the Officers and Enlisted Men, Biographies of Deceased Officers, etc: War of the Rebellion, 1861–1865.* Washington, DC: Gibson Brothers, 1871.

Cavanaugh, Michael. *The Otey, Ringgold and Davidson Virginia Artillery.* Lynchburg, VA: H.E. Howard, 1993.

_____. *6th Virginia Infantry.* Lynchburg, VA: H.E. Howard, 1988.

Clark, James H. *The Iron Hearted Regiment: Being an Account of the Battles, Marches and Gallant Deeds Performed By the 115th Regiment N.Y. Vols.* Albany, NY: J. Munsell, 1865.

Clark, Walter, ed. *Histories of the Several Regiments and Battalions from North Carolina in the Great War, 1861–1865.* 5 vols. Goldsboro, NC: Nash Brothers, 1901.

Cogswell, Leander W. *A History of the Eleventh New Hampshire Regiment Volunteer Infantry in the Rebellion War, 1861–1865.* Concord, NH: Republican Press Association, 1891.

Committee of the Regiment. *History of the Thirty-Sixth Regiment Massachusetts Volunteers, 1862–1865.* Boston: Press of Rockwell and Churchill, 1884.

Crater, Lewis. *History of the Fiftieth Regiment Penna. Vet.*

Vols., 1861–65. Reading, PA: Coleman Printing House, 1884.

Crowson, Noel, and John V. Brogden, eds. *Bloody Banners and Barefoot Boys: A History of the 27th Regiment Alabama Infantry, CSA.* Shippensburg, PA: Burd Street Press, 1997.

Cuffel, Charles A. *Durell's Battery in the Civil War (Independent Battery D, Pennsylvania Volunteer Artillery).* Philadelphia: Craig, Finley, 1903.

Cushman, Frederick E. *History of the 58th Regt. Massachusetts Vols. From the 15th day of September, 1863, to the Close of the Rebellion.* Washington, DC: Gibson Brothers, 1865.

Cutcheon, Byron M. *The Story of the Twentieth Michigan Infantry.* Lansing, MI: Robert Smith Printing, 1904.

Cutchins, John A. *A Famous Command — Richmond Light Blues.* Richmond, VA: Garrett and Massie, 1934.

Daniel, Frederick S. *Richmond Howitzers in the War: Four Years Campaigning with the Army of Northern Virginia.* Richmond, VA: Anon., 1891.

Day, William A. *A True History of Company I, 49th Regiment, North Carolina Troops, in the Great Civil War between the North and South.* Baltimore: Butternut and Blue, 1997.

Derby, W.P. *Bearing Arms in the Twenty-Seventh Massachusetts Regiment of Volunteers Infantry during The Civil War.* Boston: Wright & Potter, 1883.

Dickert, D. Augustus. *History of Kershaw's Brigade, with complete roll of companies, biographical sketches, incidents, anecdotes, etc.* Newberry, SC: E.H. Aull, ca. 1899.

Dubose, Henry Kershaw. *History of Company B, Twenty-First South Carolina Regiment (Infantry) South Carolina Volunteers; Confederate States Provisional Army.* Columbia, SC: R.L. Bryan, 1909.

Eden, Major Robert C. *The Sword and Gun: A History of the 37th Wis. Volunteer Infantry.* Madison, WI: Atwood & Rublee, 1865.

Edwards, W.H. *A Condensed History of Seventeenth Regiment S.C.V., C.S.A., From Its Organization to the Close of the War.* Columbia, SC: R.L. Bryan, 1906.

Embick, Milton A., ed. *Military History of the Third Division, Ninth Corps, Army of the Potomac.* Harrisburg, PA: C.E. Aughinbaugh, 1913.

Emmerton, James A. *A Record of the Twenty-Third Regiment Mass. Vol. Infantry in the War of the Rebellion, 1861–1865.* Boston: William Ware, 1886.

Evans, Robert G., ed. *The 16th Mississippi Infantry: Civil War Letters and Reminiscences.* Jackson: Press of Mississippi, 2002.

Flanner, Henry G. "Flanner's North Carolina Battery at the Battle of the Crater." *Southern Historical Society Papers* 5 (Jan.–Jun. 1878): 247–248.

Frederick, Gilbert. *The Story of a Regiment; Being a Record of the Military Services of the Fifty-Seventh New York State Volunteer Infantry in the War of the Rebellion.* Chicago: The Fifty-Seventh Veteran Association, 1895.

Gavin, William Gilfillan. *Campaigning with the Roundheads: The History of the Hundredth Pennsylvania Veteran Volunteer Infantry Regiment in the American Civil War, 1861–1865.* Dayton: Morningside House, 1989.

Gould, Joseph. *The Story of the Forty-Eighth: A Record of the Campaigns of the Forty-Eighth Regiment Pennsylvania Volunteer Infantry during the Four Eventful Years of Its Service in the War for the Preservation of the Union.* Philadelphia: The Regimental Association, Alfred M. Slocum, 1908.

Groom, Wendell D. *War-History of Company "C" (Beauregard Volunteers) Sixth Georgia Regiment (Infantry).* Fort Valley, GA: Advertiser, 1879.

Hagood, Johnson. "Hagood's Brigade: In Trenches of Petersburg." *Southern Historical Society Papers* (1888): 16.

Hanks, Orlando T. *History of Captain B.F. Benton's Company, Hood's Texas Brigade, 1861–1865.* Austin: Morrison Books, 1984.

Henderson, William D. *12th Virginia Infantry.* Lynchburg, VA: H.E. Howard, 1984.

Herek, Raymond J. *These Men Have Seen Hard Service: The First Michigan Sharpshooters in the Civil War.* Detroit: Wayne State University Press, 1998.

Hill, J.A., and Albert Maxfield. *The Story of One Regiment: The Eleventh Maine Infantry Volunteers in the War of the Rebellion.* New York: Committee of the Regimental Association, Press of J.J. Little, 1896.

Hopkins, William P. *The Seventh Regiment Rhode Island Volunteers in The Civil War, 1862–1865.* Providence, RI: Snow & Farnham, Providence Press, 1903.

Houston, Henry C. *The Thirty-Second Maine Regiment of Infantry Volunteers.* Portland, ME: Press of Southworth Brothers, 1903.

Hyde, William L. *History of the One Hundred and Twelfth Regiment N.Y. Volunteers.* Fredonia, NY: W. McKinstry, 1866.

Jackman, Lyman. *History of the Sixth New Hampshire Regiment in the War for the Union.* Concord, NH: Republican Press Association, 1891.

Kirk, Hyland C. *Heavy Guns and Light: A History of the 4th New York Heavy Artillery.* New York: C.T. Dillingham, 1890.

Kreutzer, William. *Notes and Observations made During Four Years of Service with the Ninety-Eighth N.Y. Volunteers in the War of 1861.* Philadelphia: Giant, Faires & Rodgers, 1878.

Little, Henry F. *The Seventh Regiment New Hampshire Volunteers in the War of the Rebellion.* Concord, NH: Ira C. Evans, 1896.

Lord, Edward. *History of the Ninth New Hampshire Volunteers in the War of the Rebellion.* Concord, NH: Republican Press Association, 1895.

Marvel, William. *Race of the Soil: The Ninth New Hampshire Regiment in the Civil War.* Wilmington, NC: Broadfoot Publishing, 1988.

Maxfield, Albert, and Robert Brady, Jr. *Roster and Statistical Record of Company D of the Eleventh Regiment Maine Infantry Volunteers, with a Sketch of Its Services in the War of the Rebellion.* New York: Press of Thos. Humphrey, 1890.

McAlpine, Charles R. "Sketch of Co. I, Sixty-first Virginia Infantry, Mahone's Brigade, C.S.A." *Southern Historical Society Papers* 24 (1896).

Mickley, Jeremiah M. *The Forty-third Regiment United States Colored Troops.* Gettysburg: J.E. Wible, 1866.

Miller, Edward A., Jr. *The Black Civil War Soldiers of Illinois: The Story of the Twenty-ninth U.S. Colored Infantry.* Columbia: University of South Carolina Press, 1998.

Morgan, William H. *Personal Reminiscences of the War of 1861–5: In Camp — in bivouac — on the march — on picket — on the skirmish line — on the battlefield — and in prison.* Freeport, NY: Books for Libraries Press, 1971.

Mowris, James W., MD. *A History of the One Hundred and Seventeenth Regiment, N.Y. Volunteers (Fourth Oneida), from the Date of Its Organization, August 1862, Till That of Its Muster Out, June 1865.* Hartford, CT: Case, Lockwood, 1866.

Mudgett, Timothy B. *Make the Fur Fly: A History of a Union Volunteer Division in the American Civil War.* Shippensburg, PA: Burd Street Press, 1997.

Nichols, James M. *Perry's Saints, or the Fighting Parson's*

Regiment, in the War of the Rebellion. Boston: D. Lothrop, 1886.

Ord, Edward O. *History of the Ninth Regiment New Hampshire Volunteers in the War of the Rebellion.* Concord, NH: Republican Press Association, 1895.

Osborne, William H. *History of the Twenty-Ninth Regiment of Massachusetts Volunteer Infantry in the Late War of the Rebellion.* Boston: Albert J. Wright, 1877.

Owen, C.W. *The First Michigan Infantry.* Quincy, MA: Quincy Herald Print, 1903.

Palmer, Abraham J. *The History of the Forty-Eighth Regiment New York State Volunteers.* Brooklyn, NY: The Veteran Association of the Regiment, Charles T. Dillingham, 1885.

Paradis, James M. *Strike the Blow for Freedom: The 6th United States Colored Infantry in the Civil War.* Shippensburg, PA: White Mane Books, 1998.

Parker, Thomas H. *History of the 51st Regiment of P.V. and V.V. from Its Organization at Camp Curtin, Harrisburg, Pa., in 1861, to Its Being Mustered Out of the United States Service at Alexandria, Va., July 27, 1865.* Philadelphia: King & Baird, Printers, 1869.

Petzold, Herman. *Memoirs of the Second Michigan Regiment.* 1897.

Pierce, Lieutenant Solon Wesley. *Battle Fields and Camp Fires of the Thirty-Eighth: An Authentic Narrative and Record of the Organization of the Thirty-Eighth Regiment of Wis. Vol. Inf'y and the Part Taken by It in the Late War.* Milwaukee: Daily Wisconsin Printing House, 1866.

Price, Isaiah. *History of the Ninety-Seventh Regiment Pennsylvania Infantry during the War of the Rebellion, 1861–65, with the Biographical Sketches of Its Field and Staff Officers and a Complete Record of Each Officer and Enlisted Man.* Philadelphia: B. & P. Printers, 1875.

Pullen, John J. *The Twentieth Maine: A Volunteer Regiment in the Civil War.* Philadelphia: J.B. Lippincott, 1957.

Rhodes, John H. *History of Battery B, First Regiment Rhode Island Light Artillery, in the War to Preserve the Union, 1861–1865.* Providence, RI: Snow & Farnham, 1894.

Roe, Alfred S. *The Thirty-Ninth Regiment Massachusetts Volunteers, 1862–1865.* Worcester, MA: Regimental Veteran Association, 1914.

Schroeder, Patrick A. *We Came to Fight: The History of the 5th New York Veteran Volunteer Infantry Duryee's Zouaves (1863–1865).* Brookneal: Schroeder Publishing, 1998.

Shaver, Lewellyn A. *A History of the Sixtieth Alabama Regiment Gracie's Alabama Brigade.* Montgomery: Barret & Brown, 1867.

Shaw, Charles A. *A History of the 14th Regiment N.Y. Heavy Artillery in the Civil War, 1863 to 1865.* Mount Kisco, NY: North Westchester Publishing, 1918.

Silo, Mark. *The 115th New York in the Civil War: A Regimental History.* Jefferson, NC: McFarland, 2007.

Simpson, Harold B. *Hood's Texas Brigade in Reunion and Memory.* Dallas: Alcor, 1983.

Stone, Dewitt Boyd, Jr., ed. *Wandering to Glory: Confederate Veterans Remember Evans' Brigade.* Columbia: University of South Carolina Press, 2002.

Trask, Benjamin H. *16th Virginia Infantry.* Lynchburg, VA: H.E. Howard, 1986.

_____. *61st Virginia Infantry.* Lynchburg, VA: H.E. Howard, 1988.

Twitchell, Albert S. *History of the Seventh Maine Light Battery, Volunteers in the Great Rebellion.* Boston: E.B. Stillings, 1892.

Vaill, Theodore F. *History of the 2nd Connecticut Volunteer Heavy Artillery, Originally the Nineteenth Connecticut Volunteers.* Winsted, CT: Winsted Printing, 1868.

Venner, William Thomas. *The Iron Brigade's 19th Indiana Regiment.* Shippensburg, PA: Burd Street Press, 1998.

Walcott, Charles F. *History of the Twenty-First Regiment Massachusetts Volunteers in the War for the Preservation of the Union, 1861–1865, with Statistics of the War and Rebel Prisons.* Boston: Houghton Mifflin, 1904.

Ward, George W. *History of the Second Pennsylvania Veteran Heavy Artillery (112th Regiment Pennsylvania Volunteers) from 1861 to 1866, including the Provisional Second Penn'a Heavy Artillery.* Philadelphia: George W. Ward, 1904.

Wilkinson, Warren, and Steven E. Woodworth. *A Scythe of Fire: A Civil War Story of the Eighth Georgia Infantry Regiment.* New York: William Morrow, 2002.

Wilkinson, Warren. *Mother, May You Never See the Sights I Have Seen: The Fifty-Seventh Massachusetts Veteran Volunteers in the Army of the Potomac, 1864–1865.* New York: Quill-William Morrow, 1990.

Zwemer, John. *For Home and the Southland: A History of the 48th Georgia Infantry Regiment.* Baltimore: Butternut and Blue, 1999.

Books and Articles

Abbot, Henry L. *Siege Artillery in the Campaign against Richmond.* New York: D. Van Nostrand, 1868.

Abel, Annie Heloise. *The American Indian and the End of the Confederacy, 1863–1866.* Lincoln: University of Nebraska Press, 1993.

_____. *The American Indian as Participant in the Civil War.* Cleveland: Arthur H. Clark, 1919.

Adams, J.C. "Battle of the Crater." *National Tribune,* June 25, 1903.

Agassiz, George R., ed. *Meade's Headquarters, 1863–1865: Letters of Colonel Theodore Lyman.* Boston: Atlantic Monthly Press, 1922.

Alexander, Bevin. *Robert E. Lee's Civil War.* Holbrook, MA: Adams Media Corporation, 1998.

Alexander, E. Porter. "Confederate Artillery Service." *Southern Historical Society Papers* 11 (1883): 99–113.

_____. *Fighting for the Confederacy.* Chapel Hill: University of North Carolina Press, 1989.

_____. *Military Memoirs of a Confederate: A Critical Narrative.* New York: Scribner's, 1907.

Anderson, Curt. *Hearts in Conflict: A One Volume History of the Civil War.* New York: Barnes and Noble, 1994.

Anderson, George Baker. *Landmarks of Rensselaer County, New York.* Syracuse, NY: D. Mason, 1897.

_____. *Landmarks of Virginia.* New York and Washington, DC: Neale Publishing, 1908.

Anderson, James. "In the Trenches at Petersburg." *Confederate Veteran Magazine* 34, no. 1 (January 1926): 23.

Andrews, J. Cutler. *The South Reports the Civil War.* Princeton, NJ: Princeton University Press, 1970.

Anonymous. *Two Hundred Years: The Military History of Ohio(1669–1865).* New York: H.H. Hardesty, 1885.

Armstrong, Hallock. *Letters from a Pennsylvania Chaplin at the Siege of Petersburg, 1865.* London: Eden Press, 1961.

Ayling, Augustus D. *A Yankee at Arms: The Diary of Lieutenant Augustus Ayling, 29th Massachusetts Volunteers.* Knoxville: University of Tennessee Press, 1999.

_____. *Revised Register of the Soldiers and Sailors of New Hampshire in the War of the Rebellion, 1861–1866.* Concord, NH: Ira C. Evans, 1895.

Bache, Richard Meade. *Life of General George Gordon Meade, Commander of the Army of the Potomac*. Philadelphia: H.T. Coates, 1898.

Bacon, James T. "Capt. George B. Lake." *Confederate Veteran* 2, no. 5 (May 1894): 153.

Badeau, Adam. *Military History of Ulysses S. Grant, 1861 to April, 1865*. 3 vols. New York: D. Appleton, 1881.

Bagby, Alfred A. *King and Queen Country, Virginia*. New York: Neale Publishing, 1908.

Ballard, Michael. *Vicksburg: The Campaign that Opened the Mississippi*. Chapel Hill: University of North Carolina Press, 2004.

Ballou, Daniel R. "The Petersburg Mine." *National Tribune*, June 5, 1913.

Baradell, Lang. "Mushroom Cloud at Vicksburg." *Civil War Times Illustrated* 44, no. 4 (2005): 50–62.

Barnwell, Robert W. "A View on the Crater Battle." *Confederate Veteran* 33, no. 1 (1925): 176–178.

Barrett, Eugene A. "The Civil War Services of John F. Hartranft." *Pennsylvania History* 32, no. 2 (1965): 166–186.

Barton, Michael, and Larry M. Logue. *The Civil War Soldier: A Historical Reader*. New York: New York University Press, 2002.

Bates, Delevan. "A Day with the Colored Troops." *National Tribune*, January 30, 1908.

Bates, Samuel P. *History of the Pennsylvania Volunteers, 1861–1865*. Harrisburg, PA: B. Singerly, State Printer, 1869–1871.

"Battle Mountain." http://www.nevadaweb.com/cnt/cc/bmtn.html.

"Battle of the Crater, July 30, 1864, Roster of the Members of the 12th Virginia Infantry, Mahone's Brigade, Who Were Engaged." *Southern Historical Society Papers* 31 (1903): 271–274.

Bausum, David F. "Personal Reminiscences of Sergeant Daniel F. Bausum, Co. K, 48th Regt., Penna. Vol. Inf., 1861–1865." *Schuylkill County Historical Society* (1914): 240–249.

Beadle, William Henry Harrison. *Autobiography of William Henry Harrison Beadle*. Pierre, SD: State Historical Society of Iowa, 1938.

Beadle, William Henry Harrison, and Doane Robinson, eds. *Memoirs of General William Henry Harrison Beadle*. Aberdeen, SD: 1906.

Beall, John B. *In Barrack and Field: Poems and Sketches of Army Life*. Nashville: Smith & Lamar, Publishing House of the M.E. Church, 1906.

Beaty, B.L. "The Battle of the Crater." *Sketches and Reminiscences*. Edited by Joshua Hilary Hudson. Columbia, SC: State Company, 1903.

Beauregard, Pierre G.T. "The Battle of Petersburg, Pt I." *The North American Review* 145, no. 371 (1887): 367–378.

_____. "The Battle of Petersburg, Pt. II." *The North American Review* 145, no. 372 (1887): 506–516.

_____. "Four Days of Battle at Petersburg." In *Battles and Leaders of the Civil War*. Edited by Johnson and Buell. New York: Castle Books, 1956.

Beller, James W. "The Mine Explosion." *National Tribune*, June 20, 1889.

Benson, Susan Williams, ed. *Berry Benson's Civil War Book: Memoirs of a Confederate Scout and Sharpshooter*. Athens: University of Georgia Press, 1992.

Bernard, George S. "The Battle of the Crater, July 30, 1864." *Southern Historical Society Papers* 18 (January–December 1890): 3–38.

_____. "Great Battle of the Crater, the Work of Mahone and Weisiger at the Fight." *Southern Historical Society Papers* 28 (1900): 204–221.

Bernard, George S., ed. *War Talks of Confederate Veterans*. Petersburg, VA: Fenn & Owen, 1892.

Beyer, W.F., and O.F. Keydel, eds. *Deeds of Valor: How America's Civil War Heroes Won the Congressional Medal of Honor*. Stamford, CT: Longmeadow Press, 1993.

Billings, John D. *Hardtack and Coffee: Soldier's Life in the Civil War*. Old Saybrook, CT: Konecky & Konecky, 1887.

_____. *Hardtack and Coffee: The Unwritten Story of Army Life*. Philadelphia: Thompson Publishing, 1888.

Blackford, Susan Leigh. *Letters from Lee's Army, or Memories of Life In and Out of the Army in Virginia during the War Between the States*. New York: Scribner's, 1947.

Blackford, W.W. *War Years with Jeb Stuart*. New York: Scribner's, 1945.

Blake, Henry Nichols. *Three Years in the Army of the Potomac*. Boston: Lee and Shepard, 1865.

Blake, Nelson Morehouse. *William Mahone of Virginia, Soldier and Political Insurgent*. Richmond, VA: Garrett and Massie, 1935.

Blanton, Deanne, and Lauren M. Cook. *They Fought Like Demons: Women Soldiers in the Civil War*. New York: Vintage Books, 2002.

Blight, David W., ed. *When This Cruel War Is Over: The Civil War Letters of Charles Henry Brewster*. Amherst: University of Massachusetts Press, 1992.

Bouton, John Bell. *A Memoir of General Louis Bell, Late Colonel of the Fourth N.H. Regiment, Who fell at the Assault on Fort Fisher, N.C., January 15th, 1865*. New York: Private Printer, 1865.

Bowley, Freeman S. "The Crater." *The National Tribune*, November 6, 1864.

_____. "The Petersburg Mine." 60 *MOLLUS*. Wilmington, NC: Broadfoot Publishing, 1995, 27–41.

_____. *A Boy Lieutenant: Memoirs of Freeman S. Bowley, 30th United States Colored Troops Officer*. Edited by Pia Seija Seagrave. Fredericksburg, VA: Sergeant Kirkland's Museum and Historical Society, 1997.

Brady, Robert. *The Story of One Regiment: The Eleventh Maine Infantry Volunteers in the War of the Rebellion*. New York: J.J. Little, 1896.

Branson, Daniel F. "The Petersburg Mine." *National Tribune*, September 13, 1911.

Brewer, Willis. *Alabama: Her History, Resources, and Public Men, from 1549 to 1872*. Montgomery: Barrell & Brown, 1872.

Brightman, Austin C., Jr. "Glory Enough: The 48th Pennsylvania Volunteers at Fort Crater." *A Journal of the American Civil War, Regimental Studies, Inc*. 2, no. 2 (1992): 141–155.

Brock, R.A. "Great Battle of the Crater." *Southern Historical Society Papers* 27 (1990): 204–221.

Bronson, Daniel F. "The Petersburg Mine." *National Tribune*, September 13, 1911.

Brooks, Noah. "Two War-Time Conventions." *The Century* (March 1895): 723–37.

_____. *Washington, D.C., in Lincoln's Time*. Edited by Herbert Mitgang. New York: Rinehart, 1958.

Brown, Augustus Cleveland. *The Diary of a Line Officer*. New York: 1906.

Brown, George H. *Confederate Veteran* 16, no. 7 (July 1908): 349.

Brown, William Wells. *The Negro in the American Rebellion, His Heroism and His Fidelity*. Miami, FL: Mnemosyne Publishing, 1969.

Bryant, Elias A. *The Diary of Elias A. Bryant, as Written by him While in his More Than Three Years Service in* the U.S. Army in the Civil War. Concord: Rumford Press.

Burbank, Horace H. "The Battle of the 'Crater.'" 16 MOL-LUS 1. Portland, ME: The Thurston Print, 1898, 283–294. Reprinted Wilmington, NC: Broadfoot, 1992.

Burton, H.W. The History of Norfolk, Virginia. Norfolk: Virginian Job Print, 36 and 38, 1879.

Burton, William L. Melting Pot Soldiers: The Union's Ethnic Regiments. New York: Fordham University Press, 1998.

Butler, Benjamin. Autobiography and Personal Reminiscences of Major General Benj. F. Butler: Butler's Book. Boston: A. M. Thayer, 1892.

Calkins, Chris, "The Presentation Report: A History of the Crater Battlefield, 1865–1992." A Journal of the American Civil War, Regimental Studies, Inc., 2, no. 2, (1992): 156–160.

Campbell, John A. Reminiscences & Documents Relating to the Civil War during the Year 1865. Baltimore: John Murphy, 1887.

Cannan, John. The Crater: Burnside's Assault on the Confederate Trenches, July 30, 1864. Cambridge, MA: Da Capo Press, 2002.

"Capt. George B. Lake." Confederate Veteran 2, no. 5 (May 1894): 153.

Carmichael, Peter S. Lee's Young Artillerist William R.J. Pegram. Charlottesville: University Press of Virginia, 1995.

Carroll, Andrew, ed. War Letters: Extraordinary Correspondence from American Wars. New York: Washington Square Press, 2001.

Carter, Captain Robert Goldthwaite. Four Brothers in Blue, or Sunshine and Shadows of the War of the Rebellion: A Story of the Great Civil War from Bull Run to Appomattox. Austin: University of Texas Press, 1978.

Carter, Solon A. "Fourteen Month's Service with Colored Troops." Maine MOLLUS 3 (1908).

Case, Ervin T. "Battle of the Mine." MOLLUS (1993): 275–307.

Case, Leverett N. "Personal Recollections of the Siege of Petersburg." Michigan MOLLUS 2 (1898).

Cashin, Joan E., ed. The War Was You and Me: Civilians in the American Civil War. Princeton, NJ: Princeton University Press, 2002.

Catton, Bruce. Glory Road. Garden City, NJ: Doubleday, 1952.

_____. Grant Moves South. New York: Little, Brown, 1960.

_____. Grant Takes Command, 1863–65. Garden City, NY: Doubleday, 1968.

_____. Mr. Lincoln's Army. New York: (1951).

_____. Never Call Retreat. Garden City, NY: Doubleday, 1965.

_____. A Stillness at Appomattox. Garden City, NY: Doubleday, 1954.

_____. This Hallowed Ground. Garden City, NY: Doubleday, 1956.

Cavanaugh, Michael A., and William Marvel. The Battle of the Crater, "The Horrible Pit," June 25–August 6, 1864. Lynchburg, VA: H.E. Howard, 1989.

Chamberlaine, Joshua Lawrence. The Passing of the Armies: An Account of the Final Campaign of the Army of the Potomac, Based upon Personal Reminiscences of the Fifth Army Corps. New York: Bantam, 1993.

Chamberlaine, William W. Memoirs of the Civil War between the Northern and Southern Sections of the United States of America, 1861 to 1865. Washington, DC: Press of Byron S. Adams, 1912.

Chamberlayne, John Hampden. Ham Chamberlayne—Virginian: Letters and Papers of an Artillery Officer in the War for Southern Independence, 1861–1865. 4 vols. Richmond, VA: Press of the Dietz Printing Co., 1932. Reprinted Wilmington, NC: Broadfoot, 1992.

Chambers, H.A. "The Bloody Crater." Confederate Veteran Magazine 31, no. 1 (1923): 174–177.

Chase, James J. The Charge at Day-Break. Lewiston, ME: Private printing, 1875.

Chesnut, Mary Boykin. Mary Chesnut's Civil War. Edited by C. Vann Woodward. New Haven: Yale University Press, 1981.

_____. A Diary from Dixie. Boston: Houghton Mifflin, 1949.

Christ, Mark K., ed. Getting Used to Being Shot At: The Spence Family Civil War Letters. Fayetteville: University of Arkansas Press, 2002.

Cisco, Walter Brian. Wade Hampton: Confederate Warrior, Conservative Statesman. Washington, DC: Brasseys, 2004.

Claiborne, John Herbert. Seventy-Five Years in Old Virginia. New York: Neale, 1904.

Clark, George. A Glance Backward, or Some Events in the Past History of My Life. Houston: Rein & Sons, 1914.

_____. "Alabamians in the Crater Battle." Confederate Veteran 3 (1895): 68–70.

Clark, Walter, ed. Histories of the Several Regiments and Battalions from North Carolina in the Great War, 1861–65. Wendell, NC: Broadfoot, 1982.

Cleveland, Mather. New Hampshire Fights the Civil War. New London, NH: University Press of New England,1969).

Cockrell, Monroe F., ed. Gunner with Stonewall: Reminiscences of William Thomas Poague. Wilmington, NC: Broadfoot Publishing, 1989.

Coco, Gregory A., ed. Through Blood and Fire: The Civil War Letters of Major Charles J. Mills, 1862–1865. Gettysburg: Gregory A. Coco, 1982.

Coffin, Charles Carleton. Four Years of Fighting: Personal Observation with the Army and Navy from the First Battle of Bull Run to the Fall of Richmond. New York: Arno & New York Times, 1970. Reprint of a copy in the State Historical Society of Wisconsin Library. Boston: Ticknor and Fields, 1866.

Coffin, Howard. The Battered Stars: One State's Civil War Ordeal during Grant's Overland Campaign. Woodstock, VT: Countryman Press, 2002.

_____. Full Duty: Vermonters in the Civil War. Woodstock, VT: Countryman Press, 1993.

Coit, James C. "The Battle of the Crater, July 30, 1864." Southern Historical Society Papers 10 (1882): 199–130.

_____. "Letter to Fitz William McMaster, August 2, 1879." Southern Historical Society Papers (1882).

Colston, R.E. "Repelling the First Assault on Petersburg." The Century Magazine (1889).

Commager, Henry Steele, ed. The Blue and the Gray. 2 vols. Indianapolis: Bobbs-Merrill, 1950.

Cook, Adrian. The Armies of the Streets: The New York City Draft Riots of 1863. Lexington: University Press of Kentucky, 1974.

Copp, Elbridge J. Reminiscences of the War of the Rebellion, 1861–1865. Nashua, NH: Telegraph Pub., 1911.

Cornish, Dudley Taylor. The Sable Arm: Black Troops in the Union Army, 1861–1865. Lawrence: University of Kansas Press, 1987.

Cowles, Calvin D. The Official Military Atlas of the Civil War. New York: Arno Press/Crown, 1978.

Crawford, Robert F. "The Civil War Letters of S. Rodman and Linton Smith." Delaware History 21 (Fall/Winter 1984): 86–116.

Cross, Thomas H. "Battle of the Crater." National Tribune, February 25, 1882.

Cullen, Joseph P. "The Siege of Petersburg." *Civil War Times Illustrated* 4, no.5 (August 1970).

_____. "The very *Beau Ideal* of a Soldier: A Personality Profile of Ambrose E. Burnside." *Civil War Times Illustrated* 16, no. 5 (August 1977): 4–11, 38–44.

_____. *Where a Hundred Thousand Fell*. Washington, DC: National Park Service Historical Handbook, Series No. 39, 1966.

Culver, J.B. "The Petersburg Mine." *National Tribune*, September 4, 1919.

Cummings, Charles M. *Yankee Quaker, Confederate General: The Curious Career of Bushrod Rust Johnson*. Rutherford, NJ: Fairleigh Dickinson University Press, 1971.

Cutrer, Thomas W., and T. Michael Parrish, eds. *Brothers in Gray: The Civil War Letters of the Pierson Family*. Baton Rouge: Louisiana State University Press, 1997.

Daly, Louise Porter Haskell. *Alexander Cheves Haskell: The Portrait of the Man*. Norwood, MA: Plimpton Press, 1934.

Dana, Charles A. *Recollections of the Civil War, with the Leaders at Washington and in the Field in the Sixties*. New York: Collier Books, 1963.

Daniel, John M. *The "Richmond Examiner" during the War*. New York: Arno and *New York Times*, 1868.

Davies, A.M. "Petersburg: The Battle of the Crater." *Blue and Gray* 3, no. 5 (May 1894): 249–252.

Davis, Burke. *Gray Fox: Robert E. Lee and the Civil War*. New York: Rinehart, 1956.

Davis, Oliver W. *Life of David Bell Birney, Major-General United States Volunteers*. Philadelphia: King & Baird, 1867.

Davis, William C. *Death in the Trenches: Grant at Petersburg*. Alexandria, VA: Time-Life Books, 1986.

_____. *The Battle of New Market*. Garden City, NY: Doubleday, 1975.

Day, W.A. "Battle of the Crater." *Confederate Veteran* 11, no. 8 (August 1903): 355–356.

_____. "The Breastworks at Petersburg." *Confederate Veteran* 24:174.

De Trobriand, Phillipe Regis. *Four Years with the Army of the Potomac*. Boston: Ticknor, 1889.

_____. "Burnside Fumbles His Chance to Take Petersburg." In *The Blue and the Gray*. Edited by Henry Steele Commager. 2 vols. Indianapolis: Bobbs-Merrill, 1950.

Domer, Ronald G. "Ohio Quaker Bushrod Johnson's Confederate military career was uneven and contradictory." *America's Civil War* 19, no. 1 (2006).

Donald, David Herbert. *Lincoln*. New York: Simon and Schuster, 1995.

Dowdey, Clifford, and Louis H. Manarin, eds. *The Wartime Papers of Robert E. Lee*. Boston: Little, Brown, 1961.

Dowdey, Clifford. *Lee*. New York: Bonanza Books, 1955.

_____. *Lee's Last Campaign: The Story of Lee and His Men against Grant, 1864*. New York: Bonanza Books, 1950.

Draper, Joseph. "We Fought in the Battle of the Crater." *Confederate Veteran* 8, no. 11 (Nov. 1900): 502.

Dunlap, William S. *Lee's Sharpshooters: The Forefront of Battle*. Little Rock: Tunnah & Pittard, Printers, 1899.

Dyer, Frederick. *A Compendium of the War of Rebellion*. 3 vols. Des Moines: Dyer, 1908.

Early, Jubal. "Early's March to Washington in 1864." In *Battles and Leaders of the Civil War*. Edited by Johnson and Buell. New York: Castle Books, 1956.

Eckert, Ralph Lowell. *John Brown Gordon: Soldier, Southerner, American*. Baton Rouge: Louisiana State University Press, 1989.

Eggleston, George C. "Mr. Eggleston Recalls When Money Was Plentiful." In *The Blue and the Gray*. Edited by Henry Steele Commager. 2 vols. Indianapolis: Bobbs-Merrill, 1950.

Eisenschiml, Otto, and Ralph Newman. *The Civil War: An American Iliad as Told by Those Who Lived It*. New York: Mallard Press, 1956.

Elliott, Charles Pinckney. "Elliott's Brigade: How It Held the Crater and Saved Petersburg." William Fitz McMaster Collection. Reprint of address before Confederate Veterans of Camp Hampton, Columbia, South Carolina, December 15, 1895.

Elliott, James Carson. *The Southern Soldier Boy: A Thousand Shots for the Confederacy*. Raleigh, NC: Edwards & Broughton Printing, 1907.

Ellis, Billy. *Tithes of Blood: A Confederate Soldier's Story*. Murfreesboro, TN: Southern Heritage Press, 1997.

Ellis, Leonnard Bolles. *History of New Bedford and Its Vicinity*. Syracuse, NY: D. Mason, 1892.

Elwell, Rev. Silas Pinckney Holbrook. *Recollections of War Times*. Bamberg, SC: Bamberg Herald Print, 1895.

Etheredge, William H. "Another Story of the Crater Battle." *Southern Historical Society Papers* 37 (1909): 203–07.

_____. "Another Story of the Crater Battle." *Confederate Veteran* 15, no. 1 (1907): 167.

Evans, Clement A., ed. *Confederate Military History*. 17 vols. Wilmington, NC: Broadfoot Publishing, 1987–88.

Featherston, Capt. John C. "The Battle of the Crater." *Confederate Veteran* 34, no. 8 (1926): 296–298.

_____. *Battle of the Crater*. Birmingham: Birmingham Public Library Press, 1987.

_____. "The Battle of the Crater, as I Saw It." *Confederate Veteran* 14, no. 1 (January 1906).

_____. "Incidents of the Battle of the Crater." *Confederate Veteran* 14 (1906): 107–108.

_____. "Graphic Account of Battle of Crater." *Southern Historical Society Papers* 33 (1905): 358–74.

Fehrenbach, T.R. *Lone Star: A History of Texas and the Texans*. New York: Wings Books, 1968.

Ferguson, Garland S. "Henry Grady's Father in the Battle of the Crater." *Confederate Veteran* 1, no. 11 (November 1893): 326.

Field, C.W. "Campaign of 1864 and 1865." *Southern Historical Society Papers* 14 (1886): 542–63.

"Field of Blood Was the Crater." *Southern Historical Society Papers* 33 (1905): 351–357.

Fitch, Michael. "We Thought the Rebellion Would Be Over Before Our Chance Would Come." In *The Blue and the Gray*. Edited by Henry Steele Commager. 2 vols. Indianapolis: Bobbs-Merrill, 1950.

"Flag Presentation to the Washington Artillery." *Southern Historical Society Papers* 12 (1884): 28–32.

Floyd, N.J. "Concerning Battle of the Crater." *Confederate Veteran* 19, no. 8 (August 1911): 387.

_____. "Concerning Battle of the Crater." *Confederate Veteran* 16, no. 4 (April 1908): 159.

Folsom, James M. *Heroes and Martyrs of Georgia: Georgia's Record in the Revolution of 1861*. Baltimore: Butternut and Blue, 1995.

Foote, Shelby. *The Civil War: A Narrative*. Alexandria: Random House, 1974.

Ford, Worthington Chauncy, ed. *A Cycle of Adams Letters, 1861–1865*. Boston: Riverside, 1920.

Fox, Wells B. *What I Remember of the Great Rebellion*. Lansing, MI: Darius D. Thorp, 1892.

Fox, William F. "The Chances of Being Hit in Battle." *The Century* 36, no. 1 (May 1888): 93–106.

_____. *Regimental Losses in the American Civil War, 1861–1865*. Albany, NY: Albany Publishing, 1889.

Frassanito, William A. *Grant and Lee: The Virginia Campaign, 1864–1865.* New York: Scribner's, 1983.

Freeman, Douglas Southall, ed. *Lee's Dispatches: Unpublished Letters of General Robert E. Lee, C.S.A., to Jefferson Davis and the War Department of the Confederate States of America, 1862–65.* New York: Putnam's, 1915.

Freeman, Douglas Southall. *Lee's Lieutenants: A Study in Command.* 4 vols. New York: Scribner's, 1944.

_____. *R.E. Lee: A Biography.* New York: Scribner's, 1934.

Friend, A. *Memorial of Colonel John A. Bross, Twenty-Ninth U. S. Colored Troops, Who Fell In Leading the Assault on Petersburg July 30, 1864.* Chicago: Tribune Book and Job Office, 1865.

Fuller, H.S. "Evacuating Morris Island." *Confederate Veteran* 11, no. 11 (November 1903): 519.

Furgurson, Ernest B. *Not War but Murder: Cold Harbor, 1864.* New York: Alfred A. Knopf, 2000.

Gallagher, Gary W. *Lee and His Generals in War and Memory.* Baton Rouge: Louisiana State University Press, 1998.

Gambone, A.M. *Major General John Frederick Hartranft: Citizen Soldier and Pennsylvania Statesman.* Baltimore: Butternut and Blue, 1995.

Garrison, Webb. *A Treasury of Civil War Tales.* Nashville: Rutledge Hill Press, 1988.

Gavin, William Gilfillan, ed. *Infantryman Pettit: The Civil War Letters of Corporal Frederick Pettit.* Shippensburg, PA: White Mane Publishing, 1990.

Geary, James W. *We Need Men: The Union Draft in the Civil War.* DeKalb: Northern Illinois University Press, 1991.

"Gen. David A. Weisiger of Virginia." *Confederate Veteran* 7, no. 8 (August 1899): 362–364.

General Assembly. *Record of Service of Connecticut Men in the Army and Navy of the United States during the War of the Rebellion.* Hartford, CT: The Case, Lockwood & Brainard, 1889.

George, Larry. "Battle of the Crater: A Combat Engineer Case Study." *Military Review* 64, no. 2 (February 1984): 35–47.

Gerrish, Theodore. *Army Life: A Private's Reminiscences of the Civil War.* Portland, ME: Fogg & Donham, 1882.

Gibbon, John. *Personal Recollections of the Civil War.* New York: Putnam's, 1928.

Glatthaar, Joseph T. *Forged in Battle: The Civil War Alliance of Black Soldiers and White Officers.* New York: Collier Macmillan, 1990.

_____. "Leaving Their Mark on the Battlefield." In *The Civil War Soldier: A Historical Reader.* Edited by Michael Barton and Larry M. Logue. New York: New York University Press, 2002.

Glenn, John F. "Brave Defence of the Cockade City." *Southern Historical Society Papers* 35 (1907): 1–24.

Goodwin, Doris Kearns. *Team of Rivals: The Political Genius of Abraham Lincoln.* New York: Simon and Schuster, 2005.

Gordon, Armistead C. *Memoirs & Memorials of William Gordon McCabe.* Richmond, VA: Old Dominion Press, 1925.

Gordon, General John B. *Reminiscences of the Civil War.* New York: Scribner's, 1903.

Goss, Warren Lee. *Recollections of a Private: A Story of the Army of the Potomac.* New York: Thomas Y. Crowell, 1890.

Goulding, Joseph Hiram. "The Colored Troops in the War of the Rebellion." *Proceedings of the Reunion Society of Vermont Officers* 2. Burlington, VT: Free Press Printing, 1906.

Gracie, Archibald. "Gen. Archibald Gracie." *Confederate Veteran* 5, no. 8 (August 1897): 429.

Grant, Lewis A. "The Old Vermont Brigade at Petersburg." MN *MOLLUS* 1. St. Paul, MN: St. Paul Book & Sta., 1887.

Grant, Ulysses S. *The Papers of Ulysses S. Grant.* Edited by John Y. Simon. 24 vols. Carbondale: Southern Illinois University Press, 1984–2000.

_____. *Personal Memoirs of U.S. Grant.* 2 vols. New York: Century, 1885–86.

Green, A. Wilson. *Civil War Petersburg: Confederate City in the Crucible of War.* Charlottesville: University of Virginia Press, 2006.

Griess, Thomas E., ed. *Atlas for the American Civil War.* Wayne, NJ: Avery Publishing Group, 1986.

Griffith, Paddy. *Battle Tactics of the Civil War.* New Haven: Yale University Press, 1987.

Hagood, James R. "Report of Campaign of 1864." *Southern Historical Society Papers* 13 (1885).

Hagood, Johnson. "Gen. P.G.T. Beauregard." *Southern Historical Society Papers* 28 (1900): 318–36.

_____. *Memoirs of the War of Secession, from the Original Manuscripts of Johnson Hagood, Brigadier-General, C.S.A.: I. Hagood's 1st 12 months S.C.V.; II. Hagood's Brigade.* Columbia, SC: State Company, 1910.

Haley, James L. *Sam Houston.* Norman: University of Oklahoma Press, 2002.

Haley, John West, and Ruth l. Silliker, eds. *The Rebel Yell & Yankee Hurrah: The Civil War Journal of a Maine Volunteer.* Camden, ME: Down East Books, 1985.

Hall, Campanion H. Seymour. "Mine Run to Petersburg." *War Talks in Kansas. MOLLUS.* Wilmington, NC: Broadfoot Publishing, 1992.

Hargrove, Hondon B. *Black Union Soldiers in the Civil War.* Jefferson, NC: McFarland, 1988.

Harrill, Lawson. *Reminiscences: 1861–1865.* Statesville, NC: Brady, Printer, 1907.

Haskell, John Cheves. *The Haskell Memoirs: The Personal Narrative of a Confederate Officer.* Edited by Gilbert E. Govan and James W. Livingood. New York: Putnam's, 1960.

Hassler, William Woods. *A.P. Hill: Lee's Forgotten General.* Chapel Hill: University of North Carolina Press, 1962.

Hastings, William H., ed. *Letters from a Sharpshooter: The Civil War Letters of Private William B. Green, Co. G, 2nd United States Sharpshooters (Berdan's), Army of the Potomac, 1861–1865.* Belleville, WI: Historic Publications, 1993.

Hattaway, Herman. *Reflections of a Civil War Historian.* Columbia: University of Missouri Press, 2004.

Hauptman, Laurence M. *Between Two Fires: American Indians in the Civil War.* New York: Free Press Paperbacks, Simon and Schuster, 1995.

_____. *The Iroquois in the Civil War: From Battlefield to Reservation.* Syracuse, NY: Syracuse University Press, 1993.

Hayden, Charles B. *For Country, Cause and Leader: The Civil War Journal of Charles B. Hayden.* Edited by Stephen W. Sears. New York: Ticknor & Fields, 1993.

Heller, J. Roderick, III, and Carolynn Ayers Heller, eds. *The Confederacy Is on Her Way Up the Spout: Letters to South Carolina, 1861–1865.* Athens: University of Georgia Press, 1992.

Henderson, William D. *Petersburg in the Civil War: War at the Door.* Lynchburg, VA: H.E. Howard, 1992.

Herbert, Hilary A. "History of the Eighth Alabama Volunteer Regiment." *Alabama Historical Quarterly* 39 (1977).

Herek, Raymond J. "First In Petersburg." *Michigan History* 74 (March–April 1990): 10–16.

Higginson, Thomas Wentworth. *Army Life in a Black Reg-*

iment. East Lansing: Michigan State University Press, 1960.

Himmelfarb, Forest Day. "Black Troops from Illinois." Illinois History, Illinois Historic Preservation Agency: Springfield, Illinois, February 1994.

Hobart, Edwin L. *Semi-History of a Boy-Veteran of the Twenty-Eighth Regiment Illinois Infantry Volunteers, in a Black Regiment: A Diary of the 28th Ill. from Organization to Veteranization*. Denver: 1909.

Hodges, Carl G., and Helene H. Levene, eds. *Illinois Negro Historymakers*. Chicago: Illinois Emancipation Centennial Commission, 1964.

Holsinger, Frank. "The Colored Troops at the Mine." *National Tribune*, October 19, 1905.

Horigan, Michael. *Elmira: Death Camp of the North*. Mechanicsburg, PA: Stackpole Books, 2002.

Horn, John. *The Petersburg Campaign: June 1864–April 1865*. Cambridge, MA: Da Capo Press, 2003.

Hotchkiss, Jedediah. *Confederate Military History: A Library of Confederate States History*. 12 vols. Edited by Clement A. Evans. Vol. 3, Virginia. Atlanta: Blue & Grey Press, 1899.

Houghton, Major Charles H. "In the Crater." In *Battles and Leaders of the Civil War*. New York: Castle Books, 1956.

Howe, Thomas. *The Petersburg Campaign, Wasted Valor, June 15–18, 1864*. Lynchburg, VA: H.E. Howard, 1988.

Howland, Henry R. "An Anecdote of the Petersburg Crater." *The Century* 2 (December 1887): 323.

Hudson, Joshua Hilary. *Sketches and Reminiscences*. Columbia, SC: State Company, 1903.

Humphreys, Andrew A. *The Virginia Campaign of '64 and '65*. New York: Scribner's, 1916.

Hurst, Jack. *Nathan Bedford Forrest: A Biography*. New York: Alfred A. Knopf, 1993.

Jackson, Harry F., and F. O'Donnell. *Back Home in Oneida: Herman Clarke and His Letters*. Syracuse, NY: Syracuse University Press, 1965.

James, George R. *Recollections and Reminiscences, 1861–1865 through World War I*. Vol. 8, *Recollections*. South Carolina Division, Daughters of the Confederacy: Columbia, SC 1992.

Jaquette, Henrietta Stratton, ed. *South after Gettysburg: Letters of Cordelia Handcock from the Army of the Potomac*. New York: Thomas Y. Crowell, 1937.

Jarrot's Hotel. *A Guide to the Fortifications and Battlefields around Petersburg*. Petersburg, VA: Jarrot's Hotel, 1866. Reprinted by Eastern National in 2003.

Jimerson, Randall C. *The Private Civil War: Popular Thought during the Sectional Conflict*. Baton Rouge: Louisiana State University Press, 1988.

Johnson, Robert Underwood, and Clarence Clough Buell, eds. *Battles and Leaders of the Civil War*. 4 vols. New York: A.S. Barnes, 1956.

Jones, Frank J. *Personal Recollections of Some of the Generals in Our Army during the Civil War*. A paper presented on December 13, 1913, before the Ohio Commandery of the Loyal Legion.

Jones, the Rev. J. William. *Army of Northern Virginia Memorial Volume*. Richmond, VA: J.W. Randolph & English, 1880.

_____. "The Battle of the Crater." *Southern Historical Society Papers* 10 (January–December 1882): 119–130.

Jones, R.W. "Mahone's Men at the Crater." *Confederate Veteran* 16, no. 1 (January 1908), iii.

Jordan, David M. *Winfield Scott Hancock: A Soldier's Life*. Bloomington: Indiana University Press, 1988.

Jordan, Ervin L., Jr. *Black Confederates and Afro-Yankees in Civil War Virginia*. Charlottesville: University Press of Virginia, 1995.

Jordan, Robert Paul. *The Civil War*. Washington, DC: National Geographic Society, 1969.

Jordan, Weymouth T., Jr., and Louis H. Manarin, eds. *North Carolina Troops: A Roster*. 12 vols. Raleigh, NC: State Dept of Archives and History, 1966–1998.

Katcher, Philip. *Lethal Glory: Dramatic Defeats of the Civil War*. London: Arms and Armour Press, 1995.

Kautz, General August, V. "Operations South of the James." In *Battles and Leaders of the Civil War*. New York: Castle Books, 1956.

Kelley, Dayton. *General Lee and Hood's Texas Brigade at the Battle of the Wilderness*. Hillsboro, TX: Hill Junior College Press, 1969.

Kenfield, Frank. "Captured by Rebels: A Vermonter at Petersburg, 1864." *Vermont History* 36 (Autumn 1968): 230–235.

Kennett, Le B., ed. "A Frenchman with Meade." *Civil War Times Illustrated* 10 (January 1972): 40–43.

Kilmer, George L. "The Dash into the Crater." *The Century Illustrated Monthly* 34 (May–October 1887): 774–776.

Kinard, Jeff. *The Battle of the Crater*. Abilene: McWhiney Foundation Press, 1998.

King, Edward. "A Ramble in Virginia: From Bristol to the Sea." *Scribner's Monthly* 7, no. 6, New York: Scribner's, April 1874, 645–74.

Kingman, Leroy W., ed. *Our Country and Its People: A Memorial History of Tioga County*. Elmira, NY: W.A. Fergusson, 1890.

Klein, Frederic S. "Lost Opportunity at Petersburg." *Civil War Times Illustrated* 5 (August 1966): 38–50.

Krick, Robert K. *Lee's Colonels: A Biographical Register of the Field Officers of the Army of Northern Virginia*. 2nd ed., rev. Dayton: Morningside Bookshop, 1984.

Lane, David. *A Soldier's Diary: The Story of a Volunteer, 1862–1865*. Jackson, MI: 1905.

Lanman, Charles. *The Red Book of Michigan*. Detroit: E.B. Smith, 1871.

Laughton, John E., Jr. "The Sharpshooters of Mahone's Brigade." *Southern Historical Society Papers* 20 (1894): 98–105.

Law, Evander M. "From the Wilderness to Cold Harbor." In *Battles and Leaders of the Civil War*. New York: Castle Books, 1956.

Leech, Margaret. *Reveille in Washington: 1860–1865*. New York: Harper & Brothers Publishers, 1941.

Levin, Kevin M. "The Earth Seemed to Tremble." *America's Civil War* 19, no. 2 (May 2006): 22–28.

_____. "William Mahone, the Lost Cause, and Civil War History." *Virginia Magazine of History and Biography* 113, no. 4: 378–412.

Litwack, Leon F. *Been in the Storm So Long: The Aftermath of Slavery*. New York: Alfred A. Knopf, 1979.

Livermore, Thomas L. "The Failure to Take Petersburg, June 15, 1864." *Papers of the Military Society of Massachusetts* 5 (1906): 33–74.

Logue, Larry M. *To Appomattox and Beyond: The Civil War Soldier in War and Peace*. Chicago: I.R. Dee, 1996.

Long, E.B., ed. *The Personal Memoirs of U.S. Grant*. Cleveland and New York: World Publishing, 1952.

Long, Lessel. *Twelve Months in Andersonville — on the March — in the Battle — in the Rebel Prison Pens, and at Last in God's Country*. Huntington, IN: Thad and Mark Butler, 1886.

Longacre, Edward G., ed. *Antietam to Fort Fisher: The Civil War Letters of Edward King Wrightman, 1862–1865*. Rutherford, NJ: Fairleigh Dickenson University Press, 1985.

_____. *Lee's Cavalrymen: A History of the Mounted Forces of the Army of Northern Virginia, 1861–1865.* Mechanicsburg: Stackpole Books, 2002.

_____. *The Man Behind the Guns: A Biography of General Henry J. Hunt, Commander of Artillery, Army of the Potomac.* Cambridge, MA: Da Capo Press, 2003.

_____. "Wilson-Kautz Raid." *Civil War Times Illustrated* 9 (May 1970): 32–34.

Loving, Jerome M., ed. *Civil War Letters of George Washington Whitman.* Durham: Duke University Press, 1975.

Lowry, Don. *No Turning Back: The Beginning of the End of the Civil War, March–June 1864.* New York: Hippocrene Books, 1992.

_____. *Fate of the Country: The Civil War from June to September 1864.* New York: Hippocrene Books, 1992.

Lykes, Richard Wayne. *Campaign for Petersburg.* Washington, DC: National Park Service, 1970.

Lyman, Theodore. "Crossing of the James River and Advance on Petersburg." *Papers of the Military Society of Massachusetts* 5 (1906): 25–32.

Lynch, J.D. "Field Of Blood Was the Crater." *Southern Historical Society Papers* 33 (1905): 351–57.

Mahone, William. *The Battle of the Crater.* Petersburg, VA: Franklin Press, 1864. Reprinted by C.W. Historicals.

Maney, R. Wayne. *Marching to Cold Harbor: Victory & Failure, 1864.* Shippensburg, PA: White Mane Publishing, 1995.

Mangham, Dana M. *"Oh, for a Touch of the Vanished Hand": Discovering a Southern Family and the Civil War.* Murfreesboro, TN: Southern Heritage Press, 2000.

Marlow, Clayton Charles. *Matt W. Ransom: Confederate General from North Carolina.* Jefferson, NC: McFarland, 1996.

Marvel, William. "And Fire Shall Devour Them: The 9th New Hampshire in the Crater." *A Journal of the American Civil War, Regimental Studies, Inc.* 2, no. 2 (1992): 118–140.

_____. "More Than Water Under Burnside's Bridge." *America's Civil War* 18, no. 6 (2005): 46–52.

_____. *Burnside.* Chapel Hill: University of North Carolina Press, 1991.

Marvin, Abijah P. *History of Worcester in the War of the Rebellion.* Worcester, MA: Abijah P. Marvin, 1880.

Matter, William D. *If It Takes All Summer: The Battle of Spotsylvania.* Chapel Hill: University of North Carolina Press, 1988.

Maurice, Frederick, ed. *Lee's Aide-De-Camp: Being the Papers of Colonel Charles Marshall, Sometime Aide-De-Camp, Military Secretary, and Assistant Adjutant General on the Staff of Robert E. Lee, 1862–1865.* Lincoln: University of Nebraska Press, 2000.

_____. *Robert E. Lee: The Soldier.* New York: Bonanza Books, 1925.

Mays, Thomas D., ed. *Let Us Meet in Heaven: The Civil War Letters of James Michael Barr, 5th South Carolina Cavalry.* Abilene: McWhiney Foundation Press, 2001.

McCabe, W. Gordon. "Defence of Petersburg." *Southern Historical Society Papers* 2 (1876).

McCady, Col. Edward. "Heroes of the Old Camden District, South Carolina, 1776–1861." *Southern Historical Society Papers* 16 (1888): 3–35.

McFeeley, William. *Grant: A Biography.* New York: W.W. Norton, 1981.

McKim, Rev. Randolph H. *The Second Maryland Infantry.* Speech delivered May 7, 1909, at the state house, Annapolis, MD.

_____. *A Soldier's Recollection: Leaves From the Diary of a*

Young Confederate, with an Oration on the Motives and Aims of the Soldiers of the South.* London: Longmans, Green, 1910.

McMaster, F.W. "The Battle of the Crater, July 30, 1864." *Southern Historical Society Papers* 10 (1882): 119–30.

McPherson, James M. *Battle Cry of Freedom: The Civil War Era.* New York: Oxford University Press, 1988.

_____. *Crossroads of Freedom: Antietam.* New York: Oxford University Press, 2002.

_____. *Drawn with the Sword: Reflections on the American Civil War.* New York: Oxford University Press, 1996.

_____. *For Cause and Comrades: Why Men Fought in the Civil War.* New York: Oxford University Press, 1997.

McQueen, Bert. *A Civil War Family (A True Story).* Hagerstown, IN: Exponent Publishers, 1987.

McWhiney, Grady, and Perry D. Jamieson. *Attack and Die: Civil War Military Tactics and the Southern Heritage.* Tuscaloosa: University of Alabama Press, 1982.

McWhiney, Grady, and Jack Jay Jenkins. "The Union's Worst General: James Ledlie." *Civil War Times Illustrated* 14, no. 3 (1975): 30–39.

Meade, George Gordon. *The Life and Letters of George Gordon Meade, Major General, United States Army.* 2 vols. New York: Scribner's, 1913.

Menge, W. Springer, and J. August Shimrak, eds. *The Civil War Notebook of Daniel Chisholm: A Chronicle of Daily Life in the Union Army, 1864–1865.* New York: Ballantine, 1989.

Michigan Adjutant General Department. *Record of Service of Michigan Volunteers in the Civil War, 1861–1865.* 46 vols. Kalamazoo: Ihling Bros.& Everland, 1903.

Miles, Nelson A. *Serving the Republic: Memoirs of the Civil War and Military Life of Nelson A. Miles Lieutenant General, United States Army.* New York: Harper & Bros., 1911.

Miller, Delavan S. *Drum Taps in Dixie: Memories of a Drummer Boy, 1861–1865.* Watertown, NY: Hungerford-Holbrook, 1905.

Mitchell, Joseph B. *The Badge of Gallantry: Recollections of Civil War Congressional Medal of Honor Winners.* New York: Macmillan, 1968.

Mitchell, Ried. *Civil War Soldiers: Their Expectations and Their Experiences.* New York: Viking, 1988.

_____. *The Vacant Chair: The Northern Soldier Leaves Home.* New York: Oxford University Press, 1993.

Mudgett, Timothy B. *Make the Fur Fly: A History of a Union Volunteer Division in the American Civil War.* Shippensburg, PA: Burd Street Press, 1997.

Naisawald, L. Van Loan. *Grape and Canister: The Story of the Field Artillery of the Army of the Potomac, 1861–1865.* New York: Oxford University Press, 1960.

Napier, W.F.P. *History of the War on the Peninsula and in the South of France from the Year 1807 to the Year 1814.* 6 vols. London: John Murry, 1828–1840.

National Park Service. "Elliott's Salient." www.crateroad.com

Nevins, Allan, and Milton Halsey Thomas, eds. *The Diary of George Templeton Strong: The Civil War, 1860–1865.* 3 vols, 3. New York: Octagon Books, 1974.

_____, ed. *A Diary of Battle: The Personal Journals of Colonel Charles S. Wainwright, 1861–1865.* New York: Harcourt, Brace & World, 1962.

Newberry, Walter C. "The Petersburg Mine." 12 *MOLLUS.* Chicago, 1899.

Newton, Steven H. *Lost for the Cause: The Confederate Army in 1864.* Mason City, IA: Savas Publishing, 2000.

Nolan, Dick. *Benjamin Butler, The Damnedest Yankee.* Novato, CA: Presidio, 1991.

Norfleet, R.E. "Reminiscences of R.E. Norfleet." *Confederate Veteran* 17, no. 1 (January 1909): 22.

O'Brien, John Emmet. *Telegraphing in Battle: Reminiscences of the Civil War.* Wilkes-Barre, PA: Raeder Press, 1910.

Oats, William C. "The Dead Cover More Than Five Acres." In *The Blue and the Gray.* Edited by Henry Steele Commager. Indianapolis: Bobbs-Merrill, 1950.

Page, Charles A. *Letters of a War Correspondent.* Boston: L.C. Page, 1899.

Page, Elizabeth Fry. "If You Love Me." *Confederate Veteran* 35, no. 4 (April 1927): 132–134.

Paige, Charles C. *Story of the Experiences of Lieut. Charles C. Paige in the Civil War of 1861–5.* Franklin, NH: Journal-Transcript Press, Franklin, 1951.

Palfrey, Francis Winthrop. *Memoir of William Francis Bartlett.* Boston: Osgood, 1878.

Palmer, Col. W.H. "General A.P. Hill Presentation of His Statue to A.P. Hill Camp, Petersburg, Virginia." *Southern Historical Society Papers* 20 (1892): 184–205.

Passarella, Lee. *Swallowed Up in Victory: A Civil War Narrative, Petersburg, 1864–1865.* Shippensburg, PA: Burd Street Press, 2002.

Patrick, Marsina Rudolph. *Inside Lincoln's Army: The Diary of Marsena Rudolph Patrick.* Edited by David S. Sparks. New York: Provost Marshall General, Army of the Potomac, T. Yoseloff, 1964.

Peabody, Frank E. "Crossing of the James and First Assault on Petersburg, June 12–15, 1864." *Papers of the Military Society of Massachusetts* 5 (1906): 125–146.

Pearce, T.H., ed. *The Diary of Captain Henry A. Chambers.* Wendell, NC: Broadfoot's Bookmark, 1983.

Pember, Phoebe Yates. *A Southern Woman's Story.* New York: G.W. Carleton, 1879.

Pennypacker, Isaac Rusling. *General Meade.* New York: D. Appleton, 1901.

Phillips, B.F. "Wilcox's Alabamians in Virginia." *Confederate Veteran* 15, no. 11 (November 1907): 490.

Piston, William Garrett. *Lee's Tarnished Lieutenant: James Longstreet and His Place in Southern History.* Athens: University of Georgia Press, 1987.

Pleasants, Henry, Jr., and George H. Straley. *Inferno at Petersburg.* Philadelphia: Chilton Book, 1961.

_____. *The Tragedy of the Crater.* Boston: Christopher Publishing House, 1938. Reprinted in 1975 by the Eastern National Park and Monument Association in cooperation with Petersburg National Military Park, National Park Service.

Pollard, Edward A. *The Lost Cause: A New Southern History of the War of the Confederacy.* Baltimore: E.B. Treat, 1866.

Pollard, Henry R. "Edward Bagby of Virginia." *Confederate Veteran* 27, no. 12 (December 1919): 453–458.

Polley, Joseph B. *A Soldier's Letters to Charming Nellie.* New York: Neale Pub., 1908.

Poore, Ben Perley. *The Life and Public Services of Ambrose E. Burnside, Soldier, Citizen, Statesman.* Providence, RI: J.A. & R.A. Reid, Publishers, 1882.

Pope, Edmund M. "Personal Experiences: A Side Light on the Wilson Raid, June 1864." *MN MOLLUS* 4. St. Paul, MN: 1898.

Potter, Henry C. "General Robert B. Potter and the Assault at the Petersburg Crater." *The Century* 35, no. 3 (1887): 481.

Porter, Charles H. "The Petersburg Mine." *Papers of the Military Historical Society of Massachusetts* 5: 222–239.

Porter, Horace. *Campaigning with Grant.* Bloomington: Indiana University Press, 1961.

Powell, Major William H. "The Battle of the Petersburg Crater." In *Battles and Leaders of the Civil War.* New York: Castle Books, 1956.

_____. "The Tragedy of the Crater." *The Century Illustrated Monthly* 34 (May–October 1887): 760–773.

Power, J. Tracy. *Lee's Miserables: Life in the Army of Northern Virginia from the Wilderness to Appomattox.* Chapel Hill: University of North Carolina Press, 1998.

Price, Isaiah. *Reunion of the Ninety-Seventh Regiment Pennsylvania Volunteers.* Philadelphia: Mollus, 1884.

Priest, John Michael. *Nowhere to Run: The Wilderness, May 4th and 5th, 1864.* Shippensburg, PA: White Mane Publishing, 1995.

Pryor, Anne Banister. "A Child's Recollection of War." *Confederate Veteran* 37, no. 2 (1931): 54–57.

Pueser, Richard W., and Trevor K. Plante. "*Cold Mountain*'s Inman: Fact Versus Fiction." *Prologue* 36, no. 2 (Summer 2004): 6–9.

Quarles, Benjamin. *The Negro in the Civil War.* Boston: Little, Brown, 1953.

Rable, George C. *Fredericksburg! Fredericksburg!* Chapel Hill: University of North Carolina Press, 2002.

Rafuse, Ethan. *George Gordon Meade and the War in the East.* Abilene: McWhiney Foundation Press, McMurry University, 1968.

Rawley, James W. *Turning Points of the Civil War.* Lincoln: University of Nebraska Press, 1966.

Ray, Joseph. "Our Indebtedness to the Negroes." *New Englander and Yale Review* 51, no. 236 (November 1889): 353–365.

Redkey, Edwin, ed. *A Grand Army of Black Men: Letters from African-American Soldiers in the Union Army, 1861–1865.* Cambridge: Cambridge University Press, 1992.

Reid-Green, Marcia, ed. *Letters Home: Henry Matrau of the Iron Brigade.* Lincoln: University of Nebraska Press, 1993.

Rhea, Gordon C. *The Battle of the Wilderness, May 5–6, 1864.* Baton Rouge: Louisiana State University Press, 1994.

_____. *The Battles for Spotsylvania Court House and the Road to the Yellow Tavern, May 7–12, 1864.* Baton Rouge: Louisiana State University Press, 1997.

_____. *Cold Harbor, Grant and Lee, May 26–June 3, 1864.* Baton Rouge: Louisiana State University Press, 2002.

_____. *To the North Anna River: Grant and Lee, May 13–25, 1864.* Baton Rouge: Louisiana State University Press, 2000.

Rhodes, Elisha H. "The Second Rhode Island Volunteers at the Siege of Petersburg, Virginia." 41 *MOLLUS* 10 (1915) (Broadfoot Publishing, Wilmington, NC, 1993): 431–449.

Rhodes, Robert Hunt, ed. *All for the Union: The Civil War Diary & Letters of Elisha Hunt Rhodes.* New York: Orion Books, 1985.

Richards, R.G. "The Blunder at the Petersburg Mine." *National Tribune,* June 18, 1925.

Rickard, James H. "Services with Colored Troops in Burnside's Corps." *Personal Narratives of Events in the War of the Rebellion: Being Papers Read Before the Rhode Island Soldiers and Sailors Historical Society* 5, no. 1 (1894).

_____. *Services with Colored Troops in Burnside's Corps.* Providence, RI: Snow & Farnham, Printers, 1894.

Roberts, W.H. *Drums and Guns around Petersburg.* Bowie, MD: Heritage Books, 1995.

Robertson, James I., Jr. *Civil War Virginia: Battleground for a Nation.* Charlottesville: University Press of Virginia, 1991.

_____. *General A.P. Hill: Story of a Confederate Warrior.* New York: Random House, 1987.

_____, ed. *The Civil War Letters of General Robert McAllister.* Baton Rouge, LA: Louisiana State University Press, 1965.

Roberston, William G. *Back Door to Richmond: The Bermuda Hundred Campaign, April–June, 1864.* Newark: University of Delaware Press, 1987.

_____. *The Petersburg Campaign:, The Battle of Old Men and Young Boys, June 9, 1864.* Lynchburg, VA: H.E. Howard, 1989.

Robinson, W.P. "Artillery in the Battle of the Crater." *Confederate Veteran* 19 (1911): 164–166.

Rodenbough, General Theodore F. "Sheridan's Trevilian Raid." In *Battles and Leaders of the Civil War.* New York: Castle Books, 1956.

Rogers, George T. "Crater Battle: Reply to Mr. Clark." *Confederate Veteran* 3, no. 5 (May 1895): 137.

_____. "The Crater Battle, 30th July, 1864." *Confederate Veteran* 3, no. 1 (1895): 12–14.

Rolph, Daniel N. *My Brother's Keeper: Union and Confederate Soldiers' Acts of Mercy during the Civil War.* Mechanicsburg: Stackpole Books, 2002.

Roman, Alfred. *The Military Operations of General Beauregard in the War between the States 1861–1865.* 2 vols. New York: Harper and Brothers, 1883–1884.

Ropes, John C. "The Failure to Take Petersburg on June 16–18, 1864." *Papers of the Military Society of Massachusetts* 5 (1906): 157–186.

Roulhac, Thomas R. "The Forty-Ninth N. C. Infantry, C.S.A." *Southern Historical Society Papers* 22 (1895): 58–78.

_____. "Forty-ninth N.C. Infantry C. S. A.: Its History from Its Organization in March, 1862, until Overpowered and Made Prisoners at Five Forks, Va., April 1, 1865." *Southern Historical Society Papers* (1895): 58–78.

Rowland, J.C. "The Petersburg Mine." *National Tribune,* July 18, 1907.

Salley, A.S. *South Carolina Troops in Confederate Service.* 3 vols. Columbia, SC: R.L. Byran, 1930.

Sandburg, Carl. *Abraham Lincoln: The War Years.* 4 vols. New York: Harcourt, Brace, 1939.

Sauers, Richard A. *Advance the Colors: Pennsylvania Civil War Battle Flags.* 2 vols. Harrisburg, PA: Capitol Preservation Committee, 1987–1991.

Saussy, George N. "Generals Lee and Gracie at the Crater." *Confederate Veteran* 17, no. 4 (April 1909): 160.

Schenck, Martin. *Up Came Hill: The Story of the Light Division and Its Leaders.* Harrisburg, PA: Stackpole, 1958.

Schiller, Herbert M., and William Farror Smith, eds. *Autobiography of Major General William F. Smith, 1861–1864.* Dayton: Morningside House, 1990.

_____. *The Bermuda Hundred Campaign: Operations on the South Side of the James River, May 1864.* Dayton: Morningside, 1988.

Schneider, Frederick. *Incidental History of the Flags and Color Guard of the Second Michigan Veteran Volunteer Infantry, 1861–5.* Lansing, MI: Winfield S. Sly, 1905.

Schouler, William A. *A History of Massachusetts in the Civil War.* 2 vols. Boston: E.P. Dutton, 1869–1871.

Scott, James G., and Edward A. Wyatt IV. *Petersburg's Story: A History.* Petersburg, VA: Deitz Press, 1960.

Scott, Robert Garth, ed. *Forgotten Valor: The Memoirs, Journals, & Civil War Letters of Orlando B. Willcox.* Kent, OH: Kent State University Press, 1999.

_____. *Into the Wilderness with the Army of the Potomac.* Bloomington: Indiana University Press, 1985.

Scroggs, Joseph J. "The Earth Shook and Quivered." Edited by Sig Synnestvedt. *Civil War Times Illustrated* 11 (December 1972): 30–37.

Segars, J.H., and Charles Kelly Barrow, eds. *Black Southerners in the Confederate Armies.* Atlanta, GA: Southern Lion Books, 2001.

Seraile, William. *New York's Black Regiments during the Civil War.* New York: Routledge, 2001.

Shearman, Sumner U. "Battle of the Crater and Experiences of Prison Life." 39 *MOLLUS* 6. Providence, RI: 1899: 387–399.

Sheehan-Dean, Aaron Charles. *The View from the Ground: Experiences of Civil War Soldiers.* Lexington: University Press of Kentucky, 2007.

Sheridan, Phillip H. *Personal Memoirs of P.H. Sheridan.* 2 vols. New York: Charles L. Webster, 1928.

Sholes, Albert E. "The Crater Fight Vividly Portrayed." *National Tribune,* January 12, 1928.

Sifakis, Stewart. *Compendium of the Confederate Armies: South Carolina and Georgia.* New York: Facts On File, 1995.

_____. *Compendium of the Confederate Armies: Alabama.* New York: Facts On File, 1992.

Simpson, Harold B. *Gaines' Mill to Appomattox: Waco & McLennan County in Hood's Texas Brigade.* Waco: Texian Press, 1988.

Skoch, George F. "Thunder from Below." *America's Civil War* 1 (July 1988): 26–33.

Small, Harold Adams, ed. *The Road to Richmond: The Civil War Memoirs of Major Abner R. Small of the Sixteenth Maine Volunteers.* Berkeley: University of California Press, 1939.

Smith, Gene. *Grant and Lee: A Dual Biography.* New York: McGraw-Hill, 1984.

Smith, John David, ed. *Black Soldiers in Blue: African American Troops in the Civil War Era.* Chapel Hill: University of North Carolina Press, 2002.

Smith, William F. "Comments on 'General Grant's Reason for Relieving General William F. Smith.'" *The Century* 33 (November 1886–April 1887): 134.

_____. "General W.F. Smith at Petersburg." *Century Magazine* 64 (1897): 318.

_____. "The Movement against Petersburg, June 1864." *Papers of the Military Society of Massachusetts* 5 (1906): 75–116.

Soldier. "The Petersburg Mine." *National Tribune,* January 17, 1884.

Sommers, Richard J. *Richmond Redeemed: The Siege at Petersburg.* Garden City, NY: Doubleday, 1981.

Sorrel, Gilbert Moxley. *Recollections of a Confederate Staff Officer.* New York: Neale Publishing, 1905.

Southern Historical Society Papers 5.

Spear, Jamin A. "Fighting Them Over." *National Tribune,* June 20, 1889.

Stackpole, Edward J. *The Fredericksburg Campaign.* New York: Bonanza Books, 1957.

Starr, Stephen Z. *The Union Cavalry in the Civil War.* 3 vols. Baton Rouge: Louisiana State University Press, 1975–1985.

_____, ed. "The Wilson Raid, 1864: A Trooper's Reminiscence." *Civil War Historian* 21 (September 1975): 218–241.

Steere, Edward. *The Wilderness Campaign: The Meeting of Grant and Lee.* New York: Bonanza Books, 1960.

Stern, Philip Van Doren. *Robert E. Lee: The Man and the Soldier.* New York: Bonanza Books, 1963.

Stevens, George T. *Three Years in the Sixth Corps: A concise narrative of events in the Army of the Potomac from 1861 to the close of the rebellion, April 1865.* Albany, NY: S.R. Gray, 1866.

Stevenson, Silas. *Account of the Battle of the Mine Explosion, or Battle of the Crater in Front of Petersburg, Va., July 30, 1864.* Ellwood City, PA: John A. Leathers, Printer, 1914.

Stewart, William H. "Carnage at 'The Crater' Near Petersburg." *Confederate Veteran* 21, no. 1 (1893): 41–42.

_____. "The Charge of the Crater." *Southern Historical Society Papers* 25 (1897).

_____. "Crater Legion of Mahone's Brigade." *Confederate Veteran* 11, no. 12, (December 1903): 557–558.

_____. *Description of the Battle of the Crater: Recollection of the Recapture of the Lines.* Norfolk, VA: Landmark Book and Job Office, 1876.

_____. "Field of Blood Was the Crater." *Southern Historical Society Papers* 33 (1905): 351–57.

_____. "Marker for Mahone's Brigade at Crater." *Confederate Veteran* 19, no. 8 (August 1911): 387.

_____. *A Pair of Blankets: War-Time History in Letters to the Young People of the South.* New York: Broadway Publishing, 1911.

Stiles, Robert. *Four Years under Marse Robert.* New York: Neale Publishing, 1910.

_____. "Their Dead and Dying Piled Higher Than the Works." In *The Blue and the Gray.* Edited by Henry Steele Commager. Indianapolis: Bobbs-Merrill, 1950.

Stine, James Henry. *History of the Army of the Potomac.* Washington, DC: Gibson Bros., 1893.

Stinson, J.B. "Mistook Each Other for an Enemy," *Confederate Veteran* 2, no. 6 (June 1894): 187.

Suderow, Bruce A. "The Battle of the Crater: The Civil War's Worst Massacre." *Civil War History* 43, no. 3 (1997): 219–221.

Sutherland, Daniel E. *Fredericksburg and Chancellorsville: The Dare Mark Campaign.* Lincoln: University of Nebraska Press, 1998.

Swift, Lt. Col. F.W. *My Experiences as a Prisoner of War.* Detroit: Wm. S. Oster, 1888.

Swinton, William. *Campaigns of the Army of the Potomac: A Critical History of Operations in Virginia, Maryland and Pennsylvania, from the Commencement to the Close of the War.* New York: C.B. Richardson, 1866.

Sword, Wiley. *Southern Invincibility: A History of the Confederate Heart.* New York: St. Martin's Press, 1999.

Sylvester, Nathaniel Bartlett. *History of Rensselaer Co., New York.* Philadelphia: Everts & Peck, 1880.

Tapert, Annette, ed. *The Brothers' War: Civil War Letters to Their Loved Ones from the Blue and Gray.* New York: Times Books, 1988.

Taylor, John M. "The Crater." In *Grinding, Relentless War.* Leesburg, VA: PRIMEDIA Enthusiast Publications, 2004.

_____. "The Crater." In *With My Face to the Enemy.* Edited by Robert Cowley. New York: Putnam's, 2001.

Taylor, Raleigh C. "The Petersburg Crater, Then and Now." *Confederate Veteran* 3, no. 1 (July 1939).

_____. "War Underground: The Petersburg Mine." *The Regional Review* 5, no. 1 (July 1940): 29–33.

Taylor, Walter H. *Four Years with General Lee.* New York: Bonanza Books, 1952.

Thomas, Benjamin B., ed. *Three Years with Grant.* New York: Alfred A. Knopf, 1955.

Thomas, General Henry Goddard. "The Colored Troops at Petersburg." *Battles and Leaders of the Civil War* 4:563–67.

_____. "The Colored Troops at Petersburg." *The Century Illustrated Monthly* 34 (May–October 1887): 777–782.

_____. "Twenty-two Hours Prisoner of War in Dixie." In *War Papers.* Maine *MOLLUS* 42. Portland, ME: Thurston Print, 1898.

Thomas, William M. "The Slaughter at Petersburg, June 18, 1864." *Southern Historical Society Papers* 25 (1897): 222–230.

Thrash, A.B. "Vivid Reminiscence of the Crater." *Confederate Veteran* 14, no. 11 (November 1906): 508–509.

Thwaites, Reuben Gold. *The Story of Wisconsin.* Boston: Lothrop Publishing, 1899.

Tower, R. Lockwood, ed. *Lee's Adjutant: The Wartime Letters of Colonel Walter Herron Taylor, 1862–1865.* Columbia: University of South Carolina Press, 1995.

Tribou, Charles E. "At the Crater." *National Tribune,* June 29, 1911.

Trudeau, Noah Andre. *Bloody Roads South: The Wilderness to Cold Harbor, May–June 1864.* Boston: Little, Brown, 1989.

_____. "Chaos in the Crater." *Civil War Times* 43, no. 3 (August 2004): 26–33.

_____. *The Last Citadel: Petersburg, Virginia, June 1864– April 1865.* Little, Brown, 1991.

_____. *Like Men of War: Black Troops in the Civil War, 1862–1865.* Castle Books, 2002.

_____. "A Mere Question of Time: Robert E. Lee from the Wilderness to Appomattox Court House." In *Lee.* Edited by Gallagher. Lincoln: University of Nebraska Press, 1996.

Trulock, Alice Rains. *In the Hands of Providence: Joshua L. Chamberlain and the American Civil War.* Chapel Hill: University of North Carolina Press, 1992.

Tucker, James M. "Kautz Raiding around Petersburg." MN *MOLLUS* 5. St. Paul, MN: Review Pub., 1903.

Tucker, Phillip Thomas. *Burnside's Bridge.* Mechanicsburg: Stackpole Books, 2000.

Turner, Charles W., ed. *Ted Barclay, Liberty Hall Volunteers: Letters from the Stonewall Brigade.* Natural Bridge Station, VA: Rockbridge Publishing, 1992.

Tuttle, Charles R. *An Illustrated History of the State of Wisconsin.* Boston: B.B. Russell, 1875.

Urwin, J.W., ed. *Black Flag Over Dixie: Racial Atrocities and Reprisals in the Civil War.* Carbondale: Southern Illinois University Press, 2004.

Vance, P.M. "Incidents of the Crater Battle." *Confederate Veteran* 14, no. 1 (1906): 178–179.

VanderCreek, Drew E. *African Americans, Race and Ethnicity in Illinois and the North during the Civil War.* Illinois during the Civil War Digitization Project. Dekalb: Northern Illinois University Libraries Digitization Unit, 2002.

Vandiver, Frank E. *Jubal's Raid: General Early's Famous Attack on Washington in 1864.* New York: McGraw-Hill, 1960.

Venable, Charles S. "General Lee in the Wilderness Campaign." In *Battles and Leaders of the Civil War* 4. New York: Castle Books, 1956.

_____. "The Campaign from the Wilderness to Petersburg." *Southern Historical Society Papers* 14 (1886): 522–542.

Venable, M.W. "In the Trenches at Petersburg." *Confederate Veteran* 34, no. 2 (February 1926): 59–61.

Walker, Francis A. *History of the Second Army Corps in the Army of the Potomac.* New York: Scribner's, 1886.

Wallace, Lee A., Jr. *A Guide to Virginia Military Organizations, 1861–1865.* Lynchburg, VA: H.E. Howard, 1986.

Walsh, George. *Damage Them All You Can: Robert E. Lee's Army of Northern Virginia.* New York: A Tom Doherty Associates Book, 2002.

_____. "Whip the Rebellion": Ulysses S. Grant's Rise to Command.* New York: A Tom Doherty Associates Book, 2005.

Ward, Geoffrey C. *The Civil War.* New York: Alfred A. Knopf, 1990.

Ward, Leo L. "City man's mine plan goes awry." *Pottsville (PA) Republican*, January 11–12, 1997.

Warner, Ezra J. *Generals in Blue*. Baton Rouge: Louisiana State University Press, 1964.

Waugh, John G. *The Class of 1846*. New York: Warner Books, 1994.

Way, D.S. "The Battle of the Crater." *National Tribune*, June 4, 1903.

Weld, Stephen Minot. "The Petersburg Mine." *Papers of the Military Historical Society of Massachusetts* 5 (1894): 207–219.

_____. *War Diary and Letters of Stephen Minot Weld, 1861–1865*. 2nd ed. Boston: Massachusetts Historical Society, 1979.

Wentz, A. "Closing Days of the War." *National Tribune*, February 11, 1904.

Wert, Jeffrey D. *The Sword of Lincoln: The Army of the Potomac*. New York: Simon and Schuster, 2005.

Wheeler, John H. *Reminiscences and Memoirs of North Carolina and Eminent North Carolinians*. Columbus, OH: Columbus Printing Works, 1884.

Wheeler, Richard. *On Fields of Fury: From the Wilderness to the Crater, an Eyewitness History*. New York: Harper-Collins, 1991.

White, Daniel. "Charging the Crater." *National Tribune*, July 3, 1919.

Whitman, William E.S. *Maine in the War for the Union: A History of the part borne by Maine troops in the suppression of the American Rebellion*. Lewiston, ME: N. Dingley Jr., 1865.

Whyte, James H. "Maryland's Negro Regiments: How, Where They Served." *Civil War Times Illustrated* 1, no.1 (1962): 41–43.

Wiley, Bell Irvin. *The Life of Billy Yank: The Common Soldier of the Union*. New York: Grosset & Dunlap, 1951.

_____. *The Life of Johnny Reb: The Common Soldier of the Confederacy*. 2 vol. Indianapolis: Bobbs-Merrill, 1943.

Wilkinson, Warren. "Bury Them if They Won't Move." *Civil War Times Illustrated* 29, no. 1 (1990): 24–25.

Wilkison, Frank. *Recollections of a Private Soldier in the Army of the Potomac*. New York: Putnam's, 1887.

William, George W. *A History of the Negro Troops in the War of the Rebellion, 1861–1865*. New York: Harper & Brothers, 1888.

Williams, Edward B., ed. *Rebel Brothers: The Civil War Letters of the Truehearts*. College Station: Texas A & M University Press, 1995.

Williams, T. Harry. *Lincoln and His Generals*. New York: Alfred A. Knopf, 1952.

_____. *P.G.T. Beauregard: Napoleon in Gray*. Baton Rouge: Louisiana State University Press, 1955.

Wilson, Joseph T. *The Black Phalanx: A History of the Negro Soldiers of the United States in the Wars of 1775–1812, 1861–'65*. Salem, NH: Ayer Company Publishers, 1968.

Wilson, Keith P. *Campfires of Freedom: The Camp Life of Black Soldiers during the Civil War*. Kent, OH: Kent State University Press, 2002.

Wise, Jennings Cropper. "The Boy Gunners of Lee." *Southern Historical Society Papers* 42 (1917): 152–173.

_____. *The Long Arm of Lee*. 2 vols. Lynchburg, VA: J.P. Bell, 1912.

Wise, John Sergeant. *The End of an Era*. Cambridge, MA: Houghton Mifflin, Riverside Press, 1899.

_____. "The West Point of the Confederacy: Boys Battle of New Market, Va., May 15, 1864." *Century Magazine* 15 (1888): 461–71.

Wolcott, Walter. *The Military History of Yates County, N.Y.* Penn Yan, NY: Express Book and Job Printing House, 1895.

Woodbury, Augustus. *Major General Ambrose E. Burnside and the Ninth Army Corps: A Narrative of Campaigns in North Carolina, Maryland, Virginia, Ohio, Kentucky, Mississippi and Tennessee during the War for the Preservation of the Republic*. Providence, RI: Sidney S. Rider & Brothers, 1867.

Woodford, Frank B. *Father Abraham's Children: Michigan Episodes in the Civil War*. Detroit: Wayne State University Press, 1961.

Woodworth, Steven E., ed. *The Loyal, True, and Brave: America's Civil War Soldiers*. Wilmington, DE: Scholarly Resources, 2002.

The Workers of the Writers' Program of the Works Progress Administration in the State of Virginia. *Dinwiddie County, "the country of the "Apomatica."* Sponsored by the Dinwiddie County School Board. Richmond, VA: Whillet & Shepperson, Printers, 1942.

Worthington, Glenn H. *Fighting for Time: The Battle of Monocacy*. Shippensburg, PA: White Mane Publishing, 1995.

W.R.S. "The Sharpshooters of Mahone's Old Brigade at the Crater." *Southern Historical Society Papers* 28 (1900).

Yeary, Mamie P. *Reminiscences of the Boys in Gray, 1861–1865*. Dallas: Smith & Lamar, Publishing House, M.E. Church, South, 1912.

Index